D1564425

THE
EIGHTH DAY

THE EIGHTH DAY

The Hidden History of the
Jewish Contribution to Civilization

Samuel Kurinsky

JASON ARONSON, INC.
Northvale, New Jersey
London

This book was set in 10 pt. Berkeley Oldstyle by Alpha Graphics of Pittsfield, New Hampshire and printed by Haddon Craftsmen in Scranton, Pennsylvania.

10 9 8 7 6 5 4 3 2 1

Library of Congress Cataloging-in-Publication Data
Kurinsky, Samuel.
    The eighth day : the hidden history of the Jewish contribution to
civilization / by Samuel Kurinsky.
        p.   cm.
    Includes bibliographical references and index.
    ISBN 0-87668-587-4
    1. Jews–Civilization.   2. Civilization, Ancient–Jewish
influences.   3. Jews–Antiquities.   I. Title.
DS112.K87   1994
909'.04924–dc20

                            92-35711

Manufactured in the United States of America. Jason Aronson Inc. offers books and cassettes. For information and catalog write to Jason Aronson Inc., 230 Livingston Street, Northvale, New Jersey 07647.

Contents

Acknowledgments

One must begin by acknowledging an immeasurable debt to all those scholars who researched and wrote the corpus of historical literature from which facts and inspiration were drawn. Their works become integral to an author's psyche; no bibliography can adequately record the ideas and impressions thus registered upon an author's subconscious, and only a small portion of the ideas consciously employed can be properly acknowledged.

An historian is essentially a re-orderer of facts who hopes that in so doing he can attain fresh and illuminative conclusions and thereby sharpen the focus of historical perspective. He may, in the course of his investigations, be fortunate in finding a few new facts and thereby add a bit to the sum of human knowledge.

I regret that I cannot list here the scores of individuals from whom I personally drew knowledge and encouragement in the course of pursuing pertinent information. Still, some of these individuals must be mentioned, in recognition of their substantive input. In Italy I met on many occasions with that remarkable, dedicated historian and chronicler of the Venetian glassmaking industry, Luigi Zecchin, who generously allowed me to tape our conversations and incorporate into my own work whatever material I needed from his vast storehouse of knowledge. Our discussions ranged far beyond the limits of the meticulous records that he had assembled on Venetian glassmaking, a monumental work amassed over a long and most productive lifetime. It is with utmost sadness and regret that I was unable to benefit from Zecchin's offer of collaboration on researching the arrival of the art to Aquileia, and on the arrival of the art to Venice from the Dalmatian coast and the Near East; our collaboration was ended by his passing from this world.

Dr. Maurizio Cassetti, director of the State Archives at Vercelli, Italy, gave unstintingly of his time, and went far beyond the call of duty in personally accompanying me in his rounds of the area on several occasions. Professor Michael Campo of Trinity College, who was honored with the title *Commenditore* by the Italian government for his extraordinary contribution to Italian cultural historiography, became familiar with and tendered valued support to my inquiries early on in the course of his research.

The indomitable Professor Machteld Mellink of Bryn Mawr University was an inspiration to me. Her quiet encouragement and personal guidance through the ancient sites that abound in Turkey provided me with a revelatory experience and invaluable background. The seas off the coast of Turkey contain ancient wrecks laden with stores of materials vital to the history of glassmaking. Credit for the revelation of much of this material goes to Professor George Bass of Texas A & M University, the pioneer of underwater archaeology, whose work I was privileged to witness as his guest on the *Virazon*, the research vessel of the Institute of Nautical Archaeology and to his proficient assistant and colleague, Cemal Pulak.

I was privileged to share experiences with Dr. David Adan-Bayewitz of Bar-Ilan University, whose parallel research in the field of pottery-making led to the identification of significant pottery-producing industries at the ancient sites of Kfar Hananiah and Shikhin in Israel. I was also privileged to employ the renowned Professor Dan Barag of Hebrew University as a sounding board for my radical view of glassmaking history. Professor Barag's cursive but incisive observations went far to direct me away from the pitfalls which await those who break new ground.

Two Americans, Steven Offerman and Mel Dubin, enthusiastically provided financial support to the Hebrew History Federation Ltd., and thus made possible the follow-up through that organization of several discoveries I had made in the course of researching glassmaking history.

Finally, I beg understanding from those whose omission from this acknowledgment should not indicate ungratefulness for their valuable contribution of encouragement and support.

Unless otherwise noted, biblical quotes are from the *Jerusalem Bible*, ed. M. Friedlander (Jerusalem: Jerusalem Bible Publishing Co., 1958).

Introduction

Ancient archaeology, as much or more than any other science, is based on theory and hypothesis more than on fact. Many historiographical constructions are hatched from a single artifact, or from a mere reference from a witness whose credibility cannot be proven. The further we probe into the past, the less we find material with which to reconstruct history, and the more subject to interpretation the reconstruction becomes. Written records are unreliable because they are for the most part written, or rewritten, by those who attain power. Such rulers or ruling institutions generally took pains to prevent the whole truth of the means by which their power was achieved and maintained from passing on to posterity. Once empowered, they employ their synthetic rendition of recorded history as a cover for the iniquitous actions by which power was commonly achieved, as a vindication of crass ambition, and as a rationale for sustaining hegemony over people and territory.

Conversely, records that present subjected peoples in a positive light are deliberately deleted or remolded and replaced to suit the interest of their conquerors. The downtrodden of society are ever at a disadvantage in having their problems and perceptions properly considered, let alone in having them preserved for posterity. Diversions from or contradictions to the official reconstructions are treated as treason or heresy and expunged. Ancient records should therefore be interpolated accordingly, but so much obfuscating lore has been transformed into standardized historiography that it becomes difficult to discern the deletions and distortions incorporated within it. The eradication of delusive lore from the corpus of historiography depends in the first place on recognition of the assimilated defects and, once recognized, on a willingness to render them visible. Unfortunately, self-interest and social, religious, and economic prejudice continue to befog the subject.

The horrific Holocaust perpetrated upon the Jewish people by the Nazis is but the most recent manifestation of an agelong series of desecrations suffered by the Jews. The human loss, the unprecedented, deliberate eradication of six million people for no other reason than that they were born of Jewish parentage, is so appalling that another ghastly aspect of the Holocaust is overlooked. Another egregious consequence that both the Jews and the world suffered as a result of Nazi bestiality was the irretrievable loss of mountains of historical data. Uncounted billions of documents were put to the torch upon the razing or confiscation of tens of thousands of Jewish enterprises, of thousands of Jewish cultural institutions, and of over six hundred synagogues. The architectural loss was the least part of the disaster that befell the world no less than the Jews; the loss of the vast corpus of documentation covering virtually the entire range of the Jewish European experience is a loss that cannot be reconstituted with the same facility with which buildings can be reconstructed. The Jews were a substantial cultural and industrial factor of Central European civilization, but the masses of documents which define that history, which demarcate Jewish identity and record Jewish accomplishments, were consumed in the flames of that secondary holocaust. Libraries of literature were reduced to ashes; a vast corpus of information regarding the Jewish contribution to art, science, and culture, worldwide in scope, disappeared.

In addition to the wholesale destruction of archival material by the Nazis, the owners and managers of tens of thousands of businesses and institutions that owed their origin or development to Jewish inspiration strove to avoid detection and desecration and themselves destroyed all traces of Jewish origin or involvement. The initiation and development of such entities cannot now be accredited to their actual initiators or animators; names were changed, conversions effected, associations obscured; the understandable need to avoid detection by Nazi persecutors resulted in a massive, indiscriminate disposal of the primary evidence with which history is redacted.

We must also take account of the loss of the cumulative memory and knowledge of six million people, a cultural treasure that descended through many generations of experiences in many lands; of the loss of tens of thousands of scholars and historians among the millions, researchers whose countless years of research are now irretrievably lost. Personal correspondence, so often the means by which the work and lives of scholars and of a people can be traced and evaluated, are gone; only wisps remain to attest to the manner in which millions of Jews wove their way through the Diaspora. The cumulative loss is both ethnic and universal, for both provinces are plainly interdependent.

Yet the twentieth-century Nazi Holocaust of four years' duration is merely the latest and not the most momentous of the recurrent devastations that have plagued the Jews for three thousand years; it is the simplest to evaluate and the gaps created are relatively easy to discern, for they do not surpass living memory. The pseudo-Marxists of the mid-twentieth century, making a travesty of the scientific formulations of Marx and Engels, rewrote history, created a new orthodoxy to bolster their bureaucracies, and employed such terms as "counterrevolutionary" as metaphors for heresy. Still, because open societies exist, because modern communication limits secrecy, and because the perversions of the modern megalomaniacs took place over a relatively short historical period, contemporary oligarchies have not wrought nearly as much historiographical havoc as took place cumulatively over two millennia under the Byzantines, the Crusaders, the Inquisition, the Counter-Reformation, and the later numerous and recurrent anti-Judaic despoliations of the Christian Era. For another millennium before the time of Christian despoliation, the historiographical havoc wrought by the Romans, Hellenes, Egyptians, Babylonians, Assyrians, and others, each in their turn, must also be accounted for in rendering a reconstruction of the history of the human experience.

Although the mass extermination of a people was not at the core of professed church policy, the extermination of a religion and a culture was patently its purpose, and the revision of history in its own image was manifestly its intention. In that latter effort the church achieved great success, for the obfuscation became worldwide in scope and continued for centuries instead of being brought to a swift end as were the Nazi perversions. Our histories are still focused on the image the church chose to present and are limited by the facts it allowed to endure. Western history is still viewed through the befogging screen of Christian literature; Western art is still dominated by the cathedrals and basilicas, many of which were built over the ruins of pagan or Jewish temples, and by the products, paintings, and sculpture produced under Christian patronage. We are left largely and blithely ignorant of the rest of a world that hosted so many great civilizations and cultures.

The Jews are presented in that Christian cosmorama as reappearing on the scene out of nowhere in the Middle Ages as usurious bankers and other unsavory characters, with little history behind them. This negative image insinuates its way through contemporary literature and, adjoined to the depiction of the Jews of an earlier time as Christ-killers, is at the heart of a continuing anti-Semitic rationale. A glance at a few raw facts, however, makes manifest the extent of the distortion by which Jewish life is depicted and of the gross deletion of the Jewish contribution to the technological evolution of civilization.

At the height of Roman hegemony over the Western world, when the empire ranged from England to the Euphrates, the total population of the Roman Empire was some fifty-five million, of which up to seven million were Jews, amounting to twelve percent or so of the entire subject population of the empire. Another million or more Jews lived outside the Roman provinces, in Mesopotamia and Central Asia. The Jews were not located in the hinterlands but concentrated at ports and productive urban centers, where they formed an even larger proportion of the population and were the driving heart of each region's mercantile and industrial force. They were, in addition, the only people who were literate *as a people*. In spite of decimation and conversion, the Jews never numbered fewer than three million, even during their darkest days. What were these millions of displaced peoples doing during the twenty centuries of the Common Era?

Jewish slaves built the Colosseum of Rome and mined the iron and copper of Sicily and the gold and silver of Spain. Jewish artisans introduced silk agronomy and industry to the West; they were smiths and dyers and weavers and tanners and shoemakers and tailors and loggers and wagoners; they minted coins for European nobility; they were merchants at the local markets; they formed the core of international trade, inasmuch as they were uniquely able to issue a letter of credit in one country and be assured of its being honored in another country months and even years later. They were doctors and accountants; they were counselors to kings. Yes, they were also money changers and bankers, occupations whose transactions were recorded and preserved, for taxes had to be paid and their business often involved the finances of the various states. The Jews who were involved in financial activity thereby became far more visible than did the millions of Jews engaged in the other mundane activities, of which records are sparse and indeterminate. Many Jews reverted to financial activities only after being proscribed from owning land and driven from a variety of trades, many of which they had introduced and developed into viable industries.

Glassmaking was one of those industries; it serves as a good example of an art and industry in which Jews were the prime factors over three millennia and for which they have been denied credit. For many years I was associated with the art of glassmaking as a marketing consultant for various Muranese glassmakers. No one associated with the art can be unaffected by it. The drama of vitric production enthralls the observer; the magical transformation of stony silicates into an ethereal material is a spectacular process, and the transformation of that material into delicate artifacts by the artistic tour de force of the masters of the art is an intriguing, even awe-inspiring event. The consummate skill with which the masters gather the yellow-hot *metal* from white-hot crucibles, the deftness with which the glowing viscous material is manipulated with the crudest of tools into exquisite works of art, captivate all attendant to the process. It is an art with which one truly falls in love; nor does the effect of the fascination ever diminish; it becomes a part of one's psyche, an enchantment to which all who have been associated with the art will willingly testify.

The process of vitrification is remarkable in that it was invented only once in all of human history; the knowledge of that process wound its way out into the world in ever-widening spirals with the people who developed it and passed their knowledge on to succeeding generations. Glassmaking is unique among the arts in this respect. Lithic craftsmanship, pottery-making, weaving, metal-smithing, basketry, and, in fact, every other art spawns independently within all human populations and defines the cultures of the divers groups of people that compose humanity. These arts were common to every culture within which they ineluctably grew in sophistication, and in a predictable evolutionary process. Cultures are measured on the time scale along which these arts evolve; the degree of cultural development is set according to the point those arts attained along that scale. The art of glassmaking is missing among these measures; its appearance among various cultures occurred at times irrespective of, and often at odds with, the magnitude of the maturity of the cultures in which it appeared.

The art of glassmaking is of a most advanced order; it involves an Iron Age pyrotechnology, the ultimate stage of technology to which human society attained until the advent of the industrial revolution. Glassmaking requires an even more sophisticated pyrotechnology than does the smelting of iron from its ore, and a chemical knowledge far beyond that requisite for mere iron-making. Well-intentioned scholars, ignoring these requisites, were drawn into a morass of misinterpretation, and until recently, placed the advent of the art of glassmaking everywhere but where it did in fact originate. Both iron-smelting and glassmaking were, in fact, being practiced in one remote corner of the world a thousand years before the twelfth century B.C.E., at which time the archaeologists officially assign the advent of the Iron Age.

The art of glassmaking came into being in ancient Akkadia during the latter part of the third millennium B.C.E. The art was associated with the progenitors of the Jewish people, a people who derived in great measure from that Mesopotamian milieu; the spread of the art into both the Eastern and Western worlds may be attributed in no small measure to that ancient association. The path of the dissemination of the art is peculiarly parallel to the dispersion of the Jews. There are yawning gaps in the histories of both the art and the people, yet it seems that wherever relevant facts emerge, that art and that people merge. I learned, to my great astonishment, that glassmaking was considered a "Jewish trade" from ancient times well into the present era. Unusual enticements were proffered to glassmakers to encourage their immigration into various realms, for it was a secret trade, and only the Semitic migrants were privy to its secrets. It was none other than St. Jerome who reported that glassmaking was one of the trades with which the Semites had "captured the Roman world"! When the two histories are placed side by side, a parallel pattern appears in which the association between the people and the art becomes plainly apparent.

The English historian W. A. Thorpe tries to be fair when he notes in his book *English Glass* that the artisans who had settled along the route of the Roman legions

> combined a willingness to migrate, a fervent sense of parenthood, a racial solidarity, a genius for selling, semitic qualities that no other glassmakers ever possessed. . . . Their activities were not confined to the black-coat business of bankers, shipowners, money-lenders, and wholesale produce merchants. They were leaders in the professions of law and medicine and in the arts of jeweler, goldsmith and silversmith.[1]

Glassmaking was only one of the manifestations of the pyrotechnical skills and knowledge of the Jews; metallurgy was the main facet of the pyrotechnology that emerged from Mesopotamian origins to transform the civilized world. Thorpe notes that the European glassmaking industry grew steadily in artistry and application until the decline of the glassmaking art, and of others introduced into Gaul by the Semites, was brought about by "the growth of anti-semitism in Merovingen Gaul during the 5th and 6th centuries. . . . High class models disappear when anti-semitic propaganda was most intense."[2]

Thus did the Dark Ages descend upon Europe. It was an oft-repeated story. Kings often implored the Jews to emigrate into their countries, offering extraordinary enticements to gain the benefits of the skills, knowledge, and literacy possessed by the Jews and lacked by those countries. Just as often the Jews were discarded, or worse, when disposal of the Jews served the ruler's purposes, or when the Jews, unbudgeable from their democratic and religious precepts, were considered a threat to authority or to rival religions. The disposal of the Jews did not suffice to satisfy the purposes of the dominant powers; the record of the substantial contribution the Jews made to the technological evolution of civilization, and with it the record of the very existence of the Jews, had to be obliterated and denied.

The historical sciences, notwithstanding pretensions to objectivity, are plagued by national, religious, and cultural strictures, infused into them by generations of subjective scholarship. Mindless parroting has transformed a mighty mass of mythology into Western-oriented, so-called classical history in which prejudiced, unipolar renditions of past events and of biographies of dominant personalities were persistently passed on uncritically to scholars and students. Recent research has produced masses of data which indicate that cultures which have long been regarded as the originators of civilization were in fact its inheritors. A problem arises as soon as classicist constructions are shown to be deficient and shot full of falsities. The classicophiles in general, and their subsidiaries the Egyptophiles, Graecophiles, and Romanophiles in particular, scholars who have passionately devoted their lives to extolling those cultures, are engaged in stubborn defense of their beleaguered domains against the mounting wave of new evidence of a world beyond their world. These echoists strain mightily to maintain a scholarly stance, become increasingly inbred, and tend to exclude the world around their world. Unhappily, they are entrenched in their fields by dint of their long and unchallenged dominance in them, and to dispute their tenets often proves pointless and, too often, academically perilous. The balance of the scale of research remains heavily weighted with dissertations on every fold in the fabric of Hellenistic sculpture and every nuance of every word in Greek and Roman rhetoric, as though the rest of the world existed only in terms of the minutiae thus examined. The archaeological community still stands agog at the mastabas and monuments of Egypt, blind to the meaning of the inscriptions emblazoned on the great pylons guarding the temples, boastful testaments that blithely attribute their construction and decoration to slaves and foreigners and list in great detail the hoards of artifacts wrested from Egypt's neighbors, most of which the Egyptians were incapable of producing.

The myth of Egyptian creativity was given great impetus as a result of the plundering of Egyptian temples and tombs, a process that gained impetus with the pillage of Egypt by Napoleon. Christians viewed the pagan artifacts with unmitigated reverence, rarely giving a thought to the fact that the Warrior Pharaohs had plundered much of this wealth from their Eastern neighbors, had received another portion from the East in tribute or taxes, and had enslaved or indentured Eastern artisans to produce the rest. It was hardly considered that the presence of the rich panoply of art and architecture preserved in an Egyptian environment no more made its creators Egyptian than its presence in European museums made its creators European.

The myth of the seminality and superiority of Greek civilization was magnified by Heinrich Schliemann, the German archaeologist who unearthed Troy and fantasied that the Greeks were blue-eyed, flaxen-haired descendants of valiant Nordic adventurers whose genius had inspired Western civilization. Western adoration of this fabulous image persists in the depictions of the Greeks, in which the black-haired, dark-eyed Asiatic Greeks are duly bleached, and in the concoction of an "Indo-European" culture which purportedly spawned European civilization, thereby bypassing the Semitic centers of ancient civilization altogether.

Aegean civilization was spawned on the island of Crete, not on the European continent. It resulted in the first place from several incursions of barbarians (termed "Achaeans" by Homer and "Mycenaeans" by archaeologists), who invaded the Aegean peninsula, subjected the indigenous populations over a period of a half-millennium, and descended upon Crete around 1600 B.C.E. The Cretan civilization (dubbed "Minoan" by Sir Arthur Evans, the British archaeologist, after their first king, Monos), was distinctly Semitic at the time, resulting from recurrent settlements of peoples speaking a Northwest Semitic dialect on the island from about 4000 B.C.E. forward. It was on Crete that the Mycenaeans first encountered a literate culture and began to develop a written language of their own. The disappearance of the Mycenaeans created a gap of four centuries in which literacy disappeared from the Aegean.

It was contact with the literate Semites thereafter, in Anatolia, Canaan, and Mesopotamia, that was responsible in large measure for the development of "Greek" civilization.

One of the greatest creative leaps civilized man ever took was to conceive a universe created by a single pervasive force. The revolutionary concept placed the Jews in contraposition to every ancient society but their own; the rejection of the divinity of idols and of rulers set the Jews apart from the precepts of the societies within which they were tolerated, and in conflict with those which felt threatened by the idea that no man-made institution was divinely inspired nor was entitled to divine rights. The roots of rationalism lay in this revolutionary perception of the way the world works, and it was from this source that the Greek philosophers drew their sustenance. Creativity is man's highest attribute, the ultimate exercise of free expression, and because it counters conformity it is anathematic to authoritarianism. The Jews obstinately held to their principles in the eras of paganism and of Christian expansion, and suffered no less thereby. The concept which accords to every individual a personal relationship with the universal spirit of God, which denies that any human has special access to that spirit or can act as an intermediary between any other human being and God, precluded the Jews from accepting the divine authority of any regime. They could not accede to laws that legitimized the arrogation of divine rights by a ruler or a priest or a church. They were in a constant state of philosophical rebellion against the imposition of such constricting concepts upon their own community.

The rebellion against authoritarianism freed the Jews from conformity and placed them in the forefront of humanism. Universal literacy, added to nonconformity, fostered creative expression throughout the Jewish community. Language is a repository of culture; the Jews shared a common language, and their shared culture was enriched by the knowledge absorbed from each of the cultures in which they were immersed. The languages of the Jews and of their progenitors of ancient times, Akkadian and Aramaic, were the instruments of international intercourse of Near Eastern civilizations for some two thousand years; Hebrew became the lingua franca for the Jews within Western civilizations for an additional two thousand years. The Jews were uniquely intercommunicative throughout the Diaspora. The dispersion of the Jews was both a boon and a bane; their nation was disjoined, but their culture was enormously enhanced. Whereas a unique omneitic outlook set the Jews apart from other peoples, a common language, literacy, and learning bound the disparate Jewish communities together and provided a firm foundation for further creativity. The exercise of this multifaceted creative propensity redounded to benefit not only the societies that harbored the Jews, but all of humankind. Jewish creativity was not restricted to the written word. The Jews reverenced work; as slaves and as freemen, as subjects within their own boundaries, and as transients within the boundaries of other nations they performed the basic functions without which civilization would be a shell without substance.

Literacy and learning were always synonymous Jewish experiences; the synagogue was the center through which these requisites for the continuity of knowledge were inclusively transmitted to the members of each successive generation. The accumulated wisdom and knowledge of all humanity was thus made accessible to the whole Jewish community. Literacy accelerated the organization of civilization, an impetus amplified by a pyrotechnological revolution that propelled mankind from the Bronze into the Iron Age.

The Latins followed in the wake of the Greeks and attained refinement largely from the rape of the East and the consequent absorption of Eastern culture and technology. Roman civilization was founded on the base of an Etruscan civilization which had arrived from the East; it was given impetus by the conquest of the Canaanites (the so-called Phoenicians or Punic people), by the assimilation of Greek culture, and soared to its zenith with the occupation of Judah and the conquest of a portion of Mesopotamia. The story of the Latin metabolization of Eastern culture comes down to us almost entirely from the Roman viewpoint, in a fabulous form which the West has happily hailed as its own.

The subsequent period of Western historiography is befogged by blatantly biased Byzantine and other Christian literature and documentation. As Christian hierarchies gained hegemony over peoples and territories they systematically obliterated the vestiges of these "alien" or "barbaric" cultures wherever and whenever possible. The zeal with which parochial Christians eradicated diverse religions, cultures, and ideologies wherever the cross was implanted, the vigor with which they destroyed evidence which was at variance with their tenets or which disturbed their historical perspective, was extended across the Old and into the New World. The records of American Indian civilizations, written in languages still vibrantly alive until a mere few centuries ago, were obliterated so completely that the surviving remnants are now less comprehensible than those written in languages that passed from use many millennia ago. From the Arctic to the islands of the South Seas and from the ancient and seminal civilizations of the Near and Far East to the Stone Age peoples of the jungles of the Amazon, the Christians performed unprecedented excisions and abridgements of history in which the record of cultures at every level of civilization were reduced to rare relics or irretrievably erased.

A realistic representation of the rise of civilization is thus handicapped by a dearth of documentation that was brought about not simply by the erosion of evidence by indiscriminate natural forces but, far more significantly, by the destruction of evidence by human agencies whose actions were deliberate and selective. The attempt to accurately reconstruct history suffers not merely from the expunging of factual evidence but also from the fabrication of false evidence by those whose interest it was to obfuscate the truth. Natural erosive forces merely leave gaps to be bridged, but self-aggrandizing human institutions substitute an artificial reality for each hiatus they create. The obfuscation has become entrenched, nurtured zealously by contemporary institutions whose legitimacy hangs on hierarchical interpretations and fabrications. The deliberate destruction that engendered the dearth of disparate evidence is conventionally ignored, whereas substituted spurious constructions have become fixed as historiographical fact.

The record of the human experience, aside from being subjected to distortion and deletion by those who control the media of communication, is also ground away by natural forces that do so erratically and randomly. Historiography is constructed largely on what was preserved and not on what existed. It is more subjective than archaeology, and because ancient historiography is constructed on the shifting sands of archaeology it is even more subject to distortion and is far more suspect. Science seeks to separate theory from theosophy, facts from philosophy; to balance self-interest against prejudice; to recognize where self-aggrandizement has led to lies, rationalization, or justification of unjust or iniquitous behavior. Something approaching scientific objectivity has only recently been applied to archaeology; it has hardly affected historiography. Which interpretation of history can we accept, the communist or the capitalist? The South African white or black? Shall we blithely accept the version of history rendered in the documents of the Inquisition, or interpolate them for the silent one of its victims?

Redacted history is, after all, merely a reflection of a perception of reality; it is, like beauty, that which exists in the eye of the beholder.

There is another lacuna that cries out to be accounted for, the absent record of the activity of the multitudes who were not to be found at the apex of power. Historians, ancient and modern alike, have devoted themselves to the plotting and planning of men and nations to obtain and maintain power, of royal fratricide and matricide and of wars and mass destruction, of towns razed and plunder taken, of dynasties created and dynasties displaced. These tales have heretofore been hailed by historians as the whole of history and promulgated as progressive stages of the development of civilization. Scarcely a glance was cast at the farmer, the artisan, and the merchant. They were treated as inconsequential figures in the background, not as the molders of civilization. They sculpted the statues that delight museums; they built palaces and temples and filled them with artifacts of gold and silver and lapis lazuli and glass; they grew food and wove cloth and fired forges; in the myopic overview of classical history, the relevance of these lowly people ceased with those accomplishments.

The Jews became literate as a people. Literacy accelerated the organization of civilization, an impetus that was amplified by a pyrotechnological revolution that propelled mankind from the Bronze into the Iron Age. The progenitors of the Jews, the Akkadians, were at the focus of this revolution; pneumatically drafted furnaces, the basic tools required for the smelting of iron from its ores, were introduced into Akkadia from the Ararat mountains during the mid-third millennium B.C.E. and employed for the esoteric art of manufacturing glass. For almost a millennium these disciplines were practiced exclusively in the Mesopotamian milieu, from which region they spread into the world at large with the migration of its peoples. The Iron Age was launched at the end of the thirteenth century B.C.E. at the time and in the area of the settlement of the Israelites in the hills of Canaan. The practice of iron-making spread quickly throughout the world, and was given an additional impetus in Europe when the Romans tore thousands of young men from *Eretz Yisrael*, the Land of Israel, to work the mines and forges of Sicily and Spain.

Archaeologists and historians, however little and late, are creditably learning to lift the cover of the self-serving tales of ambitious conquerors and despotic rulers whose chief concern was to justify the acquisition and the maintenance of power. They are learning to look beneath the megalomaniac veneer that these tales, layered with falsity, cast over the other history, the story of the growth of human understanding and use of nature's forces to elevate humanity from nature's slave to its master. They are learning to recognize that it is the muted history of human creativity that delineates the evolution of human society and civilization; that history should properly reflect the unfolding of the drama of the conquering of nature, not consist primarily of the personal stories of predators conquering their neighbors; that history should proudly feature the progressive use of the forces of the universe for construction, not abjectly recapitulate the vainglorious tales of regressive destruction; that history should celebrate the successful struggles for mutual survival and not be a reflection of the glorification of slaughter and domination; that history should properly be a record of progress brought about by human cooperation notwithstanding the disruptions caused by inhuman conflict.

Happily, the light of fuller understanding is cracking through the ancient walls, and we are beginning to perceive the countryside beyond the citadels. Archaeology has made significant advances in the last few years in this respect. The avid search for golden vessels and grandiose statues has given way in some measure to an examination of the ephemeral evidence of villages, to an attempt at reconstructing the activity of the artisans, of tracing commerce and of illuminating all the nitty-gritty of ancient daily life; historians are beginning to examine society at its roots, to seek relevance among the people who performed the creative functions of existence rather than to devote undue attention to the largely destructive affairs and ambitions of the predators.

All subjected or vanquished peoples have suffered the indignity of having the record of their contributions to civilization expunged, notably among them the Jews, who have been the perennial underdogs throughout their sojourn in the Diaspora, which is to say within every highly developed society and nation through a period of three millennia. The Jews were integral to this hitherto hidden history. The Jews have fared more fortunately in one respect than other peoples: they were literate and somehow managed to salvage their holy scriptures; thereby they preserved a critical portion of their history each time they eluded annihilation. They remained a universally literate people and so, even though Jewish literature fed the fires of ignorance again and yet again, some of the corpus of literature written by Jews survived in Greek, Latin, Arabic, and in all of the modern Western languages.

This book is frankly and consciously written from the protagonistic position of one who seeks to reassess history as it applies to the Jews, to redress distortion, to refill the voids in the substantial and significant contribution the Jews have made to Western civilization and to the world. It makes no pretense of presenting a comprehensive rendition of history but merely seeks to span particular gaps that pertain to the Jews; those gaps are considerable, enough to fill many more such volumes.

The thrust of the thesis being herein presented is to unshroud the extraordinary accomplishments of the Jews and to put into proper perspective the vast contribution the Jews have made to the technological evolution of civilization. Literacy, a learned trait, is ascribed as the reason for the extraordinary accomplishments of the Jews as a culture and a nation. Their current disproportionately prominent role in science, literature, and the arts is indisputable, albeit insufficiently appreciated even in our "enlightened" age. The Jews were, moreover, consistently literate as a people throughout the ages, and literacy was the medium through which they spurred the Western world into the Rational Age. As they taught themselves, so they taught others.

There is no doubt that the same effort should be applied to the case histories of all peoples who have suffered oppression. In the search for their roots, many people have discovered how unjustly history is written, how peoples meriting recognition have been relegated to the dustheap of history, the greatest indignity of all. Science itself has suffered in the process, for truth, the greatest leveler, is also the most effective ladder to the future.

Therein lies our story.

1

Jewish Beginnings

Urbanites and Artisans

The tribe of Abraham is popularly categorized as nomadic. This portrayal is maintained out of ignorance or as a demeaning and obscurantist image, even though such a representation has long since been shown to be false. Neither biblical representations, archaeological recoveries, ethnological research, nor documentary evidence supports the image so blithely repeated, widely disseminated, and commonly believed. The Jews stemmed from a civilization that had first domesticated wild grains; a civilization that had first made use of the wheel; a civilization that had first passed from the age of copper and stone into the age of bronze; a civilization in which the secrets of the sophisticated art of glassmaking were discovered and whose descendant peoples remained exclusively privy to that knowledge for thousands of years. The ancient Jews were the heirs of many millennia of technological development, and they became the carriers of that ancient culture into the world at large.

The seminal civilizations within which the Jewish nation evolved were ravaged time and time again by Egyptian, Persian, Hellenic, Roman, and sundry other barbarians, the pirates and warlords of antiquity who sought loot and slaves and power. Until recently, historians gave little weight to the fact that the citadels from which these conquerors ruled were generally engineered and built by war-won slaves or indentured workers, and that the cultures the barbarians thereafter manifested were absorbed, as often as not, from the peoples they conquered. Historians hardly deigned to discount the self-serving renditions of events left to posterity by the conquerers. Thus a "classical" ancient history was created, which congealed into orthodox historiographical lore, composed as much of mythology as it was of demonstrable fact.

THE NOMADIC MYTH

Recent discoveries of civilizations older than, and often underlying, those of the "classical" era have roiled the placid surface of scholarly conformity. Revelation after revelation has erupted in proof of the profundity and antiquity of the urban civilization shared by the so-called "Semitic" peoples. Classicists who berated the early archaeologists for bibliophilic bias were obliged to beat a retreat time and time again. That is not to say that the Bible must necessarily be accepted as either the ultimate or only source of fact, nor even to insist that it be taken as ever accurate; it is only to note that the hard-core classicists are as canonically rigid as the most doctrinal of religious fundamentalists.

Near Eastern archaeology has come full cycle since the period when the discipline was pursued largely by Protestant researchers digging with a shovel in one hand and a Bible in the other. The discipline thereafter passed through a period of rigid rationalist skepticism which denied the historicity of the Bible altogether; it has arrived at a time when modern scientific methods have confirmed so much of what was recorded in that remarkable text that it is again employed as a guide and as a largely reliable testament. Both literal acceptance and outright repudiation are being replaced by a recognition of its intrinsic historical value as the most complete and accurate rendition of the events covered, albeit subject to error and verification. The variant theories of a fresh generation of secularly scientific archaeologists converge in one respect: the image of the Jews as having issued from the desert with a few scraggly goats is patently at odds with the emerging facts.

Norman Gottwald reviewed the ethnological and ecological evidence of the past few decades and concluded that the characterization of the ancient Jewish tribes as nomads is grossly misleading inasmuch as the word evokes the image of present-day bedouins. Gottwald declared that this evidence "makes it utterly impossible to retain . . . the model of an early Israel as pastoral nomads who inhabited the desert and the steppe prior to their entry into Canaan."[1] In any event, life on the desert was patently impossible during the time of Abraham, inasmuch as the camel, the beast that made such life possible, had not yet been domesticated at that early date. Where, then, does the persistent characterization of the patriarchal progenitors of the Jews as desert-dwelling bedouins spring from?

THE OLDEST TESTIMONY

Let us begin with an examination of the oldest testimony extant on the subject, including that of the Bible itself. We are astounded to discover that the concept that depicts the early Hebrews as nomadic invaders of Canaan from the desert cannot be educed from biblical lore; it is contravened at the outset of Genesis and at every successive stage of the unfolding account. Even before mankind was exiled from idyllic Eden, people were engaged in sedentary occupations. We are informed in Genesis 4:2 that "Abel was a keeper of sheep, but Cain was a tiller of the ground."

Husbandry and agronomy are thus registered as the occupations of the earliest of the progenitors of the Hebrews. The transformation from a rural to an urban society occurs almost immediately, for it seems that Cain, the farmer, was not content to remain a vagabond after his exile "from the presence of the Lord." Indeed, as soon as his son Enoch was born, he founded a city (Genesis 4:17): "And Cain knew his wife; and she conceived, and bare Enoch: and he builded a city and called the name of the city, after the name of his son, Enoch."

The sole allusion to nomadism in all of the book of Genesis consists of an aside (4:20), in which Jabal is designated the "father of such as live in tents." That way of life is specified as a generality and is deferred to an unstated future, while in the same sentence emphasis is placed on the fact that Jabal was also the father "of such as have cattle." Thus nomadism is decisively counterbalanced and sharply distinguished from husbandry. Pastoralism and nomadism are, after all, not equivalent (can we classify Texas ranchers as desert nomads?). Whereas seasonal movement is associated with the pasturing of animals, tribes like that of Abraham were settled into permanent communities engaged in husbandry, agronomy, and crafts.

No further mention of "those that live in tents" occurs for well over twenty generations; furthermore, the characterization is pointedly applied not to the Jews but to their enemies. The peripheral reference to a future group of nomadic people in Genesis is immediately superseded by an emphasis on arts and crafts, which are specifically and solidly introduced into the fabric of the earliest Hebraic society. We are first introduced to Jabal's brother Jubal (Genesis 4:21) who "was the father of all such as handle the harp and organ." Music is thus the first of the arts introduced into human society and is assigned an important position immediately after agronomy and husbandry. Significantly, the instruments cited are the harp and the organ, specialized instruments peculiar to an urban society. Such instruments would likely be encountered, if not within a temple or a palace, at least within a well-ordered and substantial house. A desert environment is one in which we are more likely to come across the simple pastoral reed pipe, played for the lonely shepherd's amusement and gratification.[2]

The organ mentioned at the outset of Genesis represents, in fact, a most remarkable ancient instrument; its existence makes manifest the musical propensity and technological sophistication of the progenitors of the Jews.[3] Two mechanical versions of the organ are detailed in the Tamid and the Arakin tractates, both called the *magrephah,* which is described as being "plainly a pneumatic pipe-organ worked by twin bellows, a prototype of the kind used today. It was contained within a box, ten reed-pipes with ten holes each; some were long and thick, others short and thin."[4]

Industry immediately follows art in the very same sentence in which the harp and *magrephah* are being introduced. "And Zillah," the narrator continues, "she also bare Tubal-Cain, an instructor of every artificer in brass and iron." The literal translations of the name Tubal-Cain and the designations "instructor" and "artificer" are of a deeper significance than appears from the simple English translation given above; the original Hebrew words carry connotations of "refinement" or "sophistication."[5] The term "instructor" is also generally employed in place of the literal translation of the Hebrew term for "sharpener of tools" (of copper, brass, or iron).

Profound lessons can be gleaned from the few sentences that reflect the earliest remembrances of Hebraic society and culture. Farming requires storage and tools, and consequently sedentary life and industry. Cain's occupation represents the first of these basic facets of civilization, plant domestication. The trade of his immediate descendant, Tubal-Cain, metal toolmaking, takes agriculture to its conclusion: simple Stone Age agronomy inevitably transforms into Metal Age urbanism and industrialization. The secondary connotation of Tubal-Cain's occupation, in which he assumes the role of teacher, follows inexorably from his artisanship, and the passing on of skills acquired, which include not only the ability to shape tools but the knowledge of where to obtain, and how to smelt and forge, the required metals; thus such subjective cultural attributes as a knowledge of geology, pyrotechnology, and mathematics are implicit in the few words with which Tubal-Cain is presented. A better or more concise definition of a sedentary society, that is, of civilization, than that biblically presented in a few rich words can hardly be imagined.

The earliest recorded reference to the profession of blacksmith found to date appears in a text recovered from the time of the reign of the Assyrian king Ninurta-tukulti-Assur, dated about 1132 B.C.E. This knowledge is reflected biblically; in fact, one of the prime attributes of the promised land is listed by God himself to Moses as an inducement to observe His commandments: "For the Lord thy God bringeth thee into a good land, a land of brooks of water, of fountains and depths that spring out of valleys and hills . . . a land wherein thou shalt eat bread without scarceness, thou shalt not lack any thing in it; a land whose stones are iron and out of whose hills thou mayest dig brass" (Deuteronomy 8:7-9).

We learn from the biblical description of the process of iron-smithing that some of the Hebrews employed their skills for the production of iron idols: "The blacksmith works on it over the fire and beats it into shape with a hammer. He works on it with his strong arm till he is hungry and tired; drinking no water, he is exhausted" (Isaiah 44:12). The same familiarity is projected in Ecclesiastes 38:19-31 in which a description of the art is rendered with a gush of poetic imagery:

So it is with the blacksmith sitting by his anvil:
he considers what to do with his iron bloom.
The breath of fire scorches his skin,
as he contends with the heat of the furnace;
he batters his ear with the din of the hammer,
his eyes are fixed on the pattern;
he sets his heart on completing his work,
and stays up putting his finishing touches.[6]

The biblical account of the growth of urban civilization continues without circumscription. When the moral structure of the civilized world went awry and incurred God's bitter retribution, the good Noah and his family were selected to carry on His work by reinstituting husbandry and agronomy as soon as they had regained terra firma, where "Noah began to be an husbandman, and he planted a vineyard" (Genesis 9:20). And got drunk! One may be forgiven for noting that Noah had just concluded a successful career as a shipwright. In fact, the family of Noah must have included highly skilled artisans to have so perfectly executed God's meticulous instructions for the construction of a vessel capable of carrying pairs of all of God's faunal creation, as well as the food to sustain them all for forty days.

In Genesis 10, nations are spawned, separated, and differentiated by the creation of a babel of languages, during which time Nimrod, "a mighty hunter before the Lord," constructed a complex of cities and created a kingdom. "And the beginning of his kingdom was Babel and Erech and Akkad and Calneh, in the land of Shinar. Out of that land went forth Asshur and built Nineveh, and the city Rehoboth, and Calah" (Genesis 10, 11). The first empires were thus brought into being and urban civilization, until then confined to Akkadia ("the Land of Shinar"), began to be established throughout the world.

The biblical text proceeds to detail the development of other national entities such as Mizraim (Egypt) and Canaan and forthwith (Genesis 11:2-4), returns to Shem, whose name became the eponym of the coined term "Semites." Shem's sons "found a plain in the land of Shinar; and they dwelt there. And they said to one another, 'Go to, let us make brick, and burn them thoroughly.' And they had brick for stone, and slime had they for mortar. And they said, 'Go to, let us build a city and a tower, whose top may reach into heaven.'"

Thus, according to the Bible, the descendants of Shem, the so-called Semites, not only built sturdy structures of mortar and brick in Ur, not only did they erect an entire city which became the capital of Shinar, not only did they construct a skyscraping ziggurat, but it is thereafter recorded that they remained resident in that metropolis for nine more generations: Shem–Arphaxad–Salah–Eber–Peleg–Reu–Serug–Nahor–Terach. Thus in the city of Ur we encounter the father of Abraham, Terach, patriarch of the tribe.

ABRAHAM AND ISAAC

In this context the Jewish progenitors appear upon the proscenium of biblical history. After pausing to express our astonishment at the remarkable record of an account covering a period that must be expressed in millennia by a people who had none of the advantages of modern scientific research, no university libraries to draw from, no points of reference aside from their own tribal memory, we turn to the next question. Was the patriarch Abraham ever biblically depicted as a bedouin?

Although no physical evidence of the existence of Abraham has yet been found, there is little reason to doubt his existence. Biblical history has been substantiated in large measure from his time forward, and discounted only minimally. We are in the swing of the cycle from the iconoclastic stage of the Age of Reason, when the Bible was altogether dismissed as a true reflection of historical events, past the enthusiasm of that remarkable archaeologist Sir Leonard Woolley, who, when unearthing the ancient city of Ur, came upon evidence of a great flood, and assumed he had discovered evidence of The Flood. A number of documentary references indicate that the biblical Abraham was, in fact, something more than a mere composite memory; references that intimate the existence of an actual person.

We encounter the name of Abraham in a listing by the Egyptian king Sheshonk, the founder of the Twenty-second Dynasty (referred to as Sheshak in 1 Kings 14:25), who invaded Judea in the fifth year of Rehobeam of Judah. Sheshonk memorialized his conquest in the characteristic pharaonic manner by having his version of the events inscribed in bold relief on the wall of the temple of Karnak: tiers of bound Asiatic captives, largely Israelites, are being conducted into slavery by the god Amun who represents the pharaoh himself. Beneath the head and shoulder of each captive an oval inscription bears the captive's name, or the name of his "nation." Included are a series of biblical names: Rabbith, Taanach, Shunem, Beth-shean, Rehob, Hapharaim, Gibeon, Beth-horon, Ajalon, Megiddo, Socoh, and Arad.[7] The dean of Egyptian archaeologists, James Henry Breasted, in his monumental book *A History of Egypt,* notes that among the towns, "Sheshonk records as being taken by him is a place hitherto unnoticed called *'The Field of Abram'* in which we find the earliest occurrence of the name of Israel's eponymous hero."[8]

Josephus quotes from Nicolaus, a noteworthy historian charged with the education of the children of Anthony and Cleopatra, of King Herod, and of Herod's counselors:

> Abram reigned at Damascus, being a foreigner who came with an army out of the land above Babylon, called the land of the Chaldeans. But after a long time he got him up, and went into the land then called the land of Canaan, and this when his posterity werte become a multitude . . . and when his posterity had become a multitude. . . . Now the name of Abram is still famous in our land of Damascus; and there is a village named after him, "The Habitation of Abram."[9]

"The Habitation of Abram," attested to by Nicolaus as still existing in his time, and the "field" referred to by Breasted could not refer to the same place, for the pharaoh's armies did not penetrate as far as Damascus. Both places, however, lie along the route Abraham and his entourage purportedly traveled, and designate places where it is stipulated that they stayed. The tradition to which Josephus refers, concerning Abram's reign at "Damascus," still persists throughout the area. Jack Finegan points out that the modern inhabitants of towns near Harran, and particularly at Urfa and Ain el-Khalil, look upon Abraham as a saint and relate many legends about him.[10]

These are not the only ancient references to a physical relic relating to Abraham and his family. Josephus refers to a still extant monument to Abraham's brother,

Harran, "who died among the Chaldeans, in a city of the Chaldeans, called Ur; and his monument is shown to this day."[11]

It should be noted that not only were ancient non-Hebraic historians certain of Abraham's existence but that they had a reverent regard for his intellectual achievements and for the quality of his leadership. Josephus offers us the testimony of Berosus, a Babylonian priest and historian of Bel (281/80-262/61 B.C.E.) who dedicated his work to Antiochus I, and during whose reign Berosus wrote into his history regarding Abraham that "In the tenth generation after the flood, there was among the Chaldeans a man righteous and great, and skillful in the celestial science."[12]

The variance of these statements from the biblical rendition suggests that Berosus and Nicolaus had additional historical material to draw from that contained definitive information about Abraham. It is evident from other references as well that a considerable corpus of material was available during that early period that contained references to Abraham, material which has been lost to us. Josephus refers to Hecateus, a prolific writer dated somewhat earlier than Berosus: "But Hecateus does more than merely mention him [Abraham]; for he composed a book concerning him." Hecateus lived at the time of Alexander the Great and of Ptolemy I; he came from Abdera, and, if we can take Josephus's word for it, he had sufficient material about Abraham to devote an entire book to the Jewish patriarch. Josephus draws pointed attention to a preexisting extensive body of ancient literature concerning Abraham by taking the trouble to list some of the many sources that dealt with the life of Abraham: "In addition to those already cited, Theophilus, Theodotus, Mnaseas, Aristophanes, Hermogenes, Euhemerus, Conon, Zopyrion, and maybe many more, for my reading has not been exhaustive." [!][13]

The antiquity of the literature in which Abraham was featured is brought sharply into focus by the list of historians presented to us by Josephus. While this catalogue of ancient literature has not survived, we do know that much of it was written prior to the invasion of the Asian continent by Alexander. Aristophanes, for example, was born in 448 B.C.E. and lived to be about 64 years old. The history that "dealt with the life of Abraham" was therefore written some three quarters of a century before that watershed event, and before Hecataeus wrote his history of Abraham.

Josephus does render us the favor of describing Abraham's reputation and stature in Egyptian society during his sojourn in Egypt, an account drawn from the sources mentioned above:

[The Pharaoh] gave him leave to enter into conversation with the most learned among the Egyptians; from which conversation his virtue and reputation became more conspicuous than they had been before. . . . For whereas the Egyptians were formerly addicted to different customs, and despised one another's sacred rites, and were very angry with one another on that account, Abram conferred with each one of them, and confuting the reasons they made use of, every one for his own practices, demonstrated that such reasonings were vain and void of truth; whereupon he was admired by them in those conferences as a very wise man, and of great sagacity, when he discoursed on any subject he undertook, and this not only in understanding it but to persuade other men to assent to him. He communicated to them in arithmetic, and delivered to them the science of astronomy; for before Abram came to Egypt they were unacquainted with those parts of learning; for that science also came from the Chaldeans into Egypt, and from thence to the Greeks also.[14]

How can these accounts of early Hebraic history be interpreted as a depiction of camel-riding, tent-dwelling, homeless, *uncultured,* bedouin wanderers straggling from sandy oasis to sandy oasis with a few goats? The desert never enters the biblical scenario until Abraham and his extended family cross from Canaan into Egypt. Even then, they don't stay in the Sinai, but pass right through it to settle temporarily in Goshen, in the swampy but bountifully foliate delta of the Nile. The catalogue of advanced cultural attributes contained in the praise heaped by the Egyptians upon Abraham, as reported by Josephus, reflects the actual attributes of the Semitic peoples who recurrently infiltrated Egypt through the Nile Delta and across the intervening Red Sea. The Semites carried Mesopotamian culture and technology with them and boosted Egypt from the early Chalcolithic into the late Bronze Age, a contribution that will be subsequently addressed.

The tribe of Abraham sojourned in the lush delta while a drought was desiccating the pastoral lands in "The Promised Land," but returned as soon as the period of drought passed. Nomads move seasonally in pursuit of water, but a sedentary people digs wells; the digging of wells was the first priority of the tribe of Abraham on their arrival in "The Promised Land." Hydrologic engineering had attained a high level of proficiency in the Mesopotamian twin river alluvial basin from which the tribe of Abraham derived, and was advantageous in an area of limited rainfall like Canaan, in which the tribe of Abraham is said to have settled. The science of water management is another aspect of civilization that derives from agronomy, just as a tie to the land leads to the establishment of villages, as inadequate neolithic stone and bone are replaced by metals in the production of tools, and as the need for storage spurs the development of pottery and therefore of furnaces and pyrotechnology. Permanent housing, metal tools, fired earthenware, and hydrologic engineering are primary attributes of civilization.

So important were water resources regarded by the tribe of Abraham that each well was given an identity, a name, and the Hebrews expeditiously dug many of them even before they had settled into their new home. A growing prosperity was generated by the creation of an effective hydrologic system, which provoked envy on the part of the more primitive Philistines, depicted as an agronomically ignorant people from the sea. At first the Philistines were docile and cooperative neighbors. Abimelech, their chief, made a peace pact with Abraham after a nasty incident at one of the most important wells at Beer-Sheba. "And Abraham planted a grove in Beer-Sheba" (Genesis 21:31–33).

Beer-Sheba means either "Well of the Oath" or "Well of the Seven," referring to the seven ewes given by Abraham to Abimelech as a warrant of the amicable accord reached between them. The oasis sits at the edge of the Negev Desert and is still an important town, a crossroads where a weekly market is held at which bedouins gather for trade. Its wells still flow, and the largest is called, in Arabic, "The Well of Abraham." The groves that Abraham and Isaac presumably planted at Beer-Sheba flourish still, and the bedouins' camels find respite in their shade.

Abraham became a rancher "rich in cattle and silver and gold." So great were the herds that a tribal division had to take place because "the land was not able to bear them" (Genesis 13:2-6).

Hardly a picture of desert-dwelling bedouins!

After Abraham's passing, during another period of drought, Isaac, his son, sought permission from Abimelech to sojourn in his domain. The area was unproductive, and therefore Abimelech thought nothing of granting Isaac access to it. Isaac proceeded to dig wells and irrigate the area. "Then Isaac sowed in that land, and received the same year an hundredfold: and the Lord blessed him. For he had possession of flocks, and possession of herds, and great stores of servants." The Philistines, envious over the prosperity resulting from the technological acumen of the Hebrews, became vindictive: "and the Philistines envied him . . . And Abimelech said unto Isaac, go from us, for thou art much mightier than we" (Genesis 26:12-16).

So Isaac and his family, together with their "great stores of servants," moved into the valley of Gerar and restored the hydrologic system that his father had created and the Philistines had filled in "and he called them their names after the names by which his father called them." Running into difficulty with the local herdsmen and being a man of peace, Isaac moved again, and created a third water works, this time in a desolate area where no claimants appeared: "for that he strove not: and he called the name of it Rehoboth; and he said, for the Lord has made room, for us, and we shall be fruitful in the land" (Genesis 26:17-18; 19-22).

Thus we are reassured that the tribe of Abraham, after emigrating westward from the great urban centers of Mesopotamia, the "Land Between the Rivers," to the land bordering on what the Akkadians referred to as "The Sea of the Setting Sun," had no intention of wandering about; they strove to settle permanently in the land of Canaan with the ardent aim of becoming "fruitful in the land," of building a nation with a civilized economy. They initiated the process by establishing themselves in agronomy and husbandry, creating communities in which commerce and industry eventually evolved, in which the array of ancient skills and knowledge they had carried with them could be applied. Had this process not been interrupted by incursions of armies of rapacious Egyptian kings and invasions of the avaricious "Sea Peoples," invaders from islands of the Aegean, they might have quickly reached unprecedented heights of civilization.

No whisper of sand-dwelling nomadism is heard among the words of the ancient historians; no camels, no donkeys, no tents are accorded a passing mention; on the contrary, Abraham is depicted as a sagacious carrier of Mesopotamian culture—as are, by reflection the Hebrews, proficient in astronomy, mathematics, and logic and respected in the highest circles. At the very least, it can be said that the existence of patriarchs such as Abraham derive from the composite memory of an era, personifications of people of a period in which they wended westward from Akkadia back into the Aramaic area from which they originated and then continued a memorable odyssey toward the Mediterranean and Egypt. This momentous movement allowed a most creative people to draw deeply from many ancient cultures and to spawn and spur new civilizations. They nurtured knowledge, lifted themselves to ever higher levels of achievement. They brought an enlightened view of the nature of creation to all the peoples with whom they came into contact. The urban character of the Hebrews and of the Amorites, "Semites" who spread out from Harran along the arms of the Fertile Crescent, is strongly substantiated by the fact that the names of the family of Abraham cited in Genesis are eponyms of the towns and peoples that are known to exist or to have existed in the region.

WHO WERE THE "SEMITES"?

The term "Semite" defines neither a race nor a nation. It is used circumspectly for lack of a better designation for the peoples who spoke a family of related dialects deriving from an apparent prehistoric language spoken in the area of the biblical Aram-Naharayim or Aram (Aramea), the area in which Harran, the presumed original provenance of the tribe of Abraham, is centrally located. The term "Semitic" has no otherwise cohesive historical or anthropological foundation. Presumably the term refers to the descendants of Shem ("Sem" is the Greco-Latin form of Shem), one of the three sons of Noah (Shem, Ham, and Japheth), who are collectively designated as the forbearers of the three great divisions of mankind (Genesis 9:18). Actually the term "Semite" was "coined by a German scholar in 1781 to denote a group of closely related languages."[15]

During the fourth and third millennia B.C.E., the "Semites" fanned out from the crest of the Fertile Crescent down along both its arms, southwestward along the Mediterranean coast into Egypt in the Nile Delta, and southeastward through the headlands of the Euphrates and Tigris rivers into Sumer at the confluence of these two rivers into the Persian Gulf. The Semitic-speaking peoples of historical times came to include such heterogeneous non-Semitic-speaking peoples as Sumerians and Hurrians who melded into the Semitic culture and then employed a form of the Semitic language for spoken and written communication; they came to include Hittites and Egyptians among whom the Hebrews sojourned and who settled in Canaan for military, commercial, or diplomatic purposes and were assimilated into the fabric of Semitic Canaanite society; most certainly they came to include the "Hebrews,"[16] an amalgam of peoples who originated at the crest of the crescent, settled in Canaan, and whose tribal memory encompassed circumscriptive experiences in Aramea, Sumer, and Egypt.

The urban character of the society from which the Jewish progenitors stemmed is manifested eponymically by the unmistakable identification of the biblical figures with the centers of burgeoning civilizations. The remarkable concurrence of biblical lore with archaeological revelation substantiates this identification. The sons of Shem, named Elam and Asshur, are obviously the eponyms of the Elamites and the Assyrians; Aram is as clearly the eponym of the Aramaeans; and Lud can reasonably be related to the Lydians. Terach (Terakh), Abram's father, who died in Harran, may have derived his name from the town of Til-Turakhi, and, likewise, his great-grandfather Serug can be identified with the town of Serugi, just west of Harran.[17] Texts recovered from the ancient city of Mari also refer to the town of Peleg, which is the name of an ancestor of Abram and which town has been archaeologically identified with Phaliga, a town on the Euphrates. We learn from those records that Harran was a flourishing community and the hub of the most important trade routes from east to west. The name Harran (*al harranim*), indeed, means "caravan city." The town of Nahor is significantly referred to in the Bible as both the name of a city (Genesis 24:10: "[Abram's servant] went to Mesopotamia, unto the city of Nahor"), and of Abram's brother (Genesis 24:15: "Rebekah was born to the wife of Nahor, Abram's brother"). Such dichotomous biblical references give credence to the eponymic character of the names of Abraham's relatives, antecedent, contemporary, and descendant, and to a different aspect of the relevance of biblical legend. Ernest Wright comments:

> Here then is a remarkable situation. The identification of one name with an ancient town may be coincidence, but here are several identifications in the precise area from which Abram came. These biblical names of the brethren and ancestors of Abram were probably patriarchal clan names which were either given to the towns which they founded, or borrowed from them from cities and villages.[18]

Can such consistent concordance indeed be ascribed to coincidence? The identification of each of the progenitors of the Jews with a major urban center unmistakably stamps the intention of the biblical redactor, divine or human, to characterize these predecessors of the Jews as an urbanized people. The list can be continued for scores of such "coincidences." The appearance of biblical names of real people who were resident in Ebla, Mari, Ugarit, Byblos and other great cities, names baked into the clay tablets exhumed from such ancient communities, lends further credence to the "tribal memory" thesis. Abram appears in several such ancient documents, in texts from Mari as *Abam-ram,* for example. The outstandingly biblical name Jacob appears as *Yaacob-el* on Egyptian cartouches. There are a number of references in the Mari tablets to tribes designated as the *Benyamen,* redoubtable freedom-loving villagers whose fierce struggles for independence inflicted sleepless nights upon the governors of the metropolis of Mari.

We are biblically informed that when the tribe of Terach did finally emigrate from Ur, it had a fixed destination. It settled in the area of Harran, the ancient commercial crossroads from which its ancestors came, "and dwelt there," that is, settled permanently. Harran is located at the apex of the Fertile Crescent on the eastern bank of the Balikh river, which flows into the Euphrates some one hundred kilometers to the south. Thus the area of Harran was the hub of both river and land traffic coursing through from the east and the west, a traffic funneled through the area by the imposing Ararat mountains to the north, the Taurus mountains to the northwest and the formidable desert stretching out far into the south. The great city of Mari lay to Harran's south along the Euphrates, and past that metropolis stretched Akkad, within which the cities of Babylon, Eshnunna, Nippur, Kish, Erech, Lagash, Larsa, and Ur flourished during various ancient times. To Harran's east the trade routes crossed easily to the Euphrates' twin river, the Tigris, and to the cities of Asshur, Nimrud, and Nuzi. The trade routes extended from Harran westward through Ebla, Carcamish, and Alelakh and proceeded along the Mediteranean coast to Ugarit, Byblos, and Sidon. Branches of those same routes passed through Damascus into Jericho and stretched into Egypt along both sides of the Dead Sea.

The tribe of Abraham is depicted as wandering into Canaan on camel-back from the wastelands of Arabia only by virtue of the imaginations of scholars who consistently ignore the biblical rendition and by those who blithely follow in their wake. It was from urban, cosmopolitan Harran, one of the important epicenters of ancient civilization, that one of the sons of Terach, Abraham, and his entourage are said to have emigrated to Canaan.

The fact that, up to now, the existence of the family of Abraham can only be accepted on faith from unsubstantiated historical references, or deduced dialectically from biblical legend and tribal memory, is understandable; written records of the time were rare; the particulars of such records related essentially to the interests of the rulers who resided in the cities, essentially fortresses within which the rulers administered lands under their hegemony and from which they secured their rule. Life around these bastions is mentioned sparsely and peripherally, even though the bulk of the population resided in the scores of communities surrounding them and though the conduct of life in them depended on the husbandry, agronomy, and industry of the supportive towns and villages.

A NEW LOOK AT ANCIENT SOCIETY

Our ignorance regarding large segments of ancient society can be attributed to the fragility of village evidence. The villages, when destroyed, were generally plowed through by succeeding generations, or completely eroded away because the structures were of mud-brick, wood, straw, or other easily decomposable materials; whereas cities contained monumental structures that resisted obliteration. Cities were generally reconstructed on the foundations of precedent cultural centers, creating the *tells* or mounds that have provided the bulk of information about ancient civilizations. Modern archaeological techniques, however, allow faint traces of the smaller towns and villages to be read, and interest in village life has led to a complete reevaluation of our concepts of the civilizations of antiquity. Tens of thousands of documents recovered from the archives of administrative centers have multiplied our understanding of village life a thousandfold and have compelled basic revisions of ancient historiography. In addition, the relatively recent archaeological interest in the hinterland of ancient Anatolian, Levantine and Mesopotamian civilizations, and latterly the massive archaeological efforts being expended under the aegis of the State of Israel, have led to the exposition of hundreds of communities to modern study.

The lives of ordinary people were, until recently, of little concern to historians; scholarly treatises revolved around the lives of rulers, the concerns of ruling classes, and the wars and intrigues they conducted. Nor were archaeologists primarily concerned with the fundamental fabric of civilization. The main thrust of ostensibly scientific historiology was long the repetition of recorded history as rendered by self-aggrandizing rulers. The archaeologist's main occupation can be characterized as having been plunder, an avaricious drive to fill museums and private collections with spectacular or precious artifacts. The activities of agents for wealthy collectors, museums, and even governments were incalculably destructive of the residue of community life. In this regard most archaeologists, well into the twentieth century, were little better than the grave robbers who sought jewels and gold to melt down or dismember for sale on the open market. It remains for present-day scientists to reconstruct a true representation of society from the surviving rubble, and to avoid limiting the perception of history to one that narrowly reflects the vainglorious propaganda of potentates.

Fortunately, a fresh wind is clearing the historiographical haze. We are beginning to perceive that, outside of the ramparts of the citadels, civilization extended out across the countryside, and furthermore, that the citadels and their ramparts were but the products of that civilization.

2

The Rise of Semitic Civilization

Reading the Record

Although archaeology has undergone a significant change of orientation in the last fifty years, the hunt for precious and exotic artifacts still prejudices research to an unwarranted extent. Curators of museums remain overly devoted to decorating their institutions with lionizing statuary, idolic figures, and precious artifacts so that sponsors can feel their contributions were well served and visitors can be provided with titillating displays. The inordinate space and attention allotted to artifacts that conquerors accumulated from their victims by looting, enslavement, or indenture attributes an inflated historical importance to the culture of the conqueror at the expense of the conquered. More importantly, the misleading impression such displays inevitably generate is that the material was produced by the conquerors and not by the conquered. The booty torn from adversaries or victims, the tribute taxed from conquered peoples, and the edifices and artifacts produced by captured slaves or subject peoples are generally assumed to be the creation of the dominating power and attributed to the culture it represents. Scientific literature tends to follow suit and too often reflects the same historical deformity.

A typical example of such historiographical distortion concerns the art of primary glassmaking. Museums are proud to display "Egyptian glass," yet no ancient Egyptian ever produced glass, and probably not even glassware, the products made of that primary material. Again, no museum would feel satisfied unless it had an adequate display of "Roman glass," yet it is unlikely that any ancient Roman, unless he was an easterner who became a Roman citizen, ever produced either glass or glassware. "Provenience Egypt" would properly declare that glassware found in Egypt was not necessarily made there, and "Roman Period" would properly fix the chronology of glassware made in the Near East and not erroneously credit the Romans with its production. Such accurate labels are seldom employed, although it would appear incumbent upon museums to practice accuracy in labeling. The misleading labels that are employed inevitably lead to

15

assumptions which confound the scientific community no less than the innocent museum visitor.

A PROBLEM OF JEWISH HISTORIOGRAPHY

Jewish historiography suffers mightily by the dearth of distinguishing artifacts,
for Jews did not glorify their priests and kings with statuary; not even their
Almighty God was privy to such idolatry. The inscriptions on the monuments
from which much of ancient history are derived is therefore not available for the
reconstruction of the Jewish role in that history. Nor did the Jews normally shield
their homes or bury their dead with idolic amulets or figurines. Jewish homes
and tombs are therefore generally ethnically and culturally unidentifiable, and
their occupants are either incorrectly identified or, at best, catalogued as of
unknown ethnicity. Those who did make use of pagan talismans to provide
insurance against the unknown are likely to be registered accordingly as pagans.
Jewish unpretentious, sparsely furnished temples, meeting halls, and institutions
were almost universally leveled, and the treasures they may have housed were
plundered and recast to the specifications of the desecrators. During the Babylonian, Hellenistic, and Roman periods Jews assumed Babylonian, Greek, and
Roman names, and except for the cases in which their names incorporated a
definitive eastern reference or were of distinguishing theophoric construction,
they are prone to be classified by scholars as non-Jewish. Thus, for example, the
presence and activity of up to seven million Jews concentrated in the most creative industrial and commercial centers of Roman civilization pass by unnoticed
and unheralded. The Jewish progenitors of Canaan were among those referred
to as "Asiatics" by the Egyptians; the Jews of Judah were among those referred to
as "Syrians" by the Greeks and Romans, and they are classified with the "Palestinians" or "Syro-Palestinians" by contemporary archaeologists.

The imprint of Jewish presence is preserved in the labor Jews performed in
agronomy and husbandry, in the production of artifacts and commodities and
in the construction of temples and cities, the products of whose labor are almost
universally accredited to their oppressors. It is likewise present in other abstrac-
tions: in the leverage they exerted upon the science, philosophy, and ethics of
their times; in the services they performed as doctors, as counselors to kings,
and as local and international entrepreneurs; in the seminal influence they exerted
in the development of the technology for which they became the carriers; and
for the performance of that technology for which they were hired or enslaved.
The monuments built and the projects small and great, consummated largely or
entirely by Jews, from the Colosseum of Rome to the Manhattan Project, are legion.
We find Jewish presence among the shadows of these monumental works as well
as in the mundane attributes of civilization: in the shoes for which they tanned
leather, in the clothes for which they wove and dyed and sewed textiles, in the
iron and glass and silk of the artifacts they produced.

Ancient historiography suffers less of late from gross oversight than was the case in the rapacious past. The attempt to reconstruct as accurate a picture as possible of the lives and cultures of peoples now engages sophisticated modern technology and a multiplicity of disciplines. Attention is now paid to particles of pollen no less than to golden goblets. Concepts of ancient culture have also been deeply affected by a succession of fortunate discoveries of vast troves of written material, revelatory records of civilizations whose existence was hitherto only suspected or wholly unknown. Written records are the greatest treasures that descend through the ages, and, although they are bound to register the viewpoints and distortions of the rulers under whose aegis they were produced, if properly interpolated they provide an invaluable key to unlock a portion of the past.

The multiplicity of data made available by the application of new technologies and by the recovery of masses of documents from excavations of the last century has demanded a new perspective on the rise of civilization. The growing mountain of information has placed constraints upon the classicophiles, whose dominance in the field of archaeology still precludes an unprejudiced examination of that rise. The stones and statues so beloved of the classicists are slowly being moved to reveal the more ancient stones of precedent and seminal civilizations. The vast collections of tablets recently brought to light provide definitive information with which the parameters of those civilizations can be newly interpolated. But the gears of progress grind with excruciating morbidity, and the prejudices of the past still permeate ancient historiography. The hidden history of many conquered peoples suffers by default, and that of the Jews has suffered all the more because of religious intolerance and its heinous corollary, anti-Semitism.

The creative proficiency of the Jews resulted from immersion over many millennia in the Semitic civilization from whose matrix the Jews emerged. The first glimmerings of civilization materialized at the crown of the Fertile Crescent, the very region in which the progenitors of the Jews appeared. The term *fertile* aptly reminds us that agriculture first flourished along that arc. Agriculture provides the first sign of *civilization* in that the planting of and attending to crops and the storage of the harvest from season to season requires a cohesive community tied to the land. The world's most ancient agronomic center lay along the upper curve of the crescent around Jericho, a city which can look back upon ten thousand years of sedentary communal life. Jericho is located in a fairly dry area of the Jordan valley slightly north of the Dead Sea and west of the Jordan river.

THE ARCHAEOLOGY OF JERICHO

The modern city of Jericho rises close by the ruins of its ancient counterpart, which lie buried under a creased and weathering mound referred to as Tell el-Sultan. The ancient city was positioned near a spring, variously called Ein el-Sultan and Elisha's Well, which still, after ten millennia, gushes forth at the rate of a thousand gallons a minute and irrigates a wide swath of the surrounding farmland. It was near Jericho that the earliest cultivated wheat, emmer, einkorn, barley, and lentil were grown, where goats and sheep were evidently first domesticated[1] and where an irrigation system was developed to make effective use of available water resources.

Some of these domesticated grains were found in the caves pockmarking the cliffs of Mt. Carmel, along with the skeletons of the people whose food it was. Fragments of sickles made of bone were recovered from the el-Wad cave and a whole haft of a sickle from the Kabara cave, eloquent evidence of the horticultural capabilities of the autochthonous people of the region, a people who lived in an otherwise "hunter-gatherer" world. Domesticated cereals have been recovered from many sites around Jericho as well as from Nahal Oren on the coastal plain.[2]

The caves of Mt. Carmel overlook a small coastal basin which later witnessed another landmark of advancing civilization, the appearance of glassmaking on the Mediterranean coast. Springs flowing from the flanks of the surrounding mountains meld into a stream once known as the Belus, and now named the Na'amen. The Belus is a meager, meandering, muddy creek that squirms through a swamp and through rolling sand dunes into the sea. The dunes of sand deposited at the shore of the Mediterranean provided the basic material for glassmaking for several millennia. It was along the coast of Canaan that Iron Age pyrotechnology first reached the Mediterranean world, an event that, as we shall see, figured importantly in the unfolding story of the Jews.

The Palestine Expeditionary Society made a sounding of Tell el-Sultan under the direction of C. Warren, who concluded that nothing of value was to be found, a wry commentary on the archaeology of the time. One of Warren's exploratory shafts missed the great tower of the city by a mere meter. Dame Kathleen M. Kenyon, working out of Jerusalem in the 1950s with the British School of Archaeology, was more fortunate, and her excavation disclosed the magnitude and age of the succession of cities buried in the tell. She dug deep down through these civilizations to arrive at the most ancient walled city ever found, even to circular houses and sanctuaries of mud-brick constructions of a pastoral people predating the city itself.

The city antedates Egyptian cities by almost five thousand years, and Sumerian cities by four thousand years. "On the west side, the first town wall was associated with a remarkable structure, a great stone tower built against the inner side of the wall," Dame Kenyon reported, and, understandably awestruck by her discovery, added: "The tower is not only a monument to remarkable architectural and constructional achievement, but tower and wall together furnish evidence of a degree of communal organization and a flourishing town life wholly unexpected at a date which . . . must be in the eighth millennium B.C.[E]."[3]

The bustling community life of the burgeoning town signaled the birth of civilization. The development of sedentary agriculture stimulated the technology of housing and storage, of toolmaking, metallurgy, and irrigation. Agronomic development led to specialization, created a need for documentation and organization, and resulted in widespread trade and communication. The appearance of all of these consequences of sedentary life can be read in the ruins of Jericho. They were the harbingers of the next revolutionary stimulant to the advance of civilization, a leap forward made necessary and inevitable by sedentary existence: the ability to reduce spoken language to written symbols, thereby to conserve records on stone and clay and wood and the skins of animals. The written word permitted communication over distances far beyond the sound of a voice and over time; it made the perpetuation of ideas possible, even from a person long dead to generations yet to come.

It has long been recognized that the written word can be worth more than the finest gold; the surge in Near Eastern archaeology has added vast treasures of textual information. The rubble of the great cities of the Near East has brought to light scores of thousands of documents that delineate the composition of the ancient, seminal, Semitic-language-speaking societies. From these records and from the formerly mute records of stones and seeds and artifacts, archaeologists are bringing forth a panoramic, enhanced view of the advent and evolution of civilization. The application of an assortment of highly sophisticated analytic tools and disciplines provides a fine focus on ancient human life; hitherto invisible details now give texture and delineation to the larger images of civilization.

THE TABLETS OF EBLA: DISCOVERY AND CONTROVERSY

Agronomic technology spread slowly around the Fertile Crescent; it descended the alluvial basins of the twin rivers to the Gulf, which opened to the Far East; it crossed the Taurus mountains into Anatolia to touch upon the Aegean, and it descended the Mediterranean coast of Asia into Africa, and even to an area west of the Nile which was at that time still favored by a fairly propitious climate and arable land. Great cities and civilizations were germinated along the route and extremities of that agronomic dispersion. Jericho was joined by a number of metropolises that proliferated along the apex of the arc of Fertile Crescent, not the least of which was the recently unearthed Ebla. Ebla was already a bustling urban community at the time Egypt first emerged from the Neolithic into the Historic period. The great city was surrounded by some three hundred villages engaged in every activity attributed to sophisticated civilization. By 2400 B.C.E. the city of Ebla had a population estimated at thirty thousand, supported by suburban communities containing no fewer than a quarter of a million farmers, herdsmen, and artisans. The sumptuous palace of Ebla provided quarters for twelve thousand functionaries.[4]

Ebla lay buried within Tell Mardikh, about mid-way between Jericho and Harran. In 1974 the first of tens of thousands of inscribed tablets were exhumed from the archives of the ancient city. The great epigraphist Giovanni Pettinato was called in by the archaeologist in charge, Paolo Matthaie. It did not take long for Pettinato to realize the significance and magnitude of the unfolding information. A picture of a common cultural patrimony emerged relating Ebla and the Canaanite coastal communities, to that of Aramea (Padan-Naharaim) and Akkadia (Shinar). "The picture now emerging exceeds the expectations of even the most optimistic scholars," Pettinato excitedly reported, and emphasized the far-reaching implications of the discovery. "It is not only Ebla and its empire that are being recovered, but in a surprising fashion the world of the third-millennium Near East with all its interrelationships and differentiations."[5]

The documents found in the royal archives at Ebla detail all aspects of human activity: economic, commercial, agricultural, literary, religious, and educational. Pettinato prescribes a complete revision of our concepts of ancient Semitic civilization, hitherto viewed as nomadic. "Thanks to Ebla, [we are] able to evaluate how distorted was that vision of the known world. The area previously held to be nomadic suddenly becomes a very mature center of civilization."[6]

Among the manifestations of the maturity of Eblaite culture which most impressed Pettinato was the high level of literacy and in particular, the international character of written communication. Not only did the Eblaite students use Sumerian syllaberies, but bilingual vocabularies as well, the earliest such intercultural literature ever found. "Who would have dreamed that back in 2500 B.C.[E.] Syrian [sic] teachers and students passed their time in classrooms compiling vocabularies that the Italians would find 4500 years later? I still remember the fateful moment on that sunny afternoon of 4 October 1975 when with vivid emotion I could announce to my archaeological colleagues that tablet TM.75G.2000 was a bilingual vocabulary."[7]

Studies of the language led philologists to branch the Eblaite language off from "Northwest Semitic" (from which Canaanite and Hebrew stemmed) and to draw a line directly from it to Aramaic[8] and to Hebrew. Thus the biblical route which places the itinerary of the biblical journey of Abraham from Akkadia through Harran (linguistically related to Ebla) into Canaan is provided philologic substance. Pettinato translated an Eblaite creation epic:

> Lord of Heaven and earth:
> The earth was not, you created it,
> The light of day was not, you created it,
> The morning light you had not [yet] made exist.

"These words echoing the first chapter of Genesis have not been taken from the Bible but rather from a literary text found in three copies in the royal library of 2500 B.C." commented Pettinato, who could not contain his awe and added, "What profundity of thought, how much religious sentiment are hidden in the expression, 'Lord of Heaven and earth'!"[9] Professor Pettinato proceeds to characterize Eblaite religion as essentially polytheistic, but notes that: "the preponderance of the elements IL and Ya in the onamastica, though not authorizing the term Ur-monotheism of the semitic peoples, do suggest that the Eblaites had a quite advanced concept of the divine and were very near to Henotheism, that is, special worship of some one particular divinity among the others existent."[10]

Mitchell Dahood, in his contribution to the work of Pettinato, noted the similarity of Eblaite names to those of the Old Testament and of Akkadia, as, for example, the name of the very first man: "Till now the only attestation of '*Ādām*,' 'man,' 'Adam,' outside of the Bible appeared in old Akkadian texts from the period of Sargon the Great (circa 2350 B.C.) in the form of the personal names *A-da-mu*, '*A-da-mu*, and *Á-dam-u* . . . Now from Ebla comes the personal name *A-da-mu*, one of the 14 governors of the provinces."[11]

The revelations bursting forth from the translations of the first texts from the Eblaic trove of thousands of tablets caused a sensation. Between 1974 and 1978 both Professor Matthaie, head of the project, and Professor Pettinato, retained by Matthaie as chief epigrapher, lectured and wrote about the unprecedented lessons learned from these ancient records. The news services eagerly reported statements by both scholars. Professor Matthaie enthusiastically proclaimed: "The Ebla tablets establish the patriarchs and their names as historical realities."[12] Again, the same Matthaie announced to the world: "We have found the civilization that was the background of the people of the Old Testament."[13]

It is clear that all human cultures are correlated and interrelated, and it is necessary to emphasize the communality and reciprocity of intercultural development when treating with historical continuity; it is also essential to give credit where credit is due, and it is particularly important to be at least fair, if not scientifically objective, concerning the cultural attributes of any people. The roots of Jewish culture lie in great and advanced civilizations like that of Ebla. Unfortunately, they are located in modern Syria, Iraq, and Iran where unprejudiced evaluation of the findings of those engaged in the work is impossible to publicly pronounce.

The great philologist, epigrapher, and semeticist, Professor Giovanni Pettinato, to his bitter regret, found this unhappy fact to be true. The Syrians, incensed by the inferences, cracked down on the scientists of the mission. Matthaie abjectly acceded to Syrian pressure, backtracked to a secure position and became the Syrian whip. Pettinato also retreated, but was hesitant to deny altogether that there were historical parallels to the Old Testament and to disavow the relationship of the Jews to the ancient Eblaite culture. The Syrians set up a committee of ten whose job it was to oversee and approve translations and interpretations of the texts before publication.

The Director General of the Syrian Department of Antiquities and Museums demanded a formal "Declaration" from Pettinato outlining his position on the relationship of the inscriptions to both Syrian and biblical history. The implication was obvious: sign a disclaimer of biblical connections or be dismissed. Pettinato dutifully submitted an official "Declaration," in which he penitently wrote:

> [The documents] that I have had the honour to decipher and study, always give us more evidence of the central role of Syria in the history of the third millenary

(sic) . . . As for the pretended links with the biblical text . . . the onomastic
texts of Ebla may give way to possible comparisons to similar biblical texts of periods subsequent to the historical dating of Ebla, we are not authorized to make the
inhabitants of Ebla "predecessors of Israel."

The Syrian government lost no time in propagating Pettinato's "Declaration"
through its publication, *Flash of Damascus,* asserting that it: "refutes all Zionist
allegations aimed at defacing Syrian history, and emphasizes the antiquity of Syrian
civilization and its wide fame."

The declaration was nevertheless insufficiently supportive of the blatantly
political purposes of the Syrians. Pettinato was summarily dismissed. Conced-
ing some errors, Pettinato nevertheless continued to maintain "possible comparisons" in subsequent writings and became subjected to vicious attacks which can
only be described as a vendetta; he was accused of participation in the "Zionist
plot."

In an earlier issue of *Flash* (October 1977) the theme had already been set
with an article entitled: "Professor Matthaie refutes the Zionist Allegations About
Ebla." The web closed in upon Pettinato when Mr. Tweir, the Syrian Director of
Archaeological Research, made the Syrian position clear and attacked Pettinato
for not kneeling wholeheartedly to it: "The Zionists . . . call all studies concerning the ancient history of the whole Arab region 'biblical studies.' They faked
the archaeological, historical studies of the whole region and annexed them to
the Jewish traditions. [Pettinato] was not free from Zionist influence."[14]

Matthaie and his cohorts joined the calumnious chorus. The *Biblical Archaeological Review,* in a "recap" of the events, concerned itself with his patently unethi-
cal posture, asking, "How far will Matthaie and other scholars go to please the
Syrians?"[15]

HOW THE USE OF ANACHRONISTIC LABELS IMPEDED
THE SCIENTIFIC APPROACH TO NEAR EASTERN HISTORY

The ancient vintage of this prejudicial process is exemplified by the routine application of anachronistic designations "Syrian" and "Palestinian" to pre-Hellenistic
artifacts recovered from the Near East, thus ignoring existent cultures. "Aramea,"
"Canaan," "Israel," "Samaria," "Galilee," and "Judah" are commonly replaced by
terms which should be considered utterly inapplicable until 135 C.E., if at all. It
was only then that the Romans combined a distorted version of "Philistine," with
"Syria" into "Syro-Palestine."

An argument given for avoiding the generic designations for the provenance
of artifacts produced within the region is that such use has political overtones.
This facetious argument ignores the fact that it is the Syrians who are blatantly
political in their argument, and that it was the Romans, who, for *purely political*
purposes, substituted the name "Syro-Palestine" for the generic name of the region

in an attempt to eradicate intransigent Judah as both a cultural and a corporate entity. In a peculiar twist of logic, objections to the application of the spurious terms "Syrian" and "Palestinian" to times and places in which such entities did not exist are termed prejudicial, whereas the insistence of the Syrians on such usage for blatantly political purposes is ignored. The use of the term "Syria" is patently prejudicial in that it projects a facetious Pan-Arabic image the Syrians (and others) are promulgating for political purposes, and obscures the existence of ancient cultures which have real reason for recognition, cultures from which the Syrians and the Arabs themselves evolved.

Neither the Jews, whether atheist or orthodox, nor the Zionists reject the proposition that contemporary Syrians and Jews share a common heritage; it is the Syrians who attempt to blindfold historiology by deleting the Hebraic heritage, a cultural history every bit as valid as that of the Syrians. We are constrained to forgive the biblical scribes who, through ignorance, ascribed the "Chaldees" to the area of Ur centuries before its existence; but what can we say of scientists who consciously continue to practice deceptive anachronisms? Self-serving contemporary regional politics and national interests petrify this process and prevent a much-needed revision of ancient cultural and regional denominations. The misnomers employed by otherwise erudite scholars must be discarded if historiography is to emerge from the morass into which their usage, innocent or not, has immersed it.

Some such terms, although abstruse or not scientifically definitive, are at least not misleading. Thus the term "Semite" can be accepted when it is used circumscriptively as a description of peoples of varying cultures and histories whose language has a common genesis. The archaic designation "Mesopotamia" (Greek for "between the rivers") is acceptable as a general geographical delineation of an area, not necessarily the one restricted to the area between the Euphrates and Tigris rivers,[16] but one generally understood to include the entire alluvial basin watered by those rivers and their tributaries. However, it cannot be properly employed as a cultural epithet except as a most general reference to the commonly held precepts and practices of the divers contiguous cultures of the area.

The label "Syria" is particularly inappropriate when applied geographically or culturally to a people of pre-Hellenic times since neither such a national entity nor such a culture then existed. As a cultural label it must be used circumspectly even when it is applied to contemporary Syria inasmuch as Syria contains peoples of divers cultures. The anomalous use of this label is now being noted in some circles and adjustments are being made. Thus, in the preface to volume 3 of the *Textbook of Syrian Semitic Inscriptions* (Oxford, 1982), the author, John C. L. Gibson, in response to the criticism of several reviewers of the first two volumes, states that while the title of the third volume was retained for the "sake of consistency with the first two volumes," "Syrian" will be dropped in all future editions. Unfortunately, the term is employed so indiscriminately that it usually passes by unnoticed and unnoted. Unfortunately again, the term usually photographs through from one scholarly text to another without reference to its inaccuracy.

There are numerous proposals as to the origin of the name "Syria," all of them relating to the Hellenic period; the general consensus is that it derives from a Greek designation for a portion of the area of Aramea. One popular theory has it that "Syria" is a latinization of *Suros,* the Greek transcription of the place-name Suri, which occurs in the Nuzi tablets as the name of a town on the Euphrates in Aramea, or at best a small area around that town; that town is phonologically the closest to the name "Syria."[17] Other derivations are proposed, each with its own rationale, but no credible evidence exists that the term was originally more than a local Greek geographic designation or that such an ancient culture actually existed.

This was the region from which the Arameans stemmed, and was the provenance of the Amorites, a term which denominates the antecedents of the Arameans, if not another name for the very same people. "Amorite" is a version of the Akkadian *Amurrum,* which in turn comes from the Sumerian *Martu,*[18] meaning simply "the West," the direction from which these peoples infiltrated into Sumer and therefore became *Amurri* or "Westerners." The Bible refers to the area as Aram-Naharayim, Padan-Naharayim, or simply Aram, a reasonable rendering of the name of the region and cultural entity from which the Jews (and the later Syrians) stemmed. "Aramea," "Amurru," and the biblical variations "Aram-Naharayim," "Padan-Naharayim," and "Aram" all can be justified as labels for the cultural provenience of the Semitic-speaking peoples; Syria can not.

Therein lies the problem; present Near Eastern archaeological research lies largely within the boundaries of Syria, Lebanon, and Iraq, and scholars who work on archaeological projects within those boundaries must be circumspect about their cultural descriptions or find themselves excluded from the research. This was made abundantly clear by the removal of Professor Giovanni Pettinato from the Italian mission charged with the excavation of Tell Mardikh. The core of the controversy did not concern professor Pettinato's competency but was directed at the implications that Eblaite documents supported biblical references.

The scientific community, in the main and to its shame, stood silently aside from the issue and weakly justified the use of obfuscating Near Eastern nomenclature on the basis of "convenience." Only a few voices were raised in support of the principle of untrammeled investigation and for the right of exposing both interpretation and misinterpretation to scrutiny and criticism without fear of reprisal for views that may be anathema to the prevailing authority.

Nonetheless, the Ebla tablets do provide an unmistakable link to biblical historiography and add suggestive evidence concerning the evolution of Hebraic omneitic theology. The interrelationship between Hebraic lore and the divers "Semitic" cultures of the great urban centers of Ebla, Harran, Mari, Ur, Ugarit, and Byblos becomes ever more obvious and infinitely more intriguing as the translation of the tens of thousands of documentary inscriptions proceeds. The ramifications of the appearance of a novel concept of the divine are particularly intriguing. The texts delineate the emergence of henotheism and monotheism from the morass of primitive polytheistic practices extant in all of human society of that era. The relevance of the Bible as a historical document becomes more evident in spite of the obstructionism of the countries in which such research must be conducted.

Pettinato, in possession of copies of a large corpus of the texts, continued his work in Italy. A vivid picture of progressive concepts emerges from the texts, which herald forthcoming Hebraic theology. The panoply of Eblaite gods is headed by *Dagan,* who assumes new dimensions. To Dagan, and no other god, a newly coined, universal term, "Lord," is applied. The fact that the Dagan is conventionally not called by name impels Pettinato to ask, "[Do we] find ourselves, perhaps, in front of a religious concept, certainly different from the Mesopotamian, at the base of which the name of God is not to be pronounced . . . This question is pregnant with meaning." The manner in which the names of the Gods are listed supports the proposition that "it is permissible to conclude that the Eblaites, already in the third millennium, had arrived at a concept of divinity as an abstract entity."[19]

The incorporation of *Il* (or *El*) and *Ya* as hypocoristicons, or abbreviated adjuncts of forms of a god-name onto personal names, indicating a deity in the Eblaite onomastica, is the earliest such attested reference in any culture. The progression from *Il/El* to *Ya* shortly after 2500 B.C.E., during the reign of a certain King Ebrium, is particularly intriguing. Pettinato, while disclaiming any intentions of equating *Ya* with the Hebraic "Yahwe,"[20] compiled a suggestive listing of names demonstrating the changeover from *Il* (or *El*) to *Ya* during the King's tenure. Typical of these switches are:

en-na-il ("show favor O *El*") to *en-na-ia* ("show favor O *Ya*")
is-ma-il ("*El* has heard") to *is-ma-ia* ("*Ya* has heard")
mi-k-il ("Who *is* like *El*?") to *mi-k-ia* ("Who *is* like *Ya*?")

Whatever conclusions are to be drawn as to a possible relationship between *Ya* and the biblical YHWH, Pettinato leaves to the reader, but points out that the God *Il/El* of the tablets of Ugarit similarly changes over time to *Ya.*[21] One is left to wonder what relationship King Ebrium might bear to the biblical Ebrum.

The poem inscribed on an Eblaite tablet cited above, commencing "Lord of Heaven and earth" and designating Him creator of the cosmos and the world, of light, of morning and of day, ends with a litany of definitions and attributes of the Lord. Pettinato concludes that "the text speaks for itself; under the form of a litany the Eblaite theologians reveal their concept of God, Lord of Heaven and Earth and hence of the cosmos. God is seen as a superior being but continually present upon the earth and in daily life."

The poem was not written in the Eblaite language but in Sumerian cuneiform. The Sumerian spoken language was at this time beginning to be supplanted by Akkadian in Sumer, for it was during this period that the "Semitic" King Sargon I (that is, one who spoke an Amoritic dialect related to that of Ebla) established rule in Agade over Sumer. The written Sumerian language, however, remained for many centuries a medium of intercultural exchange, much as Aramaic and Latin were employed in later eras. That the concept of monotheism was being transmitted along the rim of the Fertile Crescent is born out by references to itinerant "prophets," holy men who subscribed to and promulgated ("prophesied," if you please) a new universalist religion. A reasonable tie between Ebla, Mari, Akkadia, and biblical tradition is established by references to these "prophets" in the tablets recovered from Ebla:

> But the most pleasant surprise is finding attested in this early period holy men not bound to the worship of a particular god but rather representing a new type of religiosity. These are the "prophets" belonging to the category of prophesiers of the divine word. These holy men, specified by the country of origin, moved from one city to another announcing the divine message.

> Existing already in the pre-biblical world, the prophets are called *nabiutum* from the root *nb'/nby,* "to call, announce," and come from Mari.[22]

Was Abraham one such prophet?

AN ANCIENT METROPOLIS: MARI

It can be reasonably presumed that if the tribe of Terach came from Akkadia it passed through the great metropolis of Mari on the way to Harran. Mari, the city from which, according to the Eblaite tablets, the "prophesiers" came, was a rival commercial city to Ebla. Its discovery came after the archaeological community was astounded by the uncovering of the ancient Canaanite city of Ugarit (Ras Shamrah), by the rich finds of tablets and artistic objects of Canaanite origin, and by the realization that a highly advanced, literate culture existed which had scarcely been noted. The tablets were inscribed in a script which proved to be a language close to biblical Hebrew. Scarcely had scholars recovered from the impact of this revelation when new, hardly less sensational, finds were made on the middle Euphrates. There, in what proved to be a great commercial center, more than twenty thousand tablets written in Semitic Akkadian were unearthed. Akkadian was the native language of the Hebrew Patriarchs.

Professor Parrot, the prestigious archaeologist in charge of the site, was ecstatic upon discovering significant biblical connotations in the translation of the tablets unearthed from the ruins of Mari. Such biblical names as Abram, Jacob, Benjamin, and Zebulun could be distinguished in the Akkadian records. The cities of Harran and Nahor, both mentioned in Genesis, were referred to as nearby, flourishing towns. Parrot was so impressed with the patriarchal flavor of the tablets from Mari that he wrote to his friend, William Foxwell Albright, "Nous n'avons pas encore trouvé la mention d'Abraham, mais presque."

The metropolis of Mari boasted a palace of hundreds of rooms devoted to, among other noteworthy municipal activities, such functions as an efficient postal system that penetrated a thousand miles in every direction. Warner Keller was properly impressed by the magnitude of the commercial activity carried on in the administrative offices of the grand palace of Mari:

> There was a foreign office and a board of trade in the great administrative palace of the kingdom of Mari. More than 100 officials were involved in dealing with the incoming and outgoing mail, which amounted to thousands of tablets alone. . . . The news services in Mari functioned so quickly and successfully that it would bear comparison with modern telegraphy. Important messages were sent by fire signals from the frontier of Babylon right up to the present day Turkey in a matter of a few hours, a distance of more than 300 miles.
> The inhabitants of Mari were Amorites who had been settled there for a long time, and preferred peace. Their interests lay in religion and ceremonial; in trade and commerce. Conquest, heroism and the clash of battle meant little to them. As we can still see from statues and pictures, their faces radiate a cheerful serenity.[23]

Among the public edifices of the city were a temple to Ishtar and a ziggurat, which, in addition to the language employed, attested to a common cultural heritage of the citizens of Mari with that of the Akkadians and of other "Semitic" peoples. The documents in the archives of the metropolis detail commissions for the construction of embankments, dams, and canals that bespoke an elaborate irrigation system, and contain the reports of government engineers who kept the system under careful, constant supervision. The trades were organized into guilds; the names of two thousand craftsmen belonging to various of these guilds are registered on a pair of tablets.

Mari was no less competent in the arts than in industry. Glassmaking was one of the arts practiced in Mari. One of the earliest intact glass vessels ever found was recovered from among a mass of fragments of glass artifacts unearthed from the ruins of the city situated on the banks of the Euphrates at the midpoint of its descent toward the sea. By the fifteenth century B.C.E. the technology was already well established in that metropolis, having spread northwestward along with the movement of peoples past it to the Mediterranean coast.

Although Mari was a relatively peaceful state at the time of Abraham, the records recovered from the ruins of the city contain numerous references to clashes between the police of the city and the free peoples of the villages around the city. Especially noteworthy were references to the Benjaminites, whose name is unmistakably biblical. The governors of Mari attempted by several ruses to control these jealously independent villagers and to incorporate them into the tax and conscription regulations of the city. On one occasion the city fathers slyly attempted to entice the villagers to come into the city as a community with the promise of free beer and festivities. By this ruse the governors intended to register the visitors and incorporate them into the official census. Evidently the thirst of the Benjaminites was insufficient to inveigle them to fall into the trap being laid, and they refused the offer, obviously savoring independence. The villages wielded sufficient strength through a common bond to give the moguls of Mari a few bad nights, as we can surmise from reading the following report of a member of Mari's police force:

> Say to my Lord: "this from Barnum, thy servant. Yesterday I left Mari and spent the night at Zuruban. All the Benjaminite villages in the Tega district replied with fire signals. I am not certain what these signals meant. I am trying to find out. I shall write to My Lord whether or not I succeed. The city guards must be strengthened and My Lord should not leave the gate."[24]

Elsewhere we read that a governor, Iahhdulum, laid hands on the territories of the Benjaminites and again that the "Davidum" of the Benjaminites was killed by one of the governors of Mari, Zimru-li. Warner Keller recalls the astonishment of the Assyriologists upon deciphering the clay tablets from the archives of Mari and translating the "reports of governors and district commissioners of the Mari Empire came across one after another of names from biblical history—names like Pelug, and Serug, Nahor and Terah—and Harran."[25]

AKKADIA, SUMER, AND UR

The descent of the Semitic-speaking peoples of Aram along the Euphrates and Tigris rivers eventually led to the imposition of Semitic culture and language over the region. The delta of the twin rivers was occupied from prehistoric times by the Sumerians, a people whose mysterious origin remains unresolved. They spoke a common language of equally ambiguous provenance and developed a cuneiform (wedge-shaped) system of writing, which spurred civilization into literacy. About 2330 B.C.E. virtually all of "Mesopotamia," saturated with Semitic-speaking peoples, was unified under the rule of Sargon I, a Semite of humble origin, and the Semites who had steadily infiltrated the area during the proto-literate era proceeded to absorb and eventually displace the Sumerians.

Sargon I established his capital at the city of Agade which became the eponym of the region Akkadia and of the Semitic dialect into which local language resolved. The Sumerian cuneiform system of writing adapted more or less conveniently to Akkadian. Some philologists suggest that cuneiform writing was employed originally for some pre-Akkadian (and pre-Sumerian) language. In any event, it is evident that a precedent literary tradition existed. "Sumerian script was not devised for the Sumerian language, as incompatibilities between the script and language show. Accordingly there was an earlier literate people from whom the Sumerians borrowed their system of writing. However, we have no clearly discernible texts in the language of that earlier people."[26]

The grandson of Sargon I, Naram-sin, reinforced the structure of this early empire and extended and strengthened its commercial ties with the world. A series of contentious struggles ensued in which various ambitious kings within the Akkadian empire sought to gain domination. The city-state of Mari became a powerful commercial center and an entity unto itself for a time with its own dynasty of rulers. At the turn of the second millennium, about 1900 B.C.E., a new dynasty was founded at Babylon, whose famous sixth-generation ruler, Hammurabi, re-established Akkadian hegemony over and beyond Mesopotamia, defeating a coalition that included Mari, which great city he sacked and destroyed in 1757 B.C.E. This period, while actually a continuation of its Akkadian predecessor and almost indistinguishable culturally from it, is alternately referred to as Babylonian.

The Sumerian language, classically employed for international intercourse in Mesopotamia, became slowly displaced by that of Semitic-speaking peoples who settled into Sumer (the biblical Shinar). The resultant "Akkadian" dialect replaced Sumerian as the lingua franca of the entire region, and became universally used for spoken and written intercultural communication not only in the area of the twin rivers, but in Anatolia and in Egypt as well. The Akkadian idiom was eventually displaced as an international medium of linguistic intercourse by a form of Aramaic, a term applied to the group of languages referred to by philologists as Northwest Semitic, Aramea being, as noted above, the very area from which all the forms of the Semitic language seem to have stemmed.

The Hebrew dialect evolved from a Semitic language spoken by the Canaanites among whom the "Hebrews" later settled; it is biblically termed Sefath Canaan, the "language ('tongue') of Canaan" (Isaiah 19:18), an identification that has been etymologically substantiated. The Hebrew tribes became differentiated from the other Canaanites through the development of unique religious and philosophic precepts; subsequently they were identified by those precepts. However, the Hebrews continued to absorb peoples from (and lose adherents to) other nations and cultures at varying rates under divers circumstances.

There are two theories concerning the provenance of the "tribe of Abraham" (and therefore of the Jews), both of which embrace an interchange of culture and of people as early as pre-Akkadian times. The "Ur of the Chaldees" was conventionally identified with the capital city of Akkadia until the recent, startling discovery of the ancient city of Ebla lent credence to an alternate theory that had been gingerly proposed by various scholars. Ebla was a great and thriving metropolis whose commercial and administrative hegemony encompassed the presumed ancestral home of the tribe of Abraham, the city of Harran and its peripheral towns. References to another "Ur" on documentary tablets unearthed from Ebla's storerooms lent support to the alternate interpretation of the biblical legend.

The provenance of the Jews is biblically given as *Ur kasdim,* conventionally translated as "Ur of the Chaldees" (but more accurately rendered as "Ur of the Chaldeans"). The original assumption of scholars was that this "Ur" was the Ur of Akkadia, since the province of the Chaldeans conjoined the area of Ur. The Chaldeans did not appear on the scene until long after the time of Abraham; the geographical reference, although an anachronistic construction, may be, however, simply and truly an identification of the intended "Ur."

The subsequent theory proposes that the Ur referred to in the Old Testament is a town near Harran. The name appears on numerous cuneiform tablets from

Nuzi, Alalakh, and Ugarit and is particularly apparent in a letter from a Hittite king to his Ugaritic counterpart. Although spelled *Ura* in the Akkadian cuneiform script of the tablet employed for this correspondence, the name would be rendered in Hebrew as Ur.[27] The theory that this "Ur" was the biblical one was convincingly propounded by Cyrus H. Gordon and repeated by him with renewed emphasis after the discovery of equally intriguing references to "Ur" in the Eblaite tablets.[28] Professor Gordon notes that the present town of Urfa near Harran retains a local tradition that boasts of being the birthplace of Abraham. Whereas the two contemporary towns of Harran and Urfa are virtually neighbors, the Akkadian Ur is a thousand miles away to the southeast.

It was noted in the previous chapter that when the tribe of Terach did finally emigrate from Ur it returned to Harran, the ancient commercial crossroads from which its ancestors came. Harran is strategically located at the apex of the Fertile Crescent on the Balikh river, which flows into the Euphrates. Thus the city was a hub of both river and land traffic coursing through from the east and the west, a traffic funneled through the area by the Ararat mountains to the north, the Taurus mountains to the northwest, and the formidable desert spreading out far into the south. The great city of Mari lay to Harran's south along the Euphrates, and past that metropolis stretched Akkadia, within which the cities of Babylon, Eshnunna, Nippur, Kish, Erech, Lagash, Larsa, Erech, and Ur flourished during ancient times. To Harran's east the trade routes crossed easily to the Euphrates' twin river, the Tigris, and to the cities of Asshur, Nirnrud, and Nuzi. The trade routes extended from Harran westward through Ebla, Carcamish, and Alelakh, and proceeded along the Mediterranean coast to Ugarit and Sidon. Branches of those same routes passed through Damascus into Jericho and stretched into Egypt along both sides of the Dead Sea.

It was from urban, cosmopolitan Harran, the epicenter of ancient civilization, that one of the sons of Terach, Abraham, and his entourage emigrated to Canaan. The stated destination was a land in which the Lord promised that they would "become a great nation."

3

The Akkadians in Anatolia

A Semitic Trading Empire

It is written that the tribe of Terach dwelt in the land of Shinar in the city of Ur, in which city Terach's son Abraham was born. Both Shinar and Ur were relegated to a mythic biblical existence until the twentieth century, a presumption that persisted even after the British Consul at Basra in southern Iraq, J. E. Taylor, blundered upon the fabulous city in 1854. Taylor was merely acceding to the instructions of his foreign office to investigate the mysterious mounds in the area at the behest of the British Museum and was unaware of what he had found, for he had no abiding archaeological interest nor scientific qualifications. The area was infested with fierce tribesmen, bands of bedouin brigands to whom tribute had to be paid for passage through or presence in their territory. A British force was assigned to protect the work force hired to excavate the mounds.

THE DISCOVERY AND EXCAVATION OF UR

One of the huge mounds thus subjected to excavation was known locally as Tel al Muqayyar, "the mound of pitch." The diggers exposed the ruins of many buildings made of bricks stamped with strange symbols that meant nothing to them or to Taylor. Among these buildings the remains of a ziggurat, a magnificent pyramidal structure, were revealed. Its stepped tiers soared to the heavens and it was constructed of the strange bricks. The stamps on the bricks happened to be the names of the original royal architect of the ancient city, Ur-nammu, and of a later Babylonian conqueror of the region, Nabonidus, who, many centuries after it had been first destroyed by invaders, rebuilt the city and the ziggurat of Ur-nammu. The excavators also scooped out scores of baked tablets covered with rows of curious incised characters. Taylor's interest was piqued by the writing on the cakes of baked clay and the characters stamped on the bricks, but having no inkling of their meaning or importance, he forwarded the queer objects to the British Museum. Cuneiform writing had not yet been deciphered, and the scholars of the museum were unaware that the peculiar inscriptions identified the site as that of the fabled city of Ur. They were deposited deep in the archival vaults of that august institution to lie dusty and forgotten for seventy-five years.

Taylor continued for a time to tear away at the mound, heedlessly scattering the bricks of ancient structures about the countryside in a frantic search for exotic statues and artifacts. Although the majestic pyramid caused some sensation in the press, no gold idols or precious jewels were found, and interest in the project flagged. The British forces considered esoteric archaeological curiosity an insufficient reason for further expenditures. Because neither gold nor gems nor impressive statues were forthcoming from the effort, funds for further investigation were denied and digging ceased.

Taylor's expedition had merely provided the villagers of the region with a mine for building material and the ancient structures were once again subjected to dismemberment. Tons upon tons of bricks baked four and five thousand years before were carted away by the villagers of the surrounding countryside until, at the end of the nineteenth century, the University of Pennsylvania made another ineffectual attempt to resume digging at Tel al Muqayyar. The new expedition was subjected to harassment by bands of brigands, and so little was accomplished that the results of the expedition were never published. The advent of World War I brought about a sizable expansion in the numbers of British troops assigned to Mesopotamia. Fortunately, a scholar who had been associated with the British Museum and was then able to decipher cuneiform script, R. Campbell Thompson, happened to be a member of the intelligence staff of the British occupying forces. Thompson, whose curiosity was aroused by the proliferation of mounds in the region, probed into them and succeeded in identifying the ancient cities of Ur, Eridu, and Larsa (al-Ubaid).

The protective umbrella of the British army afforded the British Museum an opportunity to launch an archaeological campaign in the winter of 1918-19. One of the earliest and most startling discoveries of the archaeologists was a lump of manufactured opaque blue glass at Eridu, sixteen kilometers southeast of Ur. The glass had been produced well before 2000 B.C.E., a dating which was fixed by the fact that the glass had been found underneath a pavement that had been laid down during the reign of Amar-Sin, the third king of the third dynasty of Ur. Even more ancient manufactured glass artifacts were subsequently unearthed from Ur itself, as well as from the ruins of a number of other Akkadian cities.

A STARTLING DISCOVERY

The existence of glass artifacts manufactured at such an early time brought the scientific community face to face with a fact of shattering significance whose value far exceeded that of the exotic baubles themselves: glass manufacture requires a pyrotechnology that was presumably yet a thousand years away, an Iron Age technology that had never been considered to have originated in Mesopotamia. The startling discovery that the biblical cities not merely existed, but accommodated a literate culture and a technology far in advance of the Greeks and Romans and possibly even of the Egyptians, was met by most scholars with widespread skepticism.

Scientists continued for decades to discount evidence constantly emerging in support of the upsetting concept that civilization did not originate in their favorite cultures. Many had spent an academic lifetime extolling the greatness and precedence of the "classical" cultures and now had to reexamine and reorder their premises. Prestigious scholars versed in glassmaking history continued to insist that the art of glassmaking not only did not, but could not have, reached Mesopotamia until the Roman, or, as some scholars grudgingly conceded, at best not until the Greek period. Facts found to the contrary were summarily dismissed, for the acceptance of a precedent technology would compel a revision if not an outright rejection of the romanticism with which "classical" civilization was universally regarded. Glazed pottery dating to the fourth millennium B.C.E. turned up in the lower Mesopotamian region, a chemically sophisticated technology that appeared nowhere else at that early date. The implications of the fact that glazing had been practiced in lower Mesopotamia for three millenia before the Greeks employed the process scarcely earned scholarly attention. Even the discovery of some manufactured iron objects of the same early dating did not unsettle the placid obduracy with which most of the scientific community continued to discount the persistent eruption of evidence of Mesopotamian pyrotechnology.

The evidence was of long standing: as far back as 1811, Claudius James Rich, rummaging in the rubble of the "City of the Tower of Babel," reported on the presence of masses of glass fragments among other exotic materials. In 1849, Sir Austen Henry Layard reported with unconcealed excitement on the recovery of glass vessels at the Assyrian cities of Nimrud and Kuyunjik, one of which even bore the name of the reigning king, Sargon. Still another glass bowl was recovered by Layard a few years later, clearly incised in cuneiform with the name of Sargon along with his title as king of Assyria. These and a series of other such definitive finds were assigned, with ever more circumventing logic, to imports from Egypt.

The persistence with which the dominant elements of the scientific community allowed preconceived lore to obscure the significance of discoveries that confirmed the sophistication and superiority of ancient Mesopotamian pyrotechnology was hardly shaken by the realization that the earliest appearance of copper and bronze metallurgy was also evidenced as having taken place in the same region of Mesopotamia. The earliest use of bronze is said to have occurred at Jamdet Nasr, a site near Babylon, and the earliest manufactured iron artifacts were recovered from the same region.[1] The production of both glass and iron requires the use of a pneumatically drafted furnace, a technology that goes beyond what is needed to produce copper and bronze. The production of glazes and glass depends on an advanced chemical knowledge including a familiarity with the properties of a variety of unrelated materials that have to be refined from ores mined in distant lands. The knowledge of the minerals, their sources, and the ability to obtain them bespeaks a considerable scientific and commercial capability.

The classicists were again forced to compromise some of their cherished shiboleths as a result of the efforts of Sir Leonard Woolley, who began excavation at Ur in 1922 under the combined sponsorship of the University of Pennsylvania and the British Museum and continued digging diligently at the site over a period of a dozen years. Woolley's work at Ur crowned a distinguished career in Egypt, Nubia, and Carchemish. The revelations erupting from the excavations at Ur brought about a realization that Ur and the other urban centers mentioned in the Bible not only existed, a fact which had already become indisputable, but, indeed, were as indisputably at the heart of a great and ancient civilization. They impelled Woolley to call for a radically altered view of the Hebrew patriarch, Abraham, as a citizen of a great city who inherited the traditions of an old and highly organized civilization.[2]

REGIONAL ETHNOGRAPHY IN BIBLICAL TIMES

A great and well-ordered civilization had indeed been long established throughout the alluvial plains of the twin rivers, the Tigris and the Euphrates. The delta region was by no means the site of the earliest civilization; it soon became evident that such a distinction belonged to the area at the crown of the Fertile Crescent, the hilly region from which the headwaters of the rivers flowed, and the area from which, it is written, the biblical tribe of Terach originated. The Hebrew progenitors, therefore, had been a part of a broad ethnographic movement of peoples from the land biblically referred to as Aram-Naharaim, the Land of Aram, toward the southeast. In ancient Near Eastern texts these immigrant people are referred to as being (from the land of) Martu or (from the land of) Amurru, both of which are references to "people from the West" or "Westerners," reflecting the direction from which they descended into Shinar (Sumer). At the turn of the third millennium, at the time of the Third Dynasty of Ur, Martu becomes equated with and largely displaced by Amurru as a regional designation, and the word becomes both an ethnic and occupational label. The regional context is evident, for example, in references to the Mediterranean in Akkadian texts as the Sea of Amurru or "The Western Sea." The ethnic and occupational context derives from the numbers of itinerant artisans among them, who were dubbed simply "Amurru."[3] Thus the advent of advanced technology from Aram-Naharaim is linguistically acknowledged in Akkadian texts. The word "Amurru" was transliterated into the commonly employed term "Amorite," a term synonymous with "Aramean," a term that is more specific when applied to residents of Aram-Naharaim.

The immigrant Amoritic tribes amalgamated with the other peoples of the region, notably with the Hurrians and with the indigenous Sumerians. The Hurrians (the biblical Horites) were also immigrants, having come from the higher mountains around Lake Van,[4] a region contiguous with Aram-Naharaim (Aramea). The Amorites established the first extensive empire ever known under Sargon I, who established his capital at Agade. The name of the city became the eponym of the region: Akkad. The language spoken by the immigrant Amorites, Akkadian, was a variation of that spoken in Aram, the base language referred to philologically as West-Semitic; the Akkadian "East-Semitic" dialect eventually became the lingua franca of the entire Mesopotamian region.

The term Akkad gave way by common usage to "Babylonia" after a period of decline, and the city of Babel (Akkadian, *bab-ilim,* Hebrew, *babel,* "gate of God") became the capital of one of the petty city-states of the region at the turn of the ninth century B.C.E. under what has aptly become known as the "First Babylonian Dynasty." Babylon grew to greatness under Hammurabi (1792-1750 B.C.E.), who restored Amoritic rule to some semblance of its former glory. The name Babylon remained preeminent for two millennia. The language by that time had generated a distinct new dialect which was referred to as Old Babylonian to distinguish it from its future inflections. Shinar, the common biblical term for the geographical region of Akkadia or Babylonia, appears in earlier Egyptian and Hittite documents and became the "usual name for Babylonia among the peoples west of the Euphrates during the latter half of the second millennium B.C.E., when Babylonia was under Kassite Rule."[5] Shinar thus has an equal claim to legitimacy for at least that latter period. Culturally speaking, the entire progression is part of a continuum, one that formed the matrix within which the Hebraic culture was conceived, gestated, and born.

The Akkadian Empire was essentially a commercial entity; it was established in the mid-twenty-fourth century B.C.E., coincident with the estimated time of the birth of the arts of iron smelting and glassmaking in the region, and spurred the maturation of the Middle Bronze Age. A text describing Sargon's birth includes one of the earliest documentary references to the advent of the new Bronze Age developments. "The blackheaded people I ruled," it states and cryptically continues, "and governed, mighty mountains, with chip-axes of bronze I conquered."[6]

The "black-headed" mountain people, both the Hurrians and the Amorites, were the most advanced metalworkers of the ancient world. The respect for the smithing skills of both the Amorites and the Hurrians is well recorded in more ancient documents recovered from Ebla, the great metropolis to the west of Harran. Amoritic daggers were so famed that gold replicas were used as currency in Ebla; the bronze work of the Hurrians found its way westward into Anatolia, where it became much prized by the Hittites. During the time of Sargon "the use of bronze in industrial quantities was introduced into Mesopotamia."[7] Another text refers to a victory that Sargon had won across the sea as far as Anaku, the "Tin Country," thus informing us that the import of tin, a primary material for the production of bronze, was well established. The "Tin Country" has yet to be positively identified, but the mountains of Afghanistan, the source of the prized gemstone lapis lazuli and other important minerals, were likely to have been the source of tin. The thirty-six campaigns of Sargon I recorded on Akkadian scribal records took him to "the Cedar forest and to the Silver Mountains" (The Amanus and the Taurus ranges) and to "Kaptara," that is, the Kaphthor of the Old Testament or modern Crete, and included the subjugation of Mari, Ebla, and other great centers of civilization of the times. A cuneiform tablet, a copy of "The King of Battle," the composition that describes Sargon's championing of the cause of the Akkadian merchants in central Anatolia, was found in Egypt together with the correspondence from El Amarna. Akkadian documents thus amply record the massive commercial network that expanded under Sargon and spanned some five thousand kilometers from the far reaches of Afghanistan into central Anatolia, the Mediterranean, and Egypt.

AKKADIA

Sargon I ruled for forty-five years from 2334 to 2279 B.C.E.; he built a capital city, Agade, which lent its name to the province that came to be known in a latinized transliteration as Akkadia. He held reign at an elaborate palace in which "5400 men ate bread daily before the king [Sargon]," a scribe proclaims on a cuneiform tablet. The city lay along the main overland route which penetrated Anatolia, crossed the formidable Taurus mountains through Aram-Naharaim, and descended down the Euphrates through Akkadia into southwestern Iran, a route which probably had been traveled as early as the seventh millennium B.C.E. and continued in use past the time of Alexander, when it became "The Achaemenid Royal Road from Sardis to Susa."[8] Vessels from Arabia and the far-off Makran coast of the Indus valley rested at anchor at the Agade quays. Sargon's claim to this distant trade was far from an idle boast, for among the artifacts recovered from Akkadian houses at Tell Asmar were, for example, "an Indus-type seal together with pottery, etched carnelian beads, and bone inlay of Harappan types."[9]

Akkadia, or, as it was subsequently referred to, Babylonia, the province of the "city of the tower of Babel," proved to be one of the first fountains of civilization as we know it. The Akkadian complex of cities expanded within a civilization that had already been urbanized for some thousands of years. The remarkable variety of raw materials and the extensive range and impressive distance from which they arrived to Akkadia are dramatically revealed by records that list resources already being exploited some two thousand years before the time of Abraham. The import of bitumen down river from Hit is recorded, as is copper from Oman, silver from upper Silicia, and from the hills of South Elam. Gold was imported from Elam and Cappadocia, from the Kabur district and from the Antioch region of Syria. Limestone was mined in and imported from distant Jebel Simran or the upper Euphrates Valley, diorite imported from Magan, alabaster and calcite from the northern Assyrian mountains, and lapis lazuli from the distant Pamirs, some three thousand kilometers away.[10]

The metropolis of Uruk, some thousand years later, and still a thousand years away from the time of Abraham, encompassed four hundred hectares and contained a population of "no less than 40,000-50,000. . . . The Uruk period was a time when certain artifacts entered into genuine mass production, even if the producing units in many cases seem to have been small handfuls of kilns in numerous individual settlements of all sizes rather than large centralized workshops."[11] Sir Leonard Woolley, the excavator of these ancient metropolises, calculated that some five hundred years later and still some hundreds of years before the time of Abraham, the 4,250 houses comprising the central city of Ur contained 34,000 inhabitants, and that the district of Ur had a population exceeding a quarter of a million "and may have been twice that."[12] "Ur," continued Woolley, "was a trading and manufacturing center and its business extended far afield." Seton Lloyd agreed: "The Sumerians and Babylonians were essentially town-dwellers and peasant folk. Unlike the nomads of the desert and the migratory herdsmen of the Iranian uplands they preferred to turn their backs on the open spaces."[13] Agade was the imperial center of a network of seventeen *uru-sag*, district capitals distributed within an area of 1,600 square kilometers. The entire complex can be vividly envisioned from later Neo-Assyrian annals, in which Sennacherib boasted of his conquest of "a total of 88 strong, walled cities of Chaldea, with 820 hamlets within their borders."[14]

The elaborate bureaucratic administration required to govern and control the vast complex thus created came to full fruition in the period of the Third Dynasty of Ur (2114-2004 B.C.E.). The empire was divided into some forty districts, each of which was placed under the management of a governor (*ensi*). The governors were divorced from military control, commissioned to administer civil affairs. The military establishment was composed of separate entities, district garrisons assigned to commanders, each of whom was responsible directly to the king. Courts were established to adjudicate conflicts between the military and civil administrations. Ur-Nammu, the very king who was responsible for the construction of the great ziggurat uncovered by Thompson and excavated by Woolley, was also the promulgator of one of the world's first codes of law. Breaches of contract and disputes involving property or inheritance were but two facets of the code's application. Social justice was integral to its strictures, and protection of the disadvantaged was a prime consideration. Some of the punishments prescribed for transgression would be considered harsh in a contemporary context, but the widow, the orphan, the disabled were all protected under its benign umbrella. Some of the precepts could well be incorporated in contemporary judicial law: the legal status of women, for example, was equal to that of men in both marriage and property under Akkadian law. The propensity for welding social justice to law continued to the time of Hammurabi (1792-1750 B.C.E.), the Babylonian ruler who expanded the codal structure; its precepts are reflected in the Mosaic law, which came into being shortly thereafter at Mount Sinai and has been in practice ever since.

The complex society thus created engendered the creation of an accounting system of unprecedented proportions. An administrative center was set up by Shulgi (2094-2047 B.C.E.), for example, to register the receipt and distribution of livestock. A daily balance sheet was maintained, and the records of transactions recovered from this single bookkeeping center during a single year account for over 28,000 cattle and some 350,000 sheep. Both private and royal business is recorded on such "account books," in which is also detailed the rates of pay for work in the fields, at trades, and in the services; thus we learn the relative values placed on men working in construction, digging canals, and loading or towing canal boats, or for women workers at their duties as field hands, weavers, and mill house workers. Rates of pay were established for the most menial work as well as for the most skilled disciplines: payment was effected in rations of beer, bread, oil, onions, and seed, and various other commodities according to the season and availability. Barter was not the only means of exchange or payment for services; a monetary system based on silver was employed and the metal became a standard of value. "Long lists of commodities valued in silver provide the earliest 'price index' for the staples of Mesopotamian life."[15]

Artisanship and commerce matured and thrived in Mesopotamia throughout the fourth and third millennia. The extent and importance of the development of these twin facets of urban expansion are evidenced by the development of a fully functional guild system. Guidelines for the conditions of work and trade were embodied in codes of law by Akkadian and Babylonian rulers. Artisans' guilds policed those guidelines and promoted the interests of member artisans. Traders, *tamkari,* were also associated into a guild, which was, to a surprising measure, autonomous. The city itself was essentially a military and cult center within which the ruling hierarchy and the priesthood were maintained, but the headquarters of the well-organized traders were installed outside the city proper, where they conducted business independently, deposited their assets into their own financial establishments, and enjoyed a relatively free legal status in which they managed their own juridical affairs. Business was conducted at the *karum,* or Akkadian trading colony, through barter, banking, and credit. Foreign traders, often members of an equivalent organization, were accommodated at the *karum.* The fact that meetings took place between Akkadian merchants and visiting representatives of a parallel merchant's guild of India are evidenced by engraved and stamped seals of the Indus Valley type found on Sumerian sites, and especially at Ur, dated as far back as the twenty-fourth century B.C.E. "The importers of copper from beyond the Persian Gulf transacted their business by pooling their funds and by sharing the risks, the responsibility and the profits. These texts repeatedly mention the *karu,* merchant organization with a seat and a legal status of its own, outside of the city proper."[16]

The magnitude of some of the industries of ancient Akkadia gives one pause for reflection. One tablet gives an account of 6,400 tons of wool for processing, the same tablet gives details about the workforce and indicates that nearly 9,000 slaves were employed in the textile industry at Ur. One of the weaving factories of Ur produced twelve different varieties of woolen cloth. The rations issued to each of the woman workers, the amount of wool allotted to them, and the quantity of cloth they manufactured were all carefully incorporated in the daily records of the enterprise.[17]

The copious volume of goods in transit, the size of the overland caravans, and the volume of waterway shipping are often astounding. A letter from Ishba-Erra to King Ibbi-Sin of Ur (2028-2004 B.C.E.) attests to the purchase and storage of 288,000 bushels of grain. Ishba-Erra requests that the king supply six hundred boats capable of carrying five hundred bushels each, and states that thereupon he will deliver grain to designated cities of Sumer. The idea that so many river boats of considerable size were available for the purpose suggests an ongoing traffic of considerable proportions. An even earlier letter reports a large store of barley at Emar from which a shipment of twelve thousand bushels went up the Euphrates river to Mari.[18]

Shipment by land was no less impressive. A conservative estimate (the figure accounts only for shipments listed on recovered records) of shipments over a period of fifty years in the eighteenth century B.C.E. to the *karum* of Kanesh in Anatolia totals quantities of 100,000 textiles and 13,500 kilograms of tin. The rate of export given on various records leads to an estimate of shipments of about eighty tons from Akkadia over a period of fifty years. Tin, important for alloying with copper to produce bronze, was not a local product, and the Akkadian merchants were therefore processing enough for local needs and reexporting the surplus. This commerce is even more astonishing because tin is not native to Mesopotamia. Although the exact provenance of this vital metal is still somewhat in doubt, it is certain that tin was obtained and transported from Afghanistan, three thousand kilometers east of Akkadia, some of which was shipped and delivered to clients another thousand kilometers and more to the west.

KARUMS AND THE EXPANSION OF TRADE

The Anatolian peninsula was one of the major areas into which the Semites extended their commercial activity, Egypt being the other. In Anatolia this burgeoning trade was effectuated through the medium of colonies of commercial agents, also known as *karums*, which were installed near the major centers of population. The traders, in addition to purchasing raw materials from the region, established industries in the *karum*, employing both local and imported labor to process some of these materials into semifinished and finished goods. Thus new technologies were introduced into relatively primitive cultures.

Aramaic and Akkadian culture and technology flowed alluvially along the currents of this commercial stream, together with a proliferation of material artifacts. Aram-Naharaim lay across the center of this vibrant current of interchange of goods and culture. The tribe of Abraham originated in that area, and whether it moved into Akkadia at some time before the time of Abraham (to return through it again into Canaan) or never removed from the area until its exodus (as another well-founded theory holds), its most ancient traditions clearly derive from both regions.

During the third millennium the flow of commerce swelled into a substantial stream, enriching the flourishing Semitic-speaking urban centers and extending Semitic civilizing influence out along ever-widening circles. The local overlords were generally cooperative, appreciative of the benefits accruing from the presence of the *karums*, but they sometimes grew greedy or ambitious and sought to expand their commercial take or the extent of their territory. The rulers of ancient times were, after all, impelled by the same motivations that prompt their modern counterparts. Trade is the instrument by which affluence is attained, and tradesmen are the furnishers of the means by which power is maintained. "National interests," that is, the protection of markets, provide a major incentive for waging war. Commercial concerns were no less conducive to aggression in antiquity. Quick to protect trade, rulers become the guardians of tradesmen abroad. Rulers embarked upon campaigns for economic purposes as well as for the gratification of ambitions for power and political hegemony.

The empirical Akkadian interest in protecting the unconstrained license of traders is articulated in a number of legends and is particularly pointed in an epic poem, "The King of Battle." In this poem, Sargon I, disturbed by reports that the rights of the merchants of a colony in Cappadocia are being abused by the local ruler, boasts in florid language of how he took action by heroically leading his army through strange, uncharted mountain passes (the Taurus mountains), and deep into Anatolia to Purushkanda, south of the Great Salt Lake in central Anatolia, to reinstate and preserve the abrogated rights of this colony of Akkadian merchants, and how the punishment inflicted taught the local ruler to restore and honor those rights.

Akkadian merchants on foreign location generally relied on tact, and on the economic benefits that accrued to accommodating hosts from their activity. However, when these factors failed, and an avaricious Anatolian nabob attempted to divest the resident community of Akkadian Tamkari of their privileges, Sargon was called on to intervene, and he did. Sargon I championed the cause of the Akkadian merchants precisely because his empire and its affluence depended on a flow of goods from all corners of the known world.

> On his return [from Cappadocia] he was careful to bring back specimens of foreign trees, vines, figs and roses, for acclimatization in his own land. . . . There can be no doubt that the principal motive of these foreign wars was commercial, the control of the trade routes and of the sources of supply. The kings themselves make no mystery of this. Manishtusu, the second ruler of Agade after Sargon, ends a triumphal inscription describing his victories over thirty-two allied princes of southern Elam with the statement that he thereby secured the silver mines of their land and diorite for the making of statues.[19]

Akkadian traders had a profound affect on Anatolia; the Tamkuri, the carriers of commerce, were also the conductors of culture and made a permanent imprint upon Anatolian society. Excavations in Anatolia in the last century have exposed massive evidence of fully functioning *karums* adjoining the important Hittite cities. The discovery of a substantial colony of these traders at Kültepe in the Anatolian plains of Kayseri caused a sensation, for although the Mesopotamian influence had long been suspected, few archaeologists, until then, had given much credence to the idea that a high level of civilization existed in Mesopotamia, let alone that Anatolian Hittite "Indo-European" technology and culture was largely a by-product of Mesopotamian influence. Thousands of texts were recovered from the latter two of the four levels of the Akkadian colony, which dated from 1920 to 1840 and 1813 to 1780 B.C.E. respectively, and continuing excavation has provided substantial evidence of the manner in which the primitive but powerful Hittites came in contact with, and eventually absorbed, Mesopotamian culture. The fact that the name of Sargon I and of his grandson Naram-Sin figure in recoveries from the earlier levels lends substance to what had been considered by many as mere boastful legends promulgated by the Akkadian kings.

The intrusion of the Asian "Hittites" into Anatolia in the mid-third millennium B.C.E. brought them into contact with the Aramaic peoples, who already had been trading with the indigenous peoples for several millennia before that time. Ancient Hittite historical sources, reconstituted from cuneiform records recovered from the Hittite capital at Hattusa, place the seat of the earlier Hittite princes at Nesha (Kanesh). The Akkadian traders created a substantial settlement at Nesha, the *karum* Kanesh, which may be translated as "the [Akkadian] Trader's Guild of Kanesh." Such colonies were already functioning a thousand years prior to the time of the Hittites, according to the early projections of that remarkable archaeologist Sir Leonard Woolley, and his estimates have been well borne out in recent excavations.

The antiquity, extent, and importance of the activities of the Tamkari before and during the time of the Hittites is well attested. "The commercial settlement at Ganes [Kültepe-Kanesh] in Cappadocia of which we hear in the time of Sargon of Akkad had already been long established and its origins may well go back to the first dynasty [of Ur]."[20] The one error Woolley made was in guessing that Kanesh was the Purushkanda referred to in the Sargon saga. It later became clear that both the Kanesh and the Purushkanda *karums* were among many trading posts placed at the junctions of a substantial commercial network that swept from Sumer around the Fertile Crescent and throughout the central Anatolian peninsula. Assur in Mesopotamia and Kanesh in Anatolia became the hubs from which the network radiated into their respective areas. Woolley's surmise as to the existence of an extensive Akkadian commercial empire, however, proved to be fully justified.

Their numerous letters, accounts and legal documents (amounting now to more than 16,000 texts, all but 2,000 unpublished [in 1977] have been found in Kanis, in Borghazkeui, and in very small numbers, outside of Anatolia. . . . All the texts show the merchants in at least two roles: handling the export of textiles manufactured in or traded through the town of Assur, and acting as intermediaries between mining and smelting centers and distributors in the copper and iron trade within Asia Minor. Their reports on their dealings with native rulers, and on their business activities with other merchants and with the natives, give us most of our information about Asia Minor at the beginning of the second millennium. One cannot fail to notice the freedom of movement of these traders, the security of communication without reference to any military protection, the large returns in silver and gold which their activities yielded, and, above all, the pride of the merchants in their social status, and in their high ethical standards.[21]

The Akkadian language was the standard language of virtually all of these documents. Thus, by the time of Akkadian-speaking Abraham, Mesopotamian civilization was already ancient, highly developed and well established: the tentacles of trade touched the entire known world; the quantity and diversity of goods being exchanged necessitated bustling river traffic and caravans of considerable size; the economic interests of the various kingdoms provoked them to attempt to extend their influence ever wider; the age of imperialism and colonialism was well under way.

Ancient Anatolia has long seemed an enigmatic area, a mysterious melting pot, never the center, always the detour, of history. This great eastern Mediterranean promontory of Asia, stretching around the Black Sea and encroaching on the Aegean, became a major crossroads of cultures. The annals of the first western historians, the Greeks, treated Anatolia as neither East nor West and chronicled events as Greek history, leaving few distinctions. The peoples of Europe and Asia met and mixed among its mountains. The seaways around its rockbound shores served as a commercial highway. Its numerous mountain-ringed ports became havens for pirates and piratical potentates.

MESOPOTAMIAN TECHNOLOGY IN ANATOLIA

During the latter half of the third millennium B.C.E., one of the indigenous central Anatolian peoples, the Hatti, were among those enjoying an ongoing commercial relationship with the Akkadians through a *karum* located near their stronghold at Hattus. Various central Asian elements, the so-called Indo-Europeans, were attracted to Anatolia during this period by the benefits of the burgeoning civilization. Soon after the turn of the second millennium, the indigenous peoples were overwhelmed by the newcomers. The history of this period is murky, but it seems that a certain chieftain among the infiltrators, Pithana, created a small empire by overcoming a number of other petty rulers. Pithana's son Anitta established residence at Nesha (Kanesh). The "Neshites" conquered Hattus, which name was transcribed into their form of language as Hattusa. The name Hittite derives from the name of the indigenous Hatti and became anonymously applied to the Neshites (who became powerful enough to dominate central Anatolia), and to the civilization that developed under Neshite control. Pithana and Anitta are conventionally relegated to the "Pre-Hittite" period; the "Old Hittite" period begins either from 1680 to 1650 B.C.E. according to some projections (the Middle Chronology) and from 1600 to 1570 B.C.E. according to others (Low Chronology). It is thus some 800 years after Sargon I that the "Hittite" culture appears upon the proscenium of history.

Neither the indigenous peoples nor the invaders from central Asia were literate. After the Hittites assumed power at the turn of the sixteenth century B.C.E., a new scribal tradition was instituted. The original language of the Hatti and the imported "Indo-European" languages (Luwian and Palaic) were all rendered scripturally in one or the other of two variations of cuneiform Akkadian, Semitic dialects conventionally referred to as Old Assyrian and as Old Babylonian. Old Babylonian may well have contained an Aramaic inflection, which was borrowed from the scribes of the area around Harran, "an area in the orbit of the Old Babylonian dynasty of Hammurabi."[22] A form of Luwian ("Hittite") hieroglyphs did appear in the mid-second millennium B.C.E., but whereas some historians have relegated the inception of this primitive script to an earlier period, no convincing proof of a precedent literacy has been forthcoming. Hurrian, the language of the peoples of the Ararat mountains to the east, began to intrude into texts of the later period, but, as elsewhere in Mesopotamia, the Hurrian terms appeared in Akkadian cuneiform script. Not only were the records and conduct of trade being carried on almost entirely in the language of and essentially by the Semites, but the very history of the Hittites continued to be recorded in Akkadian cuneiform, although a rare few of the records were rendered in the Hittite's own primitive hieroglyphic script. "The cuneiform records found in the sanctuaries and archives at Hattusa," sums up the Turkish historian Dr. Nurettin Yardimci, "explain the history of Hittite Anatolia between the years 1650 and 1200 B.C.E. A second site which has produced written Hittite records is that at Masa Höyük in Tokal province."[23]

The Neshites/Hittites established their capital at Hattusa (Boghazköy) from which center they controlled all of the Anatolian peninsula except for the southern coastal regions, which, protected by precipitous mountains, remained out of their grasp. The technological attainments of the Hittites (as, by custom, the Neshite culture shall be referred to hereafter) were far short of the Bronze Age, then in full flower in Mesopotamia. Yet there are insistent allusions by historians to the Hittites as expert metalsmiths, and even to their having introduced the Iron Age, a leap which is hardly credible; it is a fable that is quickly dispelled as the facts become revealed.

The disappearance of the communities of artisans working in the *karums*, or working for the traders in the *karums*, brought about the virtual cessation of the introduction of Mesopotamian technology into Anatolia. It was at this time that such sophisticated, highly developed, as yet exotic arts as iron-smelting and glassmaking began to filter across Aramea toward the Mediterranean coast. The secrets for the production of glass, born in Akkadia and retained by Semitic artisans, thus diverted, never arrived to Anatolia; the infusion of Semitic culture and technology north of the arc of the Fertile Crescent was interrupted and the movement of Semitic artisans carrying the esoteric secrets of the art of glassmaking was effectively deflected into Canaan.

The process of the intrusion of Mesopotamian culture into primitive Anatolia and the precedence of Mesopotamian metallurgy are well illustrated in the Museum of Anatolian Civilizations in Ankara, where a comprehensive Anatolian collection provides a extensive overview of the evolution of Anatolian culture and technology. One is immediately struck by the fact that the museum's earliest Bronze Age exhibits are not of Anatolian ware; they consist entirely of Mesopotamian artifacts of the Sumerian Dynastic Period (2600–2350 B.C.E.); these are followed in turn by the Ur III Dynastic and the Old Akkadian Periods (2340–2150 B.C.E.) in which bronze artifacts first appear in Anatolia, objects retrieved from the areas in which the Akkadian *karums* were installed. The Bronze Age first emerges in the Anatolian region later in the Babylonian period (2100–2000 B.C.E.). The Akkadian *karums* were active throughout these periods composing the so-called "Assyrian Trading Period."

Thus, notwithstanding the impression left by many references to Hittite metallurgic superiority in contemporary literature, Anatolian metallurgy trails the Akkadian by at least six hundred years. How, then, could they have been the initiators of the Iron Age, as many historians claim? Could they have leaped ahead of their Mesopotamian tutors?

The introduction of Eastern literacy is also well-attested to in the museum by commercial documents as well as by those that richly illustrate all aspects of the fabric of life in the region. Virtually all of the literature of the period unearthed from the ruins of Anatolia is written in Akkadian cuneiform, sometimes referred to as "Old Assyrian." Wheel-made pottery, dated to about 2000 B.C.E., among the earliest ever found, also appear in the Akkadian *karums*. The earliest writings, the earliest bronze, the earliest wheel thrown pottery. All Akkadian!

The use of "Assyrian," employed ubiquitously for the language and people of Mesopotamia in the first quarter of the second millennium B.C.E., is clearly an anachronism, inasmuch as Assyria as a viable entity did not come into existence until many centuries later. The use of the adjective "old" is a misleading designation regarding the Akkadian language employed on the tablets, and there are valid arguments offered by many scholars which even hold that, in fact, although a city of Assur existed, no such cultural or political entity as "Assyria" ever existed, old or otherwise. "Babylonia" is also habitually employed in place of Akkadia, but has legitimacy as a regional political and cultural entity, the city of the Tower of Babel being the capital of the region at the time of Hammurabi. However, properly speaking, the Babylonian period follows closely on the heels of the Akkadian period, so-named after the city of Agade, the capital of the region from the time of its founder, Sargon I.

AN ANATOLIAN EXPEDITION

My visit to the museum at Ankara took place on the occasion of a tour of ancient Anatolian archaeological sites under the guidance of Professor Machteld Mellink, a former president of the organization sponsoring the tour, the Archaeological Institute of America, of which I was a member. I leaped at the opportunity to visit the Anatolian region in the company of knowledgeable fellow-travelers and to study its sites and museums in the shadow of Professor Mellink, a distinguished scientist who has devoted her life to Anatolian studies. Newly founded Turkish museums proudly feature the artifacts she unearthed in years of patient excavation; Anatolian archaeological literature is replete with references to her discoveries; her dissertations on those discoveries are models of scientific discipline; her students adore her. Included in the group accompanying Professor Mellink were professors of various archaeological disciplines; some had been students of Mellink, some had distinguished themselves with field work in Turkey, Greece, and Crete.

Mellink is an energetic, enthusiastic woman who appears capable of conducting a safari across the most desolate desert or of trekking through the wildest jungle. Our studies began in earnest with the visit to Gordion, the site of the tomb of the fabled King Midas, whose royal tumulus, originally 80 meters high and

Machteld Mellink, right, professor of Humanities at Bryn Mawr College and past president of the Archaeological Institute of America. Professor Machteld is a distinguished excavator of many campaigns in Anatolia and is considered the dean of Anatolian studies. (Photograph by the author.)

250 meters in diameter, is now a prime tourist attraction. Midas, a poor farmer, became the fortunate successor to the childless King Gordios, the eponymous founder of Gordion. Midas, it is said, was driving a wagon-load of produce into town at the time the assembly of the city were discussing the prediction of an oracle foretelling the identity of Gordios' successor. The oracle proclaimed that a man driving a wagon into the city would become the heir of King Gordios and thereby resolve the discord over succession. King Gordios acknowledged Midas as heir and successor as the astonished farmer drove through the city gates! At least, so the legend goes.

The ruins are a short drive east of Ankara; they are the remains of the capital from which the Phrygians ruled central Anatolia after the collapse of the Hittite Empire. Although eighteen strata define superimposed civilizations dating from the Early Bronze Age, almost all the archaeological work has been devoted to the Phrygian period. The Phrygians constitute the cultural link between the Hittite and the Persian domination of Anatolia, and of the subsequent Hellenic period.

"Is there evidence of a *karum* in the Gordion area?" I asked an archaeologist at the site.

"Yes," answered the archaeologist and added, somewhat sheepishly, "but we haven't done much about that sector."

At both the Ankara and Gordion museums only a smattering of glassware was exhibited, a few odd pieces of indeterminate provenance, none earlier than the Roman period. The absence of glass or of any trace of its manufacture is of significance inasmuch as the making of glass presumes a high pyrotechnological level and presages the advent of the Iron Age. An advanced furnace is required for the smelting of iron and particularly for the production of glass, for which a pneumatically drafted, reverberatory furnace is requisite, a furnace engineered to achieve and maintain a furious temperature of 2000 or more degrees Fahrenheit. Because many scholars had written that the Hittites were the first to smelt iron, evidence of either iron or glass manufacture should exist and would be meaningful. Yet not one shred of evidence of the existence of either art appears at Gordion throughout the pre-Roman period.

"Well," I thought, "perhaps the Phrygian civilization was a step backward from that of the Hittites. At Boghazköy I may find some glass or iron, even though that Hittite capital predated this Phrygian one. After all, the Hittites demonstrated their military might by diverting the Egyptian Pharaoh Tuthmoses III at Megiddo. They defeated the Egyptians later at Kadesh and obliged Rameses II to sign a non-aggression treaty. Surely they must have had a technological potential to match their military prowess."

Boghazköy, the site of the ruins of Hattusas, is a few hours drive east of Ankara. Hattusas was the heart of Hittite hegemony, the center from which the Hittites reached the apex of their power and influence. The peace treaty of Kadesh, drawn in 1275 B.C.E. between the Hittite king Hattusilis III and Rameses II after two decades of war between the Hittites and the Egyptians, is displayed in the museum at the site, a ruddy ruin of a tablet covered by cuneiform script. It seemed too puny to be the text of one of the most important historical documents of Hittite history and of a critical turning point of Near Eastern affairs. I had seen the Egyptian counterpart at Karnak inscribed prominently and proudly in bold hieroglyphics into a 30-foot-high wall of the great temple complex. The inscription of the precedent great battle at Megiddo, in which the Egyptians touted their victory, was even more impressive. It was scrawled over much of the face of a great pylon. There, blazoning forth their message to impress the world, both texts seemed in keeping with their significance.

A translation below the modest Kadesh tablet was underlined by a curt note: "Language: Akkadian," it announced.

We were met by Dr. Peter Neve, the excavator in charge of the excavations, a gaunt figure with a weather-lined face. He devoted the afternoon to us, marching us around the vast glacis descending from the main area of temples and fortifications, flanked by Professor Mellink, who strode before us on this and each successive site with boundless energy and spirit. We tramped behind Neve and Mellink along the 6-kilometer route of the annual ritual procession of the Hittite kings, to which royal route Neve had devoted more than a year to tracing and mapping. He pointed proudly at one after another of the succession of temples being uncovered. He expounded with boyish enthusiasm on the sculptures still left on the site.

I took the opportunity of a pause in his dissertation to inquire, "Where was the *karum*?"

"It is a separate site," Neve replied.

"Are you excavating it?" I persisted.

"We have many more temples to work on."

I decided not to press further. I had in mind the revelations that had sprung out of the excavations of *karum* Kanesh at Kültepe in Cappadocia: the vast trove of thousands of Akkadian and other documents illuminating the development of Anatolian culture and commerce; the artifacts that had been recovered demonstrating a sophistication worthy of serious attention. It would appear, therefore, that the exposition of the *karum* at Hatusas should enjoy a measure of priority. It was reported subsequently that by 1988 Dr. Neve had completed the excavation of temple number 30![24]

Dr. Neve estimated the size of the *karum* as being about one third the size of Hattusas itself. It was more than mere quarters for itinerant merchants; indications were that it had been an extensive, well-ordered, urban village with settled families, artisans and a complete support system. Its influence could be judged by the fact that their language was being employed for commerce and diplomacy, and their standards of weights and measures were the ones apparently applied in the region. There was clear evidence of dozens of villages surrounding Hattusas, but since there were severe limitations on finances and staffing, the excavation of the *karum* and the villages were of necessity deferred to an indefinite future date.

Dr. Peter Neve, archaeologist in charge of excavation at Boghazköy, the site of the ruins of Ancient Hattusas. (Photograph by the author.)

That evening I reviewed the photographs in a well-documented book assembled by Nurrettin Yardimici, Director General of the Turkish Department of Antiquities and Museums, entitled *Land of Civilizations, Turkey*. During the Middle Bronze Age, so it was stated, Hittite civilization attained its pinnacle; the period was well represented by thirty-seven typical pieces found in central Anatolia. Twenty-one of the most outstanding designs, the very ones exhibiting the finest craftsmanship of all the items reproduced in the book, were from the *karum* of Kanesh. Because the *karums* were populated by foreign traders and artisans, and the sites on which these villages stood were by no means as thoroughly excavated as were the adjoining Hittite administrative and cult centers, such a disproportionate representation of sophisticated ware is, to say the least, startling. Even more puzzling was the fact that the artifacts recovered from the *karum* were the very ones employed to typify the best of "Hittite" art in Turkish brochures and publicity!

The motifs on the seals and artifacts recovered from the ruins of numerous ancient Hittite sites are easily recognizable Akkadian designs: the rayed disc, bull-men, winged griffins and raptors, sphinxes, hunting scenes, and other such characteristic subjects are rendered in typical Mesopotamian styles. "For the history of [Early Hittite] art," affirms Jeanne Vorys Canby, who has excavated at Gordion, Kültepe and Boghasköy, "we are dependant on every-day materials, such as sealings, clay ritual vessels and a few ivories, much of which come from Assyrian trade settlements in colonies outside of the small city-states of the period."[25]

The next morning we were off to Acemhöyük, south of Ankara near Aksaray. Professor Nimet Özgüc, the archaeologist in charge of excavation at the site, joined us on the bus at Ankara and, on the way down, lectured about it. Dr. Özgüc was dressed simply, her head covered by a kerchief. Professors Mellink and Özgüc obviously enjoyed a warm and long-standing relationship. Madame Özgüc's speech was as modest as her appearance, yet this was the woman who, together with her husband, Prof Tahsin Özgüc, excavated Kültepe and the Kanesh *karum*, and contributed so much to the store of Anatolian knowledge.

"This site ranked with Carchemish on the Euphrates as one of the most important centers of civilization of that early period but has not been taken as seriously as it deserves," Professor Özgüc began. "It was originally called Barush Handa, and was the seat of kings predating the Hittites by many centuries. Its potential importance is as great as Kanesh proved to be. In fact, this was the first site chosen by the Assyrians to be the capital of their enterprises in Anatolia. Later it became known as Barush Hattu. The king of Barush Hattu had an iron throne. This was, of course, well before the Iron Age, but iron was indeed being worked in small quantities. It was expensive, and worked only in small quantities.

"The kings here were more powerful than those of Kanesh. In the eighteenth century B.C. the Assyrians came to teach the local merchants to carry out their work. We have recovered thousands of bullae with cylinder seal impressions. I will show you the storeroom where most of them were found, but the seals are being analyzed at the museum. We found references to Naram-Sin and to Sargon

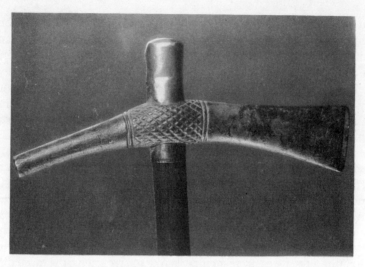

Hammer-axe of bronze and gold. This (probably ceremonial) tool illustrates two aspects of advanced technology introduced into Anatolia by the Akkadian traders and artisans, the use of bronze, and the hafting of tools and implements. (Photograph courtesy of the Andalu Medeniyetleri Museum [Museum of Anatolian Civilizations], Ankara, Turkey.)

Ceremonial vessels illustrating the high quality of craftsmanship in the Akkadian trader colonies in Anatolia. (Photograph courtesy of the Kayseri Archaeological Museum, Kayseri, Turkey.)

I. In fact, Naram-Sin was supposed to have, and I quote, 'hibernated in Barush Handa'!"

This was exciting news. Sargon I was the great twenty-fourth-century Akkadian (once again the anomalous use of "Assyrian" becomes clear) king who had inscribed on stone his concern over the abrogation of the autonomous status of the merchants of Anatolian *karums* by petty chieftains and had handily resolved the problem by a personally led punitive incursion into the area. Here was evidence that Woolley's theory that Aramaic trade relations with the pre-Hittite tribes extended back at least to the mid-third millennium stood on sound ground.

Naram-Sin, Sargon's grandson, ruled from about 2175 to 2135 B.C.E., and was equally a great administrator and innovator. Evidence of Naram-Sin's activity and of Anatolian trade had been found at Tell Brak, located in Northern Mesopotamia on the caravan route into Anatolia, where the king had built an elaborate palace.[26] Naram-Sin claimed to have followed the precedent set by his grandfather by traveling to Talhatum in Anatolia in the interests of the Akkadian merchants there on "a road which no king before had ever taken." Naram-Sin's activity in Anatolia is also known from a stele with the figure of the king found near modern Diyarbakir.[27] As early as the twenty-third century B.C.E., long before the incursion of the "Indo-Europeans," a certain Pamba, king of Hatti, was one of seventeen kings opposing the influence of the Akkadians who were dealt with by Naram-Sin.

"At Kanesh we learned much about the private lives of people from Akkadian texts," the professor continued. "For example, we have a letter from a lady who wrote from Assyria to her husband in Kanesh who had married an Anatolian lady. The Anatolian wife did not produce a child, so the Assyrian wife lent a child to the couple in Kanesh and continually forwarded beautiful clothes for the child. She writes after a while asking what the reason is that her husband does not come back to Assyria at all, and suggests that he spend six months in each city. The husband writes that he likes it in Kanesh. Thereupon she writes that he should send her money so that she can get another husband, and complains about the trouble she is having with her mother-in-law. We read her plea: 'I went to the house to sleep. She won't let me in!'"

Acemhöyük is contained beneath a low mound protected by a barbed wire fence. The site is not a tourist stop and is off limits to everyone except to groups like ours. The site was a mass of burned bricks. "These mud-brick walls on stone foundations are those of a palace of forty rooms," explained professor Özgüç. "Hundreds of stamped seal bullae were found in this room. Why used bullae were being stored is still a mystery. But finding them was a stroke of fortune for they supply hundreds of names and insignia to trace and match with others found elsewhere. We also found ivory works of art used to embellish furniture, crystal and obsidian vases and bronze objects. A very fine collection of ivories were looted by illegal diggings. They are now in the Metropolitan Museum of Art in New York. That is why we put up the barbed wire fence and posted guards."

"Where was the *karum*?" I interjected.

"It is at the first level. We have just made some soundings. We haven't excavated it yet."

"Why not?"

"We need financing. We have not been able to obtain enough to make a thorough stratified cut. Our probes tell us it is there."

"You mentioned that this site may have been even more important than Kültepe-Kanesh. Judging by the unprecedented results there and the importance you place upon the *karum* at this site, is it not reasonable to make a thorough investigation of it?"

Madame Özgüç sighed. "You are absolutely right. Perhaps . . . ?"

She left the sentence dangling.

I turned to another subject. "You mentioned an iron throne and the limited production of some iron artifacts at the turn of the second millennium. Some scholars insist that the Hittites were not only proficient smiths but carried the technology eastward. Yet it appears to me from the evidence we have seen so far that the theory that these early smiths were Hittites is ill-founded. Could that iron throne have been of local production?"

Professor Özgüç did not hesitate. "By no means. The most advanced bronze metalwork found in Anatolia is the work of the Hurrians, otherwise called the Urartians, and it was undoubtedly they who first smelted iron."

The tour of Turkey made it convincingly evident that the story of early iron-making Hittites is an unabridged fable. The technology of the Hittite metalwork, even that of the later periods when it first becomes evident, was far exceeded by that of the Hurrians; the metalwork of any note was obtained from the Aramaic and Hurrian peoples populating the mountains and hills to the east. Wherever the work in brass or iron of these Eastern artisans is absent, work by other hands is rare or non-existent. Another bubble had burst. The wonder was, upon seeing the overwhelming weight of evidence at first hand, how anyone could have proposed otherwise.

In 1970 Professor Özgüç found the remains of a metal four-wheeled vehicle, dating back to the first half of the eighteenth century B.C.E., in the burnt ruins of the palace at Acemhöyük. It was a remarkable find, for the four-spoked copper/bronze wheels of the small wagon or trolley were similar to the representations of such wheeled vehicles on Akkadian cylinder seals of the late twentieth or early nineteenth century B.C.E. found at the *Karum* II level at Kültepe. Most of the Mesopotamian seals depict such "four-wheelers with a seated driver, drawn by a team of four eguids."[28] Another, somewhat later vehicle was found at Toprak-kale, a site near Acemhöyük. It sported "four six-spoked wheels that revolved on iron axles and were comparable in size to the Acemhöyük . . . wheels. The object is considered Urartian."[29] Thus both the early use of the wheel and the production of iron is relegated to the Upper Mesopotamian region.

The judgement of Professor Nimet Özgüç that the *karum* at Acemhöyük may well turn out to rival in importance that of Kültepe-Kanesh was of deep significance, especially as new revelations continued to erupt concerning the flow of

Professor Nimet Özgüç, the archaeologist in charge of excavation of Acemhöyük. (Photograph by the author.)

trade and technology from Mesopotamia into the Anatolian peninsula from Kültepe-Kanesh. The excavations at Kültepe are being performed under the supervision of her husband, Professor Tahsin Özgüç, who wrote that evidence from Kültepe (ancient Kanesh) demonstrates that the profound interaction between southeast Anatolia and the Aramaic region was "predetermined by earlier interaction," again substantiating Woolley's similar estimate of a substantial commercial intercourse which existed long before the establishment of the *karums*, a process which "intensified during the second half of the third millennium." These new revelations justify the projections of Machteld Mellink, "who long ago pointed out that the legends of later times which tell of early Mesopotamian kings coming to Anatolia may on archaeological grounds reflect historical reality."[30] Professor Özgüç went on to cite the multiplicity of relevant finds from Kültepe which are contemporary with the Early Dynastic III, the Akkadian, and the post-Akkadian periods.[31]

A succession of types of pottery, luxury gold artifacts, gemstones and cylinder seals found at Kanesh provide the evidence for and richly illustrate the history of Aram-Naharaim (generally and anachronistically termed "Syria") and of the subsequent migrations of its peoples as much as it does that of Kültepe itself. The early Aramaic influence is reflected in the pottery unearthed from the lowest three levels (levels 13, 12, 11 and relevant subdivisions) in which large buildings were successively constructed over each other's incinerated ruins during the latter phases of the Early Bronze Age. Referring to a building of level 11b, by no means the earliest, Professor Tahsin Özgüc notes that no building of such a size can be found during the Early Bronze Age elsewhere in Anatolia, and gingerly announces that "I am inclined to think that we see here signs of ideas originating in Mesopotamia."[32]

The pottery recovered from four earlier construction levels of the Early Bronze II Age (levels 14-17) were counterparts of ware found in various sites in Aram-Naharaim, through which central Anatolia was linked to southernmost Mesopotamia. Professor Tahsin Özgüc specifically names Ur and Fara as the sites to which these ceramic linkages are most striking.[33] The ceramic connection parallels the linguistic one closely, for Ur and Fara are also two of the sites at which Akkadian names first appear in early Sumerian texts, even in texts dating to the "Ubaid" period preceding the accession to power of Sargon I. The biblical references to the very sites at which these coincidences appear are indeed curious, for Ur was referred to as the home of the tribe of Terach and Fara was ancient Suruppak, the home of the Babylonian Noah.[34] These early attestations in Sumerian documents to an Amorite population and their literacy appear throughout the region: "'Sumerian' scribes at Abu Salabikh, not far from the holy Sumerian city of Nippur, whose documents are closely comparable with those from Fara, bore largely Akkadian names. There is also evidence for the borrowing of Akkadian words into Sumerian from a very early period, whereas Semitic names appear in the Sumerian King-List for kings of city-states, especially in Akkad."[35] The Aramaic link between the two regions is evident from the presence of flasks and pots cited by Professor Özgüc which were made in imitation of metalware common to that found in a "Syrian," that is, Aramaic, context. Özgüc also cites studies by Mellink[36] that establish the chronology of the imitation metalware, and by H. Kuhne, who made comparative studies of the "metallische ware" of Tell Chuera, "a site which must form a link between Mesopotamia, Syria [sic] and Anatolia."[37]

Professor Mellink, in turn, in her annual recapitulation of the archaeological campaigns and discoveries throughout Turkey cites the reports by Professor Tahsin Özgüc on his work at the center of the Kanesh *karum*, in which well-built houses with hearths and ovens were found in the one of the most ancient levels at the site: "Notable among the pottery is a bathtub with appliqué figures of what seems to be a bearded bull-man frontally rendered, nude except for a belt. A sandstone mold for making lead figurines has a group of two frontal figures and an antelope under an eagle with wings deployed. Molds for bronze axes are for the type of shaft-hole axe known from level lb."[38]

Metal objects and weapons were common to both levels 1 and 2 of the *karum*, and the area consisted of both workshops and houses, many of which were individually identified as associated with the Mesopotamian merchants. The evidence of an influx of technology through the trading colonies has already reached an impressive level; the study of the site continues and many new revelations will undoubtedly result from both the textual as well as the physical evidence. "New plans are underway," affirms Professor Mellink, "for the study of the 11,000 tablets found in the Turkish excavations at Kültepe."[39] The prediction was made in 1987; some thousand more tablets were found less than a year later in a new area of the *karum* being investigated. The stone-paved street of the *karum* was exposed together with a stone-built drain that was part of an extensive drainage system of the entire area.

A large collection of tablets were recovered from the subsequent level 2, an "all-Assyrian quarter . . . crowded with large houses and rich archives. . . . The tablets were kept in straw matting, on wooden shelves or (often) in jars. Some of the nearly a thousand tablets found in 1988 were in their envelopes and addressed but not sent to Anatolian cities; other tablets represent unopened mail from Assür." In the tombs underneath the houses, bronze vessels, weapons, gold and silver jewelry once again attested to the prosperity of the residents. Similar inventories and "Assyrian" cylinder seals, but no tablets, were found in the houses adjoining the merchants' quarters, an area evidently inhabited by artisans. Aramaic-style axes, spearheads, and daggers found in these houses suggest additionally that a security force of Aramaic guards or soldiers was also in residence in the peripheral area. The other objects found in those houses all attest to local or Aramaic manufacture.[40]

The expansion of the Akkadian and consequent Aramaic influence is reflected in the ubiquitous appearance of the types of pottery found at Kanesh throughout the region from Akkadian Ur to Egyptian Amarna. Wheel-made pottery appears at Kanesh at a date long before it does anywhere else but within the Mesopotamian milieu where it was born. The jewelry recovered from Kanesh reinforces the evidence, established by pottery, of the intimate cultural links of Kanesh through Aram-Naharaim to Ur. An earring and gold pendant found in a grave of level 13, for example, "are made in gold-working techniques typical of Mesopotamia and the pendant is a counterpart of a small pendant found at Ur in the Royal Cemetery."[41] Beads and artifacts manufactured from lapis lazuli illustrate another aspect of Akkadian commerce, the link through Aram-Naharaim to Afghanistan: "the source of three lapis lazuli beads . . . must also be Mesopotamia, as the transshipment point from its geological source in Afghanistan."[42]

Among the *bullae*, or impressions of seals recovered by Professor Nimet Özgüç at Acemhöyük, were twenty-nine of a type which links Acemhöyük to the Akkadian trading colony of Kanesh being excavated by her husband. The broader faces of the bullae were impressed with a frieze depicting a scene similar to those frequently employed in third-millennium Akkadian cylinders, a struggle between animals and heroes. "There are three groups of figures: a bull-man grasping a lion by the chest and right front paw; a naked hero dangling a bull by its tail and hind leg while stepping on its neck; and a winged lion-dragon with open jaws standing on its hind legs, about to bite an antelope, which is seated on a small hill with its head turned back." The narrow edges of the bullae "were inscribed with the names of the seal owner, his father and the person who was to receive the goods to which the bullae were attached."[43] A large fragment of an envelope recovered at Kültepe-Kanesh bore this selfsame, unmistakable impression!

By far the majority of the impressions of hundreds of these cylinder seals unearthed from the "Bullae Depot Room of the Sarikaya Palace at Acemhöyük," depicting the struggle between heroes and animals, "are in the Old Babylonian [i.e., Akkadian] style." Similar coincidences of cylinder seal impressions of Kanesh and Acemhöyük with those found on objects in various museums and collections ranging from the mid-third millennium throughout the Akkadian Empire and the so-called "Old Assyrian Colony" periods into the fifteenth century B.C.E. are noted by Professor Özgüc. The Hittites adopted the device to a limited extent thereafter. Dr. Edibe Uzunoglu, another noted Turkish archaeologist, notes that although the cylinder seal was employed in Mesopotamia as far back as the end of the fourth millennium B.C.E., and was introduced into Anatolia in the first quarter of the second century, "very few cylinder seals have been found at the Hittite capital, Hattusas." A simple stamp seal was almost universally employed by the Hittites through this seminal Akkadian period, but after the dissolution of the Akkadian *karums* a few rare examples of Hittite adaptations of the cylinder seal do show up in fourteenth- and thirteenth-century contexts, and even in ninth-century "Neo-Assyrian and Neo-Hittite art."[44]

The next leg of our journey led us to Konya, the city of the Whirling Dervishes, and then over the Taurus mountains into Phrygian, Lydian, and Lycian areas. We wove through and over the magnificent ranges of the Taurus mountains toward the southwestern strip of Anatolia, to the area that stretched along the Mediterranean and swept around to Aegean shores. The group gloated over Phrygian and Lycian and Lydian and Carian and Hellenic and Roman tombs ad infinitum. We climbed the steps of one great Greek and Roman amphitheater after another until they blended into one great amphitheater. The intrusive Greek and Roman ruins blot out the bulk of the civilizations lying beneath them, an overlay of stone and brick which symbolizes the literary veneer which veils much of history.

The Semitic peoples sojourned in Anatolia for a thousand years and were swept away; it was not for many hundreds of years that their descendants, the Jews, were again to bring creative ideas and skills to the region.

At the time that *karums* were being established in Anatolia, Semitic traders had already penetrated deep into Africa, following the Nile through the searing desert to barter with the Nubians. Along that long river route petty Egyptian monarchs, rulers of enclaves along the Nile, demanded tribute for the privilege of passage. The Egyptian experience of the Semitic peoples was of pivotal importance to the technological evolution of Egypt, to the region, and to the Jews. Ignorance befogs that history; a strong sun of truth is needed to disperse the layers of thick mists.

No more egregious example of institutionalized obfuscation exists than that committed by historians who blithely cast history into the mold created by an Egyptian priest of the Hellenic period, Manetho, sometimes referred to as "the First Anti-Semite." The cobwebs that envelop a period in which Semitic peoples catapulted Egyptian civilization from the Chalcolithic into the Late Bronze Age in less than two hundred years must first be swept away to expose the matrix from which the Israelite nation emerged.

4

Ancient Egyptian Historiography

Setting the Record Straight

Words are often used in a way that conceals the truth by obscuring factual relationships. A word that epitomizes the concealment of truth is "Hyksos," a term often used as a pejorative reference to certain people of the southwest Asian region who immigrated into Lower Egypt, specifically those who entered Egypt during the period from the so-called twelfth through the seventeenth Dynasties, roughly from the nineteenth through the sixteenth centuries B.C.E.

MANETHO AND THE MYSTERIOUS "HYKSOS"

The term "Hyksos" is derived from words employed by Manetho (323-245 B.C.E.), an Egyptian who rose to become the High Priest of the cult of Serapis at Heliopolis during the reign of the Greek Ptolemies. Manetho was a contemporary of Ptolemy II Philadelphus (285-246 B.C.E.). He was born at Sebbynnetus (now Samannud), in the Delta region of Lower Egypt, an area that was still replete with vivid memories and traces of the period when patriarchal chieftains from Canaan ruled that area and all of Egypt and Canaan some 1,400 years earlier. Manetho's version of Egyptian history has long been the standard by which Egyptian history is written. His system of dynastic succession is still employed by the archaeological community although it has long been proven to be inaccurate, misleading, and prejudicial. Manetho's treatment of a period of several hundreds of years beginning from his "Twelfth Dynasty" forward is particularly suspect because of his sharply anti-Semitic view of a period in which Semitic peoples peacefully augmented their traditional infiltration into the Nile Delta.

We must pause to address the circumstances surrounding the Manetho rendition of Egyptian history in order to fully comprehend how it was that his account, as well as Greek and Roman renditions of history, came to be universally accepted historiography. Manetho's attitude was not uncommon. Tacitus, the Roman historian and an archetypical anti-Semite, pointed out, without the slightest appreciation of the irony of his remark, that "it is an instinct of human nature to hate a man whom you have injured."[1] Many Greek historians of that period, as well as the Roman and Christian historians who followed, became vituperative when treating with the Jews. The Greek apologists could not abide the stubborn insistence of the Jews in acknowledging only a universal God; they deeply resented the rejection by the Jews of the plethora of godly and semihuman beings that characterized Greek religion and culture. Those of the Greeks who considered themselves uniquely rational philosophers nevertheless sneered at the Jews as intransigent, stiff-necked zealots blind to the logic of Hellenic culture.

Hellenic hedonism countenanced and encouraged profligacy and sensuality and disdained moral standards that took humanitarian consideration of the interests of the lower classes, of the poor, the slave, and the disadvantaged, except as they affected Hellenic sustenance of a self-centered life-style. The Platonic society outlined in the *Republic,* a social system that reflected the supercilious stance of the Greek philosophers of the times, relegated all of humanity to a subservient role to an elitist hierarchy, who alone would enjoy democratic privilege. The ethical standards that Hebrew halachic interpretations imposed upon the Jews would, if accepted more widely, threaten the smug social mores of the Greeks; the Greeks were uncomfortable with standards of behavior within and without the family which called for sacrifice of self-interest in consideration of the needs of others. To the Greeks democracy was for elite Greeks, not for subject peoples and certainly not for peoples they considered inferior to themselves. Hebrew tenets that favored the rights of people regardless of social status and origin undercut the Hellenic presumption of an innate right to authority as rulers and reduced Greeks to an equality with commoners when they were among the conquered.

The bilious attitude of the traditionalist Greeks toward the Jews reflected a churlish feeling of inferiority. The aleph-beth that afforded the Greeks literacy, the metallurgy that provided them military strength, the nautical knowledge and acumen that opened the Mediterranean to their expansion, and a great variety of technological skills, were acquired from the peoples they had conquered, and to acknowledge that such was the case would be most disturbing to the pompous self-image they had synthesized.

Primitive mythology was, in fact, being discarded by many rationalist Greeks, who were drawn to the universality of Judaic philosophy, and, like most Jews of the time (as in modern times), deferred to basic Judaic principles, albeit they hesitated to follow all of the fundamentalist canons. Large numbers of these enlightened Greeks, in addition to recognizing a universal order, accepted the Judaic postulate of a single, universal intelligence. The adoption by large numbers of Greeks of Judaic precepts was an especially irksome irritant to the Greek nationalists. Among the rationalists were those who admired Judaic religious and social practices as well; these latter were termed variously *theosebeis* (God worshippers), *phoboemenoi* (those fearing [God]), and *sebemenoi to theon* (those reverencing God) in the Book of Acts and in other writings of Greeks, Jews, and Christians. Although they did not necessarily subscribe to circumcision or adhere to the discipline of the 613 talmudic laws, these Greeks nevertheless abjured primitive mythology, supported Judaic theosophy, and were sympathetic to the Jews. The subject of Judaization of the Gentile community of the "classical" period (as apposed to the Hellenization of the Jewish community) is a subject which will be explored further on in this dissertation in the context of its time.

Manetho wrote his history of Egypt during turbulent times in which the Jews had made a profound political, as well as a philosophical, impact. A massive immigration of Jews into Egypt began to take place under Ptolemy I, swelling the significant numbers of Semitic peoples who had traditionally inhabited the area of the Nile Delta. Ptolemy II Philadelphus ("sister-lover," who did, in fact, marry his sister) freed the Jews upon his ascension to the throne, including those who had been enslaved by his father, Ptolemy I, and those who had earlier been slaves in Egypt. Ptolemy II (283-246 B.C.E.) placed the former Jewish slaves in a social class above the Egyptians; they were granted rights the Egyptians themselves were unable to enjoy; his decrees reflected the generally superior role of the literate, technologically proficient Jews within the social order as contrasted with that of the largely illiterate, unskilled Egyptian masses. These humbling statutes were undoubtedly among the causes of the festering hatred that Manetho, who has been dubbed "the first anti-Semite," bore toward the Jews, for it was during the time of Ptolemy II that Manetho, the Egyptian priest, wrote his Egyptian history. History has not yet out-lived the effects of Manetho's virulent misrepresentations; they live on in historiological and archaeological lore.

It is expressly as a result of Greek anti-Judaic polemic that we were granted the good fortune of obtaining a partial record of Manetho's history. Manetho was first quoted (in first half of the first century B.C.E.) by Apion, a prominent and politically influential Greek writer of Egyptian origin, who gained fame as a Homeric scholar and as the author of his own work on the history of Egypt. When Greeks brought charges against the Alexandrian Jews, it was Apion who represented the Greeks before the Emperor Gaius; the Jewish philosopher Philo represented the Jews.[2]

Apion penned a poisonous polemic against the Jews, drawing much of his information from Manetho's no less biased account. Apion repeated and emphasized Manetho's most spurious misrepresentations, as, for instance, the patently fraudulent suggestions that the Jews were expelled from Egypt as lepers and that the Jews worship a golden ass that is enshrined in the Holy of Holies in their Jerusalem Temple.

Josephus wrote a powerful defense of the Jews and Judaism, *Contra Apionem,* in outrage against Apion's extraction of the most blatantly false of Manetho's allusions to support his arguments. Josephus was particularly piqued with Apion's repetition as fact of patently absurd accusations, which even Manetho himself had alluded to as rumor. In his dissertation Josephus quoted Manetho, using Manetho's own words against Apion, arguing that even as unsavory an anti-Semite as Manetho had not only conceded the antiquity of the Jews but had also recorded details of a period in which Jewish kings had once ruled Egypt.

Manetho had a triple ax to grind. As a Greek he reflected the traditionalist Greek stance toward the Jews. As an Egyptian priest he could countenance even less the revolutionary omneistic precept of the Jews. As an Egyptian nationalist he identified with his contemporary, demeaned Egyptians no less than with the ancient Egyptian barons who had rebelled fourteen hundred years earlier against the rulers of Egypt, the "Asiatics" whom Manetho specifically identified as the forefathers of the Jews. Manetho repeated as fact the slanders the conquering baronial princes seized upon to justify their actions, and, prompted to specious argument by his precarious priestly position, embellished the slanders with anti-Semitic scuttlebutt. For a long time archaeologists and historians blithely followed suit, presuming that Manetho's fabrications were authenticated by the self-aggrandizing inscriptions the warrior pharaohs had incised upon their monuments. These inscriptions may well have been among those from which Manetho had drawn his conclusions. A cycle of self-serving evidence, thus completed, became established Egyptian historiography.

Archaeologists were forewarned by the dean of Egyptologists, the great James Henry Breasted, who recognized early on that "the late tradition regarding the Hyksos . . . is but the substance of a folk-tale like . . . many other such tales from which their knowledge of Egypt's past was chiefly drawn by the Greeks."[3] The warning passed unheeded.

Not every historian of that ancient period deprecated the Jews. Manetho was a contemporary of Berosus, a priest of Marduk at Babylon under Antiochus I (281–261 B.C.E.), who, although also writing under Greek influence, became a rival of Manetho in expounding on the relative greatness and antiquity of their respective lands. Berosus lauded Semitic accomplishments and wrote sympathetically about the history of the Jews even though the religious precepts of the Jews were sharply at variance with his own.

Not a scrap of Manetho's original manuscript exists. We know Manetho's work through several fragmentary quotations by several Christian authors, but mainly from Josephus's *Contra Apion*. Josephus was the only writer quoting directly from Manetho who was sympathetic to the Jews. Josephus had been an officer in the Roman army and had participated in their wars against the Jews. He became an apologist for the Jews in spite of, and perhaps because of, his onerous military role alongside the Romans in their brutal subjugation of Jewish iconoclasticism. Christian writers who had access to Manetho's writings before they disappeared were patently anti-Semitic and their employment of spurious quotations from Manetho was designed to reinforce the universal Christian polemic against the Jews; they continued to repeat the same patently false calumnies Apion had employed earlier.

Manetho is quoted by Josephus as stating that the Hyksos were "men of ignoble birth out of the eastern parts, [who] had boldness enough to make an expedition into our country, and with ease subdued it by force, yet without our hazarding a battle with them." The force that overwhelmed Egypt consisted of 240,000 men who "burned our cities ruthlessly, razed to the ground the temples of our Gods, and treated all the natives with a cruel hostility, massacring . . . and so forth."[4]

Josephus's error in the translation of the term Manetho used to describe the chieftains of the tribes who had infiltrated into Lower Egypt, Hyk-khase, has plagued historiography to the present day. Josephus states, regarding Manetho's use of the word, "Their whole nation was called Hyksos, that is, 'King-shepherds'; for *HYK* in the sacred language means 'King' and *SOS* in common speech is 'shepherd.'"[5] Josephus's word "nation" was often translated as "race" and was blithely repeated as such by subsequent historians; the myth of a mysterious invading horde of an unknown race who came from an unknown area and disappeared just as mysteriously was thus born. The myth was promulgated throughout the corpus of scientific literature with scarcely a critical murmur to be heard.

Josephus later renders the translation of Hyksos as "captive-shepherds," in reference to their ultimate status as slaves. Historians have translated the term variously as "sand-dwellers," "desert raiders," "barbarians," "bedouin invaders," and "desert despoilers." The objections of those who questioned the existence of such a "race of sand-dwelling barbarians" passed unheeded. The fact that Manetho, Josephus, and all the Christian writers who quoted from Manetho were expressly referring to the progenitors of the Jews was ignored; a mysterious race of unknown origin composed of nomadic, sand-dwelling barbarians was concocted, an image that has pervaded literary treatment of the period.

Sir Alan Gardiner, whose philological expertise and archaeological scholarship deserves the high respect accorded to it, pointedly corrected Josephus and took Egyptologists to task: "The word Hyksos undoubtedly derives from the expression *Hik-Khase*, 'chieftain of a foreign hill country' which from the Middle Kingdom onwards was used to designate Bedouin sheikhs. It is important to observe, however, that the term refers to the rulers alone, and not, as Josephus thought, to the entire race."[6] It is also important to observe that the foreign chieftains who were reported to have come across the Sinai desert into Egypt were not dwellers of that desert; they are designated as having originated from a "hill country" and are therefore erroneously identified as bedouins. Modern scholars have often erred in this matter, and having no other explanation for who the 240,000 desert-dwelling invaders of Egypt could have been, left stand the impression that the Hyksos were a particular race of invaders who after conquering "Syria" [sic] and "Palestine" [sic] ultimately forced their way into Egypt. Nothing supports such a view.

Gardiner writes: "The invasion of the Delta by a specific new race is not out of the question. One must think rather of an infiltration by Palestinians [sic] glad to find refuge in a more peaceful and fertile environment. Some, if not most of these Palestinians were Semites. Scarabs of the period mention chieftains with names like "Anat-her" and "Yacob-her," and whatever the meaning of *her*, "Anat" was a well-known Semitic goddess, and it is difficult to reject the accepted view that the patriarch Jacob is commemorated in the other name."[7]

Gardiner re-emphasizes that Hik-khase refers not to a people in general but to individuals, the leaders or chieftains of particular groups of "hill-country" people. He points out that the term the Egyptians employed for the peoples who came into Egypt from beyond the Sinai was Aamu, which can be roughly translated as "Asiatics." The term had earlier appeared as the designation for South-west Asiatic captives and hirelings residing in Egypt as servants.[8] Satyu was another term used by the Egyptians for "Asiatics," but Aamu became the more common Egyptian word for the "Asiatics" and even more specifically for the peoples speaking a West-Semitic dialect. It has a marked similarity to the Akkadian word "Amurru" and in turn to the English word "Amorite." Significantly, the Akkadian "Amurru" means "West" or "Westerner," whereas the Egyptian word "Aam" means "right hand," or "East." From Egypt's point of view, the Aamu were clearly from the East and are as clearly none other than the Amurru.

The word Hyksos or, more properly, Hyk-khase, in fact, does not appear any-where in Egyptian literature as a designation of a people; it is used only occasionally to describe a foreign chief or ruler. A fresco adorning the wall of the tomb of Prince Khnum-Hotpe at Beni Hassan, for example, refers to Abushei, the leader of the group of thirty-seven Semitic traders passing through his home, as a "Hyk-khase" (Abushei being a Hebraic name, as, for example, that of one of King David's head generals). Yet, so engraved is the misuse of the term Hyksos to archaeological and historiological lore that cities, fortifications, and wars are attributed to this "mysterious race," which not only invaded and dominated Egypt but also invaded what is anachronistically dubbed "Palestine" as well. This nonexistent "race," hatched from a spurious translation, becomes the subject of numerous scholarly tomes. The question is repeatedly asked, "Who were the Hyksos?" as though a mystery exists, and pseudoevidence is produced proclaiming the authentication of events in the history of this fictional fierce and rapacious people.

The fortifications referred to in this literature did exist. They were quite distinctive, employing massive glacis (earthenwork embankments) against the walls. The steep incline of the embankments made access by a besieging army difficult. Numerous cities that were protected by this unique type of fortification have been identified. Yohanan Aharoni, the Israeli archaeologist, notes the ubiquitous presence of the characteristic glacis system of defense in that period:

> The remains of large towns with fortifications from this age have been discovered at Laish, Hazor, Jericho, Megiddo, Tannach, Dotham, Shechem, Bethel, Jerusalem, Beth-zur, Beth-shemesh, Gezer, Lachish, Tell Beit Mirsim, Tell Jerisheh (Gath-rimmon?), Joppa, Minat Rubin (H. Yavne Yam), Ashkelon, Tell en-Nejileh, Tell el-'Ajjul, Beth-'eglaim and Tell el-Fah'ah (Sharuhen), Tell el-Meshash (T. Masos), Tel el-Milh (T. Malhata), et al.[9]

Hazor, a main stronghold of these "mysterious" people, comprised an area of 175 acres, and was the largest city ever built in the biblical period. Tradition has it that Hazor served as the capital of Canaan. The city "appears prominently in the Mari archives," in association with Amurru, which "became the political title for southern Palestine-Syria [sic] in the Hyksos age."[10] A substantial glacis was also raised against the fortifications walls of el-Yahidiyah ("Jew-town"), in the Delta area of Lower Egypt.

How can this profusion of important urban centers continue to be ascribed to an unknown foreign race who mysteriously appeared and just as mysteriously disappeared?

While historians pay undue attention to the pejorative quotes from Manetho, they have been prone to ignore the passages which define the "ignoble people from the east" not merely as Canaanites or West-Semitic-speaking people, but specifically and unmistakably *as progenitors of the Jews*. Manetho relates that the "foreign kings," Hyk-khase, installed themselves as rulers of Egypt, making "both the upper and the lower regions pay tribute." They built a great capital walled city, Avaris, extending over an area of ten thousand acres from which successive "foreign kings" ruled for 511 years. Their departure from Egypt was occasioned by a revolt of the Upper Egyptian [Theban] kings who:

> made an attempt to take them by force and by siege, with four hundred and eighty thousand men to lie round about them; but that, upon despair of taking the place by that siege, they came to an agreement with them that they should leave Egypt and go, without any harm to be done to them whithersoever they would; and that, after this agreement was made, they went away with their whole family and effects, not fewer in number than two hundred and forty thousand, and took their journey from Egypt, through the wilderness for Syria; but as they were in fear of the Assyrians, who had then the dominion over Asia, they built a city in that country which is now called Judea, and that large enough to contain this great number of men, and called it Jerusalem.[11]

The above statement, quoted from Manetho by Josephus, can scarcely be more definitive. The word "Jew" derives from the soon-to-be-established country of Judah, a national entity created by tribes of Hebraic-speaking Canaanites whose capital, in fact, was Jerusalem. The parallels with the biblical story of Exodus are obvious. Manetho was clearly rationalizing the biblical story of the Exodus of the Israelites from his Egyptian-Greek perspective, and in glorifying his noble Egyptian heritage he counteracted the biblical tales with scuttlebutt. The reference to Jerusalem is not exceptional, for that destination is repeated in another passage in which Manetho recites the history of the succeeding Egyptian kings: "When these foreigners were gone out of Egypt to Jerusalem, Tethmosis, the king of Egypt who drove them out, reigned afterward."[12]

THE SECOND INTERMEDIATE PERIOD

The period of rule over Egypt by the "hill-country kings" has been designated by historians as the "Second Intermediate Period"; it coincides with the biblical period that commences with the time that Joseph became vizier of Egypt. John Baines and Jerome Malek attempted to put Manetho's perplexing rendition of that period into reasonable order, noting that the immigrants from Southwest Asia had been peacefully infiltrating Egypt over a long period of time, and that at least one of them, Khendjer, became king of Egypt:

> They were forerunners of the movement that was to bring foreign rule in the 2nd Intermediate Period. In the later 13th Dynasty, the eastern Delta was heavily settled by Asiatics, including the area that had been completely Egyptian in the 12th Dynasty. . . . Around 1640 the position of the 13th Dynasty was usurped by a foreign group conventionally known as the Hyksos. . . . The Hyksos, the 15th Egyptian Dynasty, seems to have been recognized as the chief line of kings in the whole country, but they tolerated other contenders. The 13th Dynasty may have continued in existence, as may also the 14th, a line of rulers in the northwestern Delta (whose existence has been doubted). There was also a parallel group of Hyksos rulers known as the 16th Dynasty, a term which may simply cover other asiatic rulers who proclaimed themselves king, wherever they may have been. The most important of these Dynasties was the 17th.[13]

The sincere attempt of Baines and Malek, and of many other reviewers of conventional Egyptian chronology, to squeeze the Manetho breakdown of a fragment of Egyptian history into rational dynastic segments is doomed to produce only a morass of contradictions. Examination of the mishmash of Egyptian history that results from Manetho's dynastic construction demonstrates that its acceptance as given is utterly naive. This is particularly true of the period in which the Canaanite kings ruled Egypt; there were no five dynasties (which infers five hereditary successions) during this period. Autonomous regional rule and not dynastic succession is made convincingly evident by the mathematics of the Manetho record itself, which consists of: sixty kings of what he designated as the Thirteenth Dynasty; seventy-six kings of the fourteenth; six Hyksos kings of the Fifteenth; thirty-two Hyksos kings of the Sixteenth; and of both forty-three Hyksos and forty-three Theban kings in the Seventeenth Dynasty. These hundreds of kings are purported to have ruled in Egypt within a period of less than two hundred years!

Other fragmentary quotations from Manetho that have been passed down to us differ in details, but all agree in one respect: according to Manetho hundreds of kings reigned during this brief period. A reasonable interpolation of this data, even without reference to supporting archaeological and documentary evidence, is that these "kings" were actually autonomous chieftains ruling under a recognized central government headed by six successive "foreign hill-country kings" of the so-designated Fifteenth Dynasty. The Fifteenth "Dynasty" itself was no dynasty at all inasmuch as the six kings were related only in that they were all foreigners, with the possible exception of two kings named Apophis. "In about 150 years some 70 kings of the Thirteenth Dynasty came and went," note Baines and Malek, somewhat bemused. "The country appears to have remained stable, even though there was no official means of replacing kings in rapid succession, but the kings themselves must have been of very little account. The most important people in the country seem instead to have been the viziers."[14]

It is easily recognized that the principle of hereditary royal succession to all-Egyptian rule had been abandoned during the "Thirteenth Dynasty," and that the continuity of the government was, in fact, vested in the hands of viziers such as is dramatically represented by the biblical Joseph. It is the only logical reconstruction of the history of Egyptian governmental authority for at least the first part of that period.[15] The influence of the administrators is evidenced by an abundance of scarabs, seals, and seal impressions found bearing their names along with their definitive titles.

The Metropolitan Museum of Art in New York has, for example, no less than eight scarabs of one official bearing the distinctly Semitic name Hur, which means "the Noble" or the "freeborn," as in the familiar Hebrew name Ben Hur, "the son of Hur." Some of these administrators or "viziers" are entitled "Sole Companion of the King," others are entitled "Overseer of the Treasury." These scarabs are found in association, for example, with those of King Sheshi, the purported founder of the Fifteenth Dynasty, and have been recovered from sites throughout Egypt ranging from Canaanite Gaza to Kermeh in Nubia.[16] Numerous other scarabs and seals of both Egyptian and Asiatic officials with similar titles testify to the importance of the office during this period.

Many of the kings bore distinctly Semitic names: Anath-her, for example, was the Egyptian rendering of the Semitic Goddess Astarte. Some had recognizable Hebrew names like Yaakov, Hiyan, and Hamudi. The king with the unmistakable Hebrew name Yaakov, as Jacob is pronounced in Hebrew, provides a parallel to the biblical name of the father of Joseph. The name Yaakov appears on numerous scarabs of the period found in Egypt, in Nubia (biblical Kush), and in Canaan, in the form of the Egyptian transliteration *Y'qb-HR*.

The most ancient of these scarabs was unearthed from a Middle Bronze Age IIB tomb at Tell Shiqmona, near Haifa, only 1.3 kilometers southwest of the Carmal Cape in the very region where glassmaking first appeared on the Mediterranean coast.[17] This Canaanite Jacob was a local chieftain of c. 1730 B.C.E., and was, according to Kempinski, "no doubt, an ancestor of the later Hyksos Pharaohs of the XVth Dynasty." King Jacob, the second of the "foreign kings" of the Fifteenth Egyptian Dynasty, ruled about 1670/1650 B.C.E.[18] Another scarab, almost identical to that of the Shiqmona, was published by Martin Pieper in 1930 and so closely resembles the Shiqmona scarab it appears to be produced by the same artisan. The single difference between the two scarabs is, however, highly significant: the name Y'qb-HR is framed on the latter scarab by a cartouche, the use of which indicates royalty and identifies that Yaakov as a king in Egypt, possibly the very Hyk-khase king Yaakov on the Manetho list.

The connection between Canaan, Egypt, and Yaakov can be readily inferred from the incorporation of the name Jacob or Yaakov into the name of a town listed by Thutmose III's roster at Karnak of 119 conquered Canaanite towns. This town was probably located in the upper Galilee,[19] the very area which extended inland from the Carmal coast from Shiqmona, where the above-mentioned scarab was found.

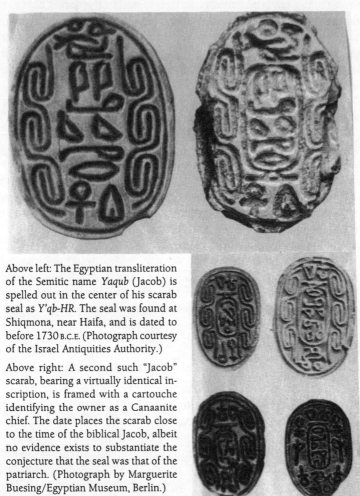

Above left: The Egyptian transliteration of the Semitic name *Yaqub* (Jacob) is spelled out in the center of his scarab seal as *Y'qb-HR*. The seal was found at Shiqmona, near Haifa, and is dated to before 1730 B.C.E. (Photograph courtesy of the Israel Antiquities Authority.)

Above right: A second such "Jacob" scarab, bearing a virtually identical inscription, is framed with a cartouche identifying the owner as a Canaanite chief. The date places the scarab close to the time of the biblical Jacob, albeit no evidence exists to substantiate the conjecture that the seal was that of the patriarch. (Photograph by Marguerite Buesing/Egyptian Museum, Berlin.)

Right: The same name appears on a number of other seals from Egypt and Canaan, roughly a century later in date and surrounded by a cartouche symbolizing royalty and a prenomen that positively identifies that Jacob as the second of the "Hyksos" kings of Egypt and Canaan. (Photograph courtesy of the British Museum.)

The case for autonomous rule does not rest on an interpolation of Manetho's simple listing of kings. The Manetho document, after describing the influx of the Hyksos, explicitly states: "Finally they appointed as king one of their number whose name was Salitis. He had a seat at Memphis, levying tribute from upper and lower Egypt. . . ." Salitis was, according to Manetho, a Hyk-khase who was *elected* by the other chiefs as a chief-of-chiefs at Memphis: "They made one of themselves king," complains Manetho, his resentment at such an unorthodox bestowal of executive power discernable through the indignant tone of his rendition of the events. During Salitis' tenure a new capital was founded at Avaris "from whence he ruled all Egypt."

It should be noted that in the language of the times, the words "chieftain," "ruler," and so forth, were often synonymous with "king"; and that the word "pharaoh" was a later, Greek version of the Hebrew word *par'oh*, meaning "great house." Pharaoh refers to the institution of kingship in the same way as the term "White House" is employed as a metonym for the president of the United States.

Cyril Aldred treats Manetho's statements with limited deference in his book *The Egyptians*, stating that "Manetho's account of the appearance of the Hyksos on the Egyptian scene as the irruption of a conquering horde spreading fire and destruction, was colored by memories of more recent Assyrian and Persian invasions in his own time, and has to be discounted."[20] Then Aldred proceeds to outline the peaceful, and often welcome, infiltration of the Delta area by the Southwest Asiatic peoples from Egypt's primitive beginnings, a thousand years and more before Joseph.

> The story of Joseph reveals how some of these Asiatics may have arrived, sold into slavery for corn in the time of famine, or offering themselves as menials in turn for food and shelter. By the Thirteenth Dynasty the number of Asiatics, even in Upper Egypt, was considerable. They acted as cooks, brewers, seamstresses, vinedressers and the like. One official, for instance, had no fewer than fourty-five Asiatics in his household. . . . It is not difficult to see that by the middle of the Thirteenth Dynasty the lively and industrious Semites could be in the same positions of responsibility in the Egyptian state as Greek freemen were to enjoy in the government of Imperial Rome.[21]

"While to Manetho the Hyksos seizure of power seemed an unmitigated disaster," adds Cyril Aldred, "we can recognize it as one of the great seminal influences in Egyptian civilization, rescuing it from political decline, bringing new ideas into the Nile Valley and ensuring that Egypt played a full part in the development of the Bronze Age culture in the eastern Mediterranean." Bronze comes into use with the influx of the Asiatics during the Middle Kingdom. It was easier to work than copper and far more durable and more effective for tools and weapons. Its introduction is signaled by its use for casting statues in the reign of Amnenemes III, a technique not possible with copper. Until then the use of metal was limited to hammering copper over a wooden core, a technique which can be seen in the only two large samples surviving from the old kingdom. Silver, too, of a purity that shows it was not of native origin but smelted from argentiferous ores, was among the new materials introduced during this period; in Egypt silver had a greater value than gold.

> A whole range of novel weapons was introduced from Asia, such as the horse-drawn chariot, scale armor, the composite bow and new designs of daggers, swords and scimitars . . . The Asiatic origin of the chariot was preserved in the different woods used in the construction, the Canaanite names for its different parts, and by the tradition of retaining Asiatics to drive and maintain some of them at least. A war helmet, probably made of leather sewn with gold metal discs, was added to the Pharaoh's regalia and is known to Egyptologists as the *Khepresh*, "the blue, or war crown." (A word similar to the Hebrew). . . . More important than these weapons of destruction were certain abiding inventions of peace, such as improved methods of spinning and weaving, using an upright loom; new musical instruments, a Iyre, the long-necked lute, the oboe and tambourine. Hump-backed bulls were imported from an Asian source, probably brought in by ship with the greatly increased trade that the Hyksos fostered.[22]

We must forgive Aldred for slipping into the use of the term "Hyksos" as though it designated a race or nation of people. He himself points out that "the Egyptians referred to the tribal chiefs of these peoples as *Hikau Khasut* or 'Princes of the Desert Uplands,' a term which Manetho by false etymology translated as *Hyksos* or shepherd kings, a name which has clung tenaciously ever since to the entire people rather than to its rulers."[23] Aldred does, after all, unlike many historians, give full credit to these Hyksos for the thankless contribution they made in boosting Egyptian civilization to a higher level within the relatively few years of their reign in Egypt.

THE ASIATIC INFLUENCE ON EGYPTIAN CULTURE

The insemination of Southwest Asian culture and technology into Egypt did not commence with Joseph; it had infiltrated continuously into Egyptian culture for several millennia before that period. The extent and value of the cultural and technological endowments that flowed from Canaan and Mesopotamia into Egypt is a subject that will be treated separately in the next chapter, for it goes to the heart of the question. Before the subject of the direction of the flow of technology can be properly addressed, however, the identification of the peoples who served as the conduits of culture must be resolved, for it is in this regard that the worst historical obfuscation exists. We must, therefore, explore the question further in order to clear away the web of misinformation woven over centuries.

Asian culture and technology penetrated most deeply into the fabric of Egyptian civilization in the period that begins with the time corresponding to that of the biblical Joseph, and continued until the time of the extinction of Asiatic rule by the Theban princes—which, in turn, corresponds to the biblical time of the enslavement of the Hebrews. This interval of less than two centuries commences with the reign of King Sebekkare (Thirteenth Dynasty, 1789-1786 B.C.E.), to the reign of Ahmose I (Eighteenth Dynasty, 1575-1550 B.C.E.).

Virtually nothing has been written about this period, one of the most critical of Egyptian history, in which fundamental changes and substantial progress took place. What little does exist is so saturated with obvious distortions, deletions, and downright falsehoods as to render it unreliable as testimony and undeserving of literal acceptance. What is even stranger, for a presumably scientific pursuit, is that Manetho's spurious stories have been promulgated as fact with hardly a demurrer as to their accuracy. The scrupulous verification to which evidence should be subjected by serious scientists was lost in the blinding glory in which Egyptian civilization was being touted. The glare of the image thus presented eclipsed the fact that the foundation of Egyptian civilization lay to the east of Egypt, and that the much maligned Hyksos represented one phase of a vast, seminal, cultural and technological intrusion.

The picture being slowly drawn by the constant accretion of archaeological and documentary evidence lends a certain credence to the biblical representation of the period. During and following the period proposed for the ascension of Joseph to the position of vizier, the Canaanite progenitors of the Hebrews, drawn to Egypt by a benign government and favorable agricultural and commercial conditions, flocked into the Delta area. Their influence continued to increase by virtue of initiatives taken that improved not only their own lot but that of the Egyptians as well. It is now well-documented that reforms were actually introduced by such viziers as the purported vizier Joseph; they reorganized Egypt's governmental structure, which had formerly revolved around the priests and a divine pharaoh, but which thereafter evolved into a temporal confederation of autonomous local governments.

The Asiatics brought to Egypt the elements of a patriarchal system that had evolved in Canaan and Akkadia, essentially a free association of clan-based local entities. The system was flexibly applied to Upper Egypt, whose local lords acceded in some respects to the new conditions. The Egyptians also submitted to the authority of a central government administered by one of the chieftains "chosen" or appointed to oversee intercommunity and international affairs. The northern and by far the most economically and technically significant section of Egypt became effectively an extension of the communities of Canaan. Its influence reached as far as the Euphrates; trade and other forms of intercourse between the African and Asian areas flourished in a period of relative freedom and peace.

The progressive developments wrought under Asiatic influence during this period have been widely acknowledged, although the implications of the events have not been fully appreciated by those who refuse to acknowledge them. "Archaeological investigations have shown that in the Hyksos period (Middle Bronze II) civilization in the country [Canaan] attained a high state of develop-

ment," summarizes Aharoni in laying the background of the period.[24] Jan Van
Seters notes the effect of the Asiatic immigrants on Egypt: "With the settlement
of Middle Bronze IIA in Palestine [sic], new sedentary culture came into the land
and brought with it a high level of urban life. . . . Only after the 13th dynasty was
there a great deal of free commercial activity between Egypt and Palestine."[25]
G. E. Wright is frankly awed by the extent of the progress made during this period:
". . . [This was a period] of the greatest prosperity that [Canaan] had seen to that
time, or would see again before the Roman peace."[26] Cyril Aldred insists that not
only was Egyptian civilization inseminated with a far superior culture, but would
probably have descended into severe decline without it.[27] Hayes expands on the
permanence of the effects of the Eastern influence:

> . . . there flowed into the Nile valley in unprecedented quantity new blood strains,
> new religious and philosophical concepts, and new artistic styles and media, as well
> as epoch-making innovations of a more practical nature . . . The Hyksos domina-
> tion provided the Egyptians with both the incentive and the means toward "world"
> expansion and so laid the foundations and to a great extent determined the charac-
> ter of the New Kingdom.[28]

A different view is taken by those who do not judge a civilization by the prosperity it attains for the greatest number or by the advances in its culture and technology but by the sizes of the statues and monuments it produces and by the
force and extent of its depredations of neighbors.

A society devoid of inscriptions boasting of conquest, plunder, and slaughter
can, however, be rated by more meaningful standards. The fact that the Second
Intermediate period was the time in which Egypt experienced its greatest leap
forward in cultural, technological, and economic affairs should be the measure
of its value, but sometimes leads to peculiar conclusions. Donald B. Redford, in
addressing the limits of objectivity in archaeology in general and Egyptology
in particular, referred to The Second Intermediate period as "a time [in which]
internal governmental weakness coincided with a period of prosperity and political
growth in Palestine and Nubia so that, for once, the Egyptians found themselves
the victims of both the political initiative and cultural momentum of others."[29]

Victims of prosperity?

The unavoidable conclusion that the seminal influence of the "foreign" Southwest Asiatic, mainly Semitic-language-speaking peoples under the rule of their
patriarchal chieftains, the Hyk-Khase, and the kings they elected to administer
the region, brought unprecedented social and economic progress to Egypt is too
often treated as an aside rather than as the essence of the historical lesson to be
learned. "Bias, a predisposition to judge matters in a certain way without recourse
to reason or evidence . . . manifests itself, at times, in a nationalistic bent, a more
or less disguised jingoism," continued Redford. This homily could well apply to
those who, enthralled with the image of a glorious Egypt and disturbed by having it disturbed by the overwhelming evidence of a preeminent Asiatic culture,
proceed to lament:

But when bias appears in the writings of scholars who have adopted a certain discipline co-extensive with an historical culture, and unconsciously construe themselves as "nationals" at a remove of several centuries, their championing of their
adopted culture becomes tiresome. The writings of these men take on chauvinism
and at times exude a heat over themes that really do not—or should not, God help
us!—matter to anybody any longer. Who cares whether a number of technical innovations were introduced into Egypt during the Hyksos period, and that they were,
thanks to Asiatic initiative, not Egyptian?[30]

It would seem that those with a biased view of history are the very ones who
refuse to "care" about the facts which must be acknowledged; it is thus that a
distorted "nationalistic" Egyptian historiography is being promulgated. Those who
are attempting to reconcile the sociology of the period with the facts are the ones
who are having difficulty making themselves heard, not least because they may
be subjected to such accusations of "chauvinism."

Redford continues: "For what honest purpose do we disseminate the baseless
nonsense that an ancient group of Palestinian tribes had developed a kind of
'primitive democracy'?"

The implication goes far beyond Egyptology, it exposes a deep-rooted antago-
nism to the acceptance of the seminal Semitic contribution to the cultural and
technological evolution of civilization, an attitude that perpetuates the very distortion of history which was being lamented.

The gravity of the matter prescribes exacting examination of the manner in
which Manetho's distorted history of the Hyksos period became standard Egyptian history. It must first be noted that the one and only Egyptian historian whose
writings encompass not merely a simple list of kings but also a description of
events touching on the period of Southwest Asiatic rule is the priest Manetho.
Unfortunately, not a scrap of his manuscript exists. What we know of his work
is derived almost entirely from quotations from or abridgements of it by four
individuals: (1) Josephus, a Hebrew historian writing about 70 C.E.; (2) Sectus
Julius Africanus, a Christian priest, in the *Chronicle* (221 C.E.); (3) Eusephius, a
Christian priest, in *Chronicon* (326 C.E.); (4) George Syncellus, a Christian priest,
called "George the Monk," in a history of the world from Adam to the Roman
Emperor Diocletian, written about 800 C.E.

The first discovery to be made on reading the various excerpts is that, although
all are purportedly quoting verbatim from the same text, none of them match.
The differences are so gross that they cannot be attributed to mere misunder-
standing. The disparities between the texts as they are given are compounded by
the circumstance that even where the quotations agree, the information given often
does not conform with known facts. Sir Alan Gardiner cites several of these discrepancies:

There are discrepancies of the most glaring kind, these finding their climax in Dynasty XVIII, where names and true sequence are now known from indisputable
monumental sources. . . . The lengths of reigns frequently differ in the two versions,

as well as often showing wide departure from the definitely ascertained figures. . . . What is even more serious, the story of Amenophis and his lepers quoted from him by Josephus, as well as the fantastic happenings ascribed to some of the kings, shows that he made use, not only of authentic records, but also of popular romances devoid of historical value.[31]

Gardiner apologizes for using such a questionable source at all in his exposition of Egyptian history, noting that "no Egyptologist has been able to free himself from the shackles imposed by the native analyst's thirty Dynasties, and these are likely to remain the essential framework of our modern expositions."

Manetho's oft-quoted account of the arrival of the Hebrew progenitors and the institution by them of rule over Egypt, the account that has become singularly the core of Egyptian history, that continues to be given credence, and that forms the basis for the creation of the myth of a mysterious new Hyksos race, is the statement quoted by Josephus:

Tutmaios. In his reign, for what cause I know not, a blast of God smote us; and unexpectedly from the regions of the East invaders of an obscure race marched in confidence of victory against our land. By main force they easily seized it without striking a blow; and having overpowered the rulers of the land they then burned our cities ruthlessly, razed to the ground the temples of our gods, and treated all the natives with a cruel hostility, massacring some and leading into slavery the wives and children of others.

Finally they appointed as King one of their number whose name was Salitis. He had his seat at Memphis, levying tribute from upper and lower Egypt, and always leaving his garrisons behind in the most advantageous places.[32]

"Unexpectedly from the regions of the East invaders of an obscure race. . . ." There are three consecutive misstatements in this single phrase:

1. The Eastern peoples were not unexpected; their presence and influence extends back into prehistory. The brick-built, stepped pyramids of the first few dynasties bear an unmistakable relationship to the ziggurats of Mesopotamia in form, construction, and materials. The stamp of Asiatic culture is evident in the Egyptian language; only the extent of the common roots shared by the Egyptian and Semitic languages are disputed, not their existence. The influx of herdsmen and farmers into and their exodus from the region of the Nile Delta (biblical Goshen or Lower Egypt) was a process that had taken place regularly for millennia, an ongoing phenomenon that depended mainly on the seasons or the conditions of weather. There were permanent communities as well, for the Delta could be considered as integral a part of Canaan as it was of Egypt, with the possible exception of the periods in which it fell under the domination of the Upper Egypt Barons. The presence of Southwest Asiatics was not restricted to the Delta, for Akkadian merchants had been constantly filtering into and through Egypt as far as and into Nubia, for which privilege tribute had to be paid to the local Egyptian grandees through whose territory they passed. Asiatic artisans were

part of the corvee and of the slave labor employed in the construction of monuments and temples. Most significant of all, the passage of technology was part of the intercourse that, in the most ancient historical periods, took place in one direction only, into and not out of Egypt, reaching the apex of its influence during the so-called Second Intermediate period.

2. The Hyksos were certainly not an obscure race. This often-repeated falsehood is easily recognized as one always applied by conquerors who justify their actions by characterizing their victims as mysterious, evil beings who deserved what they got.

3. The Asiatics did not invade by force. They were not unwelcome. That proposition is contradicted by the latter part of Manetho's own following statement: "By main force they easily seized it [our land] without striking a blow." Need one comment further?

But Manetho continues with his polemic, emphasizing that "They [The Asiatics] burned . . . , razed . . . ," and so on. Manetho is again clearly seen to contradict himself when this description is juxtaposed against the one in which he laments that the Asiatics came to rule Egypt "without striking a blow." Archaeological excavations reveal no evidence of the devastating invasion in the time of which Manetho speaks. Common sense also dictates that it is not reasonable for the Asiatics to have burned and razed cities and temples they had conquered "without striking a blow." Conquerors raze cities in retribution for resistance, not for gracious acquiescence. In the absence of resistance such counterproductive measures would have been irrational and contrary to the economic, political, and strategic interests of an occupying force, which, having established power, can peacefully obtain more tribute or taxes from a continuing rather than a crippled economy.

The facts are that many of the cities and temples of prior Egyptian regimes were left intact by the Hyk-Khase, whereas the structures of the Asiatics were the very ones ruthlessly and thoroughly demolished by the succeeding Pharaohs, until only the bare traces of a few of them remained. It is not the testimony of the victims from which we learn of this demolition, for their recorded history was effectively erased; we are apprised of the destruction of the civilization created by the Asiatics by the statements boldly and boastfully emblazoned on the monuments of the ravagers themselves. The overthrow of the Asiatic rulers of Egypt was accomplished by the members of a particular family of Theban grandees whose own words describe that destruction in dramatic detail.

THE OVERTHROW OF ASIATIC RULE IN EGYPT

The initial aggression against the rule of the Semitic chieftains was launched by Sequernenre, a Theban who was not of royal blood, but merely the second generation of a lineage that stemmed from humble roots. Sequernenre was intensely jealous of the Asiatic chieftains. He abominated Apophis, the chief-of-chiefs appointed by the other patriarchal community heads to rule Egypt and Canaan, a hatred made clear by the record of an exchange between Sequernenre and Apophis. It happened that many of the northern chieftains built winter homes in Upper Egypt where they were able to enjoy the balmier equatorial weather. Some of these estates, including that of King Apophis, were in the neighborhood in which Sequernenre resided. The latter's estate fronted on the Nile, and hosted a pool where hippopotami loved to play and to make love, which they often did, boisterously and noisily in the late evening, to the annoyance of Sequernenre's neighbors.

The Asiatics continually complained to Sequernenre of sleeplessness occasioned by the raucous nightly noise of the rambunctious hippopotami. They were given cursory, insulting responses or were entirely ignored, for Sequernenre felt that the hippopotami, being more Egyptian than his neighbors, had more right than the foreigners to freely express themselves, however loudly. Sequernenre considered it presumptuous of the Asiatics to believe that an Egyptian prince (Sequernenre fancied himself of royal blood) would interfere in the sex life of Egyptian hippopotami for the edification of Asiatic aliens. Finally, King Apophis himself sent a note to Sequernenre, complaining that his hippopotami were inconveniencing his neighbors. The story became incorporated into Egyptian folklore and was repeated in vivid detail:

> Now when the messenger whom Apophis had sent reached the Prince of the Southern City [Sequernenre of Thebes], he was taken to the Prince of the Southern City. . . . "What brings thee to the Southern City?" the messenger said to him. "It is King Apophis who sends to thee saying: "[the messenger] has come concerning the pool of the hippopotami, which is in thy city. For they permit me no sleep, day and night the noise of them are in my ear." Then the prince of the Southern City lamented for a [long] time.[33]

Ambition makes brutes of men; pseudo-princes are men, and more ambitious than most. Sequernenre envisioned himself as potentially a pharaoh seated upon the throne of Egypt; he attempted a coup, using the hippopotami affair as an excuse. Sequernenre's mummy bears the mute evidence of his failure. He suffered a number of debilitating blows, evidently from a war-club, and was finally dispatched by a massive penetration of his skull with a battle-ax whose contours match precisely those of the distinctive battle-axes wielded by the Asiatics. Sequernenre's mummy is now on display in the Cairo Museum, huge hole in head, broken jaw and all.

"They treated all the natives with cruel hostility. . . ." The second statement on the oft-quoted Manetho rendition of the Hyksos period was contradicted by Kamose, Sequernenre's oldest son, who himself dictated an inscription on a stone stele that picks up and continues the history. The inscription details the proceedings of a council meeting attended by the Egyptian hierarchy of Upper Egypt. It states that fellow Egyptian princes rejected out of hand an invasion of the north proposed by Kamose to avenge his father's demise and revitalize Egyptian pride.

The inadvisability of the adventure was argued by all the attendant Egyptian leaders because it was said that Egyptians favored the rule of the Asiatics. The Upper Egypt nomarchs attendant at the meeting hosted by Kamose insisted that the treatment they received from the Asiatics was so congenial that the southerners were welcome to pasture their cattle in the grassy north seasonally; that they were generously granted grain for their swine when drought conditions in the south created the need. "All are loyal as far as Cusae," they pointed out in their refusal to join Kamose in furthering his ambitions. Kamose reports the arguments in his inscription only to denigrate them by sneeringly remarking that the softhearted fellow princes with whom he counseled were too easily swayed by the benign treatment afforded Egyptians by the Asiatic rulers.

We must thank Kamose for setting the record straight, understanding that he did so boastfully, to prove to posterity that he was capable of overcoming all odds by thumbing his nose inscriptively at those weaklings who stood against him. He writes as a divinely invested king, an assumption belied by his second-generation tenure as a lord and by the limitations of the local lands to which he could lay claim. The text of the Kamose inscription is given by Gardiner as follows:

> In the year 3 of the mighty King in Thebes Kamose, whom Re had appointed as the real King and granted him power in very sooth. His Majesty spoke in his palace to the council of grandees who were in his suite: "I should like to know what serves this strength of mine, when a chieftain in Avaris, and another in Cush, and I sit united with an Asiatic and a Nubian, each in possession of his slice of this Egypt, and I cannot pass by him as far as Memphis. See, he holds Khmun,[34] and no man has respite from his spoliation through servitude to the Setyu. I will grapple with him and slit open his belly. My desire is to deliver Egypt and smite the Asiatics." Then spoke the grandees of his council: "See all are loyal to the Asiatics as far as Cusae. We are tranquil in our part of Egypt. Elephantine is strong, and the middle part is with us as far as Cusae. Men till for us the finest of their lands. Our cattle pasture in the Papyrus marshes.[35] Corn is sent for our swine. Our cattle are not taken away."[36]

Kamose, clearly no less ambitious than was his father, viewing himself as "the mighty King in Thebes," thus recorded his contemptuous disregard for the advice of his fellow grandees and for their desire to maintain peaceful adherence to the governmental system established by the Asiatics. Kamose, frustrated by the lack of Egyptian support, unreconciled by the cautious comments of the more circumspect courtiers, organized an army composed mainly of mercenary Medja troops, a primitive and outlaw Nubian tribe. Kamose prepared for invasion more carefully than did his father, and after a few years launched a new attack, sailing down the Nile on a flotilla of boats and rafts: "I fared downstream in might to overthrow the Asiatics by the command of Amūn, the just of counsels: my brave army in front of me like a breath of fire, troops of the Medja-Nubians aloft upon our cabins to spy out the Setyu and to destroy their places."[37]

This time the invaders succeeded in driving deep into the Delta, destroying everything in their path. Kamose found that the Egyptian communities of lower Egypt were no less supportive of the existing administration than were his southern neighbors. Flushed with initial success, anticipating ultimate victory, exulting, he brashly ordered his passion to be inscribed on stone, recording for posterity the merciless vengeance he wreaked upon his own uncooperative people, Egyptians who desired to live in peace with the Asiatics. He was particularly irate with an apparently prominent Egyptian who had shut himself up just north of Khmun, which had been "made into a nest of Asiatics. . . . I slew his people and I caused his wife to go down to the river-bank. My soldiers were like lions with their prey, with serfs, cattle, milk, fat, and honey, dividing up their possessions."[38]

Kamose continued his campaign, but was finally driven back in humiliating defeat. He wreaked wrathful retribution upon Egyptian loyalists in the path of his retreat, ravaging them even more ruthlessly than he did the Asiatic communities. "I razed their towns and burned their places, they being made into red ruins forever on account of the damage which they did within this Egypt, and they had made themselves serve the Asiatics and forsaken Egypt their mistress."[39] It becomes ever more clear from Kamose's continuing account that the Egyptians, far from being treated unkindly by the Asiatics, were enjoying the fruits of an ongoing, beneficial relationship, and regarded the ambitious Theban as an interloper who not only did not represent their interests but was acting counter to them. This fact and the consequent frustration Kamose felt in his failed attempt to appeal to them on nationalistic grounds led to his bitterly rendered account of revenge. Kamose unabashedly recorded his bloody misadventures. Gardiner stresses: "That the Theban warrior was by no means ashamed of his ruthlessness toward his own countrymen is clear from his own words."[40]

There is much documentation of the fact that not only was the period of the rule of the Southwest Asiatics one of great progress but that the Egyptian people supported the chieftains and were treated fairly and humanely. These records make manifest that the only reason for overthrowing the system of government established by the Asiatic chieftains was personal ambition, as expressed by Kamose himself, by his father before him, and subsequently by his brother Ahmose; that the rebellion took place against the wishes and advice of many of the Egyptian southerners, including the "grandees," and at the expense of the country as a whole.

Aamu administration did not end with Kamose, but it was dismantled and destroyed by his brother Ahmose, who conducted a successful invasion of the north, and embarked upon a campaign of obliteration of every trace of the presence of the Easterners, the Asiatic Aamus. Ahmose overran the Delta, ravaging the countryside even more ruthlessly than his brother Kamose had previously done. His armies looted and destroyed the cities built by the Asiatics, tearing down every remaining structure and inscription that might remind posterity of the hated Setyu, and drove the Aamus back across the eastern desert. The process was continued relentlessly by the successors to Kamose, the Warrior Pharaohs who attempted to eradicate every trace of the imprint that the Southwest Asiatic peoples had made on Egypt, to erase their very names from history. They almost succeeded.

They did not, of course, erase the knowledge they had gained nor the technology that had been introduced during the period of Asiatic rule. The rule of the Theban warriors was gained with the horses and chariots the Aamus had introduced and enforced with the improved weapons the Aamus had taught them to make and wield. The Aamus were overcome because they were unprepared for war, having ruled peacefully. No wars of any significance occurred during the period of their tenure. No great despoliations of neighboring peoples or areas took place. The period of Egyptian plunder and invasion ensued under the Warrior Pharaohs of the "New Kingdom," which commenced with incursions into Nubia and ended with incursions into Canaan.

THE RECORD OF ASIATIC RULE

Manetho's own record of the length of rule of the six Hyksos kings of the Fifteenth Dynasty weighs against the position that Egypt and the contiguous Canaanite regions were being ruled despotically. According to Manetho the "elected" Semitic chief-of-chiefs were among the longest-ruling sovereigns of Egyptian history. One of the kings named Apophis ruled sixty-one years, which, considering the average life span of the times, makes a particularly pointed statement regarding the quality of his rule. The average term of the six kings is an astonishing forty-four years! It was supposedly during the benign sixty-one year reign of Apophis that the Theban Lord Sequernenre first invaded Lower Egypt. After Apophis, according to Manetho, King Iannas ruled for fifty years and one month, and then came King Assis for forty-nine years and two months. Such lengthy terms of elected, or as Manetho puts it, "chosen" officials could hardly represent the record of an unpopular or repressive regime. We might parenthetically point out an obvious chronological discrepancy within one rendition of the Manetho account, inasmuch as Ahmose, Sequernenre's son, was the energetic prince who destroyed the "Asiatic" rule, and one of the lists would put the date of his campaign well over one hundred years after his father's death! Another historian, Africanus, however, does put Apophis at the end of Manetho's list.[41] Africanus, quoting Manetho, also ascribes an equally long reign for *six foreigners from Canaan* who seized Memphis and also founded a town in the Sethroite nome, from which base they subdued Egypt.

We conclude that there can hardly have been time for more than the six Hyksos powerful enough to have usurped the throne of the Pharaohs, and in this case Manetho's description of them as "their first rulers" was misleading, and his Dyns. XVI and XVII (in so far as the latter speaks of shepherd kings) ought to disappear. . . . Another persuasive indication is given by the fact that Manetho's 'first rulers' included an Apophis, for it will emerge that such was the name of the Hyksos against whom Amosis' brother and immediate predecessor Kamose fought, so that six kings will have embraced not merely the beginning of the foreign domination, but also its end."[42]

"Massacring some and leading into slavery the wives and children of the others." This continuation of the statement by Manetho is again a case in which one who identifies with the conqueror justifies the conqueror's iniquitous behavior by casting aspersions on his victim. It was the Asiatic Semitic chieftains who ceased erecting grandiose structures and monuments which required countless thousands of corvée and slave laborers. It was the Asiatics who limited the power of the priests and the princes, a system that minimized the advantages of slave labor. Under the rule of the Semitic chieftains no great campaigns requiring conscription were conducted against neighboring states.

It was none other than Kamose, his brother Ahmose and the pharaohs who followed who were patently guilty of such destructive behavior. They themselves recorded the process proudly and unmistakably on the monuments they built, the dismal record of what is commonly extolled as "heroic," or "glorious" adventures. Any visitor to Karnak or Luxor or Abydos or any of the other pharaonic centers of the period of the Eighteenth and Nineteenth Dynasties can bear witness to the rendition of the shameful story of the desecration of cities and enslavement of peoples by merciless armies; one does not need to decipher the hieroglyphics, the drawings are explicit enough.

In the process of describing the desecration, slaughter, and enslavement inflicted by the army of Ahmose I, a naval officer, also named Ahmose (Ahmose, son of Abana), indirectly identifies the people against whom they were campaigning as the progenitors of the Jews. The inscription on the wall of his tomb at El-Kab details his military career after he had replaced his father, who had fought under Sequernenre. Ahmose describes how, after the capture and destruction of Avaris, the Asiatics were pursued into Canaan, where they made a last stand at Sharuhen. The defenders were finally defeated after a six year campaign, three years of which were relegated to the siege of Sharuhen, which was likewise obliterated after capture. Sheruhen is listed in Joshua 19:6 among the thirteen villages assigned to Simeon as his portion of the inheritance of the tribe of Judah.

The pharaohs of the Eighteenth Dynasty placed their own native population under conditions that differed little from the slavery to which the Asiatic and other peoples were subjected. Manetho's recriminations against Asiatic rule are therefore most ironic. Manetho undoubtedly felt it necessary to divert attention from the plundering and pillaging of neighboring communities and from the cruelties and inhumanities inflicted upon the Egyptian people by the pharaonic conquerors by pointing his finger in the opposite direction. It takes little perspicacity to recognize this diversion for what it was.

"Finally they appointed as king one of their number. . . ." Does this significant statement by Manetho indicate a despotic imposition of a government by military might or does it attest to a governing body established by consensus? No claim to divine rights are here implied, no seizure of power by force. The statement is a clear indication that rule was established and maintained in the most democratic form possible in that historical period, the most democratic in existence at that time and for a long time to come.

The communality of the society instituted by the Aamus and the introduction into Egypt of a form of patriarchal society are made amply evident by analyzing the records of Manetho and others. A breakdown of Manetho's list of kings in the following table of the number and length of term of these "kings" of the purported thirteenth to seventeenth Dynasties makes this proposition manifest:

Dynasty	Theban Kings	Hyksos Kings	Total years
13	60		453
14	76		184
15		6	284
16		32	518
17	43	43	151

If we were to total the time during which Manetho's 217 kings, both Theban and Hyksos, reigned, we would arrive at a term of 1,590 years. The reign of all these rulers must have occurred within several hundred years. The kindest interpretation we can afford to this superabundance of sovereigns and to Manetho's rendition of events is that, indeed, there were no such thing as "Dynasties," but there were 179 Theban and 75 "foreign" local authorities who, during a portion of this period, appointed six "foreign" kings of the designated Fifteenth Dynasty as a central authority. The ethnic breakdown of Manetho's list suggests that the Thebans, a majority by a factor of better than two to one, willingly acceded to Aamu rule.

There is a wealth of corroborative evidence of the benign presence of the Asiatics, in spite of the destructions and erasures carried out by Ahmose and his successors. Another important list has come to light that includes the names of Asiatic "kings" of the period. It is known as the "Turin Canon of Kings" and was assembled from fragments at the Museo Egizio of Turin by the brilliant young schoolmaster from Grenoble, Jean Champollion (1790-1832), by whose genius the decipherment of the Egyptian language was accomplished.

The Turin Canon registers about one hundred kings for the equivalent "Second Intermediate period," many of whom do not appear on the Manetho list. Archaeologists have confirmed the existence of names that appear on both lists, and in addition have discovered several scores of other so-called kings who were in positions of authority during the same period. What are we to make of this plethora of princely personages, and of the discrepancies and contradictions of the various chronographers who blithely quote from the Manetho manuscript?

The dates and lengths of tenure of several scores of the hundreds of chieftains listed by Manetho and derived from other sources have been established from solid archaeological evidence. When plotted chronologically it is observed that the "kings" of the "Thirteenth Dynasty" are actually followed by those of the Seventeenth, indicating a continuity of government between those fictional dynasties.[43]

No information supplied by Africanus, Eusephius, and Syncellus, the other Christian writers who cite Manetho, adds light to the above summary. A rabid anti-Judaic bias colors their work. Given the fact that they were altogether too willing to report the worst about the Jews as manifested by the very tone of their polemics against the Jews; given their manifestly faulty, even false, adaptation of Manetho's rendition of history to suit their purposes; given the fact that their work was based on Manetho's own vituperous denigration of the "Asiatics," "foreigners," and "despoilers," to begin with; given the dearth of corroborative evidence of the truth of Manetho's statements regarding the ferocity of the Hyksos and the circumstances of their rule; given all this, it seems reasonable that scientists should have placed this antipathetic history, so replete with hearsay, fables, and vindictiveness, in proper perspective instead of constructing all of Egyptian history around it as if it represented palpable fact.

Instead, historiologists foster further obfuscation by employing the term "Second Intermediate period" disparagingly, placing emphasis on the dearth of royal gargantua or golden artifacts while peremptorily dismissing, with no more than a mere mention, the great leap forward in technology and culture Egyptian civilization took during the period.

Kent Weeks notes that the label "intermediate" is purely relative, and has no business acting as a word defining decadence.

> The word itself, in Egyptological parlance has taken unto itself a pejorative meaning: it denotes decadence, decline, anarchy, bad taste and instability. Now, regardless of how one personally regards the periods in question, such an extended use of the adjective produces a subjective nuance which is not desirable if we are to maintain empirical orientation. A term denoting a spatial relationship, like "Intermediate," is not in itself to be rejected; but it must have apt application. . . . imprecise or incorrect labels are misleading and give an erroneous cast to the discussion from the outset.[44]

"It is not too much to hope that in the future an effort will be made to avoid them [incorrect labels]," adds Kent Weeks.[45] The only reasonable interpolation of the record from the garbled recounting of Manetho's work is that it draws a picture opposite to the Alexandrian Egyptian's intention. Far from being bloodthirsty brigands, reading between the lines of Manetho points to a decentralized system of government, with a benevolent administration located at a seat of government established at a capital city, Avaris, to which allegiance was willingly granted by autonomous local authorities (chieftains, if you like), both Egyptian and Semitic.

It is also abundantly evident that during this period the panoply of mythical Egyptian gods was discarded, at least by most of the Aamus, and that the power of the priests was severely restricted. Sequernenre's rage and indignation concerning the apostasy of Apophis is documented by none other than himself, in the following inscription:

> Now it befalls that the land of Egypt was in dire affliction and there was no sovereign as king at the time. And it happened that king Sekernene was ruler of the Southern City[46] . . . while the chieftain Apophis was in Avaris and thc entire land paid tribute to him in full, as well as with good things of Timirus.[47] Then King Apophis took Sutekh, and served not any God which was in the entire land except Sutekh. And he built a temple of fair and everlasting work by the side of the house of King Apophis, and he arose every day to make sacrifice to Sutekh.[48]

It is interesting to note that Sequernenre first refers to Apophis as merely a "chieftain," although Apophis was the ruler to whom "the entire land paid tribute," and then twice refers to him as "king" in the same statement. Sequernenre's complaint that "there was no sovereign as king at the time" is an illuminating affirmation of the autonomous nature of the political structure, and his allusions to the status of Apophis, on top of this complaint, testifies to the means by which Apophis was chosen ruler "to whom the entire land paid tribute," a surprising, early reference to a government powered by the consent of the governed and a testament to the peaceful coexistence between the hundreds of patriarchal, tribal societies comprising the Near East and Egypt.

The inscription clearly designates the "Asiatics" as monotheistic. It is hardly necessary to point out that thc only people who have been mentioned as subscribing to a single deity at that time were the biblical descendants of Abraham. Other inscriptions by subsequent Egyptian rulers testify to the monotheism practiced by the Aamu chieftains, and to the erasure of reference to the principle of omneity by these Egyptian kings. John A. Wilson cites such an inscription by Queen Hat-shepsut:

> I have raised up (again) that which had formerly gone to pieces, since the Asiatics were in the midst of Avaris of the Delta, and vagabonds were in their midst, overthrowing what had been made, for they ruled without Re, and he did not act by divine command down to (the reign of) my Majesty. . . . I have made distant those who the gods abominate, and earth has carried off their (footprints).[49]

Wilson notes that "the sentence about the 'divine command' means that the God Re refused to rule Egypt until Hat-shepsut's time." Then he proceeds to quote a "folk tale written down in the Nineteenth Dynasty. . . . For King Apophis was in Avaris, and the entire land was subject to him with their dues . . . and King Apophis made him Seth as Lord, and he would not serve any god who is in the land (except) Seth."

It cannot be expected that at this early pre-Mosaic period the character of Mosaic monotheism had been fully developed. The Aamus of the Delta associated themselves omneistically with Sutekh, a god who was probably identified with Ba'al, El, or Yahweh, adapting his name from the Egyptian god Seth. It is curious and probably significant that, according to Egyptian tradition, Seth slaughtered Osiris, the central figure of the ancient panoply of Egyptian gods. Whereas the Egyptians held that Osiris rose from the dead, and by inference held out the hope of eternal life, the Aamus proclaimed Sutekh unique as creator and ruler of the Universe.[50]

It is certainly significant that none of the Semitic kings employed Sutekh in forming his personal cartouche.[51] This circumstance, running counter to Egyptian practice, suggests that the omission represented a deliberate denial of divine rights to rulers. Sacrifices to Sutekh were performed daily at a magnificent temple next to the king's dwellings at Avaris, and garlands of flowers were maintained permanently at the shrine. A few of the Aamu chieftains did, however, bow to some of the Egyptian customs, perhaps because of various levels of belief in Sutekh or in order to conciliate differences between them and the Egyptians by employing ancient trappings.

The Egyptians among the chieftains were free to serve Egyptian gods and incorporated the name of their ancient sun God Re into their names. It seems that some Aamu chieftains likewise compounded their names, thereby projecting an image of authority in deference to Egyptian and Akkadian custom. The determinative suffix *re* in such case may denote a henotheistic ascription to Re as the supreme ruler; it is also possible that it was employed in many cases as simply a sign of kingship and neither as a sign of reverence to a god nor as an indication of the assumption of divine attributes.

Manetho is not the only source for the names of the rulers in Egypt, be they patriarchal village heads or chosen monarchical administrators. Four other important lists of "kings" have been unearthed covering periods of ancient Egyptian history that overlap the period of Asiatic rule, but none are as extensive as Manetho's. The above-mentioned Turin Canon is one. The other three are: 1. The table of Abydos, in which King Sethos (1309-1291 B.C.E.) and his son Rameses are making an offering to seventy-six ancestors, depicted in the form of their cartouches. 2. The table of Sakkara, from a Memphis tomb of an overseer for Rameses II, in which fifty-seven of the king's ancestors appear. 3. The table of Karnak, in which sixty-one names of the ancestors of Thutmosis III (1490-1436 B.C.E.) are listed.

The significant aspect of these three lists is that the Asiatic "kings" or chieftains are conspicuous by absence, except for a few names which appear in garbled order on the table of Karnak. In addition, the name of the one and only Egyptian pharaoh, Akhenaten, who later rejected the Egyptian panoply of gods and turned to monotheism, and who was undoubtedly known to the inscribers of the Abydos table, is also omitted.

A few other references to foreign rule have been recovered, such as at Gebelein, upstream from Thebes, where the names of some foreign kings appear inscribed on monumental blocks which apparently came from a temple of Hathor at that location.[52] The Turin list, however, does mention six kings reigning during the same period as those on the Manetho list, and with a more reasonable time and sequence of reign. They are clearly designated as "chieftains of foreign countries." Africanus significantly refers to Manetho's six kings as "six foreigners from Canaan."

It is on the Manetho record, and little else, that the fable of a destructive invasion of Egypt by a rapacious, unknown race, the dreaded Hyksos who subjected Egypt to a black, artless period, is based. This is the fable that has been widely touted as Egyptian "history" and still permeates much of it and the search for the mysterious Hyksos remains grist for "scholarly" mills.

5

Semitic Culture and Technology Arrive in Egypt

Myths and Misconceptions about Early Egyptian History

An American engineer, Francis Cope Whitehouse, was among a group of engineers retained by the British a century ago to resolve the problem of increasing the amount of arable land in the desert wastelands of Egypt, a country then under British hegemony. Whitehouse astonished his employers by reporting that he had confirmed the existence of a vast lake artificially created by Joseph in the time of the Pharaoh Moeris, and that the most practical method of irrigating the arid Egyptian desert was to reconstruct the system of irrigation which Joseph had instituted 3,500 years ago!

EL-FAYOUM AND THE BAHR YOUSEF

Whitehouse was a distinguished technician, foresighted enough to have been an early inventor of devices to capture solar energy. In surveying the desert he found, to his amazement, that the problem of desert irrigation appeared already to have been addressed more than three millennia earlier in the time of the biblical Joseph. Tracing the remains of ancient irrigation canals, Whitehouse became intrigued by the existence of a small lake, the Birkut el-Qarun, in a deep basin of the desert known to the Egyptians as el-Fayoum some hundred kilometers southwest of Memphis. The Birkut el-Qarun, or Lake Karoun, was a freshwater lake in the midst of the vast Sahara Desert, and yet it had no visible source. His interest piqued by this peculiar circumstance, Whitehouse began an investigation that led to surprising results and to his sincere conclusion that indeed, the lake was a living legacy of a vast irrigation system instituted by none other than Joseph, vizier to the Pharaoh Moeris of Egypt.

The lake supported a fair-sized community, which was economically far better off than most of the rest of Egypt owing to the productivity of the rich agricultural lands still being served by the lake. Around the lake's perimeter, as well as at a considerable distance from its shores, Whitehouse came across the ruins of ancient dams, ditches, aqueducts, and a variety of structures that mutely testified to the existence of a vast and sophisticated irrigation system. Ancient fish bones, shells, and other signs scattered about the sands surrounding the oasis unmistakably demonstrated that the lake had once been many times its current size, that yet another lake had existed that had since dried up, and that the canal system that fed into and out of the lakes had extended the arable land far beyond its contemporary boundaries.

Growing ever more intrigued, Whitehouse delved into the archival documents in Cairo and discovered that medieval maps of the el-Fayoum region showed two lakes in the basin. He was baffled by the fact that not only was the Birket el-Qarun shown to be much larger but that the twin lake, named Lake Moeris in the aged and yellowed documents, far exceeded the dimensions of the Birkut el-Qarun at its erstwhile greatest dimensions.

Whitehouse's amazement continued to mount upon learning that the medieval maps were mere copies of maps drawn in the time of Ptolemy of Alexandria. Whitehouse dug deeper and found substantiation for the existence of an artificially created lake in the writings of the ancient historians Herodotus, Pliny, Diodorus, Strabo, and Mutianus. The lakes were already ancient at the time of the Ptolemies, and the vast expanses of fresh water astounded the ancient writers no less than it did Whitehouse. Whitehouse found the clue to the reason for the existence of the second and larger lake in the writings of Herodotus: "The water of the lake does not come out of the ground, which is here extremely dry, but is introduced by a canal from the Nile."[1]

Herodotus added admiringly that the lake was so huge that its "circumference of 3,600 furlongs (400 miles) equaled the entire length of Egypt along the seacoast."[2]

By extensive surveying Whitehouse confirmed the fact that a vast network of canals flanking the Nile had existed long before the Ptolemaic era; they had been far more extensive, and further, a huge reservoir had been created consisting of two lakes which, if the canal system had not been debased by the Greeks and other succeeding rulers, would have continued to guarantee water to a vast area. The Greeks, ignorant of the hydrology of the system, in attempting to increase acreage by reducing the extent of the lakes, had instead caused large areas of rich soil to return to dusty sand. Once fertile fields had relapsed into an arid landscape of sand, dust, and rock.

Whitehouse uncovered sections of the canal leading into the el-Fayoum basin and feeding Lake Karoun. It was a tributary canal that fed from an existing canal which paralleled the Nile for several hundred kilometers. The twin to the Nile is a canal which the Egyptians do not regard merely as an ordinary waterway but reverently refer to as the Bahr Yousef, or "The Sea of Joseph." It still waters a third of Egypt and appears on maps of Egypt under its Arabic name. Zeccarria Sitchin, a linguist and biblical scholar, reported that:

> Arab historians not only attributed the project to Joseph but reported its circumstances. It was, historians related, when Joseph was more than 100 but still held a high position in the Egyptian court. The other viziers and court officials, envying Joseph, persuaded the Pharaoh that to remain venerated Joseph should not rest on his laurels. He must prove again his abilities. When the Pharaoh agreed, the viziers suggested an impossible project—to convert the desert into a fertile area. "Inspired by God" Joseph confounded his detractors by succeeding. He dug feeder canals and created the vast artificial lake in 1000 days.
>
> Whitehouse . . . took an increasing interest in the Bible, seeking additional clues. . . . As the years went by, and Joseph loomed in his eyes ever larger, and his belief that the Hebrews possessed greater scientific knowledge than their Egyptian hosts. . . . [he became convinced that] it was Joseph, the Hebrew patriarch, who had conceived, planned and carried out the colossal irrigation enterprise.[3]

Whitehouse was also convinced that the best solution to Egypt's water needs was to reconstruct Joseph's magnificent irrigation project. Whitehouse fervently presented his discoveries in April 1883 to the Khedivial Geographical Society in Cairo; in June of the same year Whitehouse pressed his case before the Society of Biblical Archaeology in London. He pressed his views with enthusiasm with a series of lectures and pamphlets, but went unheeded and ignored. Desperate, Whitehouse even sued the authorities, but after his death in 1911 he was honored solely by a long obituary in *The New York Times*. "Thus was forgotten the discovery of an American engineer that some 3,500 years ago it was a Hebrew patriarch who had conceived, engineered, and carried out the world's largest waterworks project until the TVA."[4] The vast irrigation project was created in the time in which viziers like the biblical Joseph were the administrators of Egypt, the time in which Egypt and Canaan were ruled by chosen Asiatic chieftains, the time in which several hundreds of patriarchal progenitors of the Jews brought prosperity to their communities and to the peoples of Egypt. Whitehouse's firm opinion that it was indeed the Hebrew patriarch Joseph who had not only conceived the project, but also completed the massive work in somewhat over three years, was relegated to Egyptian folklore.

Contemporary scientists finally came to appreciate the validity of the ancient system and to reconstitute it in large measure. It was done without accrediting Whitehouse for his research or reference to the ancient tradition. Sir Alan Gardiner summarized the latest theory, almost a century after Whitehouse had presented his discoveries and recommendations to a deaf parliament:

> The original lake sank to below sea-level through the silting up of the channel until a king of Dynasty XII, by widening and deepening it, again brought the lake into equilibrium with the river. Thus was formed the famous lake of Moeris, which by functioning as a combined flood-escape and reservoir, not only protected the lands

of lower Egypt from the destructive effects of excessive high floods, but also increased the supplies of water in the river after the flood season had passed. According to the same theory, the level and consequent size of the lake were artificially reduced in early Ptolemaic times by the construction of two barrages, a portion of the submerged area being thus reclaimed.[5]

A visitor to Egypt today, if he would abjure the euphoria of viewing a mere mirage of Egypt from the deck of one of the floating hotels on the Nile, and would instead thread carefully through the countryside parallel to the Nile, could not but be impressed by the multiplicity of farms and orchards being watered by the web of canals drawn from the Bahr Yousef. This elaborate network of waterways has converted more desolate desert into rich, arable farmland than does the Aswan Dam. No electricity is produced by the Bahr Yousef, but neither does it foster the ecological damage that the Aswan dam is inflicting upon Egypt as a by-product of its function.

The mother of Egypt is, of course, the Nile; there would be no Egypt without it. It is likewise true that Egypt as we know it would not have existed without the system of canals radiating out from the Bahr Yousef across fecund fields which were once wasteland. The area east of the Nile, where only occasional pockets of agriculture exist, contrasts sharply with the area west of the Nile through which the canal flows, an area in which groves of date palms alternate with green fields of grain, verdant vegetable patches, and wide expanses of white-capped cotton plants.

It was not always so. Until the Bahr Yousef was dug, Middle and Upper Egypt was almost entirely a desert inhabited by a rather primitive society. The great constructions in Upper Egypt with which we identify Egyptian glory and power were yet to to be built. There were no great temple complexes at Aswan or Luxor, no Abydos, no Amarna. Civilization, such as it was, was centered mainly in the Delta region of the Nile. Egypt was first learning the use of metals, having yet to emerge from the Chalcolithic Age, the age of copper and stone.

MODERN EGYPTOLOGY CONFRONTS THE SEMITIC INFLUENCE

The Asiatics spurred Egyptian civilization on to higher levels on a number of occasions, beginning when it was still in pre-historic infancy. The dean of Egyptologists, the revered James Henry Breasted, to whom Egyptology is everlastingly indebted for his having spent the better part of a lifetime digging in the ruins and copying and preserving Egyptian inscriptions, took note early on of the profound impact the Asiatics had on Egyptian civilization. In 1905 Breasted wrote: "It was chiefly at the two northern corners of the Delta, that outside influences and foreign elements, who were always sifting into the Nile valley, gained access to the country. . . . The Semitic immigration from Asia, examples of which are also observable in the historic age, occurred in an epoch that lies below our remotest historical horizon."[6] Sir Flinders Petrie, whose status in Egyptology is on a par with that of Breasted, was similarly impressed by the extent of Semitic influence he was finding on his excavations in Egypt and was convinced of the fundamental Asian origin of Egyptian civilization.

These archeological pioneers pointed to the many facets of the impact of Semitic culture upon Lower Egypt. The agronomic and philological influences were cited; the brick constructions of the first pyramids and their similarity to the Akkadian ziggurats were mentioned; the advent of copper work and virtually every innovation that came into being over a period of several millennia were cited as reflections of Akkadian technology. The cylinder seal was shown to be specifically Mesopotamian and its appearance in Egypt a testimony to burgeoning trade. They also cited pictures of Mediterranean-type boats in a tomb at Hieronkopolis and a Mesopotamian-type carved ivory knife-handle recovered from Jebel el-Arak, on which a full-bearded man dressed in a typical long cloak is depicted in battle with two lions in a posture indistinguishable from that found in similar scenes on artifacts from Akkadia.

Many archaeologists rejected out of hand the evidence of these and numerous other examples and dismissed the opinions as being unduly influenced by biblical lore. Certain of the conclusions of the doughty archaeological trailblazers were indeed found to be faulty as time and archaeology advanced, but the Asiatic origin of technology and culture, central to the thrust of their theories, gained effective affirmation from an ever-growing corpus of new findings. After a period of skepticism and rejection, many contemporary scholars have come to appreciate the validity of the basis for Petrie's opinions and the value of Breasted's observations concerning the extent of the penetration of Semitic culture into Egypt. The balance of archaeological opinion has swung over to favor that of these early visionary scientists, and the foundation of their viewpoint proves to be ever more sound as new facts are revealed.

"Many scholars today accept that at some time during the Pre-dynastic period (possibly c. 3400 B.C.), a new group of people arrived in Egypt and their advent resulted in profound changes in many aspects of the civilization," stated A. Rosalie David.[7] William C. Hayes, in compiling "A Background for the Study of the Egyptian Antiquities in the Metropolitan Museum of Art," came to the conclusion that: "Over the Hyksos bridge there flowed into the Nile Valley in unprecedented quantity new blood strains, new religious and philosophical concepts, and new artistic styles and media, as well as epoch-making innovations of a more practical nature. . . . "[8] John A. Wilson agreed: "At this point there was an artistic, intellectual, and technical fructification from Babylonia, and Egypt made a great spurt toward history."[9] Percy Handcock took a cue from Breasted's early observations: "The Semites swept over Egypt and the north coast of Africa, impressing their indelible and unmistakable stamp upon the foundation-structure of the Egyptian and Libyan languages."[10] Sir Alan Gardiner concurred: "Many affinities (of the Egyptian Language) with Hamitic and in particular with Berber dialects have been found . . . on the other hand the relationship with Semitic (Hebrew, Arabic) is equally unmistakable."[11] Will Durant acknowledged the consensus: "The further back we trace the Egyptian language the more affinities it reveals with the Semitic tongues of the Near East. The pictographic writings of the pre-dynastic Egyptians seems to have come in from Sumeria."[12] W. Wendorf summed up by stating that the early Pre-dynastic cultures record the arrival of a new population in Egypt, who brought with them the cultural base from which Egyptian civilization was to develop.[13]

The more extensive the probing of the late pre-historical past in Egypt, the more probity accrued to the theories that every Egyptian attribute of civilization was fundamentally the outgrowth of Southwest Asiatic, essentially "Semitic" insemination. The growing realization by Egyptologists that the mounting evidence validated those theories brought about a bizarre result. They virtually ceased looking for new evidence!

Dr. B. G. Trigger, of the McGill University Department of Anthropology, pondered upon this peculiarity: "The conviction that Egypt was not an important centre of plant and animal domestication and a consequent shift of interest to south-western Asia are, in part, responsible for the dearth of fieldwork on Pre-dynastic sites in recent years." Dr. Trigger lamented further that the most important studies since 1952 were relegated to "restudies of earlier data."[14]

Another hiatus in Egyptological research resulted from a lack of attention to the life of common people and of the communities of artisans and merchants who lived on the periphery of the urban centers, a defect of scientific investigation that has only recently been partially rectified. This deficiency is largely responsible for the initial dismal state of archaeological research in general; the sad condition was aggravated in Egypt by the realization that indeed, most of the discoveries regarding the development of Egyptian civilization pointed to sources outside of Egypt. The "alien" communities were the creative matrix of Egyptian civilization, but they rendered little in the way of spectacular works and artifacts. "It is no wonder that the present state of studies of ancient Egyptian civilization is enormously one-sided," declares Manfred Bietak, the excavator of Tell al-Dabᶜa, or Qantir, the site on which the biblical city of Avaris was identified. "In Egypt, temple sites and cemeteries have been chosen as objects of excavation and study because they yield more museum objects and, with their imposing architecture and representations of fine arts, are far more likely to impress the trustees of institutions than the decayed mud-brick architecture of townsites with their tons of potsherds."[15]

What type of research would restore balance to the one-sidedness of Egyptological research referred to by Dr. Bietak? The main consideration is that Egypt was not monolithic but composed of diverse cultural entities each of which must be accounted for in analyzing the evolution of its development. Moreover, that during the Predynastic period the cultures were largely distinct and separate.

THE PREDYNASTIC PERIOD

The area west of the Nile (the Libyan or Nubian desert) was habitable during the Pluvial period, during which various distinguishable Paleolithic cultures succeeded each other over a period of seven hundred thousand years as cycles of moist and arid climate affected the area. At the end of that period an arid phase occurred and grew in severity and created the desert condition as it is now known. Some sporadic agricultural development began to take place west of the Nile and along the Mediterranean coast in the seventh millennium B.C.E. (the Subpluvial period), perhaps a reflection of the radical changes that were occurring in neighboring Asia, but the climatic changes of Northeast Africa were not conducive to a continuance of such activity, and during the sixth millennium B.C.E. the scattered villages disappeared, leaving behind a few ephemeral traces of their existence in the sands of the Sahara. After that time agriculture had to be confined to the area of the Delta or to the narrowing banks of the Nile as the river cut deeper and deeper through the sandstone on its long journey to the Mediterranean.

Upper Egypt was virtually isolated from the world. It had no resources conducive to the development of much more than a Neolithic culture. The sparse arable areas, crowded between the escarpments plunging down from a high desert plateau to the Nile on its eastern banks, and restricted to small, limited plots being seasonally flooded by the Nile, mostly on its western flank, were insufficient to support more than a minimal population. The area was known as the "Red Land," distinguishing the predominantly barren desert lands from the "Black Land," the fertile alluvium of the Delta area of the Nile to the north.

The Black Land had a different set of disadvantages. It is an extensive region surrounding the many-branched mouth of the Nile and down the river for a considerable distance until the desert encroaches upon the river and the arable land narrows down, to be finally contained within the rugged escarpments of the middle Nile. The Black Land was a marshy region rich with the silt carried down from the distant mountains of Ethiopia and Central Africa and deposited by the annual floods. It was a fecund area, crowded with birds and animals well adapted to the soggy environment.

The ancient historians, beginning with Herodotus, held a dim view of the Delta's inhabitability: they typically portrayed the prehistoric Delta as an all but uninhabitable swamp "whose early sites (in the unlikely possibility that they ever existed at all) would invariably be buried beneath countless meters of alluvium."[16] Herodotus was merely repeating what he and countless other historians who followed him were told by Egyptian pundits. It was said that before the reign of the first king of the First Dynasty, all of Egypt was a miserable marsh with the exception of the Theban nome.[17]

The view thus promulgated was patently an attempt by Egyptians to camouflage the true origin of Egyptian civilization. "The story is probably unfounded and was invented to enhance the fame of the unifier of the two kingdoms."[18]

Herodotus later mentioned that he was told that dikes were installed south of Memphis in the process of laying out the city to regulate the flow of flood-water, a project that took place in the time of the First Dynasty, and that these dikes first made habitation possible outside of the Theban region.[19] Although the report on the construction of dikes has a certain validity, the conclusion drawn conceals the fact that the Delta area had not only supported habitation for two millennia and more before that ancient time, albeit within the limits set by the flooding Nile, but was the very area in which civilization was implanted into Lower Egypt from neighboring Asia and through which civilization eventually gained a foothold in Upper Egypt.

The Delta was lush with foliage, a swampy quagmire of an area, which, however, dried up sufficiently during a good part of the year to support many thousands of domesticated foraging animals. The area had long been a vital reserve for the peoples of Southwest Asia who brought herds of cattle and flocks of sheep and goats across the sands of the Sinai to graze in the Delta during the recurrent periods in which drought desiccated Canaan. The area was not merely a seasonally pastoral Eden; hillocks rising from the alluvial areas provided islands of permanently dry land where agricultural settlements were established by the Asiatics. These *gezirat* (Arabic for "turtlebacks") are sedimentary relics which proliferated in the Delta in the late Pleistocene Age. The limitations of a single *gezira* were resolved by connecting it to adjoining mounds; a village and its surroundings often comprised the consolidation of a number of mounds. The settlements were situated athwart the ancient trade routes; some were close to a branch of the Nile; many were placed at the junction of the ancient land routes with one of the main waterways; others sprouted at the junctions of land routes crossing the desert, especially from Asia. Such settlements existed long before the time in which Abraham is said to have arrived with his entourage and his animals to await a better season for the completion of his *aliya* to Canaan.

Such a community was Merimde beni-Salame, situated thirty-seven miles northwest of Cairo, discovered in the winter of 1927-28 by Professor Hermann Junker, director of the Vienna Academy of Natural Science's expedition to Egypt. A large, flat area of almost fifty acres rose about two meters over the surrounding plain, strategically placed between the remaining semiarid pasturelands of the encroaching desert and the rich alluvial bottomland. It is one of the earliest known farming villages in Lower Egypt, having been settled around 4880 B.C.E. and remaining occupied thereafter for approximately 650 years. Throughout the village clusters of baskets or jars serving as granaries were buried up to their necks in the ground, and circular, clay-lined threshing floors also seemed to be associated with individual dwellings. A population of from five thousand to sixteen thousand people has been projected, although the latter figure may well be a cumulative one based on dwellings built over a span of time.[20]

It was immediately clear to the excavators that the Merimdians were radically different from both the Predynastic peoples of Upper Egypt and the Dynastic Egyptians in every respect—physically, culturally, and technologically. Their burial customs were similar to those of the Southwest Asians and strikingly different from those of the Africans. Whereas the African tradition was to bury the dead with a variety of earthly goods to sustain them and amulets to protect them in the afterlife, the graves of the Merimdians contained no grave offerings of any kind. The Merimdians lived in more or less economically independent single family units, the foundation of the same type of patriarchal system being formed at the time in the Semitic cultures of Southwestern Asia and quite unlike the autarchic systems being generated in Upper Egypt.

> [Merimde] shows none of the distinctively Egyptian characteristics. . . . In its general aspects, Merimde seems more like a village of sturdy yeoman farmers than a collection of peasants subject to the whims, avarice, and authority of a powerful man or government, although some cooperative efforts (if not centralization of food-producing tasks) are recalled by the threshing floors up to 13 feet in diameter.[21]

Merimde's pottery, although technically advanced, was plain and practical, "a theme which sets apart this and later Delta sites from the ornament-ridden and display-oriented culture of Upper Egypt."[22] The technological differences between the two regions were also conspicuous in the tools employed and particularly in agronomy and agriculture. "The site was originally settled by a people intimately familiar with the mixed herding and crop-raising techniques that dominated the Middle Eastern and Levantine worlds for 2000 years."[23] The cultivation of grain crops like wheat and barley and useful plants like flax, all foreign to and entirely unknown in Egypt until that time, were introduced from Southwest Asia into Africa by such small farming communities of the Delta. The natives of Upper Egypt were as yet Stone Age hunters and gatherers.

A second region of ancient settlement was the Fayoum basin, a natural oasis before it was artificially expanded; it accommodated agricultural settlements with many similarities to those on the hillocks of the Delta. Several sites north of the ancient lake Moeris, the lake now known as Lake Karoun, were explored by Gertrude Caton-Thompson and her geologist colleague Elinor Gardner in the winters of 1924-25 and 1925-26. The site Ms. Gardner designated as Fayoum A produced artifacts markedly dissimilar from those of the indigenous surrounding Saharan cultures as well as distinctly different from those of the cultures of Upper Egypt. The conduct of farming and husbandry underlined the unmistakable differentiation between the life-styles of this group of people from that of the indigenous Africans:

> Grains of emmer wheat and six row barley filled many of the sunken silos that clustered on the high ground overlooking the small villages. Both of these plants are Middle Eastern domesticates and their presence in fully developed form in Fayoum A underscores the speed with which Neolithic economy moved into Egypt during the middle of the Neolithic Subpluvial (ca. 5000 B.C.). Not only Middle Eastern plants, but domesticated animals abounded in Fayoum A sites, including sheep or goat, cattle and pig. . . . Contacts with other lands are attested by objects like pierced marine shells from both the Mediterranean and the Red Seas.[24]

The six row barley to which Hoffman refers requires a large amount of water such as was available in the Delta, and could not have been developed in Upper Egypt. On the other hand this hulled variety of barley has been identified at the Mesopotamian site of Ali Kosh, where it was dated to 6000 B.C.E., and where it became widely cultivated after 5500 B.C.E. as systems of irrigation expanded.[25] The appearance of this and the other equally Asiatic plants and animals which appear in the Delta within the next millennium render unambiguous testimony to the movement of the Asiatics and to the origin of the two primary facets of the inception of civilization, husbandry and agronomy. F. Wendorf compared the local terminal Paleolithic industry with that of the succeeding Fayoum A, the first stage of the agricultural communities of the basin, and found the differences so gross as to suggest the arrival of a new population who installed a cultural foundation on which not only the civilization of Lower Egypt was based, but indeed one from which all of Egyptian civilization emerged.[26]

The history of the Delta, or Lower Egypt, is quite different and separate from that of Upper Egypt. Egyptologists generally divide the latter prehistoric period of Upper Egypt into two phases of the Neolithic period; the first takes place between c. 5000 B.C.E. to c. 3500 B.C.E., a time in which a gradual adaptation to husbandry and agronomy filtered down along the Nile from the Delta and the Fayoum. The Badarian culture, so-called after its existence was disclosed at the site of el Badari, was followed by what is characterized as the Naqada culture, after the site of Naqada near Koptos. The period of the Naqada culture is subdivided into two phases, the first of which is termed the Amratian culture, after el Amri near Abydos. Animal husbandry was introduced from the north during these periods, and by the time of the historic period the raising of domesticated dogs, goats, sheep, cattle, pigs, and geese had begun to replace hunting to a considerable degree in Upper Egypt.

EARLY MESOPOTAMIAN INFLUENCES

In the Naqada II phase, distinguished as the Gerzean culture and dated from c. 3500 B.C.E. to c. 3170 B.C.E., the glimmerings of the Chalcolithic period appear. During this period the Mesopotamian influence begins to impact most powerfully upon Upper Egypt, penetrating Upper Egypt not only along the Nile but also from across the desert and the Red Sea to the east. The name that lent itself to characterize the period, Naqada, means literally "The Golden Town," a name that reflects its strategic position at the mouth of the Wadi Hammamat almost directly opposite Koptos. The gold of the eastern desert and that of Nubia passed through the town, a traffic that left the imprint of the itinerant Asiatic merchants upon the area. Similar routes led across the desert into Kom Ombo and Edfu, which centers served a similar function as crossroads of commerce. "This essentially African culture [that of the Naqada period] might have remained static at this stage of development, as it did in the Sudan for much longer, if it had not apparently been re-animated from Western Asia, whence some significant introductions now came."[27]

Sun-dried mud bricks, a building material characteristic of Lower Mesopotamia, were first employed in Egypt during this period; the use of a distinctly Mesopotamian device, the cylinder seal was introduced; and traces of writing appeared, whose images bore a marked resemblance to those of the Land of the Twin Rivers. "The first attempts at a pictographic system of writing have also been traced by some scholars ... to the Jamdet Culture [of Mesopotamia]."[28] The pear-shaped stone mace-heads found in an earlier context at the Deltic Asiatic communities such as Merimde, replications of Mesopotamian models, appear in turn in the south in the Gerzean period. The use of metal does not appear at all in Upper Egypt until the latter part of the Badarian period, at first in the form of a few pins and ornaments which may well have been trade goods. Eventually, a few crude copper tools do appear, evidently of local production.

During that very time in the latter half of the fourth millennium before the Common Era, Jamdet Nasr in lower Mesopotamia was already leaping into the next progressive phase of metallurgy, the Bronze Age. The peoples speaking "Semitic" dialects were spreading out along the entire Fertile Crescent from the great cities at the crown of the crescent; they moved south and east and absorbed Sumer, situated athwart the area where the Euphrates and Tigris rivers meld into the Arabian Gulf. Traders were ranging throughout the area and *karums*, trading villages, were being established near the burgeoning cities of Anatolia. It was during this time that Asiatic settlements in the Nile Delta expanded into urban communities and Asiatic traders began to travel down the Nile, paying their way past the enclaves of petty princes along its cliff-enclosed banks, tribute to local lords who had little else to offer but the right of passage.

During the Naqada period the Asiatic communities spread upstream; several groups of farming communities were established just below modern Cairo. In 1924 a young Egyptian mineralogist, Amin el Omari, discovered such a community in the periphery of his home town, Helwan, about twenty-three kilometers south of Cairo. Tragically, the promising young scientist died shortly afterward; in his memory the town and others which were later discovered were named after him (Omari A, B, and C), as was the distinct culture they represented. The El Omari villages were urbanized centers into which was introduced an impressive array of Asian agricultural products such as sycamore dates and figs, domesticated wild sugar, emmer wheat, and an evolved type of barley. The domesticated Omari animals, like those of Fayoum A and Merimde, were Mesopotamian varieties of pigs, goats, and cows; the bones of such animals were found in abundance, along with those of a wide assortment of the wild animals, birds, and fish that proliferated in Lower Egypt and were effectively hunted. The separate housing and facilities of the village dwellers, each of which were more or less self-contained economic units, reflect the essentially egalitarian character of Omari life. The tools, the pottery, and the method of burial of the earlier Omari periods all resemble those of Southwestern Asia as do those of the other Asiatic settlements in Lower Egypt; they are cumulatively referred to as the "Deltic tradition." In the later period the Omari culture began to absorb some of the burial and other customs of the Upper Egyptians, an evolutionary cultural trend that intensifies in both directions as intercourse increased. Grave offerings of imported ornaments begin to appear in some of the later burials, such as stone and shell beads; in one grave a staff was found clutched in the hand of the deceased, which some archaeologists interpret to have symbolized authority.

Nevertheless, the severe social stratification that is clearly evident in the contemporary Amratian and Gerzean societies of Upper Egypt is comparatively minimal among the El Omarians.[29] Perhaps one of the most significant discoveries is that the El Omarian and other Deltic peoples grew fodder vetch, a crop specifically produced for the feeding of domesticated animals and especially suitable for feeding the most common Asiatic draft animal, the Asiatic donkey. The Egyptian connection to Canaan and Mesopotamia was knit with the donkey. Whereas Upper Egypt itself had no raw materials to offer (other than stone), Nubia did, and Asiatic caravans threaded their way down the Nile by boat and donkey to trade with the Nubians. The donkey was alien to Egypt. The Egyptians, in fact, employed no pack animals at all during the Pre-dynastic period. The earliest remains of donkeys in Egypt were found in various Deltic communities and were conspicuously present in Ma'adi, an Asiatic village ten kilometers northwest of El Omari.

Ma'adi flourished at a time coeval with the southern Naqada period and lasted into the Early Dynastic times. The sprawling village covered eighteen hectares on whose northern periphery granaries consisting of meter-high jars were nested deep into the sandy soil, a system of storage reminiscent of those at Merimde. In addition, however, the Ma'adians employed substantial storage pits whose sides were reinforced with mud or basketwork; they were found to contain not only carbonized grain but basalt vases, carnelian beads, and other valuable items. The people of Ma'adi were clearly more industrially advanced and engaged in hunting and gathering to a far lesser extent than the precedent peoples of the Delta; they were not only expert in agronomy and husbandry but were accomplished craftsmen. "A copper axe-head spoiled in casting and masses of copper ore indicate that copper was being processed at Ma'adi. Ma'adi is the oldest site in northern Egypt in which copper artifacts have been found."[30] The axe heads, daggers, and other cast copper tools found in the north, and the few such tools that began to appear in the Gerzean sites to the south, may very well have been produced at Ma'adi.

Importing was an activity which is eloquently attested to by the donkey bones excavated from Ma'adi's ruins. Although Ma'adi is situated at the western end of a Wadi which leads to the copper deposits at Jebel 'Ataqa and the Sinai, it appears that the Ma'adians imported the material rather than mined it. "Ma'adi was an important entrepot handling trade between the Nile Valley, the Sinai Peninsula and Palestine [sic]." Much Early Bronze Age "Palestinian" pottery of a late coeval with the late Predynastic period was unearthed from Ma'adi;[31] this and a variety of other imported materials amplify the evidence of the function of Ma'adi as both an industrial and commercial center.

The people of Ma'adi were among the many communities of Asiatic peoples who were productively active in the north at the time it was invaded and destroyed. They suffered a cruel thanks for the technology they had introduced. "Ma'adi met a violent end as witnessed by widespread ash and human bones over the settlement. If so, then perhaps this was the 'final solution' arranged for the heterogenous society of Ma'adi by the victorious kings of the first Dynasty."[32] The legendary first king of all Egypt, Menes, established his capital at Memphis, ten kilometers north of Ma'adi.

The contrast between the Deltic agricultural communities and of both the indigenous peoples and those of Upper Egypt is evident in its many forms. Although the housing of the Asiatic communities was of different construction from the houses of the indigenous peoples, there was a striking architectural homogeneity between their structures with housing of the period unearthed near Beersheba. "Such structures are present in several sites around Beersheba but otherwise foreign to Egypt. Several ceramic types . . . , like [the] houses, have precedent in the Beersheba area,"[33] noted Hoffman.

The metallurgy of Mesopotamia had already advanced well into the Bronze Age while a crude and primitive use of copper was first appearing in Upper Egypt: "Copper tools are known from both Badarian and Amratian [Predynastic] sites, but these implements were generally small and simple (punches, drills and beads) and were hammered from natural copper, rather than smelted and cast from ore."[34] The small number of awls and pins hammered out of copper, as well as steatite beads covered with a blue-green cupric glaze, may not have been locally produced at all but were part of the goods distributed by itinerant traders traveling across the Sinai or the Red Sea. The association of these rare copper items with Red Sea shells, Sinai turquoise, Levantine pine, cedar, and other woods, and an unusual four-handled vessel leave the possibility of their local production open to serious question.[35] Copper artifacts, both cast and hammered, did not become common in Upper Egypt until the end of the Gerzean and the Early Dynastic period, when the Asiatic influence becomes pronounced. Cylinder seals then appear, of the same type as those found in the *karums* of Anatolia; Mesopotamian pottery, ivory knife handles, stone palettes, and other luxury goods were decorated with artistic motifs adopted by the Gerzean Egyptians. Interlacing serpents, serpent-necked panthers, and a winged griffin were among the characteristically Mesopotamian fabulous animals carved into the imported goods, designs which insinuated themselves into the indigenous Gerzean art. The ubiquitous Mesopotamian rendition of a carnivore attacking impassive prey and of a man dominating two animals also appears, the men wear distinctive Mesopotamian head-dresses and long robes, clearly made of fabrics strange to Egypt.[36]

The Nubians, in fact, were more advanced in the metallurgic arts than were the Egyptians, and it was to Nubia that the traffic was directed during this period.

As late as the Middle Kingdom gold and copper smelting was still being carried on in Lower Nubia.

The physical differences between the peoples of the Deltic Predynastic communities and those of Upper Egypt are perhaps even more striking than the differences in housing and technology. "The Upper Egyptian people were mostly small in stature and had long, narrow skulls, dark wavy hair and brown skin. . . . Skeletons found at Merimda, El Omari, and Ma'adi suggest that the Predynastic inhabitants of the Delta were taller and more sturdily built than the Upper Egyptians and that their skulls were broader."[37] The larger, mesocephalic peoples, whose skeletons which were found as far as Abydos by the time of the First Dynasty, were the Armenoid type of Western Asia.[38]

We must pause here to underscore a grievous source of many misconstructions of the cultural currents of the Predynastic period. Not enough account has been taken of the fact that although the Asiatic communities of the Delta flourished at the same time that the Badarian, Amratian, and Gerzean cultures were developing in Upper Egypt, the peoples were geographically distant, separate, and quite distinct. El-Matmar, the northernmost of the group of Badarian sites, was well over a hundred kilometers away from Fayoum A with virtually no habitation existing between them; an equal distance divided the Amratian sites and Merimde. The somewhat lesser separation between the Gerzean and the Asiatic sites of the period in which Ma'adi was active was due to the expansion of Asiatic communities down the Nile, but there was still a considerable distance between the closest of the two peoples.[39] Not until the imposition of Egyptian hegemony over the area did the two peoples come into continuous close contact. The relationship between the peoples was, until then, restricted to the passage of the venturesome Asiatic traders past the strongholds of the indigenous chieftains along the Nile, or to the predatory incursions of those chieftains into the north.

The primitive peoples along the Middle Nile, in fact, had little to offer other than stone. The Asiatic traders ventured far into the upper reaches of the Nile to trade with the Nubians, who did have an assortment of valuable goods to barter: gold, ivory, ebony, fancy feathers, furs, and live exotic animals fancied by the rich and powerful of Mesopotamia. The Asiatic traders penetrated Egypt from both points of the Fertile Crescent. There was a considerable traffic of shipping along and across the Red Sea, which was being navigated by vessels of an advanced design. Commercial intercourse with the Indus valley was negotiated by these seagoing ships. Encampments were established on the African coast at the western terminus of this traffic—trading posts which grew into settlements from which caravans took off across the red hills of the eastern desert. For a long time the traces of the traffic across the desert were interpreted as merely evidence of transient nomadic life, but the identification of coastal communities of considerable size and of substantial caravan stations along the arid, rocky routes from the coast to the Nile made the attribution to nomadic activity untenable. Michael Hoffman scoffed at the Egyptologists who naively echoed the fable that the Easterners who came across the Red Sea in sophisticated ships to establish trading posts in the barren hills sixty-five miles east of the Nile were analogous to nomadic bedouins, pointing out that such an idea grates against common sense:

> The Easterners . . . were transshippers—middlemen—in an exchange system that, by the middle to late fourth millennium B.C., was linking various economies of the ancient Middle East in a vast superexchange network that revolved around symbolically prestigious, exotic goods increasingly in demand by the emergent social and political elite from Egypt to India. They were neither simple Bedouin nor invaders; they were more akin to carpetbaggers: middlemen in a trade network that stretched north across Sinai into Palestine and Mesopotamia and south along the Red Sea and South Arabian coasts to the east.[40]

THE BEGINNING OF THE DYNASTIC ERA

The peaceful infiltration and settlement of the Asiatics into the Delta was interrupted by a series of incursions from Upper Egypt. The history of the period is misty and suffers from a dearth of both documentary and material evidence. Unlike the favorable conditions for the conservation of the record of human presence in Upper Egypt, the water-laden marshes and the periodic inundations of the Nile in the Delta region were hardly conducive to preservation of the relics of the pastoral villages of that distant era. It can be reasonably conjectured that as the West Asian crossroads of commerce grew in importance, and as the Gerzean nomarchs, Egyptian barons controlling small enclaves along the middle and upper Nile, grew in wealth and power from the burgeoning traffic, they sought to control the trade and to monopolize the profits accruing from it. "The desire to protect trade routes and to eliminate intermediaries in Lower Egypt may also have encouraged these rulers to try to extend their power northwards."[41]

We are dimly aware of some of the characters who engaged in raiding and eventually subduing the Delta. A king named "Scorpion" appears on a large white ceremonial macehead, wearing the White Crown of Lower Egypt, depicted in the act of ritually spading a shovelful of earth to launch the digging of a canal. The scorpion mace demonstrates the deep impression that Eastern technology had made upon Egyptian culture. Irrigation systems had been functioning in Mesopotamia for over two thousand years and had become widespread there at the time it was first being introduced into Egypt. The central importance of irrigation as an essential function of government is thus shown by the scorpion mace to have been recognized in Egypt at the turn of the Dynastic period.

The most graphic depiction of the way in which the Upper Egyptians sought to attain power is supplied by the "Narmer Palette," on one side of which the king, Narmer, is proudly wearing the White Crown of Upper Egypt and is portrayed in the act of bashing in the head of a resistant northerner; on the reverse side the scene shifts in time to the end of the campaign in which the king, wearing the Red Crown of Lower Egypt, is calmly gazing upon rows of beheaded enemies.

Other aggressive nomarchs (Ka and Aha), overlords of local principalities or nomes, are mentioned as donning the Red or White Crowns. Finally, we are told, a Theban ruler appears, Menes, who invaded the north, took firm control, and initiated the first All-Egyptian Dynasty. Whether Menes, Narmer, and Scorpion are in fact one and the same, or whether one or the other of the Upper Egypt lords was the actual conqueror of the northern communities and initiator of the Dynastic Era remains a mystery and a matter of scholarly debate. What is evident is that the nomes of Lower Egypt were transformed from a loosely organized society in which autonomous chieftains and "carpetbagging" merchants played the most significant role, to one of the two vassal states under the centralized control of an imperial king.

The homes and tombs of the wealthier Egyptians of the First Dynasty benefited from and were enriched by the artistic and technical skills that became available to them through the conquest of Lower Egypt. The skills of the Asiatic artisans of Lower Egypt, previously employed to turn out utility ware, were now engaged to produce luxury goods in wood, metal, and stone for the royal court. Large numbers of artists and craftsmen were indentured or enslaved to work in the vicinity of Memphis. "These craftsmen . . . evolved a coherent style and established artistic canons that were to remain an integral part of the elite culture of Ancient Egypt."[42] The abundance of food produced in Lower Egypt was traded for Canaanite goods; great quantities of Canaanite pottery vessels of the Early Bronze Age have been extricated from the tombs of the First Dynasty.

The rich accoutrements of the First Dynasty tombs persuaded historians that a period of prosperity had ensued. The spurt of creativity and inventiveness that resulted from the application of inherent skills to the production of luxury wares creates an illusion of progress only when the contents of royal tombs are taken as a measure of that progress. The mirage of Early Dynastic Egyptian glory is persistent, but it has become abundantly clear that far from being a period of progress, the overall welfare of Egypt and the evolution of Egyptian technology was adversely affected by the events. The passage of power to and the monopolization of trade by the Upper Egyptian barons had an immediate deleterious effect upon further technological and cultural development and ultimately resulted in stagnation. The glory which the modern-day Egyptian historians (and their more credulous disciples) have attributed to the "unification" of Egypt is belied by the record of the dire consequences of the imposition of southern rule upon what was until then a flourishing and developing economy. Manfred Bietak, the renowned excavator of the Delta region, was struck by finding that the glory attributed to the early Egyptian dynasties was but an illusory facade, and that in fact,

> . . . development was cut short after Egypt had been unified under a single monarch and a stable, centralized government had been established by the kings of the first two Dynasties. Foreign trade became the monopoly of the crown and was organized from the royal residence, a change that deprived the oldest towns, which had already been stripped of their political strength, of their economic role as well. Be-

cause of this cutting-off of former resources, the old centers, especially those in the Delta, vanished, and impetus to settle in other areas of the Delta reduced. For example, in the eastern Delta and along the land routes to Syria and Palestine [sic], we have relatively good evidence of settlement at the very end of the Predynastic Period and at the beginning of the First Dynasty. But there is almost no evidence from the Old Kingdom.[43]

Trade with Nubia also suffered with the suspension of the activity of the Asiatic itinerant merchants. Egyptian frustration over the cessation of Nubian trade led to a series of military incursions into Nubia, which, far from resulting in a healthy resumption of commerce, had a disastrous effect upon the region; the invasions "no doubt account for the eventual disappearance of a sedentary population on Lower Nubia before the end of the First Dynasty."[44] Traffic down the Nile continued sporadically, ebbing and flowing with the intensity of activist Theban militancy. The traders who traveled down the river during periods of peace established trading posts at the first cataract of the Nile on the island of Yeb and on the banks where the city of Aswan is now located; Aswan derives its very name from the Egyptian word for "trade" or "market."[45]

EGYPTIANS AND CANAANITES

For more than a millennium after Egypt was unified under the fabled Menes, the relationship between Egypt and its neighbors passed through intermittent periods of aggression and relative peace. Space does not permit entering into each of these recurrent events in detail. Suffice it to say that during the peaceful intervals the Semitic peoples of Lower Canaan flowed freely into the Delta area and that these recurrent periods are the very ones that mark whatever advances in Egyptian culture and technology ensued. The process is aptly illustrated by the biblical story of Abraham, an account which reflects a vivid tribal memory of one of the propitious times in which the Semites were warmly welcomed into Lower Egypt.

Documentary and archaeological evidence both confirm the advent of a period of peaceful relationship between the Egyptians and the Asiatics beginning at the turn of the second millennium B.C.E., some 200 years before the time Abraham and his tribe are said to have sojourned in Goshen (the Eastern Delta). One of the most renowned of Egyptian literary works stems from that time. It is a lengthy account which elucidates in personal terms and in graphic detail the positive and progressive nature of the state of affairs in the region between the two lands, Egypt and Canaan. It is called "The Tale of Sinuhe," and it relates how the said Sinuhe, an Egyptian official of high rank, believing that he had fallen afoul of the law during the reign of Egyptian king Sen-Usert I (1971–1928 B.C.E.), fled to Retenu, the name by which Canaan was referred to by the Egyptians. Hiding in bushes and creeping through the fields by day, he slipped by the Egyptian frontier guards by night, only to suffer hunger and thirst in the Sinai desert.

"I was parched and my throat was dusty. I said: 'This is the taste of death!'"

Just then Sinuhe heard the lowing of cattle and came upon the beasts being herded by a group of Asiatics, headed by a kindly Canaanite chief *"who had been in Egypt."* The well-traveled Canaanite recognized Sinuhe and rescued him, reviving the thirsty and famished fugitive with water and boiled milk. "What they did for me was good," wrote Sinuhe, thankfully.

Sinuhe went to Byblos and Qedem, where he resided for a year and a half. A certain ruler of Upper Canaan, Ammi-enshi, impressed with Sinuhe's reputation and character as given to him by *Egyptian members of the Canaanite's court,* offered to take him into his service to teach his children (presumably the Egyptian language).

"Thou wilt do well with me, and thou wilt hear the speech of Egypt," the Canaanite chieftain told Sinuhe, referring to the presence of the other Egyptians in his service. Sinuhe was treated as one of the family, which he eventually became by marrying the chieftain's daughter. Sinuhe was set up by the chieftain in style with his own estate, prospered in Canaan, and in the rendition of his experiences he describes the land of Canaan in a manner recalling almost word for word the biblical descriptions of the "promised land": "Figs were in it, and grapes. It had more wine than water. Plentiful was its honey, abundant its olives. Every (kind of) fruit was on its trees. Barley was there, and emmer. There was no limit of cattle."[46]

The story has a happy ending, for Sinuhe, nostalgic for his homeland and longing to return to be buried there, learned that he was forgiven by the Egyptian king for his imagined transgressions. Sinuhe assigned his estate in Canaan to his children, making his eldest son responsible for the administration of the property and for the extensive family he had fostered. "My tribe and all my property were in his charge: my serfs, all my cattle, my fruit, and every pleasant tree of mine." Sinuhe's "tribe" presumably lived on and prospered, living, as the ending goes, happily ever after.

The Egyptian commander at the Canaanite border informed the Egyptian king of Sinuhe's arrival, and "his majesty sent a capable overseer of peasants of the palace, with loaded ships in his train, carrying presentations from the royal presence *for the Asiatics who had followed me."* Sinuhe became a member of the royal Egyptian court and was provided with servants, fine linen clothes, and a sumptuous house with garden. He was also provided with a small pyramid set in a necropolis-garden which extended as far as "is done for a chief courtier," a suitable setting in which he could enjoy eternal rest.[47]

The amicable relationship between Egypt and Canaan so effectively attested to in "The Tale of Sinuhe" continued in the days of Sen-Usert II, the fourth king of the Twelfth Dynasty, and the burgeoning commercial intercourse proved to be a boon to the nomarchs of Upper Egypt. The nome of one such local Baron, Knumhotpe III, was posted strategically along the central Nile, 280 kilometers upstream at Beni Hassan. Knumhotpe considered the wealth which accrued to him from the passing merchants so important that, in typical Egyptian fashion, he attempted to assure the continuance of this lucrative activity after his death by having an eternal traffic of tradesmen painted prominently on a central wall of his tomb. The painting evidently registers an actual event which the prince felt worthy of eternal repetition; it depicts a caravan of thirty-seven Canaanites in full size along a wall four meters high and twenty meters long, whose leader is depicted in the act of paying customs duties to the Egyptian's officials. The black-haired and bearded Canaanite men are wearing "cloaks of many colors" and the Canaanite women and children are dressed in equally bold, brightly colored tunics. An explanatory hieroglyphic text proclaims that the Asiatics are supplying stibium, a mineral essential for preparing the eye makeup so loved by the Egyptians. Knumhotpe evidently assumed that the place he would occupy in the hereafter would lack the mineral no less than did Egypt, and its continued import from Akkadia needed to be assured.

The date given is the fourth year of Senusert II's rule or about 1892 B.C.E. The caravan leader is named Abushei, a distinctly Hebrew name appearing biblically as the name of one of King David's two top generals. The leader is referred to as a "Hyk-khase," that is, a "foreign chieftain." Metallurgy is one of the trades carried on by members of the group, a fact readily deduced from the presence of an anvil and a bellows lashed securely onto the backs of the caravan's donkeys. The laminated bows, the twelve-string harp, and the lyre being carried by the Semites are particularly meaningful, for the Egyptians had no knowledge of such bows and types of musical instruments at that time. The intricately woven and colored clothes worn by the Hebrews were woven on an upright loom, another device as yet unknown in Egypt.

EARLY CANAANITE SETTLEMENTS IN UPPER EGYPT

Such traders seem to have established a colony on Yeb now known as Elephantine Island (archaeologically: Gezirat al-Aswan), located in the Nile near Aswan close to Egypt's border with Nubia. Evidence of settlement on Yeb shows that it existed at least as far back as the Pre-dynastic period and became the capital of the first nome of Upper Egypt in the time of the Old Kingdom. It had a serviceable harbor, and reached the height of its activity by the time of Joseph, in the so-called Second Intermediate period. The artifacts of this period unearthed by the excavators of the German and Swiss Archaeological Institutes include uniquely Canaanite earthenware, which, together with other characteristic materials, indicate the ethnicity of the settlers. Similar earthenware appears elsewhere in Egypt at such sites as el Yehudiya ("Jew-town"), a Semitic settlement of the Delta around which the Hyk-khase later constructed fortifications, complete with their distinctive glacis. The pottery from Yeb is a virtual replica of earthenware of the period found at Ugarit and elsewhere in Canaan. Glass beads, rings, and perfume vials that indisputably originated from the East were also recovered from the site.[48] Although the production of such vitric artifacts was well under way in Akkadia by the seventeenth century B.C.E., the Egyptians of the time were entirely incapable of producing glass; their metallurgy was limited to melting gold or copper over an open fire; they were ages away from the pyrotechnology requisite for liquefying quartz stone.

During the period of Aamu rule, trade with Nubia (Kush) attained an unprecedented importance. Under the stimulation of peaceful trade, Kush emerged as a prominent and flourishing kingdom with close ties to the north. The Kush town of Kerma, for example, consisting largely of small brick houses spread out along the river, was the seat of a court near the Third Cataract of the Nile whose houses and burial accoutrements testify to a considerable affluence and taste for luxury

Top: The Island of Yeb, or Elephantine Island, is located just before the first cataract of the Nile at the border of ancient Nubia. Yeb served as a base from which traders from Asia conducted trade with the Nubians. Whereas the Egyptians had virtually nothing of value to trade, the Nubians were able to supply gold as well as a variety of natural products. (Photograph by the author.)

Bottom: The Elephantine Island (Yeb) Museum (seen in top photograph) displays glass artifacts dating back to the period in which the Canaanite kings ruled Egypt and Canaan. The trailed glass ring, the eye-bead pendant, the plain and festooned perfume vials were undoubtedly imported from Canaan or Mesopotamia, since the technology for producing glass objects was then absent from Egypt. They are among the earliest glass objects found in Egypt. (Photograph by the author.)

goods. The tombs were typical of Upper Egypt and Nubia, filled with fine furnishings of all kinds, which must have included many items made of gold before the tomb-robbers broke into them: a woman was interred wearing a silver crown, which somehow survived the intrusions, and the dead were laid to rest on beds, one of which was found to be made of glazed quartz.

A great assortment of seal impressions on pots, baskets and various other receptacles were extracted from the debris. The seals eloquently attest to the close and amicable relationship which existed between Kush and the Asiatics. The only names which appear on these seal impressions are those of Aamu kings: Yaacov-her,[49] Sheshi, Maatibra, and a Queen Ineni. The other seals are predominantly those of the Asiatic administrators or chieftains. Some of the sealed receptacles bore Nubian marks, and it can be reasonably assumed that inasmuch as these pots were produced locally, a considerable community of the seal owners or their representatives were resident in the city to oversee the business being conducted.

The evidence of this close trade relationship has been recovered from many Nubian sites. Almost 4,500 impressions of seals and scarabs were recovered from the ruins of Uronarti, one of which bore the name of the Aamu king Maatibra, the same king whose name appears on the above-cited Kerma seals. Juglets of a type identified with the Aamu city of el Yehudiya were recovered not only from the trading colony at Yeb, but also from the harbor cities of Aniba and Buhen. The fortress of that latter city also yielded a series of stelae whose style, epigraphy, and content are characteristic of the period of the northern chieftains.[50]

Intercourse with Nubia broke down soon after the Theban seizure of power over all Egypt, owing to the renewed attempt by the new Egyptian pharaohs to monopolize trade. The Egyptians established garrison centers at Buhen and Aniba, to control the industrial output,[51] but the productivity of Kush diminished and the commercial intercourse between it and the north slowed to a trickle with Theban centralized rule. The merchants who had served as a liaison to Kush,

The typically Canaanite vessels of the "Second Intermediate Period," found on Yeb at the same level as the glass objects, identify the occupiers of the island at the time. Documents of a later period recovered from Yeb (now in the Brooklyn Museum) describe the daily life of a colony of Jewish settlers who occupied Yeb over many centuries. The ruins of a synagogue and traces of a previous building it replaced indicate that the colony existed at least as far back as the eighth century B.C.E. (Photograph by the author.)

entrepreneurs who had brought trade goods from the north and east and had provided a market for Nubian ware, were no longer operative in the area.

The Island of Yeb continued to serve as a key Semitic trading post intermittently for more than a millennium thereafter in spite of the exigencies that affected the relationship of Egypt with Southwest Asia. An ancient, vibrant Hebrew community is known to have been active on Yeb in the sixth century B.C.E.; the date of their arrival on the island is unknown but the fact that it stretches far back into antiquity is evident. A trove of hundreds of tablets was found on the island, documenting contracts, marriage agreements, personal letters, real estate, and other business transactions thus describing the daily life of the community in vivid detail. A temple to Yahweh was found to have been constructed on the site of an earlier temple. The ritual protocol detailed on the tablets dates back to a time before the destruction of the First Temple in Jerusalem, making manifest the fact that the settlement was well established by the eighth century B.C.E., and may have been a relic of an earlier settlement. Merchants, after all, are of critical value to the conduct of an economy and have been known to be pragmatically exempted from liquidation by the most rabid of repressors.

The wife of Ammenemes I, the reputed founder of the Twelfth Dynasty, came from that island, and it is tempting to suggest that she may have been of such a community. Many Egyptian queens and princesses, as well as servants and artisans, were of distinct Semitic, even Hebrew, origin. It is one of the circumstances that may explain the benign attitude of the Egyptian kings of the so-called Twelfth and Thirteenth Dynasties to the Semites in their midst, and to the transition from imperial oligarchy to patriarchal autonomy.

Is the possibility too farfetched that the son of the patriarchal chieftain Yacobel, whose scarabs are found in both *Eretz Yisrael* and Egypt, may indeed have been a patriarch who had followed into Egypt a son who had become vizier to a king of Egypt? The substantial flow of Canaanites into Egypt during those propitious times to join those who were already established there is attested to not only by the fulminations of Manetho and the testimony of other historians but by Egyptian inscriptions and archaeological recoveries. The progenitors of the Hebrews were then, as were the Asiatics before that time, the artisans and the merchants, the carriers of a sophisticated culture and technology into a relatively backward society. Cyril Aldred describes one aspect of the process:

> The story of Joseph reveals how these Asiatics may have arrived. . . . By the Thirteenth Dynasty, the number of Asiatics, even in upper Egypt, was considerable. They acted as cooks, brewers, seamstresses, vine-dressers and the like. One official, for instance, had no fewer than fourty-five Asiatics in his household. Such people were classed as 'slaves'. . . . Their children often took Egyptian names and so fade from our sight. Asiatic dancers and a doorkeeper in a temple of Sesostris II are known, showing that these foreigners attained positions of importance and trust. It is not difficult to see that by the middle of the Thirteenth Dynasty the lively and industrious Semites could be in the same positions of responsibility in the Egyptian state as Greek freedmen were to enjoy in the government of Imperial Rome. . . . We can

recognize [the coming to power of the Semites] as one of the great seminal influences in Egyptian civilization, rescuing it from political decline, bringing new ideas into the Nile valley and insuring that Egypt played a full part in the development of Bronze Age culture in the Eastern Mediterranean.[52]

Although no physical evidence of the existence of a Joseph has been found, it must be accepted that at the very least the story represents, as does the one centered around Abraham, an indelible tribal memory of real events. The fact is that fundamental social, economic, and cultural changes did take place in Egypt during that period, and that they were as fundamental as those purportedly wrought by Joseph. The state was reconstituted from an absolute monarchy headed by a divine king to an association of autonomous communities. The confirmed contemporary existence of hundreds of patriarchal chieftains makes reasonable the truth of Manetho's sneering statement that six successive administrators who had no divine attributes were chosen chief-of-chiefs who administered both Upper and Lower Egypt by mutual consent. The Egyptians retained control of their traditional nomes, mainly in Upper Egypt, and were in the overall majority, whereas a greater proportion of the chieftains of lower Egypt were Semitic, with a sprinkling of Hurrian and perhaps other elements. Church and state were separated, and state lands were removed from priestly control. The priests were removed from civil power and derived taxes only from the lands belonging to the temples.

And while the Egyptian princes continued to serve their multiple gods, the Semites served only their one god, and the temples constructed in the capital at Avaris contained no image of him.

THE BIBLICAL CITY OF AVARIS

In 1976 the Austrian Institute of Technology in Cairo was digging at a site known as Tel el-Daba, just south of Qantir. Dr. Manfred Bietak, director of the Institute and of the campaign, found several strata that disclosed continuous occupation of the site during the Second Intermediate period by a purely Asiatic population.[53] They were the remains of the biblical Avaris, and featured among the ruins were two temples dedicated to Sutekh, a discovery which confirmed the monotheism of the inhabitants. Sutekh was depicted wearing clothes and a headdress which bore a distinct resemblance to that of the Semitic Baal.[54] In Exodus 1:12 we read how the Israelites built two great store cities in Egypt, Pithom and Avaris. Papyri recovered from ancient tombs contemporary with the times extol the greatness of Avaris. P. H. Newby relates that:

> Writers of the time were ecstatic in its praises. Its great buildings were embellished with glazed tiles the color of turquoise and lapiz-lazuli; the river, the lakes and the canals teemed with fish; vineyards produced wine of kankeme "sweeter than honey"; its granaries were full of wheat; all fruits and vegetables grew there in abundance . . .

pomegranates, apples, olives, figs—and whatever the city lacked could be brought by sea-going ships right into the busy harbor.[55]

The papyri on which these praises were written describe a great temple dedicated to the single god revered by the Semites, who was there worshiped under the Egyptian name "Setekh," and record how the king delighted to walk in the extensive gardens in back of the temple. The Austrians found a great Setekh temple in the southern quarter of the partly uncovered city, exactly where the papyri had placed it. It had pale blue walls, a favorite color of the Semites. It sat conveniently on a *gezira* mound south of a lake at the head of a semi-circular harbor. The lake was connected by canal to a bend of the Pelusiac branch of the Nile. Upstream lay Memphis and Thebes, downstream lay the Mediterranean; a canal led eastward through another lake to the penitentiary city of Tjel, from which a military road led through the Sinai, following the coast as far as Ugarit. There it connected to a transverse road leading to Anatolia, Assyria, Babylonia, Afghanistan, and India.

Rameses II and Seti I of the Nineteenth Dynasty later built a new city on the ruins of Avaris. They took full advantage of the web of drainage canals left by the defeated Semites, canals which generated the most productive area of Egypt and continue to do so until this day. Manfred Bietak reported on the temple to the International Congress on Egyptology held on Cairo in 1975:

> During the Ramesside occupation of this site, when a new town had been founded there, and re-orientated north-south, east-west under a huge planning concept, it is especially interesting to note that the axis of a large temple, which was most probably devoted to Setekh, still showed the orientation of the late Second Intermediate Period. We have reason to assume that this deviation derives from an already-existing cult installation for this god at that site.[56]

The Bible relates how, under Joseph, immigration was stimulated and indicates how the Semites came to wield great influence at the heart of Egyptian government. Many administrators, chieftains, and the "chosen" chief-of-chiefs bore distinctly Hebraic names, and such names appear widely among the slaves and artisans in Egyptian literature of the period. In a papyrus in the Brooklyn Museum dated about 1740 B.C.E., for example, thirty-seven of the ninety-five slaves listed were identified as "male Asiatic" or "female Asiatic." Almost all of the names are Northwest-Semitic, and one is similar to Shiprah, one of the Israelite midwives in Exodus 1:15.

During the time of Aamu rule Egypt leaped forward in technology and culture; the transformation of Egyptian civilization that had progressed sporadically through centuries of intermittent contact with the Asiatics now, under Asiatic control, surged forward swiftly with an inspired dynamism. The process can no longer be disputed, only the depth and extent of the cultural activation is yet to be acknowledged.

One of the earliest historians to pick up from where Breasted and Petrie left off was H. E. Winlock, who listed in 1947 an impressive array of "Hyksos" accomplishments which add up to a complete inventory of the elements of the forthcoming Egyptian civilization. Because the defeat of the Egyptians in Manetho's version of Egyptian history cannot be rationalized other than by accepting the technological superiority of the supposed invaders, scholars have no choice but to concede the introduction of basic elements by which Egypt became a mighty power in the region, such as: the horse and chariot, body armor, the new design of weapons and tools, and a new metallurgical capability. It is nevertheless difficult to dislodge the pervasive impression that the invaders were mere nomadic barbarians. A deep-rooted reluctance to acknowledge the impact of the infusion by the Asiatics persists in spite of an acknowledged, extensive array of fundamental innovations in agronomy and husbandry, commerce and industry, weaponry and tools, metallurgy, musical instrumentation, and mathematics. The innovations cannot be denied, but those who present them are accused of ruining a good case by overstatement.

In 1959, William C. Hayes compiled a catalogue of the Egyptian antiquities of the Metropolitan Museum of Art. The museum's acquisitions, obtained through its own excavations and otherwise, make up one of the world's greatest collections of Ancient Egyptian antiquities. The evidence is ample and unambiguous. Documentation of the elements of the massive Asiatic cultural and technological influence of the period may also be found distributed in all of the literature dealing with the period, even in sources which otherwise deprecate the role of the Hyksos.[57] The period of Aamu rule is regularly relegated to a cursory note on the walls of museums. The Metropolitan Museum in New York and the British Museum of London, notwithstanding their vast collections of Egyptian art, are as miserly as others are in their treatment of the period. Museums can afford no more than the display of a few minor artifacts of the period, items squeezed between the great halls exhibiting masses of monumental statuary and cases of rich accoutrements taken from the tombs of Egyptian Pharaohs, all of which is touted as "Egyptian Art." Typical of museum displays is the passage from the Twelfth to the Eighteenth Dynasties with no more than a notice which states "During the Hyksos (Second Intermediate) period, art declined." Scholarly treatises on the history of Egypt are no more expository of the seminal cultural and technological role of the Aamus than are the museums, and are equally frugal in the number of pages assigned to it.

When proper account is taken of the extent of the contribution of the immigrant Canaanite, Semitic-speaking peoples to Egyptian culture and technology, however, an astonishing picture emerges. The revelations erupting from the period of the much-maligned Hyksos are particularly striking; it proves to be a period in which one of the most revolutionary, rapid, and comprehensive cultural advances of all of human history took place.

6

The Transformation of Egypt under Canaanite Rule

The Aamu Revolution

The Aamu revolutionized Egyptian society during the short period of their rule: they taught a people who never knew the wheel, nor bronze, nor the horse; a people who worshiped idols, who prayed to a host of beasts such as the crocodile, and who adored beings with heads of jackals, and beings with beaked heads of birds.

INNOVATIONS IN MATERIALS, MANUFACTURE, AND AGRICULTURE

The introduction of the wheel wrought several changes. The potters of Egypt became more productive; they had been obliged to wind coils of clay to the form of a vessel and smooth the ribbed surfaces to shape, or to pound the resistant clay with firm fists, punching the clay into hollow bowls. Now, working on a wheel that whirled its clay burden swiftly around, the supple fingers of the potters could lightly tease the pliant wet mass to form and gently work their wares with new-won ease into elegant, harmonious shapes.

Wheeled vehicles appeared from the East, and the horses and oxen to draw them; wheels were affixed to sledges, which, until the time that it is said Joseph's people came to Egypt, had been dragged laboriously by men. Horses were introduced, and this enormous yet amenable new animal was harnessed to haul the newly created carts. The people of Egypt were astounded by the gentle, ungrudging behavior of these grand beasts, by how manageable and responsive they were. They had never seen such animals, let alone believed that such animals would do man's bidding. The donkeys upon which the Asiatic merchants had been portaging goods into Egypt over many hundreds of years were now joined by the proud, magnificent, swift horses.

Wheeled chariots were also introduced, for hunting and for war, hitched to teams of horses. The care of horses continued to rest in Asiatic hands, and Semitic charioteers continued to be employed in Egypt long after the Hyk-khase were driven from the land and their people enslaved. Chariot parts were made of different woods, all of which came from Canaan and were known in Egypt only by their Semitic names. Chariots were ill-adapted to the sands of Upper Egypt but well-adapted to war in Asia, a fact which brought great misfortune to the Aamu people, who came to suffer for having redesigned the crude and primitive Egyptian weapons.

The simple bows the Egyptians used were no more than a strong stem bent back into a single curve. They were replaced by far superior Asiatic bows that were molded into a composite curve and constructed of laminations of wood and bone cunningly layered. The reverse curves at each end of these new bows and the reinforced construction added power, range, and accuracy to the weapon, and made them durable. The Egyptians were then shown how strong sinews would accommodate the increased tension. They were taught to carry arrows in a quiver, rather than to clutch them clumsily in their hands, as arrows had been inconveniently carried by them heretofore.

The wood with which the bows were made was often of foreign import. In New York the Metropolitan Museum of Art proudly displays one such a bow, "a powerful, long-range weapon of Asiatic design which in Egypt had only recently begun to replace the old, one-piece self bow of the Middle Kingdom and earlier periods."[1] The bow is a composite masterwork in which thin layers of horn are glued to a grooved wooden core and bound throughout its length with birch bark. It is the more remarkable in that the birch tree is not to be found in Egypt, and the wood of which the body of the bow is made is also of undoubted foreign origin.

The use of scale armor was another innovation, providing protection against weapons wielded by adversaries. Asiatic armor came to good use by the Egyptian warlords when they invaded their northern and eastern neighbors. The war helmet was another Asiatic novelty which became renowned as the *khepresh*, the "Blue," or "War Crown," worn by the pharaohs. The shapes of scimitars, swords, and daggers were modified to make them more effective, and the composition of the metal was improved to make the weapons sharper and harder.

Not least among the many marvelous materials to which the Egyptians were made acquainted during the time of Aamu rule was a diversity of metals. Silver was more precious than gold in Egypt; a pure form of silver, smelted from argentiferous Asian ores, was imported from the Ararat mountains of the Hurrian land of Mitanni and from the Zagros mountains of the Hittite land of Anatolia. Copper was brought into Egypt from Alashiya, the island of Cyprus, where it was abundant and cheaper than the copper wrested from the Sinai and from the mean deposits in Egypt's desert.

The quality of copper was first improved by adding arsenic and then by alloying it with another metal, processes the Egyptians had never known. Tin was borne on the backs of asses into Egypt from the far-off mountains of Badakhshan, five thousand kilometers away. The Egyptians were taught to alloy copper with this magic metal, to transform it into a new, harder, and more durable material, bronze. Bronze tools could be honed sharper because bronze is harder; they were longer lasting because bronze resisted decay better; they were more penetrating because the tools could be lighter and wielded with more force. Other new metals were ushered into the metallurgy of Egypt by the Asiatic traders, and Egypt was thrust into the Bronze Age, a new stage of civilization.

Egyptian tools were refined and perfected. Axes and sledges were changed in structure; the Semites taught the people of Egypt how to set the helve, or handle, into a socket through the head, instead of tying the head crudely onto it. This change made such tools more enduring, and made it possible to wield them with greater force because the handle would not split as readily nor would the head fall off.

Iron was an expensive curiosity at the time of Joseph, and much time went by before it assumed its revolutionary place in the metallurgy of civilization. But the process of producing iron never arrived in ancient Egypt, for the Aamu were expelled before the furnaces required to smelt iron and form it into tools and weapons were introduced.

Lapis lazuli was brought into Egypt from the distant mountains of Central Asia; the gemstone was avidly sought by royalty and the rich and was worn proudly, even into the tomb, to impress the residents of the netherworld of its wearer's riches. So treasured was this jewelry that several extra sets were included in the paraphernalia of their tombs. Perhaps they were afraid that the gods would become jealous of their finery and ask for a share, or steal it. After all, were not Egyptian gods as greedy as men, and as subject to bribery?

For those who could not afford "lapis lazuli from the mountain," the Akkadian term by which the natural gemstone was known in Egypt, the Asiatic merchants provided "lapis lazuli from the fire," the Akkadian term by which the glass substitute became known in Egypt.[2] Lapis lazuli, whether from the fire or from the mountain, was a favored gift which the Asiatic kings would forward for the favors of the pharaohs. The first reference to glass in Egypt appears not in the Egyptian language but in Akkadian correspondence to Egypt written during the "Amarna period" in letters from Mesopotamia, for the ancient Egyptians had no word for glass and never acquired one. One of the earliest references to glass objects appears on a letter from the Babylonian king Burnaburias II (1375-1347), informing the pharaoh that his gift includes ten lumps of genuine lapis lazuli, thus deliberately distinguishing it from the artificial variety. Burnaburias added that the pharaoh's wife will also receive twenty carvings in the form of musical instruments, and assured him that they are also made of "lapis lazuli from the mountain"!

Even more sophisticated furnaces were required for the production of true glass than for the smelting of iron. Vessels of glass, rare, expensive, exquisite items, were either gifts obtained from the Eastern royalty or objects plundered from Canaan. The first glassmasters may have been brought along with the loot: the

Boston Museum of Fine Art catalog of the exhibition of "The Art of Living in the New Kingdom 1558-1085 B.C." surmises that "glassmaking may have been introduced to Egypt with the expansion of her empire during the Eighteenth Dynasty, possibly under Thutmose III, who extended his boundaries into Syria [sic] in the East . . . the quality of the glass and the skill in manufacture suggest a long tradition of working this difficult material."[3] Thutmose's passion for precious Semitic objects extended to women as well; three of the pharaoh's wives were from the East, one of whom was buried with a gold-rimmed blueglass chalice of the same provenience.

There is no evidence that the manufacture of glass vessels took place in Egypt until after the traumatic period of the invasions into Canaan by the "Warrior Pharaohs" who succeeded the Asiatic chiefs. The first trace of the manufacture of glassware appears after a respite from incursions a century later under Amenophis III (1405-1367). This gentler Egyptian married Tiy, a daughter of a foreigner who had become a lieutenant-general of chariotry, Yuya. The marriage took place while Amenophis was still in his teens, and seemed to have set a pattern, for he thereafter married two princesses from Babylonia and a princess from Arzawa. The congenial atmosphere that ameliorated Egyptian-Mesopotamian relations during his tenure encouraged Semitic traders and artisans to re-establish shops in Thebes and at Aswan. Amenophis III, enamored with the products, invited glassware makers to set up their furnaces at his palace at Malkata, the first time such an operation can be confirmed to have taken place in Egypt. The work at Malkata was highly sophisticated, the product of almost a thousand years of development in Southwest Asia. The art was subsequently transferred to el-Amarna under the aegis of Amenophis's heretic son, who became known as Akhenaten. Glasswaremaking disappeared from Egypt after the time at which the Exodus is presumed to have taken place.

The production of fabrics, made of the flax introduced from Asia in the earliest settlements of the Asiatics in the Delta, was enhanced by the introduction of Asiatic spinning devices. The upright loom, long known in the lands to the east, revolutionized the Egyptian weaving craft. As productivity was increased, the cost of fabrics was reduced and they became universally available. New fibers and new fast dyes made fabrics more durable and colorful and added another dimension to the quality of life.

One of the great benefits of trade with Nubia had been the introduction into Egypt of the cattle native to that southern land. Another great beast was brought into Egypt during the progressive period of Aamu rule, the hump-backed cattle, or zebu, from India, which was bred to be well adapted to the climate and conditions of the area. These beasts did not require extensive range, for they made efficient use of available fodder. The cows supplied milk, cheese, and meat to a hungry population and were excellent for pulling plows, an onerous labor that had been performed by men. No longer would the fellahin, back bent, straining against leather straps which leashed him to the plow, fall faint from exhaustion in his effort to grow a little grain. The zebus made excellent draft animals and performed useful work, such as the lifting of the waters of the Nile and its canals into the irrigation ditches by means of levers and turnstiles. Modern Egypt still employs the Mesoptamian *shaduf*, a counter-balanced lever, to transfer the large quantities of water from the river required by the ever-thirsty irrigation system.

The Egyptians were not altogether ignorant of the use of animals in place of men; they had learned from the Nubians that the long-horned Nubian cattle were of use in plowing, and scenes of crude plows lashed to the horns of single cows are to be found in earlier Egyptian scenes. The introduction by the Aamu of the two-handled plow, of teams of zebu oxen and of new methods of yoking made the process of plowing vastly more efficient. The largest and most explicit relief in the collection of the Metropolitan Museum of Art, which was taken from the forehall of a Theban tomb chapel, reveals the radical changes in agricultural technology. Hayes pays particular attention to the change in harnessing: "The yoke of the interesting, two-handled plow is not lashed to the horns of the beast, as was the Egyptian custom, but rests upon their necks forward of the upward-projecting humps. Even more extraordinary is the two-wheeled oxcart appearing in the [same] register."[4]

Thus, instead of carrying the wheat or barley in huge hampers slung from the shoulders of fellahin, or at best in bulging bags slung over Asiatic donkey's backs, or piled on sledges and dragged, great loads were laded onto a cart with open-latticed sides and driven to the threshing floor. The cart is provided with four-spoked wheels similar to those of chariots but is shown to be of sturdier construction.

The barnyard fowl, which, like the zebu, had been domesticated and bred in India, had been well-known in Akkadia for a thousand years and almost that long in Canaan. However, the cackling hens amazed the farmers of Egypt by their productivity as, clucking with satisfaction, the birds daily deposited another egg. So astonishing was the proliferate performance of these fertile fowl to the Egyptians that Thutmose III had inscribed in stone his perplexity and amazement at the fecundivity of this "foreign bird which gives birth every day"![5]

The contribution of the Semites to the catalogue of domesticated animals did not cease with their tenure as kings. Camels were later introduced, which few in Egypt had seen except, perhaps, in caravans from the north. These patient beasts were put to work in place of men and became the symbol of the land of Egypt; hardly a picture of a pyramid appears without a Semitic camel in the foreground!

New fruit trees were planted by the Aamu in Egypt; pomegranates and figs added sweetness and variety to Egypt's diet. Olive trees were introduced, the fruit of which improved that diet, and the oil derived from olives enhanced the culinary art of Egypt. New grains and vegetables were cultivated, plants that could survive the dry heat of the climate, plants that improved the diet of the Egyptians by adjusting the balance of their nutriment. Some of these new plants permitted the rotation of various crops, because the elements they required for good growth differed; likewise, they supplied different useful elements to the soil. Thus several crops could be planted in turn, and because the climate in parts of Egypt is warm all winter, several crops could be rotated and grown within the passage of a year. The balance of the soil was maintained, and a fuller use of the nutrients deposited by the Nile was made possible.

New and decorative floral plants from Canaan began to appear on Egyptian paintings at this time. The cornflower, a common flower of Canaan, became a favorite of the pharaohs and the tomb painters employed them lavishly. The bread-fruit tree, the carob, arrived somewhat later from Canaan and its fruit became a staple Egyptian food.

MARINE INNOVATIONS AND TRADE

The Egyptians had long sailed the Nile in *felluccas*, simple boats that were handled adeptly. These boats could not be easily managed on the high seas, however, for they lacked keels. They could ill withstand the buffeting of ocean waves or be kept on an even course, and so were restricted to plying placid river waters or to maneuvering along the shore of a peaceful sea in benign weather. The Aamu had long since learned to affix a keel to the bottom of boats, a revolutionary device that stabilized them, made them more maneuverable, safe, and seaworthy.

Seaworthy ships opened a new trading era for Egypt, for until then the activity of Egyptian merchants was largely limited to places accessible by land. Trade with the islands of the Mediterranean blossomed, and flourished, and Egypt became a more important factor in the economy of the region. Its trade with the ancient peoples of these islands, heretofore proscribed by the unpredictable winds and waves of a capricious sea, and its trade with the various peoples of the continental lands bordering that sea evolved into reciprocal commerce of substantial proportions.

INNOVATIONS IN WOODCRAFT

The camel is not the only Asiatic import that assumed a distinctly Egyptian mystique. The widespread adoption by the nobility and commoners alike of the anthropoid coffin made a noteworthy change in Egyptian burial customs. "Introduced in the last quarter of the Twelfth Dynasty [the presumed time of Joseph's administration] . . . the coffin as a sort of rectangular wooden house is replaced by the anthropomorphic case decorated to represent the deceased."[6] The dearth of good lumber restricted the Upper Egyptian provincial craftsmen to carve out coffins from the coarse-grained logs of the sycamore-fig tree, much as primitive dugout canoes are carved. The more sophisticated carpentry of the Asiatics and the availability of suitable woods quickly brought the anthropoid coffin into Egyptian popularity. The introduction of tenoning and other advanced woodworking techniques made the intricately constructed sarcophagus possible and cheap enough "so that even a moderately well-to-do citizen could afford a set or two nested one within the other."[7] The decoration of the first of these coffins incorporated a Mesopotamian motif which harks back to early Akkadia, the enveloping wing of a raptor or of the fabled griffin. Ambrose Lansing, the discoverer of four of the eight coffins of this early period now housed at the Metropolitan Museum of Art, describes them in his excavation report: "They are anthropoid in shape, with a decoration representing the wings of a vulture spread protectively over the body, and the same motive repeated on the wig."[8] Egyptologists have adopted the name Rishi, meaning "feathered" in Arabic, as the name of these first man-shaped coffins. The joinery employed in constructing the coffins was in sharp contrast to lack of any joinery in the crude, adze-carved Egyptian coffins which preceded them. The details of Rishi coffin designs were later elaborated and the decorations changed in style and theme, but the basic form of the coffin survived and are universally and ironically recognized as "Egyptian."

The tenons and dowels with which the planks of the Rishi coffins were fixed together were also employed in the construction of the furniture found in association with the coffins of the Aamu period; tables and chairs and other furnishings employing new, well-ordered cabinetry techniques appear. A typical table of the period is well-represented by one on display in the Metropolitan Museum; its top is composed of joined hardwood boards, miter-framed on four sides and supported by a crowned cavetto-and-torus cornice. Underneath the beveled cornice splayed legs are skillfully keyed into aprons with pegged tenons. Stools with plaited rush seats are also found in association with the Rishi coffins, and became popular later as footstools, "an article of furniture which did not come into use in Egypt until well along in the Eighteenth Dynasty."[9] Veneering is another sophisticated technique that was introduced during the period of Asiatic rule, and the legs of straight-backed chairs were thus overlaid with exotic woods, as well as with ivory. The use of tamarisk and ebony attests to the trade both east into Asia and south into Nubia. The same skilled cabinetry went into the improved construction of beds; even the raised wooden pillow, usually an assembly of three pieces—a base, a stem, and a curved, carved headrest—was an innovation of the period.

ON THE ABSENCE OF MONUMENTS UNDER CANAANITE RULE

The Aamu chieftains and kings built no gigantic monuments such as so often drained Egypt of its resources, for there were no godly kings among them. Their single god required no stone images to represent him on earth to compete with other jealous gods. The tombs of the nomarchs of Upper Egypt were less opulently furnished during these more modest times, a disappointment to many who show concern over the purportedly impoverished Theban overlords of the times and dismally declare that during this period, art declined. Most museums' curators seem to concur, pronouncing in the museum's descriptive material that a technological degeneration in the period of Semitic rule is indicated by the lack of imposing palaces, monumental mausoleums and mastabas, narcissistic statuary, golden goblets, and other such objects museums require to illustrate the superficial richness of a culture.

Little note is taken of the fact that in order to provide such ware for future museums, rampaging outlaw Theban armies plundered eastern cities, leveled them ruthlessly, and left little of artistic worth to posterity. Sequernenre, his two sons, and the Warrior Pharaohs who followed, were joined in this endeavor by the priests, who had been separated from civil power during the period of Aamu administration and had long longed for an opportunity to restore their ancient privilege. The priests had dreamed of the time when power and privilege would again be theirs; when the bulk of the wealth of the country would again pour into their coffers, when the resources of Egypt would again serve the priests and princes and be dispensed for the public good only as it served their own purposes. They yearned to build new temples within which idols and kings could be worshiped. They were only too pleased to support and serve the ambitious Theban barons who turned against Egypt's benefactors and proceeded to plunder their neighbors. With the encouragement of the priests, each regime in turn thereafter set out to obliterate every trace of the presence of the patriarchal society. The Aamu were slaughtered or enslaved, or driven from the land. Only the cultural and technological innovations were left, subjective items that cannot be displayed in museums.

The Aamu had built a capital city, Avaris, and other commercial and administrative centers. What was there before was respected, and not destroyed, for while the Aamu worshiped in their own way and were jealous of Setekh, their one universal god, they did not insist on imposing him upon others. The majestic works of kings who longed for eternal life, their monuments, temples, and graves were largely left intact, preserved, although replete with graven images of outlandish gods that the Aamu abhorred. These artistic renderings, therefore, still exist, and one may now gaze at them in wonder at the way things were. The works of wise men, however, more durable in essence, are far more fragile in body, and must be interpolated from the ethereal facts that cannot be displayed in a museum's case.

Wise men came and settled in the Delta area, and taught astronomy and medicine and mathematics. The greatest mathematical treatise of the times, now known as the Rhind papyrus and the proud possession of the British Museum, was copied during the thirty-third regnal year of Awesre from an earlier text. *Woserre-'Apopy* was the "Apophis" who reigned from about 1620 to 1580 B.C.E., and was, according to the Turin Canon, the fourth of the Aamu chief-of-chiefs.[10] Thus, although the chieftains sculpted no great statues of themselves, and few small ones, nor fashioned idols of fabulous gods, the arts they infused into the fabric of the culture of Egypt were of a subtler nature, and were more durable than the stone of which the idols were carved, and of benefit to all Egyptians.

The Asiatics impregnated Egypt with cultural refinement by enhancing the gentler arts. New musical forms appeared, made possible by the introduction of a rich variety of Mesopotamian musical instruments: the multifretted lute and the multistringed harp, both with elaborate systems of tuning, gave music wide scope and flexibility of tone. The lyre was regarded as a "foreign" instrument long after Asiatic rule had come to an end and was always represented in the tomb paintings of the Eighteenth Dynasty being played by a Canaanite woman. The oboe with numerous closely spaced finger holes,[11] and the tambourine and other variations of Asiatic instruments brought Aamu music rapidly into Egyptian fashion, for the beauty intrinsic to the musical arts is universally appreciated.

The names of the instruments as well as the instruments themselves were borrowed from the Semites. Thus the Egyptians call the lyre by its Semitic name, the *keniniur*. With the new music came new forms of dance, and its graceful images became forever inscribed into the graffiti of the eternal resting places of Egyptian princes and pharaohs from that time forward. Images of the new instruments being played by pretty Asiatic courtesans and danced to by sinuous Semitic slaves were thereafter incorporated into the paintings of Egyptian tombs, so that the Egyptian occupants might not lack the sweeter attributes of life in their netherworld existence.

Egyptian nobility placed Mesopotamian games with which they could amuse themselves eternally in their tombs. The *astragal*, a form of dice, made from the tarsal joint of some hooved animals (and incorrectly known as "knucklebones"), were employed in "twenty squares," a game similar to the Indian parchesi; they were also used in *senet*, "the game of thirty squares," an even more ancient Asiatic game. The back of some senet boxes sported the layout of another Asian introduction: a companion game called *tjau* ("robbers"?),[12] a game that the Akkadian traders had also introduced to the *karums* of Anatolia.

The signet ring and the earring were newly adopted by the Egyptians during the tenure of the Asiatics, and toiletry became an art. The introduction of bronze made mirrors possible, and the new, far more utilitarian alloy made a number of delicate grooming instruments possible. Bronze tweezers appear, and a "tweezer razor" comes into use in the ladies wardrobe, a hair-curling and trimming device in which a chisel-type razor is hinged to a hollow, pointed prong, allowing it to be maneuvered like a scissors or tongs. Combs, and razors, heretofore a rarity, appear with greater frequency in Theban tombs as the impact of the hirsute Asiatics' culture made itself felt up the Nile.

HOW AN AGE OF PEACE AND PROSPERITY CAME TO BE NEGLECTED

With harder, more durable metal for their arms and tools, with wheeled chariots, and with improved weaponry, the Egyptians became the equal of the nations to the north. Yet, of all the events that took place in the time of the Asiatic chieftains, the most important was one that did not occur: *there was no war of consequence in Egypt throughout the period of Aamu rule, the rule of the Semitic chieftains!*

This fact has been unfortunately misunderstood, or deliberately distorted, for it is being said that during this time the power and influence of Egypt declined. How sad it is that some still measure power by what can be enforced by arms, and not by what can be furthered by influence; that richness is measured by the quantity of loot wrested from one's neighbors, not by the number of progressive principles and productive processes absorbed from neighbors through amicable exchange. How absurd it is to gauge the wealth of a country by how many golden artifacts can be plucked from its rulers' tombs rather than by the adequate diet of the dwellers of his land. How blind is judgment when the welfare of a country is assessed according to the profligacy of its pharaohs rather than by the prosperity of its people.

How did it happen that modern historians, out of ignorance or otherwise, consistently overlooked the comprehensive contribution of those Asiatics to Egyptian civilization? It is painfully evident that plunder was too often the prime objective of scientific institutions. The accumulation not of facts but of artifacts was the driving motivation. History was incidental. The destructive tomb-robbing of natives for personal gain became the prerogative of archaeologists, museums, private collectors, and even governments. It is not surprising, therefore, insofar as few grandiose monuments or rich royal accoutrements were gathered from the period of the rule of the Asiatic chieftains, that the modern plunderers were prone to blithely pronounce that nothing of value was contributed by the Hyksos, and that, perforce, the civilization of Egypt suffered a decline during their reign. Under the pressure to acquire anything that would enhance displays or plump prestige, or that would serve to provide dramatic illustrations for scholarly treatises, items and information of great cultural significance were not only overlooked but often destroyed.

Not all the depredation and obtuseness can be attributed to an obsessive interest in the accumulation of the monuments and emoluments of royalty. Anti-Semitism, prevalent throughout the nineteenth century and into the twentieth, bolstered the credibility of those who were all too willing to deny any value gained by Egypt through Semitic rule. Anti-Semitism fostered a ready willingness on the part of historians, students, and the public at large to accept tendentious propositions uncritically. It is inexcusable, however, that in this ostensibly enlightened era of archaeology, spurious statements, terms, and attitudes are persistently repeated in the texts of historians and in the explanatory notes of the most prestigious museums. Mention of the fundamental cultural and technological advances spurred into existence by the Semites in Egypt, even where acknowledged, is often grudgingly rendered by no more than a footnote.

What is even more unjustifiable is that historians continue to confuse conquest with progress. This gross error in evaluation is not confined to the history of Egypt. In lauding the glorious achievements of conquerors, and in clucking with satisfaction over the wealth of artifacts scavenged from their grandiose monuments and tombs, historians are prone to speak of their era as having reached a "height" of cultural development simply by virtue of their military success. They skip lightly over the tens or hundreds of thousands slaughtered in the process of conquest. It seems almost blasphemous to enter into the equation the cities decimated, the countryside ravaged, the free peoples enslaved, except to laud them as acts of glory. It does not seem to be important that, under the inevitable despotic rule that follows bloody conquest, people are grievously taxed and forced into slave or corvee labor, that a great portion of their labor and their livelihood is consumed not in promoting the general welfare but in touting the glory of the conquerors through the creation of those very great works that fill modern museums.

Herodotus, one of the earliest historians writing about Egyptian history, made a leisurely journey as far up the Nile as Elephantine Island, gathering information. He was privy to information given to him by the priests of Egypt, to lists of kings, and to legends otherwise lost to us. Herodotus took cognizance of the fact that the information he received from Egyptian priests, and from available documents, was solely that which had been adulterated by the conquerors. Herodotus presents the viewpoints promulgated honestly as being those that the conquerors deigned history to have, and was thus suspect. Sober historians, forewarned to react with incredulity to the tales told by Herodotus, do so. Some inattentive historians, unmindful of his demurrers, refer to Herodotus himself as the "father of lies." But many of the same historians quote verbatim from his writings, and being blinded by monumental grandiosity, obsequiously favor Egyptian fables as fact. Yet Herodotus himself makes it abundantly clear that much of the information he gathered is based on hearsay and unconfirmable fables. He anticipated slovenly reading of his work by contemptuously addressing those who do not heed his warnings:

"Such as think the tales told by the Egyptians credible are free to accept them for history. As for myself, I keep to the general plan of this book, which is to record the traditions of the various nations just as I heard them related to me."[13]

Although the proselytizing of the Egyptians referred to by Herodotus and so flagrantly promulgated by Manetho is still persistently echoed, it is nonetheless recognized that the Asiatic chieftains shared hegemony over Egypt with Egyptian nomarchs and managed to rule Egypt in concert with them peacefully for several hundred years. It is conceded that during this amicable interlude Egypt vaulted into a new era, advancing enormously in every field of knowledge and endeavor.

Must we continue to judge a civilization by the size of its palaces, monuments, and temples? By the elaboration of its royal tombs? By the numbers of peoples it subjugated? By how affluent or profligate are its rulers?

Or do we measure a civilization by its dedication to peaceful pursuits? By the economic well-being of its people? By its cultural and technological achievements? By the freedom its citizens enjoy?

We can only conclude, in contradiction of much of what has been written, that the Manethoian period of the so-dubbed Thirteenth through Seventeenth Dynasties, the period of a pervasive influence of the Semitic peoples on Egypt, and in particular the short period in which they ruled Egypt as autonomous chieftains who funneled authority through a chosen one of their number, must be judged as the greatest of Egypt's long history. This is recognized by many historians and conceded less happily by others, but is still being ignored by those historians and scholars who, caught uncomfortably exposed, would rather revel in romantic fiction than face the facts.

In contrast with the widespread prosperity achieved in the period of Aamu rule, a prosperity acknowledged by even the most fervent of Egyptophiles, not only the foreign subjected peoples but the Egyptian population itself suffered miserably after the most glorious campaigns of the Warrior Pharaohs and during the construction of the great monuments admired so much by lovers of Egyptian pomposity.

Did the prosperity of the Warrior Pharaohs extend to the Egyptian people? The reign of Rameses II was a period of Egypt's greatest glory, in which Rameses fought to a draw with the Hittites at Kadesh (albeit he boasted of victory) and in which riches poured in from "as much of an Asiatic empire as at any other period in her history." The great Hypostyle Hall at Karnak was Rameses' most outstanding architectural achievement, and, "If the greatness of an Egyptian Pharaoh be measured by the size and number of his monuments remaining to perpetuate his memory, Sethos's son and successor Rameses II would have to be judged the equal, or even the superior of the proudest pyramid builders."[14] These numerous monuments, however, adds Gardiner in summing up, "are mostly memorials of individual persons throwing little or no light upon the state of the country as a whole."[15]

Great victories, plunder, and tribute are proudly recorded by the succeeding Egyptian kings. A passage from the famous stela that Merenptah dedicated to his victories and which includes the first mention of Israel reads: "Tjehnu-land is destroyed. Khatti is at peace, Canaan is plundered with every ill, Ashkelon is taken and Gezer seized, Yenoam made as though it had never been. Israel is desolated and has no seed."[16]

Rameses III is no less explicit; a circumstantial account of his dealing with conquered peoples and their assets is given at the end of a great and famous papyrus. After listing at length the peoples and towns destroyed or conquered, the text supplies us with details of his gains, such as in one of the campaigns against the Libyans:

> I took of those whom my sword spared many captives, pinioned like birds before my horses, their women and children in tens of thousands, and their cattle in number like hundreds of thousands. I settled their leaders in strongholds called by my name. I gave them to troop-commanders and chiefs of the tribes, branded and made into slaves stamped with my name, their women and children treated likewise. I brought their cattle to the House of Amun, made for him into everlasting herds.[17]

Who was it, then, who enjoyed prosperity under these circumstances, other than the overlords and army commanders? The state of the country becomes clear in surviving Egyptian texts that bear witness to industrial unrest in the reign of Rameses III. The dire conditions of the populace at large and of the workers on the monuments to the glory of the king provoked the first general strike in history. The workmen engaged on the royal tomb went on strike to protest their miserable condition, in spite of royal military might and of the dire consequences that might befall the protesters. The work stoppage was ended only after the intervention of a vizier, who was able to supply only half the monthly rations actually due the workmen.[18] Far from being satisfied with the slaves and plunder doled out to them, the greedy overlords of Egypt plotted against Rameses and attempted to overthrow him in a harem plot in which twenty-nine officials and six wives, an overseer of cattle, and others were involved.

Conditions went from bad to worse, and by the time of Rameses IX, social conditions had become so depressed and poverty was so widespread, that tomb-robbery, always a common practice, became an urgent subject for royal concern.[19]

SETTING THE RECORD STRAIGHT

In contrast, material and documentary evidence emerging from contemporary research continues to amass support for the great technological and cultural advances that took place during the peaceful period of rule of the Canaanite kings. Great commercial centers established during the benevolent reign of the Asiatics in Egypt have been discerned. In addition to the excavation of the capital city of Avaris at Tell el Dab'a, other important settlements were unearthed, as, for example, at Tell Makhuta, which was located directly on the route from Avaris into Canaan. Biblical history related to the condition of the Jews in Egypt is supported by the excavation of Tanis, el-Yehudiya, and many other predominantly Semitic communities that flourished during the so-called Second Intermediate period. In spite of the ruthless obliteration of the works of this period by the jealous pharaohs who followed the hated Hyk-khase, enough evidence survived to show that a vast territory was being peacefully administered from Avaris, a territory stretching over almost the entire arc of the Fertile Crescent: ". . . a vanished empire which once spread from the Euphrates to the first cataract of the Nile."[20]

The manifold innovations that enriched the fabric of Egyptian culture during the period of Semitic rule had an enormous impact on the history of the region and on Western Asia. Ancient Egypt is referred to as having been a conservative society, which infers with good reason that innovation was regarded with suspicion and creativity was squelched. Egypt was boosted into the Bronze Age during the tenure of the Hyksos, the "foreign kings from a hill country"; the size of its economy multiplied; the freedom of its people was amplified; international trade was expanded; and peaceful relations with its neighbors were established and maintained.

The regularization and expansion of trade from Egypt to its neighbors and the rationalization of commerce are unmistakably manifested by the fact that the basic standard weight used in Egypt, and other standards, were replaced by those of Mesopotamia. Egyptian correspondence was conducted with other nations in Akkadian and was continued subsequently in Aramaic, Semitic languages that were the lingua franca of their times, the standard for international trade and intergovernmental relations. The hieroglyphic picture writing on the walls of tombs and temples is beautiful to behold and it was believed by the Egyptians that its message was comprehensible to their gods. But such writing was inconvenient for conducting commerce and retaining records; nor was it universally understood by the Egyptians themselves.

The succeeding, so-called Eighteenth Dynasty, reached the stature accredited to it solely because the antecedent Semitic rulers had transformed Egypt, vaulting its technology, its economic base, and its military potential to great heights. The prowess Egyptian warlords thus gained enabled them to wrench wealth from neighboring peoples and to wrest taxes from their own, now more productive people. The radical reform of Egyptian society was redeemed by the Semitic peoples of Canaan with pain and persecution, for the very chariots, horses, weapons, and economic power they had introduced were used against them. The Egyptian princes went on vicious, merciless military campaigns, their appetite for loot whetted anew with each adventure. They behaved as brutally as Manetho accused the Hyksos of behaving, save that the brutality was no self-serving fabrication, but real. Again and again the pharaohs drove their armies into Canaan, slaughtering, ravaging, plundering.

The pharaohs tell their own tales of atrocity. Countless thousands were put to backbreaking work, erecting monuments on which the pharaoh's "glorious" conquests are inscribed. Carved into these walls are long lists of spoils stripped from the conquered peoples and deposited in the treasuries and tombs of the pharaohs and princes and priests, to which must be added the loot kept by the soldiers and officers of the pharaohs' armies. Flagrantly depicted are scenes, repeated on innumerable pillars and walls, of chains of prisoners tied by their necks, hands bound behind them, being dragged into slavery. Proudly depicted on the walls of Thebes and Karnak are images of despoliation: an army captain is shown heaping hundreds of severed hands into a huge mound before a grateful pharaoh; a commander is shown piling up penises hacked from his victims. In each case the pharaoh is shown gratefully paying in gold for each member piled before him.

The Semitic chiefs and kings did not record great battles and slaughters or riches gained by plundering, for there was little of either during their reign. Hence such scenes did not descend to historians from the period of Asiatic rule in Egypt, and that is why, on the walls of museums, otherwise erudite scholars inform an innocent public: "during the period of Hyksos domination, art declined." The depicted piles of hands and penises left a deeper impression upon Egyptologists than did the introduction of the pomegranate or of the wheel or of bronze or of a written language with which communication and trade with one's neighbors is facilitated.

We may be forgiven for conjecturing that perhaps there was among the wise Semitic viziers of the period a Joseph, who, after reorganizing Egyptian society by separating religion from state, instituted a strong civil government; that an influx of his people swelled the substantial Semitic population of Lower Egypt; that autonomy was granted the patriarchal chiefs as prescribed by ancient Mesopotamian custom; and that the land of Egypt gained prosperity and power thereby.

The most critical and important factor affecting the economy of Egypt was the engineering of an effective control of its water resources. Legends, both Hebraic and Arabic, have it that Joseph and his people made a great and everlasting contribution to Egypt in this regard. The application of Mesopotamian mathematics served in the planning of new systems of irrigation and in expanding the primitive systems previously installed in Egypt. The storage of water is even more effective as a hedge against years of drought and famine than the storage of grain, which, we are told, was a first step recommended by Joseph to the pharaoh. A reservoir would alleviate dependency on the vagaries of climate and the river, and thereby alleviate the burden of heavy taxation for the massive storage of grain during favorable climatic periods.

We can imagine that a wise vizier such as Joseph must have spent many years traversing the desert lands, measuring and calculating, making a comprehensive study of the geodesy of Egypt. Finally, he formulated a plan that transformed the face of the land of Egypt forever. Two hard days' journey from the river, resting amid the ring of a range of rugged hills, was the oasis now called el-Fayoum. It was cradled in the center of a vast depression whose level lay below that of the Nile. On the verdant shores of a small, shimmering lake in the heart of this low basin, a tribe lived coolly under the palms, unmindful of the immense, unmerciful, encompassing desert.

A canal was dug which drew the waters of the Nile into the basin of el-Fayoum. It was an ambitious undertaking, for the canal did not simply connect the river to the basin directly from the east, which would have been a massive project in itself. The canal was cut through the ridges bordering the Nile in Upper Egypt and driven northward through the desert parallel to the Nile; a twin to the Nile was thus created, extending a full third of the Nile's Egyptian length. The waters of the great canal spread out into the desert through a web of small canals branching out from it all along its length. Just before the canal reached the region of the fertile Delta, it was diverted westward into the low-lying el-Fayoum basin.

Whereas the Nile was hemmed in by rugged cliffs which gave way here and there to a few paltry parcels of flat land, the canal led through wide flat areas of the flanking desert, and, together with its feeder canals, doubled the arable land of Egypt, which had been almost entirely relegated to the Delta. Upper Egypt was integrated productively into Egypt's economy, and became something more than a mere passageway to Nubian ivory and gold.

The cold waters that had cascaded from the mountains of Nubia and Ethiopia flowed, warmed and welcomed, through the desert, which was reborn, and lived, and bloomed.

And when the water reached the basin, the small pond swelled into a voluminous pair of lakes. It is said that it was Joseph who named the great new reservoir Lake Moeris, after the king who had set the task for him. We can be forgiven for imagining that after the waters had flowed through the desert to fill the vast basin and the dream of Joseph had become a reality, the pharaoh arrived with his entire entourage, a great assemblage of all the nobles and chieftains of Egypt, to witness and to dedicate the new sweet sea set into the sands.

Of all the wonders the Aamu wrought for Egypt, none exceeds this great work for excellence, none testifies more eloquently to their genius, none bears better witness to their inspired accomplishments. Today, after more than three thousand years, the Bahr Yousef still functions vigorously and its feeder canals irrigate more territory than does the Aswan Dam. It performs its function benignly, unlike the Aswan Dam, which increases the salinity of the soil as it irrigates, a condition that portends ecological disaster.

The canal has always been and is today still called the Bahr Yousef, which translates from Egyptian Arabic simply to: "The Sea of Joseph."

It is so designated on the maps of Mizraim, the land we call Egypt.

7

Ancient Mediterranean Sea Trade

The Revelations of Modern Underwater Archaeology

The cultural and technological heritage of the Jews is drawn from four basic elements of the evolution of civilization: agronomic expertise, artisanship, literacy, and commercial entrepreneurism. The seeds of all four of these elements found sustenance in Mesopotamia, and thrived, and grew to scatter their seeds beyond the borders of that rich alluvial land to propagate abroad. The provenience of the Jewish progenitors was the area of Harran, the very hub of the ancient land trade routes radiating from the area that cradled civilization. The emigration of such tribes as that of Abraham into Canaan brought them to the coast of the Mediterranean, where commerce freed itself of the trammels of travel by land.

THE HISTORICAL BACKGROUND

Overland caravans and river crafts had been the main conveyances for commerce through the third millennium B.C.E., but as ships became more seaworthy, shipping by sea proved to be more and more economically advantageous. Piracy at sea proved to be no more perilous than predatory raids on land caravans; stormy seas brought no more incidence of disaster than did slippery rain-soaked or snowy mountain trails; wind was free, whereas beasts of burden had to be fed; the complement of sailors on a sizable ship were fewer than the handlers, guards, and scouts necessary for the safe conduct of caravans. As ships grew larger and became capable of lading an equivalent quantity of cargo to that portaged by a fair-sized caravan, sea traffic assumed a significant importance in international trade.

Geopolitical events also tended to divert the course of trade to the coasts. The Hittites had become a powerful national entity under Hattusili I, who appears to have been the ruler who unified the country and took control of its destiny, a process that ended in a certain insularity. The Hittite king incorporated the ancient Aramaic areas of northwestern Mesopotamia into his kingdom. His adopted son, Marsuli, carried the campaign of military conquest to Babylonia, which was destroyed in a conflagration about 1595 B.C.E. A series of internecine feuds thereafter weakened Hittite control and the Kassites and the Hurrians moved into the vacuum thus created.

The region was racked with a series of struggles for power over the areas controlling the trade routes around the entire arable Middle East Crescent. The *karums* disappeared in the turmoil of the times, and Akkadian traders ceased to serve as the seminal factor of Anatolian productivity in the second quarter of the second millennium. The disappearance of the communities of Mesopotamian artisans working in the *karums* or working for the traders in the *karums*, and the consequent cessation of the introduction of Mesopotamian technology into Anatolia, deprived that outlying region of much of the benefits of the Late Bronze Age and exempted it from the advent of the Iron Age. Yet Anatolian trade continued to be carried on in the language of, and largely by, Semitic-speaking merchants. The very history of the Hittites was recorded mainly in Akkadian cuneiform, although a smattering of the records were rendered in the Hittite's own primitive hieroglyphic script. The known history of the Hittites in Anatolia from 1650 to 1200 B.C.E. is derived almost entirely from cuneiform records recovered from Hattusa and from Hittite Masat Höyük.[1]

The assumption of rule by the Kassites over the Babylonian region, the creation of the Mitannian (Hurrian) Empire (whose hegemony extended over much of the rest of Mesopotamia), the parallel rise of Egypt as an aggressive military power, the turmoil created by other tribes seeking to assert themselves, and the long-standing movement of many Amurru to the Mediterranean coast, created new patterns of international intercourse. The Mediterranean assumed critical importance as an avenue of communication and trade.

THE MID-SECOND MILLENNIUM B.C.E.: A TURBULENT PERIOD

The infusion of Semitic culture and technology into the culture of peoples outside of the arc of the Fertile Crescent, northwest in Anatolia and southwest in Egypt, was effectively interrupted during the turbulent period at the end of the Bronze Age, a period in which the local rulers strove to gain imperial control over the entire region. Just as technological progress came to a halt in Egypt with the passage of the peaceful period of the rule of the Semitic chieftains in lower Egypt and the advent of the period of the Warrior Pharaohs, so progress came to a halt and a period of decline ensued with the disappearance of the peaceful period of the Semitic trading colonies, the *karums*, from the suburbs of the Hittite cities. "The cities that flourished during the period of the Assyrian merchant-colonies went into a decline from which they never recovered," noted

J. G. McQueen, "and as Hurrian pressure built up to the east the situation became more serious."[2]

It was at this very time that the sophisticated, as yet exotic disciplines of iron-smelting and glassmaking were filtering across Aram-Naharaim toward the Mediterranean coast. The secrets of glass production in particular, born and bred in Akkadia, never arrived in ancient Anatolia. The movement of artisans carrying the esoteric secrets of the art of glassmaking had already penetrated as far as Alalakh (modern Atchana in the area of Aleppo) in the eighteenth century B.C.E., but subsequent events deflected pyrotechnological progress into Canaan.

Alalakh was at that time under the rule of the great Akkadian king Hammurabi's son, Yarim-Lim, in the ruins of whose palace Sir Leonard Woolley found glazed and trail-decorated fritware, evidencing the arrival of the art in the area. In the very next level, that of the residence of Hammurabi's grandson, Niqme-epukh, a fully matriculated glassmaking technology is unmistakably evidenced by the presence of intricately wrought polychrome, true glass objects.[3] Festoonware, millefiore, elaborated inlay, and a variety of other sophisticated techniques hitherto existing only further to the east attested to the technological heights to which the art had risen in Akkadia. The fall of Alalakh to Hittite domination, about 1650 B.C.E., initiated the process of diverting the advance of pyrotechnology to the western leg of the Fertile Crescent down into Canaan.

The oldest form of the term designating the lower coastal Mediterranean region of western Asia as "Canaan" was registered in Alalakh. In the ruins of that ancient city a statue of the local ruler, Idrimi (c. 1500 B.C.E.), was recovered, on which was inscribed a text with a reference to "the Land of Canaan." The term filtered into Egypt, for shortly thereafter eleven occurrences of the place name appears in the records recovered from Egyptian Amarna, in which also appears a reference to *Ki-na-ha-u*, or "Canaanites," warranting that both a discrete land and a people associated with it existed.[4] The registration of a southwestward movement of a branch of the Amurru, "Westerners" from the Mesopotamian viewpoint, to become dwellers in the Land of Canaan and consequently, Canaanites, is further reinforced by the Amarna evidence, for both the Canaanites and the Amurru were identified by the Egyptians as "Easterners." The movement is likewise reflected in the Bible, where the terms "Amorite" and "Canaanite" are frequently used interchangeably, "Amorite" applying more consistently to peoples east of the Jordan rift. The terms "Near East," "Orient," and "Levant" all analogously identify the region as "Eastern" from the European point of view.

THE RISE OF MEDITERRANEAN SEA TRADE

Port cities flourished. The centers of civilization gravitated to the coast or to cities that could readily reach the coast by river. The *karum*, the erstwhile salient nexus of commercial intercourse on land, became displaced by harbor communities serving the coastal cities. Island peoples, already well versed in the vagaries of the sea, assumed a new importance in international commerce. The origins of the island Minoan and peninsular Mycenaean civilizations remain shrouded in mystery, but numerous philological and archaeological indications suggest an early, substantial, and ongoing intercourse with the peoples of Canaan, a relationship that laid the foundation for the development of long-distance commercial sea traffic. A substantial increase in trade and cultural interchange between the Mycenaeans and Canaan is particularly evident after the fall of Knossos, circa 1400 B.C.E. The Minoan (Cretan) influence became superseded by that of the Semitic-speaking cities prospering along the eastern coast of the Mediterranean. "In this period of Mycenaean Greek history—Late Helladic III (*alias* Mycenaean III)—the Myceneans borrowed more artistic *motifs* from Syria [sic] than from Crete."[5]

The continental population centers shifted slowly from such inland riverside concentrations as Ebla, Babylon, and Mari to the coast (Ugarit, Byblos, Tyre, Sidon, Arwad, Ashkelon). The coastal Canaanites pioneered the seaways; they converted commerce by sea from haphazard adventure to well-organized enterprise. International trade expanded. The islands afloat in the Mediterranean, and the continental lands washed by its waves, became ever more important sources of raw material and finished goods and were integrated into the widening commercial network. Regular routes were established whose timing and direction were determined by the seasonal winds. Eventually colonies were settled to service the fleet of vessels plying the sea routes. By the end of the second millennium the colonies were developing into thriving cities feeding on the hinterlands and profiting from an exchange of goods gleaned from all the lands encompassing the Mediterranean.

Canaanite participation in Mediterranean sea trade was long assumed to have been of little consequence until 800 B.C.E. This hypothesis persisted despite well-known relationships such as the intimate commercial connection between Cyprus and Ugarit, which is well-attested to in documents recovered from that bustling Canaanite city as going back as far as 1650 B.C.E. Recent physical evidence of Canaanite presence in the Mediterranean has extended its antiquity to beyond the turn of the Iron Age; quantities of eleventh-century B.C.E. Canaanite pottery were recovered, for example, from Skales, which city is located on the western side of Cyprus (near modern Paphos), and was therefore probably a staging base for Canaanite ventures out into the Mediterranean.[6] It is to be expected that traces of this ancient commercial web are to be found all along the southern Anatolian coast, yet virtually nothing is known about this critical aspect of the advance of civilization.

The most revealing evidence of the ancient movement of the Canaanites through the Mediterranean was brought about by the invention of scuba diving gear and the consequent ardent expansion of underwater archaeology. The technique of excavating ancient wrecks under stringent archaeological guidelines was pioneered by Professor George Bass, a nautical archaeologist who founded the Institute of Nautical Archaeology (INA) in 1973 at Texas A & M University. This "wet-suit archaeologist" revolutionized the technology of undersea recovery, applying approved archaeological surveying and recovery techniques.

The discovery by Peter Throckmorton in 1959 at Cape Gelidonya of a Cypriote or Canaanite ship that had foundered in the thirteenth or early twelfth century B.C.E. off the Anatolian coast, and its subsequent excavation by Throckmorton and Bass, shattered the myopic view held of East Mediterranean commerce, until then still based largely on Homer's Odyssean mythology, and activated a rapid and radical revision of nautical history.[7] The cargo consisted of more than a ton of copper ingots, evidently laded on board at Cyprus, and scrap bronze, perhaps also from Cyprus but just as likely originating from the continental area to the east. Canaanite weights and cylinder seals evidence the ethnicity of the merchants on board, and the ship's lamp, stone mortars, and other items suggest a Canaanite crew. Metalworking tools, a variety of mace-heads, and adzes of different forms suggested that one or more tinkers or smiths were on board. Two double-axes were remarkable in that they provided for a helve (wood handle) to pass through, a system that originated in Mesopotamia. A large collection of weights that matched Canaanite standards pointed to a high level of commercial competence, as did the cylinder seals, one of which was evidently carried as a decorative pendant, for it was graced at both ends with gold caps. Bronze razors were collected from the wreck, evidence of an ancient propensity for clean-shaven visages, which belies the impression that ancient men generally sported beards. An alternate use for the razors was, perhaps, to shave the head, a Canaanite practice visible in Egyptian drawings and in Canaanite glass head-beads, many of which depict goggle-eyed Semites with black beards and bald heads.

The subsequent discovery of an even older wreck off Ulu Burun, a Turkish cape near the idyllic seashore resort of Kas, and the revelation of an even more sophisticated cargo than that of the Cape Gelidonya wreck, made the revision of Mesopotamian nautical and technological history obligatory. The discovery of some sixty-five tons of glass, copper, and tin ingots on a vessel wrecked in the fourteenth century B.C.E. off the Turkish coast burst upon skeptical scholars as a bombshell. The inclusion of glass ingots was a particularly intriguing and mystifying element of the cargo. The sheer size and quantities of the glass ingots found on board was not only dramatic, incontrovertible evidence of a long-standing Mesopotamian pyrotechnology, but proof that the industry had already grown to a point at which its esoteric products had became a staple for export and had assumed considerable importance in international trade in the fourteenth century B.C.E. Yet no trace of such trade, let alone of the people who were involved in it, had hitherto made its historiographical appearance, as a diligent search through literature and the archival material of museums made plainly evident.

The production of glass objects had been ascribed to the Mycenaeans simply because a few such objects were found in a Mycenaean environment. This kind of deduction is always suspect, for provenance does not prove production. It should be clear that the fact that something is found at a site should never lead to the assumption that its possessors were its producers. Yet archaeological and historical literature is replete with such unwarranted suppositions.

AN EXPEDITION ALONG THE TURKISH COAST

It was evident to me that the limits of Mycenaean pyrotechnology precluded a glassmaking capability, and therefore the glass objects found in a Mycenaean context either must have been imported or must have been made from previously manufactured glass. Accordingly, I set out to examine the evidence at first hand and was fortunate to be able to take advantage of an intensive archaeological tour, led by the eminent archaeologist Machteld Mellink, which included an investigation of Turkish coastal sites by sea and land. The chief purpose of my participation in the expedition was to search around the coast to determine what traces of early seaborne commercial traffic around the Mediterranean had come to light. The tour afforded the opportunity to discuss the matter with the archaeologists involved in the excavation of coastal sites both on land and under the sea. In addition, Professor Bass had invited me to spend some time after the tour with the archaeologists who were diving into the depths of the Mediterranean, to observe the operation of unloading at long last the cargo of the 3,400-year-old vessel lying 140 feet and more under its surface. I had gratefully accepted an invitation to be a guest aboard the Virazon, the research vessel of the Institute for Nautical Archaeology that was anchored above the ancient wreck.

The group of archaeologists with whom I passed a portion of my Anatolian expedition began its descent toward the sea at Termossus, an impressively well-preserved Greek and Roman archaeological site perched atop the Taurus mountains off the Pamphylian coast at a height of over a thousand meters. No road led to the site, so our party had to scramble up a steep path for a kilometer and a half to reach the ruins. Alexander the Great passed peacefully by Termossus on his way across Anatolia to engage Darius in a struggle that determined the course of history. The native Solymian mountain people sat securely ensconced within the formidable mountains, and neither the Greeks nor the Romans made an attempt to subdue them. The Solymians prospered and the Roman Senate acknowledged the native Solymian mountain people as "friends and allies."

The insularity of the southern Anatolian coastal region had also kept the Hittites from overwhelming it, and the mountains that blocked access from the broad central sweeps of Anatolia effectively parted the land routes into the heart of Anatolia from the sea routes connecting east and west. Canaanite vessels had passed along this coastline in their circumnavigation of the Mediterranean over a period of more than a millennium, sailing a circular route that included visits to Cyprus and Crete and Rhodes and Egypt. They plied the Peloponnesian Archipelago, touched at the Grecian city-states, ventured up to the terminus of the Adriatic and rounded the boot of Italy to Sicily, Etruria and Rome. Eventually they established themselves upon the Iberian peninsula and sailed along the shores of the Atlantic. Traces of purported Canaanite writing have even been found in both North and South America, although their purported presence in the Western Hemisphere, if confirmed, was no doubt the result of one-way misadventures.

The Pamphylian city of Perge lies on the coast below Termossus, a city well-known from Hellenistic references. The city of the Pergians had no defensible ramparts, so they welcomed Alexander's arrival and accommodated the young warrior by guiding his army through the Yenice pass across Lykian territory, while Alexander himself and a small company marched along the coast. Two hills encompass the ancient city, one capped by an acropolis, the other crowned by a theater.

The Perge excavation was in the charge of archaeologist Dr. Jale Inan, one of a number of outstanding Turkish women archaeologists who had been freed to pursue higher education under the enlightened Ataturk regime. Dr. Inan conducted us through the monumental stadium and the theater, and rendered an impromptu dissertation on the famous frieze on the facade of the stage depicting events in the life of Dionysus. We visited the baths, the agora, the temple of Artemis, and were led through the soaring towers of the Hellenistic gate that still dominates the site. Through the gate an imposing colonnade fences a road twenty meters wide and a quarter of a kilometer long. The road is split by a decorative canal that proceeds along its entire length. The colonnade is further flanked on each side by porticos, whose converging lines focus on the Nymphaeum far off at the foot of the acropolis.

According to Strabo, a geographer and intrepid traveler born just before the turn of the Common Era near the Black Sea in Amasya, Anatolia (now Turkey), the city was founded by a group of Trojans from Argos led by the heroes Colchas and Mopsus. Dr. Anin told me that Professor Arif Mufid Mansel, who preceded her at Perge, found just such bases; the inscription on them included the names of these two adventurers. Other evidence exists that supports the legend and provides the impelling commercial reasons the Trojans had for founding a colony so far south and east of their home territory. Among the many artifacts unearthed from Troy, for example, was a potter's wheel. The use of the wheel was until then unknown in north-western Anatolia, but had been part of the eastern and southeastern Anatolia in areas accessible to the Mesopotamian traders, as far back as the fifth millennium B.C.E. Due to the rugged mountainous nature of the land separating eastern and western Anatolia it must be presumed that the potter's wheel traveled west by sea.[8]

As far back as the fourth century B.C.E. the author Scylax had mentioned Perge, and had described the Pamphylian peoples who lived along the Mediterranean trade route that led from the East. Yet I noted that there seemed to be only a limited interest in researching the Eastern origin of Anatolian civilization. No trace of the people Alexander encountered at Perge was visible in the museum at the site, and I asked Dr. Inan whether any work had been done to learn more about them. She answered that while we are only beginning to understand the advent of civilization in Anatolia, it is inevitable that a great concentration is being placed on Greek and Roman occupation of Anatolia. The reason was clear: tourism impels the government to build museums at every attractive site, and since certain civilizations provide a wealth of attractive sculpture and artifacts, it is relatively easy to obtain funds for excavating them. It is up to universities and other research organizations at work in Turkey, who have a less compelling reason for concentrating on these convenient cultures, to fund more abstract research.

A similar situation unfolded at Aspendos, our next stop. Aspendos was a most important commercial center of the Roman period, accessible to the nearby sea through the navigable Eurymedon River. Wheat, horses, wine, and salt mined from the now dry Lake Cabria were shipped throughout the eastern Mediterranean as far as Rome. Aspendos was a member of the Delian league until 425 B.C.E. The Persians used it as a naval base in 411 B.C.E., and (according to Xenophon) contributed soldiers to the campaign of Cyrus. Only hints of previous history are archaeologically extant. The archaeological guide to Pamphylia, distributed by the Turkish museums, cryptically observes that only through a systematic excavation program will the history and development of Aspendos become better known.

We wove through wooded passes down to the sea and followed the coastline toward Side, catching glimpses of brilliant blue waters here and there, and the insistent sound of surf. The ancient city of Side was situated on a peninsula. It was here that Hannibal encountered the fleet of the Rhodians, allies of the Romans, and was defeated in 190 B.C.E.

"Hannibal must have been following an ancient precedent," I mused. "This is just the type of harbor city that the Canaanites would have chosen. Perhaps the museum at Side will supply some answers." I had good reason to anticipate evidence of such a connection. Strabo and Arrian both make mention of the "settlement" of Side by Aeolians in the seventh century B.C.E. Yet the word *Side* is not Greek, but ancient Anatolian for pomegranate, an eastern fruit, and one of the favorite Israelite artistic motifs. There is no doubt as to the origin of the word, inasmuch as illustrative pomegranates appear on coins of Side from 500 B.C.E. until Roman times!

Among the proudest possessions of the museum at Side is a mysterious column with inscriptions in Sidenian and Greek, and two other texts containing Sidenian inscriptions. The Sidenian script is similar to the Semitic script of ancient times. The mystery of Side's past was not confined to the distant past. Side came under Ptolemaic and then under Seleucid control as early as the third century B.C.E. Side had gained the reputation of being an outstanding center of science and culture. The eastern Prince Antiochus came to Side to be educated and thereafter proudly adjoined the descriptive term Sidedes to his name. Side was the site of a famous library, a beautiful building whose function had been determined by Dr. Jale Inan and who had dated it to the second century B.C.E. I had learned that wherever a library existed, a synagogue was also likely to have been located close by. This was true at Sardis, at Alexandria, and at Pergamon, and Side should be no exception.

Sure enough, not one but at least two synagogues had serviced the Jewish community of Side! Where were they to be found? An aqueduct, city gates, Nymphaeum, baths, agora, temples, theater, Byzantine buildings including an archbishop's palace, and other such structures stand boldly exposed for tourists to admire. The palace of the archbishop had been constructed of materials from the ruins of other buildings, very likely that of the synagogues. The synagogues themselves are presently to be found only at the end of the description of Side in the archaeological guide:

"Two synagogues belonging to the Jewish people who lived here are also recorded, but their location is not known. Future excavations will greatly help us to learn more about the site."

Leaving Side we headed back toward Antalya, a city supposedly founded by Attalos II, King of Pergamon. The group of archaeologists boarded five motorboats and set out for three days of adventuring at sea to visit coastal sites difficult to approach by land. We were treated to some exciting moments; we sailed over a sunken city that owed its watery grave to an earthquake that had dumped the city into the sea. While marveling at the remarkable state of underwater preservation of this pseudo-Atlantis, our engine sputtered and died, and we suffered the indignity of being towed into a small seaside community, Simena, whose picturesque houses crowd up a mountain crowned with a crusader castle. Undaunted, we scaled the cliff up to the castle, and found that the ridge upon which it was located was dotted with hundreds of huge Lydian tombs; the necropolis extended as far as the eye could see.

No sooner did we reboard our revitalized vessel for departure when a violent windstorm suddenly whipped up the sea and began to toss our vessel around as if it were a cork in a Jacuzzi. The crew leaped into action, maneuvered the vessel away from the dock against which it was battering. They picked a way through the myriad of islands that checkered the bay and found refuge in a sheltered cove. We were thankful that our crews were familiar with the freakish weather we had encountered, and knew where shelter could be found. But what of the sea-farers who had wandered past these shores over 3,000 years ago? Our unnerving experience made manifest the swiftness with which an ancient ship such as that found off the Turkish coast near Kas would founder under similar circumstances. The Bronze Age vessel lay there silently beneath the sea, a playground for Aegean fish, its cargo preserved virtually intact.

The sunken vessel had been brought to the attention of Professor George Bass, founder of the Institute of Nautical Archaeology, by Turkish sponge divers who were regularly scouring the seabottom off the coast.[9] One of these spongers reported seeing strange "biscuits with ears" off a jagged promontory, Ulu Burun, mystifying objects for which Bass had instructed them to be on the lookout. The ship and its cargo proved to be sensational. The sixty-five-foot vessel, the earliest complete ship and cargo ever found, was laded with tons of copper and tin ingots in classic "oxhide" form (the biscuits with ears reported by the spongedivers), and a host of personal and commercial artifacts. An assortment of tools have been recovered from the 3,300-year-old vessel, including adzes, axes, knives, razors, chisels and drills. Weapons of bronze and stone were equally well represented, consisting of swords, daggers, and mace heads, arrowheads, and spearheads.

Professor George Bass, founder and director of the Institute of Nautical Archaeology, at Ulu Burun describing recoveries from the 3400-year-old ship to a group of visiting archaeologists. (Photograph by the author.)

Canaanite jewelry, Egyptian-type scarabs; African ebony and other types of exotic and common woods; ostrich eggshells, Cypriot cylinder seals, beads of Baltic amber; and pottery from Greece, Cyprus, and the Near East were additional attestations to the wide sweep of the ship as it circumnavigated the Eastern Mediterranean according to the season and the prevailing winds, trading goods from port to port. Exotic cargo, the ivory wing of what had been a duck-shaped cosmetic container, a magnificent gold cup and other gold objects, hippopotamus and elephant ivory were also brought up from the depth of from 150 to 200 feet of the slope down which the cargo of the ancient vessel is strewn. Pan-balance weights and cylinder seals point to the presence of one or more merchants; ceramic lamps, a faience rhyton, fishing implements, and some twenty-four great stone anchors are included in some of the more mundane accoutrements on board. Olives, figs, pomegranates, and various spices were identified to have been transported on the unfortunate vessel, as well as a large quantity of terebinthine resin.

AN UNEXPECTED DISCOVERY: GLASS INGOTS

The most exciting contents of the cargo were amphorae packed with glass beads and the scores of cobalt-blue glass ingots. The unprecedented discovery of glass and glassware being exported at this time provided indisputable proof of the fact that not only did an Iron Age glassmaking industry exist in fourteenth-century Bronze Age Mesopotamia, but it was so highly developed that it was capable of producing ingots weighing an impressive twenty-five pounds for export.

The engineering of pneumatically drafted, reverbatory furnaces capable of producing such glass hulks at this early period bespoke a sophisticated pyro-technology that shattered the assumptions of most historians. A temperature of some 1,100 degrees Celsius (about 2,000 degrees Fahrenheit) must not only be attained but unremittingly maintained by pumping a steady draft of air through the flaming furnace by means of one or more bellows for at least four days and nights to produce an ingot such as that found on board the ancient ship. Such a furious temperature is the limit of heat that could be produced by the organic fuels available to the ancient artisans. In addition to the engineering of a pneu-matically drafted furnace, a number of secret processes were involved in the pro-duction of glass. *Once glass is manufactured, however, it can readily be remelted at a reasonable temperature, and requires no knowledge of the production of the primary material.* Glass ingots, therefore, were a valuable product for resale, suitable for transformation at their destination into glassware of all kinds, while the secrets of the manufacture of the raw glass remained with its producers.

Archaeologists and historians have rarely differentiated between glassmaking and glassware-making, and were thereby subject to egregious error. The two crafts are quite distinct; whereas every glassmaker was capable of producing glassware, the reverse was by no means true. Until recently glassmaking was considered to have been born in Egypt; that proposition grated against all I had learned about the art. In my association with the industry on the island of Murano, I had deter-mined from the records of the period, in which wood was still being used on that island for firing the furnaces, that two tons or more of wood was required to produce a kilogram of glass. Considering the cruder engineering of the furnaces of three to four millennia ago, and variables such as the type of wood employed as fuel, it is clear that up to six tons of wood was required in ancient times to produce that weight of raw glass, depending on the design of the furnace and the diligence by which the pumpers of the bellows worked through day and night. The first, and by no means the only question to be answered, therefore, was "Where were the forests of Upper Egypt that supplied the necessary fuel?"

It is obvious that there were no such forests, and the importing of sufficient wood into arid Egypt to initiate and maintain such an industry would be utterly impractical. Nor was any other type of fuel available in Egypt that could substitute for wood. *Although every aspect of Egyptian technology is depicted in minute detail in Egyptian art and is described in Egyptian literature, no sign of a furnace capable of making glass appears, let alone the process itself.* The Iron Age, in fact, passed by ancient Egypt with scarcely a hint of its existence. No word for glass existed in the ancient Egyptian vocabulary, whereas *zakhukhit*, the Hebrew word for glass, traces back to an Akkadian seventeenth-century B.C.E. tablet. No developmental stages of glassware-making are apparent in the glassware recovered from Egyptian tombs; glassware suddenly appears in Eighteenth-Dynasty tombs, fully articulated, whereas the entire developmental range is found in a Mesopotamian context dating back many centuries earlier. These and other factors can only lead to the conclusion that the assumption that glassmaking existed in ancient Egypt is a myth. Nor had the Mycenaeans ever attained the Iron Age technology required for vitric production, remarkable as was the civilization they had created in other respects.

Once glass is manufactured, it can be easily remelted in a matter of minutes at little more than half the temperature required to produce it. Raw manufactured glass is therefore superbly suitable for sale and shipment, affording the primary producer a means of selling his product without relinquishing the secrets of its manufacture. Glass in ingot form, unlike goblets or bowls, is not hazardous for shipment, and its presence as a raw material, along with copper and tin ingots on the Bronze Age ship, is an indicator and measure of the direction from which technology passed to the West. The existence of amphorae loaded with glass beads in the cargo further emphasizes the convenient use of glass for export trade, for beads, like ingots, are not subject to being damaged in transportation. Beads remained a major component of trade goods carried by merchants on their adventurous rounds into the present era. From the most remote South Sea Islands to the Inuit of Alaska, glass beads have served throughout the ages as a prime medium of exchange.

THE CARGO OF A BRONZE AGE SHIP

After the tour of archaeological sites led by Professor Mellink came to a close I returned to Kas, where a member of the Institute of Nautical Archaeology team ferried me to the site of the underwater campaign at Ulu Burun. A bunk was provided for me on board the Virazon, at anchor above the wreck. At the site, and at the museum in nearby Bodrum, I was able to review the instructive array of artifacts recovered from the wreck.

The character of the cargo being raised from the depths of the sea attests to the sophistication of the maritime trade of the times. There were African ebony logs, which had originated from Nubia and were likely to have been picked up

One of the scores of glass ingots recovered from the cargo of a vessel that foundered at the end of the fourteenth century B.C.E. The bulk of the ingots (weighing more or less 25 pounds each) and the three distinct colors produced provide incontrovertible evidence of the advanced state of pyrotechnology and of the chemical sophistication of their producers. (Photograph courtesy of the Institute for Nautical Archaeology.)

in Egypt. There were tin ingots, probably cast from ores originating from the mountains of Afghanistan. The copper ingots was certainly picked up in Cyprus (which name means "copper"). Unworked Asian elephant and hippopotamus ivory on board was taken from the animals of the Levantine swamps and forests where such beasts had still not been brought to extinction, and the glass ingots and beads must have been manufactured in the thickly forested northwestern segment of the Fertile Crescent.

The meticulousness with which material was recovered from the wreck under extremely difficult conditions paid off in a number of unexpected dividends. Bits of organic matter were painstakingly retrieved from the wreck for study, resulting in a unique assemblage of plant remains, of which "all but two of the plants identified so far are among the relatively few plants named in the Bible, where scarcely more than 100 of the 2,300 species found in biblical lands are mentioned."[10] This concordance turned out to be somewhat more than a coincidence when the fruits that were part of the valuable cargo were analyzed and identified.

Over one hundred Canaanite-type jars contained terebinth resin, which, after 3,300 years, still retained a sharp, turpentine-like odor; no less than a half ton of the pungent resin was on board. In her study of the plant remains of the shipwreck, Cheryl Haldane found that clues to its provenience were provided by biblical references and by Mycenaean Greek "Linear B" tablets, Egyptian texts, Classical Greek writings, and modern ethnographic evidence. According to Pliny, terebinth was a highly valued material which was employed for the coloring and perfuming of oils and "good-smelling" emollients;[11] according to Theophratus the best such resin was obtained from the terebinth tree (*Pistaccia Terebinthus*) which grew in ancient Aramea.[12] It appears from Egyptian texts that "thousands of liters of the resin" were being imported from the Levant to Egypt each year. The Egyptologist Victor Loret identified the Egyptian word *sonter* to mean terebinthine resin,[13] and thereby was enabled to translate a number of Egyptian texts describing the import of the resin from the Canaanite coast and its use in Egyptian rituals during the fourteenth century B.C.E. "An Egyptian painting mentioned by Loret shows a Canaanite jar like those on our wreck," noted Professor Bass.[14]

Coriander fruits were stored in baskets or woven bags, an amphora was found full of olive stones. Charred cereal grains of wheat and barley, grapes, figs, safflower, almonds and sumac fruits were also among the economic plants laded on the vessel. Seven large storage (*pithoi*) jars that had contained pomegranate juice were recovered. "A preliminary sorting of a sample from the 1.4-meter-tall pithos produced more than 1,000 seeds, flower parts and fragments of skin from what were once whole pomegranates."[15] The pomegranate is native to Canaan and Mesopotamia and is mentioned frequently in the Bible; pomegranates, figs, and grapes were brought to Moses by his spies as evidence of the rich agricultural attributes of Canaan[16] and confirmed Canaan's reputation as the land of milk and honey; the pomegranate was used by the Hebrews as an architectural element, as a design motif for clothing, and was one of the earliest models for glass vessels, fine examples of which can be viewed in the Israel and Corning museums.[17]

Professor Bass noted that the sixty-seven amphoras raised by 1985 were similar to Canaanite amphoras from Mycenae, Menidi, Tell Abu Hawan, and to those from tombs near Akjko. Cemal Pulak, his able assistant in charge of the site, found similarities between these large jars and those of Meggido and Byblos.[18] A Canaanite connection to the cargo is furthermore suggested by the recovery of four gold medallions decorated in repoussé with a four-pointed star, a motif appearing on artifacts from numerous Canaanite excavations. On finding the first of these pectorals, Professor Bass recognized that it "is surely of Canaanite inspiration" and among the examples given was a reference "to earlier gold pectorals found in tombs at Byblos, a site which may in fact have influenced the techniques of goldwork at Tell el Ajjul."[19] The medallion and the motif are so typically Canaanite that the Egyptians depicted captured Canaanites wearing this distinctive symbol as an indication of their provenience.[20] The starred design originated from an earlier Akkadian period and examples were found in the ruins of Nuzi. Some of the earliest glass pendants known sport the same distinctive design as appears on the golden pectorals recovered from the wreck off Ulu Burun.

The provenance and destination of the resin suggest those of the glass ingots on board the Ulu Burun vessel; it was thus that raw glass must have arrived in Egypt for the short period in which glassware was being produced in Egypt from imported raw glass. Glassware-making (but not primary glassmaking) took place during a period of relative peace under the rules of Amenophis III and of his heretic son, Akhenaten, in the mid-fourteenth century B.C.E. Glassware-making activity then continued in Egypt, albeit in a more limited and crude fashion for a short time during the reign of the Warrior Pharaohs and then disappeared. The production of glassware in Egypt ended about the time of the reign of Merenptah in the year 1214. The Ulu Burun vessel sailed sometime within the short time during which glassware was produced in Egypt. It was during this same period that glass beads and pendants began to appear in Mycenaean and other Eastern Mediterranean and Aegean locations.

A cylinder seal that was capped with a looped gold cover at each end was found; it had evidently being used as a pendant by some sea-faring merchant on board. Another object as startling as the glass ingots was dredged from the sands covering the wreck; it was a writing tablet composed of two ivory-hinged, wooden leaves, a diptych. It precedes by a span of several centuries the earliest such writing instrument ever found. The leaves of the diptych are hollow, providing a shallow well into which wax or clay could be pressed and upon which computations could be performed by scratching into the impressionable material. The diptych evidences the literacy and commercial competence of the merchant on board the vessel to whom it belonged, and its significance is matched by that of the presence of the massive glass ingots, the products of a West Asian industrial capacity and technology that has not yet been fully appreciated.

The existence of the diptych provides evidence for the Semitic ethnicity of its possessor, for only the Semitic-speaking people of the Canaanite coast employed a so-called abecedary at the time and would find its use advantageous. Neither the Egyptians, the Minoans, nor the Mycenaeans had use for such a tablet; Egyptian hieroglyphic writing, the "Linear A" script of the Minoans, and the "Linear B" script of the Mycenaeans were all unsuitable for computation or notation on the wax surfaces provided by the diptych. The possibility of a Mycenaean origin of the vessel has been suggested, based on certain attributes of the ship and its cargo, and the alternative provenance of the merchant or merchants on board has to be considered. That such a person would be knowledgeable in Mycenaean script even if it were suitable for use on a diptych is, however, unlikely, in that the primitive script was not for general use, but a crude system restricted to a very limited group of scribes, mainly those who were assigned to the keeping of palatial accounting and administrative records.

No literary tablets have been recovered from Mycenaean sites, "and it seems probable," comments the historian Arnold Toynbee, "that none were ever made. The script was complicated and clumsy; we may guess that scribes were few; and there is not likely to have been a reading public for non-utilitarian writings."[21] In fact, the "Linear B" script was already on its way to extinction: "No 'Linear B' tablets of a later date than *circa* 1200 B.C. have been found. The widespread devastation of the Mycenean palaces about the end of the 13th century B.C. seems to have put the 'Linear B' script out of action."[22] Almost five centuries would pass before the tribes who became the "Greeks" would again enjoy the advantages of a written language; these backward peoples were never heir to Mycenaean literacy, even in its primitive form. A dark period of Aegean history ensued at the beginning of the Iron Age, made visible only by the surviving shards of the pottery of the Aegean peoples, the relics of habitation on which those peoples expressed their artistic talents and made aspects of their life indelible.

The ethnic identification of the merchant aboard the vessel that foundered off the Anatolian coast, the sea-going entrepreneur who employed a diptych at the turn of the thirteenth century B.C.E., can be interpolated from Ezekiel's account of the Tyrian Canaanites of a somewhat later period. We are reminded in Chapter 27 of the Lamentations of Ezekiel that while the ships of Tyre were piloted by "[Tyrian] wise men," the mariners came from Sidon and Arvad; the armed personnel from Persia; and the "caulkers of the vessels," as well as the fir, cedar, and oak, came from the Galilee. The merchants accommodated aboard the Tyrian vessels and participating in the fairs held in the marketplace of Tyre came from a broad spectrum of peoples from the surrounding region, including: merchants from the houses of Javan, Tubal, and Meshech who traded in servants and in vessels of brass; merchants of the house of Togarmah who participated in the fairs with "horses and horsemen and mules"; the Dedan clan, which traded in "horns of ivory and ebony," and in "precious clothes for chariots"; and the Danites, who dealt with thread and brought bright iron, cassia, and calamus to the market created by the Tyrrian seafarers.

"Judah, and the land of Israel," we are told, "they were thy merchants; they traded in thy market wheat of Minith, and dainties, and honey, and oil and balm." Merchants arrived from Damascus, Arabia, Tarshish, Sheba, and Raamach to trade for emeralds, coral, agate, and "all precious stones and gold." Chests full of rich apparel decorated with "cords and bands and chains" were being offered in the bustling Tyrian market, along with fine linen, purple textiles, and embroidered work.

The Israelites populated the Tyrrian, Arvadian, and Sidonian island hinterlands, as we are advised in Judges 11:21, 22: ". . . so Israel possessed all the land of the Amorites, the inhabitants of that country. And they possessed all the coasts of the Amorites from Arnon even unto Jabbock, and from the wilderness even unto Jordan." This event may well have taken place before the time when the ill-fated

A wooden diptych recovered from the ill-fated 3400-year-old vessel wrecked off the coast of Anatolia is the earliest ever found. Computations and notations were done on wax pressed into the hollowed sides of the hinged wooden "writing pad." The diptych attests to the literate level of the owner of the writing instrument, probably a trader on board the vessel. (Photograph courtesy of the Institute for Nautical Archaeology.)

vessel foundered off the Anatolian coast, depending on which of the several models of Israelite settlement of the area is projected.

In any event, Deborah sings in Judges 5:17 about the continued habitation of the tribe of Asher near the sea shore, and we are biblically informed many times that the tribes of Zebulun and Naphthali were equally well-rooted in the area. The children of Dan also resided near the coast (Judges 18) until they sent "five men of valour" to seek their own "inheritance to dwell in." They went to Laish, and "because it was far from Zidon" they built their own city on the site and changed the name Laish to Dan. The fact that the mainland had become essentially Israelite is evidenced in 1 Kings 9:11, in which a thankful Solomon presented Hiram with twenty cities in the land of Galilee in recompense for his friendship and assistance in the completion of the Temple.

This sampling of the composition of the population of the area suggests, as we can also infer from numerous other biblical references, that the Israelites and Judahites not only participated in the trade of the seafarers, but were likely to be found on board their vessels. The warm relationship between the Tyrians and Judah is nowhere more evident than in the account in 1 Kings 9:26-29 that after

King Solomon built a commercial navy in Ezion-Gezer with which he could navigate the Red Sea as far as Ophir, Hiram supplied sailors to accompany and teach the Judahite sailors the "knowledge of the sea." The complement of sailors who departed for Ophir every three years thereafter included both Tyrian and Judahite mariners, and we may assume that a similar mixture may well have taken place on the Mediterranean.

The merchandise on board the fourteenth-century B.C.E. vessel presages the rich roster of merchandise catalogued by Ezekiel and illustrates an industrial and cultural development whose sophistication had not been imagined before its recovery from the depths of the Mediterranean. It is within the matrix of this seminal Mesopotamian civilization that the Jews appear upon the proscenium of history.

8

The Emergence
of The Israelite Nation

The Dawn of the Iron Age

The seeding of the Iron Age in the hills and forests of Canaan, a process so dramatically documented in the Bible, is substantiated in its broad outlines by archaeological revelations, although the means by which that settlement came about are subject to considerable debate. It matters little, as far as the outcome is concerned, whether one accepts in whole or in part the biblical version of the manner in which a new cultural entity, the Israelites, emerged in the Canaanite highlands of western Asia. Two events are universally recognized as having taken place coincidently in the Canaan of the twelfth century B.C.E.: the birth of the Israelite nation and the inauguration of the Iron Age.

CANAAN FROM THE BRONZE AGE TO THE IRON AGE

Professor William Dever describes the dynamic changes taking place during the Bronze Age, in which Israelite culture gestated and from which the Israelites emerged:

> A great transformation took place just after approximately 2000 B.C.E. The brief transition between Early Bronze IV and Middle Bronze I witnessed . . . a nearly complete change in technology, economic basis, social structure, and political organization between approximately 2000 and 1800 B.C.E., as urbanism increasingly took hold. . . . The long process of collapse in the Southern Levant was halted. A sudden revival of urban life ushered in the Bronze Middle Age. By about 1800 B.C.E., 65 percent of the population lived in large fortified cities. The proliferation of these is the most characteristic feature of the period.[1]

The introduction and diffusion of tin-bronze metallurgy, an entirely new repertoire of pottery, the industrialization of ceramic technology through wheel-

147

thrown ware that "was the finest pottery ever produced in the pre-Roman period," and many other technological advances and innovations were ushered in during the following brief but seminal period of Bronze Age history in which the Semitic chieftains infiltrated the Levantine Mediterranean lands and ruled over all of Canaan and Egypt.

Hazor was one of the fulcrums of tin-bronze trade during this very period. Hazor and Dan are the only Canaanite cities mentioned in the documents unearthed from archives of Mari, and it is clear from the context in which they are cited that Hazor was a most important strategic and commercial center dominating its sector of the Fertile Crescent. We learn from the Mari documents that Hammurabi, the great Semitic king of Babylon of the eighteenth century B.C.E., maintained ambassadors at Hazor. Most illuminating is the record of at least three successive sales of tin to Abni-Adad, king of Hazor, whose name is rendered in the Mari documents in its Semitic form, Yabni-Hadad, meaning "the god Hadad has created." The director of the excavations of Hazor, Yigael Yadin, the eminent Israeli archaeologist, followed the leads given by documents from Mari, the Bible, and other sources and found confirmation in the ruins of the great metropolis.[2] The recovery from the ruins of Middle Bronze Age of many scarabs of the so-called "Hyksos" types, none of which bore royal names, serve to identify the residents of the city, and to testify to its vibrant activity during the tenure of the autonomous Canaanite chieftains.[3] Yadin was duly impressed with the town planning of the period ending about 1550 B.C.E., "particularly by the sewage systems in the houses. One of our finds was a beautiful sewage canal with an outlet made of basalt."[4]

Egyptian aggression brought technological progress to a halt. The vigorous communities were either obliterated or else reduced to being vassals of the ambitious Theban warlords. The Warrior Pharaohs ravaged the Levant, subjugated its peoples, reaped tribute from the local subservient chieftains, and proceeded to surround themselves with monumental extravagance in both life and death at the expense of the peoples within and outside Egypt. A resistance to Egyptian oppression by means of intermediary local lords engendered a tumultuous period of resistance and rebellion, a situation amply reflected in the pleas for assistance from the Canaanite lords to the pharaohs. It was during this period that fiercely independent groups, the mysterious $H_u$abiru, appeared on the Canaanite scene; these were large and small companies of artisans and pastoral peoples who appear to have accepted neither lasting national affinities nor boundaries and frequently became actively resistant to authority. They are mysterious only in that, although they were generally technologically advanced and were employed at the forefront of civilization, we learn of them entirely through the acrimonious inscriptions of overlords.

The Middle Bronze II period, corresponding to the interval in which Semitic kings ruled over Canaan and Egypt, had been one of unprecedented prosperity in which the sedentary population of Canaan west of the Jordan doubled to an estimated 140,000.[5] In the subsequent rapacious period of the Eighteenth

Dynasty Warrior Pharaohs, the mushrooming affluence of the Egyptian overlords paralleled a reduction in prosperity and decimation of the population of Canaan; many of the flourishing settlements were destroyed and the population of the region suffered a dramatic decrease; the number of residents of the area west of the Jordan was reduced in the Late Bronze period by more than fifty per cent to a total of some 60,000 to 70,000. Egyptian pugnacity and predation cannot account altogether for the attrition of economy and population during the period, some of which can undoubtedly be attributed to inner strains in the Canaanite economy, the abrasive effects of incursions by Hurrians and other geopolitical factors.

Canaan was too rich a prize to remain long uncontested. Egyptian domination of the crossroads of civilization was challenged by all of the surrounding powers. Egypt itself was invaded by the Sea Peoples and its clutch on the region shattered. Whatever other encroachments on the region are considered, the disastrous impact on Canaan of the crushing weight of Egyptian subjugation and usurpation was the overriding factor in bringing the vigorous evolution of technology to a halt. This course of events is brought into sharp focus by its reversal with the passage of the Egyptian predatory period, a no less dramatic swing to the redevelopment of new settlements in and repopulation of the Canaanite hill country. The relaxation of Egyptian control may well have occasioned a corollary insurgency of the Canaanite underclass against the local overlords. The turmoil created an administrative vacuum that was filled by a proliferation of autonomous "Israelite" settlements.

"About 240 sites of the [Iron I] period are known [to have sprung into existence] in the area between the Jezreel and Beer-Sheva valleys: 96 in Manassah, 122 in Ephraim . . . and 22 in Benjamin and Judah. In addition, 68 sites have been identified in the Galilee, 18 in the Jordan Valley and dozens of others on the Transjordanian plateau."[6] These figures are far from complete, as Israel Finklestein notes in reviewing the perplexing process of Israelite settlement, and "because sites proliferated all over the region in Iron I, no doubt more will be discovered in the future." More, indeed, have been discovered since Finklestein wrote his article in 1988, and they add substance to the question he and others ask: "From where did the people who settled the hundreds of sites in Iron I materialize?"

The occupants of the proliferating hilltop villages of Canaan in the twelfth century B.C.E. were sedentary, highly independent, egalitarian, antiestablishmentarian communities at the highest levels of metallurgic pyrotechnology and literacy that civilization had attained anywhere on earth at that time. The two contiguous events, Israelite settlement and the dawn of the Iron Age, are common to all attempts at the reconstruction of the period; all the deviant paths taken by historians and archaeologists to explain the formation of the Israelite nation converge with those events. It is incontrovertible that hundreds of Israelite villages were newly ensconced on the verdant hills of the Holy Land by the end of the twelfth century B.C.E. and that the Iron Age, as it is commonly defined, came into being in that region at that very time; all the models of Israelite settlement are conjunctively drawn to those facts. Only the manner in which those events took place is subject to debate, not the fact of their existence. Before we enter into a discussion of the metallurgical prowess of the new settlers we must first examine the various theories about the identity of the Israelites and the manner in which they arrived in the hills of Canaan.[7]

None of the arguments in the scientific community hinge on the divine origin or inspiration of the biblical narratives, even on the part of those who hold that the biblical account is rooted in history and basically accurate. The conviction that the twelve tribes of Israel conquered Canaan precisely as related in the Book of Joshua is stubbornly maintained only by the most orthodox of Jewish and Christian fundamentalists. Even so, variant sections of the books of Joshua and of Judges allow considerable latitude in the interpretation of the manner and extent of the conquest of Canaan by the Israelites.

There is a wide range of interpretations of the documentary and archaeological evidence concerning the circumstances of the appearance of a substantial, technologically advanced Israelite entity. The Exodus is denied altogether by some who deem the biblical chronology of that conquest as inconsistent with the reality of material evidence. Their argument is based chiefly on the assumption that many of the cities cited as having been destroyed by the Israelites show no evidence of having undergone devastation at the time. The discipline of "biblical archaeology" has come under criticism, on the presumption that those who practice it are employing dubious and even mythological premises rather than factual information to construct historiography, that the discipline is far too restrictive in its range, and that its dogged pursuit leads to ignoring facts or worse, the bending of facts to fit the biblical narrative. On the other hand, so many biblically cited sites and events are continually coming to the light that the supporters of the essential authenticity of the biblical account never lack for arguments to counter the skeptics.

ORIGINS OF THE ISRAELITE NATION:
THREE THEORETICAL MODELS

The numbers and rich range of discoveries resulting from excavations in *Eretz Yisrael* during the last half century have fostered three main schools of thought on the subject of the formation of the Israelite nation. The "Conquest Model," which mirrors the biblical narrative, was promulgated by early rummagers in ancient rubble, among whom were many Americans such as the intrepid archaeologist and explorer Nelson Glueck, who was intrigued by "the astonishing historical memory of the Bible,"[8] and by apologetic Protestant scholars such as the deservedly renowned and respected William Foxwell Albright. The "American School," promoters of the Conquest Model, while admitting to some dubious details, argued for the substantial historical authenticity of the Exodus and conquest narratives.[9]

An alternate "Infiltration Model" derives from a theory launched by Albrecht Alt in a set of essays published in 1925, arguing that the twelve-tribe confederacy or Amphictyony, a sacral league of the tribes formed during the period of Judges, was not the one dealt with in such detail in Exodus and Numbers but a Canaanite confederacy that preexisted Israel.[10] Alt leaned heavily upon the incursion of the Hyksos, a "Syrian" [i.e., Aramaic] people who reorganized the society of petty, autonomous Canaanite tribes into more centrally controlled city-states. Among the Hyksos was a powerful warrior class who introduced chariot warfare into the region from their Mesopotamian highlands and by whose military prowess the Hyksos gained hegemony over Egypt and Canaan and became a feudal class ensconced within fortifications from which they ruled the serfs of the country-side. The Hyksos lords were defeated by the pharoahs of the New Kingdom and subjected to Egyptian rule until the collapse of Egyptian power at the end of the thirteenth century. Egyptian debility loosed the reins on local tribes, which, reinforced by influxes of new settlers, acquired a local territorial and national consciousness.

Alt accepts details of the accounts of Israelite conquests as outlined in Joshua and Judges, but rejects that of Deuteronomy as an emendation of disparate accounts; the conquest was not viewed as a coherent event but as a series of separate encounters spread out over a long period. The tribal entities that had coalesced during this extended period were able to maintain a political independence that lasted for hundreds of years until the late Israelite monarchical period by which time the Judahites succeeded in virtually eradicating tribal allegiances.

The Alt theory was revised and expanded by his student, Martin Noth (and is hence referred to as the Alt-Noth theory), who considered Israelite occupation an essentially peaceful process in which pastoral peoples separately and independently took root in the unoccupied areas between agricultural Canaanite communities to which they had traditionally dispersed seasonally. According to this view, the twelve-tribe amphictyony came into being after and not prior to settlement.[11] With further modifications, the Alt-Noth theory found a sympathetic acceptance by a number of archaeologists, including Professor Benjamin Mazar, the dean of modern Israeli archaeologists. He held that the early Israelites were generally stock-breeders (some archaeologists persist in terming them "nomads") originating from Transjordan and the Negev, who, after coming to terms, by war or alliance with a Canaanite population composed of three ethnic strains (Hivites based in Shechem, Hittites in Hebron, and Jebusites in Jerusalem), gradually adapted to village life.[12]

Evidence continues to accumulate that suggests that the Israelites were in fact less of a pastoral people than had been assumed, let alone nomadic, and that the expertise they exhibited in their architecture, agronomy, and pyrotechnology immediately upon their arrival and settlement in the highlands of Canaan suggests that they were essentially an urban people who had arrived with a high level of literacy and technological proficiency. The series of new unwalled Iron I Israelite cities that came to light as a result of surveys and excavations impelled some archaeologists, such as Aharon Kempinski,[13] Yohanan Aharoni, and Volkmar Fritz to swing to support of the "Infiltration Model." A new version gingerly proposed by Volkmar Fritz does not completely reject the inclusion of pastoral or nomadic peoples as settlers, but leans toward their sedentary quality in its vision of the genesis of the Israelites. "The various groups that settled in the country from the twelfth century onward cannot merely be regarded as former nomads," writes Fritz, and, in order to acknowledge the shift, proposes a new name in place of the "Infiltration" model: "I would like to call the new theory the *symbiosis hypothesis.*"[14]

Professor Aharoni also views the Israelites as a pastoral people who dispersed peacefully over several hundred years into sparsely occupied areas to become a sedentary people, and expands on the scenario of a gradual process of osmosis by adding that "[In the wake of this movement] a mighty population revolution was brought about, unparalleled in the history of the country . . . The occupational center of gravity passed from the valleys to the hill country, which was henceforth the center of Israelite life down to the end of the monarchy."[15]

That dramatic vision of the creation of Israelite settlements leads into the third, "Peasants' Revolt" or "Internal Revolt" hypothesis, which was advanced by Professor George E. Mendenhall of Michigan University and subsequently modified and promoted by Norman Gottwald and Cornelis de Geus;[16] it posits a revolt of an oppressed Canaanite underclass against their feudal overlords ensconced in the citadels of the city-states. Gottwald, a fervent proponent of this theory, emphasized that "the basic division was not between agriculture and nomadism but between centralized, stratified and elitist cities, on the one hand, and the non-statist, egalitarian countryside on the other." The oppressed population of the fiefs of ruthless and ambitious overlords, probably reinforced by migrant alien elements escaping Egyptian and other tyrannies, fostered a social and religious revolutionary upheaval that generated a new sociological entity. "The shift from Canaan to Israel was primarily . . . a shift from hierarchic urban government to tribal self-management, with a corresponding transformation in religious forms, from many gods supporting the hierarchic state to one God bringing tribal peoples to birth and defending their new social system."[17]

The "Peasants' Revolt" theorists do not exclude the inclusion of Egyptian refugees among the revolutionary elements; in fact, it is proposed that it may well have been the small group of escaped Egyptian slaves, singing the praises of their liberating God, Yahweh, who galvanized the smoldering resentment of the long-suffering Canaanite and pastoralist masses into revolutionary fervor against their oppressive overlords. The Yahwehites heralded an egalitarian society in which social justice would replace exploitation, and so entire clans of the downtrodden Canaanites, identifying with the proselyting Yahwehites, revolted, and took refuge along with the erstwhile slaves in the central highlands.

The explanation that Israelite villages had proliferated because of a displacement of population from the lowlands to the hills resulting from a revolutionary movement was not entirely convincing. The total population of Canaan, after suffering decimation from the incursion of the Sea Peoples and the rapacious raids of the Warrior Pharaohs,[18] far from continuing to diminish in number, inexplicably burgeoned over an extremely short time in the transition from coastal-plain to hilltop communities. Larry Stager, at a meeting on Israelite origins, was impelled to counter Gottwald's argument by emphasizing that a massive immigration into Canaan is the only reasonable explanation for the huge increase in population from the Late Bronze Age (1550-1200 B.C.E.) to Iron Age I (1200-1000 B.C.E.), an increase which cannot be accounted for by Gottwald's thesis.[19]

In any event, each model has its fervent protagonists and there are those who, noting that each model is consistent with portions of the known archaeological record, combine suitable elements of the three models to produce variations of the themes. History, however, like the weather, results from an infinitely complex mixture of forces, which cannot be blithely reduced to a simple set of equations. Secular scholars are seen to be as palpably guilty of twisting the facts to conform to their artificial constructions as are those fundamentalists who blindly rationalize facts to conform to the Bible.

Although a literal interpretation of the Bible is proposed by few historians, many still insist that the Israelite nation came into existence much as is outlined in the Bible, and that whether that account came about through divine inspiration or was retained in an acute tribal memory is not germane to its intrinsic value as a historical phenomenon. They point to Israelite names of Egyptian origin, particularly of the priestly class, such as Moses, Pinechas, and Hophni, and the unearthing of cities such as Pithom and Avaris (Raamses), long relegated to a purely biblical literary existence by skeptics, and the numerous other sites now confirmed by sound, meticulous archaeology to be precisely where the Bible put them. Dr. Yigael Yadin, who asserts that he still approaches a dig with a spade in one hand and a Bible in the other, declares that "archaeology has increased my belief that basically the historical parts of the Bible are true. . . . I think archaeology has actually given me, if you ask me subjectively, a greater respect for the Bible."[20] Yadin's position is shared by many who have come to appreciate the inestimable historical value of the Bible, while repudiating a literal exegesis of biblical lore. Negative proofs are no proofs at all, the protagonists of the "Conquest Model" insist, but are merely gaps in the archaeological record.

Egyptian records provide ample documentation that the transition period from the Late Bronze and Early Iron Ages was indeed an era of growing proletarian unrest. Flights of slaves, convicts, and paid laborers who were required to work the farms, quarries and constructions were common. Typical of the complaints by officials of the period was one written during the reign of Merenptah: "Of the cultivators of the estate of Pharaoh which is under the authority of my lord, two have fled from the stable-master Neferhotpe as he beat them. Now look!" the official complains. "The fields are now abandoned and there is no-one there to till them."[21]

The hordes of foreigners in the Egyptian work force included a significant proportion of Semitic-speaking peoples. "Rameses IV used eight hundred 'A$_u$piru or H$_u$abiru on one of his quarrying enterprises. In all there must have been tens of thousands of foreign workers in bondage in the army, on government public works, in the temple workshops, and on the estates of the pharaoh and his nobles."²² No less than 2,607 "Syrians [sic] and Negroes of his majesty's capturing" were working on the estate of the Temple of Amon, another 2,093 on the estate of Re, and 205 more on the estate of Ptah during the reign of Rameses III (1182–1152 B.C.E.)."²³ The picture of working conditions in Egyptian records is fully consistent with those presented in the Bible. The intolerable conditions of the slaves and indentured workers reached a climax in the twenty-ninth year of the reign of Rameses III, a year in which hunger marches and the earliest historically recorded "general strikes" erupted, work stoppages in which all the artisans took part, ostensibly because they had not received their proper rations. Massive strikes occurred on three occasions under Rameses III, twice under Rameses IX (c. 1126–1108 B.C.E.), and once again about 1106 B.C.E. under Rameses X.²⁴ The socioeconomic background for a mass exodus is thus well explicated by Egyptian documentation, albeit the biblical Exodus is not specifically detailed in available Egyptian records.

Unrest was as endemic to the rest of the Near East in the Late Bronze and Early Iron Ages as it was in Egypt. It was a period in which drought afflicted the entire region; stories of famine permeate Assyrian and Babylonian records for a period of over a century. The great Mesopotamian power, Assyria, and its burgeoning rival, Babylonia, were seriously affected by inner turmoil and external aggression during the extended period of climatic crisis. The Near Eastern century of decline began in the reign of the Assyrian monarch, Tukulti-Ninurta I (c. 1244–1208 B.C.E.), and the degeneration continued without respite. The growing weakness of the central powers was exploited by the Elamites, Aramaeans, and other smaller tribes, and the raids and incursions of the Sea Peoples aggravated the general economic decline of the period.

Of particular note during this period was the activity of bands of stateless people, the H$_u$abiru (also written in Egyptian texts as 'A$_u$piru). These people, when they were not roving around the region or settled down as autonomous communities in the interstices of the city-states, were employed by all the regimes, be they Egyptian, Assyrian, or Babylonian, largely as skilled artisans. One remarkable fact emerges from the records of the independence and resilience of the ubiquitous H$_u$abiru as well as from the records of the strikes and desertions of Egyptian artisans: they were able to carry on in spite of the radical forms in which they asserted their rights and of their conspicuous disdain for military authority, as both attitudes are reflected in the very inscriptions of their overlords. The lesson to be learned is that they were skilled artisans whose services were so essential and whose skills were so unique that they were, as often as not, able to prevail despite their independent stance.

The stage upon which the appearance of the Israelite settlements took place must thus be set against the backdrop of climatic change, of incursions of smaller tribes from sea and land, of the debilitation of the great powers, and of widespread unrest. Most significantly it must be placed within an environment of resistance to exploitation and the emergence of an antiestablishment attitude on the part of a technologically advanced group, a conglomeration of people whose skills engendered a new egalitarian outlook. They learned that they could not only endure without God-kings but were better off without them. *The local gods who served the kings were useless to the stateless; their God was as universal as their skills and both their God and their skills were with them wherever they went.*

READING THE EVIDENCE—OR LACK OF IT

Although the circumstances of the emergence of an Israelite entity are clear, the mechanism by which it came about is complicated. The biblical version of the history of Israelite settlement came under serious attack when an outstanding pioneer of scientific archaeology, Dame Kathleen Kenyon, digging in the ruins of Jericho, found a civilization that dated back ten thousand years, but no evidence of Joshua's destruction of the walls of Jericho. Kenyon found that Jericho had indeed suffered seventeen catastrophic destructions between 3000 B.C.E. and 2000 B.C.E., but that no substantial new walls were constructed after Jericho's walls were destroyed by the so-called Hyksos after they had been expelled from Egypt c. 1570 B.C.E., or by the Egyptians thereafter. Kenyon concluded that no substantial occupation of the site took place after 1300 B.C.E., and that there were no walls to blow down at the presumed time of Joshua's assault.

Kenyon's conclusions were based entirely on what was not found at Jericho rather than on what was found. Her otherwise well-ordered excavation was confined to a very limited area, a poor quarter of the city where the lack of expensive ware that led to her conclusions could not in any event be expected to exist. "Dating habitation levels on the *absence* of exotic imported wares—which were found primarily in tombs in large urban centers," noted Bryant Wood, "is methodologically unsound, and indeed, unacceptable."[25] He also pointed out the untenability of the theory that the Hyksos, the Semitic patriarchal chieftains of the communities of Lower Egypt and Canaan, would destroy the cities in which they were seeking refuge in their flight from the Egyptians, and, in any event, no textual evidence exists that the Egyptians went beyond southwest Canaan in pursuit of the vanquished Semitic chieftains. Furthermore, it was suggested with good reason that Jericho was destroyed about 1400 B.C.E. rather than in 1570 B.C.E., a date that would shift forward the chronology of many events by the difference between the two dates.

The issue was not resolved by the shift in dating because the date of the Jericho destruction (at least according to archaeological evidence so far uncovered) still does not conform to that of the biblical Israelite incursion unless that date is also brought back to 1400 B.C.E., a solution offered by some scholars. Several other cities cited biblically to have been destroyed by the Israelites also appear to have been already in ruins at the time of the Israelite conquest or not to have suffered destruction at all. This was especially true of the city of Ai, the first city said to have been conquered by Joshua in the hill country. Joshua is reported to have reduced Ai to rubble and burned the ruined remnants to a crisp, but the city, a small fortified town flourishing from the thirty-third to the twenty-fourth century B.C.E., had evidently lain unoccupied for more than a millennium before Joshua's purported arrival, and was only occupied by the Israelites in a later period.[26] By shifting the date of the Exodus back by some two hundred years the discrepancy would be conveniently erased in some such cases, but this expedient solution creates other chronological incongruities. To account for the appearance of an unprecedented Israelite entity, the hundreds of villages crowning the Canaanite hills with a new, distinct, and common culture, they were proposed to have come about not as a climactic event but as the synthetic result of infiltrations into Canaan by disparate groups over a period of hundreds of years, with some of the groups coming from Egypt.[27]

A new veil was cast over the ethnogenesis of the Israelite culture by promulgators of what is termed the "New Archaeology," whose propounders suggest that archaeology should be based upon (some hard-liners insist that it should restrict itself to) facts produced by such technologies as neutron activation analysis, lead isotope analysis, magnetronomy, remote sensing, thermoluminescence, paleozoology, paleobotany, ethno-archaeology, and so on. This cramped approach did not merely counterpose the potential of both material and literary sources as evidence but fostered a refusal to accept biblical lore even as a point of departure in the absence of material evidence. It ignored the scientific premise that holds that every theory (even one based on biblical lore) is equally valid so long as no established fact proves it otherwise. The question arises: How are we to approach the study of other cultures and civilizations that are known to us only from literature? Must it be assumed a priori from the lack of artifactual data that such entities never existed and thus cease efforts to find them? The judgments of the orthodox (the term is used advisedly) artifactual centrists are often based on the delusive assumption that raw archaeological information available at any time is both pervasive and infallible.

The fact that negative conclusions so derived are as often founded on an absence of evidence as they are drawn from material data led Baruch Halpern to aptly term the intractable stance of the purists as "negative fundamentalism."[28] The conclusions of the negativists, ironically, are being toppled time and time again by factual revelations; retreats and revisions are continually forced by unanticipated discoveries that generally reinforce biblical historicity and rarely cast doubt on its verity.

A good case in point concerns the Edomites, whose existence was known only from the Bible little more than seventy years ago. "How can it be," typically began the rhetorical queries of the skeptics, "that not a trace can be found of a people saturating biblical history as the enemy of the Israelites, a people dealt with from the days of the Exodus when they refused passage to the hordes of escaping Israelites, a people with whom Saul and David fought, who rebelled and established their own kingdom and were reconquered by the Israelite king Amaziah, and who once again freed themselves and flourished until the Babylonian devastations brought both kingdoms to an end, a people upon whom the lamenting prophets Obadiah, Isaiah, Joel, Amos, and Malachi continued to vent their wrath and contumely? How can it be that no trace of the Edomites exists?"

The American rabbi-archaeologist Nelson Glueck, while serving as a secret service (OSS) agent of the United States in his surveys east of the Jordan in the 1930s, found pottery fragments and other evidence confirming that Edomite tribes had indeed dwelt in the Negev Desert. The material evidence was soon supplemented by the translation of an Egyptian papyrus in which not only were the Edomites featured, but their identification with the nomadic tribes known to the Egyptians as the Shasu was fixed. In the document, an Egyptian official reports that "[we] have finished letting the Shasu tribes of Edom pass the fortress (of) Mer-ne-Ptah . . .)."[29]

New evidence soon flowed in from the opposite pole of the ancient Near-Eastern world; victory inscriptions by Assyrian rulers Adad-Nirari (810–783 B.C.E.) and Tiglath-Pileser III (744–727 B.C.E.) were translated and it was found that they both boastfully listed Edom in their roster of conquests, as did Sargon II, who cited Edom as among the states against which he fought in his campaign of 712 B.C.E. in the region. Sennacherib recorded the tribute paid by the Edomite king Aiaramu, and another king of Edom was cited as rendering financial assistance to the erection of Esarhadon's royal palace in Eshnunna.

These and a number of other Assyrian documentations affirming Edomite existence were incontestably reinforced by the recovery by Yohanan Aharoni of Hebrew letters from the ruins of the fortress of Arad that relate to its imminent destruction in 595 B.C.E. The Judahite commander of Arad "is ordered to send soldiers to reinforce the garrison at Ramat Negeb in the eastern Negev, because an attack by the Edomites is anticipated–'Lest the Edomites come.'"[30] A flood of new evidence, material and documentary, poured in from all points of the Near East as an expansion of archaeological research took place following the formation of the state of Israel. Important among these was an excavation of what was apparently the Edomite city of Bozrah (mentioned several times in the Bible as the capital of Edom) by Dr. Crystal Bennet of the British School of Archaeology, and a substantial Edomite inscription recovered from Tel el-Kaheleifeh by Professor Joseph Naveh of the Hebrew University of Jerusalem.[31]

In 1984, a team of archaeologists under Itzhaq Beit-Arieh, after surveying the area since 1979, began excavation of Horvat Qitmit, the ruins of Qitmit, located in the heart of the Judahite settlement of the eastern Negev. The site provided the evidence of the Edomite conquest of this territory about the time of the fall of Judah in 586 B.C.E., or a few years later.[32] It turned out to be an Edomite cult center from which a wealth of clay figurines and fragments were recuperated. Two buildings and the remnants of other structures were found; they contained a platform, basin, and an altar for the performance of cultic rites and thousands of pottery fragments of a distinct type. Some of the vessels took an anthropomorphic form, familiar from similar ones found at contemporaneous sites such as at Gezer and Beth-Shemesh. Another familiar motif employed by the Edomites was that of pomegranates, which decorated several pottery chalices. The widespread use of the pomegranate in the Near East was probably related to the fact that it was a fruit pregnant with seeds and was patently a suitable symbol of fecundity, common to all Near-Eastern cultures. Dr. Beit-Arieh concludes that Qitmit "attests to the continued struggle between Judah and Edom since the peoples emerged as nations, a struggle amply reflected in the Bible."[33]

The doubts drawn by Kenyon concerning events, or rather, concerning the lack of evidence of events attested to in the Bible at Jericho and elsewhere, eventually came under criticism. Traces of mud-brick walls that Kenyon had indeed found had been eroded away almost completely together with the evidence of their destruction. A careful examination of the pottery from Kenyon's excavation convinced Bryant Wood, of Associates for Biblical Research, that not only were the walls found by Kenyon to be redated to 1400 B.C.E., but that they were found to stand at a considerable height. "Wood believes that it was this small settlement within the walls of the earlier major city that was the subject of the biblical account of Jericho's destruction."[34]

Just as historians have been prone to relegate the story of humankind to wars, conquests, and the genealogy and foibles of rulers, archaeologists have suffered egregiously from what I would term a "Disaster Syndrome." Theories constructed by archaeologists tend to be based on a record of disasters and on what has survived between disasters; little room is left for interpolating lacunae in the archaeological record. The limited dimensions of these arbitrary constructions often lead to a lack of perspective, leading in turn to errors and misinterpretations that multiply by repetition. Thus, for example, archaeologists rarely consider that the installation of a new population at a particular site does not necessarily mean the destruction of the old site and the obliteration of its population, nor the introduction of a new type of products, even if the occupation was brought about by conquest. A conquering group might well, and probably often did, take over a city without damaging a single element of its physical plant and proceed to dwell in it without making changes or additions that deviate from the existing norms. The artisans among the previous inhabitants may well have melded into the new community and have continued to produce ware in the style to which they were accustomed, even to apprentice the newcomers into that style. The presence of such artifacts, the lack of a layer of ashes or lesser evidence of destruction, the dearth of distinctively new architecture, and the continuation of old cultural modalities is inevitably interpreted as stratigraphic proof that no occupation or conquest had taken place. Scholarly literature is saturated with such negative "proofs."

Positive proofs can be as misleading as negative ones. Architecture and pottery provide much of the physical data that archaeologists employ to construct historical scenarios. This is a natural consequence of the durability of the inherent materials, but the blind application of these measures has led to the adoption of some sacred morphological shibboleths that can distort rather than clarify the record. A typical example is the inordinate use of styles of pottery for dating, a use that otherwise has a thoroughly sound basis and, when used cautiously, has inestimable value and validity. Mycenaean ware, for example, has been precisely dated by its association with objects bearing pharaonic cartouches or other objects of definitive dates. Such ware was presumably imported into Canaan until the denouement of the Mycenaean civilization about 1180 B.C.E. The assumption that the subdivisions of the styles of pottery classified as Mycenaean IIIA, B, and C were necessarily produced by artisans at consecutive times, however, can be questioned. The families of artisans who produced the Mycenaean III ware that was exported to Canaan may have been following some precedent tradition whose source has not yet been, or may never be, discovered, but whose products turned up in a Canaanite context. There may have been different populations of artisans producing similar ware at overlapping times and places. The consecutive appearance of the styles may have been due to changes in national and international marketing as much as to a progression in style. Nor does it necessarily follow that the Mycenaean artisans producing such ware, or their descendants, disappeared with the demise of Mycenaean civilization, or that artisans of other cultures who had learned from or duplicated the work of Mycenaean craftsmen did not continue the style after the disappearance of the Mycenaeans as a national entity.

The mobility of the artisans, the transference of techniques, the continuity of a family tradition both at home and in an alien environment over many generations, and changes in marketing are social considerations that have undoubtedly affected the chronology of the appearance of categories of durable goods. Thus it can be postulated that some Mycenaean IIIC pottery at one site may well predate some Mycenaean IIIA pottery at another site owing to one or a combination of such circumstances. It can also be reasonably assumed that some communities did not care for Mycenaean ware, preferring the product of its own artisans or some other type of pottery or that they simply could not afford the costly, imported Myceneaen ware. The presence or absence of such artifacts, however valuable as evidence, has sometimes been inordinately employed on occasions as chronological and cultural proof that may possibly give rise to historiographical misconstructions.

Recently applied analytical technologies, such as neutron activation and lead-isotope analyses, have made the identification of the exact provenance of elements possible, not only to a general area but even to a particular site or mine. As a result of the application of these new tools a number of sacred chronological assumptions have already fallen by the wayside, and undoubtedly many more will follow.

Dr. Yadin took issue with Kenyon's conclusions that Joshua's campaign was fabulous and unsupported by the facts. Yadin noted that the time was ripe for sociological change inasmuch as the power structure of Canaan of the thirteenth century B.C.E. was rendered economically feeble and militarily ineffectual under Egyptian dominance. The turmoil resulting from the incursions of the Sea Peoples and of neighboring powers seeking to displace Egyptian control over the strategic routes through Canaan left the Canaanites open to conquest by the relatively weak Israelite forces on the move through the area.[35] The lack of evidence of Jericho's destruction at a suitable time as cited by Kenyon was countered by the substantial evidence of conquest produced by Yadin in his excavations at Hazor.

The city of Hazor was central to the story of Joshua's conquest of Canaan. It was an ancient and mighty Canaanite city of forty thousand inhabitants, covering an area of almost two hundred acres. Its king, Jabin, was head of the Canaanite league and Joshua's victory over the forces of that coalition was considered critical to his campaign. "And all of the cities of those kings, and all the kings of them, did Joshua take," writes the biblical chronicler, "but as for the cities that stood still in their strength, Israel burned none of them, save Hazor only; that did Joshua burn."[36] Thus not merely the destruction, but the razing by fire of Hazor figures importantly in the archaeological exegesis of the times. Hazor was a vital commercial and administrative center that also figures prominently in extra-biblical literature. One of the Amarna tablets, for example, relates the activities of the $H_u$abiru, groups of independent-minded artisans and soldiers who exasperated authorities for the better part of a millennium and, as we shall see in the following chapter, were said to have been the Hebrews or to have been associated with them. The letter is revelatory of the importance of those stateless bands in the politics of the times prior to the Israelite monarchical period. One letter, for example, was written by the king of Tyre, Abi-Milki, to the pharaoh. The letter begins with the startling complaint that "the King of Hazor left his city and joined the $H_u$abiru." The city was then under the supervision of the Egyptians, and the letter concludes with a plaint and a dire prediction: "Let the King [Pharaoh] know that they [the $H_u$abiru] are hostile to the supervisor. The King's land is falling into the hands of the $H_u$abiru. Let the King ask the High Commissioner, who is familiar with Canaan."[37]

The same error of dating as was committed by Kenyon, based on an absence of evidence, had been committed at Hazor by John Gerstang, Director of the Antiquities Department of the British Mandatory Administration of Palestine, although in his case the error pertained specifically to the date of destruction rather than to both the date and the identification of the perpetrators. Gerstang correctly confirmed Tell el-Qedah to be Hazor and was the first to conduct excavations there in 1928. Gerstang based his conclusion that the last Canaanite settlement had undergone destruction by Joshua about 1400 B.C.E. on an absence of Mycanaean III pottery in the strata that ended in such destruction, a view that supported the contention that the date of the Exodus should be shifted backward by two hundred years. Mycanaean pottery of that type was commonly employed by archaeologists for dating sites and associated materials because its presence was ubiquitous throughout Canaan in the period between 1400 and

1200 B.C.E.; its absence was taken, perforce, as a negative proof of a prior date for the overlying strata. "The complete absence of Mykanean specimens, as at Jericho," wrote Gerstang, "suggests a date of destruction about 1400 B.C. . . ."[38]

Yadin reinstituted excavations at Hazor in 1955. The importance assigned to Hazor can be judged by the fact that, during the four seasons in which the main work was accomplished, 220 laborers were employed, supervised by a team of some forty-five archaeologists, architects, pottery-restorers, photographers, draftsmen, and senior students. "We can now understand the reasoning behind Gerstang's dating. Having found no Mycenaean pottery, he legitimately came to the conclusion that the occupation of the enclosure came to an end *prior* to the appearance of the Mycenaean pottery in the area, that is, roughly before 1400 B.C.E.," wrote Yadin, compassionately, and then adds, "One can readily imagine our excitement, therefore, when we uncovered an abundance of Mycenaean pottery on the floor of the topmost strata!"

Massive evidence unearthed from the ashes of that mighty Canaanite city supported the biblical record in which Joshua is said to have defeated the Canaanite league, captured the strategic site, smote its king, and burned the city. Yadin emphasized that "our very extensive excavations clearly demonstrate that a large Canaanite city was suddenly destroyed and set on fire at the end of the 13th century . . . no later than about 1230 B.C." A new settlement was found "on the thick debris of the ground of the destroyed Canaanite city."[39] "This evidence was substantiated in all the other areas of the lower city," wrote Yadin, "and is, indeed, among the most important and decisive archaeological testimonies ever uncovered in excavations concerning the date of conquest by Joshua, and, indirectly, of the Exodus itself."[40]

While the date 1230 B.C.E. has come under question due to the redating of Mycenaean IIIB ware[41] to a few decades later, the principle as stated by Yadin remains intact.

CONCLUSION

The diverse paths taken by archaeologists to determine the origins of the Israelites must converge in the inevitable acknowledgement of the existence of a cohesive and Israelite culture at the end of the thirteenth century B.C.E. Where the Israelites came from and how the settlements were created is left to the reader to choose from among the many models proposed for their appearance. Consideration might be given to the hypothesis that the story of the Exodus, although treated biblically as a single climactic event, actually represents a fusion of tribal memories of a series of emigrations from Egypt, beginning with a massive one that must have been activated by the well-documented conquest of Lower Egypt by the Theban Baron Ahmose I, and continuing with emigrations which may well have taken place under various Eighteenth- and Nineteenth-Dynasty pharaohs. Such a hypothesis has hardly been given due respect, but it is one that would resolve all of the archaeological-biblical anomalies, whereupon attention dissolves into the fundamental questions of who the Israelites were and what were their cultural and technological attributes.

The relevance of that background to this study is simply that out of it emerged the Israelites, a people who revitalized technological progress in a troubled period and spurred the advent of the Iron Age.

9

A Question of Identity

Hebrews, H$_u$abiru, and Israelites

The Hebrews wandered through the desert for forty years. So is it written.

It is written that the desert experience brought the wandering Hebrews close to their Creator; that the great band of bedraggled stragglers shuffled through the sands of the Sinai desert and survived through the miracles wrought by Him; that they learned His universal laws through the great prophet who led them through the wilderness. It is written that a covenant was entered into between the people and their Creator; that upon acceptance of His divine ordinances, the wanderers were chosen to bear the burden of delivering that Law to a wicked world of iniquity and idolatry; that they were rewarded for assuming that heavy burden by the promise of a land to dwell in from which they would wander no more.

THE BIBLICAL RECORD

The sojourn in the desert is the only period in all of the biblical account in which the Hebrews are depicted as desert dwellers, a blink in time out of some four thousand years of recorded tribal, cultural, and national existence. Even so, it is written that the Hebrews did not choose the desert as a way of life but were constrained by the force of circumstance to suffer through the period; that they quickly wearied of wandering and yearned for a sedentary life in a land of their own. It is clear that, unlike those who look to the desert as their home, they did not separate into small family units and disperse, as desert life demands, but remained a multitude that survived in mass to congeal into a nation.

After one year, one month, and one day in the wilderness of the Sinai, "Moses chose able men out of all Israel, and made them the heads over the people, rulers of thousands, rulers of hundreds, rulers of fifties, and rulers of tens."[1] They were organized into a national entity composed of twelve congregations, autonomous

163

constituencies that were administered by "the renowned of the congregation, princes of the tribes of their fathers, heads of thousands in Israel."[2]

Who were the Israelites? Who were the Hebrews?

There are no simple answers to these simple questions; the contradictory solutions offered by scholars as to the origin and identification of what were ostensibly one and the same people have done more to confuse than to clarify. "Israel" is commonly assumed to be simply a reference to the children of Jacob and their descendants, inasmuch as God, after rhetorically inquiring of Jacob, "What is thy name?" informs him that "Thy name shall be called no more Jacob, but Israel: for as a prince has thou power with God and with men, and hast prevailed."[3]

Questions immediately arise: Why is the name Israel equated with princehood, and were there princes or a class of princes who previously bore that name? The Bible continues to refer to Jacob by his original name even after his return from Aram-Naharaim with his wife and children, on which occasion God reappears to repeat "Thy name shall not be called any more Jacob, but Israel shall be thy name."[4] A peculiar dichotomy is then set up, in which the children of Israel are sometimes clearly Jacob's descendants, and at other times distinctly two different groups. In three successive perplexing paragraphs it is written that after Rachel died, "Jacob set a pillar upon her grave. . . . And Israel journeyed, and spread his tent beyond the tower of Edar. And it came to pass, when Israel dwelt in that land, that Reuben [Jacob's son] went and lay with Bilhah, his father's concubine: And Israel heard it. Now the sons of Jacob were twelve. . . . "[5] The Bible then proceeds with a genealogy of Jacob's children, not only the twelve sons of Jacob's wives Leah, Rachel, Bilhah, and Zilpah, sons who generated the "tribes of Israel," but also those of his brother Esau, who became Edomites, Amalekites, Horites and so on. With all this laid out in considerable detail we are forthwith informed that "Jacob dwelt in the land wherein his father was a stranger, in the land of Canaan."[6] Jacob [Israel?] thus is designated the first Canaanite of the lineage. The house of Jacob and the children of Israel are referred to thereafter almost consistently as parallel but separate entities linked by "and," "also," "neither," and various other connectives. For example:

> [God instructs Moses] "Thus shalt thou say to the house of Jacob, and tell the children of Israel." [Exodus 19:3]
>
> Surely there is no enchantment in Jacob, neither is there any divination in Israel; in due time it is said unto Jacob and unto Israel, what God hath wrought. [Num. 23:23]
>
> Hear ye this, O house of Jacob, which are called by the name of Israel. . . . Hearken unto me, O Jacob and Israel. . . . [Isaiah 48:1, 12]
>
> For the Lord will have mercy upon Jacob, and will yet choose Israel, and set them in their own land; and the strangers shall be joined with them, and they shall cleave to the house of Jacob. [Isaiah 14:1][7]

Jacob's sons, Judah and Joseph, were also referred to apart from Israel, as was the land of Judah distinguished from that of Israel:

[Addressing the relationship with the Tyreans]: Judah, and the land of Israel, they were thy merchants. [Ezekiel 27:17]

For Judah, and for the children of Israel, his companions . . . [Ezekiel 37:16]

Thus saith the Lord God; Behold, I will take the stick of Joseph, which is in the hands of Ephraim, and the tribe of Israel his fellows, and will put them with him, even with the stick of Judah, and make them one stick, and they shall be one in my land. [Ezekiel 37:19]

The consistency of the use of parallel entries argues against simple redundancy. It is only in the first Book of Chronicles that Israel becomes regularly substituted for the name Jacob, and the Israelites become a nation without an anomalous identity. Israel does not figure as a national entity outside of the Bible until the ninth century B.C.E. when it was inscribed on a stela authored by Mesha, king of Moab, and thereafter appears in Assyrian annals.

There is an extrabiblical document that identifies a people called Israel who dwelt in Canaan before the Exodus, an inscription on a stela found in Thebes by Sir Flinders Petrie in 1886. The stela was erected by the Pharaoh Merenptah in the fifth year of his reign (1212–1202 B.C.E.), and it refers to Israel as a people or a tribe. The coda of the inscription recounts, with the customary pharaonic hyperbole, the conquest of a number of nations that were subjected to Merenptah's ravaging campaign into Canaan. Israel is included in the list:

The Princes are prostrate, saying "Mercy!"
    Not one raises his head among the Nine Bows.
Desolation is for Tehenu; Hatti is pacified;
    Plundered is the Canaan with every evil;
Carried off is Ashkelon; seized upon is Gezer;
    Yanoum is made as that which does not exist;
Israel is laid waste, his seed is not;
    Hurru is become a widow for Egypt!
All lands together they are pacified
    Everyone who was restless, he has been bound
by the King of Upper and Lower Egypt.[8]

The discovery of the stela led some scholars to jump to the conclusion that Merenptah was the pharaoh of the Exodus. This theory was peremptorily put to rest when Merenptah's mummified body was unearthed near Deir el-Bahri on the west bank of the Nile, for the pharaoh clearly could not have been the one drowned in the Red Sea. The existence of a people or a nation known as Israel at the end of the thirteenth century B.C.E. was, however, rendered incontrovertible by the reference; Merenptah had ironically perpetuated the name of the people he had intended to exterminate.

The fact that the Merenptah stela was unique in its identification of pre-Exodus Israelites was long the only archaeological crack in the bulwark of the thesis that denied the biblical account altogether; it would seem that at the very least the existence of a people called Israel could no longer be questioned. But the testimony of a pharaoh of the biblical period was nevertheless dismissed by scholars of the antibiblical-bias school as a "literary allusion with little basis in fact, a kind of poetic hyperbole."[9] John A. Wilson, whose translation of the text appears above, prefaces it by stating that "the text is not historical in the same sense as the other two records of that victory, but is a poetic eulogy of a universally victorious pharaoh."[10] Poetic or not, the point that was being scorned by the intransigent hardliners is that a people called Israel were in fact entered upon the record that Merenptah left to posterity.

The stance of the negativists was confounded by a new discovery that filled another portion of the historical lacuna. In the winter of 1976-77 Frank J. Yurko was in Luxor as a member of the University of Chicago's epigraphic survey. He paid particular attention to a set of battle scenes on a wall 30 feet high and 158 feet long adjoining the great hypostyle hall of the Karnak temple.

Flanking the famous text of the Kadesh treaty between Rameses II (1279-1212 B.C.E.) and the Hittite King Hattusilis III are ten elaborately carved scenes, four of which are set out in two vertical registers on each side of the famous treaty, the other six stretching out farther to the right. There were successive usurpations of the scenes by the erasure and replacement of the cartouches and of the titular inscriptions that accompany them, a common practice in ancient Egypt. The cartouche and titles of Sety II (1199-1193 B.C.E.) appear on the surface as the author of the scenes, but it was clear that Sety had erased and replaced the name of a precedent pharaoh, and it was long assumed that the actual author was none other than Rameses II.

Yurko, perched precariously atop a ladder, subjected the cartouches to careful scrutiny with a mirror, which, by raking the light across the inscriptions, lengthened the shadows and made possible the reading of the underlying texts. To Yurko's astonishment he found that there were two consecutive usurpations of the scenes. Underlying the cartouche and titular texts of Sety II was that of Amenmesse (1202-1199 B.C.E.), and underlying the Amenmesse scripts was not that of the expected Rameses II, but that of Merenptah!

Corroborative evidence was found in the form of a stray block that had been removed from the wall, and that matched

> the indisputably identified visages of Merenptah from his tomb in the Valley of the Kings. . . . What all this demonstrated was that the reliefs represent the military exploits of Merenptah rather than those of Rameses II. As we will see, this makes a great difference. It will, among other things, allow us to identify the oldest pictures of Israelites ever discovered, engraved more than 3,200 years ago, at the very dawn of their emergence as a people.[11]

The discovery had many ramifications. The layout closely followed the sequence of events of the Merenptah stela text: the first scene was identified with the hieroglyph for Ashkelon and it was depicted as a fortified town, as were two others representing Gezer and Yano'am. Egyptian hieroglyphic determinatives are very specific in their connotations and the sculpted scenes were equally specific. In the Merenptah stele the determinatives for these three references were those of a city-state whereas the name of Israel was written with a determinative reserved for a people, that is, for the occupants of a region rather than of a particular city.

Bowing to the evidence of the literary determinatives, some scholars were nevertheless not to be easily dissuaded. "The argument is good," notes Wilson, "but not conclusive because of the notorious carelessness of the Late-Egyptian scribes and several blunders of writing in this stela." Other scholars, ostensibly supportive of the existence of an Israelite entity but uncertain of their ground, present a choice of both conclusions. Thus G. W. Ahlström and D. Edelman of the University of Chicago begin by stating that "the use of a determinative for people instead of land may be insignificant, resulting from the author's loose application of determinatives," but go on to add that "on the other hand, it could be an accurate record of Israel's primary association with the hill country's population, which has been used here to represent its geographical sense as well, paralleling the term Canaan."[12]

The scene mandated by Merenptah to illustrate his conquests lends considerable weight to the identification of the Israelites with the Canaanites and sharply differentiates them from the nomadic desert peoples. In sharp contrast to the setting of the other three scenes, the pharaoh is depicted in the "Israelite" scene battling with an enemy in open country with low hills. The Israelites, depicted as being dressed in the same distinctive ankle-length cloaks as the Canaanites of the three embattled cities, are indubitably being portrayed as well-organized inhabitants of the area and are identified as another group of Canaanites.

The cloaks are of the same type as those worn by the Asiatic merchants whose caravan decorates the tomb of the Egyptian nomarch Knumhotpe of the nineteenth century B.C.E., six hundred years earlier! They are also similar to the ankle-length robes worn by Israelites six hundred years later on a depiction by the Assyrian King Sennacherib of the siege and capture of Lachish, which was the earliest known portrait of Israelites until Yurko's discovery at Karnak.

Elsewhere in the last of the Karnak scenes, a file of the people known as the Shasu are shown being led away as prisoners. The Shasu were a pastoral people, shepherds who frequented the periphery of the Sinai desert, wandered about the hills of Canaan, and migrated seasonally into the Delta. They are cited in a number of Papyri as foes of the Egyptians. They are also cited by many scholars as being identified with the Hebrews or their progenitors. The Shasu do not appear in any of the battle scenes, and they are shown wearing short kilts and turban-like headdresses, an attire distinctly different from that of the Israelites and other Canaanites. The distinction between the peoples in Merenptah's 150-foot-long rendering of his adventures puts another well-worn shibboleth to rest. The Israelites were by no means to be identified with the nomadic desert dwellers.

Not only are the Israelites depicted in the Merenptah scene as an organized force, but they are shown deploying a chariot. The chariot sports six-spoked wheels, the most advanced form of the vehicle ever made. The corroboration of the historicity of the Bible in attributing such wheeled, warrior vehicles to the Canaanites is thus underscored by the specifics of the Merenptah wall. It should be recalled in this context that until the so-called Second Intermediate period, during which Egypt and Canaan were administrated by Semitic chieftains, the wheel, chariot, and the horses to pull them were all unknown in Egypt. The Exodus of the enslaved descendants of Jacob, which has been presumed to have taken place under Rameses II, may well have led them to rejoin the Israelites who had not followed Joseph into Egypt, or who may not even have been of the house of Jacob but were a cohesive Canaanite entity—other Israelites who continued to inhabit their homeland while Jacob and family went to Egypt to enjoy Joseph's beneficence. The application of the name "Israel" to Jacob symbolizes the identification of Jacob and his host with that Canaanite people, some or all of whom can be assumed to have been descendants of Abraham. Thus the "House of Jacob," that is, those who did migrate into Egypt, are consistently distinguished from those who stayed behind, a people with whom Jacob's descendants (and others included in the Exodus) integrated upon their return. The distinction is dropped after the nation of Israel is formed; after the twelve sons (and the daughters) of the house of Jacob intermarry with other Israelites, and the families fuse into one overall national entity.

The story of Moses' sojourn in Midianite territory and his marriage with a Midianite woman illustrates the tranquil relationships of Egyptian fugitives with various Canaanites before the population of Israelites swelled with the influx of an enormous group of refugees. The demographic change brought about a pressure on the land; the resultant Israelite-Midianite conflict was resolved in favor of the Israelites because, although they are identified in the Karnak scenes and not as a city-state but as a people, they were nevertheless equipped with the chariots and weapons that provided the means for the conquest of the Midianites.

"HEBREW"

What has all this to do with the "Hebrews"? The circumstances of the origin and identity of the Hebrews are as enigmatic as are those of the Israelites. The Bible employs the label "Hebrew" in a way that casts a shadow on the character of the people referred to and leaves us in the dark as to exactly who they were. We are left without a factual foundation that would validate the Hebrews as an ethnically distinct people or properly explain their association with the Israelites. The two appellations, Hebrew and Israelite, appear at times to be employed interchangeably, and yet at other times a sharp distinction is drawn between the two groups. The murky ethnogenesis of both groups is left unresolved by the biblical contexts in which they appear.

There are some tenuous linguistic connections. The Hebrews are sometimes assumed to have been the descendants of the biblical Eber (Genesis 10:21), a biblical ancestor of Abraham, but then the Arabs must also be covered by the

ıl and Jonathan put up a resistance to the Philistines, the Hebrews who were
th the Philistines left the Philistine camp to join the Israelites, and when other
aelites hidden out on Mount Ephraim heard that the Philistines were being
ıted, they came out of hiding; the Israelites and Hebrews thereafter joined forces
the Battle of Michmash. They are cited in the narration as two distinctly differ-
t groups.

The rationale for an otherwise apparently dichotomous treatment of terms may
found by comparing the biblical "Hebrews" with the H$_u$abiru (also written as
piru), a group that appears contemporaneously with the biblical "Hebrews"
texts from Amarna in Egypt and in Levantine texts as widely dispersed as Byblos
d Nuzi. These documents refer to the H$_u$abiru as bands of people who main-
ned no staunch allegiance to any state, in fact, are consistently depicted as
rcely antiauthoritarian. Most of the references to H$_u$abiru are relegated to the
riod from the sixteenth to the eleventh centuries B.C.E., but they were a distinct
:ment of the Mesopotamian population that extends back to the period of the
ird Ur Dynasty, c. 2150 B.C.E. There are mentions of the SA.GAZ in the Akkadian
cts of that period, a Sumerian appellation that philologists equate with the
mitic word H$_u$abiru, based on the consistent correspondence of the two words
Hittite treaties, Amarna correspondence, Ugaritic literature, and a wide range
other ancient texts.[19] A reference to H$_u$abiru occurs in a Cappadocian context
the first half of the eighteenth century B.C.E. at Kultepe and in a letter written
ım the Akkadian colony of Alishar concerning the rescue by ransom of the
abiru of the palace of Shalah shuwë." The reference confirms the "dependent
ıtus in which we find them throughout their history."[20] The appellation reap-
ars thereafter in texts of Mesopotamia, Egypt, and Canaan up to the period of
e Israelite kings, at which time it curiously disappears from all literature, lead-
z again to the conjecture that the H$_u$abiru had integrated into the new, Judaic
tional entity. The H$_u$abiru are regularly castigated by the rulers of the times as
ıublesome, rebellious migrants who are fiercely independent and consequently
'ficult to control. For the century after the discovery of the name H$_u$abiru in
e Amarna tablets many scholars equated the vexatious outcasts with the
:brews, whereas other scholars insisted that no connection existed between
e two. The resemblance of the pronunciation of H$_u$abiru and ^{c}ibrim, as Hebrew
pronounced in that language, the proximity of the peoples, and the chrono-
zical parallels were considered mere coincidences undeserving of credence.
The question of whether the H$_u$abiru should be equated with the Hebrews
nains a matter of debate. The matter might well be resolved by the proposi-
n that the equation is both true and untrue. A case can be made that while the
ɔlical Hebrews of the early period may have been H$_u$abiru, not all H$_u$abiru were
:brews. Both terms, H$_u$abiru and Hebrew, appear to have begun as basically
ciological rather than tribal designations; the assumption that both terms refer
displaced persons in general and not to any specific ethnic group explains
th the manner in which the H$_u$abiru are referred to in archaeologically recov-
:d texts and in which the Hebrews are alluded to in the Bible. Many of the

Hebrew umbrella, a fact which is patently excluded from other b
ations. The appearance of similar names in Ebla, Mari, and vario
texts is alternately suggested to be an adumbration of the appell
While no firm basis for any of these conjectures exists, one set
ences to such a character is particularly intriguing. It appears t
other than Sargon of Akkad who, upon subjugating Ebla in a p
tion, placed Ebrum on the throne of that mighty city. Ebrum traito
Akkad after Sargon's death, c. 2310 B.C.E., and Akkad remained
Ebla until Sargon's grandson, Naram-Sin, turned the tables by c
and putting it to the torch. The thought that tickles one's fancy i
that the descendants of displaced Ebrum did indeed become the
Hebrews of history.

In any event, the term "Hebrews" can readily be interpreted to
a sociological rather than a tribal appellation; the Hebrews of the
clearly defined as a distinct ethnic group even after they settle
become associated with Israelites. The term appears in Genesis
migrants, or of displaced slaves, servants, or artisans who served
with them wherever they went, as distinguished from citizens c
whose God was specifically attached to and a protector of a part
YHWH is alternatively referred to as the God of the Hebrews and
Israelites.[13]

The early reference to "Abram the Hebrew"[14] relates to the fac
father's house and his native country; he was presumably an Akka
origin as was his father before him and his brother and cousins wh
in Aram-Naharaim. God informs Abram that his "seed shall be
land that is not theirs" for a period of four hundred years, and fi
Abram's descendants as "servants" throughout that period.[15] Th
is thereafter employed demeaningly, as, for example, in its use
wife of Potiphar when she strikes back at Joseph by complainin
brought in an Hebrew unto us to mock us," and reporting to he
"The Hebrew servant, which thou hast brought unto us, came in u
me."[16]

Again, the Pharaoh relates that in his dream appeared "a young
servant to the captain of the guard."[17] Thus Joseph, servant, and
into a single context, with the underlying implication that he is n
a foreigner. In Exodus, the Hebrews remain specifically an alien g
Egypt. The Lord tells Moses that he has come down to deliver t
Israel" not back to their homeland but "unto the place of the Can
Hittites and the Amorites, and the Perizzites, and the Hivites, and t

The fact that the "children of Israel" were the migrants ("Hebre
in Genesis and Exodus seems well established, but after the Isra
Canaan, designated as both "the land of the Canaanites" and tl
Hebrews," other Hebrews appear. Thus the Hebrews who were
tines are distinguished from the Israelites. It is recounted that whe

biblical shifts from "Hebrew" to "Israelite" make sense only if the definition of Hebrew as "migrant" or "alien" (stranger) is taken for granted. The resemblance between the two appellations may well have etymological roots, since "H$_u$abiru" was almost universally applied to migrant or alien peoples, and at least some of the progenitors of the Jews were migrants into Canaan from Transjordan and from Egypt.

The H$_u$abiru were almost always referred to as an underclass, sometimes as enslaved or exploited workers and other times as insurgents who band together and live by brigandry. They were commonly depicted as outcasts and rebels who often attached themselves as artisans or soldiers to various regimes while zealously maintaining their identity and a measure of autonomy. As soldiers they were invariably treated as foreigners who became mercenary adjuncts to a particular army; many references concern problems arising from their immigration. Although they were consistently depicted as a stateless people, the H$_u$abiru were never equated with nomads. Just as the Israelites were pictured as separate and distinct in dress and context from the nomadic Shasu in the Merenptah scene on a Karnak temple wall, so were the H$_u$abiru set apart from nomads in another text from the time of Amenophis II (1436-1413 B.C.E.), in which the H$_u$abiru (Egyptian: 'p.rw) are distinguished from the Shasu, as well as from the Hurrians and another Amoritic group, the Nuh^{u}asse.[21] Texts recovered from an archaeological site near the crown of the Fertile Crescent, Alalakh, also made it abundantly clear that almost all of the H$_u$abiru can be identified as having been of urban origin, a heterogeneous group of divers linguistic origins, sharply contradicting the conception commonly held earlier that they were an ethnically homogeneous group originating from the desert.[22]

The term H$_u$abiru, meaning "migrant," is markedly differentiated from $p\bar{\ }t.eru$, meaning "deserter," a distinction made abundantly clear in various tablets from Mari. In one such document, the subject, an elite soldier who was accused of defection from another city-state, defended himself by claiming that he was no deserter but had migrated (verb: $h_u ba\bar{\ }ru$) four years prior to his registration. Another Mari document cites the case of a Babylonian overseer who was accepted into the Mari army together with his entire band. The overseer's answer to the demand by the Babylonians for his extradition was that he was a migrant (H$_u$abiru), and not subject to extradition.

The H$_u$abiru were similarly differentiated from runaway slaves or indentured workers, for whom the term *munnabtu* applied. Whereas both the deserters and the runaways were regularly prosecuted and extradited (all city-states having a mutual interest in discouraging such defections), the H$_u$abiru were usually regarded as independent people who enjoyed the prerogative of moving about with relative freedom unless they were under contract. It is clear that they often exercised this prerogative in their own interest and not in that of their employers, and therefore were regarded as necessary nuisances. The term H$_u$abiru is employed pejoratively and derisively by the upper-class authors of the texts of all their various employers across the Fertile Crescent region from Egypt to the lower reaches of the Mesopotamian twin rivers. The H$_u$abiru were rarely referred to without a tone of reproach or recrimination in precisely the same contexts as those in which Potiphar's wife referred to Joseph. The fact that they continued to exist and function in spite of having no organized means of defending themselves against the might of the states in whose territory they resided or against the legal power of the employer to whom they were contractually beholden prompts the question, "What factor accounts for their remarkable resilience?"

THE H$_u$ABIRU AS ARTISANS

The frequent references to the H$_u$abiru as artisans offers an oblique clue as to their identity and an explanation of the deference with which they were treated in spite of their brazen effrontery. In the Near East of the second millennium B.C.E. most workers and farmers ("plowmen") were palace dependents whose socio-economic status depended a great deal on the skills they possessed. Scribes, physicians, musicians, diviners, and artisans with specialized skills were scarce and were even able to bargain collectively for favorable conditions of employment. Typical of this quasi-guild type organizational relationship with the upper classes of Mesopotamia were such agreements as were drawn in the city of Eanna between the carpenters, metal engravers, goldsmiths, jewelers, and "all of the craftsmen" with their employers, wherein the artisans agreed to perform their specialized duties and the employers specified their obligations toward the artisans.[23] The texts of Ebla, Mari, Amarna, and Ugarit all make clear that the craftsmen of the city-states form a class of middle status in the social hierarchy. The king or ruler is at the apex of the social pyramid, underneath whom are the noblemen, who wield "considerable power even over against the crown; then there are the landowners, merchants and craftsmen (organized into 'guilds'), manual workers and unskilled laborers, and finally the slaves."[24]

The dearth of specialized craftsmen subjected them often to exchange between the kings of the city-states or to being lent out by the great king of the center city to the petty kings of provincial villages under his hegemony. "The skilled workers who were sent from one court to another were viewed as prestige goods, and their transfers are inserted into the dynamics and formal apparatus of the practice of gift-exchange."[25] One official requested that a mason and a physician be quickly dispatched; another official needed a scribe to conduct a census and to measure fields; still another official pleaded for an irrigation expert knowledgeable in sluices and dams. 226 "pluckers," evidently harvesters or unskilled workers, are requested in yet another letter, to be accompanied by some masons and chariot-builders; chariot-makers are included in an order for chariots; physicians and diviners are commonly requested in urgent pleas for assistance. A revealing letter is one in which a Babylonian sculptor was requested by H$_u$atus^{u}sili of the court of Hatti because he wished "to make some statues to put in my family house." H$_u$atus^{u}sili evidently had a record of detaining borrowed artisans beyond the agreed term. "As soon as he finishes the statues I will send him back," H$_u$atus^{u}sili promises and adds: "Did I not send back the sculptor who formerly came here? . . . Therefore do not refuse a sculptor to me!"[26]

Several factors led to the transformation of craftsmen and merchants into refugees. The turbulence of the mid-second millennium, brought about by ambitious pharaonic aggression and intense interdynastic rivalries, led to a considerable displacement of soldiers and artisans. The rapacious incursions of the Egyptian Warrior Pharaohs disrupted the social fabric of any city-state that did not submit itself to control and tribute. The devastation of a city-state in war resulted in either the capture or enslavement of its valuable personnel by the prevailing force, or their escape and consequent unemployed condition. In the first case the artisan or soldier would be likely to seek to escape; in either case, once free, he would be seeking suitable employment elsewhere. "One of the tangible results of the conflicts between the city-states was the emergence of various kinds of refugees."[27] Alternatively, the relationship between the artisan and an employer did not always work out satisfactorily, and because the artisans possessed skills that provided them with a certain security and ability to seek their fortune elsewhere, defections and migrations of specialists in search of new opportunities were frequent. They organized themselves into cohesive bands during disordered times. This was particularly evident during the eighteenth century B.C.E. in Mesopotamia (the time assigned to the biblical tribe of Terach) and during the fifteenth and fourteenth centuries B.C.E. in Canaan after the defeat and expulsion of the Semitic chieftains, Egypt's most militaristically aggressive period. The pejorative portrayal of the H$_u$abiru in the Mesopotamian and Egyptian texts as unruly outlaws reflects the patently prejudiced point of view of the dominant powers.

The mobility of artisans was defined by J. M. Sasson as a "redistributive" pattern of the times.[28] The movement of skilled workmen was particularly prevalent in the Late Bronze Age, the period in which the Exodus is said to have taken place. Many centralized, palace-controlled corporate societies collapsed during this pivotal time, and shifts into new territorial and tribal "forms of aggregation" took place throughout the Levant.[29] The proliferating, radical social changes of this period are reflected in the Mari tablets, which are replete with documentation of desperate searches in pursuit of runaway artisans (including scribes, physicians, musicians, barbers, cooks, and others). "We are told of how [after capture] they were bound, chained, and carefully watched during their journey back to the place from which they had fled."[30]

It will be recalled that the Amorite and Hurrian metalworkers, and especially the smiths, were traditionally itinerants who hired themselves out for the production of weapons or tools. The industrial requirements of the smiths were quite different from that of the potters, weavers, brewers of beer, and other proletarians whose skills were easily acquired and widely distributed, and whose activity could be confined to an urban environment. The metalworkers, especially the iron smelters, were obliged to work in densely wooded areas because of the vast amount of fuel required for their operations and needed to move their furnaces

Robert Maddin

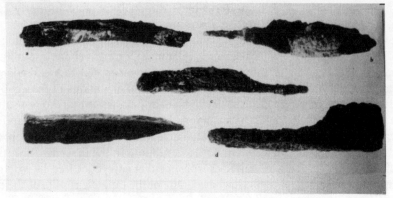

Iron tools recovered from various sites in ancient *Eretz Yisrael*: (a) knife found in a tomb at Tell el-Far'ah (south), (b) Tell se Far'ah Arrowhead, (c) Tell Jemmeh knife (south), (d) Tell Jemmeh hoe, (e) chisel from Al Mina in Aramea (northern "Syria"). (Photograph from the author's collection.)

deeper into the woods and further away from urban centers as they consumed the trees around them. The glassmakers, fewer in numbers and far more techno-logically elite, were likewise obliged to continually relocate their operations as trees, the source of fuel, became inconveniently remote. Most significantly, the techniques of metalcraft, and especially the secrets of glassmaking, were jealously confined to close-knit family groups that were dispersed throughout Canaan and Mesopotamia, throughout the area in which the artisans served the various noble masters who retained them.

EARLY MANUFACTURE OF GLASS

The process by which siliceous stone is transformed into glass was invented but once in the course of human history and remained a jealously guarded secret of privileged groups through the ages. The pyrotechnology required to produce glass is even more advanced than that of smelting iron from its ore; it is a technology that has been equalled only in the Industrial Age. The custodians of the processes employed in the production of glass were generally a family or other closely knit group who transmitted their secrets from one generation to the next, a pattern that endured for 4000 years into the twentieth century. While glass objects found in the ruins of Ur, Eridu, Eshnunna, and elsewhere in ancient Akkadia attest to the fact that the knowledge of the peculiar and particular conditions under which glass is produced goes back to between 2200 and 2400 B.C.E., the first written evidence we have of the knowledge of the art is inscribed in cuneiform Akkadian on a tablet of the seventeenth century B.C.E. The name for glass, *zaku*, and the formula by which it is made appear in that inscription. The word survives in Hebrew as *zakhukhit*. In Job 28:17, wisdom is said to be more valuable than the most costly material, such as gold or "zakhukhit."

In contrast to the antiquity of a word for glass in the Sumerian and Semitic languages, no word that literally means "glass" ever made its way into ancient Egyptian; the first literary allusion in Egypt to the product is found in the correspondence from Amarna to Babylonia and was written in Akkadian half a millennium after the word for glass and the process by which it was made was inscribed on the Akkadian tablet.

It was only after still another millennium that the Greeks first obtained its equivalent. No reference whatsoever to the manufacture of glass appears in an ancient Greek context; the first reference to the art appears on a sepulchral inscription in connection with a certain Euphrasios, a Jewish glassmaker who died in Athens.[31] Theophastrus was the first to recognize the existence of such a substance as glass, and lacking a word for it, he used the Greek word for a pottery glaze, *kyanos*. Later, Herodotus, recognizing that kyanos was an inadequate label, used the term *lithos chyte,* meaning "molten stone." Finally, the Greeks coined the word *hyalos,* which identified glass as a palpable substance different from all others.

The deep-rooted tradition of Hebrew pyrotechnology may very well have been passed on into the classical age with the transliteration of "Tubal-Cain" into *Vulcan*. No other root for the name of the god of fire is known.[32]

The Romans waited even longer; not until after the legions invaded the East did Latin acquire a word meaning "glass." At first the Romans transliterated the Greek word into *hyalus;* thereafter the Latin word *vitrum* finally appears in the mid-first century B.C.E.[33] Two thousand years passed after the invention of the process of glassmaking had taken place in Akkadia before the Romans became sufficiently aware of the vitric substance to establish a name for it. Mary Louella Trowbridge, whose philological study of the terms employed in the vitric arts stands as the definitive work on the subject, frustrated in the search through Latin literature, wrote that "in early Latin literature, one may search in vain for any mention of glass."[34] The English glass historian had long before come to the conclusion that "to the Greeks glass was something new; to the Romans something unknown."[35]

The writing on the ancient Akkadian tablet on which the glassmaking formulas were inscribed was deliberately cryptic; clearly the intention of its redactors was to conceal the knowledge recorded from all but the initiated. The translator, R. C. Thompson, did not find this literary camouflage unusual; he noted that "it has always been the outrageous custom of certain learned circles to conceal their knowledge from the lay public in a fog of jargon, a pomposity of mannerisms, due, it is hoped, less to personal vanity than to professional protection." Thompson quotes a Kassite tablet of the mid-second millennium B.C.E.: *"mudu^ muda^ likallim la mudu^ ul immar"* (let him that knoweth show him that knoweth, [but] he that knoweth not, let him not see).[36]

Sir Leonard Woolley was equally beguiled by the fact that the writer of the recipe "purposely disguised his meaning by artifices of writing which amount to a form of cryptography intelligible only to members of his guild, who were doubtless privy to his peculiar cryptograms." Woolley noted in his report on the excavations at Tell Atchana of the palace of the son and grandson of the lawgiver Hammurabi that the glassware recovered was "made according to the prescription" on the tablet. Woolley emphasized that neither the Egyptian nor the Syrian [sic] glaziers were privy to the secrets of making true glass at that time, but that the formulas described in the tablet match the analysis of the late sixteenth-century glassware recovered by him from the palace at Tell Atchana.[37]

The Kassite admonishment against teaching a trade to the uninitiated was anticipated by the Code of Hammurabi, the laws established by the Semitic Babylonian king who ruled from 1728-1686 B.C.E. The right of the maintenance of trade secrets was enforced even against the closest of family ties:

> 188: If a member of the artisan class took a son as a foster child and has taught him his handicraft, he may never be reclaimed.
> 189: If he has not taught him his handicraft, that foster child may return to his father's house.[38]

HEBREW IDENTITY, MOSAIC LAW, AND EXODUS CRAFTS

Other types of craftsmen whose secret skills, knowledge, or general irreplaceability afforded them a measure of independence may well have been included in the class of self-reliant, individualistic $H_u$abiru. We might postulate the inclusion of migrant merchants in the $H_u$abiru, traders whose allegiance to enterprise prevailed over their fealty to a particular polity. Traders had been traditionally afforded autonomous privileges in the karums of Akkadia, and their correspondence attests to the same unfettered allegiances as those of the much-maligned $H_u$abiru. The etymology of the appellation "$H_u$abiru" appears to bear out an original reference to caravaneers, for it derives from a root meaning "Dusty Ones," an apt description for the traders "trudging behind long lines of loaded donkeys."[39] The increasing use of mules and wagons during the mid-eighteenth century B.C.E. forced many of these dusty adventurers into other occupations, and the term assumed the new connotation "One from Beyond" (a river or a boundary) by "a common phonetic change and a popular etymology." William Foxwell Albright suggests that this explains why the biblical Abraham represents himself as such a traveler: "I am (only) dirt and fine dust [i.e., a Hebrew or $H_u$abiru]."[40] It was Hugo Winckler, Albright points out, who long ago identified the Akkadian word apiru/epru (as it appears in the Amarna tablets) as the source of Efer, the Hebrew word for "dust" employed by Abraham.[41]

The interlocking relationships of the scattered groups of $H_u$abiru and their insistence on independence are precisely those attributes delineated in the numerous references to the $H_u$abiru on the one hand and to the Hebrews on the other.

Some roamed around as small bands while others formed larger, settled aggregations, such as the tribes called "Sons of the South" (*Banu Yamin* = Benjamin) and "Sons of the North" (*Banu Sim'al*).[42] The common interests of these stateless people did not stem from a common ethnicity. While a large proportion of H$_u$abiru names are Northwest Semitic, others are Babylonian, Hittite, Hurrian, and Elamite; the entire spectrum of ethnicity of the Near East was represented within the ranks of the H$_u$abiru. Out of more than a hundred names appearing in the texts from Alalakh, not more than a half dozen are Semitic; of those appearing in the texts of Nuzi, at least a third were Semitic (although the area was predominantly Hurrian at the time); the Egyptian texts show a predominance of Semitic groups. Amenhotep lists among the captives taken in his second campaign into Asia, for example, the following captives: 127 princes of Retenu [Canaan]; 179 brothers of princes; 3,600 '*pr. w* [stateless H$_u$abiru]; 15,200 living Shasu [nomads]; 36,600 Kharu [settled Canaanite population]; 15,070 living Neges [Aramites]. The H$_u$abiru continued to appear in Egyptian texts as quarry workers or in other consistently menial capacities until the time of Rameses IV (1164-1157), at which time they disappear from Egyptian literature.[43] The early Hebrews of the Bible are assigned hardly less an ethnic diversity.

The numerous barbarian kings who were confined within the compounds of their city-states had to turn to the knowledgeable and proficient artisans and traders who savored independence and who recognized no boundaries. An analogy might be drawn with the employment in the Middle Ages of Jews with valuable international connections by the hierarchy of otherwise fiercely Christian governments, of the use of such specialized artisans as Jewish minters by noblemen seeking to expand their wealth and influence, and of Jewish consuls and agents employed by the Church itself. Attempts to confine and exploit the self-reliant H$_u$abiru led to defection and to their banding together to live an unfettered life, or to their migration to another state where they were retained without being subjected to the shackles commonly applied to servants of the state. The power of the petty potentates rarely extended far beyond the borders of their fiefs; the employers were obliged to suffer the indignity of putting up with the arrogance of these low-class but indispensable laborers.

The biblical Hebrews fit the H$_u$abiru mold to perfection; they were not farmers in Egypt but a work force of alien artisans who performed the technological tasks required in that land; they were the stonecutters and the sculptors, the bricklayers and the carpenters, the metalworkers and the weavers, the potters and the lapidaries, the bakers and the cooks, the scribes and artists, the musicians and dancers. The documents that vividly describe the equivalent of a general strike by the work force of Rameses III in protest against miserable and untenable conditions[44] likewise fit this Hebrew\H$_u$abiru scenario to perfection. It is reasonable to assume that groups of such artisans may well have become migrants [H$_u$abiru] by defecting from their Egyptian masters and wandering away to a land in which they would not be beholden to a king and in which they would serve no master as his property.

The Bible makes it manifest that God was fully cognizant of the technological acumen of his "chosen people," for after providing a constitutional framework with which a humanitarian society could be constructed, and instructions for creating an agronomic base upon which a sedentary society could flourish, He sets up a project in which a comprehensive array of technological disciplines are engaged. The divine discourse on the creation of a viable society follows this logical course of development. God does not dwell on survival in the desert, but launches into the fundamental Ten Commandments, creating the core of a comprehensive legal structure of 613 laws which provide not merely punishment for transgression, but for social justice within a new, progressive, *kingless* social order.

The first divinely inspired statutes significantly address limitations on slavery, the institution from which the Hebrews were divorcing themselves, and parameters of employment are established which reflect the independent standards for which the $H_u$abiru were commonly castigated. Slavery is sharply distinguished from servitude: six years is set as the limit of indenture. The Hebrew servant is not to be regarded as the property of the master but as an employee under contract for predetermined limits, after which he is free to go unless he himself freely opts otherwise. The conditions of employment are to be equivalent to those granted to a family member and protections against abuse are incorporated into the Law: "If a man smite the eye of his servant, or the eye of his maid, and causeth it to perish; he shall let him go free for the eye's sake."

The stateless status of a migrant worker is recalled in the proscription against treating such people without compassion: "Thou shalt not oppress a stranger ($H_u$abiru or Hebrew?), seeing ye were among the strangers in the land of Egypt." Not satisfied with one such admonition, it is repeated several times in more comprehensive terms: "Thou shalt not vex a stranger, nor oppress him; for ye were strangers in the land of Egypt." Sympathy and support for servants escaping onerous servitude is prescribed: "Thou shalt not deliver unto his master the servant which is escaped from his master unto thee: He shall dwell with thee, even among you, in that place which he shall choose in one of thy gates, where it liketh him best; thou shalt not oppress him."[45]

The status of a servant's wife and children are all dealt with within the terms of employment. A woman servant enjoys special protection under Mosaic law in that if the master is not pleased with her he is prohibited from selling her to "a strange nation" and must let her be redeemed. If she becomes betrothed to the master's son she is no longer to be considered a servant but to assume the same status as a daughter, and even if the son takes another wife she is to receive the same food, clothing, and treatment as before. Should the woman not be satisfied with the new arrangement, she is granted the right to freedom without any redemption payment.

Charity is central to the concept of community and was incorporated into every aspect of the social structure, an ethical standard with which the moral fabric of a civilized society was to be woven. The migrant, no less than the unfortunate, is deemed deserving of assistance and consideration: "Thou shalt not reap the corners of thy field . . . neither shalt thou gather the single grapes of thy vineyard . . . thou shalt leave them for the poor and stranger."[46]

Other statutes address internal affairs. Respect for property rights was stated as a matter of principle: "If thou meet thy enemy's ox or his ass going astray, thou shalt surely bring it back to him." Justice was to be pure and unfettered; bribery, the ubiquitous prerogative of rulers and their administrators, was anticipated and prohibited. "Thou shalt take no gift," the law stipulates, and explains, "for the gift blindeth the wise, and perverteth the words of the righteous."

Ignoring the sandy stretches of the Sinai through which the multitude of migrants must pass, sedentary life is clearly chosen as a model over nomadism. A vagabond life in which the band of thousands of refugees would fracture into family groups herding straggling goats from oasis to oasis was not to be the destiny of the chosen people. They were to form a cohesive community, a civilized nation with a fully functioning agricultural and industrial base. Every urban society is based in the first instance on husbandry and agronomy and the Hebrew wanderers were first instructed on sound practices for the conduct of both these fundamental industries.

There they were, wandering about in a sandy wasteland, yet they were already being instructed to sow for six years and to allow their fields to lie fallow on the seventh. Kind treatment for animals is prescribed, including a day of rest for the beasts, no less than for the son of the handmaid and of the stranger.

Nor does God hesitate to take advantage of the technological capabilities of the congregation, skills which encompass the entire spectrum of the arts and crafts of the times. The Israelites assembled an army of 603,550 men over twenty years of age (exclusive of the Levites).[47] Judging by their subsequent military success, we must assume that the Hebrews equipped themselves with military gear during the thirteen months of meandering through the desert, having escaped from Egypt as an unarmed horde. The logistics of this impressive accomplishment along with provision of housing, maintenance, and sustenance of two million people in their sojourn in the Sinai remains a mind-boggling mystery that can be attributed either to the performance of miracles, or to a productive association with other peoples with whom the migrants amalgamated. The varieties and vast quantities of materials required would have necessitated wide-ranging pre-existent commercial contacts that could hardly be expected of the Hebrew refugees. What they did have, however, were the skills with which such material could be worked and converted into useful goods.

The Hebrews were, after all, the very craftsmen who erected the tombs, temples, and palaces of Egypt and outfitted them with exquisite ware. A tabernacle and an ark were built to accommodate the essence of God, along with furniture and accessories that required the talents of artisans and craftsmen of every sort. The work was placed under the supervision of two men who were superbly equipped for the purpose.

Bezaleel, a master smith of the tribe of Judah, who was "filled with the spirit of

God, in wisdom, and in understanding, and in knowledge, and in all manner of workmanship," was charged with devising cunning works in gold, silver, and brass, in the cutting and setting of stone and in the carving of timber and was appointed coordinator of the project.[48]

Oholiab, of the tribe of Dan, was appointed to serve under Bezaleel; he was no less talented, a "cunning workman and an embroiderer in blue, and in scarlet, and fine linen." This Oholiab was not only competent in engraving, but an expert in all aspects of fabric production: weaving, dyeing, and embroidery.

> And Moses said unto the children of Israel, "See, the Lord has called by name Bezaleel. . . . And he has filled him with the spirit of God, in wisdom, and in understanding, and in knowledge . . . to devise cunning works, in gold and in silver, and in brass and in the cutting of stones, to set them, and in the carving of wood . . . that he may teach, both he and Oholiab. . . . Them he has filled with wisdom of heart, to work all manner of work of the engraver, and of the cunning workman, and of the embroiderer . . . and of the weaver, even of them that do any work, and of them that devise cunning work."[49]

"Thereupon," the text continues, "wrought Bezaleel and Oholiab, and every wise man in whom the Lord put wisdom and understanding to know how to work all manner of work." Under the stewardship of Bezaleel much was made of gold, including candlesticks and lamps, snuffers and snuffdishes, dishes and spoons, shovels and basins, fleshhooks and firepans and bowls. The four horns of the altar and all the vessels were made of brass. A great laver of brass was made, and mirrors of brass to satisfy human vanity.

Under Oholiab curtains were woven of "fine twined linen in blue, purple and scarlet," decorated with "cherubim of cunning work" and adorned with decorations composed of a variety of precious stones. The ten curtains enclosing the tabernacle were specified to be a generous twenty-eight cubits long and eight cubits wide. The lapidaries and leather-workers, sculptors and engravers, carpenters and smiths, weavers and embroiderers were so prolifically productive that Moses was obliged to call a halt to the artifactual cascade. "[Moses] proclaimed throughout the camp, saying: Let neither man nor woman make any more work for the offering . . . for the stuff they had was too much."[50]

Aaron, the brother of Moses, was counted among the skilled metalworkers and engravers; he had used his talents to create a golden calf, much to the discomfiture of his brother Moses and to the displeasure of God. Aaron was persuaded to perform this blasphemous act by the impatient Hebrews who would not await the descent of Moses from the mountain. "Make us gods," they pleaded, and Aaron gathered up the gold jewelry of the Hebrews' wives, sons, and daughters, "and fashioned it with a graving tool, after he had made it a golden calf."[51]

Aaron came back into favor after the tabernacle was completed; holy garments were made for him of fine linen dyed in blue and purple and scarlet, costumes with which he was to conduct services within the tabernacle. Gold was beaten, cut into threads, and woven into the fine fabric; the brooches and buckles of his ephod and girdle were encrusted with wrought onyx stones on which the names of the tribes of Israel were engraved "that they should be stones for a memorial to the children of Israel." Aaron's breastplate was even more elaborately decorated with four courses of precious stones: sardius [ruby?], topaz, and carbuncle; emerald, sapphire, and diamond; ligure [jacinth?], agate, and amethyst; a beryl, onyx, and jasper; all of which gems were engraved with the names of the tribes of Israel and enclosed, each in its own gold brooch. These precious stones were not native to the desert; we must infer from the context in which they appear and from the other raw materials required for the production of the array of artifacts listed that the Israelites were either carrying on a considerable trade with other peoples of the region, or were sending out emissaries or caravans to trade in foreign lands even while they were tenting out in the wilderness of Sinai.

The breastplate was hung with two chains wrought of gold that were attached to some of the rings that bound the breastplate to the robe. The hems of the robe were hung with alternate bells of gold and pomegranates woven of elaborately colored threads of twined linen.[52] As noted in earlier chapters, the symbolic use of the pomegranate is significant: the fruit symbolized fertility and its bud appeared as a Mesopotamian motif more than a millennium earlier in an Akkadian context and remained a distinguishing model and motif of Jewish art thereafter.

The working of gold had long been known in Egypt at the time of the Exodus; the use of brass had been introduced during the so-called Second Intermediate period, but the smelting and working of iron remained absent from ancient Egypt. The pyrotechnical and therefore the ferric and vitric expertise that had long been practiced in Mesopotamia had stopped short at the Sinai. There the Israelites are reminded of the existence and use of iron by a reference to the huge, nine-cubit-long, iron bed, on which the giant king Og of Bashan (northern Canaan) slept,[53] and it is in the Sinai that the Lord promises the Israelites not merely a land in which their agriculture will thrive with ample resources of water for irrigation but that they will have ample metallurgic resources to establish a flourishing tool and weapons industry:[54]

> For the Lord thy God bringeth thee into a good land, a land of brooks and water, of fountains and depths that spring out of the valleys and hills; a land of wheat and barley, and vines, and fig trees, and pomegranates; a land of olive oil and honey; a land wherein thou shalt eat bread without scarceness, thou shalt not lack anything in it; a land whose stones are iron, and out of whose hills thou mayest dig brass.

The wording of the reference to "a land whose stones are iron, and out of whose hills thou mayest dig brass" reveals a profound geologic knowledge, for copper ore, while occasionally found on the surface, is usually located in veins that penetrate deep into the earth, and require the digging of underground shafts and galleries for the recovery of the ore. Deposits of iron ore, on the other hand, are widely found on or near the surface, and their recovery does not necessitate an arduous mining procedure. These biblically cited circumstances, therefore, account for the fact that no ancient iron mines have to date been identified by archaeologists, whereas copper mines have been found which date back before the fourth millennium B.C.E. The familiarity of the Hebrews with iron and the

Israelite possession of iron weapons and tools again comes to our attention when the purification of all persons, objects, and weapons that touched the slain is called for after the battle with the Midianites, a battle which took place during the early, traumatic time of trial of the Exodus. The Hebrews are instructed to wash everything, even "the gold, and the silver, the brass, the iron, the tin and lead. Every thing that passeth through the fire, ye shall make it go through the fire, and it shall be clean; nevertheless it shall be purified with the water of sprinkling."[55]

An iron weapon is specifically referred to when punishment for murder is prescribed by God: "And if he smite him with an instrument of iron, so that he die, he is a murderer; the murderer shall surely be put to death."[56] Moses and the elders of Israel mysteriously proscribe iron tools from being used in the construction of an altar across the Jordan,[57] a prohibition that is no less mysteriously imposed later on in the building of the House of the Lord by Solomon "of stone made ready before it was brought thither; so that there as neither hammer nor axe nor any tool of iron heard in the house, while it was in building."[58] We are thus informed that the Israelites employed iron tools but were obliged to dress stone out of hearing range from the House of the Lord.

Moses exhorts the Israelites to "walk in his statutes," threatening dire consequences for diverting from the path of righteousness, including the making of "your heaven as iron and your earth as brass," thus making the heavens impregnable to rain and the soil resistant to tilling. The children of Israel are told that if they "hearken diligently" unto God's voice and obey his commandments they will enjoy many blessings, but warned again that if they do not strictly adhere to his statutes the enemies of Israel will "put a yoke of iron" around their necks.[59] While "breaking a [wooden] yoke" is a suitable metaphor for liberation,[60] the iron yoke here referred to represents harsh and enduring oppression.

Vessels of iron were included in the loot taken from Jericho: thus, we are informed that ironwork existed throughout Canaan at the time.[61] The Canaanites of Beth-Shean and Jezreel and all that dwelt in the surrounding villages of the valley had chariots of iron. The mountains surrounding the valley were heavily wooded, precisely the environment conducive to ironmaking and smithing.[62] Not even divine assistance prevented a disastrous defeat of Judah against the Canaanites due to their ability to deploy hundreds of iron chariots in battle.[63] The temporary setback suffered was soon rectified; although the Canaanite army had some nine hundred such iron chariots at their disposal, they were nevertheless ignominiously defeated under the leadership of the indomitable prophetess Deborah, "who judged Israel at that time" (as well as, of course, with the Lord's assistance).[64] The Israelites were later avenged by Jael, the wife of Heber, who hammered iron nails into the Canaanite general Sisera's head.[65] Joshua instructed the Manassites to divide the spoils of their campaign with their brethren, including cattle, silver, gold, brass, iron, and raiment.[66]

This record of familiarity with iron, while it may be reasonably assessed as being largely or entirely an anachronistic literary reversal, is regularly overlooked, while another biblical reference is subjected to a widely quoted misinterpretation that has fostered the idea that the Philistines were the smiths of the times and that iron-making was unknown to the Israelites. In 1 Samuel 13:19 we read that *"there was no smith found throughout all the land of Israel; for the Philistines said, 'lest the Hebrews make them swords or spears.'"* Read properly, it is clear that the Hebrews and not the Philistines are designated the arms-makers, and that they had furnished the Israelites with weapons and would have continued to do so had not the Philistines intervened. It is clear from what follows that the Philistines attempted to confiscate the weapons of one group of Israelites while they gathered up the itinerant Hebrew smiths from around the region into their camp. The intention of the Philistines is clearly laid out in the next sentence, in which it is stated that they sought to force the Israelites (referred to separately from the Hebrews) to sharpen their agricultural and industrial tools at facilities put under Philistine control, and thereby to prevent the Israelites from making or sharpening weapons. The Israelites are thus certified to have been in possession of a complete array of metal agricultural equipment, shares [plows], coulters, mattocks, forks and axes; they are attested to have been metallurgically proficient, for they surreptitiously retained their own "files" (in spite of the Philistines' attempt to confiscate all sharpening tools), and it is recorded that they continued to sharpen the weapons and tools in their possession despite the prohibition.

The inability to have or to obtain weapons applied not to all the Israelites but only to the Israelites in the villages nearby and under the control of the Philistines. Saul and his armor-bearer (Saul and Jonathan did, indeed, possess weapons) went out to Migron where Saul gathered together a troop of six hundred armed men. Jonathan, Saul's son, anticipating a battle with the Philistines, decided to go out on a foray of his own. Jonathan succeeded in demolishing a garrison of twenty Philistines by a ruse in which he and his armor-bearer exposed themselves to the garrison who, believing that the Israelites had no weapons, assumed that they were Hebrews [!] who had eluded indenture; "Behold," they are said to have exclaimed, "the Hebrews come forth from their holes."

The annihilation of the garrison caused a great stir among the Philistines, and Saul and his troops "came to the battle," whereupon we are significantly informed that *"the Hebrews that were with the Philistines before that time, which went up with them into the camp from the country about, even they turned to be with the Israelites that were with Saul and Jonathan."*[67]

This passage provides the clear confirmation that the metal-working Hebrews had indeed been rounded up and confined to the Philistine camp; that the Hebrews resented the confinement and identified their interest with that of the Israelites; and that they fled to join the ranks of the Israelites against the Philistines.

We are also informed that "likewise all the men of Israel which had hid themselves in mount Ephraim, when they heard that the Philistines had fled, even they followed hard after them in the battle." The clear implication is that the fugitive forces of Ephraim were well supplied with weapons. Thus these passages not only ascribe the possession of metal (including iron) weapons to the Israelites but clarify the anomalous use of the labels "Israelite" and "Hebrew" and resolve the apparent dichotomy.

"So Saul took over the kingdom over Israel."[68] The amalgamation of the disparate bands of Hebrews and Israelites resolved into a new entity. As the Philistines were forced to retire to their own enclave on the coast, new challenges to formation of the new nation arose and were met by Saul: the Moabites, the Ammonites, the Edomites, the Amalekites, and various "kings of Zobah," as well as new incursions of the Philistines, were all encountered and routed in turn. The host that Saul gathered together was evidently well-equipped for the purpose, as was the army of "two hundred thousand footmen and ten thousand men of Judah" that Saul assembled and employed to place all of the land of Israel under control. We are left to assume that the Hebrew artisans provided much of the expertise necessary for equipping this huge army and for the Israelite armies that conducted further campaigns.

It is written that the Philistines continued to be well equipped with armor; their champion, Goliath, sported a spear with a cast iron head weighing the equivalent of six hundred shekels,[69] and was outfitted in a brass helmet and coat of mail weighing the equivalent of five thousand shekels. David was also provided with a helmet of brass and a coat of mail, but discarded them along with his sword and chose in its place his more lethal weapon, the sling.[70] We might peripherally note for whatever significance it may have, that later on, after the Israelites were well-established, and the Hebrews were well integrated into the new nation, another conflict took place with the Philistines; they are no longer said to have been equipped with weapons of iron but of brass.[71]

While the stateless Hebrew artisans appear at this point to have melded into a newly-formed nation, the word "Hebrew" reappears pejoratively in the Bible in same sense of a troublesome outcast as the term $H_u$abiru had appeared outside of a biblical context. Thus after David's rift with Saul and his defection to the Philistines, the presence of his band is noticed and questioned by some princes of the Philistines. "What do these Hebrews here?" they ask, and are not satisfied with the assurance by the Philistine general Achish that the Hebrew band is headed by "David the servant of Saul the king of Israel," who had served him well and could be trusted.

David and his roaming band fit to perfection the depiction of the characteristics of the $H_u$abiru in extrabiblical literature. The group was composed of "every one that was in distress, and every one that was in debt, and every one that was discontented."[72] Failing in their attempts to win the favor and protection of the cities[73] they finally succeed with the above-mentioned Philistine, Achish, who "gives" them Ziklag, a town in which the erstwhile outlaws can base operations. The circumstances of this act are "precisely, for example, as Lab'ayu 'gives' Sechem to the Hapiru."[74]

The term $H_u$abiru disappears at this juncture from the literature of the times. The melding of the terms Hebrew and $H_u$abiru, and to some extent the terms Hebrew and Israelite, appears to have become effective with the formation of the Israelite nation. Nadav Na'aman notes that "when the phenomenon of the $H_u$abiru\Hebrews entirely disappeared from daily reality, the term 'Hebrew' was restricted, in the colloquial language, to individual Israelites who were either migrants or slaves."[75] Thus, the prophet Jonah, in answer to the query of a sailor: "And of what people art thou?" declares "I am a Hebrew" in his flight to a foreign country, thus emphasizing his stateless condition.[76] Na'aman concludes that "this latter stage opened the way for the post-Old Testament use of the ethnicon 'Hebrew,' in which all traces of the original meaning of the appellation disappeared, and the name simply became another term for the Israelites."[77]

The God of migrant or itinerant peoples was of necessity universal, for He was not attached to a particular city or region as were other gods. The amalgamation of the groups of migrant Hebrews with the groups of stateless Israelites and the resolution of the disparate groups into a viable nation brought about His installation in Jerusalem, where He was revered to the exclusion of all other gods. The implantation did not engender the same royal rights as were conferred by the local Gods of city-states upon kings elsewhere. The Israelite kings never got to enjoy the unequivocal patronage of God nor even of the Israelite/Hebrews; nor did any other king in whose realm the Israelite/Hebrews resided receive more than pragmatic fealty; the descendants of the Israelites remained obdurate anti-establishmentarians throughout their history, and their God and their iconoclasm remained with them wherever they went.

TECHNOLOGY IN *ERETZ YISRAEL* UNDER DAVID AND SOLOMON

The association of the Hebrews with the Israelites accounts for the integration of ferric technology into the fabric of Israelite society and the generation of the Iron Age in the forested, hilltop communities of Canaan. Although iron-making was unknown in Egypt, it had been long practiced in Mesopotamia and Canaan and was part of the metallurgy being carried on by artisans throughout the area. The earliest textual reference to the art of the blacksmith was recovered from the archives of King Ninurta-tukulti-Assur of Assyria, dated to about 1132 B.C.E.[78] When the time came to build a "house of the Lord God" on the site of a Jebusite threshing floor, David needed the services of these independent artisans, now significantly referred to as "strangers," the term that was equally applicable to the Hebrews and the $H_u$abiru: "David commanded to gather together the strangers that were in the land of Israel and he set masons to hew wrought stones to build the house of God." That smiths were prominent among these "strangers" is made perfectly clear in the next paragraph: "And David prepared iron in abundance for the nails for the doors of the gates, and for the joinings; and brass in abundance without weight."[79]

David instructed his son, Solomon, to carry on this work:

Now, behold, in my trouble I have prepared for the house of the Lord an hundred thousand talents of gold, and a thousand talents of silver; and of brass and iron without weight; for it is in abundance; timber also and stone I have prepared; and thou mayest add thereto. Moreover there are workmen with thee in abundance, hewers and workers of stone and timber, and all manner of cunning men for every manner of work. Of the gold, the silver, and the brass, and the iron, there is no number.[80]

The cultural attributes of the newly-formed nation are no less celebrated in the Bible than is its technological prowess. David's priorities included an expanded population of musicians and, per force, the production of instruments for them. "Four thousand shall praise the Lord with the instruments which I have made to praise him with.[81]

David repeated his instructions to Solomon to a gathering of the entire congregation, listing not only all the metals he had supplied for the purpose of building the house of the Lord (iron for things of iron, and so on), but onyx and precious stones and "stones to be set, glistering stones, and of divers colors, and all manner of precious stones, and marble stones in abundance." Glistering stones may well be a reference to glass gems in general; marble stones "of divers colors " may include the varicolored glass known as "agate glass,"[82] both allusions to another manifestation of the pyrotechnology which became a Judaic heritage.

After David took the royal city of Ammon "he brought forth the people that were therein, and put them under the saws, and under the harrows of iron, and under the axes of iron.[83] David's last words included the instructions that "the wicked shall be all of them thrust away, because they cannot be taken with hands: But the man that shall touch them shall be fenced with iron and the staff of a spear."[84]

Thus was the Iron Age biblically acclaimed.

Another portion of the biblical record that has been taken out of context and used to denigrate Israelite (and Judahite) technological competence is that referring to the exchange of services and supplies between Hiram, king of Tyre, and David and Solomon respectively. Such critics delight in presenting the allusions to the assistance rendered by Hiram to the newly constituted national entity as evidence of Israelite ineptitude while ignoring a wealth of references to a whole range of creative works requiring technological proficiency.

The assistance proffered by Hiram at the initial stage of Jerusalem's establishment as the seat of government was welcomely received. The assistance proffered by the king of Tyre to David in the form of some cedar trees, carpenters, and masons amounted to little more than a gesture of friendship, in that it had already been stated that the bulk of the artisans required, including skilled smiths and stonecutters, was drawn from the "strangers" [$H_u$abiru\Hebrews?] of the surrounding countryside, and a goodly supply of materials, including "brass and iron without number," had already been acquired. Hiram's gift of some timber weighed little in the logistics of the intensive recruiting and campaigning that was taking place, and of the production of the equipment needed by the forces gathered for this purpose. Hiram's assistance to David had a geo-political rationale: the Tyrian king supplied the wood and some personnel to help build David a modest palace (referred to as a "house"), while David gathered up and equipped a substantial force with which he mopped up throughout the region. Inherent in this burst of military activity was the outfitting of the forces, to which task Hebrew artisans were assigned.

David's successes can be attributed in large measure to the steadfast support of two brothers, Joab and Abushei,[85] who were at David's right hand from the time when David was yet an outlaw contending with Saul. It was under the able generalship of the two brothers that David's campaigns were conducted and the entire region from the Euphrates to Egypt was eventually placed under Israelite (Judahite) hegemony. Joab headed an extended family of master craftsmen, "the father of the valley of Harashim; for they were craftsmen."[86] It was these two men who assembled and outfitted the army with which David achieved his outstanding victories.

David carried his campaign into Transjordan, vanquishing Ammon. Then David moved around the crown of the Fertile Crescent, subduing Aram; control was established over the trade routes from Egypt to 'The River," Euphrates. As soon as David's forces took the royal city of Ammon and nearby Rabbah he returned to economic matters, putting "all the cities of the children of Ammon under the saws, and under the harrows of iron, and under the axes of iron."[87] This statement documents the artisanship of the inhabitants of Transjordan and the use and production of iron tools. A period of intense industrialization ensued, in which "David numbered the people that were with him, and set captains of thousands and captains of hundreds over them."[88] At the twilight of David's life Joab was commissioned to number the forces of Israel and Judah. The census took nine months and twenty days, and Joab reported that 800,000 valiant men drew the sword in Israel, and 500,000 more armed men were counted in Judah. Joab, master craftsman, and captain of all the host of Israel, fell out of favor with David and Solomon at the last, having backed the wrong person for succession. He was slaughtered at the command of Solomon and "buried in his own house in the wilderness."[89]

Hiram's assistance to the burgeoning state of Judah proved to have been a shrewd move. A lasting, mutually beneficial commercial and political relationship was initiated between the adventurous, seafaring, coastal Canaanites and the dynamic new nation. The stage was well set for the burst of economic development by the time David turned over the reins of government to his son Solomon. Solomon was put well on the way to the construction and outfitting of a proper House of the Lord, and for equipping a powerful military force. The most valuable of the materials David bequeathed to Solomon for those purposes was iron: the quantity of iron set aside for Solomon exceeded that of all the other metals combined! 100,000 talents of iron was included in his bequest, as compared to 5000 talents of gold and 10,000 drams, 10,000 talents of silver and 18,000 talents of brass.[90]

Solomon solidified "dominion over all the region on this side of the river" through diplomacy (much of which was accomplished by marrying princesses), and launched a massive construction program. At this juncture Hiram, who "was ever a lover of David," was approached by Solomon to establish a cooperative military and economic relationship. "Thou knowest how that David my father could not build an house unto the name of the Lord his God," Solomon advised Hiram, "for the war with the nations which were about him on every side." Implicit in Solomon's words was the supposition that were it not for an overwhelming preoccupation with war, the Israelites would have already constructed a proper "House of the Lord."

Military exigencies having been overcome, Solomon orders wood out of Lebanon, to be jointly hewn: "and my servants shall be with thy servants," flattering Hiram into supplying some of the labor by stating that "there is not among us any that can skill to hew timber like unto the Sidonians." While some "Sidonians" were clearly contributed by Hiram, since Hiram and Solomon had "made a league together," the workforce of artisans, common laborers, and the supervisory personnel that accomplished the job were predominantly Israelite, having been drawn from "*out of all Israel,*" and they were placed under the supervision not of a Tyrian but of an Israelite, Andoniram:

> And King Solomon raised a levy out of all Israel; and the levy was thirty thousand men. And he sent them to Lebanon, ten thousand a month by courses; a month they were in Lebanon, and two months at home; and Andoniram was over the Levy. And Solomon had three score and ten thousand that bear burdens, and fourscore thousand hewers in the mountains. Beside the chief of Solomon's officers which were over the work, three thousand and three hundred, which ruled over the people that wrought in the work. And the king commanded, and they brought great stones, costly stones, and hewed stones, to lay the foundations of the house. And Solomon's builders and Hiram's builders did hew them, and the stone squarers: so they prepared timber and stones to build the house [of the Lord].[91]

It was this aggregation of thirty thousand Israelite hewers who provided the wood and more than fifty thousand skilled and unskilled Israelite artisans who are said to have erected upon the crown of the Jebusite hill a composite, complex construction of monumental scale in which the Temple, the "House of the Lord," was prominently featured. The process of construction consumed thirteen years and it was only *after* the vast compound had been completed that "Solomon sent and fetched [the smith], Hiram out of Tyre." It is at this point in the narrative that we come across a crucial sentence, the only one from which the intimations that Israelite metallurgic know-how originated from Tyre are derived: "*He was a widow's son of the tribe of Naphthali, and his father was a man of Tyre,* a worker in brass; and he was filled with wisdom, and understanding, and cunning to work all works in brass."[92]

The appearance of Hiram at the end of the period of construction clearly removes him from consideration as a seminal factor in its creation; it was clearly a mere gesture of Tyrian friendship. In any event, Hiram was at least half Israelite, a fact that could not have been stated more explicitly. He may well indeed have been entirely Israelite, for the wording does not denote that his father was ethnically Tyrian or Canaanite, but merely that he hailed from Tyre. Israelite artisans and merchants were undoubtedly carrying on their disciplines in Tyre as a natural consequence of the establishment thirteen years earlier of a common league between the two nations. Hiram arrived at Jerusalem after construction had already been completed under the able supervision of Adoniram the Israelite through the 3,300 Israelite foremen under him, work which included an array of metal fittings and wood carvings elaborately detailed in the Bible. The extraordinary feat of converting the hilltop into a great compound in thirteen years can be favorably compared to equivalent constructions in Akkadia and Egypt: it required the most sophisticated labor force, one whose expertise was drawn from a deep-rooted, ancient experience in such centers as Ebla, Mari, and Thebes.

The furnishings fashioned under Hiram's supervision were indeed wondrous works. Two massive brass pillars supported the porch of the Temple; their capitals were embellished with several hundred carved pomegranates, a design established as an Israelite motif back in the time of the Exodus half a millennium earlier, a motif that the Semites had introduced into Egypt from Akkadia. The great brass basin that was placed upon twelve oxen, with borders and ledges delicately carved with lions, oxen, cherubims, and palms, was a metallurgic marvel. The entire roster of lavers and pots, of shovels and basons, of candlesticks and snuffers were not, however, the first Temple treasures made, for when Hiram completed his commission: "Solomon brought in the things that David his father had dedicated; even the silver, and the gold, and the vessels, did he put among the treasures of the Lord."[93]

Thus the string upon which the popularized idea that the technological know-how of the Israelites was mainly derived from Tyre is frail indeed, spun from a few threads of the biblical account of Hiram's contribution. Neither does such a myopic view jibe with the archaeological record of the many cities built or expanded under Solomon, the fortresses strung across the Negev, and all the other significant accomplishments effected during this short, initial phase of Israelite nationhood.

If it were true that the technology for the construction of these great works were borrowed from Tyre we would expect to find such technology in a Tyrian or in another so-called "Phoenician" environment. That is not at all the case! The somewhat limited excavations at Tyre and the extensive excavation of Byblos reveal few architectural parallels to the constructions of the early monarchical period of David and Solomon. "On the other hand," notes the Israeli archaeologist, Yohanan Aharoni, "all of the striking parallels come from northern Syria [sic], including fortifications, gates, palaces and ornamentation."[94] Such Mesopotamian cultural roots are expected, however, to have been the heritage of the migrant H$_u$abiru or the equally stateless Hebrews, and the archaeological recoveries from *Eretz Yisrael* bear out those expectations magnificently, a record that we shall examine next.

10

Architecture and Engineering

Achievements of the Israelites

Hundreds of Israelite communities mushroomed in the hill country that ridges *Eretz Yisrael*. They were implanted upon the rugged hilltops at the end of the Bronze Age, the biblical period of Judges. The region had never been extensively populated; it was a rock-strewn, wooded area that had to be laboriously cleared for habitation and farming. Other Israelite communities spread out across the Negev, a desolate, arid region. The housing and productive installations of the Israelites bore the unmistakable hallmarks of a people well versed in architecture and agriculture, a people whose knowledge and competence in crafts of all kinds reflected long and intimate urban and agronomic heritages. Many of the Israelites were literate, a cultural attribute that was not relegated to a few specialized scribes but was shared by the common people to an extent that the world at large had not yet experienced.

DOMESTIC ARCHITECTURE

The remarkable aspect of the houses that proliferated throughout *Eretz Yisrael* was their distinctive, radical, advanced type of architecture. The Israelite private houses were, for the period, ample, well-constructed habitations, and were distinguished by the use of a row of stone pillars for supporting the roof beams. This orthostatic feature was almost entirely absent from precedent private houses of the region and rare even in monumental structures. The houses were generally but not always composed of four rooms flanking a courtyard, a layout that served as a model for the structures of the subsequent "classical" period. The Israelite four-room pillared house is an ancestor and prototype of the "Roman" villa.

By the monarchical period, the privately owned Israelite houses, while never reaching palatial proportions, had become more elaborate; a second story was not unusual, and plumbing systems occasionally appeared, the earliest use of such installations outside of the palaces of kings and overlords. The architectural sophistication ubiquitously displayed by the brand-new Israelite settlers gave Professor Aharoni pause in regard to the proposal that the Israelites had arrived as an essentially pastoral people: "This technical knowledge of architecture is evidence that the tribes were not completely nomadic when they arrived in the country."[1]

The hills of *Eretz Yisrael* are saturated with the relics of a multiplicity of unwalled, that is, unfortified Israelite villages that were established during a relatively brief period. Whereas the valleys were generally well-supplied with water (some lowlands were checkered with swampy sectors), water was scarce and springs or streams were not easily accessible to the inhospitable, rocky summits on which the Israelites perched their communities. Wells had to be dug deep down to reach the water table, or cisterns had to be hacked out of the rock underlying the houses, an alternative that generally proved to be more practical. Many of the houses were provided with drains, engineered to efficiently collect rainwater from the overlying roofs and transmit it to the cisterns underneath the houses.

Whereas crude cisterns were sporadically employed by the Canaanites, new, advanced types were immediately and almost universally installed by the Israelites for water conservation and management. The Israelite cisterns were not only common to all the settlements but also engineered with innovations that marked the initiation of a new development in the storage of water and bespoke the creative propensities of the people who engineered them. Many cisterns were quarried out of the chalky layers that interspersed the limestone of which the hills were largely formed. The wet chalk generally formed an impermeable seal, but when such a self-sealing system did not suffice to do the task, or when a chalky layer was absent from the limestone, the cisterns were lined with mortar. It is a seemingly simple solution for efficient water conservation, but it was one that had rarely been applied before. A series of interconnecting cisterns were often dug under or near an Israelite house, not only to guarantee an adequate supply of water but also to form an effective filtration system, since the opening to the passage from one cistern to the other was placed at some distance above the bottoms. The cisterns were generally bell shaped, with a lidded opening just large enough to pass through for cleaning out the settled debris. Water was sometimes obtained by means of channels draining the nearby terrain as an independent water collection system or as an adjunct to the house drains; in these cases the channels led the water into a settling trap filled with gravel, from the top of which water flowed into the larger, primary cistern whose tranquility allowed finer particles to settle before the water passed on to the smaller cisterns on line. The knowledge of the engineering of such sophisticated conservational systems could only have been gained through many centuries of agricultural and technological experience.

ISRAELITE SELF-SUFFICIENCY AND INDEPENDENCE

The high degree of autonomy within the Israelite community is amply demonstrated not only by the immediate introduction and proliferation of the mortar-lined cistern systems as an adjunct to each household but by private rock-cut silos for grain and fruit storage, a precursor of the root cellar of a later era. An amicable and cooperative communal interrelationship is suggested by an interconnecting complex of cisterns found under some of the neighboring houses of ancient Ai, access to which was easily gained through cistern caps that formed part of the floor of the various houses, thus providing the inhabitants of the houses with an almost inexhaustible water supply.

By the end of the twelfth century B.C.E. the hilltop communities were already growing a variety of cereals, vines, nuts, and olives on well-ordered farms. At that early time the Israelites had already begun to develop a comprehensive system of terracing and irrigation. Small, private corrals for sheep or goats were installed, generally on the leeward side of the property from the houses so that the prevailing winds would waft the odors away from the dwellings. Professor Aharoni expressed his astonishment as to the proficiency of these presumed pastoral people and the rapidity with which sophisticated techniques were put into practice: "The tribes adapted themselves with amazing swiftness to the technological means prerequisite to settlement in the areas available to them."[2]

The agronomic expertise of the people of the area should not have come as a surprise; the earliest known evidence of the use of paired oxen for plowing is rendered by a ceramic bowl found in Samaria near Ai, the second city said to have been taken by the Israelites in their conquest of Canaan. Two earthenware yoked oxen are attached to the hollow of the bowl, posed in the act of performing their task. The bowl has been dated to the Early Bronze I period (3200–2850 B.C.E.) and registers the arrival of the plow from Mesopotamia, where it appears to have been invented some 500 years earlier.[3]

A vivid picture of an unfettered life in the early Israelite villages and of the agronomic, industrial, and cultural intelligence of their inhabitants has emerged from excavations at Ai and surrounding villages. The field work was performed under the directorship of John A. Callaway, who estimated that the towns of Ai and Raddana had come into existence about 1220 B.C.E. and that the cisterns underneath the houses were built before the houses were constructed over them. The existence of paved streets was another indication that "the new settlers had already lived a sedentary life elsewhere, and had a high degree of technical skill."[4] Callaway reported in detail on a typical Israelite dwelling of the time and region. The pillared house and divers associated structures were occupied by an Israelite named Ahilud and his family in the ancient village of Khirbut Raddana, located some four miles east of Ai.[5]

In the excavation of this house a storage jar handle turned up on which Ahilud's own name is inscribed in old Hebrew script.[6] The name Ahilud appears biblically as the father of Jehosaphat, an official recorder at King David's court. The Ahilud of Raddana, while he was unlikely to have been the sire of such an important personage, appears to have been an eleventh-century B.C.E. contemporary of his Jerusalemite namesake. Ahilud lived in a modest three-room dwelling, simpler than the usual four-room variety, although it did incorporate a row of four roof-supporting pillars. The three-roomed house, however, was but one of three houses clustered around a common courtyard, a complex of buildings that evidently accommodated Ahilud's extended family and provided facilities for a number of domestic, agricultural, and industrial activities. A silo was installed at the corner of one of the houses; three cooking pits in and near the courtyard and a large fire pit at the center of the large room of the main house provided the means for cooking for a sizable group and the means by which other processes that involved fire could be performed. The caverns of three cisterns were quarried out under the main house; an additional cistern was installed under one of the workrooms of one of the adjoining houses, and still another cistern was installed in another workroom near a hearth for metalworking. "Here, metal ingots were melted into crucibles and the molten metal was poured into molds to form the daggers, spearpoints and axe heads for Ahilud's household, as well as for other members of the community."[7]

The handle socket of an iron mattock was found within Ahilud's house. The metalworking facility, the iron tools that may well have been produced there, the terracing on which Ahilud's cereals were grown, the silo in which his grain was stored, Ahilud's personal name incised into the handle of a storage jar, and the orthostatic architecture of his house, all attest to the existence of important facets of Israelite Iron Age enlightenment within what was clearly the private dwelling of a typical, independent, accomplished family of farmers and artisans. These facets included: architectural innovation, agronomlc erudition, metallurgic proficiency (including iron-smithing), and aleph-bethic literacy. "If the village formed a microcosm, within the larger hill-country settlement area," comments Callaway, "the household functioned similarly as a microcosm within the village itself."[8]

Whereas the smelting of ores probably took place at a distance from the village communities, a variety of tanged and hafted bronze tools and weapons and well-worn grinding stones found at Raddana and Ai and at other such Israelite centers attest silently but convincingly to a well-developed cottage industry in which some of the villagers carried on local operations in which they wrought metal ingots produced in the forested areas into agricultural and other tools, or, at the very least, possessed adequate facilities to sharpen and repair them. The explanation for the evident self-sufficiency of these communities can only be predicated on a precedent capability. The incidence of Israelite iron tools from the thirteenth through the tenth centuries B.C.E. in the catalogue of metal implements employed is not substantial, to be sure, but it was widespread, and indicative of the level of metallurgy which the Israelites had attained.

All of the archaeological evidence accumulated from these villages exhibits the same clear pattern of independence and competence, which Callaway, the excavator of Ahilud's house, characterized as "isolationist and highly individualistic." Callaway then added in emphasis that this may explain why it was so difficult to establish a monarchy, for "from the beginning, Israel was self-sufficient, family-centered and characteristically independent."

> A survey of settlements in Judea and Samaria during Iron Age I—the period when Ahilud lived—reveals that the hill country was literally covered by small villages like those at Ai and Raddana. Of 102 sites identified, some 90 were newly founded. . . . Characteristically, the villages were unfortified and occupied by apparently peace-loving people. In fact, one reason they relocated in an inhospitable environment that had not previously supported anyone was to escape the better-equipped inhabitants of the more fertile lowlands.[9]

One of the important considerations supporting the "Peaceful Infiltration" model of Israelite settlement is the fact noted by Callaway, that these hundreds of Israelite villages remained unwalled and unfortified over an extended period, as much as two centuries. This propitious circumstance was true not only of the highland communities, but also of the many Israelite settlements that had been established in the dry, harsh environment of the southern desert lands. Professor Aharoni cites the case of Tel Masos as a prime example of the progressive, peaceful development and life that must have been enjoyed there in the pre-monarchical period. The village covered forty dunams, about nine acres, the largest Israelite settlement found in the Negev to the date of his report. It was situated on virgin ground on a flat mound near a wadi opposite the site of a precedent habitation of the Middle Canaanite period. The Tel Masos Israelites lived at peace in their unfortified village for more than two centuries and flourished from the thirteenth century "until the ominous rise of the Philistine military power in the mid-eleventh century."[10] The community survived those critical times into the tenth century.

The Tel Masos community sat astride the trade route that stretched from the northern Mediterranean coastal region to the Gulf of Elath, and the commercial activity of its inhabitants is well attested to by decorated pottery from the northern Canaanite littoral: Philistine ware from the southern littoral of *Eretz Yisrael*, and "Midianite ware" from the area around Elath, examples of which were found in the houses of ordinary residents of the town. Farming was an equally important occupation of the self-sufficient Masoites. Among the typical bronze tools recovered from the site were also an iron sickle and a knife, mute testimony to the existence of ferric industrial activity in *Eretz Yisrael*.

Pillared houses of the same advanced type that appeared ubiquitously as an Israelite trademark throughout *Eretz Yisrael* were found in each of the three Tel Masos strata. Although an elaborate palace and fortifications were conspicuously absent, public buildings for various productive and administrative purposes were erected within the village, a clear indication of a well-organized, self-reliant society. A stockade for harboring animals and a building with a large silo built into the courtyard were prominent among the communal structures. The walls of the

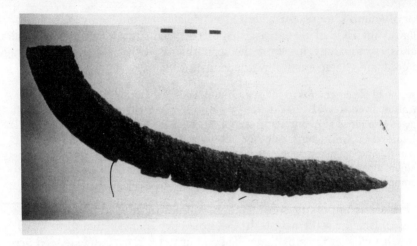

An iron sickle recovered from Tell Masos, an Israelite settlement that appeared in south-
ern Canaan at the end of the thirteenth century B.C.E. and flourished for some 300 years.
The use of iron tools throughout the area of Israelite settlement, from the Upper Galilee to
Beersheba, is evidenced by the appearance of such iron tools. (Photograph courtesy of the
Institute of Archaeology, Tel Aviv University.)

silo "were strengthened by a series of salients, at fixed intervals. This technique
is quite rare in Eretz-Israel."[11] The technique had been brought to Egypt from
Mesopotamia and appeared there in the time of the Eighteenth Dynasty; it may
therefore be an indication of the place in which the Tel Masos engineers or their
progenitors first employed it. "The tribes were not deterred by the special diffi-
culties of settling in the arid Negev," notes Aharoni with evident admiration,
"which was possible only with the help of appreciable technological skill and in
the utilization of water sources."[12]

A good example of the resourceful manner in which the Israelites acquired
and manipulated the meager water supply in the arid highlands of the Negev is
that of Ramat Matred, where water channels were dug along the slopes of the
ravine whose rim was flanked by the houses of the community. The system was
a most imaginative method of maximizing the collection and storage of water
during the rare occasions when it became available. This unique water-gathering
system was a precursor of a method of desert agriculture that "reached its zenith
in the Negev during the Roman-Byzantine period."[13] The Ramat Matred community, like that of Tel Masos and the other villages of the Negev and the central
highlands of *Eretz Yisrael*, was an integrated, self-reliant, and largely self-govern-
ing entity that lived at peace with its neighbors over an extended period of time.
Archaeology thus serves to amplify the biblical observation in Judges 21:25 that
in "those days there was no king in the land of Israel and every man did what
was right in his own eyes."

Beer-Sheba is another of the numerous sites at which a set of conditions prevailed similar to those in nearby Tel Masos, with one notable addition: the three strata of the pre-monarchical Israelite period overlaid a well associated with an earlier stratum. The well had been dug from what was then the crest of the site on which an installation of an altar and other evidence of a place of worship was also found. The well was a remarkable technical achievement of that early period, having been hewn through the bedrock to a depth of over 125 feet. It was unusual in that the effort required to place the well at that point was known to its excavators to have been unnecessary, for surrounding the rise down through which the well was driven were other wells in the vicinity of the nearby wadi that reached the water table located less than thirty feet below the surface. The well was nevertheless deliberately driven down through solid rock from the site of the altar at the crest of the hill.

> The excavating of this well on the top of the hill was, therefore, a unique project. Inasmuch as the excavations have demonstrated that the sacred cult place was on the height of this hill, it is probable that the well was somehow associated with it. Thus one may establish with considerable certainty that this is the well, the digging of which is ascribed to the patriarchs in the Bible (Genesis 21:25, 26:25).[14]

Aharoni presents the forty-meter-deep well as evidence that "the patriarchal narratives are no older than the period of the conquest."[15] In any event, the stories of Ahraham and Isaac are centered around the wells of Beer-Sheba and the region, and, whether the well excavated at Tel Masos was one of them or not, the exposed, unprotected site further attests to the settlement of a people in the area who, by and large, lived at peace with their neighbors. The archaeological appraisal that the scores of unfortified Israelite settlements were inhabited by a people who peacefully mixed and associated with the peoples of the region is reflected in the Bible, but is afforded cursory mention.

Then, as now, the events that "made the headlines" were those in which bloody conflicts took place; periods of peace rated no more space in the biblical reportage than they do in modern news-gathering. Nor are periods of peace prone to produce archaeological headlines. Extended periods of blissful prosperity are treated as mere intervals between pivotal, albeit catastrophic events. The Bible pays the most attention to times of trauma, cataclysmic events that caused radical changes in the geopolitical structure of the times, and affords minimal attention to periods of peace and progress, even in the many instances in which they extended over long passages between the conflicts and involved large sectors of the population of *Eretz Yisrael*. Read carefully, however, it becomes evident from both biblical and archaeological documentation that the struggles that marked the initial period of settlement became interspersed with, and eventually gave way to, gregarious phases in which the Israelite tribes are pictured as pursuing peaceful alternatives and even to a more or less loose amalgamation of the Israelites with other peoples.

Moses' father-in-law is said to have left Jericho together with the children of Judah to dwell "among the people" south of Arad. The Israelites did not:

> drive out the Jebusites that inhabited Jerusalem, but the Jebusites dwell with the children of Benjamin in Jerusalem unto this day. . . . Neither did Manasseh drive out the inhabitants of Beth-Shean and her towns, nor Taanach and her towns, nor the inhabitants of Ibeam and her towns, nor the inhabitants of Megiddo and her towns, but the Canaanites would dwell in that land. . . . Neither did Zebulun drive out the inhabitants of Kitron, nor the inhabitants of Nahalol, but the Canaanites dwelt among them, and became tributaries.

The same amiable relationship was established by the tribe of Asher with the inhabitants of Sidon, Akko, Ahlab, Achzib, Helbah, Aphik, and Rhob, for "the Asherites dwelt among the Canaanites." A permanent and peaceful association held as true for the tribe of Naphthali "which dwelt among the Canaanites" of Beth-Shemesh and Beth-Abnath, who became "tributaries unto them," and it held for the tribe of Dan, whose association with the Amorites was somewhat more tenuous. "Yet the hand of the house of Joseph prevailed, so that they [the Amorites] became tributaries."[16]

GROWTH AND INNOVATION IN
THE DAVIDIC PERIOD: ARCHITECTURE

Prosperity and an expanded population created a new social imperative. While the pillared, four-room architecture remained a clearly-defined Israelite standard from the wooded highlands of Dan to the dry desert of the Negev well into the monarchical period, economic and territorial growth generated new requisites. In the Davidic period, the construction of national administrative buildings, storehouses, and temples began on an extensive scale, and the architecture of public buildings and fortifications assumed their own character. The Davidic period is an exceptional one in that archaeological revelations of constructions initiated during David's tenure demonstrate that they far exceed in scale and quality the modest and peripheral mentions of such works in the Bible. The evidence of the continuation and expansion of these public works under Solomon, works detailed with some breadth in the Bible, also exceeds biblical summarizations by far. An exceptional period of accelerated growth and innovation ensued.

In the previous chapter it was pointed out that the public buildings did not follow Tyrian models, as has been so widely and uncritically assumed by an unwarranted extension of the biblical reference to Hiram's undoubtedly valuable contribution to the Temple's furnishings. Nor do more than traces of the "Egyptianizing influence," prevalent in many of the artifacts of the previous period, appear in these structures, a significant factor in the analysis of the genesis of Israelite art and engineering. The luxury goods that were previously produced for the Egyptian overlords and their local agents had been, per force, fabricated to Egyptian taste, a trend that diminished rapidly during the Israelite period. Goods produced for local use became less elaborate and more utilitarian, not because the artistic or technological competence of the Israelites was inferior, but because the artisans were catering to a humbler clientele, one with much more modest means and requirements. The goods produced for external exchange, however, continued to bear "Egyptianizing" characteristics, a modality keyed to the tastes of the clientele for whom they were fabricated.

The proscription against the making of idols and the construction of temples to house them is responsible for the dearth of Israelite objects for present-day art collectors to admire and for historians to hail as an expression of cultural excellence. The Israelites' irreverent attitude toward kings and governors likewise discouraged self-aggrandizing statues and monuments. To properly judge the level of Israelite artistry, engineering, and craftsmanship, therefore, one must look instead to the quality and appropriateness of the work actually accomplished. The Israelites adequately served their own needs and not the vanities of the oligarchs of an autocratic regime, nor were they obliged by a priestly class to produce idols to fear and adore. Judged by the criteria set for the practical purposes of an unfettered Israelite society, the level of artistry and creativity of the early Israelites can be seen to have been of a high order.

Whereas ostentation and extravagance were not important factors for Israelite village art, the competence and creativity of Israelite engineering and artisanship becomes plainly apparent in the architecture of public buildings, whose far-reaching structural and artistic innovations appeared immediately in the Davidic period, and became elaborated as the scale of construction escalated under the aegis of David's son, Solomon. Instead of the Tyrian or Egyptian models that we may be led to expect by the lore overlying Israelite history, the Mesopotamian, and in particular the Aramaic, heritage comes to the fore in the planning, stonework, and decoration of Israelite architecture.

A number of the basic structural elements employed in the Israelite monumental constructions were innovations or improvements over precedent work done elsewhere. Outstanding among these modernizations was the proficient application of ashlar masonry by the Israelite artisans. Ashlar blocks are large stones trimmed and fitted together with precision into a dry, mortarless wall. The faces of the rectangular blocks were generally smoothed to present a finished, aesthetically pleasing exterior. Although the technology of ashlar construction was not new, having been practiced in Mesopotamia as early as the third millennium B.C.E., Aharoni notes that "one must grant that thus far true ashlar masonry . . . has not been discovered in any one of the neighboring countries during or preceding the Iron Age." During the Israelite period in *Eretz Yisrael*, he adds in emphasis, "The art of building achieved one of its apogees in ashlar construction."[17]

THE ISRAELITE VOLUTE CAPITAL

One of the ironies of classical historiography is the way in which it retrospectively assigns distinctive architectural and other attributes of the Israelites to that of the later Classical period. Scholars have taken it for granted, having widely publicized "Aeolic" and "Ionic" capitals as prime examples of Greek creativity, that they are justified in terming the *Israelite volute capital,* indubitably the precursor and model for the Hellenic versions, as "Proto-Aeolic" or "Proto-Ionic"! By doing so, texts and treatises on art and architecture are enabled to blithely continue to pay homage to the purported creativity of the Greeks.

The scholarly pundits are not so generous to the Romans, readily admitting that Roman architecture and art is deeply indebted technically and stylistically to that of the Greeks. Such generosity, however, seems to stop short at the Aegean. The uniquely Israelite volute capital is a decorative ornamental treatment of the top of a pillar in which a pair of scrolls spiral out left and right from a central triangle, and is usually decorated at the crook of the scrolls by a small, stylized palm leaf or blossom. The origin of the motif itself harks back to the third millennium B.C.E. and spans the Fertile Crescent on a variety of artifacts such as cylinder seals, ivories, reliefs, wall paintings, and amulets; but its incorporation into columnar capitals must be attributed to the Israelite architects. The motif became refined and widely employed in the capitals of freestanding and relief pillars in major edifices of Hazor, Megiddo, Samaria, Jerusalem, Gezer, and at other smaller royal installations as far afield as Israelite constructions in Transjordan and Moab. "One can hardly believe it coincidental," comments Aharoni, "[that] not even one has been found in some adjacent land." The earliest appearance of an equivalent architectural feature occurs in Cyprus several hundreds of years later in the seventh century B.C.E.[18]

The incongruity of naming this distinctly Israelite architectural feature after Greek derivatives came to the attention of Yigael Yadin, who writes that while excavating at Hazor, "to our great surprise—and delight—we found two beautiful Proto-Aeolic or Proto-Ionic capitals lying on the floor," and was then constrained to explain that "they are known as Proto-Aeolic or Proto-Ionic because it is certain that the classical Ionic capitals developed from this much earlier type representing a stylized palm-tree."[19] Nor was the irony of the use of these terms lost on Aharoni, who observed with evident sarcasm that "one does not call the Phoenician script 'Proto-Ionic.'"[20] Aharoni's scorn should be extended to the fact that the script referred to is commonly designated by the Greek term "alphabet" in substitution for the original Canaanite or Hebrew "aleph-beth." The full extent of the irony seems to have escaped Ahorani, however, for he employed the Greek term "Phoenician" in place of "Canaanite" (as it should legitimately apply to those people of the tenth century B.C.E.).

OTHER ARCHITECTURAL ACHIEVEMENTS OF THE ISRAELITES

The architecture of the Israelite walled cities of the monarchical period exhibits an advance in citadel construction over the precedent models of the Middle and Late Bronze Eras, in which periods the systems of defending the approach to a walled city had already reached a high stage of development in Canaan. One of

:es (many of the ubiquitous pillared variety), and other buildings. Within
.e of the structures backed against the outer wall lay a substantial road
ng the wall. The circular road encompassed an inner city core, which was
ransversed by two roads. A public building and probably the temple were
ed on the highest point of the inner city, and other administrative build-
e sited around a city plaza. Two large courtyards were provided at one
ne plaza opposite the governmental palace, evidently areas in which visi-
ld be adequately entertained. The palace itself was approached by three
ental stairways of superb ashlar construction. The same fundamental plan
ed elsewhere, and is especially prominent in the Judahite cities Beer-Sheba,
Mirsim, Beth-Shemesh and Mizpah. Aharoni found it difficult to contain
iration for such outstanding demonstrations of sudden sophistication in
:tz Yisrael: "The rapidity and consistency of urban planning in the young
n is most surprising."[21]

.g to the drama of the popular stories of their creation and the personal
ices of countless thousands of admiring tourists, the most familiar of
engineering achievements is that of the shafts and tunnels hewn through
:k from the centers of Jerusalem, Megiddo, Hazor, Gezer, and Gibeon to
igs which furnished the life-sustaining liquid in times of both peace and
e raw statistics of these accomplishments give pause for reflection on
gic competence of the hydrological engineers of the Israelite monarchi-
d, of which these five waterworks are but the most outstanding examples.
Cole, in a study of the five magnificent works, believes that "it was at
that the Israelite engineers discovered—or rediscovered—the possibility
ng a source of fresh water outside the city, safe from an enemy during a
Gibeon (Gibeah), located seven miles north of Jerusalem, was known to
ctor of Joshua as "a great city, as one of the royal cities [even] greater
[23] and the excavators found its reputation to be well justified. Two sys-
fact, were created by the Israelite engineers at Gibeon; the earlier was
the tenth century by its excavator, the renowned archaeologist James
l,[24] and was composed of a long, stepped, 146 foot long tunnel which
i under the walls of the city to a sizable storage chamber into which water
om a spring through another 110 foot long, zigzag tunnel.
econd waterworks system at Gibeon made use of an existing cistern
ie city some thirty-seven feet in diameter and thirty-five feet deep. The
as acclaimed as the "Pool of Gibeon" in the Bible, in which it is written
.at site a dozen of David's forces under his adjutant Joab engaged in a
attle with a dozen Benjaminite supporters of King Saul commanded by
murderous hand-to-hand struggle ensued in which all twenty-four par-
slaughtered each other.[25] The Canaanite cistern was filled to its brim
rted rubble that had accumulated over a period of almost three millen-
was itself remarkable. The excavation of the rubble by the archaeolo-
ved to be a gigantic task but one that was hardly comparable to the
ended by its original excavators. "To construct it required the cutting

the outstanding architectural features of the Israelite f[...]
chambered gates. These massive, complex gate systems [...]
of pairs of guardroom chambers, usually six, arranged [...]
passage into the fortress. The immediate introduction o[...]
versions of chambered gates and of the approaches to t[...]
period of struggle ended and the Solomonic period [...]
another unmistakable manifestation of the intimate [...]
engineers with such architecture and marks the intro[...]
fortification construction throughout Israel.

The walls of the fortified Israelite cities were equ[...]
architectural expertise. They were typically composed[...]
reinforced by transverse walls. The spaces thus created[...]
wall and the inner wall were filled with rubble of stor[...]
els. At the higher levels, rooms were created for stora[...]
and even living quarters. These *casement walls,* no less[...]
make manifest the creative thinking of the Israelite p[...]
casement walls were not as unassailable as single w[...]
they did provide great strength and were far more eco[...]
use was more practical, they served peaceful purpos[...]

A number of other Israelite architectural innova[...]
palaces were not only of sound ashlar construction b[...]
windows and stone banisters. They served not merel[...]
habitations with a certain degree of civil comfort su[...]
the castles of a much later era. Wooden-banistered wi[...]
Eastern art on ivories and on various other media, b[...]
pear in Israelite *Eretz Yisrael.* The image of the wom[...]
such windows appears conspicuously in biblical lite[...]
which the mother of Sisera looked out through a la[...]
son's return from the war; in 2 Samuel 6:16, in whic[...]
said to have seen David leaping and dancing before t[...]
and in 2 Kings 9:30, in which Jezebel painted her [...]
peer out of the window properly groomed. Jezebel's [...]
appearance was of little avail, it is written, for it was o[...]
Eunuchs cast her to her death.

URBAN PLANNING

The most outstanding architectural achievement of th[...]
Aharoni, was the extent and coherence of city plan[...]
particularly evident in the Solomonic period. Beer-Sh[...]
century B.C.E. in accordance with a predetermined pla[...]
ings were incorporated into an integrated pattern. Th[...]
wall of the city was lined on the inside by a continuo[...]

reside[...]
the cir[...]
paralle[...]
in turn[...]
enscor[...]
ings w[...]
side of[...]
tors co[...]
monun[...]
is repea[...]
Tell Be[...]
his adr[...]
early E[...]
kingdo[...]

Owi[...]
experie[...]
Israelite[...]
solid rc[...]
the spr[...]
peril. T[...]
the geo[...]
cal peri[...]

Dan[...]
Gibeon[...]
of locat[...]
siege."2[...]
the red[...]
than Ai[...]
tems, ir[...]
dated t[...]
Pritcha[...]
led dow[...]
flowed [...]

The [...]
within [...]
cistern [...]
that at [...]
bloody [...]
Abner. [...]
ticipant[...]
with as[...]
nia, anc[...]
gists pr[...]
effort e[...]

and hauling away of approximately 1100 cubic feet (almost 3000 tons!) of limestone bedrock."[26]

Steps five feet wide, which spiral down around the sides of the erstwhile cistern to its bottom, were carved by the Israelites from the hard rock walling the cistern. The steps then continue on through a rock-cut shaft for another forty-five feet, deep down into the bowels of the hill to the water table. The stepped shaft leads to a kidney-shaped reservoir some twenty-two feet long and eleven feet wide which had been excavated eighty feet below the street level of the city. By means of this superb demonstration of hydrologic intelligence, the Israelite engineers enabled the city of Gibeon to achieve certain and complete independence from outside sources of water.

Gibeon was located under a tomato patch in the modern village of El-Jib. The identification of the site was assured by inscriptions on the many storage jar handles that were recovered from the debris of the water shaft together with clay stoppers and fillers. "The discovery of an extensive wine production and storage complex at Gibeon confirmed that the Gibeonites stored wine in the jars to which the handles were attached."[27] In the winter season of 1959–1960, the excavators found an extensive wine-producing facility near the cistern, composed of fewer than sixty-six circular cavities carved into bedrock, most of which were sealed with stone bungs. They were typically some two meters in diameter and two meters deep, and served several purposes. Some clearly had been used for trampling grapes, and others, protected by waterproof covers, were identified as fermentation vats. It was estimated that the comprehensive installation at Gibeon had an annual production capacity of fifty thousand gallons of wine.

Most of the jar handles date to the seventh century B.C.E. and, in addition to the word "Gibeon," scores of the handles include a phrase interpreted as "the walled (or enclosed) vineyard," along with the name or trade mark of the vintner. Some are incised with the names of Judahite towns to which wine was to be, or had been, consigned, among which Ziph, Succoth, and Jericho were the most common. The ubiquitous use of such common-place signatures reflects a level of aleph-bethic literacy in wide practice by the middle class unique to *Eretz Yisrael*.

Two tunnels of Jerusalem demonstrate the magnificent achievements of the Canaanite and Israelite hydrological engineers even more dramatically than those of Gibeon. The "Warren shaft" was named after Charles Warren, who discovered it in 1867 while visiting the famous spring of Gihon ("the bubbler") in the company of a group of pilgrims. Despite the gloom of the cave, Warren's sharp eyes detected a dark depression in the cave's roof high over the spot where the water was gushing forth from the rocky rear of the cave. Warren's curiosity was aroused. Being an experienced alpinist, he returned the following day with a ladder, climbing equipment, and a good measure of enthusiasm. Warren crawled through the tunnel to a vertical shaft, upon which he assayed his way forty feet straight up to a point at which the shaft appeared to come to an end. Undaunted, Warren poked around and found a narrow passageway through which he crawled and came to still another shaft. Recognizing that steps underlay the debris that had accumulated in it, Warren was encouraged to make his way up through it into a chamber loaded with dusty glass jars and pottery. Light shimmered through a chink of the vaulted chamber, and, barely squeezing through the narrow crack, a dusty and bedraggled Warren found himself in the midst of the city of Jerusalem.

The Warren shaft is also referred to as the "Jebusite shaft," since it may go back to a time before the establishment of Jerusalem in the tenth century. The gushing Gihon spring is located on the east side of the hill of Jerusalem and is connected by the tunnel through which Warren climbed to a sizable underground chamber, which collects and stores a substantial quantity of water. The chamber is located outside the city's walls and is reached by the combination of several tunneling elements up through which Warren forced his way. The stepped shaft just inside the city's defenses descends straight down to a slightly inclined horizontal ramp that in turn leads the water-seeker out underneath the walls of the city to a point above the underground chamber. A container can be let down from the vantage of the end of the ramp through the forty-foot vertical shaft that drops to the spring-fed collecting chamber.

This intricate system was replaced in the eighth century B.C.E. by King Hezekiah, who, based on the biblical account, was clearly responsible for its excavation. Hezekiah's tunnel leads from the spring in the Kidron Valley outside the city's walls in a gentle gradient for a distance of 1,750 feet to collect in the famous pool of Siloam. For some still mysterious reason, the two teams of stonecutters did not bore the shafts toward each other in a straight line but followed an erratic, snaking course. The Hezekian tunnelers met in the middle despite the devious route and the difficulty of plotting a path from the top of the hill. The record of this extraordinary achievement was proudly inscribed on the rock within the tunnel at the point of encounter at the behest of the tunnelers themselves. "This is the story of the piercing through," it reads, "while [the stonecutters were swinging their] axes, each toward his fellow and while there were yet three cubits to be pierced through, [there was heard] the voice of a man calling to his fellow."

The excitement of the meeting and their own awe for their magnificent accomplishment springs forth from the legend in stone: "And on the day of the piercing through," the inscription ends, "the stonecutters struck through each to meet his fellow, axe against axe. Then ran the water from the Spring to the Pool for twelve hundred cubits, and a hundred cubits was the height of the rock above the head of the stone-cutters."[28]

Megiddo's access to water was also to a spring outside the city. Several crude water systems were replaced during the Solomonic period by a system that was in turn replaced by one constructed by King Ahab in the ninth century. A deep shaft was dug down 115 feet through the rock at the center of the city; a stairway, gouged out of the shaft's wall, spirals down around the walls of a shaft to its bottom, from which a 200-foot tunnel was hacked through to the spring outside the city.

A great shaft sporting a spiralling staircase was similarly the means by which the engineers at Hazor reached the water table. If this circumstance was not accidental, notes Aharoni, "then it would appear that the hydrological engineers at Hazor had an understanding of the geology pertaining to water-bearing strata."[29] The waterworks at Hazor proved to be even more ingeniously contrived than those of Megiddo. Yigael Yadin assumed from the exposition of the system at Megiddo that Hazor would have a comparable system, based on certain similarities in the city's position, function, and type of fortifications. Yadin located the position of the shaft and began the removal of tons of debris that had accumulated and filled it over the centuries. Ninety-five feet down Yadin hit bottom, but, to his surprise, the tunnel led from the shaft eighty feet farther through the bedrock underneath the city to the natural water table 130 feet below the city's streets![30] How the engineers of ninth-century Hazor had known exactly where and how deep to drive their tunnel remains a matter of scholarly conjecture. The famous hydrological projects at Gibeon, Jerusalem, Megiddo, and Hazor were by no means unique; significant waterworks were executed in the period of the United Kingdom at Beer-Sheba, Ibleam, Gezer, and elsewhere.

The lofty level of architectural, engineering, agronomic, and pyrotechnical aptitudes of the Israelites cannot have been reached all at once by a nomadic, culturally backward people. Whatever model of the genesis of the Israelites is assumed, it must encompass their knowledge of the most advanced technological intelligence of the Iron Age.

11

Pyrotechnology in *Eretz Yisrael*

The Archaeological Evidence

The advance of civilization is appropriately measured by pyrotechnical competence. Its Neolithic beginnings are marked by the use of fire. The designations Chalcolithic, Bronze, and Iron Ages are simply reflections of the stage of pyrotechnology at which a particular culture has arrived. The ability to smelt iron from its ore and to produce glass from mineral silicates are the most noteworthy adjuncts of the shift from the Bronze to the Iron Age, and although they are by no means the only measures of a culture's sophistication, they serve as an accurate gauge of its advance. The ferric and vitric arts were important parts of the heritage that enriched Israelite culture from its Mesopotamian roots; the Jews became the carriers of those arts into the Western world.

PYROTECHNOLOGY IN OTHER NEAR EASTERN CULTURES

Among the many myths that have fallen by the wayside are those concerning the advent of ferric technology. The Egyptians, the Hittites, and the Philistines have all been proposed as the cultures from which iron-making was introduced to Canaan, but without taking cognizance of the fact that the requisite pyrotechnology was absent from all those cultures. The fact that the Egyptians were incapable of such technology has been long since, albeit grudgingly, accepted.

The only significant iron object recovered from Egyptian tombs is a Mesopotamian dagger found in the tomb of Tutankhamen. The blade has not been analyzed and in any event may have been manufactured from meteoric iron. The few iron artifacts recovered from early Hittite centers have now been conclusively shown to have been imports from Amorite and Hurrian (Urartian) territory to the east. Philistine sites have been extensively excavated, and whereas a few iron objects have been found in their ruins, no evidence of the requisite pyrotechnology has ever appeared during the Iron Age I phase (the twelfth to tenth centuries B.C.E.)

of their occupation, and the only traces of such an activity thereafter come from times and places at which Israelites were present. The Anatolian or Aegean (Mycenaean) regions from which these people stemmed had no such technology, and excavations of the colonies formed by the inaccurately dubbed "Sea Peoples" have produced no direct evidence that they brought such a technology with them.

A few iron-bladed knives have been found in tombs spotted around the Eastern Mediterranean and dated to before the tenth century B.C.E. A curved knife attached to an ivory handle with three bronze rivets turned up in a Cypriot tomb, and similar knives, found as far afield as Perati in Attica, in Philistine Tell Qasile, and Hama in Syria are cited as examples of such ware.[1] Such knives, however, were probably marketed by either Canaanite or Mycenaean traders. Some of the knives were found in association with Mycenean pottery of the twelfth century B.C.E., but there are conspicuous exceptions, items recovered from tombs in Canaan devoid of Mycenaean ware, but which significantly contain Canaanite and Israelite iron agricultural and industrial tools. Some of these latter tools predate the knives and daggers recovered from tombs in Mediterranean sites outside of Canaan. An iron pick found in 1976 in the Upper Galilee is a typical example of the earliest iron artifacts recovered from the region. "The iron pick is in a remarkable state of preservation and clearly dates to the early 12th, perhaps even the 13th century B.C."[2] This date precedes the time of Philistine settlement, or, at best, is contemporary with that event, and the iron pick was found in an area which the Philistines never reached. It is highly questionable, therefore, that the pick could have been produced by the invaders. Neither such implements, nor any other of the iron Canaanite agricultural or industrial tools, have yet been found in Mycenaean or Greek contexts, whereas both knives and agricultural implements were found in "early Israelite sites located just to the north of Jerusalem at Ai, Khirbet Raddana, and Tell el-Ful (ancient Gibeah where an 11th century plowshare was found). . . . In Palestine [sic] this same continuity [of an essentially Bronze Age culture] can be seen in the northern Canaanite cities, like Megiddo (stratum VIIA) and Taanach (period IB) in the Jezreel Valley, and at Beth Shean (stratum VI)."[3]

Yohanan Aharoni made note of the fact that "thus far no substantial archaeological evidence indicates that iron has been widely used in Philistia before it was widely used at Israelite sites."[4] All of the agricultural and industrial implements found in Canaan were absent from Mycenaean sites of the Iron Age I period and only appeared at Philistine sites when Israelites were conspicuously present, and in association with Israelite materials.

A Philistine copper-working facility was found at Tel Mor, documenting a technology that is removed from that of ferric production by 2000 years. A fifteenth-century crucible from the Greek island of Kea and the depiction of a copper-making (perhaps bronze-making) operation in the tomb of the fifteenth-century Egyptian vizier are the best that can be offered as physical evidence of the existence of Greek and Egyptian metallurgical capability. The Bronze Age, of course, goes back to at least 3200 B.C.E. in Mesopotamia, and bronze-making was unknown in Egypt until after the establishment of rule by the Semitic chieftains of the so-called Second Intermediate period. Ferric industrial facilities have so far been found only at Israelite sites such as at Megiddo and at the Galilean village of Yin'am.

The barbarian, seaborne invaders of the Levantine coast helped bring down the Hittite Empire, destroyed Ugarit, Alalakh, and Dor, and succeeded in founding permanent colonies along the southern segment of the coast on which littoral they developed their own distinct "Philistine" culture. The Aegeans arrived as a backward people whose outstanding attribute appears to have been their ferocity. Not a single Philistine text has come to light so far; it is a fair assumption that the invaders were basically illiterate. All the extant written documentation of their arrival and initial activity is second-hand. Egyptian references to the invasions from the sea are the earliest, specifically those of the time of Merneptah (of the last quarter of the thirteenth century B.C.E.) and of Rameses III (of the first quarter of the twelfth century B.C.E.). Those reports are followed by details of their incursions as given in biblical accounts and on tablets from Ugarit, Alalakh, Assyria, and Babylonia, from which the bulk of our knowledge of events is derived. The best that archaeological information can supply in regard to the history of the Philistines is a check against the tales told in those texts. Archaeological excavations do provide substantial information regarding the material artifacts of Philistine life and of the provenience of much of this material. The changes in cultural patterns are made evident by shifts from imported ware to ware produced in and around the settlements in Canaan, but iron artifacts were not among the objects from across the sea. The few iron objects found in Philistine ruins were clearly obtained from the east and north.

EVIDENCE OF IRON PRODUCTION IN ISRAELITE VILLAGES

Ferric technology was not invented at the outset of the Iron Age; objects of iron were being produced by the Mesopotamian progenitors of the Israelites a thousand years before their appearance in Canaan. The "Iron Age" does not mark the art's inception, it merely designates the period in which the proliferation of the technology was triggered in and around the Israelite villages of Canaan. The hinterlands of *Eretz Yisrael*, the thickly forested region that extended in ancient times in an arc sweeping around from the hills of central Israel through Lebanon into Aramea, is the region in which iron-smelting and forging can be expected to have been instituted. The ancient smiths did not enjoy the benefits of coal or coke or gas but depended almost entirely on wood for their fuel; the quantity of wood consumed made smelting within city limits difficult and limited casting and forging to relatively modest operations. The archaeological relics of pyroferric activity are most likely relegated to sparsely inhabited, wooded areas, or to the periphery of the urban centers, and have been largely lost through the attrition of erosion and the plow. The sparse forests and scrub of the Philistine coastal areas of southern Canaan make them implausible sites for the conduct of such an energy-demanding industry as the smelting of iron, even if the Philistines had been knowledgeable in the art.

The evidence of Israelite metalworking in the Upper Galilee dates from the outset of Israelite settlement. It was a sparsely inhabited area, hardly occupied at all until the Israelites arrived. The occupational debris of the Israelite I period was found on one of the highest Galilean ridges; in one of the rooms the remains of a kiln, ovens, benches, and vessels survived, "which proved that it served as a workshop for a metalsmith in copper and bronze." The fact that the initial habitation and workshop was sitting on bedrock and that "above this stratum was the debris of a settlement of Israelite II protected by a casement wall"[5] leaves scarcely any room for doubt that the smith was an early Israelite.

The lesson to be learned from this definitive discovery, however, remained unlearned. An example of the confusion that permeates the archaeological community regarding Philistine pyrotechnical competence and of the revelation of the true identity of the early iron producers is that of the excavations at Yin'am, just southwest of lake Tiberias. It was the region in which the biblical Rechabite metalworkers roamed, a forested area that is typical of the areas throughout the world where the art of iron-smelting is generally performed. Iron slag, evidence of an iron smeltery of the Late Bronze II period (c. thirteenth century B.C.E.) was found at the site in 1979. Seven samples of the slag were analyzed, and hematite spheres, droplets of metallic iron, showed up in them all; pieces of rusted iron in the debris of the smeltery and other evidence left no doubt that this industrial installation was indeed an iron-smelting facility. "The discovery is extremely significant," wrote Harold Liebowitz in reporting on the find, "for the history of metallurgy and the traditional view [is] that the Philistines introduced iron working into the region in the twelfth century."[6] Immersed as the discipline is in the myth of the Philistine provenience of the art, archaeologists were understandably astounded to find indisputable evidence of primary iron-making so far from Philistine territory at this absurdly early date.

In 1981, the incredulous archaeologists began to concentrate on the area of the smeltery in order "to secure a fuller picture of the major Late Bronze II building in which the iron smeltery was located."[7] The finds were indeterminate and so when the team resumed their labors the next year, they again concentrated on this area. Seven habitation phases of the site were carefully examined: a continuous occupation from the Late Bronze II entirely through the Iron Age I periods was documented, research which provided significant information regarding the architectural and other material aspects of the Israelite culture and settlement of the Lower Galilee. The earliest identifiable Israelite phase was datable to around 1200 B.C.E. and the last, seventh phase, to the late eleventh or early tenth century B.C.E., the critical period of premonarchic Israelite occupation.

"One fact of considerable importance," wrote Leibowitz, emphasizing the conclusion to which the evidence manifestly leads, "is the absence of evidence for Philistine occupation during any of the seven occupation phases."[8] Nor, it must be pointed out, does any other evidence exist that would place the Philistines in the region at that time.

The production of iron was not substantial anywhere for the first several centuries of Iron Age I, the period dating from the end of the thirteenth to the tenth century B.C.E. It was a cottage industry practiced in or near self-sufficient, basically agricultural communities by artisans who had carried the knowledge with them from wherever they had come. A good proportion of the objects recovered from such sites are agricultural: an iron plow found at Tell el-Full (an archaeological site identified as Gibeah, Saul's capital), an iron sickle recovered from Tell Masos, and several iron sickles recovered from Beer-Sheba are typical of the objects recovered from Israelite communities from the upper reaches of the Galilee to the Negev.

The exercise of such a highly advanced technology in a newly-evolving culture is, nevertheless, remarkable in itself. These formative agricultural communities were recovering from the trauma of liberation from Egyptian oppression, Canaanite feudal tyranny, or both, whichever model of emergence is assumed. The fact that the technology was unique to those communities and was but one aspect of a sophisticated agricultural and engineering intelligence (such as evidenced in terracing and the use of lined cisterns), and that the technology was accompanied by another facet of the great cultural leap forward, the use of aleph-bethic writing, provide firm underpinnings for the theory that there was among the Israelites a consequential contingent of knowledgeable migrant or refugee savants and artisans, who were, perhaps, the $H_u$abiru of literature or the Hebrews of the Bible.

The ferric industry burgeoned with the establishment of the monarchy and the formation of a cohesive nation, coinciding with the period designated by archaeologists as Iron Age II, extending from the beginning of the tenth to the end of the seventh century B.C.E., a period roughly coincident with the monarchical period to the time of the Babylonian Exile. A blacksmith's shop of the Solomonic period was uncovered at Megiddo by Gottlieb Schumacher as early as the first decade of the twentieth century. The iron ore, slag, and ash found on the site testified to an industry that had been in operation for a considerable time. A wide variety of products were being produced and survived in the substantial hoard of iron products found at the facility. It included a wide assortment of agricultural implements such as plowshares, hoes, sickles, and goads, and industrial tools such as chisels, shovels, knives, and nails. The fact that the operation was being performed within an urban environment is not unique, but unusual because, as we have seen, iron smelters are more likely to have carried on their operations deep in the forests. The discovery of the Megiddo facility provided a clear demonstration that the tradition of ironworking was well established and marked the onset of a widespread use of iron implements.[9]

The fact that iron figured prominently in the catalogue of Judahite materials with which weapons of war and other objects were fashioned is made evident by

Robert Maddin

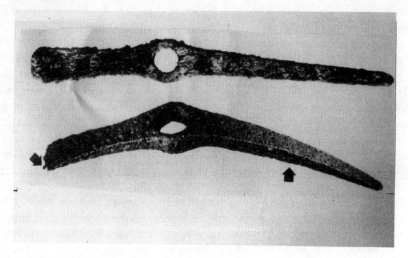

An iron pick dated to the twelfth or early thirteenth century B.C.E., the very beginning of
the officially designated advent of the Iron Age, and coinciding with the time in which
hundreds of Israelite settlements were established in the hills of Canaan. The pick was
found in the Upper Galilee in Tell Adir and is remarkable because it was composed of
carburized iron (steel). The appearance of such a hardened iron product in *Eretz Yisrael* at
such an early date attests to the advanced state of an art that had originated in the Ararat
mountains of Mesopotamia more than a millennium earlier. (Photograph from the author's
collection.)

a massive iron chain employed by the Judahites in defense of Lachish against the
Assyrians under Sennacherib at the end of the eighth century B.C.E. Four links of
this chain have survived, each link ten centimeters long. "The chain was part of
a defensive device to counter the most horrifying weapon known in ancient siege
warfare, the battering ram. . . . As the shaft of the battering ram swung close to a
wall, the defenders would lower a long chain . . . catching the shaft and raising
it, thus deflecting its direct attack on the wall."[10] The use of such a chain is evident in a relief predating the battle of Lachish by 150 years depicting the siege of
Assurbanipal (883-859 B.C.E.) upon an unidentified city.[11]

A seventh-century iron chain of another kind, complete with a four-pronged
hook, was recovered from nearby Tel Sera (Tell esh-Sharia), south of Beer-Sheba.
This site has been identified as biblical Ziklag, a city presented to David by the
Philistine King of Gath, Achish, as a refuge in his flight from Saul, and from which
David later set out to Hebron to be acclaimed king of Israel. Both glassware and
iron were found at the site. A thirteenth-century B.C.E. glass bottle of Ziklag's
Canaanite period (the sixteenth to thirteenth centuries B.C.E.) was recovered from
the ruins of the temple area, as well as two painted pottery vessels in the shape
of a pomegranate. A tenth-century iron knife of the beginning of Ziklag's Israelite
period was recovered from a typical four-room Israelite house.[12]

THE DISCOVERIES AT EKRON AND OTHER JUDAIC INDUSTRIES

Another hoard of iron farm implements, including a pair of two-headed plows, a single-headed plow, a knife, and a sickle blade, was hidden away in a storage jar under the floor of a structure at Ekron (Tel Miqne) in the seventh century B.C.E. The Philistines had displaced the indigenous Canaanite community at the site, after which it became one of the most important Philistine cities and was situated astride a strategic position on the frontier between Philistia and Judah. The relationship of Ekron with the Judahites went through several phases: at first Ekron was at the northern border of "the land that yet remains [to be possessed]," [13] but then went through cycles of conflict and cooperation with its neighbor, Judah. Ekron fell under Assyrian control at the turn of the seventh century B.C.E. and remained at peace with Judah for a seventy year period from 701–630 B.C.E. During this propitious time, Judahite influence was at its peak and Ekron reached the zenith of its economic development and growth. The city and its economy began to decline after the Egyptians displaced the Assyrians at the end of that period.

The agricultural tools were the most significant iron objects found in Ekron, although several iron knives with ivory handles were found in the city's earlier, Iron Age I settlement. It must be assumed that the agricultural implements unearthed at Ekron were produced elsewhere and had been carefully cached within the city's defenses at a time of travail, perhaps by a local farmer who intended to return to recover them. Such an event took place in 603 B.C.E., at which time Ekron was destroyed by Nebuchadnezzar in his campaign to conquer Philistia. The tools were never retrieved, a fortuitous circumstance that kept them intact until they were unearthed by Trude Dothan and Seymour Gitin, the archaeologists charged with the excavation of the site.

The association of the iron trove with a Judahite is strongly suggested by a four-horned altar, unmistakably Judahite, found in a niche of the room near the hoard of iron farm implements. The altar was but one of many that were installed in every building of the extensive industrial zone of Ekron. The installation of a four-horned altar at an industrial facility is a familiar cultic tradition from northern Israel and "may indicate that Ekron's industry was being administered by a priestly class under royal authority." [14] The iron agricultural implements were from a period in which an important, long-term economic relationship had been established between the Philistine coastal plain and Judah. A number of important industries were, in fact, obviously being operated in Ekron by Judahites, a fact made clearly evident not only from the presence of the four-horned altars, central to Judahite religious practice, but also from the presence of typical Judahite pottery, epigraphic paleo-Hebrew or Canaanite letters on a number of storage jars, and stone shekel and bekah weights characteristic of Judah. [15] An intimate relationship of Ekron and Judah continued over a considerable time; it extended back at least to the period in which Hezekiah, king of Judah, had conquered and gained control of many Philistine cities, including Ekron. Two *l'melekh* handles

(Hebrew seal impressions on the handles of storage jars, meaning "belonging to the king") were recovered at Ekron from this eighth-century B.C.E. period.

Well over a thousand handles and jars of the period bearing such definitive stamps have been recovered from throughout the Land of Israel. Four centers are specified in the stamps as the sources of the containers, of which three are known to be Judahite: Hebron, Ziph, Socoh, and the fourth, *mmst*, is a site yet to be identified. The stamps include two types of symbols: a four-winged scarab, or a two-winged sun disk, clear reflections of the Egyptian and Mesopotamian roots of the Israelite culture. It is perhaps significant that by far the great majority of stamped jar handles unearthed in the southern regions, as, for example, eighty percent of those recovered from Lachish,[16] are of the scarab types, whereas most of the handles found in the northern region are of the winged sun type. In addition to the royal seal impressions, a great number of private seal impressions have been found bearing the name of the owner or distributor and that of his father, further testimony to the sophistication of the distributive system and the level of literacy.

A four-horned altar was prominent in a room at Ekron in which a unit of a massive olive oil manufactory was installed, one of 103 olive oil production units that had been found at Ekron at the time in which only three percent of the site had been excavated. It was determined that the production capacity of those units alone was 290,000 gallons of olive oil per year, one-fifth of Israel's present production. Gitin suggests that "Thus, in antiquity Ekron was the largest olive-oil industrial center in the Near-East."[17]

Olive oil production takes place during only four months of the year, and other industries were performed during the off seasons in various rooms of the extensive industrial complex of Ekron. It appears that part of the slack time was taken up by textile production; a large number of loom weights were recovered from throughout the industrial areas, and associated with them were other four-horned altars. Evidence of extensive textile production and of another substantial olive oil facility of the late ninth–early eighth century B.C.E. was also found at Israelite Gezer.[18]

DISCOVERIES AT TIMNAH AND TEL QASILA

Still more evidence of substantial Israelite textile and olive oil production turned up in the heart of "Samson country," in Tel Batash, the biblical Timnah, located five miles east of Tel Miqne (Ekron) and six miles south of Gezer.[19] Philistine Timnah was made famous by the story of Samson, whose exploits at Timnah provide some of the most romantic as well as action-packed biblical episodes. Samson's romantic involvement with a Philistine woman from Timnah; his encounter in the fields of Timnah with a full-grown lion that he tore asunder with his bare hands; his slaughter of thirty Philistines at Ashkelon; his burning down of the Timnah grain fields by tieing torches to the tails of three hundred foxes;

the retribution he doled out in revenge for the murder of his wife and father-in-law; his slaughter of a thousand Philistines with the jawbone of an ass; the circumstances of his subsequent haircut, capture, blinding, and dramatic demise, all make the plots of the soapiest of soap operas pale by comparison.[20]

The fact is, however, that iron artifacts are notably absent from Timnah and do not appear even after it came under Israelite control in the tenth century B.C.E. A Hebrew name, however, inscribed on a pottery bowl fragment, was one of the most precious finds of the period. It is the Hebrew name Hanan, which also appears as a component of the name of one of the Solomonic districts of the Timnah region. Many of the storage jugs were found with the seal impressions of officials related to the administration of the Judahite king Hezeliah as well as royal seals, including the distinctive *l'melekh* impressions.[21] Thus the aleph-bethic competency of the Israelites is again attested to, a cultural capability that contrasts sharply with that of the people who preceded them in the area.

PHILISTINE AND MYCENAEAN VERSUS ISRAELITE FERRIC TECHNOLOGY

No evidence has been produced that attests to the ironworking propensities of the Philistines, of other "Sea Peoples," or their probable progenitors, the Mycenaeans, prior to their appearance on the Canaanite coast. No evidence exists that would indicate that they developed such a capability soon after their incursion into lower Canaan, not even in the early strata of Ashdod, the extensively excavated Philistine capital. An iron axe and a chisel were among a few iron tools found in a room of the fortifications of the city from stratum 9 of the excavation, but they date from the late seventh or early sixth century B.C.E. Evidence of iron production was found outside the city walls in the form of an accumulation of a large quantity of iron slag, which appears to have dated from about the same time,[22] some 600 years after the appearance of iron smeltery materials in the Israelite Galilee at Yin'am. A few iron objects were also found at nearby Tel Qasila, dating to the end of the eleventh century, among which was an iron bracelet of the same type recovered from earlier Israelite sites. The bracelet, notes Yohanan Aharoni, is a throwback to "a phenomenon noted in Israelite I, when the new metal was rare and costly, serving mainly for jewelry." In the excavation of an earlier temple, however, an iron blade with an ivory handle was found; it was obviously intended for ceremonial use, and was of a type similar to ones imported into Cyprus and the Aegean area from Canaan, and to those found at Ekron. "It is precisely such an exceptional find that testifies how greatly iron was regarded as a precious and rare metal."[23]

The contrast between the Philistine and Israelite metallurgic technology was drawn clearly by a team of scholars who analyzed the iron artifacts found at Taanach, and who then followed up by making a comparative survey of iron objects found in Philistine sites of the period. The Taanach objects were dated to the tenth century B.C.E., a time contemporary with that of the Megiddo black-smithing facility, and precedent by three centuries to the Ekron hoard. By 925 B.C.E. at the very latest, the producers of the Taanach implements had already achieved the carburization of iron into steel, the final elaboration of smelting technology and the climax of the Iron Age. "[The evidence] suggests that steel was being consciously produced by the tenth century B.C."[24]

The Taanach investigators researched archaeological and historical material from the entire eastern Mediterranean, including data relating to the few iron artifacts recovered from Philistine sites. Whereas "the results suggest that by the late tenth century blacksmiths supplying northern Palestine [sic] were able to produce carburized iron (steel), complementary studies of iron artifacts from Philistine sites did not reveal such consistent technical achievements. . . . There is no convincing evidence for iron production from Philistine sites, and very little for copper production."[25]

As for the Mycenaeans, not only the iron but even the bronze ceremonial dag-gers retrieved from fifteenth-century B.C.E. Mycenaean sites were either imported into Mycenae or produced by imported artisans who introduced the technology. Many were magnificently inlaid with elaborate scenes in gold, silver, copper, in alloys of these metals and in niello, a bluish-black, little-known substance that provides the clue to the origins of the technique. While the style appears to be generally Cretan, no examples have been found on that island, but superb examples have turned up at Mycenae, the island of Thera, and elsewhere. The technique did not originate in Crete, however, but in Mesopotamia about 2300 B.C.E., spread into Aram-Naharaim about 1800 B.C.E., and filtered from Aram-Naharaim to Byblos on the coast of Canaan, where an early, fine example that includes the use of niello has been found. It has been assumed that the technique then crossed over to Crete with Canaanite craftsmen after that time, during a period in which strong com-mercial intercourse developed between Byblos and Crete.[26] Mesopotamian and Canaanite goods thereafter found their way throughout the Aegean; among the indicative objects found in a palace at Thebes, for example, were cylinder seals of lapis lazuli and gems of lapis lazuli, glass, and ivory.[27]

It is significant that ferric production never appeared in Mycenaean Greece, although iron ore was easily accessible. John Chadwick puts the case succinctly: "The Mycenaeans' failure to exploit the iron ores of Greece was due to lack of technical skill."[28] This metallurgical lacuna contrasts with a considerable com-petence in working bronze, an industry that depended on copper from Cyprus and tin from either the far reaches of Anatolia or from far more distant Afghani-stan. The cargo of the fourteenth-century B.C.E. ship that foundered off Ulu Burun (discussed in Chapter 7), whose voyage appears to have originated from the Canaanite coast with tin ingots and which stopped off at Cyprus to pick up cop-per ingots, carried on board not only both these primary ingredients of brass but evidently one or more smiths, possibly an indication of where the artisans as well as the materials came from.

The earliest Greek references to iron are Homer's occasional, clearly anachronistic slips into the inclusion of the metal in place of bronze for the material of the weapons of the ancient Greeks. "Iron was of course not unknown [to the Greeks] in the Bronze Age," notes Chadwick, "it was the technique of fabrication which was lacking."[29] Whereas many biblical references are as clearly anachronistic, at least the Mesopotamian existence of the technology and its transference to Canaan is demonstrable, to whatever limited extent the art was actually practiced during the Bronze Age. The intriguing aspect of Greek metallurgical knowledge is an etymological relationship of many Greek words to those of the Semites. The normal word for gold, the most anciently worked of metals, is *khrusos,* a word that "is known to be a loan word from Semitic (Ugaritic $h_u$rs, Assyrian $h_u ura^- s^u u$).[30]

IVORY WORK IN BRONZE AGE CANAAN

The ivory handles of the Ekron knives referred to earlier are still less convincing indications of Philistine craftsmanship. Although working in ivory was being performed in the Aegean as far back as the Minoan period, it was basically one of the distinctive and well-developed Canaanite crafts of the time. The craft crossed over to Crete from Canaan in much the same fashion as did metallurgic, Bronze-Age technology. The Mycenaeans obtained ivory from Canaan, where small hippopotami were still wallowing in the estuaries of the rivers and elephants were still roaming the woods in the Bronze Age. The evidence points to a parallel importation of ivory-working craftsmen from Crete or directly from the Canaanite region of the continent: "All the ivory which has either been found by digging or is mentioned in the documents obviously came from abroad."[31] Tusks ready for carving have survived in the palaces at Phaestos and Zakro, but it has been assumed that "it may be, indeed, that most of the surviving ivories from Mycenaean sites were made by immigrant Cretan craftsmen, for ivory-working was always as much a mystery as an art."[32]

Whether the ivory handles of the Ekron knives can be considered the product of a mystery or an art, the weight of the evidence is that the mysterious artisans who produced them were of Mesopotamian origin, and that the iron blades protruding from them were indeed likely to have been forged in the highlands of *Eretz Yisrael.* A similar ivory knife handle of the pre-Philistine Early Bronze Age was recovered from Ai, predating the Ekron knives by hundreds of years. A carved ivory bull's head of the same early period was also recovered at Ai, and other such bulls' heads were unearthed at Jericho and at Khirbet Kerak near Tiberias, neither of which sites were ever graced by Philistine presence.[33] Whereas all these ivory artifacts were probably produced locally, they show strong Mesopotamian characteristics,[34] indicating that either the artifacts or the artisans who produced them, or at the very least, the progenitors of those Galilean ivory-workers, came from the East. Such a suggestion is amply reinforced by a great hoard of exquisite ivories recovered from Megiddo, by the impressive British Museum collection of ivories from ancient Nimrud, and by other Mesopotamian ivories that amply attest to the fact that the art was indeed an ancient one in the world of the twin rivers, as far back as third-millennium Akkadia. The Late Bronze Age was a period in which the art of carving ivory blossomed as an art form in Canaan to such a degree that the excellence of execution, the variety of products, and the wide practice of the art in a Canaanite context led Harold Leibowitz to employ it "as evidence for a high level of artistic achievement in this period." This artistic renaissance does not represent an isolated phenomenon, insisted Leibowitz: "Rather, the achievements in ivory-working correlate with achievements evidenced in other LB II assemblages."[35]

The repertory of Canaanite ivory work of the Late Bronze Age is indeed impressive; both incised ivory plaques and sculpture in the round are well represented: "Ivory boxes and panels decorated with complex compositions; openwork panels used in the interstices on furniture; a variety of cosmetic spoons and containers, including bowls, swimming girls, duck-shaped spoons and spoons with duck-shaped handles; combs, gaming boards. . . . "[36] A huge hoard of ivory artifacts was recovered from Megiddo, in which most of these and many other miscellaneous genres of ivory work were included. Several ivory cosmetic spoons carved in the shape of swimming girls recovered from the Megiddo treasure room were also represented in Beth-Shan and Tell es-Saᶜidi-yeh. Cosmetic duck-shaped containers were recovered from a tomb at Tel Dan, and others from tombs at Shechem, Lachish, and Tell el Farᶜah, all of which were patently Canaanite products.[37] Perhaps most indicative of the origin of the art and of the path of its transference to Canaan are the ivory gaming boards found at Megiddo, Beth-Shan, and Tell Jemmeh, on which were played the Mesopotamian games that were also introduced to Egypt during the period of Semitic rule. These game boards are virtually absent from the Aegean, and the few examples extant in faience and other media represent a totally different tradition.[38] The Canaanite ivories suggest that the LB II period, the period from 1400 to 1200 B.C.E., "was characterized by elegance and sophistication . . . a high point in the material culture of Palestine [sic]."[39]

Ivory plaques bearing figures carved in relief and *a jour* work, to which bits of gold foil still adhered, and inlaid with vari-colored glass, were recovered from the remains of buildings erected by Omri and his successors in the Arabic town of Sebaste, near Shechem. The ruins of an extensive complex of palace buildings built of fine ashlar masonry lies under later Herodian and Roman structures, surrounded by a wall through which entry was made through a most interesting gate, reminiscent of the Lion's Gate of Mycenae.[40] Reference to just such ivory work is provided in 1 Kings 22:39 in admiration of the glorious architectural accomplishments of King Ahab. "All that he [Ahab] did," crows the chronicler, "and the ivory house which he made, and all the cities he built, are they not written in the book of chronicles of the kings of Israel?"

GLASSMAKING IN THE EMERGING ISRAELITE CULTURE

Life in the Israelite communities was simple during the formative period, as one would expect in a newly-evolving culture in the process of liberation and recovery from either the trauma of Egyptian domination, feudal oppression, or from both—whichever variations of the models of Israelite evolution one chooses to accept. Nevertheless, the technological acumen of the occupants of the proliferating villages of Canaan rose to the highest level to which civilization had attained anywhere on earth at that time.

A fascinating aspect of Israelite technology was that of glassmaking. It cannot be expected that the Israelites would be greatly concerned with the production of luxury glassware in the formative period of Israelite society. The first period of the Israelite settlement in Canaan was not conducive to the production of exotic, expensive glass artifacts. Such products were produced for royalty or for the rich and powerful, and for "persons of special distinction. Since the departing Jews did not belong to this strata of society," wryly notes Frederic Neuberg, "it is hardly likely that they took any glass objects on their wanderings."[41] The Israelites turned to the production of iron and bronze tools and of agricultural paraphernalia, precisely the types of objects that have been found, but the art never disappeared, the sophisticated pyrotechnology possessed by the Israelites lent itself to the renewal of the production of glassware.

Thus, as the Iron Age generated momentum in the hills of Canaan and as Israelite society became entrenched and evolved into sovereign nationhood, objects of glass reappeared, at the very time they disappeared from Egypt. The new crop of glass artifacts were functionally distinct from Egyptian-style ware, simpler in decoration, more utilitarian or suitable for ritual purposes than lavishly executed and decorated. A jug recovered from Lachish is an example of this new category of glassware. It is decorated with a palm leaf design, a pattern that recurs continually as a standard motif of Israelite art. Glass rods, ritual scepters bearing the same type of ornamentation and topped with a representation of a pomegranate, another recurring motif of Israelite art, were found at Hazor and at Megiddo. This motif recalls the biblical references to the use of the fruit, especially those included in the instructions of God Himself.

The close association between the seafaring Canaanites and the Israelite monarchy led to a revitalized glassware industry and to the distribution of glass artifacts throughout the Mediterranean. The Belus beach was the main provider of the siliceous sand, the forests of the Galilee and Lebanon provided the fuel, and the ports of Tyre and Sidon provided the facilities through which glassware began to reach the lands girding the Mediterranean. Moses is said to have foreseen this commerce: the area through which the Belus River flows was assigned to the tribe of Zebulun, and its Galilean hinterlands were assigned to the tribes of Asher and Dan. In performing a benediction over the Belus River area, Moses predicted that "They shall profit from the abundance of the sea and from the treasures hidden in the sand."[42]

The glassmaking propensity of the Israelites lives on in legend. An Arabian folktale recalls a deception practiced by King Solomon upon the Queen of Sheba: the wily king had a pavement of glass installed in a section of his palace that deceived the visiting Queen, who believed it to be a pool of water. The legend is clearly mythical, inasmuch as an expanse of flat glass or mirror was beyond the capabilities of the ancient glassmakers, but myths often contain real elements of a tribal memory and therefore must always be considered, albeit skeptically. The Talmud does report that "white glass has ceased since the destruction of our temple,"[43] from which statement we must deduce that such glass was used in the Temple.

Familiarity with the process of glassmaking is reflected in a number of talmudic and midrashic references. Wisdom is referred to in Job as being more valuable than gold or sapphire or glass, the most costly of earthly materials.[44] The Palestinian Talmud describes the fusion of glass by rolling (the production of "agate" glass by "marvering" differently colored molten glass together), as well as the layering of glass and cutting through the layers (the production of "cameo" glass).[45] In Genesis 2:7 it is written that God formed man out of the dust of the earth, and he blew into his nostrils the breath of life. The elements of the process of this ultimate act of creation is likened in the Midrash to that of blowing glass, in which the breath of man becomes the soul of the vessel he creates just as the breath of God becomes the soul of Man.[46]

Subsequently we shall see how the exiled Israelites carried the vitric art with them into Persia; they blew soul into hot molten stone and the art of glassmaking was reborn where it had been conceived.

Let us first turn to another aspect of the Israelite culture. As we have seen, the evolution of the Israelite civilization and culture was based on an aspiration for independence that was made viable by three attributes with which the Israelite villagers of the pre-Solomonic period were endowed from their very beginning. The pyrotechnical, and perforce, the metallurgical expertise was but one facet of the remarkable progress made in a time so short that the archaeological evolution of the new society is scarcely discernible. Agronomic expertise was another facet of Israelite productive capabilities, and third, but by no means least important in the roster of Israelite cultural endowments, was the use of an aleph-bethic system that paved the way for a high degree of literacy.

12

Semitic Origins of Literacy

The Aleph-Bethic Script

The Hebrew script on the handle of Ahilud's jug at Raddana, the descriptive information on the handles found in the rubble of Gibeon, the inscriptions in the tunnel of Siloam and other such seals and inscriptions are a few of the manifestations of another stimulus of the great thrust forward into a new stage of civilization that took place at this critical juncture of history: the invention of acrophonic writing[1] and the consequent development and proliferation of the aleph-bethic writing system. The invention heralded a revolutionary advance in communication and in making knowledge available; for the first time in the world's history, universal literacy became feasible.

THE EARLIEST RECORDS

The earliest example of such writing was found at Serabit al-Khadem in the western Sinai, dating to the Middle Bronze Age about 1650-1600 B.C.E. Semitic-language-speaking slaves were put to work in the remote desert turquoise and copper mines by the Egyptians soon after control by the Canaanite chiefs was shattered and Canaan was subjugated to Theban pharaonic rule. There is no doubt that the redactors of the inscriptions were the Semitic slaves and not their Egyptian over-lords, for much of the graffiti scrawled over the rock surfaces near the mines was addressed to Semitic deities, among whom the favored ones appear to have been *El* and his consort, the "serpent lady" *Elath*. The content of the messages certify to the cultural pedigree and mark the social status of the inscribers: "Oh my God" reads a pitiful plea by one of these miserable, erudite Semitic slaves, "rescue me from the interior of the mine!"[2]

It was the great Sir William Flinders Petrie who first came across potsherd fragments on which these "Proto-Sinaitic" inscriptions appear.[3] Some twenty-two characters comprised the complete catalogue of Canaanite signs, a group of sym-

221

bols that heralded a new age of literacy, a so-called abecedary from which the parallel ancient Hebrew *aleph-beth* was directly derived.[4] This group formed, and has remained, the familiar foundation of all of the Western writing systems to the present time and has been anachronistically dubbed the alphabet. Such an actual abecedarium (aleph-beth-gimelary?) was found in an Israelite storage pit at Izbet Sartah,[5] dated to about 1200 B.C.E., the beginning of the period of Judges and probably falling within the period of the first generation of Israelite settlement. The text of five lines appears to have been written by two persons; the last line is composed of all the twenty-two letters of the Hebrew aleph-beth and was evidently written by a student practicing to write it.[6] Thus was the aleph-beth born; thus did universal literacy become feasible.

Examples of "Proto-Canaanite" aleph-bethic inscriptions, an archaic signary that may date back to the eighteenth century B.C.E., disappeared from an Egyptian-controlled environment after the sixteenth century B.C.E., when the patriarchic rulers of Egypt and Canaan were deposed by the Theban princes. The fact that the knowledge and practice of aleph-bethic writing continued through the time of upheaval, albeit that examples of such writing have not yet turned up, is evidenced by the reappearance in a more advanced form of the same aleph-beth signary in the fourteenth century B.C.E. and its use in the mid-twelfth century B.C.E. throughout the area of Israelite settlement at Megiddo, Shechem, Beth-shemesh, Lachish, Gezer, and elsewhere. The glaring gap of 200 years between the two

An inscription found at Izbet Sartah dates from the time of the Judges, between 1200 and 1000 B.C.E. It is probably a schoolchild's exercise, and its fifth line provides the oldest Hebrew abecedary ever found. The typical four-room houses, storage pits, and other evidence indicates that Izbet Sartah was an Israelite settlement that may have been the biblical Ebenezer. Another Hebrew schoolchild's inscription was found at Gezer; it dates to the tenth century and lists the months by their agricultural attributes. (Photograph from the author's collection.)

periods led S. Yeivin to ask whether it would be "too daring a hypothesis to con-nect the use of this signary with the origins of the Hebrew people, the signary having been borrowed (?) by the Patriarchs from its West-Semitic inventors in Sinai, no longer used in Canaan when the Hebrews emigrated to Egypt, and reappearing in Canaan with the first penetration of the Israelites there?"[7]

Two Canaanite aleph-bethic inscriptions were brought to light from the elev-enth century B.C.E. tomb of Ahiram, King of Byblos, and at Ugarit (Ra's Shamra·) in which city a cuneiform-derived signary attested to a new aleph-bethic development that was affirmed by subsequent discoveries at Byblos and elsewhere. It would appear that "when the Ugaritic scribes looked for a prototype on which to model an adaptation of their cuneiform signary for their documents in their own language, they invented an official alphabetic script and even made an attempt to indicate vowels in certain cases."[8] The Ugaritic script began to descend southward, even as far as Judah, when it disappeared with the destruction of the city in which it was born. The later version of the Proto-Sinaitic signary, a form of writing far more suitable for inking onto papyrus, leather, parchment, and linen, and even for marking wood and clay surfaces, became the standard for both the Canaanites and the Hebrews. Still another version of the Proto-Sinaitic signary is suggested by other finds of the late thirteenth to early twelfth century B.C.E. at Succoth and elsewhere in Transjordan, which eventually led to the development of the Southern Arabic aleph-beth.[9] Unfortunately, ink-writing is also infinitely more perishable than are inscriptions on baked clay or stone. We are therefore paradoxically subjected to a vast imbalance of the written record in that through the use of ink-writing imple-ments and the perishable mediums on which the records were written, the most literate of ancient peoples became the least documented.

The chronology of the appearance of these signaries is as curiously parallel to events in the history of the Israelites as are the signaries of the previous periods to that of their Semitic predecessors, on whatever model historiography is con-structed. We might echo Yeivin's query by asking, "Should we not assign the tim-ing of the appearance of these new signaries along the upper Canaanite coast to the spread of the premonarchical Hebrew-Israelites into the northern reaches of Canaan and to their influence upon its culture, a process that portends the ami-cable intercourse between the Tyrian king Hiram and the Israelite kings David and Solomon?"

Among the peoples who assayed the literary leap into the future were those who were simultaneously familiar with Akkadian, as cuneiform tablets unearthed in Hazor and elsewhere attest.[10] The Bible takes the literacy of the immigrating Israelites for granted. In Joshua 18:6, for example, Joshua instructed that three men from each tribe be dispatched to "describe the land into seven parts, *and bring the descriptions hither to me.*" It is this propensity for the written word that distinguished the ancient Hebrew-Israelites from all other peoples. "Israel was extraordinary," proclaims Norman Gottwald, "in being the one socially revolu-tionary people in the ancient Near East to produce a literature and to survive as a distinctive cultural and religious entity."[11] We might peripherally add that this unique characteristic endured through the next two millennia and is the single factor that provided the Jews with an advantage over all other cultures into the modern period, when universal literacy first became recognized as an essential of the Industrial Age.

No great archaeological catalog of early Israelite literature has survived. This unfortunate circumstance should not be unanticipated because in the first place, the Israelites did not create the monuments and statuary, idolic or otherwise, on which so many of the inscriptions of other cultures are commonly found and from which so much information has been gleaned. Second, the Israelites adopted the aleph-bethic system from the dawn of their appearance in Eretz Israel, and therefore, owing to the fragility of the materials employed and the moist climate to which the materials were subjected, precious little of this early material survived, and little can be expected to have survived. A notable exception to the lack of inscriptions on stone is the so-called Farmer's Calendar, discovered at Gezer and dating from the ninth century B.C.E. The tablet outlines the division of labor according to the months of the year.[12] The very existence of a stone inscription containing such mundane information stands in sharp contrast to the use to which stone inscriptions were usually put.

The durable clay tablet, so convenient and useful for the incised cuneiform system of writing, became a clumsy means of correspondence once the aleph-bethic system was invented and the pen replaced the incising tool. Cuneiform writing gradually became obsolete as a means of recording business and administrative matters. The inscriptions that have endured the exigencies of weather and wear, for example, the seals on storage jar handles and clay ostraca (shards of pottery on which letters and other texts were written), serve not only to document a considerable Israelite literacy, but have gone far to reveal the existence of persons, places, and events that had previously been known to us only from biblical references.

Because papyrus paper was not always available and was in any event costly, and because pottery shards were always available, had a smooth surface and had no intrinsic value, they were often used for correspondence and archival purposes. Accounts of receipts of taxes in the form of oil and wine were kept by officials on ostraca and stored in the palaces of the kings of Israel. Such records were recovered from the ruins of rooms of the Samarian palace dating to the eighth century B.C.E., and they provide not only the names of the officials, taxpayers, and numbers of jars of oil or wine delivered, but the names of towns, some of which are listed in the Bible, some that have been archaeologically unearthed, and some that are not otherwise known.

DISCOVERIES AT LACHISH

Thus a group of ostraca recovered from Lachish, first deciphered by Professor N. H. (Harry) Torczyner (Tur-Sinai), led Sir Charles Marston to excitedly proclaim that "it already seems quite evident that further evidence has been found that will tend to confirm the Old Testament."[13]

The preservation of ostraca at Lachish and its recovery is due to a combination of fortunate circumstances and the vigilance of the excavators. The Lachish texts stem from the time of the First Temple and reflect the precarious situation at Lachish before the Babylonians completed their conquest of Judah in the early sixth century B.C.E. The ostraca appear to be trial drafts of letters probably sent by the commander of the garrison forces stationed at Lachish, Hosha'yahu, to Jerusalem. At the time these ostraca were written only Jerusalem and Lachish remained still unconquered. The text on one ostracon includes a report that the beacon fires of Lachish are being watched over by the defendants of the city, but the fires of Azekah are no longer to be seen.[14] In Jeremiah 34:7 we read that "the king of Babylon's army fought against Jerusalem, and all the cities of Judah that were left, against Lachish, and against Azekah; for these fortified cities remained of the cities of Judah."

Whereas the shards themselves are durable, the ink employed for the writing is not, and so the texts are subject to being effaced by abrasion or to being washed off, not only by ground water but even to being accidently obliterated by archaeologists or their assistants who do not immediately perceive the presence of writing. The recovery of some eighty Hebrew inscriptions from the Israelite fortress of Arad was attributed to the "dipping method" instituted by Yohanan Aharoni to detect such writing. "Each sherd is doused in water and examined to see whether it contains an inscription that cannot otherwise be observed because of the dust and dirt clinging to it," writes Anson Rainey in reporting on the find. "If no inscription appears, a light brush is then applied to see whether such an inscription is under the dirt still stuck to the sherd."[15] The thousands of shards uncovered at a dig makes this painstaking approach a major undertaking, but the extraordinary effort proved to be well worth while, for thus were uncovered and preserved a significant portion of the files of Eliashib son of Eshiyahu, who was probably the commander of the Arad fort.

The commander's name was inscribed on a *bulla*, a clay lump that is impressed around the knot of a string used to tie a folded or scrolled document. The bullae are stamped with a signature or other identification of the party concerned with the preservation of the integrity of the textual contents. Documents such as deeds, contracts, and bills of sale were sometimes deposited in an official storeroom or library of sorts, where they were held safe and accessible in case of a dispute between contractual parties, to prove ownership of property, record the payment of taxes, register the terms of the sale of goods, and the like.

Ancient documents were typically written on papyrus, and sometimes on leather, wood, or similar materials whose period of deterioration depended greatly on the type of storage facilities in which they were deposited and the weather. A dry, sealed, massively secured Egyptian tomb provided an ideal container for the preservation of papyrus, and a large number of Egyptian documents have thereby survived. The moister climate and moribund conditions of *Eretz Yisrael* are not as conducive to the long-term endurance of papyrus or the other materials commonly used in documentation, nor even of clay, except when a conflagration takes place, in which case the clay is baked and the bullae are preserved, signature and all. The marks of the strings are usually visible on the bullae's back sides, and the imprint of the owner and other information is preserved on its face.

Three of the beautifully preserved bullae stamped "[Belonging] to Eliahib son of Eshiyahu" were found in stratum VII of Arad, dated to 620-597 B.C.E. The papyrus document that it sealed has disappeared, but the existence of such documents is attested to by a string left stuck to the backs of two of the bullae. The ostraca found in association with the bullae provide a good deal of information about the circumstances at Arad. Some are vouchers authorizing the release of provisions from the fortress storehouse: generally wine, flour or bread. Rainey notes that these items are the very basic provisions for the road mentioned in the Bible.[16] In several of the ostraca, rations are assigned to the *Kittiyim*, clearly the "Kittim" frequently mentioned in the Bible. Rainey points out that the name comes from Kition, a city on the island of Cyprus, with a population of Canaanite origin who "spoke a language akin to Hebrew, and could easily converse with Eliashib. These Kittim or Kittiyim might have been mercenaries in the service of Judah."[17]

A HOARD OF CLAY BULLAE

A fortunate find of a hoard of bullae, which first came to light in a shop of an Arab antiquities dealer in Jerusalem, goes far to expand our knowledge of the literate proficiency of the Israelites, even if it does so by indirection. Some 250 bullae have been retrieved from a hoard that first came to the attention of the renowned archaeologist Nahman Avigad of the Hebrew University when a collector came to him to evaluate four of the bullae that he had purchased from an Arab dealer in antiquities. A number of other collectors came to Professor Avigad with bullae they had purchased in Bethlehem, in the village of Beit Sahour, as well as in Jerusalem, and it became clear that they were all part of one hoard. Finally, two purchasers, a collector from Jerusalem and a philanthropist from Haifa, appeared with 200 and forty-nine bullae respectively, and Professor Avigad was able to study and publish the considerable information culled from the inscriptions.[18]

The information imprinted on the bullae was startling indeed. Included were the impressions of at least two individuals, Baruch, the son of Neriah, and Jerahmeel, the son of Jeremiah, both of whom figure importantly in an event described with considerable detail in the Bible. About the year 605 B.C.E. in the reign of King Jehoiakim, the Lord instructed Jeremiah to warn the king of Judah's destruction by the Babylonians as a consequence of Judah's alliance with Egypt. "Take thee a roll of a book," Yahweh instructs Jeremiah, "and write therein all the words that I have spoken unto thee against Israel and against Judah." Whereupon Jeremiah calls in Baruch, to whom he dictates all the prophesies transmitted through him by Yahweh. Baruch was commissioned by Jeremiah to read the dire prophesies to the people and he did so effectively, and the disturbance he created caused the king to send an emissary, Jehudi, to obtain the scroll. The officials, scribes and princes of various kinds, evidently sympathetic with Jeremiah, advised Baruch, "Go, hide thee, thou and Jeremiah; and let no man know where you are." Jehudi obtained the scroll and began to read it to the king in his winter house. "When Jehudi had read three or four leaves, he [the king] cut it with his penknife [*sic*], and cast it into the fire that was on the hearth." The king sent three officers, including his son Jerahmeel, to arrest Jeremiah and Baruch. Jeremiah, in the meantime, having heard that the king had burned his scroll, dictated another one to Baruch.[19]

Thus the physical appearance on the bullae of the names of both Baruch, son of Neriah, and of Jerahmeel, son of King Jehoiakim, was indeed a discovery of prime importance. The bullae of a number of other important high officials are included in the hoard whose names are not included in the Bible. Their titles and descriptions: "the scribe," "king's son" (a somewhat lower rank than "son of the king" and not necessarily a blood relative but an honorary court position), "servant of the king," "who is over the house" (a title, according to Avigad, reserved for the highest office of the royal court after the king), and the positive identification of two individuals among the officials who were featured in an important passage of the biblical narrative, all provide penetrating insights into the Judahite administrative structure and go a long way to confirm the historicity of much of the Bible.

THE ARAMAIC PAPYRI OF YEB

The arid climate of Egypt did serve to preserve a sizable collection of Aramaic papyri, evidence of a deep-rooted, ancient literacy that reached out to the farthest corners of Jewish life and extended back to its earliest times. They were the documents of an ancient Jewish colony that had been established on Yeb, an island situated in the Nile River at the foot of the first cataract at the border of Upper Egypt and Nubia.[20] Now known as Elephantine, the island's strategic position had made it commercially important as far back into history as has been recorded. The earliest of the documents recovered from the island dates back to 495 B.C.E.,[21] and most of the others continue the record of two families resident on that distant island for almost a century. The Yeb community centered around a substantial temple, modeled after the Temple in Jerusalem. The surprising fact that the temple was built before 525 B.C.E. is proven by a pointed reference in one of the recovered papyri that, although many Egyptian temples were destroyed, the temple on the island of Yeb was not harmed by the forces of the Persian king Cambyses on his incursion into Egypt in that year. The temple was, however, demolished about 405 B.C.E., and the manner in which the demolition came about is described in a copy of a petition by Yedoniah, the head of the community at Yeb, to Bigvai, the Persian viceroy of Judah, for the rebuilding of the temple, which had been destroyed three years earlier as a result of a plot between the "Egyptian priests of the god Khnub" and the Persian governor of the island:

In the month of Tammuz in the 14th day of Darius the king, when Arsames departed and went to the king, the priests of the god Khnub, who is in the fortress of Yeb, were in league with Waidrang who was governor here, saying, "The temple of Ya'u the God, which is in the fortress of Yeb let them remove from there. Then that Waidrang, the reprobate, sent a letter to his son Nephayan who was commander of the garrison in the fortress of Syene saying: "The temple which is in Yeb the fortress let them destroy . . . " They entered that temple, they destroyed it to the ground, and the pillars of stone which were there they broke. Also it happened, 5 gateways of stone, built with hewn blocks of stone, which were in that temple they destroyed, and their doors they lifted off (?), and the hinges of those doors were bronze, and the roof of cedar wood, all of it with the rest of the furniture and other things which were there, all of it they burnt with fire, and the basins of gold and silver and every-thing that was in the temple, all of it, they took and made their own. Already in the days of the kings of Egypt our fathers had built that temple in the fortress of Yeb, and when Cambyses came into Egypt he found that temple built, and the temples of the gods of Egypt all of them they overthrew, but no one did any harm to the temple.[22]

Yedoniah then informs the viceroy that he had applied by letter to Johanan, high priest of Jerusalem, and to Deliah and Shelemith of Samaria for permission to rebuild the temple, but had received no reply. Thus we are made aware that Yedoniah was ignorant of the rift that had taken place between Israel and Judah. Yedoniah informs the viceroy that a quantity of gold is on its way in anticipation of a positive response and that if permission is granted "we will pray for you at all times, we, our wives, our children, and the Jews, all who are here . . . and it shall be a merit unto you."

The documents show that, while the Jewish colony was organized on a mili-tary model, no military activity was being performed. The inhabitants of Yeb were devoted to commercial affairs. Thus, Aramaic papyrus no. 2, dated to c. 484 B.C.E., is a contract in which the Yebite Jews Hosea and Ahiab received from "Espemet b. Peft'onith the sailor" a consignment of beans and lentils that they undertake to deliver to the garrison at Syene. The easy familiarity with objects of iron is con-clusively demonstrated in Aramaic papyrus no. 20, in which "Menahim and Ananiah, both sons of Meshullum b. Shebonem, Jews of Yeb," refer to a transac-tion that includes "garments of wool and cotton, vessels of bronze and iron, ves-sels of wood and ivory, corn, etc."

One of the most important and interesting of the papyri is no. 21, a letter from Hananiah, a visitor to Egypt, in which instructions to keep the Passover are included, given *on the authority of the Persian king Darius.* The evident unfamiliar-ity of the community with the ceremony of Passover is an indication of the antiq-uity of the community, although there is no evidence that Passover was custom-arily performed long before the date of the Yeb Papyri.[23]

Whereas the surviving documents date to the fifth century B.C.E., they are writ-ten in a philological form that hails back far beyond the seventh century to the period of the United Monarchy, and perhaps to an even earlier period. The antique form of Aramaic in which they are written reflects that employed in northern

Canaan or Aramea and exhibits no familiarity with the Hebrew language; the contents of the documents also reveal little knowledge of the Hebrew scriptures. The Yebites did not employ the tetragrammaton YHWH, which came into use at least as far back as the ninth century B.C.E., but Yahu, an earlier form of the name of the Hebraic deity. The theophoric construction of the names of some of the Yebites reflects some former obeisance to other gods; the ancient Canaanite gods Bethel and Anath were familiar to them, just as they were to the Israelites of the patriarchal period.

Cyrus Gordon refers to the implantation by Solomon of colonies in his northern provinces and suggests that the evidence points to the Yeb colony being "an offshoot of Judah planted in Aram during the United Monarchy (prior to cultic centralization and prophetic reform) to secure the Hebrew Empire."[24] The linguistic parallels of the Aramaic employed at Yeb to that of southeastern Anatolia, from which area it is known that foreigners came to Egypt in the service of Persian rulers, and of similar social relationships to the northern provinces, particularly those detailed in a number of marriage contracts documented in the Elephantine documents which exhibit Ugaritic analogues, suggest the Aramaic provenience of the inhabitants of Yeb.[25]

The fact that no references to Greeks or Canaanites appear in the Elephantine Aramaic papyri is suggestive of a period before any of the Aegian cultures became known to Upper Egypt, that is to a period prior to the incursions of the so-called Sea Peoples. This circumstance is reinforced by an obvious familiarity with peoples from the Mesopotamian milieu as a number of references to Persians, Babylonians, Caspians, Khorazmians, and Medes make evident. A professor of the University of Sydney in Australia, E. C. B. MacLauren, offers a strong argument for such an early arrival time for the Jews at Yeb. While "there can be no doubt that Israel's position athwart the great trade routes led to prosperous trading relationships with the adjacent nations," writes MacLauren, "there is no record of Solomon establishing factories in Egypt, as elsewhere, so perhaps Hebrews were already living there."[26] MacLauren suggests, on the basis of this and other factors arising out of the documents, that the Elephantine colony can be traced to Hebrews who remained in Egypt at the time of the Exodus.

There is physical evidence to support the possibility raised by MacLauren. The museum at Elephantine exhibits pottery typical of Ugarit in northern Canaan. The pottery was unearthed on the island and was included in a stratum that dates back to the so-called Second Intermediate period, when the chieftains of Canaan were dominant in Egypt. Associated with this pottery were several glass rings, perfume bottles, and beads, which could only have been produced in Mesopotamia or Aramea at that time. The physical evidence thus unearthed from the ruins of Yeb conforms to the projection for an early date for the establishment of the "factory" on the island of Yeb referred to by MacLauren.

The period of the Canaanite kings of Egypt was preceded by that of the depiction on the tomb of Khnumhotep of a group of Hebrew artisans and traders headed by the "Hyk-khase," Abushei, traveling up the Nile in the early nineteenth century B.C.E., probably earlier than the estimated date for Abraham's arrival in Egypt. That even such an early date is not unreasonable follows from another bit of evidence cited by MacLauren. The name of the deity in the form of Bethel comes up frequently in several contexts in Yeb, especially in its theophoric application to names like Anathbethel, Eshembethel, and Herembethel. This ancient usage is noted by Bezaleel Porten, of the University of California, who points out that "the divine name Bethel has frequently been understood as a surrogate for YHWH." Cowley notes that Bethel has been shown to be another name for El, and that

> neither YHWH nor El were known by that name among the Hebrews after the time of Jacob (Gen. 28,31), so again the Yeb community seems to have been cut off from the main stream of Hebrew thought at an early stage and to have retained archaic uses . . . Thus the personnel of the Elephantine pantheon belongs to the Patriarchal period rather than to a later age, and it is quite impossible for it to have been derived from the religious systems of the time of the Kings.[27]

The Merenptah stela and the wall in Karnak provide a powerful argument for an existing Israelite/Canaanite culture of the thirteenth century B.C.E. The hardly disputable fact that the name *Isra-El* existed at the time reveals that the substitution of Baal by El was well under way by a sector of the Canaanite population before the time of the biblical Exodus. El was the Canaanite father of the divine family, and Asherah was his spouse. They relegated rule to their children, mainly to Baal ("Lord" or "master"), Anath (Baal's sister, Goddess of fertility, which attribute she shared with her mother and Ashtoreth, the distinction between the three being often blurred), and Mot (God of death), who in turn dominated some seventy other members of the divine family. The precedence of El as a Canaanite god is evidenced by its incorporation into numerous place names, and his identification with the God of Abraham is implicit in passages referred to by Cowley above (Genesis 28:19), in which Jacob renames the city Luz to Beth-El in gratitude to God for granting him and his seed title to the land; and in Genesis 31:13, in which God identifies himself in addressing Jacob: "I am the God of Beth-El, where thou anointedst the pillar, and where thou vowedst a vow unto me. Now arise, get thee out of this land, and return to the land of thy kindred." The shift from El to Yahweh occurred soon after the Exodus. Yahweh seems to have been associated with the Hebrews and their coincident biblical appearance supports the contention that a new factor entered the cultural equation, one which could very well be postulated to have been the infusion of a vast multitude who had undergone a fervent religious experience.

Following a different path, Albrecht Alt (proponent of the "Peaceful Penetration Model" referred to in Chapter 8) drew a similar conclusion: "Abraham, Isaac and Jacob came before Moses; but we can now follow the path which led from their Gods to the God of Israel."[28] The addition of a civil statutory framework within which the El/Yahweh hypostasis became biblically consolidated fits well into the process of the welding of a new national Israelite entity from disparate origins. If it is assumed that the Yeb community existed before the Exodus and was left behind in Egypt, it may have well been exempt from that consolidation, and the references to "Yahu" and the theophoric use of "Bethel," both stemming from the period between Jacob and Moses, fit well into their onomastic inheritance.

Whatever turns out to be the truth regarding the origin of the community on Yeb, one fact is abundantly clear: literacy was one of its outstanding and ancient cultural attributes. The literacy of the community as a whole is attested to by the fact that the surviving business documents, property deeds, marriage contracts, and other documents were signed by a numerous assortment of Yebite witnesses, of whom some were women. The tradition of maintaining a universal literacy was clearly a cultural attribute of the community of Yeb that extended far back into antiquity. One of the papyri is an Aramaic version of the story of Ahikar and is therefore the earliest specimen of wisdom-literature apart from biblical and cuneiform texts.[29] It is interesting that in the rendition of this originally Mesopotamian tale the names of the kings Sennacherib and Esarhaddon are not reversed as they are in later versions, one of the facts that suggest the great antiquity of the Aramaic version of Yeb. A number of proverbs are also included in the Aramaic literature recovered from the island.

A number of other indications of the antiquity of the Yebite culture are evident from their literature. One of the great philological landmarks was the decipherment of cuneiform writing as a result of the discovery of a trilingual inscription carved on a almost inaccessible rock-face at Behistun, so high up over the road from Damascus to Ectabana (Hamadan) that it was impossible to read from down below. The inscription was commissioned by Darius, the son of Hystaspes, in order to immortalize the means by which he consolidated his power. Darius thereafter ordered copies and translations to be made and distributed throughout his realm. Fragments of two versions of the "Behistun Inscription" are among the papyri of Yeb.

Although cuneiform Akkadian continued in use in Babylonian private documents in the sixth century B.C.E., Aramaic became the official language of Achemenid Persia in the time of Cyrus (559–530 B.C.E.) and was thereafter used by the Persians for official documents and governmental communication. The use of Aramaic and the expansion of Persian literacy was a direct consequence of the transference of thousands of literate Israelites and Judahites from *Eretz Yisrael* to the Land of the Two Rivers. A corollary technological renaissance was brought about in Persia by the introduction of Israelite and Judahite artisans. The impregnation of Aramaic literacy and Hebraic technology into Persia was a harbinger of the many cultural infusions Jews made into backward societies in their sojourns in the Diaspora.

13

Artisans of the Diaspora

The Jews in Persia

During the period in which the hilltop villages of the Israelites and Judahites were prospering and maturing into cohesive nations, Mesopotamia fell into a prolonged period of technological stagnation. Protracted subjugation to the Egyptians and the Hittites ended with a standoff between the great powers, but struggles ensued between the northern Assyrian and the southern Babylonian regimes in which first Assyria and then Babylonia was devastated. On the eastern flank the Elamites constantly plagued whichever of the two centers dominated the area, but most disruptive was the increasing pressure of dissident Aramaean tribes flanking the western borders of Assyria and Babylonia.

The Aramaeans were situated athwart the critical trade routes at the crown of the Fertile Crescent. During the eleventh century B.C.E. vigorous Aramaean pressures severely affected the conduct of trade along the commercial lifeline joining East and West, a threat that "seems to have encouraged the Babylonians and Assyrians to forget their differences."[1] Renewed prosperity in the region hinged on the establishment of unhindered access to the West and the Mediterranean, and on an infusion of technological skills. Mesopotamia, the region that had nurtured civilization for many millennia, had fallen far behind in industrial capability. The artisans who could help bridge this critical gap were to be found in Israel and Judah. After the Aramaeans were brought under control, the Eastern powers turned covetous attention toward the nations still blocking domination of the region's critical commercial routes: the Israelites, Judahites and their commercial allies, the sea-going Canaanites of Tyre and Sidon.

ISRAELITE PYROTECHNOLOGY

The smelting of iron and the production of glass took place in the thickly forested areas across the entire northern sector of *Eretz Yisrael*. The hardwood trees

233

of the area, and in particular, the prevalent oak trees, were the most suitable woods for attaining the fierce temperatures required for the production of these exotic products. The forests flourished in the provinces of the tribes of Naphthali (from which tribe the mother of Hiram, the biblical bronze worker stemmed), of Asher, and of Dan, but the artisans who wandered the woods in pursuit of fuel were not necessarily restricted to those tribes. Some of the Benjaminites were situated in the thickly forested hills west of lake Tiberius, and we are reminded in the Bible that the metal-working Rechabites were, in fact, Benjaminite descendants.

The technological aptitude of the Israelites is attested to by the Assyrian monarch Shalmaneser III (858–824 B.C.E.) in an inscription on a monolith in which he recorded an encounter between his forces and a coalition of enemies, among whom Ahab, king of Israel (c. 859–853 B.C.E.), was the most formidable. According to Shalmaneser, the Israelite forces of this early period mustered more chariots than did all his other opponents. More than two thousand chariots were arrayed by the Israelites against his army at the battle of Qarqar on the Orontes, by means of which they succeeded in frustrating the Assyrian king's ambitions. The Israelites continued to be harassed by the ambitious Assyrian kings after a turbulent period in which Jehu, in his fervor to purge the remnants of the Canaanite cult from Israelite religion, seized the throne of Israel. Jehu, supported by the prophet Elisha, the army, and the poor, slaughtered "all that remained of the house of Ahab in Jezreel, and all of his great men, and his kinfolks, and his priests, until he left him none standing."[2] In assuring that all possible claimants to the throne were eliminated, Jehu also murdered Ahaziah, king of Judah, and his brothers. Then, joined by the Jehonadab, the son of the zealous patriarch of the smiths, Rechab, Jehu went on a campaign to extirpate the cult of Baal from Israel. Through a duplicitous ruse, all the Baal priests were gathered in the temple of Baal. There they were ruthlessly slain, and the House of Baal and all the images of Baal and other idolic artifacts were destroyed.[3]

The Aramaeans tried to exploit the weakened condition of the Israelites, so Jehu appealed to the Assyrians for protection and attempted to keep both them and the Aramaeans at bay by paying substantial amounts of tribute to the Assyrians. Shalmaneser was pleased to be rid of Ahab and to accept tribute from heretofore troublesome Israel, a circumstance detailed on "The Black Obelisk," a four-sided monolith discovered in Nimrud by Austen Henry Layard in 1846, in which Jehu was depicted by Shalmeneser as bowing to the ground before him in abject obeisance. The inscription, dated to 841 B.C.E., provides the particulars of the acceptance by Shalmaneser of the tribute brought to him, which consisted of "silver, gold, a golden bowl, a golden vase with pointed bottom, golden tumblers, golden buckets, tin, a staff for a king [and] *purukhti* fruits."[4] The fact that tin was specified among the valuable gifts is indeed interesting and informative, for it has long been conjectured that tin came from the Anatolian mountains as well as from the mountain ranges of Afghanistan, and the offer of tin from West to East may indicate that such may indeed have been the case. In any event, the pointed inclusion of tin in the tribute, a metal not then employed alone but mainly as an essential ingredient for the production of bronze, is another indication of the metalworking attributes of the Israelites.

The Assyrian King Adad-nirari III, in a stela erected in the year 806 B.C.E., also informs us that he received payments from Jehoahaz, King of Israel [814-798 B.C.E.], as well as from the Tyrian and Sidonian rulers.[5] Thereafter we learn from inscriptions by Tiglath-Pileser and from the reliefs carved into the walls of his palace at Nimrud that after campaigning in the West he exacted tribute from Menahem of Samaria (744-738 B.C.E.). Tigleth-Pileser finally prevailed over the Israelites, at least partially, and succeeded in stripping Israel of its northern sectors. According to a fragmentary Assyrian source, 13,150 Israelites were rounded up in 733-732 B.C.E. and exchanged for Aramaean and Chaldean colonists.[6] The Bible confirms that "In the days of Pekah king of Israel came Tigleth-Pileser king of Assyria, and took Ijon, and Abel-beth-maacah, and Janoah, and Kedesh, and Hazor, and Gilead, and Galilee, all the land of Naphthali, and carried them captive to Assyria."[7]

The production of iron and glass in *Eretz Yisrael* was affected sorely by the deportation of Israelite artisans. The Israelite deportees consisted of "outstanding craftsmen [who were] resettled either in regions of Assyria that had been depopulated by the ravages of the ninth century, particularly in the area of Gozan, or on the northern and northeastern borders of the Empire."[8] Samaria was left intact for a time while the Assyrians turned against Babylon. Upon entering the ancient city on the day of the Babylonian new year in 729 B.C.E., Tigleth-Pileser "seized the hands of the god Murduk." Tigleth-Pileser died two years later. His successor Shalmaneser V (727-722 B.C.E.), strengthened by the acquisition of Babylonia and irked by the attempts of the Israelite king Hoshea to reach an accord with Egypt, turned attention to the completion of the conquest of Israel. After a three-year siege Samaria fell to Shalmaneser (or upon his death to his army commander and successor, Sargon II), in a campaign that brought about the extinction of the state of Israel. Sargon boastfully recorded that in 722 B.C.E. no fewer than 27,290 of the Israelites captured in that campaign were deported.[9] Again, the exultant blusters of the Assyrian ruler confirm a biblical account: "In the ninth year of Hoshea the king of Assyria took Samaria, and carried Israel away into Assyria, and placed them in Halah and in Habor by the river of Gozan and in the cities of the Medes."[10]

It is hardly remarkable, therefore, that coincident with the transference of artisans from Israel there was a resurgence of the pyrotechnical arts in Mesopotamia, in the very land in which those arts were conceived, gestated and born. Sargon soon took advantage of the skills of the glassmakers among the deportees; he ordered a glass vessel to be made with his name boldly inscribed upon it. The *alabastron* of Sargon II was excavated at Nimrud (near Nineveh) and is now the proud possession of the British Museum. It is a unique vessel apparently carved from a solid block of glass. It is the earliest surviving example of a vessel so manufactured, or at least to have been carved and polished from a mold-produced form. The vessel is decorated with an engraved symbolic lion together with the name of Sargon II, which blazes forth in cuneiform characters.[11]

The art of glassmaking, which had disappeared from Mesopotamia during its regressive period, reappeared soon after Tiglath-Pileser transferred thousands of captive Israelite artisans to Assyria. The illustrated vase is typical of the type that was produced in Assyria during the following period. (Photograph courtesy of the Corning Museum of Glass.)

The Israelites who had not been exiled continued to worship the God of their ancestors, and in due course many of the immigrant polytheists came to accept the Lord of the land in which they had become permanent residents. According to the Bible the shift did not come about lightly, in spite of a sincere effort to bring about universal conversion under the aegis of the king of Assyria, who gave orders that one of the priests deported from Samaria should be sent back to live there and teach the people the usage of the god of the country. One of the deported Israelite priests returned to Bethel and taught the Babylonian immigrants how to pay homage to the Lord.[12]

The Judahite chronicler of the events makes much of the fact that some of the immigrant Babylonians did not relinquish their own gods, for although they "feared the Lord," they also placed graven images of their pagan gods in the "high places which the Samaritans had made." The persistence of paganism was enjoined by the Judahite priests against the autochthonous Israelites as well as against sincere convertees, all of whom were smeared with the same broad brush and denied recognition in Jerusalem. That is not to say that pagan practices were not also pervasive in Judah: "Also Judah kept not the commandments of the Lord their God"; but it was only Israel that, according to the chronicler, was "rent from the house of David."[13] The paganization problem was dealt with by Hezekiah, who, upon becoming king of Judah, went on a rampage through Israel. Hezekiah destroyed the pagan hilltop shrines and smashed all the idols, including the bronze serpent Moses himself had presumably made, "for up to that time the Israelites did burn sacrifices to it."[14]

Having devastated Israel and reduced it to vassalage, the Assyrians were able to exact tribute from Judah. Hezekiah bought respite from Assyrian conquest with a massive amount of treasure in tribute, including the presentation of the doors of the temple of the Lord. When King Hezekiah later attempted to withhold further payment, Sennacherib, successor to Sargon II, invaded Judah in the year 701 B.C.E., and, according to his own crowing claim, decimated forty-six Judahite cities and besieged Jerusalem. We may presume that as a consequence of this campaign, additional numbers of Judahite artisans were captured and deported, swelling the already considerable Jewish population of the Land of the Two Rivers by an indeterminate but doubtless substantial amount.

The Assyrian masters did not manage to long enjoy the benefits of the inoculation by the Israelites of advanced forms of technology into their culture, for while intermittently contesting the formidable Egyptian forces over the trade routes that ran through *Eretz Yisrael*, they were simultaneously being subjected to serious conflicts with, and attrition by, other tribal powers to the south and east. The Parsuans (Persians), the Madahites (Medes), the Elamites, and especially the Babylonians and the Babylonian successors, the Chaldeans, all had to be dealt with, and the debilitating drain on Assyrian resources proved finally to be their undoing. One of the Assyrian commanders was a Chaldean, Nabopolassar, who revolted and made himself king of Babylon in 626 to 625 B.C.E. The fall of Nineveh in 612 B.C.E. to Babylonian forces sealed the fate of the Assyrian overlords, and

they passed from the royal scene forever. The Chaldean king's son, Nebuchadnezzar, sealed an alliance with the Medes by marrying a Medahite princess, thus
securing the Babylonian rear, and in 605 B.C.E. a campaign was launched against
the Egyptians. The decisive victory over the forces of Pharaoh Necho at Carchemish reduced Egypt to tenuous control over, and occasional incursions into,
Judah. Nebuchadnezzar consolidated his rear by subjecting a weakened Elam
(which had never recovered from the devastation wrought by the Assyrians under
Asurbanipal in 640 B.C.E.) to firm control, and began a reign that endured for
almost half a century from 605 to 561 B.C.E.

Some of the artisans in the forests of upper *Eretz Yisrael* had survived through
this century of shifting geopolitical currents and managed to maintain their ferric
and vitric activities and skills until the time of Nebuchadnezzar, albeit on a minimal scale. After eliminating the Egyptian presence, the Chaldean-Babylonian king,
assisted by the Aramaeans (who were only too happy to see the end of tribute to
the Egyptians and eager to share in the spoils), mopped up in the northern regions
of *Eretz Yisrael*. Some of the surviving artisans working in the woods of the region
fled to Judah, and the pyrotechnical arts virtually disappeared from the area of
the former Israel. That process is reflected biblically in recounting how, upon
witnessing the capture and removal of fellow artisans from their region to Babylonia, the descendants of the metalworking Rechabites evacuated from their beloved forests to seek refuge in Jerusalem. The motivation for the move was not
the abandoning of the tenets and way of life of their forbears; the reason given
for their sojourn in Jerusalem is explicit: "But it came to pass, when Nebuchadnezzar king of Babylon came up into the land, that we said, Come, let us go to
Jerusalem for fear of the army of the Chaldeans, and for fear of the army of Syrians;
so we dwell at Jerusalem."

The escape to Jerusalem proved to be a temporary remedy; Nebuchadnezzar
(actually as yet the crown prince of Babylon at the time) assailed Jerusalem and
forced King Jehoiakim, who had pragmatically kept Judah under the protection
of Egypt, to switch allegiance to Babylon. Nebuchadnezzar looted Judah, confiscated the treasures of the temple, and took princely Judahite hostages back to
Babylon, among whom Daniel was included.[15] The biblical rendition of the story
of that campaign is supported by a Chaldean (Babylonian) chronicle in which
the battles against the Egyptians near Hamath and at Carchemish are detailed.[16]
It was apparently in the pursuit of the defeated Egyptians that Nebuchadnezzar
besieged Jerusalem.

The death of Nebuchadnezzar's father impelled the crown prince to hurry back
to Babylon to assume the throne. The heavy burden of tribute imposed upon Judah
and the continuing struggles between Babylon and Egypt over control of the area
led Jehoiakim to attempt to play one power against another, a policy that led to
disaster; in retribution Jerusalem was again penetrated in 598 B.C.E. by the Babylonians and a total of 4,600 (or 4,897) Judahites are registered as having been
deported in successive waves to Babylon.[17] The deportees did not include King
Jehoiakim, who died a miserable death in chains.

Jehoiakim's son, Jehoiachin, assumed the Judahite throne at the tender age of 18, but after only three months he was taken prisoner by Nebuchadnezzar and transported to Babylon along with all the remaining Temple treasures and ten thousand more captives (clearly a round figure), including "all the craftsmen and the smiths."[18] Nebuchadnezzar placed Jehoichin's uncle, Zedekiah, on the throne of Judah. Zedekiah maintained a facade of loyalty to Babylon for a time and eventually allied Judah to Egypt despite forewarning by the prophet Jeremiah of the dire consequences of such an act. Jeremiah's concern proved all too accurate; enraged, Nebuchadnezzar ravaged Judah. The Lachish letters referred to above, in which the signals of Azekah could no longer be seen from Lachish, dramatize the events of the period.

Jerusalem held out for almost three years, but finally, starved, disease-ridden and bereft of its skilled artisans, it succumbed to the Babylonian forces in 586 B.C.E. The city walls of Jerusalem were systematically dismantled, the city was looted, the buildings were razed, and the city was burned to the ground in a fire that lasted for three days. Additional thousands of Judahite artisans were rounded up and deported to Babylon. Only "the poor of the land" were left to carry on as "vinedressers and husbandmen."[19] The biblical accounts of the Exilic period refer only peripherally to the numbers of deportees and provide varying figures for that number. Many must have been deported into Mesopotamia after the predatory campaign of Sennacherib in 701, for example, for although the Assyrian did not succeed in battering down the defenses of Jerusalem, thousands of Judahites must have been captured, chained, and deported from the forty-six cities destroyed by his forces. The existence of evidence from extrabiblical sources leaves no doubt that scores of thousands of the most skilled artisans of Israel and Judah were selected for deportation from these successive campaigns.

PYROTECHNOLOGY AND THE PROPHETS

The easy familiarity of the prophets of this troubled period with the pyrotechnology required to produce and work iron is richly illustrated by biblical descriptions of the tools and processes involved in the production of the metal and of the frequent metaphorical use of its unique attributes. The references can no longer be regarded as anachronisms, nor can they be ascribed to a plagiarism of such references from another culture, for they were patently acquired from personal experience or knowledge. The richness of pyrotechnical information in the biblical narratives contrasts graphically with the paucity of such information from all other sources.

The pyrotechnological heritage of the Israelites is amply reflected in the literature of the prophets. The prophets of the eighth to sixth centuries B.C.E. were already fully familiar with ferric production and metallurgy. The context of the references and the accurate descriptions of the processes, tools, and equipment involved demonstrate an intimacy with the art born of firsthand knowledge. Isaiah

declared that the Israelite is an obstinate being, whose "neck is like an iron sinew."
Isaiah castigated the smith for forging graven images of iron with hammers and
tongs,[20] but sang admiringly that "The smith with the tongs both worketh in the
coals, and fashioneth it with hammers, and worketh it with the strength of his
arms."[21] Isaiah referred knowledgeably to another process integral to the ferric
art, the use of bellows, and assigns the creation of the smith to the Lord. "Behold," Isaiah spoke for the Lord, "I have created the smith that bloweth upon the
fire of the coals, and that bringeth forth an instrument for his work."[22] Jeremiah
was no less knowledgeable and referred pointedly to the use of bellows in his
lamentations, if "the bellows are burned," Jeremiah pronounced, then the "founder
melteth in vain." The dross is not separated out, continues Jeremiah, making trans-
gressors like "rejected silver, for the Lord hath rejected them." Thus Jeremiah
demonstrates his familiarity with a method of refining silver by cupulation.[23] The
Lord God of Israel reminded Jeremiah that he brought the Israelites "out of the
land of Egypt, from the iron furnace," a metaphoric reference to the ultimate form
of tormenting heat,[24] and it is pointedly noted that smiths were among the Judeans
Nebuchadnezzar carried away to Babylon.[25] Jeremiah even referred to steel, a
sophisticated ferric product that appeared in the Judean hills in the tenth century B.C.E. Steel is equated by Jeremiah to "northern iron,"[26] thus linking the product to the very area in which it has been archaeologically confirmed. Ezekiel
accused the house of Israel of becoming as the dross of brass, and tin, and iron,
and lead in the midst of the furnace. "Yea, I will gather you," the Lord is said to
have threatened to perform as a bellows, "and blow upon you in the fire of my
wrath."[27] Job demonstrates his familiarity with the sources of raw metals, the
methods of mining, and of metallurgy by accurately describing the sources of
ores and the divers processes of recuperating various metals from ores when he
exclaimed, "Surely there is a vein for the silver, and place for gold where they
refine it. Iron is taken out of the earth, and brass molten out of the stone."[28] Job
had also referred to the use of an "iron pen" with which an inscription can be
graven on rock to last forever,[29] and to the use of barbed irons and fish spears.[30]

No other corpus of ancient literature has as rich a catalogue of ferric references as does the Bible. Even the Psalms employ iron as a common metaphor:
"Iron sharpeneth iron; so a man sharpeneth the countenance of his friend."[31]

One of the Bible's far-reaching prognostications is that of Daniel's interpretation of Nebuchadnezzar's dream. This apocalyptic narrative, although set in a
Persian environment, was probably written in the period of the Maccabees and
was undoubtedly meant to prognosticate the fate of the besieged Jews as of that
latter period as much as it did for the time in which the tale is set. In any event,
the use of the metaphor of iron as an enduring material in relation to Jewish
survival is employed in the ancient prophetic mode and is reflective of the intimacy of the narrator with metallurgy. In his dream the Assyrian king shattered a
being whose head, body, and thighs were of gold, silver, and brass and whose
legs were partly iron and partly clay. Daniel, after conferring with other wise exiled
Hebrews, arrived at an interpretation which, while it subtly satisfied Nebuchad-

nezzar, presented in its larger sense a prediction regarding the fate of the Jewish people. The Jews were captive in Babylonia, and were epitomized by the enduring iron of the shattered image. The sound part, iron, was dispersed throughout the world, but was nevertheless able to survive through all eternity:

> And the fourth kingdom shall be as sound as iron; forasmuch as iron breaketh in pieces and subdueth all things: and as iron that breaketh all these, shall it break in pieces and bruise. And whereas thou sawest the feet and toes, part of potter's clay and part of iron, the kingdom shall be divided; but there shall be in it of the strength of the iron, forasmuch as thou sawest the iron mixed with miry clay. And as the toes of the feet were part of iron, and part of clay, so the kingdom shall be partly strong, and partly broken. And whereas thou sawest iron mixed with miry clay, they shall mingle themselves with the seed of men: but they shall not cleave one to another, even as iron is not mixed with clay. And in the days of these kings shall the God of heaven set up a kingdom which shall never be destroyed: and the kingdom shall not be left to other people, but it shall break in pieces and consume all these kingdoms, and it shall stand forever. Forasmuch as thou sawest that the stone was cut out of the mountain without hands and that it brake in pieces the iron, the brass, the clay, the silver, and the gold; the great God that made known to the king what shall come to pass hereafter: and the dream is certain, and the interpretation thereof sure.[32]

The allegory of an enduring Jewish people was borne out by the ensuing events. When the Jews refused to worship the golden idol that Nebuchadnezzar had made, as did every other people, the Chaldeans convinced the king to throw Shadrach, Meshach, and Abed-nego into the fiery furnace, from which they emerged unscathed. It is perhaps significant that a furnace large enough to accommodate three men, "bound in their coats, their hosen, and their hats, and their other garments," was said to have been employed.

Impressed by the resurrection but not entirely daunted, the son of Nebuchadnezzar and the next king, Belshazzar, hosted a great feast attended by a thousand of his nobles at which they drank wine out of the gold and silver vessels that had been looted from the Temple in Jerusalem. With these holy vessels they had the temerity to toast "the gods of gold, and of silver, of brass, of iron, of wood, and of stone."[33] Thereupon the fateful fingers wrote the famous phrase upon the wall: Mene, Mene, Tekel, Upharsim, which Daniel was called upon to interpret. "Thou and all thy lords, thy wives, thy concubines have drunk wine in them [the vessels of the house of the Lord]," Daniel fearlessly castigated the company of overlords, "and thou hast praised the gods of silver, and gold, of brass, iron, wood, and stone, which see not, nor hear, nor know." Daniel presented the king with dire predictions, for which the king nevertheless thanked and rewarded him. The king was killed that night; Darius became king and set Daniel as head prince over the 120 princes of the kingdom.

Daniel had his own visions, one of which also involved a beast of many metals, including teeth of iron, representing the four kingdoms through whose reign the Jews would remain in foreign servitude. The last of these kings would cause "craft to prosper," and the rebuilding of Jerusalem. Thus the creative propensities of the captive Jews were to be released to rebuild the land from which they had been torn.

The treasures of the Temple were indeed returned by Cyrus and the rebuilding of the Temple ensued. Said to have returned are 42,360 members of the congregation together with 7,337 servants and maids. Among them were all the artisans needed to rebuild Jerusalem, accompanied by several hundred musicians. Everyone participated in the reconstruction: the priests, goldsmiths, apothecaries, and merchants are specifically cited as being among the enthusiasts who rebuilt the gates and walls of the city.[34]

> And it came to pass from that time forth that the half of my [the Lord's] servants wrought in that work, and the other half of them held both the spears, the shields, and the bows, and the habergoons; and the rulers were behind all the house of Judah; They which builded upon the wall, and they that bare burdens, with those that laded, every one with one of his hands wrought in the work, and with the other hand held a weapon.[35]

The tribes of the children of Israel then spread out across the land, some settling in Ono, "the valley of the craftsmen."[36] Ono was not the only such valley, for the valley of Harashim from which the family and descendants of Joab, captain of "all the host of Israel" stemmed, was a wilderness that was equally renowned for its craftsmen.[37] The wilderness valleys biblically alluded to are located in arboreal regions such as the ones in which the precedent Rechabites are said to have wandered about with their cattle and in which they performed their metallurgical tasks. We are biblically informed about the house of Jokim, who were potters, and whose activity presages the establishment of such great pottery-producing industries as came into being at Kfar Hananiah and Shikhin, located in the very areas biblically assigned to the house of Jokim. The peripheral references to these industrial complexes, long held to be matters of Mishnaic mythology, have now been archaeologically confirmed.[38] The Shikhin pottery works extend back into Hellenistic times, and are concrete manifestations of the extension of the tradition of craftsmanship of which the Bible and Mishnah provide mere hints.[39]

We are biblically introduced to families of scribes, and to the house of Ashbea, who wove fine linen.[40] These disciplines were to serve the Jews well, for a high degree of literacy and proficiency in the production of textiles became integral to Jewish life and, along with the pyrotechnical arts, were essential elements of the rich heritage of artisanship and creativity that was to serve not only the Jews but the world at large into the modern era. The Jewish glassmakers of Persia and the Galilee provided the glass beads and amulets that served as the medium of exchange with which Far Eastern markets were first penetrated. The Jewish producers of linen textiles and garments of the Galilean region, as we shall see, produced the finest fabrics of the "classical" era, products that provided the Greek and then the Roman hierarchy with the medium of exchange for a variety of exotic, avidly sought Far Eastern products.

THE JEWISH EXPERIENCE IN PERSIA

The creative activities of the Jews, in both artisanship and commerce, gained great impetus within the Persian matrix and became the driving industrial and commercial force by which a succession of regimes advanced themselves. Jewish bankers of Persia made finance capital a viable factor of industrial development and initiated an international system of credit that intrepid Jewish travelers wove into the world economy. The industrial, commercial, and financial skills the Jews cultivated in the Persia Diaspora served the Jews no less than Persia and continued to serve them and the other societies into whose Diasporas they were hurled throughout the next two millennia.

Cuneiform documents recovered from the ruins of Nippur and elsewhere, the records of the banking families of Egibi and Murashu recovered from the ancient ruins, and other such records, make it clear that the biblical references to deportations from Judah are but a glimmer of a much larger process of deportation and resettlement that took place during the period. The references in the Assyrian document to the 13,150 deportees under Tiglath-Pileser, and the annals of Sargon II, which indicate that in his campaign alone over 27,000 Israelites were deported,[41] reveal but part of the process of expansion of the Jewish Mesopotamian population through the Babylonian, Persian, Achaemenid, and Seleucid periods to total some million persons. This population doubled to as much as two million with the additional influx of Jews after the Roman destruction of the Second Temple.

The end of the history of Israel marks the beginning of multiple Jewish histories in the Diaspora, of which that of Persia was but the first. The remarkable aspect of the Jewish suffusion into disparate societies is that almost invariably the Jewish communities were concentrated in the productive commercial centers at the forefront of technological evolution, and their dispersion also occasioned the dispersion of the technologies at which they were the most adept. Although the dispersion of the Jews was disruptive of immediate circumstances and even disastrous to great numbers of Jews, it also activated the establishment of a worldwide commercial network. Although they were repeatedly buffeted by storms of prejudice and intolerance, they gained the commercial advantage of access to each other across borders, one which no other people possessed. Being a literate people, they were able to maintain communication with their peers and relatives in foreign lands. Having a common interest, they were able to establish commercial liaisons of mutual benefit and to issue letters of credit that were certain to be honored. A worldwide commercial network was seeded in Persia, in which international contact and travel became part and parcel of Jewish life. Persia was the pivotal point around which the trade of the Far Eastern and Western worlds revolved, and the Jews became the common denominator between those two worlds. The commercial network eventually became epitomized by the activity of the world-girdling Rhadanites, whose itinerary spanned Eurasia from Gaul and North Africa to China and India, and whose erudition and literacy enabled them to become the couriers of the canons of Judaic philosophy from the Jewish universities along their route to the Jewish communities throughout the vast tricontinental region. They were at once the postal system by which the Jewish communities maintained contact and the carriers of culture into the Diaspora at large. They maintained an exchange of halachic precepts within the dispersed Judaic communities and established the links by which trade and technology were exchanged between East and West.

The progenitors of the Jews had been literate in Akkadian cuneiform and they had adapted to the dialect of the coastal Canaanites in the creation of Hebrew. Aramaic was at the root of the culture of a large proportion of the Jews in the Persian Diaspora and became the lingua franca of the region. It was the Jews who, more than any other population, were accordingly able to communicate in all of those languages and who thereafter became equally proficient in Greek and Latin. Universal literacy became a requisite for the Jews in the Persian Diaspora, and it was in Persia that great universities were established for this purpose and where students speaking all the languages of the Western world converged.

The development of international commerce is contingent on available credit and capital. Financial institutions are a natural result of such needs. The records of two banking families are among the most revealing documents of the Persian period. Olmstead, author of an early comprehensive study of the history of the Persian Empire, took special note of the fact that in the development of its economy, "without any doubt, the most important economic phenomenon was the emergence of the private banker and the consequent expansion of credit."[42] Credit had been carried on in Assyria into the seventh century B.C.E. mainly as temple loans to dependents, to be repaid to the temple in kind or equivalent, or as advances of grains or other foodstuffs from landlords to their peasant tenants in off season, to be repaid at harvest time. Although such loans were interest free, a penalty, generally amounting to some twenty-five percent, was imposed if payment was not made at the due date.

Soon after the settlement of the Israelites into the area, the Jewish financiers instituted a reformed system of credit whereby interest-bearing capital was also offered privately for seminal secular or nongovernmental purposes. By the midseventh century the Babylonian banking houses of Egibi and the Persian house of Murashu were actively engaged in such enterprise on a private basis, extending the previously agrarian nature of credit to industry and commerce. The records of these two banking houses are valuable not only in what they reveal of their own operations over specific periods, but in what they indicate of the kind of investments that must have been made by similar banking establishments operating during the period whose records have not had the good fortune to be recovered.

The origins of both the powerful banking houses of whose records a substantial part has been fortuitously recovered, that of Egibi and Sons of Babylonia and of Murashu and Sons of Persia, are shrouded in mystery, and we must interpolate their inception from the context of the portion of their archival records that have been found. The Egibi records date from the mid-seventh century B.C.E. and survived mainly because their cuneiform inscriptions were incised upon clay tablets that were baked in a conflagration. Although the event surely occasioned an unfortunate loss for the banking family, it served to enrich history. The records concern credits issued and loans granted, bills of exchange, the founding and financing of commercial enterprises, the purchase of goods (including slaves), and the acquisition, management, and sale of considerable tracts of land.

The name Egibi is an Akkadian transliteration of Jacob. The ethnicity of the family was brought into question because of the name of the head of the firm, Itti-Marduk-balatu, who also proudly employed the fine old royal name of Isin.[43] The theophoric inclusion of the god Marduk in the name is likely, however, to have been either a deference to the prestigious position the family held in Babylonian society, a fashionable acceptance of Babylonian norms without religious overtones (as many other Jews are known to have pragmatically assumed such names), or, indeed, an indication that the individuals who bore that type of name had apostatized. For an example of another such anomalous name we might cite that of Sheshbazzar, the governor of Judah to whom the temple utensils brought back from Babylon were handed over; he was, as it turned out, a Jewish prince, the father of Zerubabbel.[44] A study of the Murashu documents brought to light an indicative pattern: whereas many of the older members of this unquestionably Jewish family assumed pagan names, they reverted to the employ of Yahwist names for their children. This consistent reversion suggests that in the century following the fall of Jerusalem (586-486 B.C.E.) extradited Jews were either forced to suspend allegiance to Yahweh, or found it politic to do so while secretly adhering to their faith. They returned to its open practice as official attitudes grew more tolerant. The examples in more modern times of that very practice by the Spanish Marranos and others lend credence to this theory.

The Babylonian name of the most active member of the Egibi family during the period of the particular set of documents was, in fact, a secondary name. The family name of the banker's father was Shirik, an Aramaic name, and what must have been his first name is given as Iddina, which is rendered in Hebrew as Nathan. The ancestor of another member of the family was named Bel-iau, a name which indubitably invokes the Israelite God, yet in contrast, a number of the descendants of Egibi appear to have deferred to the Babylonian deity Nabu. It seems evident from the record that the family was of Israelite or Judahite origin, and while its members generally continued to identify themselves as a family with the other Jews of the Babylonian Diaspora, some of its members may have assimilated through the descending generations or deferred to Babylonian religious norms.

The Murashu family was thoroughly Jewish, clearly having been among those deported from Judah. After rooting in Nippur they became one of the most important banking families of Mesopotamia, an institution that was central to the region's economy for at least a period of a century and a half. 730 tablets of the banking house of Murashu and Sons were recovered from Nippur, which was a commercially important city lying just southeast of Babylon. These documents survived because the clay jars in which these were stored were carefully sealed with asphalt. Although the documents from the archives of the business houses are those of the three sons and three grandsons of the founder, covering a half century between 455 and 403 B.C.E., it is clear that the firm had a precedent history in the region. The records provide a piercing view into the economy of the times.

The city of Nippur was located on the Chebar, an important irrigation canal of the Euphrates (Akkadian *na^ru kabari*), and the Jewish settlement of Tel-Abib (a precursor of modern Tel Aviv), the community in which the prophet Ezekiel resided,[45] was located on the same "grand canal" of the region. The satrap of Egypt, Arsames, made his headquarters there at the end of the fifth century. His mail-pouch containing Aramaic letters to his Egyptian bailiffs was unearthed from Nippur[46] and he is referred to in the Aramaic papyri written by the Jews of Elephantine Island. Tel-Abib was one of twenty-eight such Jewish settlements in the immediate Nippur area alone that are mentioned in the Murashu records. The documents attest to the widespread activities of the exiles—deeds for land acquisitions, contracts, and conveyances of all kinds, insurance, and the provision of capital, even securities for imprisoned debtors were dealt with by the prestigious banking house. The Murashus managed estates for absentee landlords, hiring the labor, paying taxes to the state exchequer and remitting the profits to the landlords. They provided collectives of small holdings with the machinery to raise water from the irrigation canals around which the small farms were clustered as well as with draft animals, seed, and farm implements.

The Murashu documents make evident that many forms of such collectives existed. In addition to groups of agrarian workers, the system encompassed "various groups of artisans, for example, carpenters, tanners, ferrymen and shepherds, as well as merchants, scribes and so on."[47] Many Jews are featured in the documents, some of whom owned land in the Nippur neighborhood, and others were employed by high-placed Persians and Babylonians or were servants of the crown. There was, for example, a certain Hannani, son of Minahhim, who held the post of "one who is over the birds of the King (Darius II)," that is, who attended the flocks of fowl belonging to the crown.[48]

Whereas many Jews assumed Babylonian names, as is inevitably the case, at least eight percent of the clients of the banking families can be identified as Jews from their names alone. This percentage corresponds roughly to that of the proportion of Jews among the official population, which, before the influx of deportees from Judah, amounted to somewhat over six percent of the total. The Aramaic form of other names and other hints from names or activities, however, indicate that the actual percentage of Jews among managers and officials was considerably higher. Some Jewish entrepreneurs made out well with the assistance of Murashu capital. Thus a certain Jedaiah mortgaged his land to the Murashu banking house at an annual fee of thirty thousand liters of barley; three years later Jedaiah in association with other partners expanded his holdings, paying three times the amount in rent. In 419 B.C.E. Jedaiah's son, Eliada, formed a partnership with a Persian to become the agents of the steward of the royal domains in the Nippur area.[49]

It is clear that although the Egibi and Murashu families were wealthy Jews, and while others did well at court and in the service of the hierarchy, many were busy at agriculture and crafts. There are a number of references to Jewish engineers who earned their livelihood as irrigation experts. All fourteen canal managers known to us through the documents by name were Jews; they were responsible administrators who exercised a technical trade central to the economy of the region.[50] Some Jews participated in the military establishment; thus the son of a feudatory, Gadalyaw Gedaliah, "volunteered to serve as a mounted and cuirassed archer in place of a son of Murashu. This Gedaliah was the earliest, individually known predecessor of medieval mailclad and mounted knights."[51]

Most of the Jews referred to in the Murashu documents, however, were of the "lower classes." Some were slaves, and come to our attention because slaves of those times were not treated as mere property but as persons who privately retained both individual privileges and responsibilities, and could independently enter into legal agreements. Two such slaves, one clearly Jewish, were contracted by the head of the house of Murashu to repair the dam of the irrigation canal passing through Murashu property or be assessed damages if they failed to exercise their commitment! Other credits were extended to persons of meager resources. An impoverished Jewish woman who made a living at home by spinning and selling her product was assisted in her endeavors. A Jewish guide was hired for a journey and was promised, in addition to wages and expenses, a bonus upon the successful completion of the trip. A certain Zebadiah was one of five fisherman who leased nets for a period of twenty days.[52]

JEWISH MERCHANTS AND ARTISANS AND FAR EASTERN TRADE

The Babylonian economic and technological renaissance that began with the influx of the Israelites and accelerated with the additional infusion of masses of Judahites into the socio-economic fabric of the region is visible in the records of the banking houses. The activity of the Egibi bankers in Susa, gateway to India, presages the expansion of trade along the land and sea routes to the Far East. The Mesopotamian Jews were concentrated in the fertile irrigated heart of the land between the two rivers, a region that formed the very hub of the greater Asian land routes. Jewish merchants and artisans established themselves in the principal commercial centers along the trade routes fanning out from that region. Jewish merchants infiltrated the communities along the through routes being newly cleared to China and to Southeast Asia.

Trade between the two extremities of the Eurasian continent had been heretofore topographically circumscribed in central Asia by the Pamirs, a north-south mountain range joining the Hindu Kush and the Himalayas, on the south, and by a vast desert stretching out beyond the Pamirs. The formidable mountain chains and the severe stretches of scorching sands effectively segmented the immense Eurasian land mass. The most stringent limitation on East-West trade was, however, the control over sectors of the passage from east to west by tribes typified by the *Hsuing Nu,* the so-called Huns, one of the Turkic-speaking peoples through whose good offices the caravans had to be cleared for passage. East-West commerce could not be conducted without the intervention of such peoples until the second century B.C.E.; goods had to pass through several hands to reach their final destination.

Glass beads were the first important sign of a burgeoning contact between East and West. The earliest glass objects recovered from Chinese tombs exhibit strong Near Eastern affinities. The characteristic *eye-beads,* which had become staple trade goods for the Canaanites around the Mediterranean, suddenly appear among Imperial Chinese grave goods during this period. Such intricately wrought glass beads, as well as beads of plainer varieties, have been found in central and western Asia only along the ancient routes to and from Persia into China and India. The provenience of glass artifacts of this early period found along the route to the Far East is attested to by a Persian-period blue-glass lion seated royally upon a rectangular base, one of three almost identical lions, the other two of which were found in Teheran and Egypt.

During the Achaemenian period (550-330 B.C.E.) the glassmaking art reached a new height of sophistication in Persia. The finest examples of the art have been recovered from Nippur, Nimrud, and Ctesiphon, precisely the areas of heaviest concentration of Jewish communities. A particular style of shallow hemispherical bowls, molded on the bottom in relief with a fluted rosette of leaves, was characteristic of the area and the period. They were widely distributed. Examples of these unmistakable objects were found as far afield as Ephesus and Gordion in Anatolia, Jerusalem, Persopolis, and elsewhere. One such bowl, complete with an eighteen-leafed rosette molded into its bottom, appeared on the London market and is inscribed in Aramaic with the name *Tryphon,* probably the name of its original owner.

The very first mention of glassware in Greek literature relates to the experience of Greek ambassadors to the Persian court. Aristophanes reported in 425 about the amazement of the Greek dignitaries on being served drinks in bowls made of this brilliant, crystallike material, for which no word yet existed in their language.[53] One can well imagine the value set by the enraptured Greek emissaries on such crystal bowls, but it could hardly have been more than that set at a Sotheby auction, where an Achaemenid bowl was sold on July 13, 1976 for sixty-two thousand English pounds!

The arrival of the glassmakers in China some time during or after the fifth century B.C.E. is attested to by the fact that whereas the earliest imported glassware was composed of the same elements as those of Near Eastern glass, much of the second-century B.C.E. glassware found in the royal graves at Lo-yang contains an unusual amount of lead oxide, and especially barium, an element that was unique to the Chinese and absent from Near Eastern glass. The cemetery at Lo-yang is near the former capital of China, Kaifeng. In the heart of that city at the end of the "silk route," a substantial colony of Jews was established, the genesis of which may stem back to this early period.

A favorite Chinese tale, which appears in numerous Chinese literary works, concerns the claim of traders who arrived from the West at the court of the Emperor Tai Wu that they could imitate precious colored stones by melting together certain secret minerals, and offered to do so if the Emperor would grant them mining privileges. The Emperor, enamored with the imitation jades, crystals, and intriguing eye-beads that had hitherto been imported into his realm, and delighted with the prospect of an infinite supply of precious material, eagerly accepted the offer of the traders and granted them permission to obtain whatever minerals they needed from the nearby hills. According to an often-quoted version of the story given in the *Pai-shih,* a historical work of the fifth century c.e., the glass gems produced by the enterprising traders were of exceptional beauty and brilliance, even superior to the imported variety.

The second sign of escalating Chinese contacts with the Near East was the appearance of ferric production in the heart of China at the end of the transcontinental trade route soon after 500 b.c.e. The Chinese civilization was advanced in many respects, and pyrotechnology was a discipline in which they excelled. Chinese bronze work was outstanding, the result of more than a thousand years of experience in casting the compound metal alloy. Pneumatically drafted furnaces were not unknown to the Chinese; some of the massive bronze castings were only possible through the use of such furnaces. The Chinese could have produced iron but, perhaps because their proficiency in brass made iron almost redundant, they had never turned to its production. The escalation of intercourse with Mesopotamia in the fifth century b.c.e., however, brought iron manufacture as well as its pyrotechnical corollary, glass manufacture, to China.

The first iron producers in China did not pass through any developmental stages of iron production, but launched directly into casting the metal. This leap into an advanced state of the art signals the arrival of artisans who installed themselves in China or taught the trade to the Chinese. Primitive ferric technology is restricted to the production of wrought iron, which can be achieved at a temperature of just under 1,100 degrees Celsius. The spongy mass that results from the smelting process (the "bloom") is composed of a disoriented mass composed of iron granules and impurities. By means of continued reheating, hammering, and quenching the iron is hardened and shaped, because the repeated pounding and heating compacts the iron granules into a homogeneous mass and removes the slag. Casting iron, however, requires a melting temperature of over 1,400 degrees Centigrade, at which temperature the slag can be skimmed off from an already homogenized raw material. The technique of casting bronze by pouring the molten metal into molds is a technique at which the Chinese were already adept. Upon arriving in China, the Near Eastern smiths were able to take advantage of the exemplary competence of the Chinese in metal-casting; they were enabled to hurdle over the more primitive processes of iron production and immediately launch into an advanced stage of metallurgy, the production of cast iron.

The intimate involvement of Judahite Jews in the production of iron was warranted by the historian Dio Cassius (c. 150-235 C.E.), castigating the Jews for their duplicity during the period leading to the Bar Kochba rebellion. Dio Cassius accuses the Jewish armorers of sabotage by having deliberately fabricated defective weapons. In doing so the Jews gained an additional advantage, for the discarded weapons were then appropriated and reworked for use by the Jewish saboteurs![54] No better testimony to Judahite familiarity with the mining, smelting, and smithing of iron can be had, however, than the fact that among the slaves the Romans soon thereafter took and transported from *Eretz Yisrael* to the Roman Diaspora, were 4,000 stalwart young Judahites who were assigned to the iron mines and forges of Sicily, where their descendants remained as miners, smelters, and smiths into the Middle Ages. Many more thousands of Judahite slaves were delegated to dig and work the gold and silver from the mines of Spain, and other Jewish metalworkers were dispersed behind the Roman legions deep into the Diaspora. It is no mere coincidence that "Ferro," "Fierro," "Herriero," and "Ferriere" (literally "iron" or "smith") were Italian, Spanish, and French Jewish names through the Middle Ages, and that names deriving from "Goldsmith," "Silver," and "Glass" continue to suggest the ethnicity of their bearers to the present day.

China had its own unique manufactured product to offer the West: silk was a wondrous filament with which the most elegant materials could be woven. The farming of silkworms, the technique of reeling off strands of silk hundreds of meters long from their cocoons, and of weaving the incredibly strong filaments into exotic fabrics, date back to the earliest period of Chinese civilization. A silk fabric found in Zhejiang Province dates back to the astoundingly early date of 2700 B.C.E., a time when, according to accepted archaeological chronology, China was still in the process of emerging from its Neolithic period.

> Silk, the finest of all natural fibers, has three crucial qualities: strength, elasticity and extremely long fibers. A silk thread made of seven filaments has a tensile strength of 65,000 pounds per square inch. . . . As the wealth and power of the aristocracy increased, beginning in the latter part of the Warring States period (475-221 B.C.) preceding the Han, the market for luxury goods led to the production of embroidered cloth and fabrics woven in complex patterns. The drawloom, a special type of horizontal hand loom, was designed for this purpose.[55]

The invention of the drawloom revolutionized Chinese silk manufacture and by the time of the Han period the industry had attained exceptional sophistication. The weaving of complex embroidered patterns with as many as 400 to 600 threads per linear inch were made possible by the drawloom and the embroiderers were enabled to reproduce freehand any design they could imagine. Consummately skilled Chinese embroiderers took full advantage of the drawloom's capability by executing the most intricate designs in shimmering silk. The *feng-huang* bird, the dragon, and other stylized versions of mythical creatures, as well as magnificent faunal and floral patterns were woven into the garments of the wealthy Chinese. Emperors clad themselves luxuriously in silken masterpieces while alive and were buried in them after death. Little wonder that Western aristocrats soon avidly sought the sumptuous silken fabrics being flaunted by their counterparts in the East.

Western civilizations were ignorant of the remarkable attributes of silken fibers until the Hellenic period, when silk produced from wild Asia Minor silkworms first appeared among the Near Eastern civilizations. Sericulture, however, was peculiarly, uniquely, and anciently a Chinese industry until the raising of silkworms and the production of silk textiles were added to the roster of Jewish arts. Just as the Persian Jews were central to the process by which ferric and vitric production reached the Far East, so they became the medium through which the ancient, esoteric Chinese art of sericulture penetrated into the West.

The quality of Chinese silk made from the cocoons of cultivated silk worms was so superior that it displaced the use of locally produced silk as soon as it became available. One of the important centers of this East-West trade was Damascus. The import of silk into Damascus and the production and export from that city of silk products that appropriately became famous as *damasks*, were largely in the hands of Jewish entrepreneurs, and glassware was an integral element of the process of exchange. L. Boulnois, piecing together scraps of data concerning the traffic to the Far East, came to the conclusion that the Jewish merchants:

> were celebrated for their work in glass, byssus [linen] and silk, as well as for their dyeing. Silk—dyeing—glass—caravans: the combination of these four elements might well lead us to suppose that they had some part in the far-eastern silk trade. . . . From its arrival on Roman territory to its purchase by the consumer, silk passed through relatively few hands; often enough it was one family that bought the silk from the Persian middle-man, wove it, dyed it and re-exported it to other parts of the Mediterranean. And that family was as likely to be Jewish as it was to be Tyrian or Greek. As expert glass workers, the Jews had on hand one of the means of exchange used as payment for silk—especially the famous glass beads.[56]

BETH SHEAN AND BETH SHEARIM: JEWISH LINEN AND JEWISH GLASS

The exchange of products, as Boulnois emphasizes, was not limited to iron, glass, and silk; the Chinese were as avidly interested in Western linen fabrics (*byssus*) as the West was of silk fabrics, and linens figured as importantly in the freight flowing eastward as silk did among the goods moving to the West. By the Hellenic period, the Jews had became pre-eminently proficient in the weaving of linens. One of the earliest centers of weaving was the town of Beth Shean, one of the Canaanite towns that had fallen to the forces of David. The biblically attested weavers of fine linen of the house of Ashbea, which was referred to previously, were located at nearby Beth Shean. By the third century B.C.E. Beth Shean had already achieved fame as a producer of fine fabrics, an attribute that was reflected in numerous talmudic references; the Jerusalem Talmud places great value upon the "fine linen vestments which come from Beth Shean."[57]

Beth Shean, a city situated at a strategic point along one of the main routes linking East with West, was second only to Samaria in importance in northeastern *Eretz Yisrael*. It was one of the first communities overrun by Alexander in the campaign that carried the Macedonian and his mercenaries across Judah, Mesopotamia, and Persia to the banks of the Oxus and Indus rivers. The town was dubbed "Scythopolis" by the Greeks and its workshops supplied the Chinese with linens, one of the most important products with which the Greeks, and subsequently the Romans, redressed the balance of payments for merchandise from further East. Joseph Needham, who compiled a most comprehensive and authoritative western work on Chinese technology, concluded that: "The byssus (fine linen) mentioned as being brought to China by merchants or embassies from the 1st century onward is likely to have come from Scythopolis (Beit Shean) in the Jordan Valley."[58]

The Jewish linen weavers of Beth Shean achieved worldwide recognition for the superiority of their textiles and for the quality of the garments produced from them. The flaxen products of Beth Shean commanded the highest prices, prices reflecting the reputation for excellence that they had achieved. This value was not only determined by market constraints but was eventually confirmed by the Roman Emperor Diocletian. The Roman ruler, in an attempt to curb runaway inflation, fixed ceilings on prices and wages throughout the Empire in the year 301 C.E. in an "Edict of Maximum Prices." The value of the woven products of Beth Shean (Scythopolis) was placed at the top of the various categories in which they figured, including:

> Tunics without stripes, dalmatics (upper garments) for men and women, short and light mantles, short cloaks with hoods for women, kerchiefs and sheets. The textile goods are divided into three qualities: first, second and third. In each group the produce of Scythopolis appears in the first class. Only the produce of Tarsus competes with it occasionally.[59]

The synagogue of Beth Shean was rebuilt at the end of the third century. The fact that the community was observant of Hebraic law is evidenced by the size and importance of the synagogue; the involvement of the Jews in international trade is furthermore evidenced by such incidents as the refusal of Beth Shean Jews to leave for Sidon on a Saturday to conduct business. Sidon was the main port through which glass was exported and through which many of the minerals for the production of glass were imported. Beth Shean, in addition to being a center of weaving and garment production, was also involved in the production of glassware; it was one of the vital centers whose ancient workshops, in addition to providing a valuable range of imports into Europe, supplied the Greeks and then the Romans with glass, fabrics, and other finished products with which to redress the balance of payments for merchandise from the East.

It happens that in the same edict in which the linens of Beth Shean are classified by Diocletian as the most worthy, the existence of only two categories of glassware is specified. The two types of glassware listed in the edict are *vitri Ijudaici* ("Jewish glass"), and *vitri Alexandrini* ("Alexandrian glass").[60] The implication is clear that by far the main sources of glass products were *Eretz Yisrael* and Alexandria, and that products from any other source were so similar, being "Jewish glass" produced elsewhere in the Roman Empire, that they did not require distinguishing tariffs. The name Judah had been officially expunged by Hadrian in 135 C.E., and the area incorporated into the newly constituted *Provincia Syro-Palestina*. The Diocletian edict, however, makes it abundantly clear that despite the attempted obliteration of the Jews as a national entity, the term "Jewish glass" had become so endemic that the term persisted for centuries after Judaea was no longer officially in existence as such. "Jewish glass," in fact, persisted into the mid-nineteenth century as a generic designation of lead glass.

"Sidon" and "Phoenicia" are conspicuously absent from the edict, although "Sidonian glass" and "Phoenician glass" are common epithets modernly applied to glassware of the region produced during the classical period. Although the ports of Sidon and Tyre were the major ports from which glassware was being shipped, the main manufacture of "Jewish glass" was being carried on in the hinterlands, an industry now in evidence from the scoria (glass, crucible, and furnace fragments) of ancient glassmaking furnaces emerging from *kibbutz* farmland throughout the upper and lower Galilee.

"Alexandrian glass" was fixed in the Diocletian edict at a higher price than that of "Jewish glass," reflecting the fact that the Alexandrian industry was devoted to the production of elaborate, exotic, and expensive glassware directed at the upper class market, whereas the glassware of *Eretz Yisrael* was of a commoner type, and was turning up in substantial quantities throughout the Roman Empire. It so happens, however, that the glassmakers of Alexandria were as Jewish as were the glassmakers of *Eretz Yisrael*.

The art of glassmaking spread from the Galilee and Judah to Alexandria soon after that Ptolemaic city was founded. The Romans became the city's rulers during the period when glassmaking matured from an industry restricted to the supplying of exotic artifacts for the rich and powerful to an industry capable of satisfying a wide market. The Jews, constituting about forty percent of the Alexandrian population, were at the forefront of the skilled crafts of that bustling city, and were preeminently the glassblowers. Hadrian Augustus, in the course of a vituperative critique of the Alexandrian Jews, paid them some backhanded compliments, crediting them with carrying on the skilled crafts of the city and placing the revolutionary process of glassblowing pointedly among them. In an epistle to Servianus the Consul, the Roman emperor states that the Alexandrian Jews were "prosperous, rich and fruitful, and in it [Alexandria] no one is idle. Some are blowers of glass, others makers of paper, all are at least weavers of linen or seem to belong to one craft or another; the lame have their occupations, the wounded have theirs, the blind have theirs, and not even those whose hands are crippled are idle."

Thus two Roman emperors identify glassmaking as uniquely Jewish industries of *both* Judea and Alexandria, the major producers and exporters of glass and glassware of the Roman Imperial period. The selfsame emperors also assign the production of the finest fabrics and garments to the Jewish communities of the Near East. Accordingly, the two most important products that figured in trade to the Far East, glassware and linens, are attested to as the products of Jewish artisans. Indeed, the production of paper, noted by Hadrian Augustus as being another Jewish industry, had already become another specialty of the Jews, one in which the production of papyrus ("paper") was followed by what became more commonly referred to as "paper," yet another Chinese product that was introduced into the West by Jewish merchants.

The importance of the linen-weaving industry of Beth Shean is further attested to in a Latin geographical work of the mid-fourth century, *Totius Descriptotus Orbis*, in which Beth Shean is described as preeminently one of the cities that supply textiles to the whole world. The Mishnah, that rich repository of Jewish tradition and law, plies us with anecdotes that elucidate halachic ethical and legal issues. The tales in this indirect exegetical process serve to peripherally document many Jewish activities, including the intimate involvement of the Jews with the production and distribution of glassware and textiles.

The Mishnah was compiled at Beth Shearim, which became the seat of the Sanhedrin after the fall of the Second Temple. It was to Beth Shearim that Judah Ha-Nasi ("the Prince," 135–219 C.E.) first came back on his return from Babylonia. He is among the many sages who now lie buried in the catacombs riddling the hills around the village. Each of the great scholars earned his living at a trade, abjuring compensation for his role as teacher. The work ethic of the Mishnaic scholars contrasted sharply with the disdain that the Greeks and Romans, and indeed all conquerors, placed upon manual labor.

Just as Beth Shean was notable as the center of linen production, so Beth Shearim was notable as a center for glassmaking. A great 8.8-ton slab of solid glass can still be seen in Beth Shearim in a museum situated at the entrance to the final resting places of the great sages. The massive glass slab is the wonder of the glassmaking world, being exceeded in bulk only slightly by the two-hundred-inch lenses made by Corning glass for the Mount Palomar telescope.[61] To have brought fifty thousand or more pounds of raw minerals up to a temperature of 1050 degrees centigrade or higher, and to have incessantly maintained this fierce temperature for a period of a week or longer, necessitated the engineering of a gigantic reverbatory furnace, the continuous stoking of the furnace with tons upon tons of wood, and the manual forcing of powerful drafts of air day and night throughout the period by an unremitting pumping of a series of bellows. The production of such a monumental mass of glass presumes a technology that, with all the expertise and knowledge we have gained over the past two thousand years, remains a tour-de-force of the first magnitude, a feat that has never been duplicated with the use of the materials and fuel then available.

There is evidence that Beth Shearim was only one of the sites in the region at which huge masses of glass were being produced. At nearby Arsuf in 1950, Drs. P. P. Kahane and Immanuel Ben-Dor found "glass floors" that match the description of the monumental slab of Beth Shearim. Unfortunately, only a few glass fragments were saved from the Arsuf excavation, relics that were examined by Robert Brill of the Corning Museum, who concluded that "there might be a connection between the 'glass floors' at Arsuf and the Beth She'arim slab."[62]

There are indications that other facilities were producing massive amounts of raw glass nearer the coast. I made a survey of surface evidence of such facilities from Tel Aviv to Haifa, and found numerous sites worthy of further investigation. Near the modern city of Herziliya lie the ruins of ancient Appolonia, where so much glassmaking debris was left in the area by the ancient glassmakers that it was used for building material by the Crusaders in erecting their coastal fortifications. Other sites where large quantities of furnace slag and vitric scoria were evident were seen, for example, at Hadera, Caesarea, and near Akko, further up the coast. Unfortunately, much of the coastline is being subjected to development, and that evidence that is not being plowed under in the *kibbutzim* along the coast is fast falling subject to urban expansion.

Judah Ha-Nasi moved to Beth Shean, where he was joined by Rabbi Chiyya bar Abba, a scholar who is among those mentioned in the Mishnah as traveling widely in the conduct of his business. Rabbi Chiyya dealt with four of the basic goods being traded along the route into China: spices, and products of glass, silk, and linen. Rabbi Chiyya was not only a trader, but was also one of the growers of flax, an agricultural product whose demand was nourished by the booming business in linen.[63]

It is related, for example, that Rabbi Chiyya, together with the son of Judah Ha-Nasi and a Rabbi Simeon ben Gamliel had just come from Tyre, where they had completed a business transaction involving bales of raw silk. "Let us emulate the example of our forebears," they said, referring to an ancient double-checking tradition that they had evidently neglected to follow. "Let us see if we have left anything behind." They returned to Tyre, and sure enough, found that they had left behind a bale of silk.[64]

One of Rabbi Chiyya's duties in his travels among the towns of Israel was to determine which of them were lacking teachers and scribes and then to provide them. He was on such a mission together with several other rabbis, when they came to a town that had neither a scribe nor a teacher. "Bring us the guardians of the town," they asked the people, who dutifully brought citizens of the senatorial class before them. "Do you think that these are the guardians of the town?" Rabbi Chiyya asked, and added, "they are none other than the destroyers of the town."

"Who, then, are the guardians of the town?" the puzzled townspeople inquired.

"The scribes and teachers."[65]

The ramifications of Rabbi Chiyya's Judaic philosophy and the teaching of the sages are definitively characterized by the following passage:

My task is to make provision that the Torah be not forgotten in Israel; thus I bring flax seed, sow it, spin thread, twist ropes and prepare snares by means of which I catch deer. The flesh of these I distribute among orphans, and I use the hides to prepare parchment, on which I write the Torah. Provided with these I go to places where there are no teachers and instruct the children.

Rabbi Chiyya was a humble man, and when a question of ethics regarding his own conduct arose, he reverted to Judah Ha-Nasi. Some ass drivers came to buy some flax from him. He told them that he was not thinking of selling it at that time but later, when the demand would be greater and the price higher. "Sell it to us now at the price you will get if you sell it later," the ass drivers said to him. He came to consult with Ha-Nasi, who told him that such a transaction was forbidden.[66]

Rabbi Chiyya turned to Ha-Nasi for practical as well as ethical advice, as on the occasion when his flax crop became worm-infested. This inquiry establishes that Rabbi Chiyya's references were "not just hyperbole."[67] Rabbi Chiyya's business trips took him to Beth Shean, to Laodicia (another weaving center), throughout the Galilee, and Nabatea. There are references to dealing in spikenard, a spice imported from the Himalayas whose import was controlled by the Nabatean Arabs.[68] Thus the Mishnah reflects the involvement of Jews like Rabbi Chiyya in all the elements that composed the China trade. It was this tradition that expanded into a world-girdling network of Jewish trade exemplified by the Persian Radhanites, and under the doughty Jewish traveling entrepreneurs who followed in their wake.

Beth Shean was a mixed community, but the linen-weaving and garment-producing industries were clearly Jewish industries. The textile industries followed the emigration of Jews from *Eretz Yisrael* to the West where, significantly, the products of the Land of Israel were held up as standards for excellence. Thus at the end of the second century C.E., when Jewish artisans had established themselves in Anatolia and Greece, Clement of Alexandria took to task the spendthrifts who luxuriated in rich trappings. Egyptian garments made of coarse linens were not good enough for these profligates, chided Clement, "they have to deck themselves out in fabrics imported from the *land of the Hebrews* and from Cilicia [in southeast Anatolia, where a colony of Jews had established itself]."[69]

Greek textile products were gauged against those produced by the Jews in *Eretz Yisrael* by Pausanius, who commented after visiting Palestine in 175 C.E. that the products of Greece were not inferior to those made by the Jews in that ancient land.

The Jewish textile industries were not confined to luxury goods. Not far from Beth Shean was the thoroughly Jewish town of Arbel, nested near the shores of Lake Tiberias. Rabbinic sources refer to the coarser garments produced in Arbel as well as to the finer vestments of Beth Shean.[70] The styles of textiles developed in Tarsus, capital of Anatolian Cilicia, were duplicated by Galilean craftsmen. The fashions became so popular that the producers, called *tarsim* after the city that had given birth to them, were organized into special cooperatives, or guilds. The story is told that when the Romans arrested Rabbi Eliezer ben Partha and Rabbi Joshua ben Teradyon for ignoring the prohibition against teaching Torah, Rabbi Eliezer denied the charge, whereupon the Romans inquired as to why he was being called *Rav* (master, rabbi, or teacher). "Because I am a *tarsim* (master of weaving)," the good rabbi retorted, undoubtedly with tongue held firmly in cheek.

Gedaliah Alon points out that the title *Rav*, or master, serves in a number of Semitic languages as "the technical designation for the chief of a company of tradesmen or artisans."[71] There were at least two towns in which the tarsim guilds maintained their own synagogues. A controversy is recorded to have taken place in a synagogue in Tiberias at a time before the Bar Kochba Rebellion, and another account places such a weaver's union in Lydda.[72]

The intimacy of the Alexandrian Jewish artisans with various arts and their organization into guild-like organizations is made explicit in a passage of the *Diplostoön* ("The Double Colonnade"), in which the congregation of the great synagogue of Alexandria is described: "[In the synagogue] the people did not sit at random, but rather grouped by trades: goldsmiths in their own section, silversmiths in theirs, weavers [*tarsim*] in theirs. So that when a newcomer entered, he sought out the members of his own craft, and on applying to that quarter, received his livelihood . . ."[73]

JEWISH DYERS AND THE ROYAL PURPLE

The production and use of dyes was another set of industrial secrets the Jews carried with them throughout the Diaspora, and the involvement of the Jews in silk traffic coupled them even more intimately to the art of dyeing. The Jews had long been privy to the process of producing purple dyes, which were employed for coloring wool textiles. Although the ancient purple dyes were not suitable for linens, they were admirably applicable to silk.

The association of the Jews with these dyes stems back to their Akkadian progenitors; the oldest record of purple dyeing goes back 3,500 years to Mesopotamian Nuzi.[74] The mention of the two classic shades of purple and blue first appears in a sixteenth-century B.C.E. cuneiform text.[75] For a brief period the word *takiltu*, its Akkadian form, shows up in the el Amarna correspondence between Babylonia and Egypt. References to *takiltu* appear in the business records of the Cassite kings "and became current in Babylonia after the sixteenth century [B.C.E.],"[76] but the word seems to disappear from the region and does not reappear in the Assyrian language before the eighth century, that is, until after the deportation of the Israelites from the Canaanite coastal regions to the interior of Mesopotamia.

The royal purple (*argaman* in Hebrew) and the biblical (or ritual) blue (*tekhelet* in Hebrew) were two of the most important colors in the culture of ancient Israel.[77] The familiarity of the Jews with *tekhelet* and *argaman* and their appreciation of the value of these mollusc-derived dyes is biblically evidenced by their immediate introduction into religious ritual by God Himself. The first instructions given to Moses during his sojourn of forty days on Mount Sinai was that the children of Israel must willingly bring him an offering of "gold, and silver, and brass, and blue, and purple, and scarlet. . . ."[78] *Tekhelet* in particular is thereafter employed in sacerdotal vestments, tabernacle awnings and is specified as a color for inclusion in *tsitsit*, the fringes of prayer shawls and undergarments:

> And the Lord spake unto Moses saying, "Speak unto the children of Israel, and bid them that they make them fringes in the corners of their garments throughout their generations, and that they put upon the fringes of the corners a thread of blue [*Tekelet*], and it shall be unto you a fringe, that ye may look upon it, and remember all the commandments of the Lord, and do them. . . ."[79]

Violet, purple, and crimson wools are prescribed in Numbers 4 for the covering of sacred vessels being transported from the sanctuary of the Temple.

The production of these colors (ranging from crimson to "royal" purple) from Mediterranean molluscs had evidently been introduced to the Canaanite coast in the Iron Age, during the period of Israelite settlement. Ezekiel refers to Elishah (Cyprus) as a source from which the inhabitants of Tyre obtained *tekhelet* and *argaman*,[80] a reference that implies that the secret of producing the exotic colors may well have been known on that island as well as in the city that became world famous for its royal purple dye (Tyrian purple). In 1980, archaeologists unearthed a commercial purple dye installation near Acco (Acre). Massive layers of crushed murex shells were superimposed upon burials of the so-called "Hyksos" and "late Canaanites," dating the industry to the end of the thirteenth or beginning of the twelfth century B.C.E. Further evidence of pottery production and the reworking of metals was also found being performed at that level. The settlement of one of the "Sea Peoples," the Shardan, along the northern coast of *Eretz Yisrael* also helps to fix the date of the industrial installations, especially because one of the artifacts they left behind was a scarab seal bearing the name of Queen Teo-Sret, dated to circa 1200 B.C.E. Nira Karmon and Ehud Spanier point out, in their review of the archaeological evidence of the purple dye industry from Israel, that the Shardan "are mentioned in one of the Egyptian sources in connection with the Israelite tribe of Asher."[81]

The continuity of the industry under the inhabitants of the Acco area and especially at Tel Shikmona (at the southern perimeter of Haifa), through the Persian into the Hellenistic period, are confirmed by a number of other recoveries of purple-stained pottery and large quantities of crushed murex shells in and around the tells throughout the coastal area biblically assigned to the tribes of Asher and Zebulun. "The toponymy of the area in the Hellenistic period seems to recall activities connected with purple dye, as Haifa was known as 'Purphurion.' In addition, talmudic tradition mentions that purple snails were fished on the coast extending from the ladder of Tyre to Haifa."[82]

The involvement of the Jews with the production of purple dyes in the area is attested to by another talmudic tradition, which asserts that the "poor of the land" who were left behind by Nebuchadnezzar's captain of the guard to be the "vine-dressers and husbandmen" of depopulated Judah were also engaged in fishing the purple-producing snails off the Canaanite littoral from Haifa to Tyre.[83] Nor did Jewish knowledge of dyes remain limited to those derived from various murex molluscs of the Mediterranean; another scarlet-purplish or crimson dye, for example, was produced from a red insect, the kermes, which thrives on a certain species of oak, and was used to color wool. The continuing familiarity of the Jews with the art of dye-making is attested to no less by the knowledge of imitations of the authentic purple dyes as by the real thing. Samples of imitation purple wool were recovered, for one example, from the Judean Cave of Letters of the Bar-Kochba period.[84]

Purple reappears in Persia on the royal insignia of Assyria and on garments worn by Assyrian kings soon after the extradition of Israelite artisans from the region of Canaan. Ezekiel was well aware of the Assyrian propensity for purple, for he informs us that Oholah the harlot doted on the Assyrian "captains and rulers, all of them desireable young men, horsemen riding upon horses," who were "clothed in purple."[85] Chapter 27 of Ezekiel goes into great detail regarding the producers and traders in the many products that flowed between East and West overseas from the Tyrian coast and overland from Damascus. Purple (blue) goods are featured in several places and are included with other valuable export products: firs and oaks for the building of ships; benches of ivory; fine linen with embroidered work; iron, silver, tin, and lead; horses and mules; emeralds, purple [the dye?]; embroidered goods, white wool, and fine linen; coral and agate; "wheat of Minith"; dainties and honey; the wine of Helbon; lambs and rams and goats; spices, precious stones, and gold.

The remarkable feature of the lengthy catalogue of products provided by Ezekiel, by which the Tyrian shippers "enriched the kings of the earth," was that the purple goods are said to have come not from the Canaanite coast at this time but from Assyria; it was "Harran, and Canneh, and Eden, the merchants of Sheba, Asshur, and Chilmad" who were the "merchants in blue clothes, and embroidered work, and in chests of rich apparel"; Ezekiel also informs us that Dan and Javan attended the Tyrian fairs with "thread, bright iron, cassia, and calamus," the very products that bespoke a commercial relationship with the Far East.

The biblical reference to the poor Judaic dye-producers left behind by Nebuchadnezzar on the shores of *Eretz Yisrael* is easily related to the archaeological evidence of the production of purple dye being practiced at many ancient sites along the coast, especially from Ashkelon to Tyre. The vestiges of a substantial dye industry were found at Tel Dor, Shikmona, Acco, and other locations, an industry that was already in full flower in the Hellenistic period.[86]

Until the first century of the Common Era, purple dye was used mainly for dyeing woolen textiles, for textiles made of flax (linen) did not take the dye well. The various dyes obtained from the different varieties of the murex and other purple-producing molluscs were among the fastest dyes known. They were extraordinarily expensive, and purple fabrics were used most frugally. Purple clothes became a mark of prestige, and restrictions placed on the wearing of purple made it the mark of noble status. Only the Roman censors and generals on campaign were allowed clothing entirely of purple, and the generals were permitted to continue wearing such clothing on their return only if they had been triumphant! Consuls and praetors were relegated to trimming their togas with purple, and the practice of employing purple woolen roundels or other small trimmings was more or less followed until the third century, when silk became acceptable for men's attire and silken garments replaced woolen ones among the rich and powerful.

It is clear by now that the term "silk route" does not adequately describe its function. The term was coined in the nineteenth century and represents a Western point of view. Without the flow of linens and glassware from the West there would be no return of spices and silks from the East. Silk, skins, iron, lacquer, rhubarb, and cinnamon are among the products arriving overland from China, and household slaves, pets and arena animals, exotic furs, cashmere wool, raw and finished cotton, and some silks arrived overseas from India. Other spices and dye substances such as cochineal and indigo were picked up along the southern route, and slaves and animal skins were added on the northern route. Flaxen and woolen textiles, lamps and glassware, carpets, amber and coral, asbestos, bronze vessels, wine, and papyrus were the main products traveling east. The Jews were the couriers of Eastern products such as camphor, jade, and a rich variety of spices, profitable items whose sources often remained secrets confined to the traders; and such secrets as glassmaking and dye-manufacture long remained privy to the Jewish artisans wherever they were located.

Both India and China were sources of exotic spices, products valued for disguising the taste of rancid food and for preserving food in an era when refrigeration was as yet more than two millennia away. Spices were valued not only for the enhancement of the taste of food but also for their medicinal properties. Cinnamon, and the raw bark from which it was ground, cassia, were the most important among the spices traded to the West. Sri Lanka (Ceylon), India, and Southern China are the areas in which varieties of the evergreen trees whose bark is stripped for this purpose grow. The twin products were in high demand for use as condiments, employed at first to enhance the flavor of wine and later as a flavoring for food. The aromatic spice was also an ingredient of valuable perfumes for overpowering body odor at a time when plumbing was a rarity, as well as of fragrant unguents to be applied not only to living bodies but also for the scenting of corpses. Not the least of the value of these products lay in their pharmaceutical application; Greek physicians began early on to prescribe potions that included cassia or cinnamon, alone or in combination with other ingredients, as antidotes against poisonous bites, and ended up by making them popular cure-alls. "As it happens, cinnamon and cassia do possess genuine pharmaceutical properties: as carminatives, antiseptics, and astringents, they still maintain a place in the pharmacopoeia."[87]

The intimate association of the Jews with Far Eastern spices predates the birth of Western classical civilization. Long before the Greeks had learned the word "cinnamon," in fact, long before the Greeks had even employed the aleph-beth to commit their vernacular to writing, both cinnamon and cassia had already figured prominently in the second Book of Moses.[88] It is written that the Lord Himself gave Moses instructions (Exodus 30:23-25) on compounding an olive oil ointment in precise proportions "after the art of the apothecary," with the inclusion of "three principal spices, of pure myrrh five hundred shekels, and of sweet cinnamon half so much, and of sweet calamus two hundred and fifty shekels." To this mixture Moses was advised to add five hundred shekels' worth of cassia.

In Psalms (45:9) we encounter the word *ḳeṣiāh*, clearly the model for the Greek word *kasia*. *Kiddāh* as clearly becomes the Greek *kittō*, a cheap grade of cassia. It is not only reference to the Bible that provides the etymological roots of the precedence of Jewish familiarity with these aromatics; the historian Herodotus (*Persian Wars* 3:107-111) was the first among the Greeks to identify the derivation of the Greek word *kinnammōmon* from the Canaanite (so-called "Phoenician") language. The form of the ending, speculated Lionel Casson, "possibly arose by association with the spice *amōmon*."[89]

Thus, by interpolating from the etymology as given by Herodotus and by the occurrence of the original terms in the Bible and in Jewish Aramaic literature, we perceive that the names of the oriental spices come down to us through the contact of the Greeks with people who spoke Aramaic and were the intermediaries of the trade to the Far East. The exotic spices were transported from Southeast Asia to the Canaanite coast, from whence they were distributed into the Mediterranean region. The Greeks were entirely ignorant of the original source of these spices until a late date. It is not surprising that the well-traveled Herodotus (485-425 B.C.E.) and Theophrastus (372-286 B.C.E.), for example, believed at that early period that cinnamon and cassia came from trees that grew in Arabia. The fact is that "there is not a trace of cinnamon or cassia there, nor could there be: the plants require a degree of moisture not to be found in that parched peninsula."[90] It is even stranger that Strabo (60 B.C.E.-21 C.E.), and other Greeks of a period in which the Seleucids were solidly installed in Persia, who were bound to know that India was a source for cassia and cinnamon, still cite Arabia as a source of these forms of the spice and labored under the illusion that they also came from East Africa. Strabo, in fact, refers to the region he considered the southernmost inhabited part of the world, Somalia and Ethiopia (Sudan) as "Cinnamon Country"!

A mythology grew out of Western ignorance of the sources of such biblical aromatic standbys as myrrh and frankincense no less than that of cassia and cinnamon. Herodotus informs us, for example, that winged serpents were charged with the protection of the frankincense trees (3:107), and that they were assisted by winged batlike creatures which stood guard over the cassia trees (3:110). The fifth-century B.C.E. "Father of History" was quite unaware that cinnamon was no more than ground up cassia and believed that the products came from two different trees. Western ignorance about spices continued into the Late Roman period. Two other Greek writers, erudite physicians who discoursed at great length on the substances, Dioscorides (first century C.E.) and Galen (c. 130-201 C.E.) still believed in separate sources for cinnamon and cassia.

Although Pliny, Ptolemy, and a number of other Greek scholars had become aware that Arabia was not the region in which the evergreen that produced cassia grew, they were still convinced that not only India but also East Africa was an important source for cinnamon and cassia. Ignorance regarding the source of spices so widely used in the West extended to other Eastern spices. There was an equally ancient traffic in the leaves of the cinnamon trees known as *malabathron*. Neither the Greeks nor the Romans were aware of any connection between the aromatic *malabathron* leaves and the tree from which they were plucked. The leaves also had pharmaceutical application and the physician Dioscorides presumed that they came from the spikenard plant of Mesopotamia. The spikenard plant in the Mishnah also figures predominantly in the Bible, and numerous references evidence the familiarity of the sages who redacted the work with the plant and to their trade in its products.

The appetite for exotic goods from China and India in Rome caused a severe drain on the Roman economy. The emperor Tiberius, alarmed, warned in the first century that precious gold was being drained from the treasury to pay for "articles that flatter the vanity of women; jewels and those little objects of luxury which drain away the riches of the empire. In exchange for trifles, our money is being sent to foreign lands and even to our enemies." Pliny the Younger later pointed out that the annual drain on the Roman treasury amounted to "55 million Sesterces paid to India and 45 million to Seres (China)." The glassware, metalware, and linens produced by the Jews in the land of Israel went a long way to ease Rome's balance of trade, but did not resolve the problem resulting from the gluttonous appetite of the Roman hierarchy for exotic and expensive goods.[91] Two methods of alleviating the problem were instituted by the Romans and their successors, the Byzantines, as time went on: nationalizing the industries and/or importing the artisans.

Metallurgy, silk and linen weaving, (purple) dyeing, glass and glassware-making all appeared in Roman Italy and Byzantium coincident with the implantation of Jews, primarily at first as slaves and thereafter as independent entrepreneurs. In 1867 a Strasbourg professor, Oskar Schmidt, found the remains of *Murex bradaris* and *Murex trunculus* on the site of a former dye-house in Aquileia.[92] This interesting discovery was only the first of a number of revelations, all of which point to the presence of substantial Jewish communities around the northern Adriatic in the Roman period, and especially in Aquileia. Ferric, vitric, and textile-producing industries were all introduced into that primitive area at that same time.

"Tyrian" purple was considered so important a product that Roman emperors began to place the production of the dye under their control. During the reign of Diocletian (284–305 C.E.) the Tyrian dye-works were made Imperial property, and control over the industry was retained by the rulers of the area through the Byzantine period. The dye-workers, however, were Jews, and the industry continued to flourish on the coast of *Eretz Yisrael* until it disappeared as a consequence of the destruction of Tyre wrought by the Arabs in 638 C.E. and the exile of the Jews from the Golan Heights. The Jewish dye-workers were transplanted into Byzantium, and the purple dye industry disappeared from Tyre as the area came under Islamic rule.

The dye-workers were a portion of the corpus of skilled Jewish craftsmen transplanted into Byzantium. The glassmakers, metallurgists, and weavers were also conspicuous among the artisans who carried their arts into Constantinople, Thebes, Thessalonica, Corinth, and other cities of Byzantium, where their knowledge and efforts provided the Christians with a substantial industrial base. Jewish artisans remained the industrial core of Byzantium until the Crusades, at which time entire communities of craftsmen were again rounded up by Roger II and transplanted into Southern Italy and Sicily. Benjamin of Tudela, who visited the communities in 1165, reported that Jewish artisans were still active in the Greek peninsula at that time. The dye-making craft did manage to continue in the Byzantian Mediterranean basin until it ceased altogether in the Levant with the fall of Constantinople in 1453 C.E.

14

The Hidden History of the Diaspora

A Matter of Numbers

The Roman Forum! Aphrodisias! Ephesus! Sardis! Corinth! Thessalonica! Fabulous names, names that evoke vivid visions of grand ruins and dazzling art. Names that contain mysteries to be unraveled, events to be recaptured, peoples to be resurrected from obscurity. Apparitions of the Jews can be discerned among the ashes and ashlars strewn about the ruins of these ancient communities, nebulous but insistent, dim but demanding revelation.

The term "classical" was coined to infer "of the highest class," and is customarily applied to the period of Greek and Roman hegemony over the Near East. The civilization the Greek and Roman mercenary armies encountered in that area was indeed of the highest order, one that they captured and absorbed and made their own. The world was ripe for Judaic egalitarian precepts, and their universal appeal led to a rapid and massive multiplication of the number of Jews by those who were attracted to and identified with Judaic ethical, moral, and, to a significant extent, religious principles. The threat that those principles posed to rulers and ruling classes proved to be the undoing of the existence of a Judahite national entity.

HOW POPULOUS WERE THE JEWS IN THE CLASSICAL ERA?

The Greek author of the *Sibylline Chronicles* puts the total population of the Jews of the Roman empire at 6,944,000, a figure that was derived from a census taken by the Emperor Claudius in 42 C.E.[1] The sheer numbers of Jews of that time bespeak the importance of Jewish culture in the life of the Greeks and Romans far beyond that commonly accredited to them. The astonishing size of the figure exposes the abysmal depth of our ignorance of the seminal role such a number of Jews must have played in Western civilization.

265

The validity of the figure of seven million has been questioned, but the preponderance of evidence strongly supports the growth of the Jewish population to an impressive size during the "classical" period. The Jewish population of the Roman Empire has in any event been assessed at having reached many millions of people during the time in which Rome dominated the Western world, and the figure of seven million is not unreasonable. The number of Jews translates to a bewildering ten percent or more of the entire European and Near Eastern population under Roman rule at the height of Rome's power, a population that totaled between fifty and sixty million inhabitants in an area that spanned portions of three continents from England to the Euphrates.

It has already been noted in discussing the Persian experience that up to two million additional Jews can be readily discerned to have resided outside of areas under Roman rule, including Jewish descendants of those uprooted previously from Israel and Judah, and those fleeing the Romans after the Bar Kochba revolt. Nissim Rejwan, in an authoritative work on the history of the Jews of Iraq, stated that estimates based on cumulative figures from various documentary sources, including interpolations from the Babylonian Talmud:

> would show that about the year 70 A.D. the Jews of Babylonia numbered about a million. They continued to increase, both by birth and by immigration from Palestine; in Roman times, indeed, Jews beyond the Euphrates are said to have been counted by the millions. The most important and populous communities were those of Nehardea, at the junction of the Euphrates and the Royal Canal; Nisbis and Mahosa on the same canal; and Sura, to the south of Mahasia. But Jews of course lived also outside the large cities, in villages and hamlets. It is estimated, therefore, that between A.D. 200 and 500 the number of Jews in Babylonia approached the two-million mark.[2]

Persia was central to the trade routes that splayed out westward and eastward. In the astigmatic Western view of that bustling intercontinental web it is regarded as though the commercial initiatives that created it originated from the West (the Marco Polo adventure, et al). The fact is that Babylonia was the center of international trade long before the Romans tied into the network, and remained the fulcrum for land traffic long after the Roman Empire faded from the scene. "Babylonian trade routes took the Jews to every corner of the known world, making them men of commerce and international trade."[3] The sea also became a major highway connecting the Eurasian continental extremities, and new Jewish communities mushroomed along, and at the destinations of, the trade routes along the land-based "silk route" into the hearts of China and India and at the ports that accommodated the growing sea traffic.

The population figures are all the more striking and significant when considering that these burgeoning Jewish communities were rarely located in the hinterlands; they were solidly implanted in the heart of the Western world's most productive centers. Jews were as often as not the primary productive elements of the populations at the ports and commercial crossroads of the known civilized world.

In those hyperactive towns and cities they were a considerably larger, more significant proportion of the population than they were in the Western world at large. They comprised a major element of the artisans and merchants, they constituted the most literate segment of the local populations, and they carried with them their own laws and their own religion, both of which achieved an international legitimacy by which each Jewish community became integral to a worldwide cultural network with common interests and purpose.

The importance of this dynamic element of Western civilization has never been properly evaluated. The evidence of its existence, notwithstanding the sheer numbers involved, has been largely ignored. And yet, tantalizing bits can be glimpsed through the veneer that has been overlaid on ancient history. Once assembled, and despite a multiplicity of missing parts, the disparate pieces form a mosaic that demonstrates that the course of history cannot be rationalized without the inclusion of the Jews as a far more seminal and forceful factor in the development of civilizations throughout the Near East and Europe than is generally acknowledged.

WHY HAS THE JEWISH PRESENCE BEEN MINIMIZED?

There are many reasons for the ephemeral appearance of the many millions of Jews during the "classical" era in the historical record. Let us examine four of them.

(1) Fascination with the blanketing accoutrements of Egyptian, Greek, and Roman civilizations has diverted the attention of the scholarly community from the underlying dynamics that made them possible. The production of structures, statues, and artifacts is attributed to the conquerors although it was the conquered peoples who performed the menial tasks of empire. The toil of construction and production was considered beneath the dignity of the conquering peoples. In the case of the Jews, for example, the only "Jewish" objects exhibited in museums, Jewish museums no less than others, are cultish articles classified as "Judaica," whether or not they were produced by Jews. The only structures considered the product of Jews are the simple remains of synagogues.

An anti-Judaic cultural bias saturates the scientific community so thoroughly that it has been unaware of its own astigmatism. As far as museums are concerned, the Israelites and Judahites never produced a pot, for virtually every pot exhumed from the ancient ruins of *Eretz Yisrael* is labeled "Phoenician," "Philistine," "Syrian," "Palestinian," "Syro-Palestinian," or, at best, "Near Eastern" or "West Asian"! No matter that the Judahites were a discrete culture for over a thousand years and a sovereign nation for a good portion of that time.

Nor does it seem to matter that fourteen thousand Jewish slaves engineered and built the great "Roman" Colosseum, a fact hardly heeded by historians. That gigantic amphitheater and the majestic Arch of Titus were erected in Rome as permanent memorials to the triumph of the three Flavians over the very people who were consigned to construct them.[4] Many other buildings of ancient Rome owe their existence to the labor of Jewish slaves. Among the buildings lost to posterity, along with its precious contents, was a building sardonically dubbed "The Temple of Peace" by the Romans, a building erected by Jewish slaves torn from "Captive Judah" to house the contents of the Jerusalem Temple, the sacred vessels, and other booty looted by their Roman overseers from the Temple before it was demolished. The fact that "Roman" architectural structures of its most glorious period were not built by Romans is not unique. The same obfuscation applies to the assignment of credit for sophisticated artifacts filling the museums under deceptive labels. No ancient Roman ever made "Roman" glassware, for example, no more than any ancient Egyptian ever made "Egyptian" glassware, facts that are not only ignored but come as a revelation to all who are so informed.

(2) In classifying "Jews," many historians proceed on the assumption that Jews were homogeneously cultish, and that the only distinguishing characteristic of an ancient Jew was a strict and unwavering adherence to and practice of the rituals and precepts of the priests and prophets. National, cultural, and genealogical attributes are regarded as non sequiturs and the fact that millions of nonobservant or partially observant Jews, then as now, nevertheless regarded themselves unequivocally as Jews is dismissed. These anomalous peoples were, however, treated as Jews when they were enslaved, dispossessed, or dispersed until they thereafter disappeared into the Diaspora, uncounted and unaccounted for.

Historians who confine themselves to cult as a criteria for classifying Jews ironically align themselves with the most sectarian of priestly precepts, blithely accepting a narrow definition of a Jew, which they reject for every other national or cultural case. Would the same scholars confine the ethnic label "Greek" to those who venerated the Olympian panoply of Gods? How would an "American" be defined within such a limitation? Cannot a "Jewish-American" also be an atheist?

(3) The very stipulation that religious adherence be the criteria of being considered a Jew precludes estimating the numbers of Jews from articles retrieved from ancient garbage and graves, the two most productive mines of archaeological and ethnographical information. Jewish garbage and graves were not likely to contain distinguishing amulets or objects that identified the religion of the householder or the interred until well into the Common Era, when the menorah and other nonidolic symbolic objects or emblems came into occasional use. Idolic objects that mark the religious inclination of the deceased or of his family are per force absent from an Orthodox Jewish environment. It cannot be denied that many superstitious Jews did employ pagan artifacts to assure fertility or their tranquil passage into and existence in the afterworld, but in such cases they would not likely be counted among the Jews. That such pragmatic practices were indeed performed is evident from their appearance in the thoroughly Jewish catacombs of Rome. Nor are many Jews to be counted among the overlords whose entombment was enduring; by far the most Jews were among the masses whose shallow graves and brittle bones dissolved into their earthen surroundings. Only a few Jewish entombments fortuitously survived two thousand years of Christian des-

ecration; the catacombs of Rome in Italy and of Beth Shearim in Israel are no more than notable exceptions.

(4) Because artifactual evidence is lacking from Jewish entombment and because those who engaged in the construction of buildings, monuments, and other architectural and engineering projects can only be anonymously acclaimed, we are virtually restricted to religious references and suggestive names appearing in literature or inscription. In the latter case we are again confined to positively identify as Jews only those who employed a name that incorporated a form of the name of the Judaic God or who was specifically declared to be, or to have been, a Jew.

Certain clues can sometimes be used as indicative of Jewish origin: patronymic or geographic references can sometimes serve as persuasive inferences if not as conclusive evidence of ethnicity. In this regard we run across an idiosyncratic contradiction between the ancient and modern methods of identifying a Jew of the "classical" period: only the place of origin was documented in Greek and Roman records—religion was irrelevant. The use of the reverse criteria as a standard for Jewish identification is clearly inconsistent with ancient records.

A NEW LOOK AT EARLY RECORDS

Elias J. Bickerman cites the case of the earliest Ptolemaic papyrus in which a man was officially qualified as a Jew. He was a cavalryman, "Alexander, the son of Andronicus," whose name and paternal pedigree was far from "Jewish." Another cavalryman with the Greek name of "Theodoros, son of Theodorus" turns out to be a Jew, since we incidently and accidentally learn that he was also known as Samuel [Samu-el]. An Egyptian village contract of 201 B.C.E. exceptionally but specifically identifies all of the six signatories as Jews, yet five of the six names are distinctly Greek, ranging from Theodotus to Democrates; only the sixth name, Sabbattaios, bears a religious imprint. "We have to first know," points out Bickerman, "that all immigrants, of whatever origin, were assigned to the class of 'Hellenes,' in order to distinguish them from Native Egyptians. 'Hellenes' were aliens residing in Egypt."[5]

It can be assumed that "Hellenes" of the Ptolemaic period who worked as artisans or at any work considered to be menial were not ethnic Greeks. The Greek overlords would no more demean their haughty stature by performing the most skilled, albeit still undignified, work of an artisan than they would by engaging in the basest of physical toil, the type relegated to Egyptians. The laboring "Hellenes" held higher and better-paid positions than the Egyptians, for they were brought to Egypt for their specialized skills or came to work in Lower Egypt on their own because of the opportunities such skills afforded them.

The technological and social span between the non-Greek "Hellenes" and the native Egyptians was true in agriculture no less than in industry. The Egyptians were still using wooden plows and hoes as late as the Ptolemaic period, for ancient Egypt had never passed from the Bronze into the Iron Age. The shallow soil deposited annually by the flooding Nile was easily worked with the primitive plows of the native Egyptians, and there was little incentive for improving their wooden equipment. In stony Judah, however, "iron plow-points, shovels and axes and other implements [of iron] had been in use since the time of King David."[6] The "Hellenes" who introduced this technology into Ptolemaic Egypt were largely to be found in managerial tasks and not among the "plow-men," the peasantry relegated to its physical application.

There are numerous contemporary witnesses to an anthropographic portrait of the times that make a re-ordering of assumptions based on the classicist syndrome mandatory. An examination of this testimony makes clear, first of all, that the figure of a total population of seven to nine million Jews at the turn of the Common Era is not only plausible but that it is likely to approach the higher amount.

Philo Judaeus, the Jewish philosopher and historian who was born in Ptolemaic Alexandria, stated emphatically that there was no city in Asia or Syria that did not contain Jews.[7] Although Philo was nurtured in a Greek ambience, he remained steadfastly proud of his Jewish heritage. His testimony has been borne out by his contemporaries, those derogatory of the Jews as well as those more kindly disposed toward them.

Cicero, the wealthy Roman patrician, orator, statesman, and man of letters of the first half of the first century B.C.E., had occasion to discuss a proclamation favoring the Jews published by the Roman consul. The declaration was distributed throughout the lands of the Empire and to the Greek cities where Jews resided. Among the various regions and cities of Asia Minor cited were Caria, Pamphylia, Lycia, Halicarnassus, Myndos, Cnidus, Phaselis, Side, Amysos, and the islands of Delos, Samos, Laodiciea, Adramyttium, and Pergamum. Cicero also relates that Flaccus, the governor of the Roman province of Asia, confiscated Jewish money at Apameia, Laodiciea, Adramyttium, and Pergamum.[8]

This lengthy roster of Jewish population centers is hardly adequate. The Roman proclamation, issued during the time of Simon Maccabee Hasmonean, also alludes to a sizable Jewish community in Rhodes of 139 B.C.E. and goes on to mention the Jews in Cos, Sparta, Sicyon, in the town of Gortyn on the island of Crete, and on the island of Cyprus,[9] where Jewish coins have indeed been found, evidence of a Jewish commercial presence of some note. Josephus, the Jewish historian who participated on both sides of the wars between the Romans and the Jews, cites resolutions taken by Greek cities and documents drafted by the Romans mentioning populations of resident Jews in many other towns, such as Miletus, Pergamum, Halicarnassus, Tralles, Laodiceia, Sardis and Ephesus, and on the islands of Paros, Delos, and Cos.

The New Testament is replete with references to Jewish communities in the Anatolian and Greek Diaspora: Smyrna, Philadelphia, Antioch in Pisidia, Tarsus, and Iconium, are among the important centers mentioned that can be added to the impressive list of the Jewish communities of the times. The Acts of the Apostles add Phillipi, Thessalonica, Beroia, Athens, and Corinth. When Barnabas, Saul, and John came to Salamis in Cyprus, they preached at the synagogues [note the plural!] of the Jews. The synagogues of the Ichetlines, Cyrenaians, and Alexandrians all figured in the visits of these proselyting Christians, preaching to Jewish communities large enough to maintain one or more synagogues.

LOOKING BACKWARD FROM SICILY, SPAIN, AND VENICE

Inscriptions testifying to Jewish presence appear peripherally in places not even mentioned in the sources that have survived the ravages of time and man. Two such, dated years 150 and 157, were discovered at Delphi, announcing the emancipation of Jewish slaves. Slaves are, however, rarely classified into discrete ethnic groups in ancient population statistics; ethnic information must be culled from the rare, incidental referrals to their existence. We are informed that the Emperor Tiberius wrested four thousand sturdy young Jews from war-racked Judah and consigned them to mine and process the ores of Sicily. Jews were engaged on that island from that time forward in mining silver and iron and in metalworking (not to mention the sericulture and textile industries) until the early Middle Ages, when Spanish persecution of the Jews penetrated into the island. Hardly a trace of the substantial Jewish communities of Roman Sicily has trickled down to our times.

It becomes clear that Sicilian mining and metallurgy were exclusively Jewish occupations for more than a millennium after the Romans implanted the Judahite artisans only because they remained so into the Middle Ages, at which time the Spanish persecution of the Jews reveals the predominantly Jewish ethnicity of Sicilian miners, smiths, sericulturists, weavers, and dyers. The metalworking industry was so dependent on the skills of the Jewish artisans that despite the opposition of local ecclesiastic and other authorities, a royal decree of 1327 ordered Sicilian officials to support Jewish mine prospectors and miners. As late as "the beginning of the 15th century two Jews of Alghero received special authorization to exploit the resources of the region, on condition that half the output be turned over to the crown."[10]

Jewish artisans had also been central to the metal-crafts industry of Spain from the time sixty thousand slaves, largely Jews, mined gold and other metals, crafted gold artifacts under the Romans, and continued in the industry under the various ruling hierarchies until well into the fifteenth century.[11] It has already been noted that such names as Gold, Goldman, Goldsmith, Silver, Silverman, and Silverstein persist as recognizable Jewish surnames into contemporary times, and that Ferro, Fierro, and Herrero, and other names identifying a family's involvement in ironwork, were at the same time common Jewish surnames into the Middle Ages. The latter names continue to appear in a Sephardic context through the period of the Inquisition, as, for example, Acach de Fierro, the name of a prominent and influential resident of a *juiverie* ("Jewish quarter," equivalent to the Italian *giudecca*), of Barbastro, approximately 150 kilometers northwest of Barcelona. Acach appears as one of the guarantors of the payment of taxes and imposts for that Jewish community.[12] Luisa Ferro, whose family name is spelled in the familiar form in which it appears in Italy, was the widow of a wealthy magnate, Manuel Cotizos de Villesante, and was listed in an Inquisition proceeding of the year 1554 in which Luisa suffered trial by the Inquisition, as did her prestigious husband before her.[13]

The exodus of the Jews from Spain taking place from the twelfth century to the final expulsion of the Jews from Castile and Portugal in 1492, from Sicily in 1493, from Naples in 1540 and 1541, from Tuscany in 1571, and from Milan in 1597, fostered the spread of a superior form of ferric technology eastward through the Mediterranean. Sultan Bayezid II avidly invited the expelled Jews to settle and work in his dominions, and issued firmans to ensure the protection of the "talented Sefardim." The Ottoman sultan "considered Ferdinand of Spain a fool" for pursuing a blind policy of expulsion, which, first of all, impoverished his own kingdom while enriching the sultan's and secondly, allowed such vital secret arts as munitions-making to escape from Spain to its enemies.[14] In Salonica and Constantinople the newly arrived Jews established, among other trades, iron-mongery shops,[15] and built the first wheeled gun-carriages for the army of Suleiman the Magnificent, a form of field artillery that contributed in no small measure to his military successes. The models for these gun-carriages were the ones employed by Charles VIII in Italy, in 1494.[16] The Jews established numerous industries on both sides of the Bosporus; they located the iron manufactories just south of Galata, on the other side of the "Golden Horn" from Constantinople, "where they make powder and artillery."[17]

When the Spanish expulsion of the Jews was extended to Sicily on 18 June 1492, the Sicilian officials as well as the Christian leaders in Palermo and in other cities complained bitterly that "in this realm almost all the artisans are Jews. If all of them will suddenly depart there will be a shortage of many commodities, for the Christians are accustomed to receive from them many mechanical objects, particularly iron works needed for the shoeing of animals and for cultivating the soil; also the necessary supplies for ships, galleys and other maritime vessels."[18]

Nevertheless, in spite of cynical attempts to retain the vital services of the Jewish metalsmiths and other skilled artisans, the pressures of oppression drove the Sephardim from Sicily and southern Italy; the practitioners of vital trades resettled into the northern republics. Metal-smithing, silk production, dyeing and weaving were still being carried on by the wandering Jews throughout the Levant and North Africa.[19] Sephardic artisans swelled the communities in northern Italy that had already absorbed an influx of Jews driven out of most of the manual trades of western Europe.

Venice was one of the first states to promote patent legislation. The statutes protected inventors for a period of ten years, on condition that the invention be put at the service of the state. Jews were among the inventors who applied for patents, not the least important of which involved the casting of cannons employed for bombardment. Sigismondo Alberghetti, a member of a Ferrara family famed for engineering skills, presented a request to the authorities of the city soon after he became established as an official of Venice. Needing the assistance of the specialists in the casting of cannons, he asked for a special confirmation of the patent laws to make possible the hiring of the Sephardic masters of the art so that they could be brought to Venice. The request was made on 9 June 1490 and was granted.[20]

Alberghetti was eager to obtain the Jewish smiths from Spain, who had become famous throughout Europe for their casting skills, having already become aware that the Turks were eagerly welcoming and benefiting from the Jewish experts in foundry technology. Disturbing information reached Venice through official correspondence that the Turks were equipping their navy with advanced forms of artillery as a consequence of the arrival in Turkey of the Jewish metallurgic technicians. In a letter written from Constantinople to Venice and included by Mario Sanuto in his "Chronicles of Venice," the writer emphasizes the great impetus given to the rearmament of the Turkish navy by the munitions and artillery supplied by the newly immigrant Sephardim. "They all work like Gauls (a pejorative reference to the primitive, despised enemy) to produce munitions, artillery and so on, but it is the Jews who produce it on a grand scale."[21]

The Jews contributed more than metalworking technology to Venice's war machine: the arming of the Venetian flotilla was financed in large measure by the Jewish community. The war against the Turks in 1480-81 was the occasion of extraordinary financial assistance, and in 1483 the Jews supplied no less than ten thousand ducats for the war against Ferrara. These contributions did not weigh heavily in the balance against ecclesiastic pressures for the expulsion of the Jews. In 1573, when the Jews were again threatened with expulsion from Venice in accordance with a decision of 14 December 1571 (which had previously been revoked), a certain Soranzo, who represented Venice at Constantinople as bailo, and had there observed at close range the seminal role of the Jews in various technologies and most particularly iron manufacturing, appeared before the Venetian governing body, the Council of Ten, where he is reported as asking:

> What pernicious act is this, to expel the Jews? Do you not know what it may cost you in years to come? Who gave the Turk his strength and where else would he have found the skilled craftsmen to make the cannon, bows, shot, swords, shields and bucklers which enable him to measure himself against other powers, if not among the Jews who were expelled by the Kings of Spain?[22]

Thus the morphology of the name of Ferro, a family that rose to prominence in the annals of both Venetian and Altarese glassmaking, does not merely manifest a family's ancient activity; it also provides a clue to its ethnic origin. Glassmaking and iron-smithing were both among the professions that became proscribed to Jews later on. In both cases notable exceptions were made, as in the cases of the Cologne glassmakers and the Silesian (Polish) and Sicilian ironsmiths, but generally the dire circumstances that were brought about by that proscription forced Jewish artisans to move about, seeking a better life wherever relative freedom allowed the pursuit of their trades. In most of Europe such freedom had become unattainable; a change of location, however, served to enable the camouflaging of Jewish identity and permitted Jews to surreptitiously enter a guild or to practice an art in areas and under circumstances that otherwise would have proved futile. The workers, as well as most of their employers, were thereafter obliged to maintain their new *Christian* facade. As time and generations passed, the memory of the ethnic origins of the workers as well as the employers of these early capitalist institutions faded into oblivion.

We are specifically informed about the transference of four thousand young Judahites to Sicily, but there is no way to determine how many Jews were among the sixty thousand slaves working the gold and silver mines of Spain or among the scores of thousands consigned to the mines, furnaces, and forges throughout the Roman Empire. The number of Jews is difficult to assess, for more often than not they are referred to anonymously as "Orientals" or "Syrians," and only an interpolation of the later data makes them visible.

OTHER JEWISH COMMUNITIES UNDER GREEK AND ROMAN RULE

Ancient Jewish communities circled the central and southern reaches of the Adriatic, notable among which were Naupolis, Spolato, Ragusa, and Dubrovnik on its eastern shores and Oria, Bari, and Ancona on its western shores. Jewish communities ringed the Grecian peninsula at metropolises such as Thessalonica, Thebes, Corinth, and Castoria and they were found in the smaller centers of central and southern Asia Minor such as at Amorium, Attaleia, and Seleucia.[23] Many of these communities existed when the Hellenic expansion was yet in its infancy and they endured into late Byzantine times; each in its own way contributed not only to the Roman but also to the ensuing Byzantine economy, and thereafter to the growth of the Venetian Republic.

Such communities were also installed behind the Roman legions as the Roman soldiers bludgeoned their way westward and northward through Nordica, Pannonia, the Seine-Rhine valleys and Spain. In the opposite direction and outside the area under Roman hegemony, there were communities that had remained and flourished in Babylonia, although freed from the exigencies of exile by the edict of Cyrus in the mid-sixth century B.C.E. On the Roman side of that eastern border, significant populations of Jews occupied military-commercial centers such as those at Palmyra and Duro-Europus.

Sizable and influential Jewish communities come continuously and unexpectedly to light, such as that of the Anatolian city of Aphrodisias, where a stela was accidentally found with the names of fifty-two Jews and an even greater number of sympathizers (including four city councillors), who were officials of and donors to a charitable institution of significant importance.

The sheer numbers of Jews in areas under Greek and Roman domination bespeak an importance of Jewish culture in those civilizations far beyond that commonly accredited to them. The profound impact of Jewish culture must be deduced from the manifold multiplication of their numbers during the Greek and early Roman periods despite recurrent repressions, restrictions, massacres, Hellenization, dislocations and dispersion. The population of the Jews increased at a rate far greater than that of any other peoples, including that of the Greeks and the ethnic Romans. This increase cannot be attributed to a higher birth rate, for studies show no discernible differences in that regard. Nor can a normal peacetime growth be ascribed as a reason for the extraordinary expansion of Jewish population; the Jews had more than their share of military devastation and massacre.

A massive number of Jews can also be discerned in the events that shaped the "classical" period. At the time of the destruction of the First Temple in Jerusalem, the greatest concentration of Jews was in Judea. The population of Judah at that time has been estimated at somewhat more than 150,000 out of a world population of Jews that was certainly considerably less than 500,000.[24] The rise to a figure that indeed may have approached ten million by the mid-first century C.E. can clearly not be attributed to natural increase.

What was the dynamic, then, by which such a phenomenal increase occurred? When did it occur? And why do we find so little reference to Jewish presence in extant literature and so few representative archaeological relics in the garbage and graves of these past civilizations? These perplexing questions wax even more persistent when, in addition to the conspicuous explosion in the spread and size of Jewish communities, which was evident through the Hellenic period and continued well into the Common Era, account is taken of the caliber of those communities and of the strategic sites in which they were located. How does it happen that we find Jewish communities always solidly ensconced within the creative heart of the societies to which they were exiled? Why, in an essentially agrarian age, were Jewish slaves rarely among the millions tilling the soil but were systematically implanted within urban centers, at all of the important ports and at all of the commercial crossroads?

Slave, liberated, and free Jewish activities throughout the Diaspora were basically artisan or commercial in nature. Many Jews were part of the military forces. Jews, slave and free, were consistently found at the forefront of civilization. The proportion of Jews of the population in the seminal centers of civilization must have been significant indeed, far exceeding the already astonishing figure of more than ten percent of the overall population of the Roman Empire. Philo's pronouncement that there is no part of Asia or Syria without its Jews is demonstrably true of Europe as well. No part of Roman Europe was devoid of a significant and productive Jewish population. We should therefore graciously accept the fact that a great gap exists in our knowledge and understanding of ancient times, and when subjected to close scrutiny, the Jews are prominent among those who are found occupying that historiographical vacuum.

A massive immigration of Jews into Egypt occurred under Ptolemy I about the year 312 B.C.E. Aristeas relates that some ten years later one hundred thousand Jews were enslaved and brought to Egypt by Ptolemy. The thirty thousand most stalwart young Jews of military age were assigned to man the fortresses, no doubt positioned at the most vulnerable posts, being considered expendable. The other seventy thousand Jewish slaves were distributed among the soldiers, and we may well assume that they served by performing all the skilled labor required, for the available Egyptian labor force was more than adequate for menial work, and manual labor was beneath the dignity of the Greeks.

Corroboration of a scenario in which the magnitude of Jewish penetration of Lower Egypt is far greater than that given in individual accounts is evident from the numbers of Jewish slaves freed by Ptolemy II (283–246) upon ascending the throne. The price of redeeming the slaves was set at twenty drachmae per slave, and a calculation from the sums provided for the purpose would place the numbers of liberated Jewish slaves from a minimum of 120,000 to as many as 198,000, to which number must be added the considerable number of Jews already resident in the region. The figures on the number of freed slaves are supported by a recovered papyrus of the period.[25]

The Jews made up a significant proportion of the population of other areas of Lower Egypt; many Jews also lived and worked in the Fayoum, in Fustat (Old Cairo). Others lived in the rural Delta area, where some owned farms and others managed the farms of Greek landowners. Philo states that the population of Jews in Egypt reached 1,000,000 during this period, out of a total population of 7,500,000 Egyptians of both Upper and Lower Egypt. It is a round figure, but not unreasonable. Although ghettoization had not become a common practice, the groups tended to live in separate districts and in Alexandria alone two out of the five districts that made up the city were Jewish.

The social status of the Jews under Ptolemy II, even that of former slaves, placed them above the Egyptians. The Jews were generally skilled artisans or engaged in pursuits that reflected their literacy. In recognition of their superiority in the arts, sciences, and commerce they were granted rights that the Egyptians, employed for heavy compulsory work as common laborers, were unable to enjoy. Egyptians who were not at work in the fields were engaged in the construction of dikes, road building and maintenance, canal repair, and performed as porters and the like. Native Egyptians were thus degraded to the lowest level, a people without status or rights, while one set of aliens ruled their land with a heavy hand and other aliens enjoyed the special privileges accruing to artisans and entrepreneurs. It was during the time of this very Ptolemy II Philadelphus that Manetho wrote his Egyptian history. The irksome favoritism shown the Jews was surely one of the causes of the festering hatred that Manetho bore toward the Jews.

Jewish colonies were established under Greek rule in Lydia and Phrygia. The military character of the settlements, called *katoikia* by the Greeks, usually became muted with the passage of time. Other Jewish communities appeared, termed by the Greeks variously as *laos*, *synodos*, and *synagoge*. The autonomous status of these communities is attested by reference to a Jewish community in general as a *politeuma*, which denotes a foreign version of the Greek *Poli*, in which Greek citizens exercised "democratic" government. Aristeas uses this term and it appears in two inscriptions from Berenice in Cyrenaica. A *katoika* in Phrygia was characterized as *Judeni*. Such communities became permanent establishments throughout Anatolia, and were well rooted by Roman times.

Jewish presence was by no means restricted to the colonies created for military purposes. Many records make manifest the integration of significant populations of Jews into every important production and trade center of Asia Minor. In thriving Smyrna (now Izmir), a seaport central to the Anatolian Coast, a certain Solomon, using the Greek translation of his name: "Eirenopoios," donated seven pieces of gold for a balustrade of a synagogue. In Phocaea, a Jew named Tation erected a synagogue and a colonnade "at his own expense." In Ephesus, a Jew was on the staff of "chief physicians," evidently appointed by the city officials.

In *Wars of the Jews*, Josephus describes the massive yearly pilgrimage to Jerusalem for the Passover festivals at which an attendance of three million Jews took place. He also states that 204 Jewish towns and villages existed in the Galilee, none of which had a population of less than fifteen thousand people. Although these figures are patently inflated, inasmuch as a total Jewish population of more than three million in the Galilee alone would result, they do bespeak a dense and numerous Jewish presence whose influence can be accordingly postulated. From India to the shores of the Black Sea, throughout the Balkans and the Mediterranean, Jewish artisans, merchants, and sages made themselves felt by their presence and by the establishment of houses of study, that is, synagogues. The precepts of the Jews promulgated within these establishments were often regarded as dangerous by the reigning powers. The Jews acknowledged submission to power as pragmatically necessary, but the unshakable Jewish tenet that man owed ultimate allegiance only to God was a persistent irritant to jealous rulers. They feared the influence of such an insidiously revolutionary concept; they feared that it would infect the populace and foster disaffection.

Significant Jewish communities existed in places that are entirely absent from literature or are merely mentioned in passing. A prime example of such omission, and yet not an untypical one, is that of the sizable Jewish community that flourished in Aquileia, a major Roman metropolis and port implanted on the Adriatic Sea, halfway between present-day Venice and Trieste. Not even the *Encyclopedia Judaica* offers a hint of the existence of this bustling community, which numbered in the thousands and was vital to the development of Roman traffic to the East and to the exploitation of Central Europe.

AQUILEIA

Aquileia was a major Roman gateway to imports from the East, both of goods and artisans. The city assumed increasing significance as the legions established themselves along the routes laid down along the river valleys that traverse the Alpine Dolomites, wind over lofty passes through Pannonia and Nordica into Central Europe, and stretch out to the Baltic coast. The port of Aquileia served as a funnel through which products of the East and of Central Europe reached Rome itself.

The Jewish community of Aquileia is among the multitude of Jewish communities of substantial size and importance whose history has escaped the attention of almost all historians,[27] one of the rare exceptions being Yves-Marie Duval. "There can be no doubt," she wrote after studying the voluminous writings and correspondence of St. Jerome and others, "that one can abstract the existence of thousands of Jews in Aquileia and in the region."[28] The Aquileian Jewish community may have been one of the largest and most influential communities of the Diaspora, exceeded only by that of Rome and Alexandria. A few other scholars have noted the many references to the notable Jewish influence on Christian affairs in Aquileia and nearby towns.[29] A Jewish population of many thousands is also manifested by numerous Hellenicized inscriptions of Eastern immigrants.[30] Aerial surveys show the existence of a pre-Roman city, one that could not have been created by the rather backward indigenous tribes of the area but could only have been instituted by entrepreneurial adventurers from the East. Many of the inscriptions indicate that the great Roman port did indeed harbor a significant Jewish population from the earliest incidence of Roman influence, long before the Christians made themselves felt in the area.[31]

Many of the inscriptions identify the deceased by vocation; the bulk of the industries thus documented are those in which the Jews were dominant. The textile industry is well represented among these inscriptions, and the complexity and sophistication of the industry is delineated by the fine distinctions of the categories of arts involved in the industry, both in materials (wool, linen, or silk) and in quality. The *vestiarii*, the practitioners of the art of garment manufacture in general, were composed of *tenuarii* (the producers of fine quality garments) and *centonarii* (the producers of crude fabrics used for slaves' clothing and for putting out fires!). Women were part of the labor force, as exemplified by an inscription that identifies the deceased as *lanifica Trosia Hilara*, a weaver-tailoress of woolen clothing.

The art of dyeing textiles was inscriptively represented by an *infector* (dyer) and by several *purpurii* (specialists in the colors ranging over purple and blue to crimson).[32] The art of dyeing at the stage of development at which it was practiced in Aquileia continued to be virtually an exclusively Jewish occupation throughout Europe into the modern age. There can be no question that the weaving and dyeing industry of Aquileia was composed principally or exclusively by Jewish immigrants. The pre-Roman indigenous population of the region were backward tribes whose capabilities were far short of the sophisticated operation which was being performed in the great Adriatic port.

The metalworking industry in Aquileia was similarly complex and was separated into lead-, iron-, gold- and silver-smithing, performed at first by imported

Eastern slaves. Lead was used largely for conduits and one slave left a leaden tube to be used as his headstone, which he inscribed: *Aq(uileiae) Iuvinalus f(acit)*, which translates to "Iuvinalus of Aquileia made this." By the Roman period, bronze and ferric metallurgy had long since spread across Europe, and so the fact that it was being performed in the region of Aquileia does not of itself indicate the ethnicity of the smiths. However, as in the case of the weaving and dyeing industry, the state of the Aquileian metallurgy as well as some of the inscriptions weighs in favor of it being performed by the Easterners who formed the bulk of the industrial work force. The names of slaves are common among the industrial workers, and two of the most intriguing of these individuals are those of glassware producers, one of whom was a woman. Glassmaking was, of course, entirely a mysterious art in Europe at the turn of the Common Era, and even glassware-making had barely been introduced into Rome from the East at this early period.

The introduction of glassware into the area, another industry in which Jews were predominant, is evidenced by Aquileian artisans' signatures molded into vessels. Two glass vessels were found in Linz, an Austrian city on the Danube that lies along the Roman route across the Dolomites. The vessels bear the inscription *Sentia Secunda facit Aquileiae vitra*, which is interesting not only because it informs us that glass vessels were being made in Aquileia but also because the feminine form of the producer, *Sentia Secunda*, marks it as being the name of a woman. She was also clearly a slave, as was another such glassmaker who proudly molded both his name and his slave status into his vessels: *C. Salvius Gratus*. Salvius was a name that first identified its owner as a slave, and carried on to become the proud name of many Venetian and other families of high status and repute. The shards of glassware bearing the name Ennion, a glassware producer of *Eretz Yisrael,* have also turned up in the ruins of Aquileia. Ennion, whose signature appears on some thirty samples of his work, is a Greek transliteration of the Hebrew name *Anania* and is the best known of the few glassware makers whose names we know.

Christianity reached Aquileia early on in apostolic times before the end of the third century. St. Peter dispatched St. Mark to Aquileia from Rome, where it is presumed he wrote or translated his gospel into Greek. St. Hermagoras was born in Aquileia and was consecrated the first bishop of Italy over a diocese that ranks next only to Rome in antiquity. By the end of the fourth century, Valerian presided in Aquileia over the bishoprics of Venetia, Istria, Noricum, Pannonia, Como.[33]

The Jewish community suffered through an early and particularly virulent persecution in the area of Aquileia. The destiny of the Jews awaited the resolution of the initial struggle of the church against the Arians and Pagans, both of whom regarded Jesus as human. Chromazio, the episcopal head of the church in Aquileia, after crushing these heretical groups, turned malignant attention to the Jews. A most malevolent repression ensued and Jewish institutions were demolished. From this period forward the presence of the Jews in Aquileia and the contribution they had made to the development of the port was deliberately and methodically eradicated.

No Jewish structure is known to have survived into the fifth century, and traces of the considerable Jewish presence are relegated a few inscriptural, morphological, and indirect references. The existence of at least one great synagogue is attested to by a funerary inscription of the third to early fourth century dedicated to the daughter of the head of the elders of the synagogue.[34] "There cannot be any doubt that in Aquileia . . . at least until 388, a synagogue existed," unequivocally states Luila Cracco Ruggini, a writer who delved into Chromazio's campaign against the Jews and their influence.[35] The fact that a great synagogue existed cannot be denied, however, because of the survival of a peripheral reference to it by St. Ambrose (Ambrogio) after its destruction. Christian arsonists had been accused of deliberately bringing about its destruction. Stung by the accusation, Ambrose penned a letter to Emperor Theodoric in December 388, in which the event was characterized as "an act of providence."[36]

Ambrose resided in Aquileia, as did St. Jerome. It was very likely that St. Jerome's Aquileian experience led him to complain bitterly and resentfully that the Semitic artisans, mosaicists, and sculptors were everywhere, and that not only was retail trade in their hands, but that they also controlled the export of industrial products such as those made of glass, silk, and leather. He cited glassmaking as one of the trades "by which the Semites captured the Roman world."[37]

At Monastero (near Aquileia), a museum designated a "Paleo-Christian" museum was built over a mosaic floor that the author and other scholars are convinced was not a Christian structure at all but that of a synagogue, perhaps the one on record as having been burned down by Christian arsonists in the fourth century C.E. (Photograph by the author.)

At Monastero, a suburb of Aquileia within sight of the Roman ruins of Aquileia itself, stands a simple but substantial modern structure whose facade bears a bold inscription that proclaims it to be a "Paleo-Christian Museum." The museum is essentially a great hall housing a magnificent mosaic floor composed of a complex of geometric patterns, many of which encompass the names of its donors. Intruding upon the integral design of the floor is the stubble of the walls of an ancient building. The crude ashlar blocks rip through the masterfully wrought mosaic patterns and through the names of the donors. It is clear that those responsible for the walls were not merely indifferent to but contemptuous of the mosaic remnants of a building that had stood on that very spot.

The mosaic floor was clearly that of a synagogue, complete with a dedication to the Sabbath and replete with a recurrent interwoven motif known variously as the *nodo di Salomone*, "Solomon's knot," or "Solomon's seal." This symbol of Solomon appears in many Jewish structures of the period, not only in Israel but far afield, as, for example, in Sicilian remnants of Jewish architecture to which "Jewish elements, such as the 'seal of Solomon' were added."[38] Some fifty donors are acknowledged as financiers of various sections of the mosaic, many of whose names are of distinctly Semitic origin, one of whom dedicated fifty meters to the Sabbath.[39] It appears that the altar table did survive; it stands proudly bearing a label that identifies it as being "of eastern design." Adjoining the ruins is a platform on which are exposed the mosaic floors of rooms of private houses unearthed

Above left: The walls of a Christian structure rip through a mosaic floor of a precedent building whose identification as a synagogue is evidenced by the predominantly Hebraic names of the donors, a dedication to the Sabbath, and the prolific use of the "Seal of Solomon" as an integrated design element. (Photograph by the author.)

Above right: The floors of the small houses found near the mosaic floor housed by the "Paleo-Christian" museum all employ the "Seal of Solomon" as a prominent design element. The mosaic floors of the larger Roman villas at Aquileia contain no such design, although elaborations of the design and other characteristics show that the floors were laid by the same artisans. (Photograph by the author.)

near the erstwhile synagogue. The mosaics of these floors are imaginatively arranged in different patterns, but each is even more densely spotted with the "Solomon's knot" than is the floor of the synagogue and it is the feature they carry in common.

Nearby, in a separate area of Aquileia, the more elaborate floors and stumps of the walls of the sumptuous houses of the former Roman overlords lie exposed. Many such Roman houses have already been brought to light; their floors are composed of magnificent mosaics obviously laid by the same group of skilled workmen who laid the synagogue floor at Monastero, but they show no evidence of the singular design, the "Solomon's knot" so ubiquitously integrated into the floors of the smaller houses unearthed near the synagogue.[40]

It is my opinion that not only is the large mosaic floor preserved in the Paleo-Christian Museum of Monastero the remnant of a synagogue, an opinion shared by others, but that the floor of an even greater synagogue, perhaps the main synagogue of ancient Aquileia, lies beneath the great basilica of Aquileia and is more likely to be the one referred to in the Ambrogio correspondence. The basilica rises above a vast and magnificent mosaic floor, which lay more than a meter below the floor of the basilica and extends under the presbytery of the basilica and out to an undetermined end. The interior columns of the basilica were implanted indiscriminately across the mosaic panels,[41] whose major feature is a grand tripartite depiction of the story of Jonah being swallowed by, then regurgitated from, the sea monster, and finally resting thankfully and prayerfully upon terra firma.[42]

Jonah being expelled from the belly of the sea monster, the center of three scenes illustrating the story of Jonah, which together form a great central panel of the great mosaic floor discovered under the Basilica at Aquileia. (Photograph by the author.)

The *campanile*, or bell tower, which rises majestically at a short distance from the basilica, was also thrust crassly through another set of superb mosaic floors of a complex of buildings with which the synagogue was associated. The buried mosaics lay long hidden under the area adjoining the basilica until accidentally discovered in 1962. The base of the bell tower cuts across through the designs of the magnificent mosaic panels with the same utter disregard as do the columns of the basilica in their march across the underlying mosaics. The design of the mosaic is a configuration of multiple panels, in most of which appears an exquisite faunal figure and the whole of which is interwoven with imaginative floral tracery. Brilliant glass tiles are included in the tesserae, and the colorful renderings attest dramatically to the artistic and technical competence of the mosaicists. The panels are interspersed with the seal of Solomon, the *nodo di Salomone*.[43] The vast and superbly wrought mosaic expanse around and within the bottom of the tower had evidently conjoined with that of the basilica. The entire system of buildings delineated by the layout of the floor is reminiscent of other such assemblages of ancient structures adjoining ancient synagogues (such as at Duro-Europos, for example, in which the layout and function of the synagogue and its associated rooms are remarkably similar to those of the Aquileian complex).[44] The additional building(s), in addition to serving as administration quarters, provided accommodations for passing pilgrims and merchants. The area of the floor under the basilica alone rivals, and may prove to exceed, the expanse of the hitherto largest known synagogue of the period at Sardis; the exposed area alone measures some eight hundred square meters!

Implanted into the mosaic floor under the basilica is a dedication to Theodoric, the fifth bishop of Aquileia (308-320 C.E.), which evidently refers to the construction of a structure about to be built upon the site. It was so crudely imposed upon the overall design that no one doubts it was a later insertion, not even those who vehemently deny any association the floor might have had with a synagogue. It is undeniable, moreover, that the basilica was a later construction. The implant does, however, indicate that the mosaic floor had to have been in existence well before the year 320 C.E. One writer assumes that the implant was inserted by the (Christian) faithful after Theodoric's death.[45]

The proposition that in the third or early fourth century an installation of this immensity and magnificence could have been accomplished by a newly-formed church organization, still in the throes of divorcing itself from Arianism, strains the imagination. A number of labored attempts have been made to relate a few of the subjects of the various mosaic panels of the complex to Christian hierology. The scene of an encounter between a rooster and a turtle is cited; such roosters, however, are also found in both pagan and Jewish contexts.[46] An imposing figure of Victory and a simple figure of a shepherd boy appear the most credible evidence of Christian orientation,[47] but the figure of Victory also appears in the Jewish catacombs of Rome and the simple shepherd boy is relegated to a panel in an inconspicuous far corner of the mosaic, hardly a place in which the central figure of Christianity would be placed.

The absence of credible Christian symbols carries over to the imported and locally produced glassware, in which "Old Testament" themes are molded into a number of glass relics: one plate is decorated with an incised depiction of "Daniel in the lion's den";[48] another fragment features Abraham and Isaac in the foreground and the facade of the Jerusalem Temple in the background just as it appears in the context of Jewish art;[49] a third "gold glass" bottom of a bowl pictures Moses about to strike a huge desert rock to produce a miraculous flow of water.[50] That particular theme is unlikely to have been chosen by a Christian, and the representation of the Jerusalem Temple facade would not have been included in Christian art, yet all these renderings have been hitherto presented as Paleo-Christian art.

Between the buildings that once stood in the place of the bell tower and the structure underlying the basilica lie the ruins of what was apparently a sizable marble-lined Jewish ritual bath, a *mikvah*, constructed six steps down and supplied by a conduit that fed fresh-flowing waters as prescribed in Mosaic law. It replaced an even older bath, one that probably predated organized Christian presence; yet both have been assumed to have been baptismal founts.[51] The fact that the two structures are oriented toward Jerusalem, and other significant features of the structures, lend credence to the conjecture that here stood the cultural and administrative center of a Jewish community of impressive size and

The remains of an octagonal bath located in a building flanked by the present basilica and the bell tower, labeled a baptismal fount. The size of the bath, the fact that it was sunk into the floor, its position between the basilica and the bell tower (and not within one of them), the number of steps leading down to it, and the fact that it was fed by a running stream all attest to its probable function, that of a Jewish ritual bath or *mikvah*. (Photograph by the author.)

importance, just the sort of structure we would expect to find serving the populous Jewish community of Aquileia. The baptistery, rising close in front of the basilica, is likewise constructed on the ruins of a so-called heathen temple.[52]

Underneath still another basilica at Beligna di Aquileia, referred to as the "Basilica del Fondo Tullio," a mosaic floor was found which, again, seems to have been devoid of Christian identification.[53] A beautiful apsoidal mosaic section was removed largely intact and is also featured in the "Paleo-Christian" museum at Monastero. Its shape, design, and execution are remarkably similar to the semi-circular section of floor laid at the foot of the seats of the elders at the far end of the synagogue at Sardis, so much so that it seems almost possible to substitute one for the other. No accounting of the excavation is extant; it probably took place soon after 1900 and leaves us with a lack of information, but much ground for speculation as to whether this mosaic floor could have been yet another of the hundreds of the missing pre-Christian meeting places of Jewish communities—that is to say, synagogues.

The barbarian invasion under Attila "the Hun" was no less destructive of the suffering remnant of the Jewish community of Aquileia than it was of the Christians who suppressed them. The devastation of the area obliterated whatever traces of Jewish presence were left by the Christians. The city was destroyed in 452, and in 552 the citizens who returned were again driven away and the area ravished.

15

The Classical Era

Hellenization or Judaization?

From the twelfth to the seventh century B.C.E., the "Greeks" were a collection of disparate, contentious, illiterate, barbarian societies.[1] The insular Minoan and the peninsular Mycenean civilizations that preceded the formation of a "Greek" or "Hellenic" culture in the Aegean region had passed from the scene together with their writing and much of their technology. A period of literary darkness spanning more than four centuries intervenes between the passage of the Mycenaeans and the beginning of the process of the coagulation of the disparate tribes into a new cultural entity.

The ancient communities of the region did not continue the use of the primitive "Linear A" scripture of the Cretan island Minoans nor of the somewhat more advanced "Linear B" system that the peninsular Mycenaeans had developed, let alone participate in their evolution. The tribes that descended from Central Asia at the end of the twelfth century to meld with the autochthonous tribes of the region had no literate tradition whatsoever. Virtually all that is known of both the peninsular and the insular peoples strewn about the Aegean in that interim period has been gleaned from relics retrieved from the area and from their iconography.

An oral tradition did exist in the Aegean region, insular and peninsular, consisting of poetic narratives containing traces of the memory of the glorious civilizations that had burst into being in the region and had faded from the scene. The vestiges of the Minoan and Mycenaean civilizations are discernible in the *Iliad* and the *Odyssey*, the Homeric sagas that have descended through the centuries by oral repetition and refinement, to be finally committed to writing after the Greeks had absorbed the Semitic aleph-beth. The *Iliad* does provide a single, anomalous hint of an awareness by the Homeric poets of the art of writing, a single mention of a message on a *folded* tablet, and we must assume that it was a diptych that was being described with that phrase.[2] The diptych cannot have been either Mycenaean, Minoan, or Greek at the time. "The poet was aware of

287

the existence of the art of writing, but he may have known of it only as a contemporary foreign technique."³ A diptych recovered from a late fourteenth-century vessel that foundered off the coast of Turkey was discussed in Chapter 7; it predated the Homeric legends by many centuries and the Greeks acquisition of the aleph-beth by some seven centuries. The cargo, largely glass, copper and tin ingots, bespoke an highly developed pyrotechnology as well as a background of literacy.

EARLY CONTACTS BETWEEN JEWISH AND GREEK CULTURES

Once the Greeks had adopted the aleph-beth, they advanced rapidly in literary and artistic proficiency and achieved the cultural virtuosity that became the envy of the Western world. How much of this cultural leap forward was due to an absorption of culture from the ancient island civilizations to the south? How much was derived from Greek contact with the peninsular Anatolian peoples to the east? How much was due to their interaction with the Israelites of Judah and Babylonia? In order to evaluate the cultural interchange of the Greeks with the other eastern Mediterranean peoples we must first account for the impact of the ancient Semitic cultures on the Anatolian and Egyptian cultures, a process we have already examined, and adduce the consequences of the Greek encounters directly with the Canaanite and Judaic cultures, both of which had *already experienced more than two thousand years of literacy.*

The fact that such a cultural exchange did take place is obvious from the very adoption of the Semitic aleph-beth, the so-called *abecedary*, by the Greeks, possibly the single most important factor in the elevation of Greek culture to its enviable heights. Many of the Greeks were Mediterranean sailors, competitors of the coastal Canaanites on that great sea's European shores. Jewish merchants were associated with the intrepid sea-faring Canaanites, and other Jewish merchants had plied the land routes into areas where Greek incursions undoubtedly brought the two peoples into close contact. The Jews were among the Persian forces that came into military conflict with the Greeks; Jewish slaves must have been included in the spoils of war captured by the Greeks. Greek mercenaries were also among the Persian forces at a time when Persian culture was itself being influenced by a significant Jewish presence. Greek mercenaries enlisted with the Egyptians, and undoubtedly encountered Jews of Lower Egypt in the Delta and the Fayoum, and must have had some contact with the island community of Jews at Yeb.

Kittim (Greek mercenaries) were stationed at the southern border in Arad even at the end of the Jewish monarchy, under Josiah. At about the same time the Saite dynasty in Egypt enlisted Greek mercenaries who were settled in the country, and Greeks fought earlier from the beginning of the seventh century B.C., in Assyrian armies. A brother of the Lesbian poet Alcaeus, named Antimenidas, served under the king of Babylon, presumably Nebuchadnezzar, and perhaps took part in the siege of Ashkelon in 604 B.C. Later Greeks were highly valued by the satraps of the western Persian provinces . . . the long-drawn-out war over the independence of Egypt in the fourth century B.C. was carried out principally with Greek mercenaries on both sides, who from time to time went through Palestine.[4]

Attic and other "Greek" pottery unearthed from archaeological sites throughout the land of Israel render silent testimony to the fact that intercourse took place between these peoples from the seventh century B.C.E. forward to a degree far greater than is discerned from literature. Until then, the bulk of imported pottery into Judah was Corinthian, Rhodian, or generally "East Greek." Contact intensified during the fifth and fourth centuries and Attic ware began to predominate.[5] Greek artifacts have been found as far as Elat, the port at which Western wares were bartered for spices from the East.[6] In addition to pottery painted in the inimitable Greek manner, Athenian coins bearing a distinctive rendition of an owl have been unearthed from several sites in Israel, even from Jerusalem itself.[7]

The Greeks came into closer contact with Babylonian science and astronomy during the Achemenid period, an ongoing experience that was recorded in great detail by Herodotus, who visited Babylon around 450 B.C.E. Herodotus acknowledged in his great work that the Greeks had learned their science of astronomy from the Babylonians. Great advances were made in astronomy during the Persian period of Jewish exile, a period of cultural florescence due to no mean extent to the presence of erudite Israelites and Judeans among the erstwhile deportees and their descendants. Scientists among the Babylonians systematically registered summer solstices and lunar eclipses; astronomical tabulation led to the formulation of a calendarial cycle in which seven additional months were inserted after every nineteen years. Ancient authors refer to the Babylonian astronomer Nabaunus, who presumably discovered a method of calculating the phases of the moon, and of Kidenas, many of whose works may be those that survived under the name Kidinnu. The Achaemenides inherited the "Babylonian" scientific and cultural achievements of the Persian period, *and they continued to employ Aramaic as their standard language.*

THE JEWISH INFLUENCE ON GREEK PHILOSOPHY AND SCIENCE

The centuries-long contact of the Greeks with the Jews and other Semitic peoples of *Eretz Yisrael*, Anatolia, Egypt, and Mesopotamia encompassed not only technological but also subtler influences such as that of literary composition and of music and musical instrumentation. Judaic metaphysics was not least among these influences, and in the Achaemenid environment, indeed, in the world at large, it was uniquely the Jews who rejected paganism in favor of an omneitic (unitary) view of creation. It is nonetheless apparent that from Thales (640-546 B.C.E.), Socratic Plato (c. 427-347 B.C.E.), and Aristotle (384-322 B.C.E.), to St. Augustine (354-340 C.E.) and Aquinas (1225-1274 C.E.), the omneitic Judaic principle was the foundation upon which all the abstruse unitary concepts of creation and of existence were based.

It has been said that the roots of the tree of knowledge that bore fruit in Athens lay in Jerusalem. The *physikoi*, the Greek secularist philosophers, and the Mosaic prophets performed parallel philosophical functions: the demystification of a plethora of mythical gods, demons, and devils and the introduction of a universalist principle to creation. Moses taught the unity of creation and of the creator; Thales (fl. 580 B.C.E.), born in Anatolian Miletus and founder of the aptly named "Milesian School of Philosophy," taught that *everything is one*. Thales was the earliest of Ionian Greek philosophers. He became immersed in Babylonian mathematics and philosophy while in that region on commercial visits. It was in Babylonia that the merchant Thales acquired his knowledge of land-surveying techniques and astronomy. The application of this knowledge made him reputedly the inventor of "geometry," a discipline that the merchant is said to have developed by refining the Babylonian techniques with deductive reasoning.[8] How much was original with the Thales and how much the erstwhile trader had absorbed from his Babylonian mentors remains a matter of conjecture, but that he absorbed the basics in Babylonia is evident from references to his activities.

Pythagoras (582 B.C.E.) was born on the island of Samos off the western coast of Anatolia and, after becoming acquainted with the teachings of the early Ionic philosophy originated by Thales, likewise encountered Eastern wisdom and knowledge in his travels. There is no question that Babylonian mathematics was at the root of Pythagorean mathematical constructions. As long as two thousand years before Pythagoras set foot into Babylonia the circle had already been divided into 360 degrees, the day into twenty-four hours, and the Pythagorean theorem had itself been anticipated in its basic form in Akkadian Eshnunna. Just as Pythagoras drew on Babylonian mathematics, so he was said to have derived substantial portions of his philosophy from the Jews. Pythagorean precepts constituted more of a way of life than a philosophy. The introduction of ethical and moral regulations reflect their counterpart in biblical directives, albeit the aristocratic institutions promulgated by the Pythagoreans are not in concordance with the fundamentally egalitarian principles of Judaism.

Josephus quotes from a book by Hermippus of Smyrna in which Hermippus baldly stated that Pythagoras had plagiarized Thracian and Jewish concepts, accusing Pythagoras of the "imitation of the doctrines of the Jews and Thracians, which he transferred to his own philosophy."[9] Josephus then adds a pointed emphasis of his own: "For it is truly affirmed of this Pythagoras, that he took a great many of the laws of the Jews into his own philosophy." Aristoxenus of Tarentum, a pupil of Aristotle and a writer on music, concurred in presuming that Pythagoras had obtained his basic knowledge from the East. The opinion was shared by still another Peripatetic (follower of Aristotle), the Jewish writer Aristobolus, who referred to Hermippus as "a careful researcher" and claimed that "Pythagoras, when speaking of the Deity, followed Jewish books."

Pantheism, the doctrine that holds that God is not human-like, but is a pervasive manifestation of all the laws, forces, and attributes of the natural universe, evolved out of Judaic universalist principles. The strands from which are woven the theories professing that the universe taken as a whole is God, were obtained in the visits to Athens by Easterners who brought that revolutionary concept to that forum, or were obtained by Greeks traveling in the East from Eastern philosophers.

Leucippus (c. 400 B.C.E.) was a philosopher who purportedly inspired the atomic school of Greek philosophy. Leucippus was born at Anatolian Miletus, and he likewise derived from "Eastern" philosophers the principles on which his works, *The Great World System* and *On Mind*, were based. Democritus, renowned as the principal promulgator of the atomist school (albeit he followed Leucippus and therefore could not have been, as has been widely proclaimed, the originator of the atomic theory), was born at Abdera in Thrace between 470-460 B.C.E. Again we learn that Democritus traveled extensively in the East, where he diligently collected the works of numerous philosophers, among whom were those who were pursuing the universalist concepts that were being generated as a by-product of Judaist iconoclasm. It was undoubtedly among these unnamed and uncredited [Judaic?] philosophers that Leucippus and Democritus found the inspiration for, if not the elements of, the atomic theory, in which Democritus proposed that law prevailed but was not instituted by design.

We know of Democritus' works only from the collection of fragments of his voluminous physical, mathematical, ethical, and musical works that were first compiled by Mullach of Berlin in 1843. Democritus never deigned to identify his Eastern mentors by name as originators of the works he had collected, works that were passed on to posterity under his name through the efforts of Mullach and others. Nor were any of the other Anatolian and Greek sojourners in the East specific about where and how they acquired information other than in the most general terms.

The theory that the universe is composed of an infinite number of atoms invested with a primary motion, and that what is termed *nature* is but an aggregate of the multitudinous combinations that evolve from that activity, is in no way in conflict with Judaic precepts. The principle promoted by Democritus digressed from Judaic precepts only in that it held that nature derives from no higher principle, whereas Jewish tradition held that God created the physical universe with both the particles and their motion inherent in its fabric.

We can readily presume that the Eastern philosophers from whom Democritus drew his inspiration were as varied in their concept of creation as are those of the modern Jewish community, a large proportion of which acknowledges and reveres Judaism for its seminal egalitarian, moral and ethical principles and traditions while allowing for a less atavistic, but nonetheless universalist rationale for creation. Albert Einstein, for example, neither accepted nor rejected the concept of a greater principle underlying creation, and similarly measured agnosticism can be attributed to the Einsteins of the pre-Hellenic period of *Eretz Yisrael* and Babylonia from whom Democritus and other visiting Greeks drew their sustenance. The fact that Jewish philosophers who promulgated such concepts existed survives in part by virtue of the reproval and renunciation of such ideas accorded it by the biblical, talmudic, and Mishnaic redactors who grouped such deviationists with Canaanite or Persian paganists and subsequently condemned them as Hellenists.

The Stoic school of philosophy was founded by Zeno (342-270 B.C.E.), who was evidently not Greek at all but a Canaanite born in Citium, a town on the island of Cyprus. Zeno went to Athens about the year 320 B.C.E., where he made the rounds of the philosophical schools, and opened one of his own about twelve years later. The Stoics believed that "virtue" is intrinsically good, and that all attributes of life that are the subjects of desire, not only physical goods, but yearnings for wife and children, and even aspirations for honor, can merit at best a morally indifferent value.

The Stoics did not deny God but taught the doctrine that a god or gods were not separate entities, but that the universe itself and all that it represents, including life, is the embodiment of divine law. Thus the Stoics attempted to rationalize creation by making man part of the divine. The philosophy is thus an extension of the concept that God is not anthropomorphic but an omnipresent, pervasive entity.

The Epicureans, that is, those who followed the doctrines of Epicurus (c. 341-270 B.C.E.), sought to deprive the world of divinity altogether, teaching that pleasure is the only good and the essence of all morality, qualifying the hedonism integral to that philosophy by holding that prudence, honor, and justice must pertain to the pursuit of pleasure. Epicurus was born in Samos, visited Athens at the age of 18 and then returned to Asia where he encountered Eastern philosophy. He opened a school in Mitylene in 310 and taught there and at Lampascus, returning to Greece to found his school of philosophy at Athens in 305.

Epicurus warned that "when we say that pleasure is the end of life, we do not mean the pleasure of the debauchee or the sensualist, as some from ignorance or malignity represent, but freedom of the body from pain and the soul from anxiety." While temperance and simplicity were practiced by Epicurus and his close followers, the philosophy was exploited by the Cyrenaics and others who extended it into a suitable rationalization for self-indulgence and wanton licentiousness. Epicurus was an atomist of the school of Democritus; he envisioned the universe as infinite in extent, eternal in duration, and as composed of vacuum and invisible elements (atoms) and compounds. As an atomist, Epicurus reasoned that the world was produced by the collision and whirling together of these invisible but corporeal elements.

Thus, the antiquity and sophistication of Eastern civilization came as news to the Greeks, reflecting their entrance into the civilized world as novices. The fact that concepts that have been credited to the Greeks were revealed to them in their intercourse with Eastern sages was stated unequivocally by Megasthenes, who served as an ambassador to India under Seleucus from 306-298 B.C.E. Megasthenes reported that "all that has been written on natural science by the old Greek philosophers may be found in philosophers outside of Greece, such as the Hindu Brahmans and the so-called Jews of Syria."[10] The identity of the Eastern sages whose sciences were appropriated by the Greeks was, however, lost to posterity as a consequence of the conquest of the region by Alexander and the imposition of Seleucid rule. The lingua franca of commercial correspondence and cultural intercourse, which had been Aramaic for the better part of a millennium, was displaced by Greek.

The Ptolemaic city of Alexandria in Egypt served as a school of Eastern philosophy for the Greeks from the very beginning of its existence. The Jews constituted forty percent of the population of that port city, and a considerable number of Jewish sages were to be found alongside the Judaic artisans and entrepreneurs who composed the city's industrial core. It was at Alexandria that Hecateus of Abdura undoubtedly obtained the information that spurred him to write a history of the Jews. It was written about 300 B.C.E., just a first few decades after the founding of the Ptolemaic city. Although the broad outlines of that history were correct, the inaccuracies are significant, for they reflect the malevolent tales told by the Egyptians regarding the Exodus and misconceptions regarding Judaic religious practice. The main thrust of Hecateus's history, however, includes valuable lessons gleaned from Judaic historiography and an appreciation of the iconoclastic attitude of the Jews toward government.

Hecateus related, for example, that the Jews founded a sovereign nation that lasted for centuries after their great leader, Moses, "famed for his wisdom and valor," led them from Egypt. Moses chose men of the highest character and ability and instructed them in the law, priests who then performed sacerdotal, judicial, and governmental duties and served as guardians of law and morality. For this reason, Hecateus pointedly (but incorrectly) emphasized that the Jews never had a king, but continued to appoint the learned and the wise to rule over them. Hecateus gathered his information from Babylonian, Egyptian, and Jewish sources (now lost), for the ancient scriptures had not yet been translated into Greek at the time. The omission of reference to the glorious reigns of David, Solomon, and others may have been engendered by the contemporary irreverent attitude of the Jews toward kings in general, a stance anciently reflected in the Bible.

Hecateus was cognizant of the strictures and obligations of the law as given to the Jews by Moses. The first four of the Ten Commandments contain a prescription for the rejection of earthly gods. The last six commandments and the subsequent directives formulate a corpus of discrete restrictions for the conduct of an ordered and orderly society. When transcribed into the form of governmental statutes, the commandments, together with the subsequent 613 directives, form the basis of a society that is deferential neither to class nor to birthright. Many intellectual Greeks were ripe to discard the plethora of traditional gods and myths in favor of a unitary creative force, and were open to the democratic precepts inherent in Judaic law. These Greeks were impressed with the universal literacy promulgated by the Jews and were intrigued by the atmosphere of inquiry that attended Jewish studies.

Hecateus claimed that two Greek heroes, Cadmus and Daneus, were exiled together with the Jewish aliens who had been expelled from Egypt because they had offended the Egyptian gods. It was Daneus who, according to a mythological tradition, formed the Greek nation. Hecateus thus places the purported founder of the Hellenic culture as emerging from within a Judaic matrix. Whether Cadmeus and Daneus were fictional characters or not, they symbolize the process by which fundamental Judaic precepts arrived on the Greek scene.

The Alexandrian Jewish author of the latter half of the second century B.C.E., Aristobolus of Paneus, like Hermippus of Smyrna before him, charged Pythagoras as well as Plato of plagiarizing Jewish scriptures, and added insult to injury by putting down in Greek a version of the poem concerning Orpheus, the seminal poet and prophet of the Greeks. In this Orphic poem, rendered in fine hexameter and employing a vocabulary gleaned from classic Greek epics and oracles, it is a Jewish Orpheus who sings of a "rush-born" Moses and of Abraham, the founder of astronomy. Artapanus, the Alexandrian historian of the same period, was another writer who stretched polemics to fanciful heights. He bestowed on Moses the classic Greek name of Musaeus and reported that attributed to the said Musaeus was "the invention of military science, navigation, architecture, philosophy and even hieroglyphics."[11]

The reputation of the Jews as mathematicians and astronomers is emphasized in a number of references to Abraham's mastery of those disciplines, references that appear to have originated in Babylonia and were thereafter repeated by the Greeks. As noted in Chapter 1, the close association between Jewish and Babylonian science was drawn by Berosus, a Babylonian priest and historian who wrote about Abraham that "in the tenth generation after the flood, there was among the Chaldeans a man righteous and great, and skillful in the celestial science." Josephus recalled these traditional attributes of Abraham in relating how Abraham was welcomed into Egypt as a great scientist, and was encouraged by the pharaoh to enter into debate over metaphysical questions with the Egyptian sages. Abraham's sagacity confounded the Egyptians; he introduced them to the complexities of mathematics, "and delivered to them the science of astronomy; for before Abram came to Egypt they were unacquainted with those parts of learning; for that science also came from the Chaldeans into Egypt, and from thence to the Greeks also."[12]

In that chapter it was also noted that Josephus drew his information from many sources, including an extensive body of ancient literature that provided information about Abraham and the Jews, most of which has since vanished. "My reading has not been exhaustive," modestly admits Josephus in citing this literature. "In addition to those already cited, Theophilus, Theodotus, Mnaseas, Aristophanes, Hermogenes, Euhemerus, Conon, Zopyrion, and maybe many more."[13]

The antiquity of these references extends to pre-Alexandrian Aristophanes (c. 448–388 B.C.E.), a playwright whose masterpieces have survived. The idea that mathematical and astronomic knowledge stemmed generally from the Babylonian East and, in many cases, specifically from the Jews, was rife among the ancient Greek authors, and lasted into the third century of the Common Era. The extent of the influence of the Jews acknowledged by Hecateus was further amplified by the Neoplatonic philosopher Porphyrius (233-304 c.e.) in his work of about 275 c.e. Porphyrius was likewise impressed with the extent of Jewish astronomic wisdom; he quoted the pupil and successor of Aristotle, of Lesbos: ". . . inasmuch as they are philosophers by race, they discuss the nature of the Deity among themselves, and spend the night observing the stars."

The ontological approach of the rationalists, that is, the investigation of the existence of a creative force in the very nature of being, among Greek and Judaic philosophers alike, stems directly from the Judaic concept of the universality of the creator and of creation. The dismissal of a multitude of superhuman beings and demons and, per force, of the possibility of their interdiction into human affairs—and its corollary, the rejection of the power of idolic representations of these mythical beings; the substitution of the conscious exercise of free will for immutable fate: these concepts were basic to the "scientific" or logical investigation of the nature of the physical universe. The iconoclastic Judaic concepts impacted upon the Greeks early on, at least upon those few who sought, and were ready to accept, a rational explication of existence and natural processes.

REJECTION OF JEWISH EGALITARIANISM
BY GREEK AND ROMAN RULERS

As time passed and as the Greeks grew powerful, they haughtily disavowed Judaic inspiration; the denial was part of an introspective process by which Greek philosophers forged an attitude of racial superiority. This supercilious attitude was co-opted by the Romans, albeit the Romans always felt their debt to the Greeks and never overcame a certain feeling of inferiority in acknowledging that heritage. In the process of counteracting Aristotelian precepts the Christians had to dismiss both Greek rationality and its seminal Judaic underpinnings.

The egalitarian concepts inherent in the teachings of those such as Moses and Thales and those who followed were pragmatically discarded by Greek, Roman, and Christian rulers in seeking priestly sanctification of conquest and domination. Oligarchic power can only be philosophically justified by the interdiction of divinely ordered privilege, and so democratic principles were discarded or ignored in the process of the assumption of divine rights as princely prerogatives. Only stiff-necked Judaic faith in primary principles survived, and the Jews suffered miserably thereby.

The Diadochi, the Macedonian generals who divided up the territory conquered by Alexander the Great after his death, began the process of deification by certifying Alexander as a god after his death and setting up official cult centers in Egypt and Asia. A number of the Ptolemies set up statues in the temples of Egypt, consecrated altars to themselves and appointed priests to attend to the resultant cult centers. Some of the Seleucids actually assumed the names of Gods; Seleucus I made himself known by the name of Zeus and Antiochus I as Apollo. The Jews stubbornly refused to recognize divinity in any human, rulers included.

When rulers, intent on reinforcing their authority and perpetuating their name, invoked divinity and demanded obeisance, the Jews were obliged to act counter to royal mandate. Ordinarily, the rulers ignored such transgression; the Jews were, after all, commonly granted the right to conduct themselves under their own religious precepts and often to govern themselves autonomously within their own communities under their own laws. But Jewish philosophical and religious precepts were bound to affect the surrounding peoples in which they were immersed, and, even worse, to "corrupt" members of the hierarchy with dangerous anarchistic principles. Many Greeks were indeed inspired by the revolutionary Judaic tenets; some were ready to acknowledge the infinite intelligence and power of the Jewish God. Thereupon rulers began to look askance at the extraordinary liberties afforded the Jews and to take steps to limit or remove the privileges under which the Jews existed and to bend the Jews to conform. Some Jews did assimilate, but many Jews did not. Resistance to pressure led to repression and then to conflict or pogroms, the eternal cycle in which the Jews found themselves embroiled.

It was not merely the denial of the Son of God that later led to Christian inquisition, repression, and expulsion; Jewish metaphysicians were the translators and promulgators of Aristotle's "First Theology" dealing with the nature of being, with cause or genesis, and with the existence of "God," the unique creator. Inherent in that philosophy was the denial of divinity in whole or in part to any earthly being, a precept that neither the papal-structured Church nor the kings upon whom the Church invested divine rights could abide.

In the process of reordering basic principles, a significant and continuous cultural cross-fertilization did nevertheless take place between the Jews and their Greek and subsequent Roman hosts. Aristotle (384–322 B.C.E.), the father of formal logic, was said to have derived wisdom from a Jew. Clearchus, Aristotle's disciple, quotes his master regarding this encounter:

> This man [said Aristotle] was by birth a Jew, and came from Celesyria; these Jews are derived from the Indian philosophers; they are named by the Indians *Calami*, and by the Syrians *Judaea*, and took their name from the country they inhabit, which is called Judea; but for the name of their city it is a very awkward one, for they call it Jerusalem. Now this man, when he was hospitably treated by a great many, came down from the upper country to the places near the sea, and became a Grecian, not only in his language, but in his soul also; insomuch that when we ourselves happened to be in Asia about the same places whither he came, he conversed with us and with other philosophical persons, and made a trial of our skill in philosophy; and as he had lived with many learned men, he communicated to us more information than he received from us.[14]

Many of the later Greeks were eager to accept egalitarianian precepts; they were attracted to the stability of the extended-family-oriented Jewish society; they found the institution of self-sustaining humanitarian and charitable processes most appealing. Even agnostics were sensitive to Jewish philosophy and expressed respect for the derivative social tenets while abjuring an outright acceptance of the Judaic tribal concept of God. One such Greek was Numenius of Apomea (c. 250 B.C.E.), a disciple of Plato, who was characterized in ancient sources as "the Pythagorean." The Alexandrian Jewish philosopher Aristobolus stated that Numenius "the Pythagorean" expressed Judaic philosophy: "For what is Plato but Moses speaking in Attic."[15] The remark is reported by Theodoretus and repeated by Eusebius (fourth century B.C.E.): "Thus then speaks Numenius, explaining clearly both Plato's doctrines and the much earlier doctrines of Moses. With reason therefore is that saying attributed to him, in which it is recorded that he said, For what else is Plato than Moses speaking Attic Greek?"[16]

Jewish precepts proved to be pervasive. Origenes (184-254 C.E.), probably born in Alexandria, was a Christian apologist of an early period who is considered the most learned, profound, and seminal of the early church fathers. Origenes ties Pythagorean concepts to those of the Jews through Numenius:

> How much better than Celsus is Numenius the Pythagorean, a man who showed himself in many works to be very learned and who by studying several doctrines made from many sources a synthesis of those which seemed to him to be true. In the first book on "The Good" where he speaks of the nations that believe God to be incorporeal, he also included the Jews among them and did not hesitate to quote the sayings of the prophets in his book and to give them an allegorical interpretation.

This statement of Origines focuses on the main difference between Celsus "Philosophus" (second century C.E.) and Numenius. Celsus did not accept an allegorical interpretation of the prophets as did many Jews and Greeks of his time. He looked upon Christianity as a threat to society and blamed the Jews for fostering such an aberration! Although Celsus conceived of God as transcendental and abstract, he acquiesced to polytheism, believing that he who worships the many deities ultimately worships the Supreme Being. He was unequivocal in his denunciation of the acceptance of Jesus as the Messiah but accepted Judaism as a national Jewish expression. He approved of, even admired, the way Jews conducted themselves under Mosaic law. His main thrust was against orthodox Mosaic cosmography *for the Greeks* on nationalistic rather than on rational grounds. Celsus complains of the deep impression that Judaic principles, if not Judaic lore, had made on the Greeks. Greek "sympathizers" are the target of his bitter reproval:

> Now the Jews became as an individual nation, and made laws according to the customs of their country; and they maintain these laws among themselves at the present day, and observe a worship that may be very peculiar but is at least

traditional. . . . If indeed according to these principles the Jews maintained their own law, we should not find fault with them but rather with those who have abandoned their own traditions and professed those of the Jews.[17]

HELLENIZATION VERSUS JUDAIZATION

Historians, Jews and Gentiles alike, harp on the "Hellenization" of sections of the Jewish populace; the Talmud focuses on that process. Little attention has been paid to the reverse phenomenon, the Judaization of Gentiles. A veil is cast over the vital impact that Jewish philosophical, social, and religious concepts had upon archaic Hellas[18] and how they continued to affect Greek culture ever more profoundly as contact between the two peoples became more intimate. It is true that numbers of Jews became attracted to Greek hedonism, a process that may have peaked during the time when Jason bribed his way into the post of High Priest in Jerusalem.[19] Affluent Jews were prone to indulge in the hedonism of Greek culture, but the emphasis on the process of assimilation glosses over the immensely more important, magnetic attraction that Jewish philosophy and religion had for large masses of Greeks and subsequently for the Romans.

Jewish hedonism was a minor element in the cultural tides of the times. Judaization was pervasive and was viewed as an inherent threat to authority until its advance was stemmed by the substitution of Christianity. The Christians, while professing a rejection of paganism, were nonetheless amenable to conferring divine rights upon rulers, and thus constituted an acceptable alternative to Judaism. Christianity quickly became an operative part of governmental authority and the main weapon in the siege upon Judaic influence. In the process, the records and writings of the Jews were relegated to the dustheap: documents were destroyed, centers were razed, synagogues were demolished, massacres took place, people were displaced.

Historians have paid scant attention to the remaining ephemeral evidence; the statues, temples, and other artifacts of pagan idolatry are far more conspicuous than are subjective concepts. They make attractive illustrations of scholarly texts and provide museums with valuable, crowd-pleasing assets. Ancient Greek literature and art reflected the reality that upper-class, traditionalist Greeks created for themselves, and historians complacently follow, idealizing the ancient Greeks and treating pagan Greek mythology as the epitome of culture. Modern literature is loaded with sympathetic poetic and allegoric references to Greek gods and to their fabulous struggles and human failings. Hellenophiles are enthralled with the magnificent artistry of paintings and statuary produced at the behest of the hierarchical Greek adorers of the ancient gods, many of whom identified themselves as, or at least as the offspring of, such gods. They are blinded by the artistry of idolatry to the spiritual beauty of a theosophy without idols and to the creativity of the artisans who left little but their unsigned products to posterity. They readily join the conquerors in the denigration of the people subjected to them. They disregarded the fact that it was the subjected peoples who provided the very fountain from which the Greeks drew their knowledge and their strength. They ignored the fact that it was the subjected and enslaved peoples, and not the Greeks or Romans, who constructed the temples and were the executors of the art so warmly admired.

Enraptured by Muses and myths, the classicophiles were oblivious to the verity of the proposition that far more Greeks (and others) were affected by Judaic precepts than was true of the reverse. The theistic preachings of the rabbinic hierarchy were only part of the attraction Jewish philosophy held out to the world. Halachic prescripts also consecrated and promulgated egalitarian precepts with universal application. Their humanitarian appeal was so profound that, in spite of massacres, repression, opportunism, displacement, *and Hellenization* the numbers of Jews and their sympathizers multiplied many times faster than the numbers of the surrounding peoples. An age of humanism and of reason was begging to be born. Josephus summarized that appeal: "Moses did not make religion a part of virtue, but he saw and ordained other virtues to be part of religion."

The rejection by Jewish sages of mystical and magical superstitions impressed such historians as Hecateus of Miletus. As a significant illustration of Judaic rationalism, Hecateus reported an event that he witnessed while accompanying Alexander the Great on his campaign. Many Jews went along as auxiliary forces, we are told, and among them was a Jewish horseman, Mosollam, "a person of great courage, of a strong body and the most skillful archer that was among either the Greeks or barbarians." The entire entourage was stopped in its tracks by the "augur" or soothsayer, who accompanied the expedition as a reader of signs. The augur took his cue from a resting bird, saying that if the bird did not move from the spot it would be a sign that Alexander's troops should not go on for fear of ill fortune befalling them. If the bird did get up and fly away, that would be the sign that it was safe for the troops to proceed. No sooner had the augur pronounced this fateful procedure when Mosollom drew his bow and shot the bird. The augur and others rose, enraged, and cast imprecations upon the Jew who then calmly turned to them and asked:

"Why are you so mad? For how can this bird give us any information concerning our march, which could not see how to save himself? For had he been able to foretell the future he would not have come to this place."[20]

On the other hand, Cornelius Tacitus, the Roman historian, could not abide the blanket refusal by Jews to accept such portents and omens, and, in a peculiar twist of logic, accuses the Hebrews of "superstition" and takes them to task because they did not heed such supernatural warnings before the siege of Jerusalem. "Portents had happened," Tacitus rails, "which a race prone to superstition, opposed to religious observance, does not think it right to expiate either by sacrifice or prayer." The Jews were therefore, in the eyes of the rabidly anti-semitic Tacitus, responsible for their own demise because they were proscribed from reverting to the Sibylines or other soothsayers for divination, nor would they sacrifice to the gods to whom all other peoples turned for protection. Tacitus was correct, Leviticus 19:26 is specific on the subject: "You shall not practice divination or soothsaying." Jeremiah (10:2) likewise warns against being swayed by the arguments of such as Tacitus: "Do not fall into the ways of the nations, do not be awed by signs in the heavens."

The scraps of Judaic literature that have endured indicate that Judaic philosophy was not limited to unidimensional interpretations of the Bible. The fundamentalists, whether Essene, Samaritan, Saddusaic, Pharasaic, or of their canonically orthodox descendants, represented small, albeit politically and socially influential, proportions of a Jewish population of many millions. The doctrinal hyper-orthodox of the past can be compared with the Hasidic and other ultra-Orthodox communities of modern times who are respected and even revered for their role in preserving a critical portion of the Judaic heritage, but who do not reflect the attitudes of most of the considerable corpus of Jewish scientists, artists, artisans, and intellectuals in modern society. Rationalism, a natural extension of Judaism, was regarded by many conservative elements of the ancient rabbinate as a dangerously erosive Hellenization. The abysmal ignorance regarding the numbers and influence of Jews of the times is not merely the result of the obliterations of Jewish communities and their records by successive ruling regimes, or of the changes, deletions, and obfuscations effected by Christians and Muslims over a period of two millennia. While the Rabbinate throughout the Christian Era must be gratefully accredited for the preservation of holy and halachic literature, often heroically rescued under the most horrendous circumstances, they must also bear part of the responsibility for the expurgation of science and technology from Jewish historiography.

Some scraps of these facets of ancient Jewish culture have survived, often by virtue of individuals being mistakenly assumed to have been non-Jews. An outstanding example of an early Jewish scientist-philosopher who won a significant place in the history of Greek literature is Caecilius of Kalakte in Sicily. His works are known only from fortuitously preserved scraps, but the list of his works is extensive and his influence was clearly pervasive: his lexicon, his historical works, and his treatise on historiography were made use of by later writers and were referred to by them as authoritative. He was a close associate of Dionysius of Halicarnassus, both having studied rhetoric in Rome. Both employed a scientific approach to aesthetic criticism: "His method was scientific in the best sense." Caecilius was born a slave, and it is "explicitly stated that he was a Jew, whether born such or a proselyte to the faith is not certain." He is the first to cite the Bible and "to consider and criticize biblical expressions from the aesthetic and the literary point of view. . . . The Jew Caecilius belongs to the Graeco-Roman world as the Alexandrian Jew Philo a generation or two later."[21]

The operative link between the Jews dispersed throughout the Diaspora and their tradition has always been the humanist philosophy inherent in that tradition: charity above all; the dignity of the individual; reverence for learning; a questioning, even agnostic skepticism regarding all knowledge; denial of divine attributes of any human, even of kings and priests; the universality of egalitarianism; the unitary relationship of man to his creator without need of, and indeed with a proscription against, a human intermediary. Atheist Jews can relate to these precepts no less than can deists, for, in their case, a human interloper is per force proscribed. The relationship between each individual and God is a personal one; all else pertains to the relationship between man and his fellow man.

Just as many of these haughty principles were condensed and restated eloquently in the eighteenth century by Thomas Paine (in spite of Paine's vituperations regarding God's biblical activities), revered by Jefferson and Adams, and their essence subsequently incorporated into the American Declaration of Independence and the American Constitution, so a process of cultural osmosis filtered them into segments of Hellenic philosophy. The Greeks encountered these concepts first in Anatolia into which area they arrived as basically barbarian marauders. Then, having tasted Eastern literacy and civilization, some found their way into *Eretz Yisrael*, Mesopotamia, and Lower Egypt, where they became immersed in Semitic culture.

Literacy was, of course, the primary implant of Semitic culture into that of the barbarian Greeks. After the Greeks had adopted the Semitic aleph-beth, the concepts promulgated by the Semites in general, and the Jews in particular, became widely disseminated; the social concepts now so highly acclaimed as the foundations of modern democratic society were absorbed by the Greeks and became integrated into what is euphemistically termed "Hellenism." The term "Hellenism" carries a different connotation from the term "Hellenic"; it designates a mixture rather than a source. The present significance of the term derives from a doctoral thesis presented by J. G. Droysen in 1831, in which he expands on the symbiosis of cultures that took place during the epoch of Greek expansion into the Orient. The cross-fertilization and metamorphosis that took place during that period of cultural flux came about as a result of the two "disciplines most deeply involved in the history of Hellenism": philology and theology.[22]

> The Hellenizing of Judaism was welcomed by the Jews of Egypt and included both the interpretation of Judaism to the Greeks and the interpretation of Hellenism to themselves, stretching it upon the canvas of historic Jewish traditions. The Jews sought to demonstrate that their own religion could be acceptable to the Greeks as a universal wisdom and insight into the truth while they endeavored to see historic Judaism in universalistic and humane terms.[23]

PHILO, JOSEPHUS, AND OTHER JEWISH WRITERS OF THE PERIOD

The later Greeks could not, however, accept the corpus of Jewish philosophy in its entirety, for equality was central to it and to accept that precept would require them to abjure their haughty status as conquerors. Therein lies the rub. We are fortunate in inheriting much of the writings of Philo Judaeus, an Alexandrian who sought to promulgate the concepts contained in the above quotation. Philo is referred to as the archetypical Hellenized Jew on the one hand and as an apologist for the Jews on the other. For Philo, "historic Judaism was a world view which demonstrated all that the Hebrew virtues, epitomized by the Patriarchs and heroes of the faith, were really the ideals subsequently perceived by the Greeks and established as the roots and foundations of their admirable humanism."[24] Philo's writings contain expositions upon the structure of the universe and the nature of the human mind that are drawn from Judaic scripture and culture. Philo employed the "Delphic" maxim upon which scientific inquiry is based, proclaiming that "this is nature's law: know thyself."[25] It has been said that Philo's speculation upon these fundamental questions has parallels in Hellenistic natural philosophy: "Philo had used a lost compilation of speculations concerned with heaven, the stars, the moon, and the nature, origin, continued existence and seat of the soul, which was also drawn by Aetius (c. 100 C.E.). Such a source had already been posited by Deals for Aetius, who gave it the title *vetusta Placita* and dated it to the mid-first century C.E."[26]

Such may be the case, but Philo also drew from a vast fund of Jewish literature now lost to us. Philo discoursed upon the effect of Judaic canons and precepts upon the Greek/Roman community, proclaiming, "All those who have seen fit to worship the Creator and Father of the Universe, if not from the beginning, at least later, and have embraced the idea of one [divine] ruler instead of many, must be considered our dearest friends and closest kin." The arguments posed by Philo and other Jewish rationalists of the times have suffered the scorn of fundamentalist Jews no less than that of the Gentile scholars who refused to acknowledge, or were blind to, the Judaic foundations of the enlightened philosophy they expressed. As a result, the arguments the Jewish rationalists posed were left in limbo over the centuries, notwithstanding the fact that Philo and others were not merely attempting to introduce the Gentile community to that heritage, but were equally concerned with drawing back to the fold such Jews as had begun to question the worthiness of their heritage and faith. "In fact, Philo referred ruefully to those of his fellow Jews living in the Graeco-Roman milieu who had cultivated 'a dislike of the institutions of our fathers and make it their constant study to denounce and decry the Laws.'"[27]

Joseph ben Matthias was another Jewish writer of renown from whom we have quoted abundantly under the name (Flavius) Josephus, the name he assumed after serving an [ignoble?] stint as a Roman officer in the campaign against the Jews. He named himself Flavius Josephus in deference to the Flavian dynasty to which he had devoted his talents. Josephus' works, in addition to being a comprehensive exposition on the history of the Jews and, in particular, on that history as it unfolded during Roman times, was apologetic in favor of the Jews while at the same time glorifying Titus and the imperial Flavian dynasty. His works serve to illustrate the attitude of that body of Jews who, although proud of their heritage and cognizant of the contribution the Jews had made and were making to civilization, did not necessarily accede to the political nor the philosophical stance of fundamentalist Jewish groups.

During that period many Greek and Roman historians wrote inaccurate and even crassly falsified histories of the Jews as a consequence of the conflicts between the Romans and the Jews. Josephus felt it necessary to contradict the calumnious fictions being promulgated. Josephus recast his Aramaic works into Greek, in which form they have managed to survive. His facts are, in the main, accurately presented and are universally employed by historians of the period. The authenticity of his rendition is attested to by the fact that his seven books of the "Jewish War," despite having been admittedly written as an apologia for the Jews, were reviewed and recommended by Vespasian, the general who had conducted the war against the Jews and became emperor of the Roman Empire, and by the Emperor Titus, King Agrippa, King Archelaus, and Herod. Vespasian and Agrippa had read and approved the work even before its publication.[28] The books received no recommendation but were rather resented by the Rabbinate; at least they were not regarded with favor by its orthodox hierarchy.

Josephus unequivocally contended that the roots of Greek science and philosophy lay in the Mosaic tradition: "Our earliest imitators were the Greeks," he wrote, emphasizing the persistent penetration of Judaic precepts into Greek culture, "though ostensibly observing the laws of their own countries, yet in their own conduct and philosophy [the Greeks] were Moses' disciples, holding similar views about God."

The existence of a substantial body of Judaic literature upon which not only Philo and Josephus but also the Greek philosophers drew is a subject for scholarly inquiry that has yet to be fully explored. A few remnants of this corpus of literature have survived, mainly those that had attained limited sanction by some Jewish congregations, the so-called *Apocrypha* and *Pseudepigrapha*. These were preserved not so much because they had been accepted by some Jews but because they became a component of the literature of Christian communities that succeeded the Jewish congregations.[29]

It is clear, however, that a substantial corpus of Jewish philosophical and scientific literature existed even by extrapolating its extent from the references to and selections from it by Greek and Roman authors, almost all of which are written in unfriendly, even malicious contexts. The wide scope of Jewish literature can readily be interpolated from the rabble-rousing, anti-Semitic frothings of Manetho, Lysimachus, Apollonius, Molon, Posidonius, and Chaeremon; from the fulminations of Polybius, Strabo, Diodorus of Sicily, Cicero's orations, Suetonius, and the particularly vituperative Tacitus,[30] no less than from the now-lost sources to which Philo, Josephus and other sympathetic writers refer.

Only a few of the works of Philo the Alexandrian have been preserved, and it may well be that their providential survival is due to the fact that church scholars, seemingly oblivious to the fact that Philo was the rabbi of the great Synagogue of Alexandria, mistakenly revered him as one of the earliest of the Church Fathers! Philo's works, ironically, were thereupon preserved not by the Jews but by the Church Fathers Clement of Alexandria (d. c. 215 C.E.) and Eusebius (fourth century). It was not until the sixteenth century that Azariah dei Rossi, an Italian Jewish humanist, "rediscovered Philo for what he actually was: a devout Jew!" Nathan

Ausubel, in his incisive review of Jewish Hellenists, cannot but contain his aston-
ishment at the irony that not only did theologians of early Christianity like
Eusebius, Clement, and Origen consider Philo to have been one of the Church
Fathers but "even more wry is the knowledge that he profoundly influenced
Christian theology and yet left no trace of his thinking on Jewish religious and
intellectual history."[31]

The historical writings of Justus of Tiberius, who was a contemporary of
Josephus, and of many other Jewish writers and philosophers who preceded him
did not enjoy such good fortune and have disappeared. Surviving fragments of a
few of these works constitute a smattering of the large body of writings that have
been lost, mutilated, or destroyed and are otherwise known only by peripheral
references to them. These were not oracular or revelationary works but the reasoned disquisitions of educated, highly-cultured men who, in the best tradition
of halachic and exegetical argumentation, extended inquiry beyond creation and
covenant into the way the world works. Many of them were apologetic expositions of Jewish religious precepts, devoted to two propositions: the validity of
ethical monotheism and its superiority over animistic paganism; and the magnitude of the debt Greek philosophy owed to Mosaic tradition and Judaic philosophy, social and scientific.

The Jewish rabbinic sages banned the works by Jewish "Hellenists" as well as
most of the works designated as Pseudepigrapha, not so much because they were
heretical but because the Christian church had adopted them as their own; thereby
they contributed to the loss of a vital and seminal section of Judaism and to the
hiatus in Judaic philosophical history. The Greek and Roman upper-class historians and philosophers certainly had no strong imperative to conserve Judaic
literature and the Byzantines and other Christians, more often than not, strove
to obliterate it. Because knowledge of the Jewish input into the evolution of civilization must, *per force*, be derived from literature and from architecture and artifacts, the dearth of extant material on all counts unfortunately relegates the question of how much "classical" culture owes to the Jews to dialectic arguments, which
always remain subject to skepticism.

The preponderance of extant Greek, and especially of Roman, literature of the
period is due in no small measure to the survival of administrative archival records,
a privilege not obtained by the Jews of the times. Cicero's speeches to the Roman
Senate alone make up a substantial corpus of historical material. The rhetoric
and writings of such aristocrats provide not only the information but also the
perspective with which "classical" history has been formulated. The Jews have
no such governmental archive to draw from; their literature was esoteric, and its
endurance was incidental to the times. The documentary evidence concerning
the effect that Judaic perceptions, both sacred and secular, had upon the Greeks
and Romans must therefore be interpolated from surviving literature and relics,
which represent only a tiny part of what existed. We are compelled to comb the
biased literature of the conquerors for a rational explanation of the phenomenal
increase in the Jewish population of the classical era, an explosive expansion in

numbers and influence that took place despite the severe exigencies Jews were recurrently forced to face.

THE FLOURISHING OF JUDAISM IN THE CLASSICAL ERA: DOCUMENTARY AND ARCHAEOLOGICAL EVIDENCE

Greek merchants were scarcely strangers to the eastern Mediterranean mainland. Demosthenes (c. 383-322 B.C.E.) discusses the presence of Greek merchants at Acco for about a decade around 460 B.C.E., at which time the city paid tribute to the predatory Attic sea alliance.[32] Later, between 380 and 374 B.C.E., the Athenian general Iphicrates (419-353 B.C.E.) was also in Acco, this time to prepare for an attack on Egypt. We learn that subsequently Egypt fomented a rebellion in Sidon in which Greek troops played a critical part: the sacking of Egypt by the Persian king Artaxerxes III (Ochus, son of Artaxerxes II, 359-338 B.C.E.) that followed was largely a war fought between Greek mercenaries in the employ of the kings.[33] Thus the Greeks were brought into close contact with the Canaanite and Judaic cultures both by commercial contact and through their role as mercenaries for various of the region's royal employers.

Alexander's campaigns through the Near East brought him into close contact with the revitalized Jewish communities of Judah and with the million or so Jews who by then inhabited the "Land of the Two Rivers," the land into which the cream of Israeli and Judean society had been thrust. Alexander treated the Jews with considerable respect, and the Alexandrian generals who split up Alexander's empire between them, the *Diadochi*, treated them, at first, with no less reverence. The main body of Babylonian exilic Jewry had remained in Persia, and it was from this body of Jews that Antiochus III (the greatest of the Seleucids, referred to as Antiochus the Great) transferred two thousand families, or some ten thousand literate people, to Lydia and Phrygia, into the very heart of Anatolia. Thus a colony of Jews was again implanted in the very area in which the Akkadian *karums* had nurtured civilization among the Hittites two thousand years earlier.

The instructions with which Antiochus effectuated the resettlement bespeak the special regard the Greek ruler had acquired for the trustworthiness of the Jews, the respect he held for the halachic principles under which the Jews conducted their lives, and the admiration he bore for their cultural achievements. Antiochus commanded Zeuxis, the general in charge of his forces in Anatolia, to proceed as follows:

> Having been informed that a sedition is arisen in Lydia and Phrygia . . . it has been thought proper to remove two thousand families of Jews, with their effects, out of Mesopotamia and Babylon, unto the castles and places that lie most convenient; for I am persuaded that they will be well disposed guardians of our possessions, because of their piety toward God, and because they are faithful, and with alacrity do what they desired to do. I will, therefore, though it be a laborious work, that thou remove these Jews; under the promise that they shall be permitted to use their own

laws . . . thou shalt give every one of their families a place for building their houses, a portion of land for their husbandry, and for the placement of their vines; and thou shalt discharge them from paying taxes of the fruits of the earth for ten years. . . . Take care likewise of that nation, as far as thou art able, that they might not have any disturbance given them by anyone.[34]

This event, which took place between 210–205 B.C.E., was one of several occasions in which trusted Jewish forces were employed far afield from Jerusalem by the Greeks. Josephus reports that Samaritans accompanied Alexander into Egypt, a story that was once subjected to skepticism. A village in the Fayoum named Samaria is, however, described in a papyrus dated to the time of Ptolemy II ("Philadelphus," d. 247 B.C.E.) with no indication of how a village with such a distinguishing biblical name got there. The fact that the Egyptian town of Samaria was an explicitly Jewish habitation is crystal clear; prominent among the settler's names listed in the papyrus are theophoric Greek names commonly employed by Jews, distinctly Hebraic names of Jewish males such as Shabbatai, Johanan, Jacob and Jonathan, as well as of females such as Sabbatis and Miriam.[35]

The conquering Greeks disdained physical work and exercised their right to relegate what they considered menial activity (which included that of the artisan no less than of unskilled work) to foreigners and slaves. During the period of Hellenic expansion, however, Greek stonecutters could still be found as far as Susa working at the palace of Artaxerxes III (359–338 B.C.E.). The transformation of the Greeks from a conglomeration of contentious tribes, predators, and mercenaries to arrogant rulers brought about the imposition of new standards of comportment. "Greek citizens," the Greek historian, essayist, and military commander Xenophon (435–354 B.C.E.) was already proclaiming to his fellow citizens at this early period of Greek cultural development, "are prohibited from practicing crafts where Greeks are in military control."[36]

Xenophon had pursued an exemplary military career before he became a prolific author of historical works. He campaigned brilliantly in Anatolia and Armenia in the command of the "Ten Thousand Greeks." The army fought its way against ferocious mountain tribes, marched through an icy, inclement winter and arrived triumphant at the shores of the Black Sea. The principle expressed by Xenophon was no mere dilletantish expression of a pompous military adventurer, it was the policy thereafter instituted by the Greeks wherever they imposed their hegemony.

Xenophon was a follower of Socrates and reflected the haughty attitude of Socrates and of Socrates' famous pupil Plato, regarding the ignoble status of artisanship. Artisans, in Plato's representation of the structure of an ideal society, are restricted to its lowest social strata; artists are to be given applause but must be instantly deported from Plato's projected Republic. Aristotle inculcated his pupil Alexander with the same principles. "The finest type of city will not make an artisan a citizen,"[37] Aristotle proclaimed, a wry commentary on the democratic ideals vaunted as the Greek contribution to civilization. The Greeks, no less than the conquerors of all ages, sought to certify their noble status by the acquisition of works of art and luxurious surroundings, but whereas they esteemed artisanship, they had nothing but contempt for the artisan.

Greek antipathy toward physical labor is reflected in the way Greeks perceived the god of the forge, Hephaestus: an ugly cripple hobbling lamely about Mt. Olympus. The unfortunate divinity was continuously subjected to derision for his base occupation no less than for his deformity. The Homeric tales melodramatically portray the manner in which the grotesque empyrean smith served the gracious, gloriously handsome divinities Apollo, Hermes, and all the other exquisite creatures of the Greek pantheon as a source of "unquenchable laughter."[38]

It was the Jews, therefore, who became the mainstay of a number of industries and of technology in general, practicing occupations that were considered not merely mundane but beneath the dignity of the Greek overseers. The presence of Jews was pervasive throughout the Hellenic world but the record of their accomplishments lies less in inscriptions than in anonymous production. They multiplied, and their influence spread despite their lowly station, a fact that confounded and often enraged authority.

Outright conversion of significant numbers of Gentiles to Judaism is the only process that can account for the phenomenal increase in Jewish population during the "classical period." Philo hailed this movement, rejoicing that "[the laws of Moses] attract and win the attention of all, of Barbarians (i.e., non-Greeks), of Greeks, of dwellers on the mainland, of nations of the East and West, of Europe and Asia and of the whole inhabited world from end to end."[39]

There was a substantial body of Gentiles who did not consider themselves Jews per se, but accepted Judaic tenets to a lesser or greater degree. They contributed to the synagogues and participated in synagogue activity. These pious Gentiles were termed *sebomenoi*, that is, "worshiping ones." "There was an increasing number, perhaps millions by the first century, of *sepomenoi*, Gentiles who had not gone the entire route toward conversion."[40] Then there were the *phobomenoi* or "fearing ones" (i.e., "God-Fearers"). These followers of the Jewish universalist concept were not necessarily circumcised, nor did they necessarily subscribe to the 613 Mosaic laws. The "God-Fearers" are distinct from the ethnic Jews who are generally referred to as *theosebeis* or "God worshipers," a distinction that appears in divers literary contexts. In the New Testament we find Paul in Antioch addressing the crowd at the synagogue, among whom are "men of Israel *and* you that fear God" (Acts 13:16). In Athens, Paul "argued in the synagogue with the Jews *and* the devout persons" (Acts 17:17).

Jesus, most ironically, is said to have himself bitterly complained about the pervasive spread of Orthodox Judaism into the Gentile world, and to have predicted dire consequences for those who persisted in its spread: "Woe unto you scribes and Pharisees, for you compass sea and land to make one proselyte."

Louis H. Feldman addressed the question in some depth in the *Biblical Archaeological Review*. He assembled a number of classical references to "sympathizers," including one attributed to Seneca ("the Younger," c. 5 B.C.E.-65 C.E.) by St. Augustine. "After deriding the Jews for their laziness in wasting one-seventh of their lives in idleness through observance of the Sabbath, Seneca declares that 'the custom of this most accursed race has gained such influence that it has now been received throughout the world.'"[41]

In fact, Seneca goes much further in his polemic. "The vanquished," Seneca goes on to complain bitterly about the prodigious impact of Jewish mores, "have imposed their laws on the conquerors." The resentment of a member of the ruling class over a weekly unproductive day can well be understood. Both Seneca and his father (the Elder) were born in Cordova, Spain, where scores of thousands of slaves were toiling in the mines and other thousands of slaves and laborers were tilling the farms, firing the forges, and attending to the needs of their masters. Should conversion to Judaism become widespread and rest and prayer on the Sabbath become widespread, the rate of production and accretion of wealth would be reduced by some fifteen per cent! Seneca's fears are revealed by his next remark: "At least they [the Jews] know the origins of their ceremonies: the greater part of our people have no idea of the reason for the things they do." Seneca's grudging concession to a religious rationale for Jewish observance of the Sabbath is thus overridden by his concern that Gentile followers may employ the holiday as an excuse to beg off from productive work.

Epictetus was born in Hieropolis about 50 C.E. and was at first a slave in Rome. Upon being freed Epictetus became a Stoic philosopher, and his anecdotal maxims were preserved in the works of his pupil Arrian. In these illuminating expressions of the mores of the times, Epictetus expressed his chagrin over the pervasive Jewish influence and resultant Gentile indulgences in Jewish practices such as Sabbath observance: "Why," asks the philosopher, "do you act the part of a Jew when you are a Greek?" Epictetus then adds, "Whenever we see a man halting between two faiths we are in the habit of saying, 'he is only acting the part.' But when he adopts the attitude of mind of the man who has been baptized and has made his choice, then he is both a Jew in fact and is called one."[42]

The attraction of Judaism to a broad spectrum of the population was of concern to Christian poet and priest alike. "The third-century Christian Latin poet Commodianus likewise alludes to Judaizers who seek to live both ways '... that is, partaking of both Judaism and Christianity. Commodianus makes the same point when he exclaims: 'What! Are you half a Jew?'"[43]

In this regard it is significant to note that there were a large body of Gentiles who had a good financial reason to conceal their sympathy to the Jewish faith, whatever the degree of their adherence to it, for special taxes were imposed on professed Jews. "A similar distinction is implied in Suetonius ... who declares that two classes of people were persecuted by the Roman Emperor Domitian ... for evasion of the special tax on Jews, namely, those that lived as Jews without acknowledging that faith ... and those who concealed their origin."[44]

Suetonius (75-160 C.E.) was a Roman biographer and antiquarian who was in an excellent position to observe that process when he was employed as secretary to Hadrian. He forfeited his position at age fifty, having been compromised by his involvement in a court intrigue. His largely biographical work is marked by its impartiality and frankness, attributes well attested to by the above remark, one that provides us with evidence of the considerable number of secret Jews of his time. The precarious position of these clandestine practitioners of the Jewish faith reminds us of the similar position of the Marranos of Spain, and of the tests applied to the exposition of proselyting "New Christians."

Josephus remarks that each city, though believing that it had rid itself of its Jews, still had its Judaizers, sympathizers who mixed Jewish customs with that of the pagans. These elements aroused suspicion, and the Syrians feared them as much as proclaimed aliens. Another passage alludes to "sympathizers," a large "multitude" of Greeks attracted to Jewish religious ceremonies in Antioch that the Jews had "in some measure incorporated them with themselves." A key passage is the one in which Josephus describes the great wealth of the Temple in Jerusalem, noting that Asian and European Gentiles who worshiped [the Jewish] God had contributed to it for a very long time. Josephus refers to the wife of Nero as a worshiper of God who pleaded on behalf of the Jews.[45]

Numerous other such references from Josephus attest to the many "Jewish customs that have now found their way to some cities"; to many "customs that have penetrated the world"; to the fact that "the masses have long since shown a keen desire to adopt the Jewish religion." Josephus singles out the abstinence from work on the Sabbath and the lighting of candles as practices that are observed everywhere.

Talmudic and midrashic references to Gentiles practicing or actively sympathizing with Judaism are numerous, and lest such sources should be taken as biased, Christian sources may also be tapped for corroboration of the spread of Judaic influence. St. Justin refers to the charge of the Jew Typho that Christians neither keep the feasts or Sabbaths nor practice the rite of circumcision, whereas all God-Fearing persons (sympathizers) do so.[46] St. Justin (c. 100–165 c.e.) was a Jew born in Samaria who became one of the "fathers" of the Church after he was successively a Stoic, Platonist, and Christian. Justin addressed two *Apologias* for Christianity to the emperor before his purported martyrdom, and his resentment of Gentiles who not only are drawn to Judaism but actually practice circumcision can be easily understood from the circumstances of his own conversion.

We are treated to numerous insights into the pervasive influence of Jewish precepts from Christian sources, especially from notable converts to Christianity. Perhaps no better example of such a source is Tertullian (c. 160–220 c.e.) who was born a pagan in Carthage and was converted to Christianity in Rome. It is said that no other theologian between St. Paul and St. Augustine had a greater influence on the Latin Church. A great number of his works were heated polemics directed at heathens, heretics, and Jews, from which we learn that indeed, a great host of Gentiles not only followed but conformed to Jewish liturgical rites and ceremonies. Conversion or adherence to Judaism by pagans was a major concern of Tertullian's work.

The name *Sambathian* was commonly given to children of Sabbath-observing parents:

The name "Sambathian" . . . in 20 Egyptian papyri ranging in date from the early first century A.D. to the fifth century apparently refers to adherents of a sect of Sabbath observers, since their kinsmen seem to be non-Jewish and the papyri were found in villages that are non-Jewish as far as we know . . . we may consider every Sambathian as representing a whole family and the total number of Sabbath observers was consequently not inconsiderable.[47]

A symptomatic reference to the Judaizing "problem" among the Gentiles, as seen from the vantage point of the satirist Juvenal of the early second century C.E., is his bitter complaint:

Some who have had a father who reveres the Sabbath, worship nothing but the clouds and the divinity of the heavens and see no difference between eating swine's flesh, from which their father abstained, and that of man; and in time they take to circumcision. Having been wont to flout the laws of Rome, they learn to revere the Jewish Law and all that Moses handed down in his secret Tome.[48]

Juvenal (c. 55–140 C.E.], a Roman attorney, was notorious for his hatred of both women and Jews, the subjects of the last of his six satires. His vicious fulminations serve to confirm the prevalence of Jewish mores among the Gentiles. It also expresses clearly the concern of society for whom Juvenal speaks: Gentiles who accept Jewish precepts in part begin by renouncing idolic worship and rejecting the mythical gods. They are then beguiled into following the Jewish law and end by endowing their children with a will to become full-fledged Jews, that is, even to become circumcised. His statements make manifest that the process is nothing unusual; it is a social problem that cannot be ignored and is therefore deserving of the biting comments of the author.

Archaeological sites are not altogether barren of the evidence of the presence of a substantial Jewish population and of a large retinue of Gentile followers. Although Jewish structures were devoid of durable effigies, they often incorporated the names of donors into the design of the mosaic floors of their otherwise plain and simple meeting halls, the synagogues. Many of these names were of Jews who had assumed Greek or Roman names, but the great numbers of such occurrences indicate that among the financial supporters of the houses of Judaic study were Greek or Roman sympathizers. Unfortunately, mere traces remain of most of the hundreds of synagogues which were destroyed between the third and fifth centuries. In many cases churches were built over the ruins of the synagogues. Here and there, portions of a mosaic floor come to light, and occasionally, as at Sardis in Anatolia, an extensive, virtually complete mosaic floor is exposed, with the various donors' names integrated into the design.

A few commemorative plaques associated with a synagogue have survived, but most such inscriptions have disappeared along with the structures that housed them. Some can be found in buildings constructed with the elements of the razed structures they replaced. Even rarer are indicative names that were inscribed into the stones of pagan structures and survived. In Anatolia at Miletus, for example, one such inscription did endure the ravages of time; emblazoned across a stone embedded in a tier of the city's great Roman theater is such a rare inscription, rendered in Greek, which proclaims that the section of the arena is the "Place of the Jews, Who Are Also the God-Fearers [theosebeis]"!

At Monastero, the suburb of the Roman glass-importing and manufacturing city of Aquileia referred to in Chapter 15, the ruins of the mosaic floor of the synagogue contain no less than thirty-two Latin and four Greek inscriptions interwoven into the overall design of the floor, providing some fifty donors' names.[49] The fact that the mosaic floor was that of a synagogue is borne out by one insertion in which the donor dedicates his gift to the Sabbath [*Sabaot*]. Three of the donor's names can be identified as definitely Jewish; many others are clearly of Eastern origin. There appears, however, one inscription that reads "*Victor Theosebes*," proclaiming clearly that the donor was a God-Fearer, and a Jew by choice.

The term *theosebeis*, used in this fashion, and other equivalent terms demonstrate that there are classifications of proselyte Jews as well as of Jews by ethnic origin. Feldman pointed out that a second-century inscription uses the phrase *theon sebon*, which also translates as "God-Fearers." The inscription indubitably separates Jews from proselytes in assigning *both* Jews and the God-Fearers as guardians of an enfranchised slave.

A spectacular find at Aphrodisias leaves no room for doubt. The inscription was unearthed in 1976; it unmistakably registers the existence in Aphrodisias of about 210 B.C.E. of two discrete communities, Jews and "God-Fearing" gentiles, *both* of whom were active supporters of and adherents to the synagogue. The excavator, Kenan T. Erim of New York University, assigned the publication of the inscription to Joyce Reynolds of Newnham College, Cambridge University. The stone appears to have been employed as a doorjamb.

Two separate lists are inscribed on the stone, characterized by the heading *ktistai*, designating "donors." The distinction between the two lists is unmistakable. The first, composed of fifty-five unmistakable, typically Jewish names such as Jacob, Manasses, Judas, Joseph and Reuben, are further identified as candymaker, bird seller, cattle fodder purveyor, and so forth. A space between the first and second list leads to the definitive heading *kai hosoi theosebeis* (*and* those who are God-Fearers), followed by a list of fifty-two names such as Zeno, Diogenes, Antiochos, Polychronios, Chrysippos, Appianos, Eutropios, Valerianos, and Athenogoras. All the names on the latter list, with the possible exception of one, are nonbiblical names. The first nine members are designated as city council members; the rest are professionals and artisans such as mason, marble worker, athlete, portrait painter, fuller, tax collector, carpenter.

The reverse side of the stone has a similar inscription, placed there as if to convince us of the accuracy of our interpretation of the obverse side. Three categories of donors are thereon inscribed: the eighteen names provided are of fourteen Jews, of two gentlemen named Samuel and Ioses who are separately described as proselytes, and two more, Emmonius and Antinonus, who are significantly characterized as *theosebeis*!

The synagogue at Sardis, located in the heart of Anatolia, was another spectacular find. It owes its survival and recovery largely because it stood at the heart of the Roman city and adjoined one of the greatest libraries of ancient times. The names of the donors in the mosaic floor and the shops lining one of the synagogue's outside walls testify to a dynamic, sizable Jewish community.

> The importance of the discovery of the Sardis synagogue is simply that it reveals a Jewish community of far greater wealth, power and self-confidence than the usual views of ancient Judaism would give us any right to expect. The older consensus ... (1) tends to concentrate on ancient Palestine, (2) bases itself on the abundant *literary* evidence, and (3) often assumes that after Jesus, Judaism is compromised and drops into the background, unimportant, impotent—an ancient Christian bias still marvelously alive today ... The abundant Sardis evidence challenges this consensus at nearly every point. ...[50]

The propensity of scholars to nit-pick at the understandably sparse evidence of a pervasive Jewish influence in the "classical" period can hardly compare to the vehemence with which ancient Roman and Greek writers railed against an influence which loomed threateningly large in their times. The pagan poet Claudius Rutulius Namatianus was, at the beginning of the fifth century, one of the last of the pagan writers to give vent to antipathy towards the Jews:

> Would that Judaea's folk had never at all been conquered,
> Would that Pompey and Titus their victories ne'er had won!
> Dead is the pest, yet onward creeps ever its poison.
> *And so the folk that was conquered now over its victors prevails.*[51]

16

The Jews under Roman Rule

The Second Diaspora

The ancient Jews did proselytize; therein lay the threat to authority, for the philosophy of the Jews was anti-autocratic at heart. Evidence of a missionary outreach of some importance has come down to us from a variety of sources. This "subversive" activity was persistent, and its libertarian effect was felt in Rome at an early period, a continuation of the rampant Judaization of the Greeks.

THE ROMAN RESPONSE

Rome reacted early and harshly to the insidious antiestablishmentarian influence of Jewish precepts. In 139 B.C.E. the praetor of Rome, Cornelius Hispalus, "compelled the Jews to return to their homes because they attempted to corrupt Roman morals through their cult of Jupiter Sabazius."[1] This event took place about a year after Simon, the Hasmonean ruler, delegated Numenius, son of Antiochus, and Antipater, son of Jason, as envoys to the Roman Senate to plead on behalf of the Jews. The confusion exhibited by the praetor regarding distinguishing the Sabbath and the Phrygian god (Jupiter) Sabazia may well have arisen from the circumstance that some of the proselytizing Jews came from Phrygia, where Sabazius was a god identified with Dionysus and Jupiter, and the similarity of the name induced a mistaken identification with the Jewish God. Whatever the reason for the confusion displayed by the praetor, clearly he, as well as the consuls of Rome, already felt at this early date that their social structure was being undermined by insidious Jewish ideology.

The Jews, however, were absolutely essential for the health of the Roman economy; the technology of the Near East was vital to Roman industry, and Jewish slaves and free artisans were a prime factor in the provision of the technological disciplines required for the maintenance of the Roman establishment. As Jewish numbers grew, so did their philosophy filter out into Roman society.

313

By the time of Seneca "The Philosopher" (end of the first century B.C.E. to 65 C.E.) the attitude of the defenders of Roman society had become vitriolic: "Meanwhile the customs of this accursed race have gained such influence that they are received throughout the world. The vanquished have given laws to their victors."[2]

The Roman poet and satirist Horace (65-8 B.C.E.), whose father began as a manumitted slave and rose to become a tax collector and thereby a rich estate owner, identified his interests at first with the Roman ruling class. After a stint in the army at the side of Brutus in Athens and as an officer at the disastrous battle of Phillipi, Horace fled back to Italy to find his property confiscated. Horace's poverty drove him into civil service and, as he himself reveals, to writing verses. Horace's misfortunes dampened his ardor for the Roman establishment and he turned to satire, which became so popular that he acquired the position of poet laureate. He expressed the compelling power of poets and poetry with that of Jewish proselytizing, and thereby bore witness to its effect:

> If you don't grant this,
> A great band of poets—for we are many—
> Will come to my aid and like the Jews
> Will just force you to join our crowd.[3]

The process of sympathizing with Judaic precepts did not diminish with the passage of time. About the end of the first century C.E., the Roman lawyer, satirist, and poet Juvenal, who despised Orientals in general (including "Greeklings"), and Jews and women in particular, was particularly vituperative regarding the Jews. Juvenal berated the "God-Fearers among the Jews," that is, those Gentiles who sympathized with Jewish ideology and supported Jewish institutions; he warned that this kind of cultural defection would inevitably lead to the full loss of their children to Judaism:

> Some have a father who reveres the Sabbath day,
> And worship nothing but the clouds and the heavenly spirit.
> They see no difference between the flesh of man and swine,
> Of which their fathers would eat, and presently are circumcised.
> Taught now to scorn Rome's laws,
> They learn, observe and honor Jewish law alone which Moses handed down to them
>   in secret scrolls,
> So as not to show the way to one of different faith
> And lead none but the circumcised to a fountain sought.
> This is the father's fault, who every seventh day rested and gave no other thought to
>   other things in life.

The impact of Judaic precepts persisted and began to penetrate all of Roman and Greek society. The Greek historian Dio Cassius (c. 155-230 C.E.) moved to Rome about 180 C.E. and became the legate, or military governor, of Dalmatia and Pannonia during a most critical period, after which he retired to the city of

Nicaea in Bithynia, where he had been born. Cassius was in a perfect position to observe the influence of Judaism in the Roman provinces as well as among the Romans. The nineteen of Cassius' eighty books on the *History of Rome* that have survived cover the critical period of 68 B.C.E. to 10 C.E. In them, Cassius describes with awe and with more than a modicum of admiration the self-destructive obstinacy of the Jews in refusing to defend themselves on the Sabbath even in defense of their holy city of Jerusalem.

> For it was on high ground and was fortified by a wall of its own and if they had continued defending it on all days alike, he [Pompey] could not have gotten possession of it. As it was, they made an exception of what are called the days of Saturn, and by doing no work at all on those days afforded the Romans an opportunity in this interval to batter down the wall.

What was even more significant in his account is the tenor of his continuing observations that Jewish tenets had become so pervasive "even among the Romans," that they identified themselves as Jews:

> The country had been named Judaea, and the people themselves Jews. I do not know how this title came to be given them, but it applies to all the rest of mankind, although of an alien race, who affect their customs. This class exists even among the Romans, and though often repressed has increased to a very great extent and has won its way to the right of freedom in its observances.[4]

Dio Cassius then relates with undisguised satisfaction on the one hand that "as the Jews flocked to Rome in great numbers and were converting many of the natives to their ways, he (Tiberius) banished most of them."[5] Cassius ruefully reports on the other hand that in the later onslaught against Jerusalem by Titus, much support and assistance was given to the Jews not only by Jews but by the Gentile sympathizers the Jews had won to their side both inside and outside the Roman Empire:

> Titus, who had been assigned to the war against the Jews, undertook to win them over by certain representations and promises; but, as they would not yield, he now proceeded to wage war upon them. The first battles were indecisive; then he got the upper hand and proceeded to besiege Jerusalem. . . . The Jews were also assisted by many of their countrymen from the region about *and by many who professed the same religion*, not only from the Roman Empire but from beyond the Euphrates; and these, also, kept hurling missiles and stones . . .[6]

Thus the process of Judaization, which had made great strides throughout the Hellenic Era, became a factor in the Roman military confrontation with the Jews. The God-fearing ones, the *theosobeis* and other sympathizers, joined the Jews in their endeavors to free themselves from foreign domination. The appeal of Jewish precepts remained effective even after the Romans had crushed the revolt of the Jews, and sympathetic ears were found at court no less than among the people. Passing on to the time of Domitian, Dio Cassius reports in another account:

> Domitian slew, along with many others, Flavius Clemens the Consul, although he was a cousin and had to wife Flavia Domitilla, who was a relative of the Emperor. The charge brought against them was that of atheism, a charge on which many others who had drifted into Jewish ways were condemned. Some of these were put to death, and the rest were deprived of their property.[7]

We have seen in the preceding chapter that the Roman biographer Suetonius concurred with that account, adding that the "atheists" were Gentiles who lived as Jews without acknowledging their faith and concealing it in order to evade the special tax on Jews. The talmudic version of this event is that the "God-fearing" senator confounded the intention of the decree that called for the execution of the Jews, first having himself circumcised and then committing suicide by taking poison. By killing himself, Flavius Clemens the proselyte negated the effect of his conviction inasmuch as a decree of the Senate could not be executed if a senator died between the passing of the decree and its execution. This account is one of several such conversions among the Roman hierarchy, as for example, another one that records that "Onkelos ben Klonikos, son of Titus's sister, embraced Judaism."[8]

By such accounts it is clear that Jewish influence was felt not only among the Gentile masses but on Gentiles in high places. Women could afford to be more open about their convictions, and so we find women scattered throughout the literature of the times, such as the above Flavia, who professed sympathy for, if not adherence to, Judaism. In Phrygia, we encounter a member of the aristocracy of Acmonia, Julia Severa, whose husband was L. Servinius Capito, as well as another member of the latter's family, L. Serninius Cornutus, who was a senator in Nero's time. Both were "sympathizers," if not outright proselytes. Another patrician woman, Fulvia, the wife of Saturninus, who was a close friend of the emperor Tiberius, became a proselyte. Pompinia Graecina, the wife of Aula Platis, the conqueror of Britain under Claudius, was "judged by her husband" as being a proselyte. Still another upper-class woman, Plautia, the wife of Publius Petronius, who was a proconsul of Asia and governor of Syria, was a proselyte. Other such converts are similarly recorded in talmudic and midrashic literature.[9] Andrew Sharf, who produced a scholarly study on Byzantine Jewry, found that at Antioch the pagan interest in Judaism carried on well into the Christian Era: "In the fourth century, listening to Jewish preachers became fashionable among the upper classes, particularly among the women."[10]

Porphyry (233–c.305 C.E.), a native of Tyre and a Neoplatonist, had an intense interest in Judaism. After studying in Athens and Rome he concluded that asceticism and knowledge of God would bring about purification of the soul and salvation. While far from being a proselyte, his writings are replete with amazement at the staying and swaying power of Judaic precepts while expressing utter bewilderment at non-Jews who accepted Christian deviation from basic concepts.

JEWS, CHRISTIANS, AND THE EMPEROR JULIAN

Porphyry's admiration for Jewish comportment if not Jewish philosophy is matched by none other than that of Julian (331-363), the "apostate emperor." The teacher and the emperor present parallel arguments regarding the deviationist Christians; while both criticized many of the precepts of Judaism, they admired the principled deportment of the Jews and credited the Jews with being a legitimate nation, albeit a subjected nation within a nation. Their polemics are largely directed at the "Galileans," or Christians, who had achieved official status under Constantine.

Julian was born in Constantinople, studied Greek philosophy for a few months in Athens, from which city he was summoned to Italy to marry Helena, the emperor's sister, and to assume the rank of Caesar. His personal courage and severe simplicity of life endeared him to the soldiers under his command to such a degree that the emperor considered him a threat. An attempt to split up the army under Julian's command led to their insurgency; the soldiers proclaimed Julian Augustus, and followed him into Constantinople. Along the way Julian declared himself a pagan, and in the reforms he instituted at Constantinople the Christians were stripped of some of their privileges, and some of the restrictions that had been placed on the Jews were removed.

Although Julian practiced tolerance, he was frank in expressing profound disdain for the Christians:

> Why is it, I repeat, that after deserting us you do not accept the laws of the Jews or abide by the sayings of Moses? . . . Why in your diet are you not as pure as the Jews, and why do you say we ought to eat everything "even as the green herb," putting your faith in Peter . . .[11] If you had not at any rate paid heed to their teachings, you would not have fared altogether ill . . . but now it has come to pass that like leeches you have sucked the worst blood from the source and have left the purer.[12]

The Christian attribution of the woes of the Jews to a refusal to accept Jesus spurred Julian to respond cryptically for the Jews: "Nay, the Galileans answer, they refused to hearken unto Jesus. What? How was it then that this hard-hearted and stubborn-necked people hearkened unto Moses?"

In a letter written from the East to Theodorus (*Ad Theodorum*), Julian lamented about the weak hold traditional Roman religion had on his Gentile subjects, expressed a profound perplexity at the potency of Judaic religious canons, and exhibited a lack of understanding regarding Jewish rejection of "other gods":

There is among us a great indifference about the gods and all reverence for the heavenly powers has been driven out by impure and vulgar luxury. I always secretly lamented this state of things. For I saw that those whose minds were turned to the doctrines of the Jewish religion are so ardent in their belief that they would choose to die for it, and to endure utter want and starvation rather than taste pork . . . these Jews are in part god-fearing, seeing that they revere a god who is truly most powerful and most good and governs this world of sense, and, as I well know, is worshiped by us under other names. They act, as is right and seemly, in my opinion, if they do not transgress other laws; but in this one thing they err in that, while reserving their deepest devotion for their one god, they do not conciliate the other gods also.

It is important to realize that Julian was brought up as a Christian, and his reaction reflected the attitude of a large proportion of Roman society, which accepted his reforms with equanimity. These reforms were, however, inimical to the newly created Christian hierarchy. Julian's letter to the Alexandrians (_Ad Alexandrinos_) expresses his chagrin at the ready acceptance of some Romans of the Christianity imposed previously upon Rome by his brother, Constantine:

I am overwhelmed with shame. I affirm it by the gods, O men of Alexandria, to think that even a single Alexandrian can admit that he is a Galilean. The forefathers of the genuine Hebrew were the slaves of the Egyptians long ago, but in these days, men of Alexandria, you who conquered the Egyptians—for your founder was the conqueror of Egypt—submit yourselves, despite your sacred traditions, in willing slavery to men who set at naught the teachings of their ancestors.

It is not surprising, therefore, that sympathetic Julian acted to relieve the Jews of the odious burdens placed upon them. His letter to the community of Jews apologizes for his brother's actions and attributes them to the influence of the Christians, whom he depicts as "barbarians in mind and godless in soul."

By far the most burdensome thing in the yoke of your slavery, even more than in times past, has been the fact that you were subjected to unauthorized ordinances and had to contribute an untold amount of money to the accounts of the treasury. Of this I used to see many instances with my own eyes, and I have learned of much more, by finding the records which have been preserved against you. Moreover, when a tax was about to be levied again I prevented it, and compelled the impiety of such obloquy to cease here; and I threw into the fire the records against you that were stored in my desks; so that it is no longer possible for anyone to aim against you such a reproach of impiety. My brother Constantinus of honored memory was not so much responsible for these wrongs of yours as were the men who used to frequent his table, barbarians in mind, godless in soul. These I seized with my own hands and put them to death by thrusting them into the pit, that not even a memory of their destruction might still linger among us. And since I wish that you should prosper yet more, I have admonished my brother Iulus your most venerable patriarch that the levy which is said to exist among you should be prohibited, and that no one is any longer to have the power to oppress the masses of your people by such exactions; so that everywhere you may have the security of mind, and in the enjoyment of my reign . . . may offer more fervid prayers for my reign to the Most High God, the Creator, who has deigned to crown me with his own immaculate hand.[13]

History twists and turns. It was the record of the Judaic impact on civilization, the record of the vast contribution these harried people had made to the technological—no less than to the religious, moral, and ethical—evolution of civilization that was finally consigned to the fire, and not the record of their oppressors. The ruling class, and such bureaucratic hierarchies as had been created with the Christian church, are not prone to engaging in the exceptional unbigoted indulgence that Julian exhibited. Unbridled, driving ambition has molded more history than has passive tolerance; greed overwhelms charity. The voracious appetite for lavish luxury, the avid aspiration for wealth, and in particular, the insatiable lust for power, drive men inexorably from dominance to intolerance. Rulers cannot long endure precepts that question the legitimacy of their power. Divine rights are ultimately invoked, mandating unequivocal obeisance, and a priestly class amenable to legitimizing the ruler's divine rights in turn gains royal legitimization. The Christians accepted the principle of secular power by divine right by investing it into a church and a papacy, which was in turn empowered to impart it to kings. Kings, therefore, expediently accepted and then promoted Christianity.

It is Constantine, therefore, who should be considered the "apostate emperor" and not Julian, who insisted that in the process of abandoning his pagan principles, his brother had expediently legitimized a deviant, bastard religion which, in order to gain sanction, discarded the basic tenets it had professed as its foundation. The Christians, however, had obtained a winning position in the arena of power. The interests of emperors and ruling classes cannot be sustained on egalitarian principles, and those rulers who succeeded Julian found Constantine's apostolic acceptance of Christianity to their advantage.

IN THE AFTERMATH OF JULIAN'S RULE

The assumption of human divinity was fundamentally anathematic to the Jews; it was regarded not merely as unacceptable but as blasphemous. The rejection of the principle of rule by divine right was corollary to that precept. The venomous repression of the Jews returned, accompanied by a ruthless attempt at the obliteration of all traces of Jewish influence. Hundreds of synagogues were destroyed throughout the Roman Empire along with their archives. Churches were erected over their ruins, the better to bury the incipient threat of a religion that denied the inherent right of any king or class to rule over others, a philosophy that promulgated universalism and projected the concept of an unknowable creative universal force that refused to relegate power to any human being over another.

In spite of the Christian and Byzantine repressions that followed the emperor Julian, the evidence of a vibrant, productive Judaic presence breaks through the calumny heaped upon a long-suffering people. The testimony of the emperor Hadrian Augustus regarding the grudging tolerance that had to be granted to the Jews because of the dependence of the Roman economy on their skills will be recalled from his communication to his consul at Alexandria. From "Hadrian Augustus to Servianus the Consul, Greeting," it begins, and characterizes the Jews of Alexandria as:

> A folk most seditious, most deceitful, most given to injury; but their city [Alexandria] is prosperous, rich and fruitful, and in it no one is idle. Some are blowers of glass, others makers of paper, all are at least weavers of linen or seem to belong to one craft or another; the lame have their occupations, the wounded have theirs, the blind have theirs, and not even those whose hands are crippled are idle.

The obstinate adherence to their God and to tradition served to deliver the Jews from religious and cultural destruction; their inordinate skills and erudition delivered them from national destruction. Had their participation in industry not been vital and often indispensable, their religion and culture would have perished along with their national existence. Attempts at the utter obliteration of the Jews were continually foiled by a deference to the need for their expertise, a pragmatism only too well expressed by Hadrian in the above-quoted communication to his consul. It was not merely Judaic diligence that was in demand; the despised Jews possessed unique skills to which other peoples were not privy and which the conquerors, even if they were so endowed, could not deign to exercise.

ROMAN ATTITUDES TOWARD THE ARTISAN

Conquerors do not aspire to artisanship; conquering peoples disdain to engage in manual labor. Arts and crafts are regarded by "master races" as odious occupations relegated to inferior peoples. The product is admired; the practice is scorned. Among the privileges accruing to conquerors is the power to oblige the vanquished, whether as slaves, serfs, or freemen, to toil at manual labor. The Romans were no different in this regard than were the Greeks, whose culture they had absorbed. When it became desirable to maintain a facade of superiority over subject peoples, Roman laws were instituted to preclude the Roman upper classes from engaging in crafts and to dissuade any Roman citizen from so doing, for to do so was to stoop to the level of a slave or, at best, to the demeaning social status of a foreign laborer.

The rigorous, sweaty toil to which the smiths bent their backs, the malodorous trade of the slaughterers and tanners, the dangerous activity of miners, the ceaseless patience of the weavers, and of all the other arts and crafts that constitute industry, were relegated to slaves and foreigners. The Roman disinclination to soil one's hands was especially true when it came to abjuring participation in as difficult a discipline as making glass and glassware. The art of glassmaking is a prime example of the many skills and technologies introduced from the East by artisans who arrived as slaves or indentured workers or as entrepreneurs who followed the Roman legions into primitive regions.

The Romans, in fact, were entirely ignorant of the process of making glass at the time their armies thrust into the Near East. Despite the "Roman" label ubiquitously applied to glass of the subsequent period in archaeological collections and museums everywhere, even the glassmakers of the later Roman period were unlikely to have been Romans. The best that can be claimed for the ancient Romans is that glass and glassware was produced in the Roman provinces during the period of Roman rule; it was produced in Rome itself by foreigners during the last half of Rome's existence as an imperial power. Consumption, not creativity, was the concern of Roman gentlemen. Their primary objective was the accumulation of luxurious surroundings and ostentatious accoutrements befitting their noble status; they had, after all, loosed rivers of blood for the right to have the world support their privileged position.

The distinction between plebeian Romans and foreigners dimmed with the development of the Republic, but lower-class Romans nevertheless strove for noble similitude as befits a Roman, if not a nobleman. A Roman household was considered unworthy of the name without its retinue of slaves. Each middle-class household harbored a staff of at least eight servants, and the upper classes engaged hundreds and even thousands of slaves and other laborers. The *familia Caesaris* numbered no less than twenty thousand souls. Even the Roman proletariat retained servants, and one of the bitter complaints of professionals of low status was that they were unable to retain enough of a corps of servants to sustain their Roman station in life. Libanius, the head of a philosophical school in Antioch, complained that the teachers under his wing were so poorly paid that they could afford no more than three or four slaves apiece.

Roman society was based on slavery. Traffic in slaves was one of the largest and most profitable of Roman enterprises. Up to 50,000 captives were taken in a single campaign; they were considered booty to be shipped off for sale throughout the empire. No less than ten thousand slaves were daily sold off the auction blocks of the slave clearing houses at Delos and later at Ostia, which impelled the Roman lawyer and satirist Juvenal to remark that "the Syrian Orontes [river] has poured into the Tiber." Caesar is said to have taken nearly half a million captives in his nine years of campaigning in Gaul. Other Roman campaigners were no less avaricious slave-takers: sixty thousand Carthaginians were taken in the year 146; Epirotes enslaved one hundred fifty thousand in the year 167.

The list goes on. It has been computed that the slave population in Italy alone during the reign of Claudius amounted to as much as twenty million, of which approximately four hundred thousand served in the city of Rome. As with the Greeks, Roman intellectuals would have nothing to do with anything that had practical value. The aristocrats, the members of the ruling classes, would have nothing to do with the grimy, sweaty folk who built their houses, made their shoes, fashioned their armor, and ground their grain.[14] The Romans harbored no greater regard for the status of the artisan than had the Greeks, nor did they regard commerce (unless it was on a grand scale) as a enterprise to be undertaken by Romans. Roman riches were earned in the first place by the looting of the peoples they conquered, by taxing the subjected peoples, and thereafter by exploiting them both as freemen and slaves. Romans became soldiers, administrators, or the owners or landlords of farms. A proper Roman was obliged to abjure participation in both production and the marketplace. Land-management was recognized as a suitable occupation of a Roman, but only so long as slaves or serfs, or on occasion, hired help, sweated at the work to be done. In Roman, as in modern times, only "gentlemen farmers" are accorded a berth in "genteel society"; no place is provided in it for "gentlemen merchants," "gentlemen artisans," "gentlemen manufacturers," or even of "gentlemen capitalists."

Hiring help to produce a product or profit was strictly off limits for a patrician. Even the propriety of a land-owner to contract for the sale of minerals, timber or clay was brought under question, particularly if the products so sold were processed into saleable products. The *Theodosian Code* addresses the very question of usufructuary rights and brings it into focus. The code was intended to exempt estate management from taxation, but when Constantine introduced the *collatio Lustralis*, a tax on sales, "Even the Roman bureaucrats and lawyers were uncertain about its status; witness the disagreement among the jurists . . . as to whether claybeds were counted among the *instrumenta* of the estate.[15]

A Roman landowner could grant usufructuary rights to brickmakers or potters to clay deposits found on his estates, for example, but to contract for the purchase and sale of the products made of that clay raised the question of whether the clay was a product of the soil, in which case the sale of products made from it was an acceptable Roman activity, or whether its sale constituted a commercial enterprise unrelated to farming, in which case such sale had to be renounced as being incompatible with Roman status. It was only in farming that Romans legitimately entered into the productive process, in which case the labor was still performed by slaves, indentured workers, or on occasion, by hired help. Roman "gentlemen farmers" would under no circumstance be caught wielding tools other than weapons of war.

There were, in fact, laws prohibiting Roman aristocracy even from hiring craftsmen for the purpose of selling their products. Members of the senatorial class were disbarred altogether from participating in commercial activities by a law passed as far back as 218 B.C.E. A noble Roman who would stoop to such lowly enterprise could be stripped of his plutocratic privileges. Such prohibitions did not, however, prevent greedy Roman aristocrats from surreptitiously participating in equestrian corporations as silent partners, nor even from investing secretly "in the name of a freedman or other client."[16]

The aristocrats delighted in taking to task others of their class whom they caught engaged in mundane commercial activities. Sometimes this activity took a bizarre turn, as in the case in which Plutarch reported on certain unsavory commercial activity on the part of Cato, whom he decries as "given much to the desire of gain." Plutarch declares that Cato was "of the opinion that the greatest cause of misbehavior in slaves were their sexual passions," in satisfaction of which Cato stooped so low as to arrange "for the males to consort with the females at a fixed price."[17]

The Roman upper classes, or orders, were warrior officers, bureaucrats, plantation owners, noble and pseudonoble parasites. The native Roman lower classes were uneducated, impoverished, and unskilled. The slaves captured in foreign campaigns were of diverse levels of technical competence: those captured in England, Gaul, and elsewhere in Western Europe were suited for simple labor, primitive crafts, or work on the farms, few being literate, educated or possessing sophisticated skills; among those captured in the East were literate, educated men of high achievement, and artisans of all kinds.

Among plebeians no less than patricians, Roman sentiments regarding manual work were comparable to those of modern Americans toward ditch-diggers or stoop farm labor, occupations consigned to immigrants from starving nations or to illegal immigrants from Mexico. Cicero wrote a didactic treatise in 44 B.C.E. for his 21-year-old son in which he apposes Roman precepts to those of the Greeks:

> Now in regard to trade and other means of livelihood, which ones are to be considered becoming to a gentleman and which ones are vulgar, we have been taught, in general, as follows . . . .: Vulgar are the means of livelihood of all hired workmen whom we pay for mere manual labor, not for artistic skill; for in their case the very wages they receive are a pledge of their slavery. . . . These privileges Xenophon, a pupil of Socrates, has set forth most happily in his book entitled *Oeconomicus*. When I was about your present age, I translated it from Greek to Latin.[18]

Cicero emphasized that any Roman engagement in manual labor was demeaning, for "all craftsmen are engaged in a lowly art; for no workshop can have anything appropriate to a free man." Cicero reluctantly concedes that large-scale, wholesale trade and such professions as architecture, medicine, and teaching are permissible for a "gentleman." Archimedes (287-212 B.C.E.), one of the most celebrated of ancient mathematicians, is an apt example of the fact that even those professions were regarded with distaste by the supercilious Greeks and Romans. Archimedes created catapults that hurled monstrous boulders capable of crushing defensive walls as well as the people who manned them, engineered cranes whose "huge claws fastened upon ships and lifted them right out of the water, even a brobdingnagian burning glass that could set them on fire from a distance."[19] Archimedes was reticent to boast of his considerable accomplishments as a designer of these fiendish war machines. It was not their destructive capabilities that disturbed Archimedes' conscience but the fact that designing worldly items was beneath the dignity of an intellectual!

The modern world proclaims its appreciation of the Greek scientist's magnificent accomplishments. Archimedes was, however, thoroughly ashamed of his engagement in a lowly exercise of his intellect, albeit one that advanced imperial ambitions. Plutarch reports that "[Archimedes] never wanted to leave behind a book on the subject but viewed the work of the engineer and every single art connected with everyday needs as ignoble and fit only for an artisan. He devoted his ambition only to those studies in which beauty and subtlety are present uncontaminated by necessity."[20]

Equestrians, just under senators in rank, and all other classes or "orders" of middle and upper Roman society, were constricted as to the type of gainful occupations they could employ while maintaining their dignity and social standing. Cicero, in his above-quoted *On Duties*, makes the circumscriptions clear; not only can no artisan's "workshop have anything liberal about it" but carrying on service of any kind is to be especially spurned: "Least [gentlemanly] of all are those trades which cater to sensual pleasures: Fishmongers, butchers, cooks, and poulterers, and fishermen."

Slaves were not relegated merely to menial tasks nor restricted to crafts; they performed as trusted stewards, musicians, geometricians, grammarians, managers of farms and estates, masters of ships, and even as money-lending bankers.[21] Virtually all the creative work of the Roman realm was performed by foreigners, whether slave or free, and their activity extended to the conduct of daily business in all its aspects. The station of a noble Roman citizen was no less compromised by his engaging in common trade than by engaging in manual labor.

"CAPTIVE JUDAH" AND THE MONUMENTS OF ROME

The vainglorious Roman conquerors established themselves as masters by flaunting their prowess immediately after Roman forces under Pompey took Jerusalem on the holy Jewish Atonement Day in 63 B.C.E. The Jewish king Aristobolus and his family were paraded ignominiously through Rome in a triumphal procession, along with a host of other captive Jews. Thousands of the Jewish slaves brought from "captive Judah" (as an inscription emblazoned on a Roman coin boastfully memorialized the defeat and enslavement of the Jewish population) were set to work erecting great structures dedicated to the memory of the defeat of the nation from which they had been torn.

At least two of these impressive monuments still stand as witness to the engineering skills and craftsmanship of the Jewish slaves who were consigned to their construction under the whips of their Roman masters. The majestic Arch of Titus was erected at the focal point of the Roman Forum as a permanent memorial to the triumph of the three Flavians over the Jews. Carved three-dimensionally onto its face is the dramatic scene in which the Romans are hauling away the rich booty looted from the Temple of Jerusalem.

No fewer than fourteen thousand stalwart Jews are recorded as having built the colossal amphitheater renowned worldwide as the Colosseum, and having erected it in a phenomenally short time. Countless millions of admiring tourists have been enthralled by the magnificent structure, marching around its tiers, imagining the gory scenes that took place in its arena, but giving no thought to the hapless Jews whose blood, sweat, and tears are soaked into its stones.

At least one more splendid structure was known to have been built under duress by Jewish slaves for a dedication to their defeat; it was a building that was specifically built to house the great collection of sacred vessels and other artifacts looted from the Jerusalem Temple. It was sardonically dubbed the Temple of Peace by the Romans, and no longer exists, for it was destroyed by fire, and the treasures of the Temple disappeared in the flames of the conflagration.

Millions of Jewish artisans did leave their imprint throughout the Roman Empire, and their identity is no more evident there than it is in the structures dominating ancient Rome. Jews had already been part of the scene on the Italian peninsula from time immemorial, as traders accompanying the Canaanite seafarers on their rounds of the Mediterranean and as residents of the communities established on its shores. The Severians were an ancient congregation clearly established during the time of the Severi in Rome itself, dating back to about 200 B.C.E.[22] An early documentary reference to Jewish presence in Rome in 151 B.C.E. derives, ironically, from having been banished out of Rome and Italy, an event that took place at a time "in which an embassy from the Jewish prince Simon was honorably received by the Roman Senate and dismissed with assurances of friendship.."[23] It was the "corrupting influence" of Roman morals by Jewish religious propaganda that brought about the exclusion of the Jews from Rome, a consideration the Romans did not apply to the import of Jewish slaves thereafter.

TRASTEVERE: THE JEWISH QUARTER OF ROME

Some scholars have estimated that by the first half of the first century the free Jewish population of Rome was at least twenty thousand.[24] Other sources appraise the numbers of free Jews resident in Rome at the turn of the Common Era to as many as forty thousand. Josephus related that when the Jewish embassy made a petition to the Roman emperor to remove Herod's dynasty after the tyrant's death in 3 B.C.E.: "It was escorted on its way to the imperial palace by a crowd of eight thousand Jews." To this resident population some tens of thousands of slaves were added after the Roman victory. The Jewish population continued to grow rapidly for the next century as a result of continued manumission and immigration.

> It was from this stratum that the Roman proletariat and its petty bourgeoisie for the most part was recruited. It was from this stratum that the Roman Jews predominantly belonged . . . these humble immigrants settled by the Tiber and especially in the Trastevere, or right bank. There the boats which brought goods from Ostia docked; there lived harbor and transport workers, boatmen, shopkeepers, numerous artisans. There were sailor's taverns and all trades and industries which could not be admitted into the city.[25]

At least thirteen congregations dating from the time of the early Roman Empire have been identified, chiefly from Greek inscriptions found on the tombstones. One of the oldest of these synagogues stood in the heart of the area of Rome known as *Trastevere* (Transtiberis), literally "across the River Tiber." Trastevere was the Jewish quarter in the southeastern part of Rome, a dreary, sooty slum area with crooked streets and dingy workshops. This was the area in which industry was concentrated, an area in which smoke from the furnaces of the smiths and the glassmakers blackened the skies, where the odoriferous industries of unguent manufacturing and the tanning of leather assailed the nostrils of the Roman overlords who had to pass over a bridge that spanned the Tiber and then through the Jewish quarter to reach the gardens of Caesar outside the city.[26]

The bridge was known as the *Quattro Capi* but was more commonly referred to as the *Pons Judaeorum*, "The Jew's Bridge," a name it retained through the Middle Ages. The road over the bridge led to the aptly named *Via del Pianto*, the "Street of Lamentation," which rammed through the heart of the *Vicus Judaeorum*, "The Jewish District," the area that later became referred to as the Ghetto.[27] The road terminated at the *Porta Portese*, or "The Gate to the Port," in the foreground of which and still within the Trastevere district was an area known as the *Campo Judaeorum*, or "Jew's Field," until the seventeenth century. Industrial traffic passed from and through the Jewish quarter, for the district was traversed by the Appian and Latin roads, and was the bridgehead for communication "with the great harbors of Puteoli and Brunisium, with Capua and Naples, with the seaside resorts and country estates at Baiae and its environs."[28]

The district endured continuously as both the center of Jewish life and as the craft center of Rome for a millennium and a half. Even when the Jews were proscribed from engaging in their traditional occupations elsewhere in Christendom the arts were allowed to linger in the Jewish quarter of Rome, and Jewish vocations endured in that squalid environment.

In the year 1019 Pope Benedictus VIII designated the area *fundum integrum, qui vocatur Judaeorum*, "the whole district, named after the Jews,"[29] and chartered it to the bishopric of Portus, whose jurisdiction extended over the islands of the Tiber and Trastevere. Although the Jews were not confined to a special quarter until the institution of the Ghetto in 1556, the majority had always inhabited and labored in Trastevere. In that year all the Jews of Rome were forcefully confined to a portion of that quarter by the cruel Paul IV Caraffa, a pontiff hated by the Christians hardly less than by the Jews, who referred to him as the reincarnation of the biblical Haman. It was not until 1885, under King Victor Immanuel, that the first steps toward the abolishment of the ghettos were taken.

THE JEWS IN OTHER REGIONS OF THE EMPIRE

The ports that served Rome harbored active Jewish communities: an ancient synagogue that served a sizable Jewish proletariat community was uncovered at the port of Ostia. The Jewish workforce was an important factor in the importing and industrial activities of the area, just as it was at the Adriatic end of Italy at Aquileia. A great number of Jews are known to have been buried at the Roman harbor cities of Puteoli and Portus by virtue of their distinguishing names, although such evidence is scarcely indicative of the total population, inasmuch as the Jews who assumed Greek or Roman names are thereby indistinguishable. Most of the trade with Alexandria and the East into the Roman area took place through the ports of Puteoli. The burials "indicate callings which have to do with commerce and navigation."[30] In Puteoli still another synagogue existed in the first century of the Christian Era,[31] and the important seaport had a street of glassmakers and a quarter for incense makers, another distinctly Jewish trade.

Mining and metalworking were two of the industries in which Jews were heavily involved from the time the emperor Tiberius sent four thousand Jewish youths as slaves to work the mines of Sicily, as described in Chapter 15. Many of the Jewish slaves were manumitted, according to Philo, "for having been brought to Italy as captives, they were freed by their owners and [were] not forced to violate any of their ancestral customs." Jews were engaged on Sicily from that time forward in mining silver and iron and in metalworking until the early Middle Ages, when Spanish persecution of the Jews penetrated into the island. It is only by virtue of that persecution that we learn how inclusive was the involvement of the Jews in the metallurgy of the region from the Roman time forward, for the laborers who toiled for more than a millennium to supply the Romans with metal weapons, tools, and other artifacts remain faceless and nameless.

Roman soldiers who had completed their stint in the military were rewarded for service by grants of land on which they could establish their estate. The slaves they captured in war, or purchased in the marketplace, provided the labor forces of the small farms no less than of the *latifundia*, the Roman plantations. The autochthonous population, who were in large measure peasants or backwoodsmen, were put to tilling the soil and serving both the newly enfranchised Roman landowners and the local officials whose allegiance to Rome was purchased with a bribe of Roman citizenship and a continuation of their privileged social position. The needs of the new nobility stimulated an increase in imported goods, for a market was created that could not be served by the local, unskilled population. In addition to the supply of army gear for the military garrisons that were implanted throughout the Roman Empire, the villa furnishings, clothes and the accoutrements of luxurious living were in great demand by the members of the reconstituted establishment.

Jewish presence in the areas that had been opened for settlement by the Roman legions begins with the importation of slaves.

According to a chronicle the most ancient Jews in the Rhine district are said to have been the descendants of the legionnaires who took part in the destruction of the Temple. From the vast horde of Jewish prisoners, the Vangioni had chosen the most beautiful women, had brought them back to their stations on the shores of the Rhine and the Main, and had compelled them to minister to the satisfaction of their desires. The children thus begotten of Jewish and Germanic parents were brought up by their mothers in the Jewish faith, their fathers not troubling about them. It is these children who are said to have been the founders of the first Jewish communities between Worms and Mayence. It is certain that a Jewish congregation existed in the Roman colony, the city of Cologne, long before Christianity had been raised to power by Constantine.[32]

An immigration of artisans whose sophisticated skills were novel to the backward hinterlands of Europe ensued, and Easterners became conspicuous in the transalpine regions leading across the Dolomites from Aquileia into Pannonia and Nordicum, and up through the Seine and Rhine valleys as far as Cologne. Worldly-wise entrepreneurs trained in the Persian and Alexandrian milieus, whose contacts were indispensable for the purpose, and Eastern artisans set up their enterprises in strategic market areas and supplied their wares to the burgeoning class of Roman and non-Roman overlords. Communities of Near Eastern artisans and merchants sprang up along the routes through the Roman-occupied territories, reaching as far as Cologne. The ruins of two early synagogues in that city situated on the banks of the Rhine at the limit of the Roman Empire, attest to the importance of the Jewish presence.

Even Jewish warriors were part of the flotsam and jetsam of Jews who were captured, enslaved, and indentured into the Roman legions, but the most notable effect of the dispersion of the Jews was the appearance of a host of sophisticated disciplines coincident with the establishment of Jewish colonies and communities. They became the doctors and the accountants, the smiths and the weavers, the miners and the engineers, the tradesmen who traveled the Roman roads and the navigators who plied the seas.

> The Jewish merchants whose business pursuits brought them from Alexandria or Asia Minor to Rome and Italy, the Jewish warriors whom the emperors Vespasian and Titus, the conquerors of Judea, had dispersed as prisoners throughout the Roman provinces, found their way, voluntarily or involuntarily into Gaul and Iberia. . . . The Gallic Jews, whose first settlement was in the district of Arles, enjoyed the full rights of Roman citizenship, whether they arrived as merchants or fugitives, with the peddlers pack or in the garb of slaves. . . . In the Frankish kingdom founded by Clovis, the Jews dwelt in Auvergne (Arvena), in Carcassonne, Arles, Orleans, and as far north as Paris and Belgium. Numbers of them resided in the old Greek port of Marseilles, and Beziers (Biterrae) and so many of them dwelt in the province of Narbonne that a mountain near that city of that name was called *Mons Judaicus*. . . . The Jews of Frankish and Burgundian kingdoms carried on agriculture, trade and commerce without restraint; they navigated the seas and rivers in their own ships. They also practiced medicine, and the advice of the Jewish physicians was sought even by the clergy, who probably did not care to rely entirely on the miraculous healing powers of the saints and of relics. They were also skilled in the use of weapons of war, and took an active part in the battles between Clovis and Theodoric's generals before Arles (508 c.e.).[33]

New technologies were introduced and those skills that existed in primitive forms were enhanced. In Gaul, for example, the Germanic peoples had fired their pottery on open wood fires until the Celts, moving across the continent, introduced the use of kilns from the East. Ironworking had also been introduced, and owing to the ubiquitous presence of iron ore throughout northern Europe and the vast forests that provided an abundant supply of charcoal, almost every village built small, crude, but adequate facilities for the smelting and working of iron, mainly for the production of tools and decorative ware. The advent of Eastern artisans brought about a dramatic increase in the production of ironworking at the turn of the Common Era, and especially during the first century c.e. Glassmaking was introduced, first as imports from the East, and finally by artisans who settled in the area.

W. A. Thorpe, the English glass historian, reports that the Semitic artisans who had settled along the route of the Roman legions established "their quarters in the great industrial cities . . . they combined a willingness to migrate, a fervent sense of parenthood, a racial solidarity, a genius for selling, semitic qualities that no other glassmakers ever possessed." Thorpe made a study of these communities and found that by the late Roman period:

> [In] Nice, Marseille, Orleans, Bourges, Treves, and above all, Paris, industrial capital was controlled by the Semites. . . . Their activities were not confined to the black-coat business of bankers, ship-owners, money-lenders, and wholesale produce merchants. They were the leaders in the professions of law and medicine and in the arts of jeweler, goldsmith, and silversmith.[34]

The equally prestigious German glass historian, Axel von Saldern, concurs with Thorpe, noting that an efficient industry was established by Jewish glassmakers who had emigrated from Palestine in the first century in "Naples, Rome, northern Italy, south-eastern France, Cologne and other cities along the Rhine.[35]

Thorpe points out that the decline of the art of glassmaking and that of the numerous other disciplines introduced into Gaul by the "Semites" was brought about by

> the growth of anti-Semitism in the Merovingian Gaul during the 5th and 6th centuries. This movement had been made familiar in its religious aspect as a conflict of the Christian church with the Jews, but the real issue was racial and commercial. The Germans who invaded Gaul discovered that the capital of the country was largely in the hands of the orientals, in some trades their superiors as craftsmen, and invariably their superiors as men of business. . . . The glass industry suffered with the other rackets [crafts controlled by the Jews] of the Semites [and] high class models disappear when anti-semitic propaganda was most intense.[36]

The dependence of the Roman establishment on Jews for both locally-made and imported artifacts led St. Jerome to complain bitterly that the skilled trades were the means by which the Semites "captured the Roman world."[37] This humiliating dependency spurred the church to propose a humbler attitude toward manual labor; a new policy was established and a program was launched to replace the stiff-necked Eastern artisans. Monasticism was fostered and a regimen of manual labor introduced, a process that served as one of the means by which the manual arts could be placed under church control. The intention was not only to restore respectability to the artisan but also to remove the disrepute under which manual labor had suffered through all of ancient times. From the beginning, however, the monks had been mindful of the Hebrew tradition that work was in accordance with God's commandments.[38]

Manual labor finally achieved a modicum of respectability in the Christian period. The guilds were formed and put under the "protection" of specialized Christian saints; members were required to be, or to become, Christians. The church did not relish dependence on Eastern artisans who stubbornly refused to relinquish their religion or who practiced it surreptitiously when circumstances forced them to assume a Christian facade. The Jews were driven from most manual trades; whatever Jewish artisans remained in the guilds ostensibly converted to Christianity. Conversion was, however, unevenly enforced because no substitutes existed for certain skilled artisans. Jewish glassmakers were given specific exemption from conversion as a condition for continuing in their occupation:

> In Cologne . . . where the guilds succeeded in ultimately barring Jews from almost all of industrial occupations, they still allowed them to become glaziers, probably because no other qualified personnel was available. This exception was reminiscent of the Greek glassblowers in seventh-century France who claimed to produce glass as well as the Jews did.[39]

Glassmaking was a unique exception to the otherwise rigidly enforced restrictive edicts that issued forth with insistent regularity from a church that had become powerful enough to impose its strictures upon society and to bend the nobility to its purpose. The dark age that descended upon Europe was accompanied by recurrent repressions of the Jews; time and time again Jews were expelled from various areas, only to be recalled when the economies of the regions suffered adversity by their absence. Some of the glassmakers eventually converted; others sought more favorable conditions elsewhere, and never returned.

THE JEWISH ATTITUDE TOWARD LABOR: A FINAL WORD

The Jews, far from decrying engagement in physical labor, esteemed all creative vocations: physical, mental, and spiritual. The admonishment recited repeatedly in every Jewish household and in every synagogue, "Forget not that we were all once slaves in Egypt," serves as an enduring reminder of the dignity of labor and as a rebuke to those who would set themselves above the "common" laborer. The sages proclaimed that "work is a great, strong foundation of Torah, a precondition to the study of Torah, and of greater value than God-fearing." This maxim was illustrated in no uncertain terms by Rabbi Yohanan Ben-Zakai, who declared that "if a man is planting a tree and is told that the Messiah has come, he must first complete the planting and only then go to meet the Redeemer."

The *Tannaim* (scholars of the Mishnah) and the *Amoraim* (scholars of the Talmud) not only preached combining work with Torah study, they practiced it. The sages of the great universities of Babylon and Jerusalem labored proudly at various trades to earn their daily sustenance. Teaching was not considered an activity for which compensation was required; teaching the Torah was a privilege for which remuneration was unnecessary. This principle was woven permanently into the body of talmudic practice. "Torah is not a spade" was the precept practiced by the sages as they eked out a living by creative labor. Prospective scholars were enjoined to engage in even such menial trades as skinning carcasses in the *shuk*, the ritual slaughterhouse, over dependence on public funds. An ancient and oft-repeated rabbinic maxim placed man within the context of divinic, continued creativity: "He who is productive so that the world's work might go on, has a share in God's creation."

"God, after all," it was argued, "was the ultimate artisan; it was through His *labor* that the world was created; He earned a rest on the Sabbath, setting an example for humankind."

Abbreviations Used throughout Notes and Bibliography

AA	Antichita Altoadriatiche (journal published in Udine, Italy)
AJA	American Journal of Archaeology
AN	Aquileia Nostra (journal published in Udine, Italy)
ARE	Ancient Records of Egypt
ASOR	Annual of the American Schools of Oriental Research
BA	Biblical Archaeologist
BAR	Biblical Archaeology Review
BASOR	Bulletin of the American Schools for Oriental Research
IEJ	Israel Exploration Journal
INA	Institute for Nautical Archaeology
JAOS	Journal of the American Oriental Society
JNES	Journal of Near Eastern Studies
JPS	Jewish Publication Society of America
NGM	The National Geographic Magazine

Notes

INTRODUCTION

1. W. A. Thorpe, *English Glass* (London: A. & C. Black Ltd., 1935), 76.
2. Ibid., 77.

CHAPTER 1

1. Norman Gottwald, "Were the Early Israelites Pastoral Nomads?" *BAR* 4 (June 1978): 2.
2. Reeded pipes were among the instruments the Hebrews employed. A double-reeded pipe, the *chalil*, was particularly loved, as its name (sweetness) indicates. The Talmud says of the instrument: "The pipe is called the chalil because its sound is so sweet." The name of the traditional Sabbath bread, the *challah*, derives from the same root word.
3. Harps and lyres are among the most intriguing recoveries from the ruins of Ur, dating back into Sumerian times. A harp and a lyre, instruments otherwise unknown to the Egyptians at the time, are included in a full-scale drawing of a group of thirty-seven Semitic traders in the tomb of an Egyptian prince of the nineteenth century B.C.E., a time which could be contemporary with that of Terach, father of Abraham. The hieroglyphic inscription informs us that the patriarchal head of the traders is named Abushei, a Hebrew name (as, for example, the name of one of King David's generals).
4. Nathan Ausubel, *The Book of Jewish Knowledge* (New York: Crown Publishers, 1964), 310-311.
5. "Tubal" is rendered by the great commentator Rashi as "refined." "The word *Tubal* . . . is an expression of "spices"–*tavlin* . . . [which refine and improve the taste of food]." Pinchas Doron, *The Mystery of Creation According to Rashi* (New York: Maznaim, 1982), 109.
6. James D. Mulhy, "How Iron Technology Changed the Ancient World, *BAR* 7 (December 1982): 6. Mulhy corrects the *Jerusalem Bible* translation by reading "bloom"

instead of "pig iron." For the advent of the Iron Age in connection with the Israelite settlement in Canaan see Yohanan Aharoni, "The Israelite Occupation of Canaan," *BAR* 8 (May-June 1982): 3.

7. Jack Finegan, *Light from the Ancient Past* bk. 1 (1946; reprint, Princeton, NJ: Princeton University Press, 1974), 126.
8. James Henry Breasted, *A History of Egypt* (1910; reprint, New York: Bantam, 1964), 443.
9. Flavius Josephus, *Antiquities of the Jews*, vol. 2, *The Works of Flavius Josephus*, trans. William Whiston (1974; reprint, Grand Rapids, MI: Baker Book House, 1983), 86.
10. Finegan, *Light from the Ancient Past*, 68.
11. Josephus, *Antiquities of the Jews*, 85.
12. Ibid., 86.
13. Flavius Josephus, *Against Apion*, vol. 1, *The Works of Flavius Josephus*, trans. William Whiston (1974; reprint, Grand Rapids, MI: Baker Book House, 1983), 181.
14. Josephus, *Antiquities of the Jews*, 87-88.
15. S. D. Groitein, *Jews and Arabs*, rev. ed. (New York: Schocken, 1974), 2.
16. Ezekiel 16:3: "Thus saith the Lord God unto Jerusalem; Thy birth and thy nativity is of the Land of Canaan; Thy father was an Amorite, and thy mother a Hittite."
17. G. Ernest Wright, *Biblical Archaeology* (1957; reprint, Philadelphia: Westminster Press, 1979), 41.
18. Ibid., 41.

CHAPTER 2

1. Dame Kathleen M. Kenyon, *Archaeology in the Holy Land* (1960; reprint, New York: Norton, 1979), 5.
2. Andrew Sillen, "Dietary Reconstruction and Near Eastern Archaeology," *Expedition* 2 (1986):19.
3. Dame Kathleen M. Kenyon, "Jericho," in *Encyclopedia of Archaeological Excavations in the Holy Land*, vol. 2, ed. Michael Avi-Yonah (Englewood Cliffs, NJ: Prentice-Hall, 1976), 554.
4. Carol G. Thomas, *The Earliest Civilizations* (Boston: University Press of America, 1982), 40.
5. Giovanni Pettinato, *The Archives of Ebla* (Garden City, NY: Doubleday, 1981), 3.
6. Giovanni Pettinato, *Nuovi orizzonti della storia* (Milano: Rusconi, 1985), 12.
7. Pettinato, *Archives*, 65.
8. Sabatino Moscati, ed., *An Introduction to the Comparative Grammar of the Semitic Languages* (Weisbaden: O. Harrassowitz, 1964). See also the chart, pp. 10-11, in the introduction by Harvey Weiss to *Ebla to Damascus*, the catalog of the exhibition of that name by the Smithsonian Museum, Washington, DC, 1985.
9. Pettinato, *Archives*, 244.
10. Ibid., 249
11. Mitchell Dahood, in the afterword to Pettinato, *Archives*, 272.
12. *The Washington Post*, August 16, 1976.
13. *The New York Times*, October 25, 1976.
14. Quoted from "Ebla Scholarship 'á la Syrienne'," *BAR* 8:1 (January 1982).
15. Editorial in *BAR* 6:3 (May-June 1981): 49.

16. Seton Lloyd, *The Archaeology of Mesopotamia*, rev. ed. (London: Thames and Hudson, 1984), 12: "The Greek translators of the Old Testament thought of [Mesopotamia] as the homeland of the Patriarch Abraham around the ancient city of Harran, which lies between the middle courses of the Euphrates and Tigris. Strabo also used the term to denote only the northern part of the interfluvial lowland, and referred to the southern part as 'Babylonia.' It was Pliny who extended its limits to the Arabian Gulf."

17. John A. Tvedtnes, "The Origin of the Name 'Syria'," *JNES* 40:2 (April 1982): 139-140.

18. John Oates, *Babylon* (1979; reprint, New York: Thames and Hudson, 1986), 55.

19. Giovanni Pettinato, *Ebla. Nuovi orizzonti della storia* (Milano: Rusconi, 1985), 333.

20. Giovanni Pettinato, "Ebla and the Bible," *BAR* 6:6 (November–December 1980): 38. Pettinato, in disclaiming the implication that Ya is equivalent to the biblical Yahwe, proposes that Ya is simply a divine element. It is "a general term for a Deity," and the transition from Il to Ya "may have been something of a religious revolution because the names ending in Il were largely replaced by Ya."

21. Pettinato, *Ebla*, 334.

22. Ibid., 259.

23. Warner Keller, *The Bible as History* (1955; reprint, New York: William Morrow, 1980), 62, 64.

24. Keller, 64-65.

25. Ibid., 66.

26. Cyrus H. Gordon, *The Ancient Near East* (New York: Norton, 1965), 34.

27. Jean Nougayrol, "Textes Accadiens des Archives Sud (Archives Internationales)," *Le Palais Royal d'Ugarit* 4 (1956), 103-105.

28. Cyrus Gordon, "Abraham of Ur," *Hebrew and Oxford Studies* (Oxford: Oxford University Press, 1963); "Where is Abraham's Ur?," *BAR* 3:2 (June 1977), 20.

CHAPTER 3

1. Ernest Mackay and Stephen Langdon, "Report on Excavations at Jamdet Nasr," in *Field Museums: Anthropological Memoirs 1-3* (Chicago, 1931), 37.

2. The history of glassmaking, other aspects of the vitric arts and the association of the Jews with the arts are continued in Samuel Kurinsky, *The Glassmakers: An Odyssey of the Jews* (New York: Hippocrene Publishers, 1991).

3. E. A. Speiser, "Amorites and Canaanites," *The World History of the Jewish People*, vol. 2, ed. Benjamin Mazar (New Brunswick, NJ: Rutgers University Press, 1970), 164-65.

4. The Hurrians later formed the kingdom of Uriatri, or Urartu, which, according to an inscription of Shalmanaser I, was established in the ninth century B.C.E.

5. Ran Zadok, "The Origin of the Name Shinar," *Zeitschrift für Assyriologie* 74:2 (1984): 240, 244. Zadok notes that the earliest occurrence of the Egyptian equivalent to Shinar occurs in Thutmos III's thirty-third year (1457 B.C.E.) [J. H. Breasted, *Ancient Records of Egypt 2* (Chicago: University of Chicago Press, 1960, 484], and appears in topographical texts from the reign of Amenhotep III down to that of Tirhaka; in a Hurrian letter sent from Mitanni to Egypt; in the Amarna letter sent from Alasia (Cyprus) to Egypt; and in Kassite documents thereafter.

6. J. B. Pritchard, *Ancient Near Eastern Texts Relating to the Old Testament,* 2d ed. (Princeton, NJ, and London: Princeton University Press, 1975), 119.

7. Emanuel Anati, *Palestine before the Hebrews* (New York: Alfred A. Knopf, 1963), 363.

8. Joan Oates, *Babylon* (1979; reprint, New York: Thames and Hudson, 1986), 10.

9. Ibid., 38.

10. Sir Leonard Woolley, *The Sumerians* (1929; reprint, New York: Norton, 1965), 45.

11. Robert McCormack Adams, *Heartland of Cities* (Chicago and London: University of Chicago Press, 1981), 85. See also Carl G. Thomas, *The Earliest Civilizations* (Boston: University Press of America, 1982), 12.

12. Sir Leonard Woolley, *Ur of the Chaldees* (1929; reprint, London: Herbert Press, 1982), 213.

13. Seton Lloyd, *The Archaeology of Mesopotamia,* rev. ed. (London: Thames and Hudson, 1984), 20.

14. Adams, *Heartland of Cities,* 137.

15. Oates, *Babylon.*

16. A. Leo Oppenheim, *Ancient Mesopotamia* (1964; reprint, Chicago and London: University of Chicago Press, 1977), 91.

17. Jack Finegan, *Light from the Ancient Past,* vol. 1 (1946; reprint, Princeton, NJ: Princeton University Press, 1974), 52.

18. A. Leo Oppenheim, *Letters from Mesopotamia* (Chicago: University of Chicago Press, 1967), 98-99.

19. Woolley, *The Sumerians,* 79-80.

20. Ibid., 49.

21. Oppenheim, *Ancient Mesopotamia,* 92

22. Gregory McMahon, "The History of the Hittites," *BA* 52 (June-September 1989): 65.

23. Nurettin Yardimci, *Land of Civilizations, Turkey* (Japan: Heibonsha Limited, 1985), 38.

24. Machteld J. Mellink, "Archaeology in Anatolia," *AJA* (January 1990): 126.

25. Jeanne Vorys Canby, "Hittite Art," *BA* 52 (June-September 1989): 111.

26. M. E. L. Mallowan, "Excavations at Brak and Chagar Bazar," *Iraq* 9 (1947): 1ff.

27. Oates, *Babylon,* 36.

28. M. A. Littauer and J. H. Crouwel, "The Earliest Known Three-dimensional Evidence for Spoked Wheels," *BA* 52 (June-September 1989): 395.

29. Ibid., 397, citing M. J. Mellink, "Bronze Wagon," *AJA* 75 (1971): 165.

30. Professor T. Özgüc is referring to the projections formulated by M. J. Mellink as long ago as 1962 in "The Prehistory of Syro-Cilicia," *Bibliotheca Orientalis* 19: 5-6: 225-226; and in "Archeology in Asia Minor," *American Journal of Archaeology* 69 (1965): 135.

31. Tahsin Özgüc, "New Observations on the Relationship of Kültepe with Southeast Anatolia and North Syria during the Third Millennium B.C.," *Ancient Anatolia* (Ankara: Tarih Kurumu Bulletin, 1986), 31.

32. Ibid., 34.

33. Ibid., 37.

34. Oates, *Babylon,* 22.

35. Ibid., 22

36. Machteld J. Mellink, "The Pre-history of Syro-Cilicia," *Bibliotheca Orientalis* 19:5-6 (1962).

37. Tahsin Özgüc, "New Orientations," citing H. Kuhne, *Die Keramic von Tel Chuera und ihre Beziehungen zu Funden aus Syrian-Palestina der Turkey und dem Iraq* (Berlin, 1976), 33-72, and numerous other references.

38. Machteld J. Mellink, "Archaeology in Anatolia," *ALA* (January 1987): 3.

39. Ibid., 30.

40. Ibid., 129.

41. Tahsin Özgüc, 42.

42. Ibid., 43

43. Nimet Özgüc, "Seals of the Old Assyrian Colony Period and some Observations on the Seal Impressions," in *Ancient Anatolia* (Ankara, 1986), 48.

44. Edibe Uzunoglu, "Three Hittite Cylinder Seals in the Istanbul Archaeological Museum," in *Ancient Anatolia*, 77.

CHAPTER 4

1. Tacitus, *Agricola*, 1.42.

2. Flavius Josephus, *Antiquities of the Jews*, vol 2, *The Works of Flavius Josephus*, trans. William Whiston (Grand Rapids, MI: Baker Book House, 1983), 257ff.

3. James Henry Breasted, *A History of Egypt* (1905; reprint, New York: Bantam, 1964), 179.

4. Flavius Josephus, *Against Apion*, vol 4, *The Works of Flavius Josephus*, trans. William Whiston (Grand Rapids, MI: Baker Book House, 1983), 163.

5. Ibid.

6. Sir Alan Gardiner, *Egypt of the Pharaohs* (1961; reprint, Oxford: Oxford University Press, 1979), 156-157.

7. Ibid.

8. Ibid., 157.

9. Yohanan Aharoni, *The Land of the Bible, A Historical Geography*, trans. Anson F. Rainey (Philadelphia: Westminster Press, 1979), 148.

10. Ibid., 150.

11. Josephus, *Against Apion*, 163.

12. Ibid., 165.

13. John Baines and Jerome Malek, *Atlas of Ancient Egypt* (New York: Facts on File Publications, 1980), 40.

14. Ibid., 41.

15. B. G. Trigger, B. J. Kemp, D. O'Connor, and A. B. Lloyd, *Ancient Egypt, A Social History* (1983; reprint, Cambridge: Cambridge University Press, 1986), 154.

16. William C. Hayes, *The Scepter of Egypt, Part II: The Hyksos Period (1675-1080 b.c.)* (1959; reprint, Metropolitan Museum of Art, 1968), 8.

17. Michael Avi-Yonah and Ephraim Stern, *Encyclopedia of Archaeological Excavations in the Holy Land*, vol. 4 (Cambridge: Oxford University Press, 1978), 1101.

18. Aharon Kempinski, *Encyclopedia of Archaeological Excavations in the Holy Land*, vol. 1 (Cambridge: Oxford University Press, 1978), 45.

19. Aharoni, *Land of the Bible*, 163, see item 102.

20. Cyril Aldred, *The Egyptians* (1961; reprint, London: Thames and Hudson, 1984), 139.

21. Ibid., 139, 141.

22. Ibid., 142-43.

23. Ibid., 139.

24. Aharoni, *Land of the Bible,* 148.
25. John Van Seters, *The Hyksos* (New Haven: Yale University Press, 1966), 20.
26. G. E. Wright, "The Archaeology of Palestine From the Neolithic through the Middle Bronze Age," *JAOS* 91 (1971): 276-293.
27. Cyril Aldred, *The Egyptians,* 141.
28. Hayes, *The Scepter of Egypt,* 4.
29. Trigger et al., *Ancient Egypt,* 172-173.
30. Donald B. Redford, "The Historiography of Ancient Egypt," *Egyptology and the Social Sciences* (Cairo: The American University of Cairo Press, 1979), 9, 10. (Redford is a member of the faculty of the University of Toronto, an archeologist who served as Director of the Akhenaten Temple Project of Karnak.)
31. Gardiner, *Egypt of the Pharoahs,* 46-47.
32. Ibid., 155-156.
33. Breasted, *A History of Egypt,* 186-187.
34. Hermopolis Magna, the modern Ashmunen.
35. The Delta area of the Nile.
36. Gardiner, *Egypt of the Pharaohs,* 166.
37. Ibid., 166.
38. Ibid., 167.
39. Ibid.
40. Ibid.
41. Africanus states that the Hyksos rulers and their tenures were: (1) Saites, nineteen yrs.; (2) Bnon, fourty-four yrs.; (3) Pachman, sixty-one yrs.; (4) Staan, fifty yrs.; (5) Arcles, 49 yrs.; and (6) Apophis, sixty-one yrs.
42. Gardiner, *Egypt of the Pharaohs,* 159.
43. Trigger et al., *Ancient Egypt,* 150-151.
44. Kent R. Weeks, ed. *Egyptology and the Social Sciences* (Cairo: The American Museum in Cairo Press, 1979), 17.
45. Ibid.
46. Thebes.
47. A name of Egypt.
48. Gardiner, *Egypt of the Pharaohs,* 163.
49. John A. Wilson, *The Culture of Ancient Egypt* (1951; reprint, Chicago: University of Chicago Press, 1963), 160, quoting A. H. Gardiner in the *Journal of Egyptian Archaeology* 32 (1946), 43ff.
50. Gardiner adds (Ibid., 164-165): "Their version of Seth, now written in Babylonian fashion as though pronounced as Sutekh, was certainly more Asiatic in character than the native original, bearing in his garment and head-dress a distinct resemblance to the Semitic Ba'al."
51. Trigger et al., *Ancient Egypt,* 158.
52. Ibid.

CHAPTER 5

1. Herodotus, *Persian Wars,* 2.149.
2. Ibid.
3. Zaccaria Sitchin, in *The Jewish Week and the American Examiner,* July 22, 1983. (Sitchin is a linguist and biblical scholar and author of *The Twelfth Planet* and *The Stairway to Heaven.*)

4. Ibid.
5. Sir Alan Gardiner, *Egypt of the Pharaohs* (1961; reprint, Oxford: Oxford University Press, 1979), 35.
6. James Henry Breasted, *A History of Egypt* (1905; reprint, New York: Bantam, 1964), 4, 20.
7. A. Rosalie David, *The Ancient Egyptians* (London: Routledge & Kegan Paul, 1982), 12.
8. William C. Hayes, *The Scepter of Egypt, Part 2: The Hyksos Period and the New Kingdom (1675-1080 B.C.)* (1959; reprint, Metropolitan Museum of Art, 1968), 4.
9. John A. Wilson, *The Culture of Ancient Egypt* (1951; reprint, Chicago: University of Chicago Press, 1963), 39.
10. Percy S. P. Hancock, *Mesopotamian Archaeology* (New York: Kraus Reprint & Periodicals, 1963), 5.
11. Gardiner, *Egypt of the Pharaohs*, 19.
12. Will Durant, *Our Oriental Heritage* (1935; reprint, New York: Simon & Schuster, 1954), 135.
13. F. Wendorf et al., "Egyptian Prehistory: Some New Concepts," *Science* (1969): 1161-1171.
14. B. G. Trigger et al., "The Rise of Egyptian Civilization," in *Ancient Egypt: A Social History* (1983; reprint, Cambridge: Cambridge University Press, 1986), 3.
15. Manfred Bietak, "Urban Archaeology and the 'Town Problem' in Ancient Egypt," *Egyptology* (1979): 97.
16. Michael A. Hoffman, *Egypt Before the Pharaohs* (London: Routledge & Kegan Paul, 1980), 27.
17. Herodotus, *Persian Wars*, 2.4.
18. Hermann Kees, *Ancient Egypt* (1961; reprint, University of Chicago Press, English Translation by Faber and Faber, Phoenix Edition (1977), 24.
19. Herodotus, *Persian Wars*, 2.99.
20. Trigger et al., *Ancient Egypt*, 23; Hoffman, *Egypt Before the Pharaohs*, 169.
21. Hoffman, *Egypt Before the Pharaohs*, 177.
22. Ibid., 181.
23. Ibid., 169.
24. Ibid., 186, 189.
25. G. E. Wright, "The Archaeology of Palestine from the Neolithic through the Middle Bronze Age," *JAOS* 91 (1971): 276-293.
26. Wendorf et al., "Egyptian Prehistory," 1161-1171.
27. Aldred, *The Egyptians*, 77.
28. H. J. Kantor, "The Relative Chronology of Egypt and Its Foreign Correlations before the Bronze Age," in *Chronologies in Old World Archaeology*, ed. R. Ehrich (Chicago: University of Chicago Press, 1965), 1-46.
29. Hoffman, *Egypt Before the Pharaohs*, 196.
30. Trigger et al., *Ancient Egypt*, 25-26.
31. Trigger, 26, citing Kantor, "Relative Chronology of Egypt," 9.
32. Hoffman, *Egypt Before the Pharaohs*, 214.
33. Ibid., 201.
34. Ibid., 207.
35. Trigger et al., *Ancient Egypt*, 29, citing A. J. Arkell and P. J. Ucko, "Review of Predynastic Development on the Nile Valley," *Current Anthropology* 6 (1965): 145-46, and Kantor, "Relative Chronology of Egypt," 9.

36. Ibid., 37, citing H. Frankfort, *The Birth of Civilization in the Near East* (1956), 121–137; J. Vandier, *Manuel d'archéologie égyptienne*, vol. 1 (1952), 280–281.

37. Ibid., 12.

38. Ibid., 13, citing D. E. Derry, "The Dynastic Race in Egypt," *Journal of Egyptian Archaeology* 42 (1956): 80–85.

39. See map, Trigger et al., *Ancient Egypt*, 28.

40. Hoffman, *Egypt Before the Pharaohs*, 246.

41. Trigger et al., *Ancient Egypt*, 49.

42. Ibid., 60.

43. Bietek, "Urban Archaeology," 129.

44. Trigger et al., *Ancient Egypt*, 62f.

45. Aldred, *The Egyptians*, 28.

46. Exodus 3:8; Deuteronomy 8:8.

47. James B. Pritchard, ed., *The Ancient Near East* (1958; reprint, Princeton, NJ: Princeton University Press, 1973), 5–11.

48. These items, recovered from a Second Intermediate period strata of the excavations on Yeb, are on display at the Museum on Elephantine Island.

49. Hayes, *The Scepter of Egypt*, 5, 6. The Metropolitan Museum has four Jacob-el scarabs, written as "Y'akub-her" in Egyptian. Hayes notes that a seal of King *Ma'-yeb-Re'sheshi* was also found at Kerma (Kermeh), another was found at Elephantine Island and still another at Deir el Bahri in an Eighteenth-Dynasty rubbish pit. The seals of this Aamu chief and that of Jacob-el are numerous and widely distributed. The close association "in time and in the geographic area" that the two kings controlled leads Hayes to suggest that the two were one and the same and "the second of the Great Hyksos rulers."

50. Barry Kemp, *Ancient Egypt: Anatomy of a Civilization* (London: Routledge, Chapman, and Hall, 1989), 161–167.

51. Bietak, "Urban Archaeology," 128.

52. Aldred, *The Egyptians*, 139, 141, 142.

53. Bietak, "Urban Archaeology," 116.

54. Gardiner, *Egypt of the Pharaohs*, 165.

55. P. H. Newby, *Warrior Pharoahs* (London: Faber & Boston, 1980), 166.

56. Bietak, "Urban Archaeology," 119.

57. William C. Hayes, *The Scepter of Egypt*. References are scattered throughout the work.

CHAPTER 6

1. William C. Hayes, *The Scepter of Egypt, part 2; The Hyksos Period and the New Kingdom (1675–1080 b.c.e.)* (1959; reprint, Metropolitan Museum of Art, 1968), 29.

2. A. L. Oppenheim, "The Cuneiform Texts," in *Glass and Glassmaking in Ancient Mesopotamia*, rev. ed. (Chicago: University of Chicago Press, 1970), 10, 1–102, 230–231.

   Gemstones born in a furnace were then, as today, considered less valuable than original stones mined from the mountains. Akkadian and Sumerian are the earliest languages which differentiate real gemstones from their imitations in glass. The Akkadian word for lapis lazuli was *ugnū*, for fire or furnace was *kūru* and mountain *šadû*. Thus *ugnū-kūri*, literally means "lapis lazuli from the kiln," and denotes lapis lazuli colored glass, and *ugnū-sadî* literally means "lapis lazuli from the mountain," the genuine stone.

The Akkadian word *šadû* for "mountain" originated from the word for breast (i.e., a woman's breast). The Hebrew word for mountain is *šad*, and is still colloquially in use to designate a woman's breast.

3. *Egypt's Golden Age*, catalog of the exhibition "The Art of Living in the New Kingdom 1558–1085 B.C." (Boston: Museum of Fine Arts, 1982), 16, 161.

4. Hayes, *The Scepter of Egypt*, 165. The scene is in two registers, and is dated to the Thutmoside period of Queen Hatshepsut.

5. *Egypt's Golden Age*, 48.

6. Cyril Aldred, *The Egyptians* (1961; reprint, London: Thames and Hudson, 1984), 143.

7. Hayes, *The Scepter of Egypt*, 414.

8. Ibid., 29, 30.

9. Ibid., 27.

10. Sir Alan Gardiner, *Egypt of the Pharaohs* (1961; reprint, Oxford: Oxford University Press, 1979), 158; Hayes, *The Scepter of Egypt*, 6.

11. Hayes, *The Scepter of Egypt*, 25.

12. Ibid., 25–26.

13. Herodotus, *The Histories* (New York: Penguin Classics, 1972), 178.

14. Gardiner, *Egypt of the Pharaohs*, 255.

15. Ibid., 268.

16. Ibid., 273.

17. Ibid., 287.

18. Ibid., 288.

19. A. Rosalie David, *The Ancient Egyptians* (London: Routledge & Kegan Paul, 1982), 140.

20. James Henry Breasted, *A History of Egypt* (1905; reprint, New York: Bantam, 1964), 182.

CHAPTER 7

1. Nurettin Yardimci, *Land of Civilization, Turkey* (Catalog of an Exhibition by The Middle East Culture Center in Japan: Heibonsha Limited, 1985), 38.

2. J. G. McQueen, *The Hittites* (1975; reprint, London: Thames and Hudson, 1986), 20–21.

3. Sir Leonard Woolley, *Alelakh, An Account of the Excavations at Tel-Atchana in the Hataq* (Oxford: Oxford University Press, 1955), 297–302.

4. E. A. Speiser, "Amorites and Canaanites," in *The World History of the Jewish People*, vol. 2., ed. Benjamin Mazar (New Brunswick, NJ: Rutgers University Press, 1970), 162.

5. Arnold Toynbee, *The Greeks and Their Heritages* (Oxford: Oxford University Press, 1981), 19.

6. Patricia Maynor Bikai, "Cyprus and the Phoenicians," *BA* 52:4 (December 1989): 204.

7. Peter Throckmorton, "Thirty-three Centuries Under the Sea, *NGM* 117: 5 (May 1960): 682–703; George Bass, "Cape Gelidonya: A Bronze Age Shipwreck," *Transactions of the American Philosophical Society*, no. 57, pt. 8 (Philadelphia: The Society, 1967); Cemal Pulak and Donald A. Frey, "The Search for a Bronze Age Shipwreck," *Archaeology* (July–August 1985): 19; George Bass, "Return to Cape Gelidonya," *INA Newsletter* 15:2 (June 1988): 3–5.

8. *The Anatolian Civilizations*, an archaeological guide to Pamphylia distributed by the Turkish museums.

9. George Bass, "The Ulu Burun Shipwreck," *Kazi Sonuclari Toplantisi* (May 1985): 20-24; "A Bronze Age Shipwreck at Ulu Burun (Kas), 1984 Campaign," *AJA* 90 (1986): 269-296; "Oldest Known Shipwreck Reveals Splendors of the Bronze Age," *NGM* 172 (1987): 692-733; George Bass et al., "The Bronze Age Shipwreck at Ulu Burun: 1986," *AJA* 93 (1989): 1-29; Cemal Pulak, "The Bronze Age Shipwreck at Ulu Burun, Turkey: 1985 Campaign," *AJA* 92 (January 1988): 37; "Excavations in Turkey: 1988 Campaign," *INA Newsletter* 15:4 (December 1988): 12-17.

10. Cheryl Ward Haldane, "Shipwrecked Plant Remains," *BA* 53 (March 1990): 57, citing *Interpreter's Dictionary of the Bible* (1962), 285.

11. Ibid., 57, citing Isaiah 6:13; Hosea 4:13; Pliny, *De Materia Medica* 1.71-76.

12. Ibid., 57, citing Theophrastus, *Enquiry into Plants*, vol. 2, trans. A. Hort, Loeb Classical Library (New York and London: Putnam's Sons and Heinemann, 1916), 223.

13. Ibid., citing V. Loret, *La résin de térébinthe (sonter) chez les anciens Égyptiens* (Cairo: L'institut Francaise d'Archeolgie Orientale, Recerches d'archéologie de philologie et d'histoire, 1949), 19.

14. George Bass, "Civilization Under the Sea," *Modern Maturity* (April-May 1989): 60.

15. Haldane, 58.

16. Pomegranates, grapes, figs, and olives were among the agricultural products introduced into Egypt in the Second Intermediate period by the Canaanite chieftains who ruled Egypt during that period (c. 1730-1570 B.C.E.). The earliest Egyptian mention of the pomegranate appears in a funerary text of Tuthmosis I, c. 1530 B.C.E.

17. Numbers 13:17-27; Exodus 28:33-34, 39:24-25; 1 Kings 7:18, 20, 42; the juice was used in spiced wine (Song of Solomon 8:2); Haldane notes that "Two charred seeds were recovered from the early third millennium B.C.E. at Arad; seeds and skin fragments from Bronze Age Jericho " [citing M. Hopf, "Plant Remains and Early Farming in Jericho," in *The Domestication and Exploitation of Plants and Animals*, ed. P. J. Ucko and C. W. Dimbleby (London: Duckworth, 1969), 355-59; Dame Kathleen M. Kenyon, *Jericho* (London: British School of Archaeology, 1960), 371, 392-93 and Plate XVII.4].

18. Cemal Pulak, "The Bronze Age Shipwreck at Ulu Burun, Turkey: 1985 Campaign," *AJA* 92:1 (January 1988): 10.

19. George Bass, "A Bronze Age Shipwreck at Ulu Burun (Kos): 1984 Campaign," *AJA* 90 (1986): 287.

20. Cemal Pulak, "Excavations in Turkey: 1988 Campaign," *INA Newsletter* 15:4 (December 1988): 15.

21. Toynbee, *The Greeks and Their Heritages*, 28.

22. Ibid., 29.

CHAPTER 8

1. William G. Dever, "The Middle Bronze Age, the Zenith of the Urban Canaanite Era," *BAR* 50:3 (September 1987): 149-153.

2. Yigael Yadin, *Hazor* (New York: Random House, 1975), 15, 16. Yigael Yadin, Professor of Archaeology at Hebrew University of Jerusalem, was the director of its Institute of Archaeology. In 1955 Yadin initiated the five-year search which proved to be the key to the understanding of much of biblical chronology. Within five years

no less than twenty-two cities were identified, including Hazor, which dates back to 2500 B.C.E. Yadin directed the excavations at Hazor in 1955-58; he led the exploration of the Judean Desert caves where the Bar Khochba documents were discovered in 1960-1961, and directed the excavations of Masada in 1963.

3. Ibid., 39.

4. Ibid., 37.

5. Magen Broshi and R. Goiphna, "Middle Bronze Age II Palestine Settlements and Population," *BASOR* 261 (1986), 73–90. In Middle Age II B (c. 1750-1650 B.C.E.) the population crested. Some 200 sites have been identified in the central hill country (more undoubtedly existed), and a lesser number identified in the northern and southern areas of Canaan. Most of these centers, both fortified and unfortified, were destroyed by the end of MB II (c. 1550 B.C.E.).

6. Israel Finklestein, "Searching for Israelite Origins," *BAR* 14:5 (September–October 1988): 39-40.

7. The metallurgical transformation taking place at the time in Canaan is dealt with in Chapter 11.

8. Albert A. Soggin, *A History of Ancient Israel: From the Beginnings to the Bar Khochba Revolt AD 135*, trans. John Bowden (Philadelphia: Westminster Press, 1984), 96.

9. The "Conquest" school includes William F. Albright, "The Israelite Conquest of Canaan in the Light of Archaeology," *BASOR* 74 (1939): 11-23; Yehezkel Kaufman, *The Biblical Account of the Conquest of Palestine* (1953); G. Ernest Wright, *Biblical Archaeology*, 2d ed. (London: Duckworth, 1962); Paul Lapp, "The Conquest of Palestine in Light of Archaeology," *Concordia Theological Monthly* 38 (1967): 283-300; Abraham Malamet, "Israelite Conduct of War in the Conquest of Canaan," in *Symposia Celebrating the Seventy-fifty Anniversary of the Founding of the American Schools of Oriental Research, 1900-1975* (1979), 35-55, and "How Inferior Israelite Forces Conquered Fortified Canaanite Cities," *BAR* 8.2 (March–April 1982), 25-35; [with qualifications] Yigael Yadin, *Hazor* (1975), esp. 29-41; Yadin, "The Transition from a Semi-Nomadic to a Sedentary Society in the Twelfth Century B.C.E." *Symposia . . .* [see above], 57-68; Yadin, "Is the Biblical Account of the Israelite Conquest of Canaan Historically Reliable?" *BAR* 8.2 (March–April 1982): 16-23; John Bright, *A History of Israel* (London: SCM Press, 1972), 69-84 [John Bright subsequently shifted toward the internal revolt theory in the 3d edition of his work (1981)].

10. The "Peaceful Infiltration Model" was developed by Albrecht Alt, Martin Noth, and Manfred Weippert. Albrecht Alt, "The Settlement of the Israelites in Palestine," *Essays on Old Testament History and Religion*, trans. G. W. Anderson (Oxford: Basil Blackwell, 1966) of *Die Landnahme der Israeliten in Palästina*, 1925; Martin Noth, "Grundsätzliches zur geschichtlichen Deutung archäologischer Befunde auf dem Boden Palästinas," *Palästinjahrbuch* 37 (1960): 7-22; Noth, *The History of Israel, Geschichte Israels* (London: A. & C. Black, 1960); Manfred Weippert, *The Settlement of the Israelite Tribes in Palestine* (1971); Weippert, "The Israelite 'Conquest' and the Evidence from Transjordan," in *Symposia Celebrating the Seventy-fifth Anniversary of the Founding of the American Schools of Oriental Research, 1970-1975* (1979), 15-34.

11. Martin Noth, "Studien zu den historisch-geographischen Dokumenten des Josuabuches," *Zetschrift des deutschen Palastina-Vereins* (1935): 185-255; *The History of Israel*.

12. Benjamin Mazar, *The Early Biblical Period, Historical Studies* (Jerusalem: Israel Ex-

ploration Society, 1986). The first three of fifteen articles relate to the Israelite settlement period.

13. Aharon Kempinski, "Israelite Conquest or Settlement? New Light from Tell Masos," *BAR* 2:3 (September 1976): 25–30.

14. Volkmar Fritz, "Conquest or Settlement?" *BAR* 50:2 (June 1987): 98. See also by Fritz: "The Israelite 'Conquest' in Light of Recent Excavations at Khirbet el-Meshash," *BASOR* 241 (1981): 61–73; "The Conquest in the Light of Archaeology," in *Proceedings of the Eighth World Congress of Jewish Studies* (Jerusalem, n.d.): 15–21.

15. Yohanan Aharoni, *The Archaeology of the Land of Israel* (Philadelphia: Westminster Press, 1982). See also: "Nothing Early and Nothing Late: Rewriting Israel's Conquest," *BA* 39:3 (May 1976): 55–76.

16. George F. Mendenhall, "The Hebrew Conquest of Palestine," *BA* 25 (1962): 66–87, a revised version subsequently appeared in *The Biblical Archaeologist Reader*, vol. 3, ed. E. F. Campbell and D. N. Freedman (Garden City, NY: Doubleday), 100–120. See also: *The Tenth Generation: The Origins of Biblical Tradition* (Baltimore: Johns Hopkins University Press, 1973).

17. Norman K. Gottwald, "Were the Early Israelites Pastoral Nomads?" *BAR* 4:2 (June 1978): 6.

18. Israel Finkelstein, *The Archaeology of the Israelite Settlement* (Jerusalem: Israel Exploration Society, 1988), 341.

19. "Origin of the Israelites," a report in *BAR* 14:2 (March–April 1988): 54, on the annual meeting organized by Dr. William Dever entitled "New Perspectives on the Emergence of Israel in Canaan."

20. Hershel Shanks, "*BAR* Interviews Yigael Yadin," *BAR* 9:1 (January–February 1983): 16–21. The *BAR* pursued a discussion of the subject with articles by the proponents of the various models of Israelite settlement, a sampling of which are here referred to.

21. Hermann Kees, *Ancient Egypt: A Cultural Topography*, trans. Ian F. D. Morrow (Chicago: University of Chicago Press, 1961), 73.

22. John A. Wilson, *The Culture of Ancient Egypt* (Chicago and London: University of Chicago Press, 1951), 257.

23. Ibid., 257.

24. James Henry Breasted, *A History of Egypt* (1905; reprint, New York: Bantam, 1964), 496; Sir Alan Gardiner, *Egypt of the Pharaohs* (1961; reprint, Oxford: Oxford University Press, 1979), 288–289, 297, 299; Kees, 73, 74, 277–280.

25. Bryant G. Wood, "Did the Israelites Conquer Jericho?" *BAR* 16:2 (March–April 1990): 50.

26. Joshua 8:28.

27. Kathleen M. Kenyon, *Digging up Jericho* (London: Ernest Benn Limited, 1957); *Archaeology of the Holy Land* (London: Ernest Benn Limited, 1965).

28. Baruch Halpern, *The First Historians* (San Francisco: Harper & Row, 1988), 4.

29. Itzhaq Beit-Arieh, "New Light on the Edomites," *BAR* 14:2 (March–April 1988): 30.

30. Ibid., 35.

31. Ibid., 35.

32. Ibid., 29.

33. Ibid., 41.

34. "Origin of the Israelites," a report in *BAR* 14:2 (March–April 1988): 55.

35. Yigael Yadin, *The Art of War in Biblical Lands* (London: Weidenfeld & Nicolson, 1963).
36. Joshua 11:12, 13.
37. Yadin, *The Art of War*, 18.
38. Yigael Yadin, *Hazor* (New York: Random House, 1975), 34, quoting Gerstang.
39. Yigael Yadin, "Is the Biblical Account of the Israelite Conquest of Canaan Historically Reliable?" *BAR* 8:2 (March–April 1982): 19.
40. Ibid., 36.
41. The date of 1230 B.C.E. was based on the dating of Mycenaean IIIB ware by A. Furumark in 1941 to the reign of Rameses II, which ended in 1234 B.C.E. The same ware was found at Ugarit in association with a sword incised with the cartouche of Merenptah, whose reign ended in 1203 or 1204 B.C.E. V. R. d'A. Desborough in 1964 proposed on the basis of Aegian examples that the transition from Mycenaean IIIB to Mycenaean IIIC occurred around 1200 B.C.E.; others suggest an even lower date of 1190. These postulated dates are good examples of fixing a chronology to incidences of the appearances of particular material that do not take into consideration the relative factors discussed above.

CHAPTER 9

1. Exodus 18:25.
2. Numbers 1:16.
3. Genesis 32:28, 29.
4. Genesis 35:10.
5. Genesis 35:20-22.
6. Genesis 37:1.
7. "And" is almost universally applied in distinguishing [?] between Jacob and Israel; in addition to the above we can add:

> Who can count the dust of Jacob, and the number of the fourth part of Israel? [Numbers 23:10]
> How goodly are thy tents, O Jacob, and thy tabernacles, O Israel! [Numbers 34:5]
> The Lord sent a word into Jacob, and it hath lighted upon Israel. [Isaiah 9:7]
> Therefore the Lord heard this, and was wroth: so a fire was kindled against Jacob, and anger also came up against Israel. [Psalms 78:21]
> Who gave Jacob for a spoil, and Israel to the robbers? [Isaiah 63:24]
> Yet hear now, O Jacob my servant; and Israel, whom I have chosen. Thus saith the Lord that made thee. . . . Fear not, O Jacob, my servant, and thou, Jesurun, whom I have chosen. [Isaiah 44:1, 2]
> Hearken unto me, O house of Jacob, and all the remnant of the house of Israel . . . [Isaiah 45:3]
> Israel also came into Egypt; and Jacob sojourned in the land of Ham. [Psalms 105:23]
> [The Lord instructed Isaiah] to bring Jacob again to him, that Israel be gathered unto him . . . thou shouldst be my servant to raise up the tribes of Jacob, and to restore the preserved of Israel. . . . [Isaiah 49:5, 6]
> But fear not, O my servant Jacob, and be not dismayed, O Israel. [Jeremiah 46:27]
> For the transgression of Jacob is all this and for the sins of the house of Israel. [Micah 1:5]
> Oh that the salvation of Israel were come out of Zion! When God bringeth back the captivity of his people, Jacob shall rejoice, and Israel shall be glad. [Psalms 53:7]
> For this is a statute for Israel, and a law of the God of Jacob. [Psalms 81:5]

[The covenant made with Abraham and Isaac was confirmed] unto Jacob for a law, and to Israel for an everlasting account. [Psalms 105:10]

When Israel went out of Egypt, the house of Jacob from a people of strange language; Judah was his sanctuary and Israel his dominion. [Psalms 94:1]

For the Lord hath chosen Jacob unto himself, and Israel for his peculiar treasure. [Psalms 135:4]

8. The text as given by John A. Wilson in *The Ancient Near East*, vol. 1, ed. James B. Pritchard (1958; reprint, Princeton, NJ: Princeton University Press, 1973), 231.
9. Frank J. Yurko, "3,200 Year-Old Picture of Israelites Found in Egypt," *BAR* 16:5 (September–October 1990): 27.
10. Wilson, *The Ancient Near East*, 31.
11. Yurko, 25–26.
12. G. W. Ahlström and D. Edelman, "Merenptah's Israel," *JNES* 44:1 (January 1985): 60–61.
13. Exodus 5:1, 3.
14. Genesis 14:13.
15. Genesis 15:13.
16. Genesis 39:14, 17.
17. Genesis 41:12.
18. Exodus 3:8.
19. Moshe Greenberg, "The Hap\biru," in *Ancient Times–Patriarchs and Judges*, in *The World History of the Jewish People*, vol. 2 (1955; reprint, New Haven: American Oriental Society, 1970), 189.
20. Ibid.
21. Siegfried Herrmann, *A History of Israel in Old Testament Times*, 2d ed. (Philadelphia: Fortress Press, 1980), 54 n. 41.
22. Greenberg, "The Hap\biru," 3.
23. Carlo Zaccagnini, "Patterns of Mobility Among Ancient Near Eastern Craftsmen," *JNES* 42:4 (October 1983): 261.
24. J. Alberto Soggin, *A History of Ancient Israel: From the Beginnings to the Bar Khochba Revolt* A.D. *135*, trans. John Bowden (Philadelphia: Westminster Press, 1984), 14.
25. Zaccagnini, "Patterns of Mobility," 250.
26. Ibid., 253.
27. Soggin, *A History of Ancient Israel*, 15.
28. J. M. Sasson, "Instances of Mobility among Mari Artisans," *BASOR* 190 (1968): 46–54.
29. Zaccagnini, "Patterns of Mobility," 258.
30. Ibid., 247.
31. Mary Louella Trowbridge, *Philological Studies in Ancient Glass* (Urbana: University of Illinois, 1930), 114, 133, citing E. Gersprach, *L'Arte de la Verrerie* (Paris: Bibliothèque de l'Enseignement de Beaux-Arts, 1885).
32. According to Isaac Mozeson, author of *The Word* (New York: Shapolsky, 1989).
33. The Latin word *vitrum* appears first in a speech by Cicero in 54 B.C.E. (*Pro Rabirio Postumo*, 14.40); and then in Lucretius' *De Rerum Natura*, 4, 145ff.
34. Trowbridge, *Philological Studies*, 59.
35. W. A. Thorpe, *English Glass* (London: A. & C. Black Ltd., 1953), 2.
36. R. Campbell Thompson, *A Dictionary of Assyrian Chemistry and Geology* (Oxford: Clarendon Press, 1936), xii.

37. Sir. Leonard Woolley, *Alalakh; An Account of the Excavations at Tel-Atchana in the Hataq 1937–1949, 1955* (Oxford: Oxford University Press, 1955), 297–302.
38. James B. Pritchard, ed., *The Ancient Near East*, vol. 1 (1958; reprint, Princeton, NJ: Princeton University Press, 1973), 160.
39. William Foxwell Albright, *Archaeology, Historical Analogy, and Early Biblical Tradition* (Baton Rouge: Louisiana State University Press, 1966), 40, citing studies by E. Dhorme and R. Borger.
40. Genesis 8:27.
41. Albright, *Archaeology*, acknowledging the reference to Dr. M. Gertner of London.
42. Ibid., 39.
43. Greenberg, "The Hap\biru," 194, 195.
44. Gardiner, *Egypt of the Pharaohs*, 228–229.
45. Deuteronomy 23:16–17.
46. Leviticus 19:9–10.
47. Numbers 2:32–33.
48. Exodus 31:2–5.
49. Exodus 35:30–35.
50. Exodus 36:1–7.
51. Exodus 32:4.
52. Exodus 39:1–31.
53. Deuteronomy 3:11.
54. Deuteronomy 8:7–9.
55. Numbers 31:22–23.
56. Numbers 35:16.
57. Deuteronomy 27:4–5.
58. 1 Kings 6:7.
59. Deuteronomy 28:48.
60. Jeremiah 2:20.
61. Joshua 6:19, 24.
62. Joshua 18:16, 18.
63. Judges 1:19.
64. Judges 1:19–4:15.
65. Judges 4:21; 5:26.
66. Joshua 22:8.
67. 1 Samuel 13:19–23.
68. 1 Samuel 14:47.
69. 1 Samuel 17:5–7.
70. 1 Samuel 38–40.
71. 2 Samuel 21:15–16.
72. 2 Samuel 22:2.
73. 1 Samuel 23.
74. Greenberg, "The Hap\biru," 279 n. 12, citing J. Bottéro, *Le Probléme des Habiru*, 1954.
75. Nadav Na'aman, "H$_u$abiru and Hebrews: The Transfer of a Social Term to the Literary Sphere," *JNES* 45:4 (October 1986): 288.
76. Jonah 1:9.
77. Na'aman, "H$_u$abiru and Hebrews," 288.

78. James D. Mulhy, "How Iron Technology Changed the Ancient World," in *Archaeology and the Bible* (Washington, DC: Biblical Archaeological Society, 1990), 234.
79. 1 Chronicles 22:2, 3.
80. 1 Chronicles 22:14-16.
81. 1 Chronicles 23:5.
82. 1 Chronicles 29:2.
83. 2 Samuel 12:31.
84. 2 Samuel 23:6, 7.
85. 1 Chronicles 1:16.
86. 1 Chronicles 4:14. Abushei, it will be recalled, was also the name of the Hyk-khase who headed the group of thirty-seven artisan-traders down the Nile some seven hundred years earlier.
87. 2 Samuel 13:31.
88. 2 Samuel 17:1.
89. 1 Kings 2:34.
90. 1 Chronicles 29:7.
91. 1 Kings 5:27-32.
92. 1 Kings 7:13-14. Italics appear for emphasis.
93. 1 Kings 7:51.
94. Yohanan Aharoni, *The Archaeology of the Land of Israel,* trans. A. F. Rainey (Philadelphia: Westminster Press, 1982), 212.

CHAPTER 10

1. Yohanan Aharoni, *The Archaeology of the Land of Israel*, trans. A. F. Rainey (Philadelphia: Westminster Press, 1982), 161.
2. Ibid.
3. Thomas E. Levy, "How Ancient Man First Utilized Rivers in the Sand," *BAR* 16:6 (November-December 1990): 29.
4. J. Alberto Soggin, *A History of Ancient Israel From the Beginnings to the Bar Khochba Revolt A.D. 135*, trans. John Bowden (Philadelphia: Westminster Press, 1985), 363.
5. Joseph A. Callaway, "A Visit with Ahilud," *BAR* (September-October 1983), reprinted in *Archaeology and the Bible* (Washington, DC: Biblical Archaeological Society, 1990), 65-75.
6. Ibid., 65-66; Yohanan Aharoni, "Khirbet Raddana and Its Inscriptions," *IEJ* 21:3 (1971): 130-135.
7. Callaway, "A Visit with Ahilud," 69.
8. Ibid., 75.
9. Ibid., 75.
10. Aharoni, *The Archaeology of the Land of Israel*, 167; a variety of goods were found in the Tel Masos houses; besides locally produced wares, there were vessels from the northern coast, Philistine ware from the southern coast, Midianite ware from the region of the Gulf of Elath, and luxury goods such as the: "lion's head carved from ivory in the best Canaanite tradition."
11. Ibid., 163.
12. Ibid., 167.
13. Ibid., 171.

14. Ibid., 168.

15. Ibid., 168–169.

16. Judges 1:21–35.

17. Aharoni, *Archaeology of the Land of Israel*, 213, 214.

18. Ibid., 215.

19. Yigael Yadin, *Hazor* (New York: Random House, 1975), 166.

20. Aharoni, *Archaeology of the Land of Israel*, 214.

21. Ibid., 217–219.

22. Dan Cole, "How Water Tunnels Worked," in *Archaeology and the Bible* (Washington, DC: The Biblical Archaeological Society, 1990), 257.

23. Joshua 10:2.

24. James B. Pritchard, *Gibeon, Where the Sun Stood Still* (Princeton, NJ: Princeton University Press, 1962), 64–74.

25. 2 Samuel 2:15–16.

26. Cole, "How Water Tunnels Worked," 259.

27. Ibid., 257.

28. A Cubit, an ancient unit of length, is based on the distance from the elbow to the tip of the middle finger, roughly eighteen inches.

29. Aharoni, *Archaeology of the Land of Israel*, 237.

30. Cole, "How Water Tunnels Worked," 251–252.

CHAPTER 11

1. James D. Mulhy, "How Iron Technology Changed the Ancient World," in *Archaeology and the Bible* (Washington, DC: Biblical Archeological Society, 1990), 230–242.

2. Ibid.

3. Ibid.

4. Yohanan Aharoni, "The Israelite Occupation of Canaan," *BAR* 8:3 (May–June 1982): 14.

5. Aharoni, "The Israelite Occupation of Canaan," 160.

6. Harold Liebowitz, "Tel Yin'am, 1980," *IEJ* 32:1 (1982): 64–65.

7. Harold Liebowitz, "Tel Yin'am, 1981," *IEJ* 33:1-2 (1983): 65.

8. Ibid., 65.

9. Yohanan Aharoni, *The Archaeology of the Land of Israel*, trans. A. F. Rainey (Philadelphia: Westminster Press, 1982), 156.

10. Yigael Yadin, "The Mystery of the Unexplained Chain," *BAR* 10:4 (July–August 1984): 65, 66.

11. Ibid., 66.

12. Eliezer Oren, *Explorations in the Negev and Sinai* (Catalog of the Bethsheba Sinai Museum, 1976), showcase I, item 2; showcase IV, items 1, 4.

13. Joshua 13:2, 3.

14. Seymour Gitin, "Part II: Olive-Oil Suppliers to the World," *BAR* 16:2 (March–April 1990): 39.

15. Ibid., 38–40.

16. Aharoni, *The Archaeology of the Land of Israel*, 254–259.

17. Ibid., 39.

18. J. D. Seger, "Tel Gezer," *IEJ* 23:4 (1973): 250–251.

19. George L. Kelm and Amihai Mazar, "Excavating in Samson Country, *BAR* 15:1 (January–February 1989): 37–49; id., "Three Seasons of Excavations at Tel Barash-Biblical Timnah," *BASOR* 237 (1982): 1–36; id., "Tel Batash (Timnah) Excavations, Second Preliminary Report (1981–1983)," *BASOR Supplement* 23 (1985): 93–120.
20. Judges 13–16.
21. Kelm and Mazar, "Tel Batash (Timnah) Excavations, Second Preliminary Report," 93–120.
22. M Dothan, "Tel Ashdod," *IEJ* 22:4 (1972): 244.
23. Aharoni, *The Archaeology of the Land of Israel*, 156.
24. T. Stech-Wheeler et al., "Iron at Taanach and Early Iron Metallurgy in the Eastern Mediterranean," *AJA* 85:3 (July 1981): 255.
25. Ibid., 260.
26. Reynold Higgins, *Minoan and Mycenaean Art* (New York: Praeger, 1981), 136–141, figs. 169–173.
27. Ibid., 80.
28. John Chadwick, *The Mycenaean World* (Cambridge: Cambridge University Press, 1977), 139.
29. Ibid., 185.
30. Ibid., 144.
31. Ibid., 156.
32. Higgins, *Minoan and Mycenaean Art*, 129.
33. Jericho: R. Cleveland, "An Ivory Bull's Head from Jericho," *BASOR* 163 (1961): 31, 34, figs. 1, 2; Khirbet Kirak: P. Bar-Adon, "Another Ivory Bull's Head from Palestine," *BASOR* 165 (1964): 46; Ai: A. Ben-Tor, "An Ivory Bull's Head from ᶜAi," *BASOR* 208 (1972): 47, fig. 1.
34. Harold Leibowitz, "Late Bronze Ivory Work in Palestine: Evidence of a Cultural Highpoint," *BASOR* 265 (1987): 4.
35. Leibowitz, "Late Bronze Ivory Work," 3.
36. Ibid., 5.
37. Ibid., 14, 15.
38. Ibid., 16.
39. Ibid., 16, 18.
40. E. L. Sukenik, "History in Jewish Archaeology," in *The Jewish People, Past and Present* (New York: Central Yiddish Culture Organization, 1946), 35.
41. Frederic Neuberg, *Ancient Glass* (London: Barrie & Rockcliff, 1962), 51.
42. Deuteronomy 33:19.
43. Palestinian Talmud, ch. 4, 59b.
44. Job 28:1–17.
45. Palestinian Talmud, ch. 4, 59b.
46. A glass vessel, it is related, begins with the breath (*neshimah*) of the glassblower, which flows as a wind (*rauch*) through the glassblowing pipe, and finally comes to rest (*nafash*) as an ethereal element within the vessel. Man's soul or "disposition" (*neshamah*) stems from the same root, *neshimah* (cf.: Exodus 23:12, 31:17) and refers to that element of the soul that is bound to the body and "rests" there. *Rauch*, which means a wind, is the part of the soul that binds the *neshamah* and *nefesh* [Moshe Chaim Luzzatto, *Derech haShem* ("The Way of God"), trans. and annotated by Aryeh Kaplan (Jerusalem, 1983), pt. 2, 347–348, referring to the Midrash *Bereishis Rabbah* 14:9, *Devarium Rabbah* 2:9, and *Shaar haGilgulim*].

CHAPTER 12

1. Acrophony is the use of a symbol to phonetically represent the initial sound of the name of an object previously represented by a pictorial sign or hieroglyph. Thus a picture of the owl, used at first to represent the bird itself, comes to denote simply the initial sound: O.

2. William Foxwell Albright, *The Proto-Sinaitic Inscriptions and their Decipherment*, Harvard Theological Studies (Cambridge, MA: Harvard University Press, 1966).

3. A. E. Cowley, "The Sinaitic Inscriptions," *The Journal of Eastern Archaeology* 15: 2, 4 (1929): 200–218; S. Yeivin, "The Canaanite Inscriptions and the Story of the Alphabet," in *The World History of the Jewish People*, vol. 2, ed. Benjamin Mazar (New Brunswick, NJ: Rutgers University Press, 1970), 24–33.

4. W. F. Albright identified twenty-seven *Proto-Sinaitic* and subsequent *Proto-Canaanite* phonomes employed between the seventeenth and twelfth centuries B.C.E., some of which resolved into a single phonome, reducing the Hebrew aleph-beth to twenty-two symbols.

5. Trude Dothan, "In the Days When the Judges Ruled—Research on the Period of the Settlement and the Judges," in *Recent Archaeology in the Land of Israel*, ed. Hershel Shanks (Washington, DC: Biblical Archaeological Society, 1981), 35.

6. Aaron Demsky and Moshe Kochavi, "An Alphabet from the Days of the Judges," *BAR* 4:3 (September–October 1978): 23–25.

7. Yeivin, "The Canaanite Inscriptions", 26–28. Typical examples of aleph-beth signary are inscriptions on a shard of an incense stand found in Gezer, a fragmentary stele found in Shechem, and a dagger found in Lachish, all of MB II period; on a jar-sherd at Tel Nagila of the MB II-III period; on an LB ostracon at Hazor; on an ostracon of the fourteenth century at Tel Hasi; on a gold ring assigned to the mid-thirteenth century B.C.E. at Megiddo; on a bowl and handle of the thirteenth–twelfth centuries B.C.E. at Beth Eglaim; on an ink-inscribed ostracon from the early twelfth century B.C.E. at Beth Shemesh. Israelite examples will be given along with their context further on.

8. Ibid., 32.

9. Ibid., 30.

10. B. Landsberger and H. Tadmor, "Fragments of Clay Liver Models," *IEJ* 14 (1964): 201–218.

11. Norman Gottwald, "John Bright's New Revision of A History of Israel," *BAR* 8:4 (July–August 1982): 60, citing Norman Gottwald, *The Tribes of Yahweh: A Sociology of the Religion of Liberated Israel, 1250-1050* B.C.E. (Maryknoll, NY: Orbis, 1979), 592-599.

12. E. L. Sukenik, "History in Jewish Archaeology," in *The Jewish People, Past and Present* (New York: Central Yiddish Culture Organization, 1946), 55.

13. Oded Borowski, "Yadin Presents New Interpretation of the Famous Lachish Letters," in *Archaeology and the Bible* (Washington, DC: Biblical Archaeological Society, 1990), 314.

14. Ibid., 317. "Watching for the beacon of Lachish" was the previous translation, which seemed to indicate that the ostraca was sent to Lachish. Yigael Yadin made an updated interpretation of the text, in which he pointed out that "watching over" was meant, and that this ostraca and the others were all written at Lachish.

15. Anson F. Rainey, "The Saga of Eliashib," in *Archaeology and the Bible* (Washington, DC: Biblical Archeological Society, 1990), 318.

16. Ibid., referring to: Genesis 14:18; Joshua 19:19; 1 Samuel 10:3, 16:20, 25:18, 2 Samuel 16:1-2.
17. Ibid., 321.
18. Hershel Shanks, "Jeremiah's Scribe and Confidant Speaks from a Hoard of Clay Bullae," in *Archaeology and the Bible*, vol. 1, ed. Hershel Shanks and Dan P. Cole (Washington, DC: Biblical Archaeological Society, 1990), 306-313.
19. Jeremiah 36:2-23.
20. See Chapter 5, the section entitled "Early Hebrew Settlements."
21. A. Cowley, *Aramaic Papyri of the Fifth Century* B.C.E. (Oxford: Clarendon Press, 1923), Aramaic papyrus no. 1.
22. Ibid., papyrus no. 30.
23. The earliest mention of the Passover is in Deuteronomy 16. In 2 Kings 23:21-23 we read that "the king commanded all the people, saying, 'Keep the Passover unto the Lord your God, as it is written in the book of this covenant.' Surely there was not holden such a passover from the days of the judges that judged Israel, nor in all the days of the kings of Israel, nor of the kings of Judah; but in the eighteenth year of king Josiah, wherein this passover was holden to the Lord in Jerusalem." It is therefore probable that the Passover was not practiced as an annual national event earlier than 622 B.C.E.
24. Cyrus H. Gordon, "The Origin of the Jews in Elephantine," *JNES* 14 (1955): 56, referring to 2 Chronicles 8:2-6.
25. Ibid., 57.
26. E. C. B. MacLauren, "Date of the Foundation of the Jewish Colony at Elephantine," *JNES* 87:2 (1968): 89. MacLauren uses the term *factories,* as "they were called a couple of centuries ago, in the countries with which a trade existed; such colonies with their permanent homes and warehouses and substantial financial reserves, were the only means for providing for the requirements of international trade before the full development of the modern type of banking system."
27. Ibid., 91-92.
28. Albrecht Alt, "The God of the Fathers," *Essays on Old Testament History and Religion,* trans. G. W. Anderson (Oxford: Basil Blackstone, 1966), 66.
29. Crowley, *Aramaic Papyri,* 204.

CHAPTER 13

1. John Oates, *Babylon* (New York: Thames and Hudson, 1986), 107.
2. 2 Kings 10:11.
3. 2 Kings 10:15-28.
4. Erika Bleibtrau, "Grisly Assyrian Record of Torture and Death," *BAR* 17:1 (January–February 1991): 58-59.
5. Stephanie Page, "A Stela of Adad-nirari III and Nergal-eres from Tell al Rimah," *Iraq* 30 (1968): 143.
6. Hayim Tadmor, "The Decline, Rise and Destruction of the Kingdom of Israel," in *A History of the Jewish People*, ed. H. H. Ben-Sasson (Cambridge, MA: Harvard University Press, 1969), 133-134.
7. 2 Kings 15:29.
8. H. H. Ben-Sasson, *A History of the Jewish People* (Cambridge MA: Harvard University Press, 1976), 135.

9. Sargon claims to have conquered Samaria in 722 B.C.E., although it is likely that Samaria's capture and destruction was brought about under Shalmaneser V in 723 B.C.E. Hayim Tadmor, "The Campaigns of Sargon II of Assur," *Journal of Cuneiform Studies* 121 (1958): 33-40.

10. 2 Kings 17:6.

11. Harold Newman, *An Illustrated Dictionary of Glass* (London: Thames and Hudson, 1977), 271-272.

12. 2 Kings 17:25-29.

13. 2 Kings 17:21.

14. 2 Kings 17:1-8.

15. Daniel 1:6.

16. Donald J. Wiseman, *Chronicles of Chaldean Kings (626-556 B.C.E.) in the British Museum* (London, 1956), 67, 69.

17. Jeremiah 52:28-30. Three thousand three hundred and twenty "were carried away captive" in the seventh year of Nebuchadnezzar's rule, 832 in his eighteenth year and 745 in his twenty-third year, which add up to 4,897 rather than the 4,600 total given in Jeremiah.

18. 2 Kings 24:14.

19. 2 Kings 25:12.

20. Isaiah 44:12.

21. Isaiah 44:12.

22. Isaiah 44:16

23. Jeremiah 6:28, 29; Morris Silver, *Prophets and Markets* (Boston: Kluwer-Nijhoff, 1983), 17.

24. Jeremiah 11:4.

25. Jeremiah 24:1: "Shall iron break the northern iron and steel?"

26. Jeremiah 15:12.

27. Ezekiel. 22:18-22.

28. Job 28:1, 2.

29. Job 19:24.

30. Job 40:31.

31. Psalms 27:17; see also 2:9; 149:8.

32. Daniel 2:40-45.

33. Dan. 5:1-4.

34. Ezra 2:64, 65; 2:7; Nehemiah 3:1-38.

35. Nehemiah 4:10, 11.

35. Nehemiah 11:35.

37. 1 Chronicles 4:14.

38. David Adan-Bayewitz and Isadore Perlman, "The Local Trade of Sepphoris in the Roman Period," *IEJ* (January 1991): 153-167. The final report on the Kfar Hananiah excavations is expected to be published by David Bayewitz under the title *Excavations at Kefar Hananya: A Galilean Manufacturing Village of the Roman Period.*

39. A final report on the excavations are expected shortly in a book by David Bayewitz: *The Products of Shikhin: A Galilean Town of the Late Hellenistic and Roman Periods.*

40. 1 Chronicles 3:55; 4:14; 4:23.

41. James B. Pritchard, ed., *Ancient Near East in Pictures*, 3d ed. (Princeton, NJ: Princeton University Press, 1969), 284-285; 60.

42. Albert Ten Eyck Olmstead, *History of the Persian Empire* (Chicago: University of Chicago Press, 1948), 83.

43. J. M. Cook, *The Persian Empire* (New York: Schocken, 1983), 88-89; W. D. Davies and Louis Finklestein, eds., *The Cambridge History of Judaism*, vol. 1 (Cambridge: Cambridge University Press, 1984), 336-337, 340; Olmstead, *History of the Persian Empire*, 565, 74, 83, 192.

44. Olmstead, *History of the Persian Empire*, 58; Haggai, 1:12, 14; 2:2, 4. Zerubbabel is designated as the son of Shealtiel, governor of Judah, in turn identified as Sheshbazzar.

45. Ezekiel 3:15.

46. Davies and Finklestein, *The Cambridge History of Judaism*, 344-345.

47. Ibid., 334.

48. Ibid.

49. Ibid., 347.

50. Ibid.

51. Ibid., 346.

52. Ibid., 347-348.

53. Aristophanes, *Acharnians*, 5:74; Mary L. Trowbridge, *Philological Studies in Ancient Glass* (Urbana, IL: University of Illinois Press, 1930), 151.

54. Dio Cassius, *Historia Romana*, 69, 12.

55. Jean M. James, "Silk, China and the Drawloom," *Archaeology* 39:9 (September–October 1986).

56. L. Boulnois, *The Silk Road* (New York: Dutton, 1966), 88, 89.

57. *Qiddushin* ii, 5-62 c.

58. Joseph Needham, *Science and Civilization in China*, vol. 2 (Cambridge: Cambridge University Press, 1965), 192.

59. Avi Yonah, "Scythopolis," *IEJ* 12:2 (1962): 128-189.

60. Dan Barag, "Recent Epigraphic Discoveries Related to the History of Glassmaking in the Roman Period," *Annales du 10th Congress* (an annual congress on glass, held that year in Madrid-Segovie, 1985): 113-116. Professor Kenin Erim of New York University, excavating at Aphrodisias in 1970-72, recovered over 150 fragments of the record of tariffs fixed by Diocletian in his edict, including those on glassware.

61. Robert Brill and John F. Wosinski, "A Huge Slab of Glass in the Ancient Necropolis of Beth She'arim," paper submitted to Section B of the 7th International Congress of Glass (Brussels, 1965), 2, 3.

62. Ibid., 92.

63. *Baba Metzia* 24b.

64. Midrash, *Genesis Rabbah* 77, 2.

65. *Hagigah* 1:7, 2.

66. *Baba Metzia* 5:6.4.

67. Anita Engles, *Readings in Glass History*, vol. 4 (Jerusalem: Phoenix Publications, 1974), 10, quoting from the Babylonian Talmud, *Ketubot* 103b; *Baba Metzia* 85b; Palestine Talmud, *Megillah* 4:1.74d.

68. Engles, *Glass History*, 11-15.

69. Gedaliah Alon, *The Jews in Their Land* (Cambridge, MA: Harvard University Press, 1989), 169.

70. Ibid., 169; references also given: *Yerushalmi Ketuvot*, 7:31c; *Sefer ha-Yishuv*, 17; *Genesis Rabbah*, 19:1.

71. Ibid., 170, citing *Avodah Zarah* 17b.
72. Ibid., 170, citing *Yerushalmi Shekalm*, 2:47a; *Bavli Yevamot* 96a.
73. Ibid., 171, citing *Tosefta Sukkah* 4:6; *Bavli Sukkah* 51b; and *Yerushalmi Sukkah* 55b.
74. I. Irving Friedman, "Seashells and Ancient Purple Dying," *BAR* 53:2 (June 1990): 98.
75. Isaac Herzog, "Proceedings of the Belfast Natural History and Philosophical Society, Appendix B," in *The Royal Purple and the Biblical Blue*, ed. Moshe Ron and Ehud Spaniel (Jerusalem: Keter, 1987), 145.
76. Ibid., 50.
77. "Introduction," *The Royal Purple and the Biblical Blue*, ed. Moshe Ron and Ehud Spaniel, 9.
78. Exodus 21:1-4.
79. Numbers 15:37-39.
80. Ezekiel 27:7.
81. Nira Karmon and Ehud Spaniel, "Archaeological Evidence of the Purple Dye Industry from Israel," in *The Royal Purple and the Biblical Blue*, 151.
82. Ibid., 155, citing Rheinhold, "The History of Purple as a Status Symbol in Antiquity," *Collection Latomus* (Brussels, 1970), 59, 169.
83. Herzog, "Proceedings," 144.
84. Yigael Yadin, *The Finds from the Bar-Khochba Period in the Cave of Letters* (Jerusalem: Israel Exploration Society, 1963), 182-187.
85. Ezekiel 33:5, 6.
86. Karmon and Spaniel, "Archaeological Evidence," 151.
87. Lionel Casson, *Ancient Trade and Society* (Detroit: Wayne State University Press, 1984), 230-231.
88. Exodus 30:23-25.
89. Casson, *Ancient Trade and Society*, 226.
90. Ibid., 234.
91. John E. Vollmer, E. J. Keall, E. Nagai-Berthong, *Silk Road–China Ships* (Toronto: Royal Ontario Museum, 1983), 29.
92. Isaac Herzog, "Hebrew Porphyrology," in *The Royal Purple and the Biblical Blue*, ed. Moshe Ron and Ehud Spaniel (Jerusalem: Keter, 1987), 25.

CHAPTER 14

1. Pococke, ed. and trans., "Bar-Hebraeus," in *Historia compeniera dynastiarum* (1985), 73, 116.
2. Nissim Rejwan, *The Jews of Iraq* (Boulder, CO: Westview, 1986), 28-29.
3. Ibid., 24.
4. Hermann Vogelstein, *The Jews of Rome* (Philadelphia: Jewish Publication Society, 1940), 65.
5. Elias J. Bickerman, *The Jews in the Greek Age* (Cambridge, MA: Harvard University Press, 1988), 82, 83, 85.
6. Ibid., 85, 86.
7. Judaeus Philo, *Flacco*, 43.
8. Marcus Tullius Cicero, *Pro Flacco* 28, 68.
9. See also 1 Maccabees 15:16-24. Jewish merchants from Ashkelon were active at the islands of Rhodes and Delos and at Athens at least as far back as the third cen-

tury (E. Schurer, *Geschichte des judischen Volkes im Zeitalter Jesu Christi*, vols. 1-3, [Leipzig: J. C. Hinricks, 1901-09], 124f); one of the earliest known synagogues, dating back to the first century B.C.E., was uncovered on Delos. (P. Roussel, *Delos, colonnie atheneienne*, Bibliotheque des écoles francaises d'Athenes, et de Rome, vol. 3 [Paris, 1916].)

10. Nachum Gross, ed., *Economic History of the Jews* (Jerusalem: Keter, 1975), 174.

11. Jose Ramon Onega, *Los Judios en la Reino de Galicia* (Madrid: Editora Nazional, 1981), 65-66.

12. "Jews in the Kingdom of Aragon," in *Hispania Judaica* (Barcelona: Encyclopedia Brittanica Publishers, 1990), 493.

13. Jose Ramon Onega, *Los Judios*, 486.

14. Norman A. Stillman, *The Jews of Arab Lands* (Philadelphia: Jewish Publication Society, 1979), 87.

15. Pierre Belon (Belon du Mans), *Les Observations de plusiers singularitez et choses memorables trouve en Grece, Asie, Arakie et autres pays estranges* (1553), 182.

16. Fernand Braudel, *The Mediterranean and the Mediterranean World in the Age of Philip Second* (New York: Harper & Row, 1973), 760-761.

17. Ibid., 349.

18. Gross, *Economic History of the Jews*, 40.

19. To cite only a few examples: In the ninth century the Karaite Benjamin Nahawendi refers to Jews who "like the tailor and the launderer, the worker in iron, in copper, tin and lead, the dyer and the weaver as well as every other artisan." These trades were considered menial activities by the Muslims, fit only for slaves and Jews (ibid., 147). In North Africa, between 1016 and 1260, the Jews were "concerned with gold and silver-smithing and other metal work . . . dyeing . . . the manufacture of glass vessels . . . weaving . . . silk work . . . the making of wine . . . and cheese and sugar factories." (S. D. Goitein, *A Mediterranean Society*, vol. 1 [Los Angeles: University of California Press, 1967], 362.)

20. G. Mandich, "Primi riconoscementi veneziani di un diritto di privativa agli inventori," *Rivista do diritto industriale* 1:7 (1958): 101, and *Le privative industriali Veneziane, 1450-1550* (1936): 517, citing patents registered in the Venetian State Archives (Archivio di Stato, Senato, parte I terra 7:34, fo. 32a, and Collegio, Notario 14, fo. 17b).

21. Ibid., *Diarii*, col. 147: "ognuno si fatica si de le galie come di le munitione, artillerie etc., ma praesertim hebrei spagnoli se operano grandemente."

22. Braudel, *The Mediterranean*, 808.

23. Andrew Sharf, *Byzantine Jewry* (London: Routledge & Kegan Paul, 1971), 2.

24. Salo Baron, "Population," *Encyclopaedia Judaica* (Jerusalem: Keter, 1972), 896.

25. Moses Hadas, *Aristeas to Philocrates* (Hoboken, NJ: Ktav, 1990), 104.

27. Aquileia is missing from all Jewish atlases, as, for example, from the authoritative atlas of Martin Gilbert, *Atlas of Jewish History*, rev. ed. (New York: Dorset Press, 1976).

28. Yves-Marie Duval, "Aquilee et la Palestine entre 370 et 420," *AA* (1978): 263: "Il ne fait pas de doute qu'on ne peut faire abstraction des milieux juifs d'Aquilée et de la region."

29. Luila Gracco-Ruggini, "Ebrei e Orientali in Aquileia," *AA* (1977): 352-382.

30. B. Forlati Tamaro, "Iscrizioni greche di Siriani a Concordia," *AA* (1977): 383-392.

31. Giovanni Brusin, "Orientali in Aquileia romana," *AN* 24, 25 (1953-54): 56-70.

32. Silvio Panciera, *Vita Economica di Aquileia in eta Romana* (Aquileia, 1957), 24-25.

33. F. Hamilton Jackson, *The Shores of the Adriatic* (London, 1906), 24.

34. Luila Gracco-Ruggini, "Il vescovo Cromazio e gli ebrei di Aquileia," *AA* 8 (1975): 363.

35. Ibid.

36. Ibid.

37. St. Jerome, *Comm. in Exekiel*, xxvii, in *Pat. Lat.* 25, 313, "Orbe, Romano Occupato."

38. M. I. Finley, *Ancient Sicily to the Arab Conquest* (New York: Viking Press, 1968), 167.

39. Francesco Vattioni, "I nomi Giudaici delle épigrafi di Monastero di Aquileia," *AN* 43 (1972): 126-132; Giovanni Brusin, "Grande edificio culturale scoperto a Monastero di Aquileia," *AN* 20 (1949): 26-30: "Both the latin and the Greek epigraphs here in evidence make manifest their Semitic origins"; F. Cassola, "Aquileia e l'Oriente mediteraneo," *AA* (1977): 74: "They are partly composed of 'classic' names, Greek and Latin but are predominantly of semitic origin."

40. Luisa Bertacchi, "Nuovi mosaici figurati di Aquileia," *AN* 34, (1963): 20-84.

41. Paolo Lino Zovatto, "Architettura e decorazione nella basilica Teodoriana di Aquileia," *AN* (1961-1962): 42.

42. Giovanni Rinaldi, "I tre quadri di Giona nel mosaico dell'aula Teodorina," *AA* 8 (1975): 109-130.

43. Luisa Bertacchi, "Il mosaico Teodoriano scoperto nell'interno del campanile di Aquileia," *AN* 32-33 (1961-62): 32. Dr. Bertacchi is the director of the museum of Aquileia and of the "Paleo-Christian" museum at Monastero.

44. Ann Perkins, *The Excavations at Duro-Europus*, Final Report 4, Part 5 (New Haven: Yale University Press, 1963). See Plan 5, "House H and Synagogue, Field Plan."

45. Antonio Carlini, "L'epigraphe Teodoriana di Aquileia," *AN* 55 (1984).

46. Elisabeth Jastrzebowska, "Les Origines de la Scene du Combat entre le coq et la Tortue dans les mosaics chretiennes d'Aquilee," *AA* 8 (1975): 93-107.

47. Franca Mian, "La 'Vittoria' di Aquileia," *AA* 8 (1975): 131; Giovanni Brusin, "I mosaico paleocristiani di aquileia e il libro di un Parocco inglese," *AN* 34 (1963): 108-132.

48. Rosa Barovier Mentasti, "La coppa incisa con 'Daniele nella fossa dei leoni,' al museo Nazionale Concordiese," *AN* 14 (1943): 157-172.

49. Luisa Bertacchi, "Due vetri paleocristiani di Aquileia," *AN* 38 (1967): 142-150.

50. M. C. Calvi, "Il miracolo della fonte nel vetro dorato del museo di Aquileia," *AN* 30 (1959): 38-48.

51. Bruna Forlati Tamaro, "Ricerche sull'aula teodoriana nord e sui Battisteri di Aquileia," *AN* (1963): 86-100.

52. Jackson, *The Shores of the Adriatic*, 25.

53. Luisa Bertacchi, "Nuovi elementi e ipotesi circa la Basilica del Fondo Tullio," *AN* (1961-1962): 48-76.

CHAPTER 15

1. For the sake of brevity the anonymous label "Greeks" is here being used to encompass all the peninsular and insular groups of the Aegean region, including the Dorians who invaded the peninsula from the north together with the indigenous peoples such as the Achaeans, Aeolians, Ionians, Pelasgians, Macedonians, Epirotes, and others.

2. Homer, *Iliad*, 6.168-169.

3. Arnold Toynbee, *The Greeks and Their Heritages* (Oxford: Oxford University Press, 1981), 32.

4. Martin Hengel, *Judaism and Hellenism*, trans. John Bowden (Philadelphia: Fortress Press, 1974), 12-13.

5. Ephraim Stern, *Material Culture of the Land of the Bible in the Persian Period, 538-332 B.C.* (English ed., Warminster: Aris & Phillips Ltd., 1982).

6. Nelson Glueck, "The Other Side of Jordan," *BASOR* 82 (April 1941): 3f; *BASOR* 80 (December 1940).

7. Victor Tcherikover, *Corpus Papyronan Judaicanam III* (Cambridge, MA, 1964).

8. Thale's purported prediction of the solar eclipse in 585 B.C.E. was based on astronomical information he had acquired from the Babylonians.

9. Flavius Josephus, *Against Apion*, vol. 4, *The Works of Flavius Josephus*, trans. William Whiston (1974; reprint, Grand Rapids, MI: Baker Book House, 1983), 174.

10. Max Radin, *The Jews Among the Greeks and Romans* (Philadelphia: Jewish Publication Society of America, 1915), 86. Megasthenes had previously resided at the court of Sibyrtius, satrap of Southern Afghanistan.

11. Nathan Ausubel, *The Book of Jewish Knowledge* (New York: Crown Publishers, 1964), 215.

12. Flavius Josephus, *Antiquities of the Jews*, vol. 2, *The Works of Flavius Josephus*, trans. William Whiston (1974; reprint, Grand Rapids, MI: Baker Book House, 1983), 86.

13. Josephus, *Against Apion*, 181.

14. Josephus, *Against Apion*, 176.

15. Clemens Alexandrinus, *Stromata*, 1.22.150-154.

16. Eusebius, *Praeparatio Evangelica*, 11.10.14.

17. Celsus, in Origenes *Contra Celsum*.

18. Robert Brown, *Semitic Influence in Hellenic Mythology* (Clifton, NJ: Reference Book Publishers, Inc., 1966), 83-87.

19. 2 Maccabees 4:8-9: The brother of Onias, Joshua, changed his Hebrew name to Jason. Jason deposed his brother by journeying to Antiochus, and pledged sixty and a further eighty talents above the usual tribute of 300 talents for the position of High Priest. Jason promised an additional 150 talents if Antiochus would grant permission to build a *gymnasion* and *ephebeion* in Jerusalem and to "register the people of Jerusalem as Antiochenes."

20. Josephus, *Antiquities of the Jews*, 180.

21. Hermann Vogelstein, *The Jews of Rome* (Philadelphia: Jewish Publication Society, 1940), 47-49.

22. Hengel, *Judaism and Hellenism*, 2.

23. J. Harold Ellens, "Philo Judaeus and the Ancient Library of Alexandria," in *Seminar Papers of the Society of Biblical Literature* (1987), 440.

24. Ibid.

25. There are differing translations of this maxim from Philo, *de Somniis* 1.57; the one quoted is their essence.

26. Hilgert, "De Somnis 1-2," in *Seminar Papers of the Society of Biblical Literature* (1987), 399.

27. Ausubel, *The Book of Jewish Knowledge*, 214.

28. Vogelstein, *The Jews of Rome*, 61; also Flavius Josephus, *Dissertation*, vol. 3, *The Works of Flavius Josephus*, trans. William Whiston (1974; reprint, Grand Rapids, MI: Baker Book House, 1983), 281-282.

29. Radin, *The Jews Among the Greeks and Romans*, 19.
30. Manetho's work has already been examined. The succession of writers mentioned all stemmed from the upper class and were typically as contemptuous of Greek and Roman lower classes as they were of subject peoples.

    Lysimachus (281 B.C.E.) was a Macedonian general under Alexander who became King of Thrace. It will be recalled that Hermippus accused Pythagoras of plagiarizing Thracian and Jewish concepts.

    Polybius (c. 205–123 B.C.E.) was a Greek historian who wrote his histories after a military stint alongside of Scipio at the destruction of Carthage. His histories were designed to demonstrate how and why all civilized countries of the world fell under Rome's hegemony.

    Posidonius (c. 135–51 B.C.E.) was born in Apimea, a region in which a heavy concentration of Babylonian Jews had settled. He was appointed envoy to Rome, became a close friend of Cicero and Pompey, and reflected their supercilious upper-class attitude.

    Cicero (106–43 B.C.E.) was the ultimate aristocrat in his social philosophy, an attitude fully explicated in his orations in the Roman Senate and in his works on rhetoric and philosophy.

    Strabo (c. 60 B.C.E.–21 C.E.), a Greek geographer, drew copiously upon his predecessors such as above, and reflected their attitudes.

    Apollonius of Tyana (3 B.C.E.–c. 97 C.E.) was said to have been a zealous neo-Pythagorean teacher who met the "magi" of Babylonia on his way to India, and earned a reputation of having divine attributes and of being a worker of miracles; it was doubtless Judaic skepticism that spurred his reaction.

    Tacitus (c. 55–120 C.E.), Roman historian and attorney who expressed his hatred of the Jews in no uncertain terms, repeated unfounded calumnies and barefaced lies in the process.
31. Ausubel, *The Book of Jewish Knowledge*, 215, 216.
32. Demosthenes, *Orations*, 52, 20; Isaios (420–350 B.C.E.), the Athenian teacher of Demosthenes, also mentions this colony of Greeks: *Orations*, 4, 7.
33. Hengel, *Judaism and Hellenism*, 13.
34. Josephus, *Antiquities of the Jews*, 168.
35. Josephus, *Antiquities of the Jews*, 145; Victor Tcherikower, *Hellenistic Civilization and the Jews* (New York: Atheneum, 1985), 336.
36. Xenophon, *Oeconomicus*, 4.3.
37. Aristotle, *Politics*, 3.3.2.
38. Homer, *Iliad*, 1.599.
39. As quoted under "Hellenists, Jewish," Ausubel, *The Book of Jewish Knowledge*, 214–15.
40. "Jewish Identity," *Encyclopaedia Judaica* (Jerusalem: Keter, 1972), 10:55.
41. Louis H. Feldman, "The Omnipresence of the God-fearers," in *BAR* 12:5 (September–October 1986), quoting St. Augustine, *The City of God*, 6.11.
42. Arrian, *Dissertationes*, 2.19–21.
43. Arrian, *Dissertationes*, 2.19–21; Commodianus, *Instructiones*, 1.24.11ff, 1.37.
44. Ibid., quoting Suetonius about the life of Domitianus in *Lives of the Caesars*, 12.2.
45. Flavius Josephus, *Wars of the Jews*, vol. 1, *The Works of Flavius Josephus*, trans. William Whiston (1974; reprint, Grand Rapids, MI: Baker Book House, 1983), 2.463, 745; *Antiquities of the Jews*, 14.110, 20.195; Justin Martyr, *Dialogue with Typho*, 10.2.
46. Martyr, *Dialogue with Typho*, 10.2.

47. Victor Tcherikover, *Corpus Papyronan Judaicanam III* (1964), 54-55, 63.
48. Juvenal, *Satires*, 6:14.96-99.
49. Francesco Vattioni, "I Nomi Giudaici delle epigrafi di monastero di Aquileia," *AN* 43 (1972): 126.
50. Andrew R. Seager and A. Thomas Kraabel, "The Synagogue and the Jewish Community" [of Sardis], in George M. A. Hanffman, *Sardis* (Cambridge, MA: Harvard University Press, 1983), 178.
51. Claudius Rutulius Namatianus, *De Reditu Suo.*

CHAPTER 16

1. Valerius Maximus, *Facta et Dicta Memorabilia*, 1.3:3.
2. Seneca, *De Superstitione*; Augustinius, *De Civitate Dei*, 6.2.
3. Horace, *Sermones*, 1.4.139-143.
4. Dio Cassius, *Historia Romana*, 37, 15.2-17.4.
5. Ibid., 7, 18.55A.
6. Ibid., 66, 4-7.
7. Ibid., 67, 14.1-3.
8. Hermann Vogelstein, *The Jews of Rome* (Philadelphia: Jewish Publication Society, 1940), 71.
9. Menahem Stern, *Greek and Latin Authors on Jews and Judaism*, vol. 2 (Jerusalem: Israel Academy of Sciences and Humanities, 1976), 383-384.
10. Andrew Sharf, *Byzantine Jewry* (London: Routledge & Kegan Paul, 1971), 33.
11. Julian, *Contra Galileos.*
12. Julian, *Ad Theodorum.*
13. Julian, *ad Communitatem Iudaeorium.*
14. Lionel Casson, *Ancient Trade and Society* (Detroit: Wayne State University Press, 1984), 140-42.
15. M. I. Finley, *The Ancient Economy* (Los Angeles: University of California Press, 1985), 188-189.
16. Naphtali Lewis and Meyer Reinhold, *Roman Civilization* (New York: Harper & Row, 1966), 227.
17. Plutarch, *Life of Cato the Elder*, 21.
18. Cicero, *On Duties*, 1:150-151.
19. Casson, *Ancient Trade*, 142.
20. Plutarch, *Marc*, 17.3-4.
21. Philo Judaeus, *Quod imnis Probus Libus Sit*, 157.
22. Vogelstein, *The Jews of Rome*, 27.
23. Ibid., 9-10.
24. Ibid., 17.
25. Ibid., 17-18.
26. Ibid., 25.
27. David Philipson, *Old European Jewries* (1894; reprint, Philadelphia: Jewish Publication Society, 1943), 122.
28. Vogelstein, *The Jews of Rome*, 77.
29. Philipson, *Old European Jewries*, 122.
30. Vogelstein, *The Jews of Rome*, 43.
31. Acts 28:13, 14

32. Heinrich Graetz, *History of the Jews*, vol. 3 (Philadelphia: Jewish Publication Society, 1967), 41.
33. Ibid., 35.
34. W. A. Thorpe, *English Glass* (London: A. & C. Black Ltd., 1953), 7, 8, 11, 75, 76.
35. Axel von Saldern, *Glas von der Antike bis zum Jugendstil* (Mainz am Rhein, 1980), 19.
36. Thorpe, *English Glass*, 77.
37. St. Jerome, *Comm. in Exekiel*, xxvii, in *Pat. Lat.*, 25, 313, "Orbe, Romano Occupato."
38. Casson, *Ancient Trade and Early Society*, 147.
39. Salo W. Baron et al., *Economic History of the Jews* (Jerusalem: Keter, 1975), 40.

Bibliography

Adams, Robert McCormack. *Heartland of Cities*. Chicago and London: University of Chicago Press, 1981.

Adan-Bayewitz, David, and Perlmon, Isodore. "The Local Trade of Sepphoris in the Roman Period." *IEJ* (January 1991): 153-167.

Ahlström, G. W., and Edelman, D. "Merenptah's Israel." *JNES* 44:1 (January 1985): 60-61.

Aharoni, Yohanan. "Khirbet Raddana and Its Inscriptions." *IEJ* 21:3 (1971): 130-135.

——. "Nothing Early and Nothing Late: Rewriting Israel's Conquest." *BA* 39:3 (May 1976): 55-76.

——. *The Land of the Bible*, A Historical Geography. 1962. Trans. A. F. Rainey. Philadelphia: Westminster Press, 1979.

——. "The Israelite Occupation of Canaan." *BAR* 8 (May-June 1982): 3, 14, 160.

——. *The Archaeology of the Land of Israel*. Philadelphia: Westminster Press, 1982.

Albright, William Foxwell. "The Israelite Conquest of Canaan in the Light of Archaeology." *BASOR* 74 (1939): 11-23.

——. *Archaeology, Historical Analogy, and Early Biblical Tradition*. Baton Rouge: Louisiana State University Press, 1966.

——. *The Proto-Sinaitic Inscriptions and their Decipherment*. Harvard Theological Studies. Cambridge, MA: Harvard University Press, 1970.

Aldred, Cyril. *The Egyptians*. 1961. Reprint. London: Thames and Hudson, 1984.

Alon, Gedaliah. *The Jews in Their Land*. Cambridge, MA: Harvard University Press, 1989.

Alt, Albrecht. "The Settlement of the Israelites in Palestine." In *Essays on Old Testament History and Religion*, trans. G. W. Anderson. Oxford: Basil Blackwell, 1966.

——. "The God of the Fathers." In *Essays on Old Testament History and Religion*, trans. G. W. Anderson. Oxford: Basil Blackwell, 1966.

Anati, Emanuel. *Palestine before the Hebrews*. New York: Alfred A. Knopf, 1963.

Aristophanes. *Acharnians*.

Aristotle. *Politics*.

Arrian. *Dissertationes*.

Augustinius. *De Civitate Dei*.

Ausubel, Nathan. *The Book of Jewish Knowledge*. New York: Crown Publishers, 1964.

Avi-Yonah, Michael, and Stern, Ephraim. *Encyclopedia of Archaeological Excavations in the Holy Land*. Vol. 4. Cambridge: Oxford University Presss, 1978.

Baines, John, and Malek, Jerome. *Atlas of Ancient Egypt*. New York: Facts on File Publications, 1980.

Bar-Adon, P. "Another Ivory Bull's Head from Palestine." *BASOR* 165 (1964): 46.

Barag, Dan. "Recent Epigraphic Discoveries Related to the History of Glassmaking in the Roman Period." In *Annales du 10th Congress*. Madrid-Segovie, 1985.

Baron, Salo. "Population." In *Encyclopaedia Judaica*. Jerusalem: Keter, 1972.

———. *Economic History of the Jews*. Ed. Chaim Gross. New York: Schocken, 1975.

Baron, Salo W., et al. *Economic History of the Jews*. Jerusalem: Keter, 1975.

Bass, George. "Cape Gelidonya: A Bronze Age Shipwreck." In *Transactions of the American Philosophical Society* no. 57, pt. 8. Philadelphia: The Society, 1967.

———. "The Ulu Burun Shipwreck." *Kazi Sonuclari Toplantisi* (May 1985): 20-24.

———. "A Bronze Age Shipwreck at Ula Burun (Kas), 1984 Campaign." *AJA* 90 (1986): 269-296.

———. "Oldest Known Shipwreck Reveals Splendors of the Bronze Age." *NGM* 172 (1987): 692-733.

———. "Return to Cape Gelidonya." *INA Newsletter* 15:2 (June 1988): 3-5.

———. "Civilization Under the Sea." *Modern Maturity* (April-May 1989): 60.

Bass, George, et al. "The Bronze Age Shipwreck at Ulu Burun: 1986." *AJA* 93 (1989): 1-29.

Beit-Arieh, Itzhaq. "New Light on the Edomites." *BAR* 14:2 (March-April 1988): 30.

Belon, Pierre. (Belon du Mans): *les Observations de plusiers singularitez et choses memorables trouve en Grece, Asie, Arabie et autres pays estranges* (1553).

Ben-Sasson, H. H. *A History of the Jewish People*. Cambridge, MA: Harvard University Press, 1976.

Ben-Tor, A. "An Ivory Bull's Head from ᶜAi." *BASOR* 208 (1972): 47.

Bertacchi, Luisa. "Nuovi elementi e ipotesi circa la Basilica del Fondo Tullio." *AN* (1961-1962): 48-76.

———. "Il mosaico Teodoriano scoperto nell'interno del campanile di Aquileia." *AN* 32-33 (1961-1962): 32.

———. "Nuovi mosaici figurati di Aquileia." *AN* 34 (1963): 20-84.

———. "Due vetri paleocristiani di Aquileia." AN 38 (1967): 142-150.

Bickerman, Elias J. *Chronology of the Ancient World*. New York: Cornell University Press, 1968.

———. *The Jews in the Greek Age*. Cambridge, MA: Harvard University Press, 1988.

Bietak, Manfred. "Urban Archaeology and the 'Town Problem' in Ancient Egypt." *Egyptology* (1979), 97.

Bikai, Patricia Maynor. "Cyprus and the Phoenicians." *BA* 52:4 (December 1989): 204.

Bleibtrau, Erika. "Grisly Assyrian Record of Torture and Death." *BAR* 17:1 (January-February 1991): 58-59.

Borowski, Oded. "Yadin Presents New Interpretation of the Famous Lachish Letters." In *Archaeology and the Bible*. Washington, DC: Biblical Archaeological Society (1990).

Boston Museum of Fine Arts. "The Art of Living in the New Kingdom 1558-1085 B.C." In *Egypt's Golden Age*. Catalog of the exhibition, 1982.

Boulnois, L. *The Silk Road*. New York: Dutton, 1966.

Braudel, Fernand. *The Mediterranean and the Mediterranean World in the Age of Philip Second*. New York: Harper & Row, 1973.

Breasted, James Henry. *Ancient Records of Egypt* 2. Chicago: University of Chicago Press, 1960.

———. *A History of Egypt*. 1905. Reprint. New York: Bantam, 1964.

Bright, John. *A History of Israel*. London: SCM Press, 1972.

Brill, Robert, and Wosinski, John F. "A Huge Slab of Glass in the Ancient Necropolis of Beth She'arim" (Paper submitted to Section B of the 7th International Congress of Glass). Brussels, 1965.

Broshi, Magen, and Goiphna, R. "Middle Bronze Age II Palestine Settlements and Population." *BASOR* 261 (1986): 73-90.

Brown, Robert. *Semitic Influence in Hellenic Mythology*. Clifton, NJ: Reference Book Publishers, 1966.

Brusin, Giovanni. "Grande edificio culturale scoperto a Monastero di Aquileia." *AN* 20 (1949): 26-30.

———. "Orientali in Aquileia Romana." *AN* 24, 25 (1953-1954): 56-70.

———. "I mosaico paleocristiani di aquileia e il libro di un Parocco inglese." *AN* 34 (1963): 108-132.

Callaway, Joseph A. "A Visit with Ahilud." *BAR* (September-October 1983). Reprinted in *Archaeology and the Bible*. Washington, DC: Biblical Archaeological Society, 1990.

Calvi, M. C. "Il miracolo della fonte nel vetro dorato del museo di Aquileia." *AN* 30 (1959): 38-48.

———. *I Vetri Romani*. Aquileia: Associazone Nazionale per Aquileia, 1969.

Canby, Jeanne Vorys. "Hittite Art." *BA* 52 (June-September 1989): 111.

Carlini, Antonio. "L'epigraphe Teodoriana di Aquileia." *AN* 55 (1984).

Cassola, F. "Aquileia e l'Oriente mediteraneo." *AA* (1977): 74.

Casson, Lionel. *Ancient Trade and Society*. Detroit: Wayne State University Press, 1984.

Chadwick, John. *The Mycenaean World*. Cambridge: Cambridge University Press, 1977.

Cicero. *On Duties*.

Cicero, Marcus Tullius. *Pro Flacco*.

———. *Pro Rabirio Postumo*.

Claudius, Rutulius Namatianus. *De Reditu Suo*.

Clemens, Alexandrinus. *Stromata*.

Cleveland, R. "An Ivory Bull's Head from Jericho." *BASOR* 163 (1961): 31, 34.

Cole, Dan. "How Water Tunnels Worked." In *Archaeology and the Bible*. Washington, DC: Biblical Archaeological Society, 1990.

Commodianus. *Instructiones*.

Cook, J. M. *The Persian Empire*. New York: Schocken, 1983.

Cowley, A. E. *Aramaic Papyri of the Fifth Century B.C.E.* Oxford: Clarendon Press, 1923.

———. "The Sinaitic Inscriptions." *The Journal of Eastern Archaeology* 15, parts 2, 4 (1929): 200-218.

David, A. Rosalie. *The Ancient Egyptians*. London: Routledge & Kegan Paul, 1982.

Davies, W. D., and Finklestein, Louis, eds. *The Cambridge History of Judaism*. Vol. 1. Cambridge: Cambridge University Press, 1984.

Demosthenes. *Orations*.

Demsky, Aaron, and Kochavi, Moshe. "An Alphabet from the Days of the Judges." *BAR* 4:3 (September-October 1978): 23-25.

Dever, William G. "The Middle Bronze Age, the Zenith of the Urban Canaanite Era." *BAR* 50:3 (September 1987): 149-153.

Dio, Cassius. *Historia Romana*.

Doron, Pinchas. *The Mystery of Creation According to Rashi*. New York: Maznaim, 1982.

Dothan, M. "Tel Ashdod." *IEJ* 22:4 (1972): 244.

Dothan, Trude. "In the Days When the Judges Ruled—Research on the Period of the Settlement and the Judges." In *Recent Archaeology in the Land of Israel*, ed. Hershel Shanks. Washington, DC: Biblical Archaeological Society, 1981.

Dupree, Louis. *Afghanistan*. Princeton, NJ: Princeton University Press, 1980.

Durant, Will. *Our Oriental Heritage*. 1935. Reprint. New York: Simon & Schuster, 1954.

Duval, Yves-Marie. "Aquilee et la Palestine entre 370 et 420." *AA* (1978): 263.

Ellens, J. Harold. "Philo Judaeus and the Ancient Library of Alexandria." In *Seminar Papers of the Society of Biblical Literature* (1987).

Engles, Anita. *Readings in Glass History*. Vol. 4. Jerusalem: Phoenix Publications, 1974.

Eusebius. *Praeparatio Evangelica*.

Feldman, Louis H. "The Omnipresence of the God-fearers." *BAR* 12:5 (September–October 1986).

Finegan, Jack. *Light from the Ancient Past.* Vol. 1. 1946. Reprint. Princeton, NJ: Princeton University Press, 1974.

Finklestein, Israel. "Searching for Israelite Origins." *BAR* 14:5 (September–October 1988): 39–40.

———. *The Archaeology of the Israelite Settlement.* Jerusalem: Israel Exploration Society, 1988.

Finley, M. I. *Ancient Sicily to the Arab Conquest.* New York: Viking Press, 1968.

———. *The Ancient Economy.* Los Angeles: University of California Press, 1985.

Friedman, I. Irving. "Seashells and Ancient Purple Dying." *BAR* 53:2 (June 1990): 98.

Fritz, Volkmar. "The Israelite 'Conquest' in Light of Recent Excavations at Khirbet el-Meshash." *BASOR* 241 (1981): 61–73.

———. "Conquest or Settlement?" *BAR* 50:2 (June 1987): 98.

———. "The Conquest in the Light of Archaeology." In *Proceedings of the Eighth World Congress of Jewish Studies* (Jerusalem, n.d.).

Gardiner, Sir Alan. *Egypt of the Pharaohs.* 1961. Reprint. Oxford: Oxford University Press, 1979.

Gersprach, E. *L'Arte de la Verrerie.* Paris: Bibliothèque de l'Enseignement de Beaux-Arts, 1885.

Gilbert, Martin, *Atlas of Jewish History.* Rev. ed. New York: Dorset Press, 1976.

Gitin, Seymour. "Part II: Olive-Oil Suppliers to the World." *BAR* 16:2 (March–April 1990): 39.

Glueck, Nelson. "The Other Side of Jordan." *BASOR* 80 (December 1940) and *BASOR* 82 (April 1941): 3f.

Goitein, S. D. *A Mediterranean Society.* Vol. 1. Los Angeles: University of California Press, 1967.

———. *Jews and Arabs.* Rev. ed. New York: Schocken, 1974.

Gordon, Cyrus. "Abraham of Ur." In *Hebrew and Oxford Studies.* Oxford: Oxford University Press, 1963.

———. "Where is Abraham's Ur?" *BAR* 3:2 (June 1977): 20.

———. "The Origin of the Jews in Elephantine." *JNES* 14 (1955): 56–57.

———. *The Ancient Near East.* New York: Norton & Co., 1965.

Gottwald, Norman. *The Tribes of Yahweh: a Sociology of the Religion of Liberated Israel 1250–1050 B.C.E.* Maryknoll, NY: Orbis, 1979.

———. "John Bright's New Revision of a History of Israel." *BAR* 8:4 (July–August 1982): 60.

Gottwald, Norman K. "Were the Early Israelites Pastoral Nomads?" *BAR* 4:2 (June 1978): 2, 6.

Gracco-Ruggini, Luila. "Il vescovo Cromazio e gli ebrei di Aquileia." *AA* 8 (1975): 363.

———. "Ebrei e Orientali in Aquileia." *AA* (1977): 352–382.

Grant, Michael. *The History of Ancient Israel.* New York: Charles Scribner and Sons, 1984.

Graetz, Heinrich. *History of the Jews.* Vol. 3. Philadelphia: Jewish Publication Society, 1967.

Greenberg, Moshe. "The Hap\biru," in *Ancient Times–Patriarchs and Judges.* In *The World History of the Jewish People.* Vol. 2. 1955. Reprint. New Haven: American Oriental Society, 1970.

Gross, Nachum, ed. *Economic History of the Jews.* Jerusalem: Keter, 1975.

Hadas, Moses. *Aristeas to Philocrates.* Hoboken, NJ: Ktav, 1990.

Haldane, Cheryl Ward. "Shipwrecked Plant Remains." *BA* 53 (March 1990): 57–58.

Halpern, Baruch. *The First Historians.* San Francisco: Harper & Row, 1988.

Hancock, Percy S. P. *Mesopotamian Archaeology.* New York: Kraus Reprint & Periodicals, 1963.

Hayes, William C. *The Scepter of Egypt.* Part 2: *The Hyksos Period (1675–1080 B.C.).* 1959. Reprint. New York: Metropolitan Museum of Art, 1968.

Hengel, Martin. *Judaism and Hellenism*. Trans. John Bowden. Philadelphia: Fortress Press, 1974.

Herodotus. *Persian Wars*.

———. *The Histories*. New York: Penguin Classics, 1972.

Herrmann, Siegfried. *A History of Israel in Old Testament Times*. 2d. ed. Philadelphia: Fortress Press, 1980.

Herzog, Isaac. "Proceedings of the Belfast Natural History and Philosophical Society, Appendix B." In *The Royal Purple and the Biblical Blue*, ed. Moshe Ron and Ehud Spaniel. Jerusalem: Keter, 1987.

Hispania Judaica. Barcelona: Encyclopedia Brittanica Publishers, 1990.

Historia compeniera dynastiarum. "Bar-Hebraeus." Ed. and trans. E. Pococke, 1985.

Higgins, Reynold. *Minoan and Mycenaean Art*. New York: Praeger, 1981.

Hilgert. "De Somnis 1-2." In *Seminar Papers of the Society of Biblical Literature*, 1987.

Hoffman, Michael A. *Egypt Before the Pharaohs*. London: Routledge & Kegan Paul, 1980.

Homer. *Iliad*.

Hopf, M. "Plant Remains and Early Farming in Jericho." In *The Domestication and Exploitation of Plants and Animals*, ed. P. J. Ucko and C. W. Dimbleby. London: Duckworth, 1969.

Horace. *Sermones*.

Jackson, F. Hamilton. *The Shores of the Adriatic*. London, 1906.

James, Jean M. "Silk, China and the Drawloom." *Archaeology* 39:9 (September–October 1986).

Jastrzebowska, Elisabeth. "Les Origines de la Scene du Combat entre le coq et la Tortue dans les mosaics chretiennes d'Aquilee." *AA* 8 (1975): 93–107.

Jerome, Saint. *Comm. in Exekiel*.

Josephus, Flavius. *The Works of Flavius Josephus*. Vols. 1–4, *Wars of the Jews*; *Antiquities of the Jews* (*Antiquitates Judaicae*); *Dissertation*; *Against Apion* (*Contra Apionem*). Trans. William Whiston. 1974. Reprint. Grand Rapids, MI: Baker Book House, 1983.

Julian. *Contra Galileos*.

———. *ad Communitatem Iudaeorium*.

———. *Ad Theodorum*.

Juvenal. *Satires*.

Kantor, H. J. "The Relative Chronology of Egypt and Its Foreign Correlations Before the Bronze Age." In *Chronologies in Old World Archaeology*, ed. R. Ehrich. Chicago: University of Chicago Press, 1965.

Karmon, Nira, and Spaniel, Ehud. "Archaeological Evidence of the Purple Dye Industry from Israel." In *The Royal Purple and the Biblical Blue*. Jerusalem: Keter, 1987.

Kees, Hermann. *Ancient Egypt: A Cultural Topography*. Trans. Ian F. D. Morrow. Chicago: University of Chicago Press, 1961.

———. *Ancient Egypt*. 1961. Trans. Faber and Faber. Reprint. Chicago: University of Chicago Press, Phoenix edition, 1977.

Keller, Warner. *The Bible as History*. 1955. Reprint. New York: William Morrow, 1980.

Kelm, George L., and Mazar, Amihai. "Three Seasons of Excavations at Tel Barash-Biblical Timnah." *BASOR* 237 (1982): 1–36.

———. "Tel Batash (Timnah) Excavations, Second Preliminary Report (1981–1983)." *BASOR Supplement* 23 (1985): 93–120.

———. "Excavating in Samson Country." *BAR* 15:1 (January–February 1989): 37–49.

Kemp, Barry. *Ancient Egypt: Anatomy of a Civilization*. London: Routledge, Chapman, and Hall, 1989.

Kempinski, Aharon. "Israelite Conquest or Settlement? New Light from Tell Masos." *BAR* 2:3 (September 1976): 25–30.

———. *Encyclopedia of Archaeological Excavations in the Holy Land*. Vol. 1. Cambridge: Oxford University Press, 1978.

Kenyon, Kathleen M. *Digging up Jericho*. London: Ernest Benn Limited, 1957.

Kenyon, Dame Kathleen M. *Jericho*. London: British School of Archaeology, 1960.

——. "Jericho." In *Encyclopedia of Archaeological Excavations in the Holy Land*. Vol. 2. English edition, ed. Michael Avi-Yonah. Englewood Cliffs, NJ: Prentice-Hall, 1976.

——. *Archaeology in the Holy Land*. 1960. Reprint. New York: Norton, 1979.

Kuhne, H. *Die Keramic von Tel Chuera Chuera und ihre Beziehungen zu Funden aus Syrian-Palestina der Turkei und dem Iraq*. Berlin, 1976.

Kurinsky, Samuel. *The Glassmakers: an Odyssey of the Jews*. New York: Hippocrene Books, 1991.

Landsberger, B., and Tadmor, H. "Fragments of Clay Liver Models." *IEJ* 14 (1964): 201-218.

Lapp, Paul. "The Conquest of Palestine in Light of Archaeology." *Concordia Theological Monthly* 38 (1967).

Liebowitz, Harold. "Tel Yin'am, 1980." *IEJ* 32:1 (1982): 64-65.

——. "Late Bronze Ivory Work in Palestine: Evidence of a Cultural Highpoint." *BASOR* 265 (1987): 3-5, 14-16, 18.

——. "Tel Yin'am, 1981." *IEJ* 33:1-2 (1983): 65.

Lewis, Naphtali, and Reinhold, Meyer. *Roman Civilization*. New York: Harper & Row, 1966.

Levy, Thomas E. "How Ancient Man First Utilized Rivers in the Sand." *BAR* 16:6 (November-December 1990): 29.

Littauer, M. A., and Crouwel, J. H. "The Earliest Known Three-dimensional Evidence for Spoked Wheels." *BA* 52 (June-September 1989): 395.

Lloyd, Seton. *The Archaeology of Mesopotamia*. Rev. ed. London: Thames and Hudson, 1984.

Loret, V. *La résin de térébinthe (sonter) chez les anciens Égyptiens*. Cairo: L'institut Francaise d'Archaeolgie Orientale, Recerches d'archéologie de philologie de et d'histoire, 1949.

Lucretius. *De Rerum Natura*.

Mackay, Ernest, and Langdon, Stephen. "Report on Excavations at Jamdet Nasr." In *Field Museum Anthopological Memoirs 1-3*. Chicago, 1931.

MacLauren, E. C. B. "Date of the Foundation of the Jewish Colony at Elephantine." *JNES* 87:2 (April 1968): 89, 91, 92.

Malamet, Abraham. "Israelite Conduct of War in the Conquest of Canaan." In *Symposia Celebrating the Seventy-fifth Anniversary of the Founding of the American Schools of Oriental Research, 1900-1975* (1979).

——. "How Inferior Israelite Forces Conquered Fortified Canaanite Cities." *BAR* 8:2 (March-April 1982): 25-35.

Mallowan, M. E. L. "Excavations at Brak and Chagar Bazar." *Iraq* 9 (1947): 1ff.

Mandich, G. "Primi riconoscementi veneziani di un diritto di privativa agli inventori." *Rivista do dritto industriale* 1:7 (1958): 101.

Martyr, Justin. *Dialogue with Typho*.

Maximus, Valerius. *Facta et Dicta Memorabilia*.

Mazar, Benjamin. *The Early Biblical Period, Historical Studies*. Jerusalem: Israel Exploration Society, 1986.

McQueen, J. G. *The Hittites*. 1975. Reprint. London: Thames and Hudson, 1986.

McMahon, Gregory. "The History of the Hittites." *BA* 52 (June-September 1989): 65.

Mellink, Machteld J. "The pre-history of Syro-Cilicia." *Bibliotheca Orientalis* 19:5-6 (1962): 225-226.

——. "Archaeology in Asia Minor." *American Journal of Archaeology* 69 (1965): 135.

——. "Bronze Wagon." *AJA* 75 (1971): 165.

——. "Archaeology in Anatolia." *AJA* (January 1987): 3.

——. "Archaeology in Anatolia." *AJA* (January 1990): 126.

Mendenhall, George F. *The Tenth Generation: The Origins of Biblical Tradition*. Baltimore: Johns Hopkins University Press, 1973.

——. "The Hebrew Conquest of Palestine." *BA* 25 (1962): 66-87. In revised version *The*

Biblical Archaeologist Reader, vol. 3, ed. E. F. Campbell and D. N. Freedman. Garden City, NY: Doubleday, 1990.

Mentasti, Rosa Barovier. "La coppa incisa con 'Daniele nella fossa dei leoni,' al museo Nazionale Concordiese." *AN* 14 (1943): 157-172.

Meyers, Carol L. "Of Drums and Damsels." *BAR* 54:1 (March 1991).

Mian, Franca. "La 'Vittoria' di Aquileia." *AA* 8 (1975): 131.

Moscati, Sabatino. *An Introduction to the Comparative Grammar of the Semitic Languages.* Weisbaden: O. Harrassowitz, 1964.

Mozeson, Isaac. *The Word.* New York: Shapolsky, 1989.

Mulhy, James D. "How Iron Technology Changed the Ancient World." *BAR* 7 (December 1982): 6. Reprint, *Archaeology and the Bible.* Washington, DC: Biblical Archaeological Society, 1990.

Na'am, Nadar. "H$_u$abiru and Hebrews: The Transfer of a Social Term to the Literary Sphere." *JNES* 45:40 (October 1986): 288.

Needham, Joseph. *Science and Civilization in China.* Vol. 2. Cambridge: Cambridge University Press, 1965.

Neuberg, Frederic. *Ancient Glass.* London: Barrie & Rockcliff, 1962.

Newby, P. H. *Warrior Pharaohs.* London: Faber & Boston, 1980.

Newman, Harold. *An Illustrated Dictionary of Glass.* London: Thames and Hudson, 1977.

Noth, Martin. "Studien zu den historisch-geographischen Dokumenten des Josuabuches." *Zeitschrift des deutschen Palastina-Vereins* (1935): 185-255.

——. "Grundsätzliches zur geschichtlichen Deutung archäologischer Befunde auf dem Boden Palästinas." *Palästinjahrbuch* 37 (1960): 7-22.

——. *The History of Israel.* London: A. & C. Black, 1960.

Nougayrol, Jean. "Textes Accadiens des Archives Sud (Archives Internationales)." *Le Palais Royal d'Ugarit* 4, 1956.

Oates, Joan. *Babylon.* New York: Thames and Hudson, 1986.

Olmstead, Albert Ten Eyck. *History of the Persian Empire.* Chicago: University of Chicago Press, 1948.

Onega, Jose Ramon. *Los Judios en la Reino de Galicia.* Madrid: Editora Nazional, 1981.

Oppenheim, A. Leo. *Letters from Mesopotamia.* Chicago: University of Chicago Press, 1967.

——. "The Cuneiform Texts." *Glass and Glassmaking in Ancient Mesopotamia.* Rev. ed. Chicago: University of Chicago Press, 1970.

——. *Ancient Mesopotamia.* 1964. Reprint. Chicago and London: University of Chicago Press, 1977.

Oren, Eliezer. *Explorations in the Negev and Sinai.* Catalog of the Bathsheba Sinai Museum, 1976.

Origenes. *Contra Celsum.*

Özgüc, Nimet. "Seals of the Old Assyrian Colony Period and some Observations on the Seal Impressions." In *Ancient Anatolia.* Ankara, 1986.

Özgüc, Tahsin. "New Observations on the Relationship of Kultepe with Southeast Anatolia and North Syria during the Third Millennium B.C." In *Ancient Anatolia.* Ankara: Tarih Kurumu Bulletin, 1986.

Page, Stephanie. "A Stela of Adad-nirari III and Nergal-eres from Tel al Rimah." *Iraq* 30 (1968): 143.

Panciera, Silvio. *Vita Economica di Aquileia in eta Romana.* Aquileia, 1957.

Paul, Shalom M., and Dever, William G., eds. *Biblical Archaeology.* Jerusalem: Keter, 1973.

Perkins, Ann. *The Excavations at Duro-Europus, 1963.* Final Report 4, part 5. New Haven: Yale University Press, 1964.

Petrie, Sir Flinders. *Researches in Sinai.* 1906. Reprint. Ed. Benjamin Mazar. New Brunswick, NJ: Rutgers University Press, 1970.

Pettinato, Giovanni. "Ebla and the Bible." *BAR* 6:6 (November-December 1980): 38.

——. *The Archives of Ebla.* Trans., 1979. Ed. *Ebla. Un Impero inciso nell'argilla.* New York: Doubleday, 1981.

——. *Ebla. Nuovi orizzonti della storia.* Milano: Rusconi, 1985.

Philipson, David. *Old European Jewries.* 1894. Reprint. Philadelphia: Jewish Publication Society, 1943.

Philo, Judaeus. *Flacco.*

——. *Quod imnis Probus Libus Sit.*

Plutarch. *Life of Cato the Elder.*

——. *Marc.*

Pritchard, James B. *Gibeon, Where the Sun Stood Still.* Princeton, NJ: Princeton University Press, 1962.

——. *Ancient Near East in Pictures.* 3d ed. Princeton, NJ: Princeton University Press, 1969.

——. *The Ancient Near East.* 1958. Reprint. Princeton, NJ: Princeton University Press, 1973.

——. *Ancient Near Eastern Texts Relating to the Old Testament.* 2d ed. Princeton, NJ, and London: Princeton University Press, 1975.

Pulak, Cemal. "The Bronze Age Shipwreck at Ulu Burun, Turkey: 1985 Campaign." *AJA* 92:1 (January 1988): 10, 37.

——. "Excavations in Turkey: 1988 Campaign." *INA Newsletter* 15:4 (December 1988): 12-17.

Pulak, Cemal, and Frey, Donald A. "The Search for a Bronze Age Shipwreck." *Archaeology* (July-August 1985): 19.

Radin, Max. *The Jews Among the Greeks and Romans.* Philadelphia: Jewish Publication Society, 1915.

Rainey, Anson F. "The Saga of Eliashib." In *Archaeology and the Bible.* Washington, DC: Biblical Archaeological Society, 1990.

Redford, Donald B. "The Historiography of Ancient Egypt." In *Egyptology and the Social Sciences.* Cairo: The American University of Cairo Press, 1979.

Rejwan, Nissim. *The Jews of Iraq.* Boulder, CO: Westview, 1986.

Rinaldi, Giovanni. "I tre quadri di Giona nel mosaico dell'aula Teodorina." *AA* 8 (1975): 109-130.

Ron, Moshe, and Spaniel, Ehud, eds. *The Royal Purple and the Biblical Blue.* Jerusalem: Keter, 1987.

Rosenthal, Monroe, and Mozeson, Isaac. *Wars of the Jews.* New York: Hippocrene Books, 1990.

Roth, Cecil. *The Jewish Contribution to Civilization.* London: East and West Library, 1956.

Roussel, P. *Delos colonnie atheneienne.* Vol. 3. Paris: Bibliotheque des écoles francaises d'Athenes, et de Rome, n.d.

Saint Augustine. *The City of God.* Trans. Henry Bettenson. New York: Viking Penguin Books, 1986.

Saldern, Axel von. *Glas von der Antike bis zum Jugendstil.* Mainz am Rhein, 1980.

Sasson, J. M. "Instances of Mobility among Mari Artisans." *BASOR* 190 (1968): 46-54.

Schurer, E. *Geschichte des judischen Volkes im Zeitalter Jesu Christi.* Vols. 1-3. Leipzig: J. C. Hinricks, 1909.

Seager, Andrew R., and Kraabel, A. Thomas. "The Synagogue and the Jewish Community" [of Sardis]. In *Sardis,* ed. George M. A. Hanffman. Cambridge, MA: Harvard University Press, 1983.

Seger, J. D. "Tel Gezer." *IEJ* 23:4 (1973): 250-251.

Seneca. *De Superstitione.*

Seters, John Van. *The Hyksos.* New Haven: Yale University Press, 1966.

Shanks, Hershel. "*BAR* Interviews Yigael Yadin." *BAR* 9:1 (January-February 1983): 16-21.

——. "Jeremiah's Scribe and Confidant Speaks from a Hoard of Clay Bullae." In *Archaeology and the Bible,* vol. 1, ed. Hershel Shanks and Dan P. Cole. Washington, DC: Biblical Archaeology Society, 1990.

Shanks, Hershel, and Cole, Dan P., eds. *Archaeology and the Bible*, Vol. 1. Washington, DC: Biblical Archaeology Society, 1990.

Sharf, Andrew. *Byzantine Jewry*. London: Routledge & Kegan Paul, 1971.

Sillen, Andrew. "Dietary Reconstruction and Near Eastern Archaeology." *Expedition* 2 (1986): 19.

Silver, Morris. *Prophets and Markets*. Boston: Kluwer-Nijhoff, 1983.

Sitchin, Zaccharia. Article in *The Jewish Week and the American Examiner*, July 22, 1983.

Soggin, J. Alberto. *A History of Ancient Israel: From the Beginnings to the Bar Khochba Revolt A.D. 135*. Trans. John Bowden. Philadelphia: Westminster Press, 1985.

Speiser, E. A. "Amorites and Canaanites." In *The World History of the Jewish People*, vol. 2, ed. Benjamin Mazar. New Brunswick, NJ: Rutgers University Press, 1970.

Stech-Wheeler, T., et al. "Iron at Taanach and Early Iron Metallurgy in the Eastern Mediterranean." *AJA* 85:3 (July 1981): 255, 260.

Stern, Ephraim. *Material Culture of the Land of the Bible in the Persian Period, 538-332 B.C.* English ed. Warminster: Aris & Phillips Ltd., 1982.

Stern, Menahem. *Greek and Latin Authors on Jews and Judaism*. Vol. 2. Jerusalem: Israel Academy of Sciences and Humanities, 1976.

Stillman, Norman A. *The Jews of Arab Lands*. Philadelphia: Jewish Publication Society of America, 1979.

Sukenik, E. L. "History in Jewish Archaeology." In *The Jewish People, Past and Present*. New York: Central Yiddish Culture Organization, 1946.

Tacitus. *Agricola*.

Tadmor, Hayim. "The Campaigns of Sargon II of Assur." *Journal of Cuneiform Studies* 121 (1958): 33-40.

——. "The Decline, Rise and Destruction of the Kingdom of Israel." In *A History of the Jewish People*, ed. H. H. Ben-Sasson. Cambridge, MA: Harvard University Press, 1969.

Tamaro, Bruna Forlati. "Richerche sull'aula teodoriana nord e sui Battisteri di Aquileia." *AN* (1963): 86-100.

——. "Iscrizioni greche di Siriani a Concordia." *AA* (1977): 383-392.

Tcherikover, Victor. *Corpus Papyronan Judaicanam III*. Cambridge, MA, 1964.

——. *Hellenistic Civilization and the Jews*. New York: Atheneum, 1985.

Theophrastus. *Enquiry into Plants*, vol. 2, trans. A. Hort. Loeb Classical Library. New York and London: Putnam's Sons and Heinemann, 1916.

Thomas, Carol G. *The Earliest Civilizations*. Boston: University Press of America, 1982.

Thompson, R. Campbell. *A Dictionary of Assyrian Chemistry and Geology*. Oxford: Clarendon Press, 1936.

Thorpe, W. A. *English Glass*. London: A. & C. Black Ltd., 1953.

Throckmorton, Peter. "Thirty-three Centuries Under the Sea." *NGM* 117:5 (May 1960): 682-703.

Toynbee, Arnold. *The Greeks and Their Heritages*. Oxford: Oxford University Press, 1981.

Trigger, B. G., et al. *Ancient Egypt: A Social History*. 1983. Reprint. Cambridge, MA: Cambridge University Press, 1986.

Trowbridge, Mary Louella. *Philological Studies in Ancient Glass*. Urbana, IL: University of Illinois Press, 1930.

Tvedtnes, John A. "The Origin of the Name 'Syria'." *JNES* 40:2 (April 1982): 139-140.

Uzunoglu, Edibe. "Three Hittite Cylinder Seals in the Istanbul Archaeological Museum." In *Ancient Anatolia*, 1986.

Vattioni, Francesco. "I nomi Giudaici delle épigrafi di Monastero di Aquileia." *AN* 43 (1972): 126-132.

Vogelstein, Hermann. *The Jews of Rome*. Philadelphia: Jewish Publication Society, 1940.

Vollmer, John E., et al. *Silk Roads–China Ships*. Toronto: Royal Ontario Museum, 1983.

Weeks, Kent R., ed. *Egyptology and the Social Sciences*. Cairo: American Museum in Cairo Press, 1979.

Weippert, Manfred. "The Israelite 'Conquest' and the Evidence from Transjordan." In *Symposia Celebrating the Seventy-fifth Anniversary of the Founding of the American Schools of Oriental Research, 1900-1975* (1979).

Wendorf, F., et al. "Egyptian Prehistory; Some New Concepts." *Science* (1969): 1161-1171.

Weiss, Harvey. "Introduction." In *Ebla to Damascus.* Washington, DC: Catalog of the exhibition, Smithsonian Museum, 1985.

Wiseman, Donald J. *Chronicles of Chaldean Kings (626-556 B.C.E.) in the British Museum.* London, 1956.

Wilson, John A. *The Culture of Ancient Egypt.* 1951. Reprint. Chicago: University of Chicago Press, 1963.

——. *The Ancient Near East*, vol. 1, ed. James B. Pritchard. 1958. Reprint. Princeton, NJ: Princeton University Press, 1973.

Wood, Bryant G. "Did the Israelites Conquer Jericho?" *BAR* 16:2 (March-April 1990): 50.

Woolley, Sir Leonard. *Alalakh, An Account of the Excavations at Tel-Atchana in the Hataq 1937-1949, 1955.* Oxford: Oxford University Press, 1955.

——. *The Sumerians.* 1929. Reprint. New York: W. W. Norton, 1965.

——. *Ur of the Chaldees.* 1929. Reprint. London: Herbert Press, 1982.

Wright, G. E. "The Archaeology of Palestine From the Neolithic Through the Middle Bronze Age." *JAOS* 91 (1971): 276-293.

Wright, G. Ernest. *Biblical Archaeology.* 1957. Reprint. Philadelphia: Westminster Press, 1979.

Xenophon. *Oeconomicus.*

Yadin, Yigael. *The Finds from the Bar-Khochba Period in the Cave of Letters.* Jerusalem: Israel Exploration Society, 1963.

——. *The Art of War in Biblical Lands.* London: Weidenfeld & Nicolson, 1963.

——. *Hazor.* New York: Random House, 1975.

——. "The Transition from a Semi-Nomadic to a Sedentary Society in the Twelfth Century B.C.E." In *Symposia Celebrating the Seventy-fifth Anniversary of the Founding of the American Schools of Oriental Research, 1900-1975* (1979).

——. "Is the Biblical Account of the Israelite Conquest of Canaan Historically Reliable?" *BAR* 8:2 (March-April 1982): 16-23.

——. "The Mystery of the Unexplained Chain." *BAR* 10:4 (July-August 1984): 65-66.

Yardimci, Nurettin. *Land of Civilizations, Turkey.* Catalog of an exhibition by The Middle East Culture Center in Japan: Heibonsha Limited, 1985.

Yeivin, S. "The Canaanite Inscriptions and the Story of the Alphabet." In *The World History of the Jewish People*, vol. 2, ed. Benjamin Mazar. New Brunswick, NJ: Rutgers University Press, 1970.

Yonah, Avi. "Scythopolis." *IEJ* 12:2 (1962): 128-189.

Yurko, Frank J. "3,200 Year-Old Picture of Israelites Found in Egypt." *BAR* 16:5 (September-October 1990): 25-27.

Zaccagnini, Carlo. "Patterns of Mobility Among Ancient Near Eastern Craftsmen." *JNES* 42:4 (October 1983): 247, 250, 253, 258, 261.

Zadok, Ran. "The Origin of the Name Shinar." *Zeitschrift für Assyriologie* 74:2 (1984): 240, 244.

Zovatto, Paolo Lino. "Architettura e decorazione nella basilica Teodoriana di Aquileia." *AN* (1961-1962): 42.

Index

Language (*continued*)
  Hittite, 43
  Indo-European, 43
  name of God, 25, 229, 230
  of Near Eastern archaeology, 22-26
  references to H_uabiru, 171
  Semitic, 29, 35, 91-92, 126
  Sumerian, 25-26, 28, 29
  translation of Hyksos, 63-64
  translations of Manetho, 73-74
Lapis lazuli, 115
Lebanon, 24
Legal system
  Babylonian, 37
  Hebrew, 178-179, 293-294
  of sedentary societies, 178
Leibowitz, Harold, 210-211, 218
Leucippus, 291

MacLauren, E. C. B., 229
Manetho, 57, 276
  Dynastic chronology of, 65-70, 74,
    79-82
  Hyksos and, 62-65, 73, 85
  translations of, 73-74
Mari, 26-28, 29
Matthaie, Paolo, 19, 21, 22
Matthias, Joseph ben. *See* Josephus
Mazar, Benjamin, 151
Mediterranean Sea
  in Akkadian texts, 34
  sea trade in, 131-133, 134
Megasthenes, 292-293
Mellink, Machteld, 45-46, 47, 49, 53,
    54, 134
Mendenhall, George E., 152
Merenptah, 165, 166-168, 209
Merimde beni-Salame, 94-95
Mesopotamia
  Anatolian technology and, 42-44
  Bronze Age, 208-209
  as cultural/epochal designation, 23
  early influence in Egypt, 96-101
  Early Iron Age social unrest, 154-
    155
  iron artifacts in, 207-209, 215-217
  peoples of, 34-36
  Sumerian rule of, 28
  trade in, 39-42
Metalwork. *See also* Bronze-making;
    Copper; Ironmaking
  Aamu in Egypt, 114-115
  in Akkadia, 35-36

of biblical Hebrews, 180-183, 185-186
biblical references, 3-4, 239-242
Chinese, 249-250
in Diaspora Aquileia, 278-279
Diaspora Jews in European Middle
    Ages, 272-274
earliest Egyptian, 97
in early Israelite settlements, 194
Egyptian Second Intermediate Period,
    65-70
Jewish surnames and, 271, 273-274
Mesopotamian, 33
Mesopotamian influence in Anatolia,
    43-44, 46, 52
requirements for, 173-174
in Temple of Solomon, 188-189
Tyrean, 186-187, 188-189
Midas, King, 45-46
Midianites, 168
Military science
  Aamu bows in Egypt, 114
  David, 187
  Hebrews, 179, 183-184
  Israelite-Assyrian confrontations, 234
  Jews in Middle Ages, 272-273
Minoa, 287
  Canaanite trade in, 132
Mishnah, 255-256
Monotheism, 24-26
  of Asiatics in Egypt, 83-84, 109
Moses, 163, 168, 182, 197, 219, 258, 261,
    290, 293
Mt. Carmel, 18
Musical instruments
  Aamu in Egypt, 120-121
  in Genesis, 3
Mycenae/Mycenaeans, 287
  Canaanite trade, 132
  glassmaking, 133-134
  ironwork, 208, 215, 216
  ivory artifacts, 217
  Linear B script, 143-144
  pottery, in archaeological dating, 159,
    160-161

Nahor, 11, 26
Naqada culture, 96, 97
Naram-Sin, 28-29, 41, 49-51, 169
Nebuchadnezzar, 213, 238, 259
  his dream, 240-241
Neshites, 42-43
Neve, Peter, 47
Noah, 4-5

About the Author

The work of Samuel Kurinsky, author of *The Glassmakers: An Odyssey of the Jews*, has spurred an entirely new perspective on the history of glassmaking and the Jews. Through extensive research, he identified previously unrecognized glassmaking sites in Israel, opening the door to a new perception of the history of the Jewish people as well as glassmaking and other technological advancements. Currently the executive director of the Hebrew History Federation, Ltd., Kurinsky is also a member of the Biblical Archaeological Society, the Archaeological Institute of America, the Institute of Nautical Archaeology, and the American Archaeological Society for Oriental Research.